Introduction

In this third omnibus volume of my series, we continue following our soldiers across Europe and back again to the Pacific. We begin with the storytellers from the Italian campaign and the Normandy and Bulge campaigns.

THE STORYTELLERS (IN ORDER OF APPEARANCE):

ABBOTT L. WILEY
WILLIAM A. MILLETTE
HARRY ROSENTHAL
JACOB N. CUTLER
SYDNEY COLE

WORLD WAR II GENERATION SPEAKS III

THE THINGS OUR FATHERS SAW SERIES,
VOLUMES VII & VIII/MISC.

VOL. VII: ACROSS THE RHINE
VOL. VIII: ON TO TOKYO

MATTHEW A. ROZELL

WOODCHUCK HOLLOW PRESS

Hartford · New York

World War II Generation Speaks III

Copyright © 2024 by Matthew A. Rozell. WW2 GEN 3 VOLS 7-8. 2.6.24. All rights reserved. No part of this publication may be reproduced, distributed, or transmitted in any form or by any means without the prior written permission of the publisher. Grateful acknowledgment is made for previously published material used with permission and short quotations credited to other previously published sources. Please see author notes throughout the following works.

Maps by Susan Winchell.

Front Cover, "Then came the big day when we marched into Germany-right through the Siegfried Line.", ca. 1945. Unknown photographer, United States Army. Office of War Information. National Archives, public domain. Cover layout by Matthew Rozell.

Back Cover: "U.S. Marines in Landing Craft head for the beach at Iwo Jima on Feb. 19, 1945, during the initial landings." U.S. Marine Corps Historical Center. Public Domain Photographs, National Archives.

Any additional photographs and descriptions sourced at Wikimedia Commons within terms of use, unless otherwise noted.

Publisher's Cataloging-in-Publication Data

Names: Rozell, Matthew A., 1961-
Title: World War II generation speaks 3 /Matthew A. Rozell.
Description: Hartford, NY: Woodchuck Hollow Press, 2024. | Series: The things our fathers saw: the untold stories of the World War II generation, vol. 7-8. | Includes bibliographical references.
Identifiers: | ISBN 978-1-948155-41-0 (pbk.) | ISBN 978-1-948155-42-7 (hbk) |
Subjects: LCSH: World War, 1939-1945--Personal narratives, American. | World War, 1939-1945 --Biography. | Military history, Modern--20th century. | BISAC: HISTORY / Military / Veterans. | HISTORY / Military / World War II.

matthewrozellbooks.com

Table of Contents

ITALY

THE BATTERY COMMANDER	11
THE CANNONEER	41

D-DAY/BULGE

THE CRYPTOGRAPHER	51
THE MILITARY POLICEMAN	63
THE ARTILLERY SPOTTER	72

ACROSS THE RHINE

AUTHOR'S NOTE	93
PART ONE	99
THE ROAD TO THE REICH	99

TO LIBERATE A CONTINENT	101
THE RANGER	103
A BRIDGE TOO FAR	139
THE PARATROOPER I	143
THE RECON MAN I	169
PART TWO	187
SETBACKS	187
THE CAVALRYMAN I	189
THE PARATROOPER II	199
PART THREE	215
CROSSING OVER	215
'THE WAY IT WAS'	217
THE INFANTRY SERGEANT	219
THE GIVER	235
THE FORWARD OBSERVER	251
THE ROCKET MAN	265

THE PARATROOPER III	275
THE CAVALRYMAN II	295
THE RECON MAN II	307
THE MEDIC	321
THE FALL OF BERLIN	335
THE PARATROOPER IV	337
JUDGMENT AT NUREMBERG	343
THE JEWISH GUARD KEEPER	347
THE COURTROOM SENTINEL	363
PART FOUR	387
LAST THOUGHTS	387
THE PARATROOPER V	389
DACHAU AND THE QUESTION	395
WAR STORIES	405
AMERICANS CAME TO LIBERATE	423

ON TO TOKYO

PART ONE	443
THE PACIFIC	445
THE PEARL HARBOR SURVIVOR	453
THE MARINE RIFLEMAN	471
THE INVASION RADIOMAN I	499
THE MARINE MECHANIC I	529
PART TWO	557
THE RUNNER	559
THE MARINE GUNNER I	583
'REVENGE FOR THE DEAD'	601
PART THREE	615
THE INVASION RADIOMAN II	617
THE BAR MAN	643
THE MARINE GUNNER II	657

THE B-29 RADIOMAN	665
PART FOUR	685
HACKSAW RIDGE	687
THE NAVY CORPSMAN	709
THE INVASION RADIOMAN III	733
PART FIVE	741
OCCUPATION DUTY	743
THE INVASION RADIOMAN IV	757
THE RESTING PLACE	771
ACKNOWLEDGEMENTS	783

ITALY

[ORIGINAL SELECTIONS FROM VOLUME 4:
UP THE BLOODY BOOT]

In Volume IV, *Up the Bloody Boot: The War in Italy*, the men and women veterans of the Italian campaign opened up about a war that was so brutal, news of it was downplayed at home, one that for many Americans is shrouded in mystery and murkiness. Yet it was here that the United States launched its first offensive in the west on enemy soil, just a year after Pearl Harbor, and it was here that Allied forces would be slogging it out with a tenacious enemy fighting for its life in desert passes, against fortified beachheads, across swollen and angry rivers, up and over punishing mountain ridges, and through mud-rutted valleys in the longest single American campaign of World War II, lasting for five hundred long, bloody days until the week before the end of World War II in Europe.

Here men would be asked to do the impossible, and get it done.

The Battery Commander

Abbott Lansing Wiley was born in 1916 and raised on a farm outside a small village on the Hoosic River in Rensselaer County, New York. In 1942 he was commissioned as a 2nd lieutenant and sent to North

Africa, and from there to Italy, landing south of Naples as part of the Fifth Army. He was promoted to captain and made a battery commander in the 347th Field Artillery Battalion of the 91st Infantry Division, seeing action in Anzio, Civitavecchia, Grosseto, Pisa, Florence, Bologna, Treviso, Udine, and Trieste. Some of his stories from the war are harrowing, others hilarious—'[The wartime experience] sure changes your life. It's funny seeing the guys from Iraq come back and they have stress, but I never had stress. I always wondered about this...[but] my wife has never seen me laugh and never heard me cry. That's kind of a funny thing, how do you figure that out? It's a mystery. So [the war] changed me.' He was honorably discharged at the end of the war as a major, and as a recipient of the Bronze Star. This interview took place at his home in Valley Falls, New York, in 2013.

Abbott L. Wiley

I attended a district school, which had about twelve, thirteen, or fourteen kids. Then later I went to Lansingburg High School, which involved a trip four miles to the railroad, and then thirteen miles on the railroad to high school. I graduated in 1934. [Instead of college], I worked on a farm; we lived on a dairy farm from age 17, when I got out of high school, to 24. I intended to be a farmer, but in 1940 Congress passed the draft. We had just built a new cow barn on the side of the milking herd, but I decided I wanted to get the year training over with. So on April 3, 1941, I joined up; that year lasted until February 6, 1946. [*Laughs*]

'You're all goddamn Yankees'

I enlisted in the Army—I'd always done rifle shooting, hunting and trapping and all that, so I think it was natural for the Army. For basic training I went to Camp Wheeler, Georgia. They were just building the camp. Our company, half Tennesseans and half New

Yorkers, was the first company there. I remember that because a whole bunch of us got sick and we had to go to the hospital, and the hospital was just being built. We were in a big room on cots. I was really sick.

I said to one of the orderlies—it was about 2:00 a.m.—'Boy I don't think I can make it till morning, is there a doctor here?'

He said no.

'Is there a nurse here?'

He said, 'No, I'm the only one.' He'd probably been in the Army a couple of weeks too; he was a medic.

I said, 'I'm in tough shape,' but he said, 'I'll tell you, I shouldn't do this, but when I left home, my grandmother gave me a bottle of medicine'—she was in the mountains of Tennessee— 'and she told me if I ever got sick, to take a couple of teaspoons of this.'

He went and got the medicine and gave me a couple of teaspoons. I don't know what it was, but I went to sleep and didn't wake up till the next morning. So that ended that deal; the next day I went home.

We got along good with those boys from Tennessee. I remember one Sunday, one of the guys said, 'All you guys really ain't that bad, the only trouble is you're all goddamn Yankees.' [*Laughs*] The training was normal, all the rifle training, you know. I always remember—and they talk about women getting into combat today—but when we were at bayonet training, [they taught us that] if you stick a guy with a bayonet, you'd turn it 90 degrees and pull it out. Did you know that?

We were training with the old World War I Springfields back then.[1] We shot with a Springfield, and of course we had a lot of map reading, a lot of night marching, compass reading, and so forth.

---

[1] *old World War I Springfields*-Model 1903 Springfield Rifle, clip-loaded, 5-shot, bolt-action. It 'kicks like a mule' because the 30.06 cartridge is very powerful. Used in WWI and WWII, one WWI veteran recalled that U.S.

Next, they sent me to the 113th Infantry [Regiment] at Fort Dix, New Jersey. The commander was Colonel Schwarzkopf, the father of General [Norman] Schwarzkopf, from the 1991 [Gulf] War. While there, they made me a radio operator, which I didn't really know much about. Then after there, we went to the Carolinas for maneuvers. We were there for quite a while; I think that was in the summer. So on the way home from maneuvers, we stopped, I think, in West Virginia overnight. Me being on the radio, I got the message that the Japs had bombed Pearl Harbor. Of course, you write out a notice and give it to the commanding officer. But while we were eating, I couldn't keep it to myself, so the guys got mad at me for starting a rumor. But then we were called out after eating chow on the side of a hill, and a major explained to us what happened, that the Japs had bombed Pearl Harbor, and we probably wouldn't be going home—which we didn't.

'I don't want to be an officer'

Then we went fast back up to New Jersey, walking guard [duty] on the Jersey coast. This is the funny thing about walking guard. See, in January, Hitler's submarines were working off the coast. We were walking guard without any guns, and I wanted to bring my deer rifle from home so we'd have a gun; that's how well-off we were. [*Laughs*] But I remember walking guard one night and seeing five fires out to sea. The Coast Guard tried to get their boats through a six and seven-foot surf, to go out and pick up what I presumed would be people.

Well, then, this was the headquarters battery that we were in. My job was just the radio. They were lousy radios compared to

---

troops in France could operate the '03 so rapidly and accurately that the Germans thought Americans had machine guns. Army Times, www.armytimes.com/legacy/rar/1-292308-269297.php.

today. I was a corporal; our first sergeant was Sergeant Monaghan. He'd been in the Army six years—a short Irishman with black hair. He wanted me to be a corporal. To do that I had to take a test—a written test. Then I had to go before a board of officers. I took the written test, and then I went before four officers. There was a captain, and the rest were field officers. So because they were all from the city, they found out I was from the farm, and they were kidding me about making hay and milking cows and that kind of stuff.

Finally they said, 'What do you think of the outfit?' I said, 'Do you want me to really tell you what I think of the outfit?' They were all for that. I said, 'The first thing, we're walking guard and it's so cold, [but] we don't have any clothes. I wear everything that's issued to me, and half of some other guys' [clothes when I'm] on guard. The eats are leftovers from World War I, and they're also small. And another thing—I have an engineer in our company, and if we're going to win the war he should be in the engineers. There's also a telephone man, and he should be in the Signal Corps.'

Then, I shouldn't have said this, because these guys were all field officers so they were a little out of shape—

I said, 'We're really not in shape for an infantry outfit, we should be doing more calisthenics and walking.'

So I was dismissed.

When I went back, First Sergeant Monaghan said, 'How'd you make out?'

I said the written test wasn't too bad, but then they asked me what I thought of the outfit.

He said, 'Well, what'd you tell them?'

When I finished, I thought he was going to have a stroke. He sat down in a chair and for two minutes he couldn't stop laughing.

He said, 'In all my life, that's the funniest thing I've ever heard, you telling them what you thought of the outfit.' He said, 'You know what you've done? You made'—you know what it is—'the shit list. I've got to get you out of here.'

I said, 'Well, get me in the Marines.'

He said, 'No, I ain't going to get you in the Marines. I'm going to put you in for Officer School.'

I said, 'I don't want to be an officer!' He said, 'You let me handle it.'

Well, I had learned enough from being a private in the Army that if a captain or a lieutenant tells you to do something, you could always get out of it by telling them you didn't understand it. But if the first sergeant tells you to do something, you better do it, because he could make life so miserable for you the next two days you'd wish you'd never been born.

A couple of days later somebody said, 'The first sergeant wants to see you.'

I went up and he said, 'I got some papers here for you to sign. You better read them over.' It was for me to go to school at Fort Knox for Armored School. I signed the papers and that went along for two or three days. Then he wanted to see me again.

He said, 'Now this afternoon, you've got to be down to 113th headquarters. You've got to meet Colonel Schwarzkopf. And for gosh sake, get the mud off your shoes, and if you have a clean pair of pants put them on, and be shaved, and you'd better brush up on your 'Yes sirs' and 'No sirs'.'

At two o'clock I was down at headquarters. There was a corporal there and he said, 'What do you want?'

I said, 'I was told to report here.' He stuck his head in the door and said, 'Go on in.' I went in, and standing behind the desk was this rather medium-sized man, and he had a mustache under his nose just like Adolf Hitler's.

I said, 'Private reporting as ordered, sir.'

He said, 'Sit down.'

I sat down, and he stood up and said, 'The other day you took a test for corporal. You took a written test'—I found out the written test was what he used to give the New Jersey State Police when they were trying to get in—'You passed the written test, very highly. But on the oral test before the officers you didn't do so good. Tell me about it.'

So I told him exactly what happened, and he probably already knew it. But after, he said, 'Well, you're dismissed,' so that was it. I was glad to get rid of that. But then three days later, the first sergeant wanted to see me again.

He said, 'Here, I have a pass for you. You can go home for three days, and when you come back you're going to Fort Knox.'

So it took a day to get home, and I was home a day, and then I went back. When I reported back, he said everything changed. The Army said I was too high in math! [The first sergeant] said, 'You're going to Fort Sill. I've got your train tickets here, I've got your meal tickets here, pack your stuff and we'll take you up to the railroad and you'll be off.'

That was the last I was on the East Coast. I don't know how long I was on the train, but it probably took a day or more to get to Officer School at Fort Sill. I remember when we got there, the officer said, 'We've got a year's worth [of work] to do in three months. The day starts at five, and ends at eleven. You never walk; if you're going anywhere, you will run!'

That was it. So three months later I got out of there, as a second lieutenant. Then I came home, and I had orders to go to Oregon. They were activating the 91st Infantry Division, and all the new guys were going in there. They had jobs for second lieutenants and captains and everything else. I went there and this is a funny thing. They took me out of the infantry and put me in the artillery because of my math [score]! But when I got to the artillery, because I was from the infantry, they put me in service battery, which I was upset about. But later in combat, I realized that I had the best deal; I was on the go, by my own self, and not staying in one place.

Overseas

[They sent me overseas] in the first part of '44. I know [in] the 346th and 347th Battalions, we had all the guns and equipment on one train. It came straight through to Newport News, [Virginia]; it never stopped. There, a couple of days later, they brought all the troops in and they had to check all the equipment on the boat. Then in 21 days the whole division landed in Oran. [We went over in a convoy]; it was a lot of ships. The captain would let us go up in the lookout, and as far as you could see to the front, right, left, and rear, there were ships. I think they went down to the West Indies, and across to Africa, up along the coast of Africa, through the Strait of Gibraltar, to Oran. What we were supposed to do there was train for landing operations, and of course the rumor was that we were going to land in southern France. We were there a month or so. Oran had been taken, between the British and Americans.

One little incident happened there. Our army had to capture Oran from the French. I know when the guys were unloading our guns they dropped one, so it bounced. The colonel was looking overboard and yelled about it. Well, they dropped the next one so it bounced a little bit more, and I remember the colonel grabbed a carbine and shot four or five times over their heads; that ended the dropping.

From there, the Navy took us across the Mediterranean to Italy. We thought we were going to southern France, but in the middle of the Mediterranean, they opened the orders, and we were to go to Italy. Another little incident I remember was the captain of the boat said the officers could eat in the officers' mess—I was a captain. He said when we did, we needed ties. Our Colonel Lynn said to him,

'Just where in the hell do you think we got ties? Everything we have is on our backs.'

I remember climbing down that big rope ladder—it was a hundred feet wide—down to the landing craft. This was near Naples; the British army had taken Naples. So we got in the landing craft and I always thought the guy was afraid of getting mud on his boat, because he let us out in about four feet of water. When we got to shore we were all pretty wet.

Nothing really happened until we got north of Rome; the [Allies] had taken Rome [on June 4]. I remember north of Rome we got news that the landing on June 6 from England to northern France had started.

Then we were really on the Italian Campaign. The war in Italy was mainly artillery and sniper fire; there was a lot of artillery. The British had the line, and it takes a little while to prepare for battle—you've got to get a lot of ammunition up and that stuff, you know. The British Eighth Army had a lot of different nationalities; there were Canadians, Gurkhas, Sikhs. The Gurkhas were from northern India, and the Sikhs were big, tall guys with beards. There were Hindus. The Gurkhas, their religion said nothing would happen to them until the time came. I remember one instance, I was going across this bridge, and the Germans were shelling it, so we stopped and didn't get through. But the Gurkhas came up and walked right through it! They didn't believe anything would happen because everything was predetermined. The Sikhs had their own live goats with them and they didn't have utensils, just a big bowl where everything was cooked; you used your fingers. They asked me to have something to eat with them one night—you just reach in the bowl and pick something out, and that did away with all the extra utensils!

Three Strikes

 I don't know how much time elapsed there, but we were to take over for another division that had been on the line. I'll tell you this, this is a funny story. [For] a new outfit going on the line, the custom was for the new officers to go up for a day with the other guys, the old outfit. I think it was the 34th Division we were replacing. An officer from the 34th took us out, and we were driving through the countryside—no noise, no nothing. Finally he stops. He said, 'This is as far as I'm going, but that ridge over there'—about half a mile away—'that's German territory. If I were you, I would sit around here and listen to see what's going on.' There was no battle noise. It's different than on TV when they've got guns and racket, bombs bursting—there was no sound, no nothing. I was with another captain, Captain Ben, from our headquarters battery.

 So we sat there probably for an hour and there was nothing there. Between us and that ridge, there was a house. We thought we'd go over. So we went over to the house and were there maybe a half hour—again, no noise, nothing. This house was dug into the side of a hill and it slanted out, so I thought I would go around the back of the house and climb up on the roof to see what was going on. There was a red chimney there, I remember. I just scrambled up the house on my belly and got up next to the chimney; my ear was up against the chimney, looking around, still no noise, nothing. All of a sudden near me on the chimney there was a little ping, and little bits of mortar hit my cheek! Then I heard a sound—I didn't need an education to tell me that was a bullet! So I scrambled back down the roof and went inside and told Ben what happened. We stayed there for a while. Then there was a little window in this house that had little panes, about four or five inches square. So after a while I thought I had to see out of them, so I got along the right side of the window to look out. That went on for four or five minutes. All of a sudden, the next pane over from me disappeared! So I got out of there.

Captain Ben said, 'Did you ever play baseball?'

I said yes, I'd played a lot of baseball. He said, 'If I were you, I'd watch for the third strike.' So anyway, we didn't do much else; that was the first time I was under fire.

That afternoon we wandered around a little and ran into a squad of Japanese out of Hawaii, the 442nd Regiment.[2] They had been on patrol that night, I think, and were all sleeping in a ditch—they had their blankets over them, and had one guard. This guy was sitting on the chest of a big, dead German, eating his K-rations. The German had been hit with a shell, and the little [guy] said to me, 'Boy, this guy really got hit, didn't he?' I thought to myself he must be pretty hungry to be sitting there [on top of the dead body], eating that K-ration.

Afterwards we went on back to our Jeep, and that night, we were going to sleep in a ditch by the Jeep. I was pretty near sleep and I looked up, and silhouetted by the sky is somebody who says something. I look up and I can see he's got an M1 rifle, so I knew I was okay.

He said, 'Look, guys, you'd better get out of here. Intelligence tells us the Germans are supposed to attack here today, we've got it covered with artillery and mortar fire. We're pulling out and leaving it to them.' So we pulled back and then the next day we went to our outfits.

Strafed

Maybe I should tell you about Sergeant Riley and the German Messerschmitt. One day—Sergeant Riley was one of my better

---

[2] *the 442nd Regiment-* A highly decorated unit made up of mostly Japanese Americans, some of whose families were in internment camps.

men—one day I remember asking him to do some detail. I said, 'Take your friend Rayban to do this.'

He said, 'Oh no, I can't take Rayban, he's reading the Bible.'

I said, 'Reading the Bible?'

He said, 'Yes, last night while he was sleeping a shell hit terribly close to him, so ever since daylight he's been reading the Bible. I can't use him.'

I said, 'Okay, get somebody else, I'm glad somebody's reading the Bible.'

Then one day I was talking to Sergeant Riley out along the road. He's got his back up the road. About half a mile up the road, around a bend, comes a German fighter. They had two machine guns in each wing and [the pilot] had the tracers lined up on the road, so there's just a sheet of flame coming down the road. I jumped in the ditch and Riley jumped on top of me. It was only seconds when bullets were hitting around us and digging up the dirt. This is the funny thing about the mind: while I lay in the ditch, my mind returned to when I was nine or ten years old, and we had a terrible hailstorm at home. The wind was blowing at about the same angle as these bullets were coming. Every time a hailstone would hit the ground, it would splash water; the only difference was these bullets were splashing dirt. Anyway, after probably forty seconds, I said to Riley, 'Get off of me.' So he stood up. Knowing that he had his back to the plane, he couldn't see it; and since it was traveling the speed of sound, he probably couldn't hear it. I said, 'What the hell did you jump in there for?' He said, 'I jumped because you jumped.' That's a trained soldier.

Shelled

Another time, my battery was in this area about two or three acres. Between Florence and Bologna was all mountains, and there was one road—Route 65, it was a good road—and going up it were three infantry divisions: the 85th, 88th, and 91st. When we moved into this area, the firing batteries were off to the right, in front of us was a big hill, and to the left of the hill was what used to be a path—probably for cattle, but the infantry used it for their Jeeps—then off to the left there was a river. Across the river on the other side were other divisions. When we moved in there, I got a message at ten o'clock at night that nobody's on your left, and Route 65 was behind us. So I got up and looked out, and boy, it was terribly dark. You couldn't see anything. So I thought, 'I don't think the Germans can see anything more than I can.' I knew my sentries would be holed up in the cab of a truck, and they didn't like guys running around who weren't supposed to be there. So I thought we could wait till morning, so I went to sleep.

Everything went along, but one thing I did after being there for a few days: I looked in some of the foxholes and they had snow and mud in them, so I gave the first sergeant orders that I would be around before dark, and every man should have a full foxhole. That was one of the best orders I ever gave. I had a tent, probably six feet wide and eight feet long. There were two lieutenants and I, and we were playing some kind of foolish game with matches. We had a candle. We had about probably six or seven months of good artillery fire, so we were pretty well-tuned to artillery. While we were playing there, we heard a heavy gun sound, and then we heard the shell. I'll never forget, all three of us froze, because there was no use in running. It seemed like it almost skidded against the tent and went into the ground; it was a dud. I always said if I ever ran into the slave-laborer that made that fuse, I would kiss his rear end in St. Peter's Square. [*Laughs*]

Then they started shelling us, and that went on for six minutes; boy, that was heavy stuff. After a little while there was a pause, and then I thought I'd better see what's happening. But then they started shelling us again, another six or seven minutes. After that, there was a stop, and I thought, I'd better get out of this hole, you're a damn coward, you've got to get out and see where your men are. I started out on the right side of my area and I passed a couple [of men] who were in foxholes. You know when you're being shelled in a foxhole, you only take up about six inches of the bottom. So as I went on, a shell landed in front of me—now this is big stuff—and dirt went all over me, shrapnel went past my ear, and I don't really know what happened.

The next thing I know, there was a light shining in my eye and I came to after a while. It seemed like dawn was breaking in the east. I realized I was in a hole with another man. He was a Montana sheep herder. He was snoring, and I couldn't believe that; how could he be snoring with all the shelling going on? Finally, I came to a little bit more, and I went out across the battery area and I ran into one of my sergeants. He tried to tell me something; his lips moved but I remember no noise. So I went on and ran into more people and had the same problem: they tried to tell me things but there was no noise. I thought, 'Boy, these guys are really shook up.' Finally I found a guy that could talk, and he said—one of the sergeants had dragged me back into the hole with the other guy who must've been knocked out—they shelled us two more times for six or seven minutes, and only one guy was wounded and we got him to the hospital. I thought, boy, somebody knew we were behind that hill.

Finally I got my Jeep driver and I went up and told Colonel Lynn I had to move, so he said find a better place if you can. So I looked around but couldn't find a better place, so I sent a truck back to pick up sandbags. I told the guys we were going to stay here, but we're going to sandbag ourselves in. After a while, probably ten o'clock, the truck came back with sandbags. We started sandbagging where we slept. Some of them we dug into the hill. I said I wanted three feet of sandbags around the sleeping tents. I got right in and helped them. I probably didn't let anybody sit around because I thought work would be the thing to do. I remember it was noon, or afternoon, and this Corporal Slater was holding a sandbag and I had a shovel pouring in the sand. He looks up at me and says, 'Now we know why you've been such a son of a bitch all morning. We feel better already.'

After that we did pretty well, but a day or so later, down the corner of this hill comes an infantry Jeep and they've got a German officer as a prisoner. I couldn't believe my eyes—here's a German officer in full dress, with a hat on, full uniform, everything, a monocle in his right eye, his boots are as black and polished as could be. I looked at my boots, they were mud and snow, I'd probably had my trousers on for three weeks, but anyway, I thought I must be in the wrong army. [*Laughs*] They went on with him, but a day or so later a platoon of infantry had been brought back to go get some new clothes. The quartermaster had an exchange back there, where you'd get a gallon of water and you could shower and change your clothes with some other outfit that'd had it done before. Anyway, when they came back through, the platoon was all jumbled up, and I ran out and told the lieutenant to spread his men out, because when they turn that corner they may get a shell from German artillery. He came back with the dumbest answer I'd ever heard—he said, 'We're not afraid.' Twenty minutes later, the medics brought four guys out of there on litters. Whether they were killed or just wounded I never knew, but that lieutenant was really nuts not to spread those guys out. You should never take a chance if you're an officer; if you have any little bit of information, use it. I had told him what might happen, but now there were four guys gone.

Money

Two-thirds of the way through the Italian Campaign, our battalion had fired a million shells. I know the Germans fired half that many back at us. Another time, in December [1944], the Army set up the payroll, which was real silly, because there was nothing to buy. It would be Italian lira they would pay us with. I went around and paid all the guys, because you couldn't call them together—you kept them separated as much as possible. The guys were dug in the side of the hill with their tents, so I went down to them. When I got near the next-to-the last tent—you've got to always play your hunches—I was in the tent and got those guys paid, and said to them, 'Now you scram out of here and tell those guys in the last tent to come on over here.' So they came over and I paid them. One guy was missing, and it happened to be Corporal Slater. He'd been on guard that night and he was sleeping in the tent. So I sent his sergeant over to get him. So he goes in the tent, wakes him up, brings him outside the tent, and they're about eight feet outside the tent when a shell hit directly inside that tent. Because the guys were protected by those three feet of sandbags outside the tent, they didn't get hit with any shrapnel. So Slater came over to me and said, 'Captain, you keep the money.'

I said, 'No, I want to tell you something—this is the luckiest money you will ever have. Please don't spend it, just keep it.'

[This brings me to] the value of money and another story. When I played baseball [before the war], there were six of us, and we had an old car [to get around in], and we had an accident. The guy [we collided with] wanted some money because we had bent his fender. Between six guys, we had six quarters and one fifty-cent piece which we gave him to fix up his car. The opposite of that was when we got to the Po River to try to cross it. The engineers had been trying to work to build a pontoon bridge. The Germans had three fighters and they kept strafing them, so they had to quit during the daytime and wait until night; we were all waiting to cross for a mile around there. The Germans had [left] a lot of equipment there, but they'd gotten their troops across [before the bridge was destroyed]. So each one of my men either had a German horse or German car that they were monkeying around with. But there was one big covered truck there, and the doors were closed. I remember one of the guys started opening it, and I yelled, 'Don't touch it! It may be booby trapped.'

We hooked a rope on it, tied it to my Jeep, got a hundred feet away, and opened it. It was full of money, Italian lira—the same money Uncle Sam was paying us! The guys had piles of it three feet high, burning it to warm their hands! There were Italian citizens there going crazy, like 'here's these crazy Americans burning money to warm their hands!' This I learned: money, if you can't use it for something, it's not worth any more than the *Troy Record*.[3] We better leave it at that.

Peach Pie

I'll tell you a funny story. Going up Route 65, through the Apennine Mountains, there was no motorized stuff, just infantry and artillery. Of the three divisions, there would be two on the line; the artillery would stay in line, but they would change the infantry. This one time, for one reason or another, in the 91st, the artillery came back, and the next morning one of my lieutenants—we must've been five or six miles behind the line—said, 'There are orchards here, and they've got peaches.'

So I beat it over to the mess sergeant and said, 'Suppose I got some peaches, could you make peach pie?'

---

[3] *Troy Record*-local newspaper

He said, 'I think I could. I might have to substitute something but I'll try it.'

So I said to Nick Marcella, who spoke Italian, 'Take some trading stuff and go get some peaches.'

He came back with about a bushel and a half of peaches. The kitchen help went over to start peeling them, and I went over and sat down with my jack knife and was helping them peel peaches. It didn't take as long as I thought, because everyone would come over and say, 'What are you guys doing?' and I'd say, 'Can't you see we're peeling peaches? Don't you have a knife?' So they'd help us. It wasn't long before we had all the peaches peeled. Sergeant Hall, the mess sergeant, had them all in the square pans, ready to put in the ovens.

So probably twenty minutes later he came to me and said, 'I can't bake the pies, because I got orders that the general is going to inspect the kitchens.' We were in the back. He said, 'What'll I do?' I figured we might have a few hours, so I said bake the pies. So he started baking the pies. Then probably twenty or thirty minutes later, who comes driving in the yard but the general, my Colonel Lynn, and of course one of the general's staff and the driver. The general drives up to my kitchen, hops out, walks up to the kitchen, and is met by Sergeant Hall, the mess sergeant, an old army man. The general says, 'Sergeant, I've come to inspect your kitchen.' Sergeant Hall says, 'But I'm baking pies.' The general says, 'Baking pies?' He turns to Colonel Lynn, and by that time I'd appeared on the scene, and he said [to Colonel Lynn], 'Didn't you tell this man I was coming to inspect the kitchen?' He said yes, there was no argument. Then he turned to me and wanted an explanation. I told him just what happened. He seemed a little bit perturbed. Now this general was a full-blooded Iroquois Indian, and I don't think he was known for his humor. I think he was really perturbed. I would say on a number one to ten, he was perturbed about a ten.

Anyway, he went back to his Jeep and got in. Colonel Lynn got in and he wasn't smiling either. Then when they drove out, even the driver spun the wheels. I always think the reason the general was so perturbed, that morning he probably got up and went to get a cup of coffee, and a new man on the job gave him lukewarm coffee and the dried eggs weren't up to swath; he couldn't find his kitchen inspecting gloves; his staff told him he had to inspect the kitchens; he gets out and there's dust on the star; and he's driving over three miles to the 347th Battalion over roads that Julius Caesar had built and no one had done anything with them since. He picks up the colonel and probably thinks, 'Of the 300 or 400 kitchens in the Fifth Army, I had to pick this dummy who's baking pies.' Well, the next day Colonel Lynn says, 'Well, you came the nearest to getting court-martialed of anyone I ever knew.' I know the general was after the colonel three different times—I learned through the grapevine—to relieve me of command. I always wondered why the general didn't relieve me. But you know around a general's headquarters, there's usually a *Stars and Stripes* reporter, or one from the Fifth Army. I can see the front page of *Stars and Stripes*— 'Captain gets relieved of command for giving his men peach pies.' [*Laughs*] Well, I never heard more about the peach pies till Colonel Lynn—he and I had always exchanged Christmas cards—said coming back on the boat—he came from the upper crust of the Army—that the funniest thing that happened during the whole Italian Campaign was the peach pies [incident]! It must've been a tale the colonel told, because on the Christmas cards, his wife would write out, 'Merry Christmas to the man who thought enough of his men to give them peach pies.'

On the Road

I'll tell you a little story about my Jeep driver. He was about 18 or 19 years old, and I think the reason First Sergeant Weiss talked me into using him was because he could never find him to do any work. But anyway, we got along well. When we moved, my job was to get everybody organized—the kitchen, the latrine—and see that was done and that they were spread out, and he would find a place for our Jeep. Anyway, this little town where Highway 65 went through, on the outside of it, [the road] went around a hill. Out at about eleven o'clock across the way, about three quarters of a mile, the Germans had an 88mm gun dug into the middle of the mountain. The 88 was probably the best gun of any army in all of WWII. It was a 3-inch gun, and they used it for anti-aircraft, they used it against tanks, and they would shoot at a man with it, because they figured if there was one man there was usually another. Well, they had an area outside this town that was under observation and had a man on this gun. Whenever a truck would go across this 200 to 250-yard area, he would shoot at them. After a while, we knew what that area was. So when we got up there we would stop, look for shell holes, and then go as fast as we could over that area. But this morning, for some reason or another—I must've been asleep—the sun was out bright and early, and we were about a quarter of a mile across there when I woke up. My driver was only about a quarter of the way across, and I said, 'Get this damn Jeep moving.' Just then, about thirty or forty feet ahead of us, a shell landed in the road. Edge [the driver] says, 'Look, if we'd been going faster, we'd have caught that one.' So we got to the other end and we had a one-way discussion that never again would a shell land in front of us while we were going over there.

    I got even with him a few days later. Now down below us was a house. Edge and I had taken it over—it was right near the shelling but it was near the front. The Italian houses were built in the side of a hill. There would be an entryway and a middle room, then another room, I guess a bedroom. The Germans did a lot of stuff that seemed to be by clockwork. One day, below this house at about four o'clock, they dropped in one shell. Then they moved up to the road with the whole battery shelling. So this one shell would give them an idea of where they were hitting, and of course the other guns would move their sights with that gun. The second day the same thing happened at about four o'clock—why I happen to remember that, I don't know. But then another day, later, for some reason or another, I was either reading or doing some paperwork in this house, in the room to the front—it was the most open. I looked at my watch and it was about four o'clock. I thought, maybe the German data is a bit better today; they'd been eighty yards below the house, then they were forty. So I moved out of that room and Edge was in the middle room, and I said, 'Edge, come on out of this room, maybe this guy's data is a little better today.' But he didn't move. So I got to the entrance room, which was right off the ground. I got there, and who runs by me but Edge, and he's covered in mortar. He said, 'You can't believe it, that room you just left ain't there anymore.' That was pretty lucky. Just playing hunches, I guess.

When we were attacking or something there would be more artillery from the Germans. During one period, I think the maintenance unit of our battalion changed 155 tires in eight days, from Monday to Monday. See, a shell could come and hit near a truck and not do too much damage, but it would blow the tires from the shrapnel. One little thing I probably should've had, but this Sergeant Riley—the one that was with me with the strafing incident—I remember him this one day, too. Our trucks used to go down through Florence, then on to Leghorn, the depot, to pick up ammunition for the artillery. They would have four or five tons on the trucks. Coming back through, the first one got hit with a shell—it blew his tire and the driver jumped out and left the truck there. So the guys behind him were all stacked up, although they'd been spaced. They were all there and the Germans had been doing quite a bit of shelling in that area, right at the spot where the trucks were.

So I looked and I thought when it got dark we'd get the trucks out of there—the other drivers had to go out too because they couldn't move. After a while, I got a note from headquarters to move the trucks. Well, I took a look again, and the shells were coming in pretty heavy. I thought, 'If headquarters wants the trucks moved, they can come right out and move them themselves.'

So that didn't last very long—half an hour later they said I had to move the trucks because they wanted to get tanks through. Not thinking—Sergeant Riley happened to be there—I said, 'Sergeant, we've got to move the trucks.'

And he said, 'Captain, I don't have the guts to send a man in there.'

I said, 'Sergeant, if I go, suppose you can find a couple of men?'

He said yes. So, he came back with a couple of men—they weren't too enthused about it.

But I said, 'We'll go over as near as we can, because you know with shelling in an area, there's dispersion.'

So we got as near as we could, and I picked out what trucks we were going to take. Now these Germans do everything by clock; we had to check them. So I took my watch out, and for two minutes, the shells would be coming in real fast, and for two minutes, they'd be slack. Then two more minutes there'd be shells coming in fast, and two minutes they'd be slack.

So I said, 'The next time after shelling, I'm going to yell 'Go!' We've got two minutes to get the trucks.' And we got the trucks. I should've written up a citation for those guys, but we were so happy to get out of there we didn't bother with any citations.

*

New Officers

At the end of the war we were crossing the Po [River]. The 10th Mountain [Division] was on the other side, along with the 92nd, which was Eleanor Roosevelt's division, the all-colored troops. Most of the officers were white, but it was a colored division. The 10th Mountain was over on our left. At the end of the war, we were combat teams, and I remember we had a regiment of infantry and a battalion of artillery. The orders were to go up this road and go as fast and far as you can. Pay no attention to anybody on the right or left and just get through the German army; if you can get behind them, the war will be over. Well, in front of us it seemed like there was a bigger unit of Germans retreating, and they would leave out units of rear guards once in a while. They would stop us with firefights. This one time, they stopped for a little firefight. Of course, the artillery is in a line, one behind the other. I remember talking with the guys, bullshitting with them, you know. I had new lieutenants and new replacements. This new lieutenant had been in the Pentagon all during the war.

Everybody knew the ones you had the most trouble with were the ones who'd just come in. The old soldiers knew to stay right on that road. Out about ninety degrees to the road was this windbreak, out probably a hundred yards. Out at the end of this windbreak to the right this lieutenant called me out. He'd heard something back at the Pentagon about living off the land and thought there was a pig or a sheep or something. He had his pistol out and he calls me up, so I'm thinking that there's some animal out there. I walk right out of the hedgerow, a little unconcerned. I get to the end of the hedgerow, and off to my left, probably twenty-five or thirty yards, is a German gun emplacement manned by two German soldiers, each with a light machine now aimed at me. Now, there's 2,500 to 3,000 men within a quarter mile of me, and [these

Germans] really didn't want to start a war. But the only thing I could think of, I remember sliding into second base when I played baseball and the umpire would stretch out his hands, and that's what I did. [*Gestures with arms out*] They laid the guns on the edge of the earthworks, and I waved this lieutenant back to our column. When we got back, I explained to him that if he wanted to go get himself killed that was his business, but to call me out there, that was a different thing. I said he should stay in line there or I might shoot him myself!

I hadn't gotten over that, then this other new guy was of German descent. He hands me this German Luger, and says, 'You're a captain, here's a gun for you.' It's all engraved with gold.

I said, 'Where in the devil did you get a gun like that?'

He said, 'Over here in the gully.'

He said there was a German colonel that wanted to surrender to an officer. You know there were two departments of the German army, the old German Army and the Nazis.

So I said, 'Did you bring him in?'

He said, 'No, I shot him.'

I felt bad about that. I was all ready to ball him out for shooting a guy when I realized they had sent him over from the States to shoot Germans; so that was that.

'*A column of German infantry*'

I no more than got over that and the firefight had stopped. Up the road, there was a town about three miles up. Colonel Lynn, the artillery commander, said, 'I think we'll be up to that town. I want you to go up there and pick out a spot for the battalion to come in.'

So I went out to the right of this main road, found a dirt road, and got to the town. There were some civilians there and they were glad to see us, but I went outside the town, found a good place for the battalion, and after looking that over, I went back to the road, and who comes by but an infantry scout. He's all alone and he's coming back—we were on kind of a ridge. He said, 'Watch it, guys, that valley there is full of Germans.' So we went back to the town.

The road I came in on and the main road come together in a Y. So I situated there because I had been told to stay there till the battalion got there. The townspeople wanted to talk, but it started getting late. I told them to get inside and stay inside, because I had a machine gunner on the Jeep, and if we saw anything move [after dark] we may shoot. I told them to stay inside and if there was any firing, to get in the cellar or something. It's pretty dusky, and who comes in to pick us up but this Captain Ben. He calls me up and says, 'Wiley, what the hell are you doing up here? Follow me.' Captain Ben was a guy who always smoked cigars, which I thought was a funny thing. Actually, most of the time he was out of cigars, but he had about a third of it in his mouth.

I said, 'What the hell are you so excited about?'

[Captain Ben] said, 'Here I was trying to get something to eat and the colonel [ordered me to head out and look for you]. I went back and found out which way you went. I got my Jeep and driver and started up the road. In front of me was a column of vehicles, so I told my driver to pass them. In the dusk, we got about halfway up the column, and I looked up and everyone had a German helmet on. I told my driver to jump this ditch and we went around and got up to you!' That was probably a [whole] column of German infantry. Can you imagine? I always wondered what happened to that cigar in his mouth. [*Laughs*] They were still moving north to the Alps. I think about three or four days later we got word that they were surrendering.

*

No Flags

At the end I was at Gorizia, which is on the Yugoslav border. There was just a little creek between us and Yugoslavia. Everything was as quiet as could be. It was a funny thing, no celebration, [no flag waving]. Everyone wonders about flags; I don't ever remember seeing an American flag in all of combat because you were just telling the Germans where you were.

I think they were planning to send us to Japan. That's what happened to me. They had an order that the captains who had so many points could go home. I had about a hundred more points, so I said to my colonel, 'Well, it looks like I'll be going home.'

He said, 'No, you won't be going home. If I have to go to Japan, you're going to go.'

But this I never understood either. I was a captain all the time. We were still in Italy, getting ready for a boat to come in and pick us up to go to Japan. I remember I'm sitting on a cot talking to Captain Ben. A German prisoner walked by. He said the war was over.

I said, 'How the hell do you know?'

He said, 'It came in on my radio.'

The boat had come in to take us to Japan, and he was two days late because he'd stayed in New York to wait for milk to arrive from Wisconsin. The next day we loaded on the boat and it turned around and brought us home. [So, in late] 1945 I was home and on furlough. Then I had to go back and help deactivate the division. I met Ruth and then thirty days later we got married. That was 67 years ago. [*Laughter in room from wife and others*] Then we went back to deactivate the division and get all the stuff that we took overseas. Somebody had to sign for it, you know; the battery commanders and so forth had to go back.

Rank

I'm getting out of the Army and on my papers they have, 'Major.' I said, 'Jesus, don't put me down as major! In New York State if I'm a captain I get $250, if I'm a field officer I don't get anything.'

He says, 'You've been a major for a long time.'

I said, 'I have?'

He said, 'I got the orders right here.'

I never got the orders. But the only thing I can figure is when my colonel said I wasn't going home, a major wouldn't get to go home. I was probably in for major then and didn't even know it! The paperwork going overseas would be separated from us and was all screwed up. Then again I owed the [government] some money because my sister was getting an allotment from home and they paid me $250 for my allotment. The finance officer down in Camp Rucker, Alabama, said, 'Here's all the papers where you owe the Army.'

I said, 'Is this all the paper?'

He said, 'Yes.' So I threw them in the wastepaper basket and never heard from them again. That must've been the orders.

*

I got discharged February 6, 1946. I came back to New York, I stayed around the farm. It was about Thanksgiving time, I guess. Then this guy that owned this business in Valley Falls, New York, he and his partner wanted to sell the thing and came to the house two or three times to see if we wanted to be involved in buying it. Of course, there were sixteen million guys in the Army and there weren't going to be too many jobs [when they got out]. That's when we bought this business in Valley Falls. It was a feed and coal business, something new. This is a funny thing. When I got out of the Army I came to Albany, got a bus up to the end of the bus line, and walked home. Then I stopped at my brother's place at the farm in the morning for breakfast. I said to him, 'Boy, these eggs don't have any taste.' He was quite insulted. Of course, the eggs we had had in the army were probably six months old; they were dried.

*

I've been a life member of the VFW and the Legion. I had so many new things with being in business. Then I was in politics. First they wanted me to run for supervisor, so I was supervisor of the town for six years. Then we were running this business with my brother, and I was president. Then we moved over to where we are now with what was a wholesale hardware and lumber center. That was a lot of work. Then I got involved in the county legislature, I was finance chairman. Then I was a Hudson Valley [Community College] trustee. According to my wife, I spent a lot of time away from home.

[The wartime experience] sure changes your life. It's funny seeing the guys from Iraq come back and they have stress, but I never had stress. I always wondered about this. When I went to district school they used to call me the 'laughing fool.' When I went to high school, under my picture they had a bit of mirth, and in the history they said, *'Whenever there was a bunch of guys having a lot of fun and raising a deuce and laughing, Ab would be there.'* And probably two years ago, I met a girl working in the bank whose grandmother had been a friend. I said, 'Remind your grandmother you saw me.' She came back a couple of weeks later and said her grandmother was so happy, that I was always the one laughing and having a good time. Now, my wife has never seen me laugh and never heard me cry. That's kind of a funny thing, how do you figure that out? It's a mystery. So it's changed me.[4]

---

[4] *So it's changed me*-On the day that Mr. Wiley passed, his grandson wrote: 'For the rest of his life, he would see the world through the lenses of that experience of the war. He believed that every issue could be addressed through the application of some lesson he'd learned in the army or would

Mr. Wiley passed away at home at the age of 100 years and eight months in August 2017.

---

draw parallels to an experience during the war. He treated that experience as the source of wisdom that guided him throughout his life. He was even shaped in his personality: he had had a reputation as something of a joker before the war, but afterward, although a wry comment might drop from his lips from time to time, he had taken on a much more serious, stoic demeanor.'

The Cannoneer

William Millette was born on August 8, 1925, in Oneonta, New York. He attended Christian Brothers Academy but was forced to graduate early in three years due to the draft quotas. He was drafted into the Army in 1944 and became an artilleryman as part of a task force with the 86th Infantry Regiment of the 10th Mountain Division. 'When we jumped off on April 14; our orders were to go like hell, pell-mell, and not to let anything stop us, get over the Po River and seal the Brenner Pass to prevent the Germans from getting back in there. At that time, there was a great deal of concern that if the Germans got back into those mountains, we'd be ten years digging them out.' He gave this interview in 2004 at the age of 78.

William A. Millette

I received basic training at Fort Sill, Oklahoma, in the pack artillery. Pack artillery is a special arm of the army's artillery. Their weapon is the 75-millimeter pack howitzer, which can be broken down and disassembled into ten individual pieces and mounted and carried by six army mules. To qualify to get into the pack artillery, when you went through the reception center at Fort Sill, a sergeant stood at the top of the line and measured everybody going through. Anyone 5'10" or taller went in the pack artillery. Everyone less than that went to the regular artillery.

It was very strenuous training. Our PT was ongoing constantly to keep us in top physical shape. As I recall, the only time we ever rode was the time that the trucks picked us up at the train and the time the trucks took us back to the train when we left Sill. After our second or third week of basic training, we never walked less than 14 miles a day.

Basically, in a pack artillery section, there are 13 people. There was a chief of section and six cannoneers and six mule handlers. It took approximately a minute to disassemble that howitzer and pack it onto a mule or take it off the mule and assemble it. We could have that howitzer off a mule in less than a minute, ready to fire. That's a well-trained crew. Due to the type of our training and the type of weapon we're training on and the potential for where we would be serving, we had to qualify in all types of weapons, because most of the pack artillery battalions were then serving in the South Pacific. Most of them, a lot of them, were the Merrill's Marauders.[5]

I finished my basic training, was sent to Camp Carson, Colorado, and assigned to the 613th Pack Artillery Battalion. Fortunately for me, when I got to Carson, the 613th had already shipped out to the West Coast, heading for the South Pacific. At that time, they didn't know what to do with us. After about two or three days of doing nothing, they sent us over to a place called Cheyenne Mountain at Camp Carson for rock climbing. We got our shipping orders to go to Camp Hale, Colorado, with the 10th Mountain Division.

While at Carson, while we're rock climbing, as each day progressed and we ascended higher into the rocks and so forth and looked down, I was not particularly happy with what I saw below me. Upon our return to our barracks, there was a big bulletin issuing a call for immediate volunteers for the airborne.

I said to this one fella from Chicago, 'I've had enough of this rock climbing.' We went over and volunteered to join the paratroopers.

---

[5] *Merrill's Marauders*- specialized Army force that conducted deep-penetration missions behind Japanese lines in the China-Burma-India Theater of Operations.

Took our physical, passed with flying colors. We're all set. Unfortunately, at that time, we got shipping orders to go to the 10th Mountain. Got to the 10th Mountain, informed the sergeant at wherever we were at, some headquarters, that we wouldn't be staying with the 10th Mountain. We were going to go in the airborne. We were very politely but firmly informed that our days in the airborne were over—'You're now in the 10th Mountain and you're going to stay here.' That was it.

Then, we went from Camp Hale to Camp Swift, Texas, for flat land training, the main purpose being that the difference in altitudes from firing weapons and mortars and artillery at 11,000 and 12,000 feet elevation is a lot different from firing at ground level. Your ballistics are a lot different. We had to be trained for that.

We also had to be proficient in some skiing and be able to move around in the snow, because many times, we had to [break a path] for the mules going through the snow. Sometimes the snow was crusted and it would eat into their skin. Snowshoes were [necessary] and we had to be proficient in using them.

*

The 10th was made up of three mountain infantry regiments, the 85th, the 86th, and 87th mountain infantry regiments. These were supported by the 604th, the 605th, and the 616th pack artillery battalions into regimental combat teams.

We left the United States in December of '44. We got over there early January. [Our destination was] Naples, which we didn't know at the time until we got on board the *USS Meigs*. I asked one of the crew members where we were heading. He said this, and I always remember his remark. He said, 'This tub has been nowhere but Naples.' We knew we were heading for Italy.

We got to Italy. We disembarked, walked down the quay, and got on an LCI.[6] The LCI was supposed to take us up the coast of Leghorn. On our way up, we had a tremendous storm in the Mediterranean. I might add that an awful lot of our guys were seasick. It was unbelievable. The storm was so bad that the fantail back where the latrine was cracked right in half! We had to turn around and put into port.

We went into a staging area around Pisa Lucca, where we had to get the howitzers and get cleaned up and oriented. Then, we were trucked up to a place called Lizzano in Belvedere, where we put our weapons in and began our firing missions prior to the infantry assault on Belvedere and Riva Ridge. Then, we went from there up through the campaign with the rest of the division.

My particular assignment, while I was not assigned to a particular gun section as a cannoneer or whatever, was as a security person with a BAR to provide perimeter security for the battery. That meant being out two, three, 400 yards in front of them to intercept enemy patrols and that type of thing. Also, to provide security for our forward observers in the observation point. As a result, I was up on the OP when we supported the 86th when they went up the Riva Ridge, to provide security for our forward observers. We had incidents where the Germans counterattacked and sought out weak spots. I loved the BAR, contrary to a lot of people, who hated it. The only reason I could think they hated it, they didn't know how to handle it or they didn't maintain it, or keep it clean. I kept mine immaculate at all times. I never had a problem with it, [but the bipod] got an early death. [*Laughs*]

*

---

[6] *got on an LCI*- Landing Craft, Infantry

Pack Mules

We had 5,000 mules in our division. It was basically our organic transportation. I know every artillery battalion had a service battery. That was where the shoers were and the saddle makers; these guys were really good. The mules carried their own food. On those mules, they had what they call a Phillips pack saddle. They were common for every mule and they had a rack, an adapter on the top of the saddle, which was to put different parts of the howitzer on, plus carrying hay, oats, and grain and that type of thing or water, ammunition, whatever.

At that time, they had nothing but the best of leather. Civilians couldn't get leather. These guys had the best leather you could get. The mules shied [when the cannon was fired]. They're very sensitive to noise and so forth. But believe me when I tell you, there is nothing on this God's earth as ornery as a Missouri mule. They are intelligent. They're hard. They're tough. A mule is a lot smarter than a horse will ever be. I've seen them do stuff that was unbelievable. I had one take off on me and I'm holding the holds and I can't hold them. He ran me up towards a tree; he ran so close to that tree, I had to let go of the halter. They're just bad news. I've been kicked by one. We had a stable sergeant, a Southern boy from South Carolina. Mules were his specialty. He said, 'I don't want to see you boys smoking.' He got some of the guys' chewing tobacco, me included. I chewed tobacco until I was cleaning out the hoof of one of our mules. He just drew back that hoof and kicked me square in the butt and sent me flying. When he did that, I swallowed the cud. I'll tell you. I was sick for two days. [*Laughs*] That was one amusing incident about the mules, but they were an amazing animal. They're sure-footed and just as nice as any horse. They're really, really tough.

Obviously, they weren't the only ones we had. The Italian Alpini did a lot of service for the 10th.[7] In fact, they had an Alpini mountain company pack unit attached to each regiment. All the regiments in their service companies had pack platoons and used mules. They had to; that's the only way they could get ammunition and water up in the mountains. The problem was that although we were a pack artillery and trained with mules, we didn't get our own mules. In fact, we were one of a very few units, the only unit that I know of, that used the mules when we jumped off on April 14 on our final offensive out of the Apennines. Our G.I. mules were big animals. These were a little bit smaller.

When we jumped off on April 14, we were part of a task force with the 86th Infantry. Our orders were to go like hell, pell-mell, and not to let anything stop us, get over the Po River and seal the Brenner Pass to prevent the Germans from getting back in there. At that time, there was a great deal of concern that if the Germans got back into those mountains, we'd be ten years digging them out.

*

The Tunnels

Our combat ended on May 2, 1945. Today is the anniversary of one of our big campaigns, April 30th, up on Lago di Garda in Northern Italy, when our battery went in on an amphibious assault in DUKWs to go around blowing out tunnels on the lake to support our infantry. We disassembled the howitzers, put them on the DUKWs with the ammunition, and went up the lake. Then, when the DUKWs pulled into a disembark area, where we were under fire, we hand-carried those pieces up a steep embankment onto the road.

---

[7] *Italian Alpini-* an elite mountain warfare troops of the Italian Army.

Lago di Garda is a very beautiful lake. In fact, Mussolini had one of his palaces up there. The road was built right into the side of the mountain and a series of five or six tunnels. The Germans, in their retreat, blew some of these tunnels to halt our progress. As a result, we had to go around them in DUKWs to support our infantry. In fact, the Germans had a couple of 88s up at the head up in Torbole that were firing into our troops. We went up and we duked them out. This is where I got my Bronze Star, and we duked them out, then knocked the 88s out.

Some of our infantry were actually trapped up there because, even if they had to, they couldn't get back down because the tunnels were blowing up behind them. The Germans, in their haste to blow these tunnels, had prematurely blown one and trapped one of their own trucks full of engineers. I think there were 15 or 20 German soldiers in that truck that were killed.

Lago del Predil

Then, our infantry went into Torbole. We went in behind them. The war ended [in Italy] on May 2.

We were there for a little while up in Torbole. Then, we got orders to move to the east coast; they were having some problems in Trieste with the Yugoslavians. The Yugoslavs moved into Trieste and claimed that port city as their own, which was an Italian city. We had orders to go across the top of Italy to Trieste, which we did.

We were over there with the British. Finally, the British conned the Yugoslavs into surrendering. They invited them into a huge soccer field. These guys were armed right to the teeth. The British colonel invited them to lay down their arms. The war was over. 'Go home to your farms, your homes, and leave your weapons here.' When he said that, the Yugos became a little restless. Then—and I always remember the colonel saying this, he had an interpreter—'If you chose not to lay down your weapons, look behind you or around you.' The place was completely surrounded with British and American troops with automatic weapons. They got the message and dropped their weapons and filed out.

We went up into a little place called Lago del Predil, right in the corner of Yugoslavia, Austria, and Italy. Beautiful little valley, and there we were. We stayed on occupation until we came home. We visited over and over and got a chance to go over to Austria, do some skiing, did a lot of road work, exercising; life was good then.

[On one of our excursions], we came across huge, huge caverns, with doors, I don't know, 15-feet wide probably. [These huge chambers] were dug into the mountain. Fortunately, we had engineers with us; we probed them for mines and booby traps. The first one we went into was a cavern loaded with brand-new Pratt-Whitney airplane engines from Ohio; I remember they were made in Ohio somewhere. Another of the big caverns we went into was just loaded with kegs of German beer, German brandy, and champagne that you would not believe. Fortunately, our division people got the trucks and we got that stuff out of there before one of the other divisions from southern France was to come up to meet us in the Brenner Pass. As a result, when we went up into Predil, everybody got a huge ration of champagne, brandy, and whatever. We had a good time. [*Laughs*]

Civilians

We had some contact with the Italian people. Our relations, as far as I know, were excellent. I know we were in one position, and there's a little farmhouse down to our right. We watched this woman come out every once in a while; we were there for a while. She came out, obviously very, very pregnant, and that's the first time I ever realized how the Italians made spaghetti; they rolled it out. They brought it out and laid it over the clothes line, and that's where there's a loop in it to dry.

She had her baby while she was there, our medics were there to help her and so forth. The biggest problem we had was with the children, the kids. God! They were just so poor, it was unbelievable. As a result, you had to watch your equipment, because they would come in and take whatever they could get. They were just completely poverty-stricken. When we finished [our missions], our mess sections were in operation, we were getting hot food and so forth. They'd stand at the end of the mess line and take your scraps any way they could get them. Coffee, they'd take coffee. They were begging for cigarettes and candy and so forth. They were not above taking something if you laid it down; if it had any value, it would be gone.

I had a very fortunate experience. When we were in Predil, we used to bring our clothing up to the Italian family up in the northern end of the lake. When we got ready to leave, they invited three of us up to have a farewell dinner on a Sunday. I think it was a 12 or 13-course dinner. My God, they had pasta, they had all kinds of stuff. One of the items they had, which I didn't recognize at first, was snails in sauce. They treated us very well. Obviously, they did our washing, our clothes, and so forth, which we paid for. That was a nice experience for them. They were very nice people.

[The war in Italy was over], but the war was still going on in the Pacific. We were informed that since we were actually the last division to arrive in Italy, we were going to be redeployed to the United States, refitted, and shipped to the Pacific. I have the plans. I came by some plans some years ago of our position in the final assault on Japan.

Another interesting point about our unit's artillery that was top secret at that time was that they shipped all of our artillery to the

Greeks to use in their army. We sent something like 20 or 24 of our artillerymen along with them to train the Greek army in their use. The Greeks were fighting for their independence against the communists in Greece. They were having a real battle; they asked for help. Officially, President Roosevelt, being the liberal that he was, thought he could control Joe Stalin and didn't want to offend the communists. That never came out. It was never made public until many years later.

When we found out we were heading for the South Pacific to go heading for Japan, [it was tough]. When [the war in the Pacific ended], we were very relieved that we had survived, as obviously a lot of our guys did not. There were some bittersweet moments. We had our memorial services and that type of thing. In our division association, we had many, many annual, semi-annual meetings and so forth. We chat personally. We have never, ever, ever forgotten these people who we lost over there; there's a huge cemetery in Florence where they're buried. We have the division association that goes back to Italy every two or three years, and it's always a stop at the Florence cemetery. We have a memorial service. Whenever we gather the group, they're always remembered. And I think World War II made me appreciate more of what life is all about.

Mr. Millette passed away at the age of 92 in 2017.

D-DAY

[ORIGINAL SELECTIONS FROM VOLUME 5:
D-DAY AND BEYOND]

On June 4, 1944, Rome, the first formerly Axis capital, fell to the American Fifth Army. On the five-month push from Cassino to Rome, 100,000 Americans had been killed or wounded. Not long after the first celebratory bottles of wine were emptied on the streets of Rome, the Allied cross-channel invasion in the early hours of June 6 knocked Mark Clark's Fifth Army off of the front pages. Overnight, the conquest of Italy became a sideshow; for over a year the needs of Operation Overlord siphoned off top commanders, men, and materiel from the Italian campaign.

The Normandy front had opened.

The Cryptographer

Harry Rosenthal was drafted in 1943 out of high school. From an inauspicious start, he rose to being selected as a courier and decoder aboard an important Navy flagship, the USS Bayfield, *during the Normandy landings and afterwards. He was anxious to sit for this 2002 interview.*

Harry Rosenthal

I was born on March 20, 1924 in Brooklyn. I had a high school education; I didn't go beyond that, and I had plenty of jobs up until the time the war broke out, then you couldn't get any jobs because you were eligible for the draft. Oh, I remember Pearl Harbor, but I didn't know it was a U.S. possession. I didn't know what it meant, Territory of Hawaii, until I got to Pearl Harbor. This is about three years later. I was stationed there for a year from 1944, I think, September to September '45. I was in the streets when I heard about it, but I don't know what I was doing. Maybe I was playing ball or... I know it was a Sunday, I remember that. And when we heard that we said, 'Where's that?' So we found out later where it was.

So, I waited [for my turn]. And then when it came my turn, they sent me a letter, 'Greetings and salutations.' At the time, Grand Central Terminal was the induction center, so we went there, the big station, and there was an Army officer, lieutenant, and a young second lieutenant from the Navy, a JG, junior grade. And there was a Marine lieutenant. When they saw all the blue marks on my health chart, they [wanted to] put me in the Marines or the Navy. And I said to them, 'No,' I said, 'I want to go to the Army.'

He said, 'I'm sorry, son, you have no choice. You can either enlist in the Navy or the Marines.'

I said, 'I can be drafted?'

He says, 'No, not at this time.'

So I went to the Navy, and I enlisted. They gave me a week off and we went down to, I think it was 20 Whitehall Street, not far from where the World Trade Center was. It wasn't there then, of course. And then they had the people, the inductees... in the Navy there's regular Navy, I think there's USNR Naval Reserve, and there were Seabees. So, I didn't know what to do. And I found out later, never volunteer. I raised my hand. I said, 'I want to go into this

Seabees,' which is construction battalion. And I found out that there, you fight and you work. Well, if I have to fight, why should I work? So I got out of it, took me two hours before another lieutenant says, 'You're in here now, you stay in this group here.'

I said, 'No, I want to go in the Naval Reserve.'

So he said, 'Okay, get back with the other bunch.' By that time, I was regular Navy, so I didn't go to the Seabees, because I knew the Marines and the Navy were in the Pacific, and it was pretty bad there. I didn't know I was going to go to Normandy. I got my share, anyway.

I think it was February '43. February 19, they sent us up to a boot camp in Sampson, New York, right near the Canadian border. And we were in boot training for about three months, but they were well equipped. We went around the drill field with a full sea bag, and that was pretty heavy walking around there and marching cadence. And then what we had to do was learn how to use whaleboats, which are aboard ship, and they're used for safety when a ship is going under. Well, we didn't have any whaleboats to practice on, so we had beams to sit on and something in the shape of a boat that was arched like a whaleboat, it was about 25 feet long, I think. And then we had two by fours used as oars, so eight of us on one side of the two by fours and eight on the other side. And it was snowing, and the guy at the helm was hollering, 'Heave-ho,' something like that, and it looked like Washington crossing the Delaware with the snow coming down. We were on grass that you couldn't see, and it's full of snow, and here we were, 'Heave-ho,' just to get the idea.

So we did that a few times, and then I wasn't used to that kind of life, washing clothes. [It was my first time] away from home. Well, there were some good times in it, but that came later on. But over there in boot camp it was very cold, and I wasn't used to eating that kind of food. I don't know. I don't know what SOS was. Oh, you know what that is, right? So, and then I never had any of that food before. I used to go to the PX. Well, the Army closed the PX. We didn't call it that. We called candy 'pogey-bait' and ice cream 'gedunk.' We had that. I used to go there to eat the candies and the ice cream instead of the food. Whenever I had money in my pocket, I went over there to eat. I couldn't stand the food, unless sometimes on a Sunday they'd bake cake or they gave you eggs, but I got used to the food later on in different parts of the world.

We stayed three months, and then they shipped us to the *USS Alcor*, a training ship. That was in Norfolk, Virginia. The ship never left port, it stayed there. And well, we were on there for about three months, I think. We used to get liberty weekend passes or liberty by the day. Place was full of sailors, loaded with sailors; nobody liked sailors there. They couldn't wait for us to leave, couldn't wait to get rid of them, and then another batch would come in from different training stations. So yeah, I stayed there, and then they shipped us out.

Crossing the Atlantic

They sent us from there on an LST pulling out of Norfolk, Virginia, to Halifax, Nova Scotia. Well, we don't know what we were going into, but there were ten or so LSTs. I was on LST 531, and there were six British corvettes convoying a 72-ship convoy across the North Atlantic. There were German U-boats there, and it was freezing. The guy in the forecastle along the bow of the ship, he had about 40 pounds of gear on him, and you couldn't even see his face and his eyes. And he was always at it, he's looking out there for subs. And then they would give us duty, 24 hours on and 24 off on the watch. We had about a 30-foot tower to scale, it's like the firemen use. It's a long pole, and it's got bars on the side to grab on. Out in the North Atlantic it was stormy and ice cold, and you couldn't see anything at night. I don't see how you could see a sub with a periscope then, impossible. And the weather was bad, and the ship would pitch at a 25, 30-degree angle, and you're up there and knocking on the door, and he's a lieutenant JG. He says, 'All's well below, sir.' 'Aye-aye.' And you climbed back down there, and you go below decks, you know, where it's warmer.

The LST was loaded with tanks, trucks, jeeps, ammo, everything. So about 500 miles out, two LSTs turned back, they had problems. Well, we were now about 1500 miles, the point of no return. And we had to hobble into Glasgow, Scotland, because the rudder was broken. They had three of us, they were calling down degrees of where to steer the ship, and we'd all take turns. So we did that, 1500 miles into Glasgow, but we stayed and dried out overnight.

*

We went down the English Channel via the Irish Sea, and we went to Plymouth, England. That was March of 1944, and when we got there, well, we saw a bombed-out city. They put us in Quonset huts or barracks, and we saw these balloons up there with cables attached and realized they were filled with hydrogen. And that was for the German Luftwaffe, so they would not come in and strafe the city, which they did [anyway].

We stayed there, and I was a courier there, but I didn't know how to drive, and I didn't want to learn how to drive. So there's this other sailor, he was from upstate New York, and I used to wake him, Haran. I used to wake him up every hour as long as I was on duty, because I needed a car driver. So he got disgusted, and he says, 'I'm going to teach you to drive. So I got behind the jeep with him, and I didn't know how to shift with the clutch and all that. And we were jerking. We had to go about two or three miles away, just a little letter, but it was high security, and it was [for] the British about two miles away. Well, I stepped on the gas, and he almost flew out. And I was going fast and slow, and I finally got there and he was with me. Then he says, 'Next time, don't wake me up anymore.'

So I was really nervous: Don't wake him up anymore. So I got the .45 on my hip, and I got a jeep. I used to go to the motor pool, and each gate was about 20 feet wide because they have trucks and weapons carriers. So one day he didn't have any jeeps, and he doesn't know anything from anything, this guy on duty. I give him my pass and he gives me a weapons carrier, and that thing... well, they look amphibious, they're huge, and 10 forward speeds. I says, 'Where do I start?' And I was embarrassed. I couldn't wait for him to go inside. I feel he was hidden from my view. So I got up, I drove there, but I was really nervous with that big thing. And I got there and I got back, and as I progressed, you know, I got to be a little bit better. So I ended up learning to drive, not too well over there, but we stayed there about three months. And the city was all bombed out, and they ran dances in the local church, and we didn't have too many good times. And you couldn't get any sweets, no candies, nothing at all. And I love the sweets.

So after that March, April, May... the LST 531 went out for maneuvers, and it was sunk by a tin fish, a torpedo. It hit the LST midship and the thing went down because that thing is hollow. I knew some of the men on board, I met them when I was going across on the LST, but they were assigned. I was lucky I was off, because I was that courier. They told me it sunk immediately, and then I saw the names on the roster, and they were in burning oil, I heard.[8]

Now we didn't know where we were going, but it was June. When it came early morning, it was June 6, [but we may have] left June 5 and we were in the English Channel. I know it was June 6 because I was assigned to Admiral Moon's staff. There were forty

---

[8] *LST 531 went out for maneuvers, and it was sunk by a tin fish, a torpedo-* His former shipmates were killed when LST 531 was sunk by German torpedo boats during the ill-fated Exercise TIGER in April 1944.

of us, and we were assigned to the *USS Bayfield*. It was a hooligan ship. A hooligan ship [in our lingo] means it's a Coast Guard ship. And we were passengers, and they were ship's company because they were attached to the ship. So we were doing our jobs decoding messages. They called it a HAG machine, H-A-G, and we were doing whatever we were told to do.[9] There were other Coast Guard guys on the *Bayfield* with the .50 caliber firing at the planes. And someone said, 'They're ours!' So the guys [shooting] said, 'Who knows whose it is? They just [better not] fly over here.' And they kept shooting at them, no matter who came over.

Omaha Beach

When we were attached to that ship we were in the Channel, and we hit the Omaha Beach. I never left the ship, but there were big water mines with tentacles. They were huge. They looked like eight to 10-feet-tall ones; you could see that half of it with the tentacle sticking out. Some of the men didn't even get a chance to go down those ropes to get onto the small crafts. But they weren't hitting us with the shells because we were about three to five miles off the shoreline.

But [later] we were pulling up the American soldiers, sailors out of the Channel. On these small craft where they were wounded, they would put six or eight stretchers and they put a cable or a rope, like a V, and they'd lower the boom with a hoist and pick up eight at a time and put them on the quarter deck towards the bow of the ship. And there was hardly any room to stand. You couldn't stand there. So we had everybody aboard.

---

[9] *They called it a HAG machine-* The U.S. used a portable rotor-based encrypting device, the Hagelin C-38, which they designated the M-209. Designed by Swedish cryptographer Boris Hagelin, it worked on the same principle as the German Enigma machine.

[Later we were transporting German PoWs] and one of the Germans, he had a hole in his back as big as your fist, and he was asking others for a cigarette. I says, 'Nope, I don't'—I wasn't smoking. And [there were so many] aboard, there was no room for anything. And I realized later—I saw them baking bread before, I don't know if it was on land or aboard ship, but they were baking bread and putting it in the freezer—one day we were sewing these stiffs up in canvas, and they were putting them in the freezer and I realized the bread is there. So I lost my appetite for the bread, but men did what they had to do.

And finally it was D+5, I think, and we left the English Channel, and we thought it was over. Now my case, I don't think my experience was so severe as some of these men who hit the shoreline, they really got it bad. I felt bad for that, I really did. And the guys aboard ship [had it rough too] if they were sunk or they hit a mine, [and soon after] was the worst storm of the channel at the time. They had these big anchors with these chains—they're as big as my forearm, each side of the ship—and they were breaking loose from the moorings, and the ships were floating loose in that channel with the mines. So it was dangerous, but these guys who hit the beaches, they really took a beating.

The Flagship

Our ship was a pretty big size ship, it was the flagship. They had a few flagships, but Admiral Moon, he was the flag on the flagship. And they had medical people doing whatever they could but not nearly enough. We pulled out with the wounded. But it was D plus three or four when they sent over the V-bomb, I saw it on the HAG machine. We didn't know what the V-bomb was yet, but it was jet-propelled, [and] they could hit Britain. So you know, we started to realize that we're not [shooting back at] anybody who was firing a gun, and whatever they hit, they hit.

We ended up pulling out, we went down through the Mediterranean Sea and we stayed in Oran, North Africa. And it was stifling, like the desert. Our sheets, the Arabs were buying them for $25 a sheet if you wanted to sell. We stayed there about a month and we were walking in the streets around there, and [my friend] had his sunglasses stolen. An Arab kid runs over, picks it off him, and he started to chase the Arab kid. I says, 'You better not.' I says, 'Look behind you,' because you don't know what they're carrying in under those sheets.' So he stopped running. I says, 'Let him keep the sunglasses.' So he stopped. But we didn't know where we were at because it was new for everybody. Five cents a beer, but I don't drink. What a shame. [*Laughs*]

So we stayed there about a month in the heat, sweating into our sheets, and they put us aboard ship, and we went to Southern France. There was another invasion there. And we didn't know that, they told us later, but that was easier because it was only about two days because the Germans were moving inland. We already hit them from Utah and Omaha Beach and on the Cherbourg Peninsula.

When we got to Southern France, I got off the ship. We stayed there, I think it was about three or four days only. They anchored, and then they let us swim off the ship. They tied a line out to a life preserver at about twenty-five feet out. And you can jump off the side of the ship and swim in the Mediterranean and then you come back. And we did that and we got aboard ship and we went to Naples.

We stayed in Naples about two months, I think. And Admiral Moon, we were still on his staff... I was a courier and I used to go with an LCVP, a landing craft vehicle personnel. It was a square type of thing, probably 30, 40 feet long, I think. And I used to go get the mail. Well, at one time while aboard ship Admiral Moon put a gun to his head, and he committed suicide. They called it battle fatigue. We don't know if it was or not, but that's what I was told.[10]

So we stayed there for a time and I remember cartons of cigarettes were 50 cents a carton. So now I'm going to make a confession. I was selling cigarettes maybe for $3 a carton if it was Raleigh, Lucky Strike; I got $5 for Camels and Chesterfield. I had a mailbag. I gave the guys a buck a carton. So I would wait inside a public toilet in Naples, and I had the Italian customers I sold to for three to five dollars a carton. I was making a profit, the start of being a businessman. And when I got enough, I used to go shopping, I forgot the name of that fancy street, but I bought the leather gloves for my relatives back home, ladies, and I bought tortoise shell combs, $5 a comb. Well, when you don't pay much for it, sell it pretty cheap. I came back with some prizes.

And after a while I got tired of eating the food aboard ship, so I wanted to go have some eggs, and you couldn't get eggs nowhere. Ah, some girl offered me eggs. I says, 'Yeah, where's the chicken?' She took me to the building, they're big courtyards, the houses there, the tenements, and she says, 'You stay here.' She went, I don't know if she got a frying pan and she gave me two eggs. I think it was a penny, a lira. I got $5 worth, two eggs, 500 lira. And I got eggs and it was a real treat.

And there were girls around, plenty of girls, but you don't know what you were getting. You took your chances. Well, I didn't get anything, I wasn't sick. But brothers were pimping their sisters. The mother and father would be in the living room, not caring, offering

---

[10] *Admiral Moon put a gun to his head*-(1894-1944) On August 5, 1944, Rear Admiral Don Pardee Moon shot himself in the head with his .45 aboard his flagship *Bayfield* in Naples harbor. Some attributed his personal hell to the ill-fated Exercise TIGER disaster that had occurred under his watch back in April.

you wine. If one British or American would go with the daughter, the other one would be waiting, and it wasn't like a typical turnstile, but it was war. So people were very hard up for money. Grandmothers were picking bricks out of the streets for pennies a day just to make ends meet. Getting something, some money. An American dollar meant a lot.

Harry Rosenthal passed on September 25, 2012, at the age of 88.

The Military Policeman

Jacob Cutler became a military policeman with the First Army. He participated in the Normandy landings on Omaha Beach and elsewhere, as you will read. In this 2002 interview, Mr. Cutler also talks about the appearance of a new secret weapon, the German V-2 rocket, a last-ditch effort by Hitler to terrorize England.

Jacob N. Cutler

I was born on February 17, 1924 in Brooklyn. Pearl Harbor was a Sunday afternoon; I had finished one year of college. I was listening to the New York Giants football game on the radio. They interrupted and announced that Pearl Harbor had been bombed. I said, 'Where the heck is Pearl Harbor? I never heard of it.' Of course, later we learned it was Hawaii, and the war was on. I was 18. I enlisted in the Army Signal Corps. I was interested in electronics and radio. I used to build radios as a kid and whatnot, so I thought that would be something good. Of course, I didn't know what the Signal Corps did. Not what I expected... I was called into active service in April 1943. I reported to Fort Dix, New Jersey, reception center. There I was collared by someone who asked me if I play a musical instrument. I was drafted into the Army reception center band only for about two weeks because it was a temporary thing. I was shipped out to Signal Corps camp in Camp Crowder, Missouri, where I took basic training for about four weeks. Then, I was shipped to Fort Monmouth, New Jersey, for Signal Corps training. I was there for about three months or so, I guess with all the training and whatnot, and I was assigned to a unit to go overseas. I landed in England in November 1943.

We crossed in a tub that had been a former cruise liner, the *Capetown Castle*. The food on it was absolutely awful. The ship rocked and rolled because it was a small tub. We crossed in a convoy escorted by one of the ships, which I'll always remember was the battleship *Texas*. I have a reason for remembering it. At one point, they thought there were some submarines. The convoy stopped and the battleships and other escorts got in closer, but it turned out to be a false alarm.

I believe we landed in Southampton, England. Then, I was assigned to a Signal Corps battalion, 59th Signal Battalion with V Corps, First Army. We were stationed in Taunton, England. That was south of Bristol, which was a large city. Bristol was bombed very, very heavily by the Germans. We heard them regularly. Almost every night we could hear the bombers coming over; we could actually hear the bombs coming down. They took a terrible beating. The people of England were very friendly, very nice. If you found the pubs in the back roads, they would give you liquor, which was not available. I wasn't much of a drinker, but I started to drink gin and soda there. Gin and lime was what they drank. That hooked me on that.

I believe it was the 1st or 2nd of June, they told us, 'Pack up. The invasion is coming. The intel is just where, when. We're moving out.'

I forgot to mention it. While I was in this Signal Corps camp, a new military police platoon was being formed to be security for the V Corps headquarters. They asked for volunteers, and I volunteered. They say you should never volunteer in the Army, but I thought it would be a good change for me, so I volunteered. Actually, when the invasion came, I was in the military police.

I believe it was very early, June 1 or 2 or maybe the last days of May, when we moved out to a marshaling area where they then briefed us as to exactly what was going to happen. We were scheduled for D-Day H+3. We couldn't understand why they needed MPs there on D-Day, but they explained to us that you'd take positions on the road and guide all the straggling troops and whatnot to their units. Just didn't work out that way.

I crossed the channel on an LST, tank landing ship. The invasion was supposed to be June 5. We started out on June 5. The Channel and the weather was so bad that it was canceled. We went back to the ports. Of course, we were terrified because at this time we thought, 'How could the Germans not have seen us?' We expected an attack any minute. I slept on deck under a truck. I figured that would be the safest place.

The next day, we started out and we got to within wherever we were supposed to get off and get on to small landing craft. They had these big nets over the side of the ship, had to climb down with a 60-pound pack carrying my tent and food and rifle and whatnot and climbed down to get to the landing boat. The water was still very rough. When I thought the boat was down, I jumped from the net. Then, a wave lifted the boat up. I just hit and my legs just buckled under me, but I was unhurt.

The Landing

Then, we started in towards shore, at about the early afternoon, I would say somewhere between 1:00 and 2:00 p.m. We were supposed to land probably at 8:00 or 9:00 a.m., original plan, but we didn't complain about that. We were briefed and told we would land, at most, knee-high water they would let us off, that we'd have to wade in. Didn't work out that way. Partway across, again, our boat got pounded so hard by the waves and there was a lot of shelling around us. Other boats were being hit, and our boat got a leak. They took us back to the tank ship; we had to climb back up the nets. We thought we were probably lucky because we were delayed a couple of hours till another boat came to get us.

The same procedure; down we went. This time we made it except that the Navy guys were afraid they would get trapped near the shore or get hit by shellfire or whatever, so they dropped us off in chest-high water. A lot of guys were floundering—they didn't know how to swim, and they were so taken by surprise, some went under. Fortunately, nobody in my group drowned. We all managed to get ashore. We just raced across that beach, Omaha Beach, Easy Red sector, just to the left of the cliffs that the Rangers had climbed to try to take out the pillboxes.

The beach was a horrible mess—bodies and bodies all over the place, bleeding and bloody, dead bodies. They didn't have time to remove them. We just ran. On the end of the beach was like a little bluff, maybe eight feet high or whatever; we took cover under there and had to clean our rifles. We didn't have any dry clothes, so we just stayed wet. Luckily, it was warm.

Later in the afternoon, we moved up the road; the Germans had been pushed back a couple of miles. Along this road off the beach, the Germans had built a long trench with interior dugouts that they had been using as a headquarters. We stayed about two nights in this area. We started moving inland in Normandy very slowly, through the hedgerow areas. We were bogged down for quite a while until July. Troops are moving very slowly. The Germans were putting up very fierce resistance.

Finally, the time came when I guess they felt they had enough armor and big guns. Incidentally, going back to the invasion, they had these amphibious boats that were called DUKWs, which was an acronym for something, had to do with landing amphibian. They were carrying most of our artillery for the first day. Almost every one was sunk, so we had no guns on the beach. The battleship *Texas* cruised back and forth shelling the German positions. I think they and the other ships that were shelling saved the day, but I always remember that battleship just cruising back and forth, back and forth, from about five miles out, firing shells into the German positions. The aircraft did a very bad job. I think the weather, they couldn't see the targets. They didn't take out everything they were supposed to.

Anyway, we started moving inland. We were bogged down. Saint-Lô was the big strong point for the Germans. Finally, the time came for the breakthrough. I was sleeping in a, I guess you'd call it a trench. I was about a foot underground, below ground or so. About 5:00 in the morning, the shelling of the German position started. It was so intense, the ground was vibrating. These shells came overhead, sounded like a subway train screeching around a corner, it's the shrieks.

It was so heavy that the Germans finally broke. Many of them surrendered and they were shaking and terrified. They thought we had invented automatic cannons because there were so many guns being fired in sequence non-stop, just rapidly like it was a machine gun. They broke. Then, the big breakthrough came. The troops moved through.

We were always a few miles behind the front. We never got into real combat. D-Day was our worst day, but I was lucky that way. We moved through. We eventually reached Paris. The infantry marched through the famous march. We were right behind them. We stayed in the outskirts of Paris for one night and then continued to move on. We went through France. At this point, we began moving fairly rapidly compared to before. Finally, France was completely liberated.

We went into Luxembourg. Then, we went down into Belgium. We went through and we stayed one night overnight in Bastogne, which was later under siege. It was never captured by the Germans. We moved south into this village in Belgium a few miles, maybe two, three miles from the German border. It was the first place we finally had indoor quarters. The first night we spent in a movie theater. We slept on the floor. I was really very thankful for it. The floor was a great comfort.

The next day, we moved into a building nearby, which had apparently been some kind of a school, and they had dormitories. We moved into there. We slept on folding cots, which, as far as we were concerned, were the most comfortable things in the world at that time. We're just waiting to break through into Germany.

Mostly, [my responsibility as an MP] was security guard duty. We took over outposts and just did guard duty watching out for German patrols that might break through and to sound alarms if that happened. We were called 'combat MPs' because we never were in the villages with the white hats and whatnot. Never had those. We wore camouflage nets on our helmets. More or less, we were security troops.

The 'Vengeance' Rockets

A week after D-Day, the Germans began launching a new type of weapon—a small, medium-range cruise missile—from bases in northern France, the Netherlands, and western Germany. It was the forerunner to the modern rocket; indeed, some of the German scientists involved in the program later worked on the U.S. space program. The loud noise that made by the primitive pulsejet engine of the V-1, or 'Vengeance Weapon 1', could be heard approaching from more than ten miles away. Over 9500 were launched at England through the next five months, sometimes more than one hundred a day until the launch sites were knocked out by the advancing Allies on the continent.[1]

Hitler kept saying he had a secret weapon, a secret weapon that was going to destroy us and win the war. We had reason to believe that the Germans were working on an atomic bomb. We were fortunate we beat them to it. [The German] buzz bombs were small, I have a picture of them. They did have a cockpit which could hold one man, but I don't think they were ever piloted that I know of. They were like robots. They went up and they just landed almost at random at areas in France. I think they were more of a terrorist thing than anything else. If they hit anything, of course they were powerful bombs.

One went over a hill where I was on guard duty in Belgium and exploded. I heard it and I hit the ground. I didn't know where it was coming down because you heard this awful noise. When it stopped, you know the engines died and it was coming down. It came down and whistled like a bomb, just shrieked coming down.

[Another time] I was on guard duty near a field where we had stopped. One of them came down and it hit the field and didn't explode; it kind of pinwheeled across the field. It crashed into a barn and then it exploded and blew up the whole barn. It was maybe 50 yards or so from where I was.

They just came over and it got to a point where they were pushed back far enough where they really couldn't do anything anymore but then they discovered the first rockets. The Germans were way ahead of us in rocket launching. They had these V-2 rockets that were really huge. I have a picture of that, too. They were huge. They would take off, all you would see was a vapor trail, a blue vapor trail. Then, they just disappeared. You couldn't hear them coming because they were faster than sound. They were actually hitting London till they got pushed back too far where they couldn't reach anymore.

Mr. Cutler passed away in 2018 at the age of 95.

THE BULGE

[ORIGINAL SELECTION FROM VOLUME 6:
THE BULGE AND BEYOND]

Allied forces moved rapidly after the Normandy breakout, but five months after the D-Day landings, the Germans launched an all-out surprise counterattack against scantily defended American lines in the Ardennes Forest. In the frozen early morning hours of December 16, 1944, six hundred German tanks broke through the thinly manned American lines after a tremendous artillery barrage, creating a 'bulge' or pocket they hoped to exploit to the sea, sowing desperation, panic, and confusion in the blitzkrieg's wake. Allied soldiers found themselves in a desperate struggle for survival as temperatures plunged to the coldest in European memory during the winter of 1944–45. Many had little experience, having replaced those killed and wounded in the Normandy campaign thus far. The average American replacement was nineteen years old, and in this battle, the second bloodiest in United States military history, just over 19,000 were killed.[11] More than 700,000 Americans would eventually be engaged in yet another death match that would herald the outcome of World War II in Europe, and many would be taken as prisoners of war.

---

[11] *the second bloodiest in United States military history-* 19,276 Americans were killed between December 16, 1944, and January 25, 1945. The bloodiest campaign/battle was World War I's Meuse-Argonne Offensive from September 26 to November 11, 1918, with 26,277 Americans killed. Source: List of battles with most United States military fatalities, en.wikipedia.org/wiki/List_of_battles_with_most_United_States_military_fatalities#Campaigns

The Artillery Spotter

Sydney Cole's service in World War II begins in Canada. The Buffalo, New York, native was anxious to join the Army Air Corps, but a series of incidents brought him instead to Toronto, Canada, to join up with the Royal Canadian Air Force. After the attack at Pearl Harbor, he managed to get released to return to try to become a pilot for the United States. He would wind up in the glider program, which he disliked; eventually he hit his stride flying 126 missions in Europe as a field artillery spotter. On his final mission, he survived being shot down and became a prisoner of war during the Battle of the Bulge; in his captivity, he became an eyewitness to the Holocaust.

In an interview in 1989, he emphasized, 'I wouldn't have come normally, but when you mentioned it would go in the archives of the Holocaust, then that just changed my mind completely. Now, this is something that I put in the back of my mind many, many years ago. I didn't want to think about it too much… but that's the only reason I'm doing this, because of the Holocaust. If one person in the entire world gets anything out of this interview, I'll be happy about it. Just one. I want people to remember what really happened back in the old Nazi days.'

Sydney Cole

I was born on September 1, 1914. I attended grammar school in New York City, then moved to Buffalo with my family while I was young. My father did architectural maintenance on buildings, whenever they were in need of repair, and he got a call from someone in Buffalo for a mansion on Delaware Avenue that needed work, and that is how we got to Buffalo. I went to high school in Buffalo, Madison Park, and graduated in I think 1932. Then I went to Buffalo State.

I knew eventually, with war in the upcoming, that I would be drafted. I did not want to be a foot soldier. I wanted to be a pilot; I had just made up my mind to do that. I tried and tried to get into service and couldn't get anywhere; I tried to get into the Army Air Corps, but it was a big deal to get in; they told me that I'd have to go to New York City for my physical, just to be physically able to get into the Air Corps. I finally made connections in New York City. So I went to New York City. They had said, 'Go try to join a YMCA, get in the best shape you can,' and I went from there. I took the physical and there were about 70 people at that area from Buffalo, from New York, from New Jersey, and Pennsylvania. Just everybody trying to get into the Air Corps. I did pass the physical, and then they sent me to the University of Syracuse a couple of months later to take what they called a mental. Not your mental capacity, just your knowledge and everything else, and there again about 70 or 80 from different parts of the country. New York, New Jersey. And we all failed the test, couldn't comprehend it one bit the mental exam. But I didn't give up.

Canada

So, I went to Hamilton, Canada, [to see about the aviator program there]. They didn't know anything about getting me in, they sent me to Toronto. And I took the physical and the mental exam there in one day and passed everything, and I think it was a month later they called me. I went there, got sworn in and started, and graduated in their flight school training.

And then when the actual war broke out with Pearl Harbor, I, as an American volunteer, had signed a contract with the Canadian force that I could leave at my will. And later, they gave me an extremely hard time, because we had gone through this training which was very expensive. I had gone through it with a group that came from England, because they were bombing around London [before Pearl Harbor] and they were sending groups here to be trained for the Royal Canadian Air Force. I went up there and we checked into Manning Field, which is the exhibition grounds of the Canadian National Exhibition. And after many inductions and shots and programs and so forth, I didn't see an aircraft or anything for three, four months. It was all ground work. Then we started our fighter pilot training. We finished up with Spitfires, graduated with that Spitfire kind of training, and I finally got through with the paperwork and everything else. In the interim, when I was up there, I was called to the office one day, and because I had had two FBI men track me to Canada, and they thought I'd went to Canada to avoid the military, which [was not the case]. And they left with joy in their hearts because I was in the military, and that helped me get back into the American forces and get through with my contract with the Canadians.

When Pearl Harbor happened, I decided I wanted to come back to the United States. Being a volunteer with the USA patch on my shoulder, and the enlistment papers that I had signed when I entered the Canadian service, I could ask for a discharge at my will. Well anyhow, I put in for a request to be discharged from the service, and it finally came through after a few months. I reported to the United States, went to the draft board, and waited there because they didn't know what to do with me and that particular time, with the qualifications I had, just coming out of service. They weren't set up yet for any type of enlistment and so forth and so on. Then they called me and they asked me if I would be interested in taking glider pilot training. Now, in order to be qualified to do that, you had to have power shift training, which I had just completed in Canada.

So I agreed to it, I went into service here as an enlisted man. They sent me to Miami Beach to round up the thirty that were going to be the first class for glider pilot training in the United States. Well, from there we went to Santa Fe, New Mexico. We went to Janesville, Wisconsin. We rode flying power shifts right along, and then we were checked out by some of the Army Air Force pilots that came from West Point. They were a very, very small organization at that time. The complete thirty that took the first glider pilot training course did pass. There wasn't one failure. Now we went to Twentynine Palms, California, for our first glimpse of gliders. But from the moment I got into a glider, I knew I didn't like it. It was so quiet that the noise was deafening. I can't describe it, and I was always reaching for a throttle that it didn't have. I just knew that they wanted to use gliders in combat, and it would never work. I just knew it couldn't. Well anyhow, we graduated in 1942.

Field Artillery Spotting

One night I was OD, which is Officer of the Day. At midnight, a telex came through. They were looking for liaison pilot instructors. Now, liaison pilot people are ones that spot field artillery shells for field artillery battalions. They have forward observers that are on the ground, and they have them in the air. I felt that's what I would want to do because it's flying and not glidering. I went to my commanding officer the next morning, after reading this telex, and he refused to release me. I went over his head and finally made connections, and went down to Fort Bragg, North Carolina, which is one of the largest field artillery training camps in the United States. They said, 'Fine. Your qualifications are fine, but you have to be a field artillery officer.' I was in the [Army] Air Force. I had nothing to do with a gun. I never took a basic training, where I had to march and go through all the other equipment that a normal soldier does. Well, anyhow, I said I would, so they discharged me with the convenience of the government. They then sent me to Fort Sill, Oklahoma, which is a field artillery training camp, and that's OCS. It's a 90-day course. Everything is double time. I was in that group. I was probably 26 years old at that particular time. And I was in with a group of VMI students that were 21, 22, fresh out of school, and had to keep up with them.

I then became an instructor in liaison pilot training. After three or four months of that, I tired of it and asked for overseas duty, which they gladly recommended and okayed. I was assigned to a separate field artillery battalion, not with a large group or anything; we were by ourselves. We were sent where we were needed. We were like a SWAT team with a police department. Wherever there was a problem, our battalion went.

We got into combat in the middle of '44; I got to Paris right after the Germans vacated Paris.[12] We were waiting for aircraft. They finally came into Orly Field in Paris and then we went over, and then we were sent on separate missions, wherever they needed us. That's when I started my combat flying.

Then we were assigned to the Battle of the Bulge. We had been around Bastogne in early December. The push started December 16th, and everything was amassed there.

The weather was horrendous. It was mid-winter. Incidentally, I'll never forget, I was sent out on a mission Christmas Eve, and when I came back, my special turkey dinner was gone; they had used everything up, there was very little food left, outside of C-rations

---

[12] *I got to Paris right after the Germans vacated Paris-*This was actually probably September 1944.

and canned food. I missed Christmas dinner, I missed New Year's Eve dinner. I was out on a mission at that particular time, too.

The Last Mission

I had flown 126 missions. The last mission was the 126th, and that happened January 2, 1945. I had 125 missions with no parachute. We didn't have them available at that particular time; the shipments never arrived from the States. We were very short of materials at that particular time. Well, you see, we weren't fighter pilots or bomber pilots. I was flying in an observation unit. These were specially built with a large 360-degree cockpit, to see all around you. It was a low-flying propellered craft; the only thing I carried was a .45. That was it.

We could take off and land and be back in six or eight minutes, and that's considered a mission. That's why we acquired so many, that's how we could do it. But this particular mission now, January 2nd of 1945, I was ordered into the air at three o'clock in the morning. The temperature was hovering right around four or five degrees. The snow was [at least] eight feet high in drifts. The runways were completely blocked. We need runways to get off, we need a lot of room because of the ice and everything else, and we didn't have concrete. It was all mud and field, just open field. It was just done by the engineers in a rush, because everything was frozen. We just couldn't start the aircraft. We had to drain the oil out of the aircraft, heat it with blow torches, pour it back in, and finally take off. Now, with these types of aircraft, the only heat in the aircraft is a manifold heater, and that throws very little heat. You can't wear boots because the rudders and everything are small, and you have to operate with just your feet, and you have to wear very normal shoes. Luckily, that day I put on a bomber jacket, which was warm.

Normally, you would wear just flight clothes, which was a thin nylon jacket and suit.

I was ordered into the air. I had been up around two and a half hours, and my fuel was getting low. We couldn't spot too many of the field artillery shells because of the snow-covered ground. We finally called for smoke bombs—when a shell hits the ground with a smoke bomb, it sends up a column of smoke. Then you can zero in and observe what you're doing and be able to get aircraft and field artillery shells where you want to put them.

At that point, though, there was so much confusion. Our own planes were strafing everybody. They were just letting bullets fly from wherever they could. Anywhere they thought the enemy might be, even on our side of the battle line. It was just a state of confusion. The Germans were confused, our forces were confused, but everything was going, you just couldn't believe what was happening there. My field artillery officer directing the ground fire would not let us come down. When I told him our fuel was getting low, he said, 'Go within six minutes and try to get back.' And of course, we needed a lot more time. All of a sudden, our aircraft was hit by anti-aircraft fire. We are sitting tandem in the aircraft with a very small door. The parachutes we were wearing that particular morning, they were seat packs. Now, there are two types of parachutes. One is a backpack, but that puts you forward in the aircraft, where you can't control the aircraft too sensibly. The seat pack raises you up where your head is hitting the canopy. But we had them on, [although] our parachute training instruction was [just] two hours; they showed us how they fold the parachute and how to pull the cord. Period. That was my instruction.

When the aircraft was hit and I lost control, I had put it in a glide position; the engine was shot out, so I had no power, but when we were taking glider pilot training, our instructor would take us out five or ten thousand feet, reach over—he was in the back—shut the ignition off, and you'd have to land in a circle; that was part of the training to be a glider pilot. Well anyhow, it came in very, very good stead with me, but to get back to the story, I ordered my observer out. Out of the plane, because we were both going to jump. We couldn't stay in the plane, it was disabled. So he had to go first because he was behind me. We opened the door, which was a very narrow door, and he got tangled up in his headsets and all these radio wires. He was leaning out; he couldn't budge at all. I took my foot and shoved him out. I saw his parachute open. In the three or four minutes between the time he got out and by the time I bailed out, he landed on the American side, and I landed on the enemy side. Minutes, just minutes, because we were right sort of in the center.

I was wounded by shrapnel and I saw the Germans shooting at me coming down in the parachute; I could see the holes popping up in the parachute. Now evidently, I was hit in my arm and I was hit in the leg. Now, I don't know if I was hit when the aircraft was disabled or when they were shooting at me when I was coming down in the parachute; I didn't feel it. When the aircraft was hit, I had a funny smell in the aircraft. I can't describe it, what it was, but it was not normal in that aircraft. After I bailed out and saw these bullet holes... You know, you can guide yourself coming down with the shroud cords, and anyhow, I got away and landed at the edge of a forest. Completely wounded and bleeding profusely. I grabbed the parachute, wrapped it around me, then I lost consciousness.

I woke up intermittently, back and forth. I think the second time that I woke up, I remembered my dog tags. The dog tags had an 'H' on them, for Hebrew. I knew I was in German territory; I knew that the Germans were starting to retreat through there, so I took my dog tags and just flung them as far as I possibly could.

Now, I passed out, and I was in and out [of consciousness], perhaps 36, 48, 72 hours. I have no way of knowing, but it may not have been more than 48 hours, because the Germans were retreating. There was a tank that passed by me, manned by German officers, and they were running for their lives. They spotted me, stopped, didn't take me into the tank at all, but threw me on top of the tank, just threw me on, without the parachute or anything, just physically grabbed me and threw me on.

The bleeding had stopped because the blood had crusted over, scabbed over. I was taken back to some small town or village. They turned me over to the Hitler Youth. Kids. They were in full uniform, with the Nazi thing across their chest, with the brown pants, with the brown shirts, with everything. They were just like you see in the movies, just like you see anywhere where they show in these horror pictures. These were anywhere from 12 to 19, 20 years of age. They started interrogating me, but they could speak very little English and not enough to convey anything that I would understand. When I didn't answer properly, every time I didn't give them a right answer, I would get hit. They never would hit me in the face, it was always in the body, in the groin, on the shins, and so forth. They were just so incensed they were [totally indoctrinated], being born and raised in that era. Their families, their fathers, their mothers, they just hated us, American [airmen] especially, because we bombed their cities, we ruined their beautiful Berlin, all the buildings were shut down, all their culture—they just had a hatred for pilots like you couldn't believe.

When they got through with me, they threw me down in a cellar, locked the door. Now, there were no windows in the cellars in the way these little houses were built in these German villages; you could just see the stone. It was extremely damp down there, and there was a mound of old, rotten potatoes, [and I had not eaten in probably three or four days]. The next morning, for some reason, I was thrown in the back of a truck, and taken to a Red Cross tent, where they were treating German soldiers somewhere in Germany.

This German doctor was just treating the Germans first. When he got to me—I was, of course, the last one he looked at—he did wrap my arm and my leg with some paper bandages and gave me a tetanus shot. Now why I don't know, but actually, it helped.

From there, I was sent to some other place where they tried to interrogate me. I couldn't answer. I was put on a train and taken somewhere else, and they tagged me severely wounded. Of course, on the train, there was a bowl of soup. There was some food. On this particular train, there was an English doctor who was captured a long time before. He was a major, a medical man, but he had very little equipment. He had rusty tweezers, he had a little black bag with nothing in it, paper bandages, perhaps some Mercurochrome. He might have had some sulfur powder, I don't know, but anyhow, he was picking this shrapnel out of my leg. He couldn't do anything with my arm because the fragments were too small and they were embedded too deep—the shrapnel in my left arm is still there, 26 very small pieces of shrapnel, and the calf on my leg from my ankle to my knee had been split wide open—and he couldn't open up the scar on a moving train. And there were other prisoners on the train. There was no such thing in those days as pain pills or anything to alleviate it.

I went from camp to camp to camp. Everywhere I went, I remember lying somewhere for a day or two, in a large room with a wooden floor, and perhaps a hundred prisoners, just lying on the floor, awaiting orders, awaiting to be shipped out. And finally, I got to a stalag, which was a prisoner of war camp. The stalag was ironically named IV-F; I think it was on the German-Polish border, somewhere there.

In the meantime, they had wired a dog tag on me, a German dog tag, when I got to that camp, on my bad leg. It has the numbers that were assigned to me as a prisoner of war. Now somewhere, if the records are still available in Germany, it would show Stalag IV-F, a date I was brought there, my name and number. Now where, when, I don't know.

The Stalag

When we got to the stalag, there was a captain who was a senior ranking officer, and three other officers, including myself and two other officers. Of course, the first thing we did was to have a meeting of the officers to see how we were going to handle ourselves, and our escape routes, what would happen if we were ever liberated, what would happen if we ever overcame the German guards. We were split up into different battalions, and I was in charge of battalion three. There were possibly eighty prisoners under my command, mixed. There were English, Italian, American, and so forth. We were the only ranking officers there; the rest were enlisted men. Now, incidentally, anybody who was Jewish was called and taken out of this particular Stalag IV-F, and I never saw them come back, four or five, six at a time—Rosenberg, Finklestein, whomever it may have been; one day I asked the guard what happened to these soldiers that were picked, and he said, 'They are out doing work.' But they never came back. Whether they were killed, whether they were transferred to another stalag, I don't know. I presumed they were dead, executed.

Now I didn't go around saying, 'I'm a Jew.' I was as discreet as could be. I was in that camp possibly two and a half, three months. When I threw my dog tags away, when I was interrogated and they started registering my name, I told them that I was Protestant but they didn't bring up religion with me whatsoever, beyond, 'What is your religion? What's your age, your name, your rank, your serial number, where were you born? What outfit were you with? How many airplanes and aircraft do they have? How many tanks? How many field artillery battalions? How many infantrymen?' All those questions, which I did not answer, except the pertinent questions to my own personal views.

The treatment in the stalag was horrible. There was no hot water, there was little food, there was no medication, there were no showers. There was an outside pump with well water that was rank, filthy, rotten, rusty, smelly water. There was no shaving equipment. There was one in the morning, one at night, and both meals were alike—a potato soup with grass in it, anything they could make to try to make it a little thick. One of the German guards and I tried to converse, and we sort of got a little bit friendly. He brought me a loaf of bread. Now, this loaf of bread was baked in 1939. It was in a wooden box, completely sealed. It was a replica of a little coffin, and it was made out of wood, like balsa wood. It was very light, and you could just rip it open, and there was a fresh loaf of bread, four or five years old; they had produced maybe millions of loaves of bread. It was just amazing, how they had prepared all this, scheming ahead for food and so forth.

My mother did get an MIA telegram, and my sister still has it to this day. Everybody lost weight, and I went down to 95 pounds, from 145, in five months. They didn't ever issue clothes. My clothes were tattered, absolutely tattered. The bomber jacket I was wearing had been penetrated by fire. I was shot, I was shot in the leg and shot in the arm. My left arm, where I was shot, my left sleeve of this bomber jacket was completely tattered. The socks I was wearing were rank, the shoes, everything. And you know, you'd try to wash them, you'd try to do this, but you're using cold water. And it can't dry. It's the wintertime, too. You can't believe the cold; it's just almost impossible to describe the conditions there.

Liberated by the Russians

We had a formation in April, and the Germans did announce that President Roosevelt had died, they did tell us that. We had heard that the Russians were coming, by the Germans. [And] we knew that that particular night, that the camp was going to be vacated by the German guards. We had gathered everybody—nobody went to sleep, everybody was alerted—we were all awake, and we heard the Russians coming and they came in by horse-drawn carts, very few vehicles. The Russians came in like at 4:30, 5:00 in the morning, but the guards had left. Most of [the liberating soldiers] were Mongolians. The pots and pans were rattling on the back of the two-wheel carts. Just like the old days. You couldn't believe it, it took you back in history, it was primitive.

The first thing the Russians did was rip out all the barbed wire, the complete barbed wire encampment around the whole camp. And then, of course, we four officers were taken to meet the Russian major. The Russian major was a graduate of the University of Minnesota and could speak English. He took a liking to me. We became buddies, and wherever he went, I went.

Now, this is May of '45. April is when they announced that the president had died. The Russians came in with medical personnel also. They assigned a female doctor to handle me; they had perhaps three or four doctors with them and they were all female, incidentally. And this girl was very young. I assumed she was around 23, 24. She couldn't speak good English, but she examined me, she saw the condition I was in. There was a lot of infection there, which she treated. Then they went out and they slaughtered cattle, they brought in chickens, they brought in eggs and started cooking and having feasts and everything. We got excellent treatment by the Russians. I couldn't believe it. Now, the major also explained to us that we were going to be kept by the Russians approximately one to two months, to build us up, because we were the first Americans that were ever liberated in the Russian zone by the Russians. They were awaiting Russian prisoners liberated by the Americans to have an exchange.

'I Just Couldn't Believe What I Saw'

In the meantime, I had gained some strength. The Russian major and myself and a party went scouring the country; we needed medical supplies badly. We broke into pharmacies and just took what we wanted. That's when we ran into some of these satellite concentration camps where Jews were kept. And the first Jews I ever saw were in a barn, just inside the camp, away from the big dormitories and from the big compounds. There were yellow stars on them. They were in the pajama-type stripes. Of course, they start talking in [Yiddish], which I could understand. Then, of course, the Russian major knew I was Jewish. And then, of course, everybody knew I was Jewish after that. It didn't make a bit of difference, no, and I never denied the fact after that, because we were liberated.

I think there were possibly anywhere around twenty-five of these prisoners, the most horrible sight I ever saw in my life, with heads that had swelled up to the size of a soccer ball, or a volleyball. And their limbs, you can't describe it—they were just bones covered with skin, no flesh whatsoever. No flesh in the cheek, nothing on the hands, no flesh at all, just skin and bones. You could just see their groin just sticking out, the bones. They looked like a skeleton. I think [the Germans] put them wherever they could find room.

We tried to feed these people. We tried to give medication, water, hot drinks, whatever. No [effect]; they all died. They just could not consume food, they were too far gone. In other words, they were living death. They didn't want to shoot them because it would waste a bullet.

It was so confusing there... I think it was Auschwitz, and there was another one not too far from there—Bergen-Belsen, I was just going to say Belsen.[13] Now, I saw the trenches there. They hadn't been covered yet, with thousands, literally thousands of bodies, just helter-skelter, just thrown in there, and they were all skeletal-type people in there. I just can't even really describe it anymore. They had a grave at least two football fields wide and long with empty bodies in there—men, women, and children—both male and female, naked, lying there just like this one on top of the other. Unbelievable. It was a scene that I can't describe fully, and it just boggled my mind right to this very day. The horrible, horrible conditions, and it didn't improve my [mental] condition much either.

These prisoners were now freed. There were no Germans around there, either, but these people couldn't maneuver, they were just too ill. You couldn't believe what you saw! You thought it was something that... I can't describe it. Emotionally, I was just gone, with seeing something like that, and knowing these people were all Jewish people, I just couldn't believe what I saw.

That was it for me, to just then realize how you were a prisoner there for five, six months, with this type of [perpetrator], and to come through it—I'm really surprised they didn't just wipe out the prisoner of war camp. The Germans didn't have enough food

---

[13] *It was so confusing there*-Mr. Cole was prompted to speculate that he may have been at Auschwitz, which was liberated by the Red Army on January 27, 1945, and then perhaps at Bergen-Belsen, which was liberated by the British Army on April 15, 1945, quite a distance from the eastern German-Polish border where Mr. Cole states he was held. Uncovered mass graves were indeed a spectacle at Belsen for a few weeks after liberation, but it is unclear if this is what he refers to; the author finds it unlikely that a Russian-held prisoner would have been in the vicinity of Bergen-Belsen, in the west, before the graves were covered. That is not to say that Mr. Cole did not witness these mass graves, just probably not at the most infamous mass grave site, Bergen-Belsen. See my 2016 book, *A Train Near Magdeburg*, for a more complete Holocaust liberation timeline/discussion.

themselves, they didn't have enough water, they didn't have enough fuel for their aircraft, for their tanks, for their vehicles. They didn't have enough food for their soldiers, they didn't have medical supplies. Everything the Germans had was ersatz. There were no such things as gauze bandages, everything was paper.

In July [we left Russian control]. They had a tremendous ceremony with bands and music and speeches. It was like a light opera. There were Russian songs, Russian dancers, and there were American generals. Right after the ceremony, they turned the American prisoners over to the Americans, and the Americans turned the Russians over to them. I was flown right to Paris, to be interrogated by our own people, because we were the first prisoners to be liberated by the Russians. We were the first stalag to be liberated by Russians. They wanted to know what treatment we got, what the Russians did, how they acted, and everything. Of course, we were allies at the time. There were only good words for them.

I had built up my strength a little bit. There's no question about it. I wouldn't let myself lie down and say, 'I'm ill. I'm going to act ill and be ill.' I just fought mentally to keep my strength and to keep going.

After I was interrogated by the generals in Paris, I was sent to a camp to be built up some more, with the eggnogs and cocoa and all the medical things that you could think of. There were psychiatrists there, there were psychologists there, there were legal people there, there was a PX. Of course, they stripped me immediately, 'Go into the PX. Pick out whatever you want, as far as clothes are concerned.'

But there was no happiness there. It was a feeling of elation that I'm free, but how am I, really? How am I going to act? What's going to happen to me? I don't know. Because myself, being a POW didn't affect me as much as going into these concentration camps. That's what really set me off. I couldn't believe this was happening.

They had decided, me being one of the first prisoners of war liberated by the Russians, that they wanted to fly me back to get me back to the Pentagon to be interviewed by some of the generals about how the Russians treated me, an American officer, because we weren't really on good terms with Russia—there's still an enigma there. They put me on a liberty ship, instead of flying me—I could be home in twelve hours or whatever; it took seven days. They put me on the deck, 8:00 in the morning to 8:00 at night with the sun shining and bringing me eggnogs and milkshakes and sandwiches; the food was so rich I couldn't eat it, I would just toss a lot of it overboard, but drank some of [the liquids] trying to gain back some weight. Now, when I was shot down, my weight was 145 pounds. When I was liberated, I weighed 95 pounds. I never really got my weight back, right to this very day. My top weight was 120, right now I'm right about 115.

Home

My mother had gotten the telegram that I was an MIA, [and she did not find out I was alive until] probably when I was on my way home. 'Your son, blah, blah, blah, missing in action, we will give you further notice, blah, blah, blah.' And my whole family said, 'He's gone, he's dead.' They all believed I was dead! My mother was the only one who said, 'He'll be home. He's coming home.'

[We landed in New York], and there were people waiting for us; I was taken right down to Savannah, Georgia. I was still in bad shape, not in the greatest shape at all. I had to go be rebuilt; they treated me there for about two weeks, hospitalized and everything else. Then I went for my interview and was released home. I went back and they wanted me to hold PoW meetings with soldiers who were going overseas, and they kept me there for a while. How I was treated, how to be treated, how to treat the guards, how to talk to them, how to act if you are a PoW.

[I was discharged] at the end of 1946. I got a telegram and a letter and a phone call that I will be serving for the next 20 years in the Air Corps Reserves. Never called for duty or anything, but I kept up my flying status in the reserves.

I did not take advantage of the GI Bill because I had fulfilled one of the things on my mind when I was young—number one was medicine; the second was aviation. Once I had completed [my dream of] aviation, and given the condition I was in when I came out, I had no desire to go back to school or anything else. I just thought, what am I going to do with my life now? Of course, when I got released the first thing I did after I was out of uniform was to join the downtown YMCA for a fitness program to get back in shape. Mentally and physically I was still bad. Now this was in 1947, and I needed transportation. They were not making many vehicles then, the automobile business had been suspended, so there were no used car lots or anything else. I didn't know where to start and where to go, and I needed transportation. I couldn't take a bus; they didn't have any buses or streetcars. One day, I decided to take a bus ride to Lackawanna. I got off at one of the residential stations, and just roamed around the streets. I'd knock on a door of a house and I introduced myself and said I was looking for a used vehicle, do you know where I can get one? Because a lot of these people, their husbands were drafted, went into service, and a lot of them, of course, didn't come back. And one woman, 'Yes, we have a car.' I think it was a Chevy at that time. Flat tires, everything else. Her husband was killed in service. He worked at Bethlehem Steel, went into service, had a family. And they didn't know what to do with the car, but I knew what to do. Flat tires, no battery, won't start. In the meantime, I had lined up a mechanic that I knew, and I had the car picked up. They couldn't tow it, they had to put it on the lift, brought it in. In those days the tires had tubes in them, because you couldn't buy tires, you couldn't buy anything. But there was an auto parts store on Broadway in Buffalo, and they had tubes. I put the car in shape, and cleaned it up, and used it.

One day there was a note on my car that someone wanted to purchase it. So I called this number, and I told him I wouldn't sell it right away because I needed it. Then something clicked, maybe this is something I should do. So I went back to Lackawanna, and through this woman, and I got her neighbor, the neighbor gave me another person. And I started buying cars, putting them in shape, and selling them. All of a sudden, it turned into a business—that's how I got started in the car business. I couldn't do everything myself; one of my fraternity brothers was back from service. I called him and asked him if he'd be interested in working for me. I sent him out to do what I was doing. And we started, and then I rented a lot on Franklin Street to store these vehicles. It was close to downtown, it was close to the YMCA where I was going every day. That's how I started my car business.

Then, of course, they started building cars again. Then I decided to go into the new car business when they did build the cars, and I acquired an English Ford franchise. I flew to New York, met with the English people there and asked them about becoming a dealer for their English Ford. They said yes, they are contemplating opening up franchises in America. The English Ford was owned by Ford Motor Company, but it was all American-style parts and not English parts, metric and so forth. So I made a deal with them. They asked me, 'What's your bank, how are you going to finance, how are you going to pay for all this?' I said, 'Well, we got the price and everything else. How many can you put on a truck to transport now?' He said, 'We have a unit that has nine, we can put nine units on it.'

I said, 'Well, I'll give you a check for the first batch, the first carload.' I hadn't been paid for about three years in the service, [due to my MIA/POW status], and when I was released, I had little money. So that's how I started in the car business.

'I Had to Get On'

I have no idea what happened [to the fellow who went out of my airplane]. My entire squadron, every single one, including my major, my colonel, everyone else is gone now. I had no contact whatsoever with them at all, and now they are all passed away.

I went to a couple veterans organization meetings, but actually it depressed me a little bit. I could get nothing out of it. I did go through Post-Traumatic Stress, but that didn't help me at all. Just one or two meetings, and I canceled out; I did it all on my own. Oh yeah, I had my own problems. But [the Army] was more interested in knowing how the Russians acted toward me, if they were violent or anything else, or if they tried to get information out of me on how the Americans are. On a scale of 1 to 10, I would give the Russians a 10.

I had to get on. I was single, I was not married at the time. I just wanted to get on, to try to forget and put everything in the past.

And like I told you before, I wouldn't have come [but for what I saw regarding] the Holocaust, that this would be [read by] some person, somewhere in the future… If one person ever remembers this and gets some good out of it, then I'm very, very happy about it, because this is bringing back things that I didn't want to bring back—things that I put in the back of my mind, that I hadn't thought about in years.

Just remember, being a Jew is one of the best things that could ever… If you were born and raised as a Jew, stay a Jew. Never deny it. Be proud and remember. Remember there are people in this world today that I know do not believe there was ever a Holocaust. They think it's a fiction by the Jews. Believe me, it is true; [I saw it].

At one time the oldest living veteran in New York, Captain Cole returned home to open a series of car dealerships in western New York. He passed at the age of 107 in November 2021.

MATTHEW A. ROZELL

THE THINGS
—— OUR ——
FATHERS SAW

THE UNTOLD STORIES OF THE WORLD WAR II
GENERATION FROM HOMETOWN, USA

ACROSS THE RHINE

VOLUME VII

THE THINGS OUR FATHERS SAW

THE UNTOLD STORIES OF THE
WORLD WAR II GENERATION
FROM HOMETOWN, USA

VOLUME VII:
ACROSS THE RHINE

Matthew A. Rozell

WOODCHUCK HOLLOW PRESS
Hartford · New York

Copyright © 2021,2024 by Matthew A. Rozell. Version 6.30.23. All rights reserved. No part of this publication may be reproduced, distributed, or transmitted in any form or by any means without the prior written permission of the publisher. Grateful acknowledgement is made for the credited use of various short quotations also appearing in other previously published sources. Please see author notes.

Information at matthewrozellbooks.com.

Maps by Susan Winchell. Cover design by Mary R. Rozell.

Front Cover: "Crossing the Rhine under enemy fire at St. Goar, March, 1945. 89th Infantry Division." US Army, Office of War Information. Public Domain Photographs, National Archives.

Back Cover: "Then came the big day when we marched into Germany-right through the Siegfried Line.", ca. 1945. Unknown photographer, United States Army. Office of War Information. National Archives, public domain.

Any additional photographs and descriptions sourced at Wikimedia Commons within terms of use, unless otherwise noted.

Publisher's Cataloging-in-Publication Data

Names: Rozell, Matthew A., 1961- author.
Title: Across the rhine : the things our fathers saw : the untold stories of the World War II generation, volume VII / Matthew A. Rozell.
Description: Hartford, NY : Matthew A. Rozell, 2021. | Series: The things our fathers saw, vol. 7. | Also available in audiobook format.
Identifiers: LCCN 2021922786 | ISBN 978-1-948155-28-1 (hardcover) | ISBN 978-1-948155-14-4 (paperback) | ISBN 978-1-948155-26-7 (ebook)
Subjects: LCSH: World War, 1939-1945--Campaigns—Netherlands. | World War, 1939-1945--Campaigns--France--Normandy. | World War, 1939-1945--Campaigns—Belgium. | World War, 1939-1945--Campaigns—Germany. | World War, 1939-1945--Personal narratives, American. | Veterans--United States--Biography. | Military history, Modern--20th century. | BISAC: HISTORY / Military / World War II. | HISTORY / Military / Veterans. | BIOGRAPHY & AUTOBIOGRAPHY / Military.

matthewrozellbooks.com.

Created in the United States of America

*~To the memory of
The World War II Generation~
and
Tom Warner, Sr.
1931-2021*
✳✳✳

'To survive ten months was to survive a hundred years. I could not even remember my former life. I was a fugitive from the law of averages.'

— U.S. TANK COMMANDER, RECOUNTING HIS BATTALION'S ADVANCE ACROSS THE RHINE

✳

'Heroes are important—they exist, and can help you to know who and what you are. Tell the children that I was a warrior.'

— U.S. PARATROOPER, MOHAWK NATION, SIXTY YEARS AFTER THE WAR

THE THINGS OUR FATHERS SAW VII:

ACROSS THE RHINE

THE STORYTELLERS (IN ORDER OF APPEARANCE):

NICHOLAS F. BUTRICO
ALBERT L. TARBELL
RICHARD M. MAROWITZ
TIMOTHY J. HORGAN
LAWRENCE E. BENNETT
AUGUSTINE J. DIFIORE
ROBERT C. BALDRIDGE
RUDOLF F. DRENICK
CHARLES J. ZAPPO
ALVIN M. COHEN
EMILIO J. DIPALMA
TONY HAYS
DOUGLAS VINK

THE THINGS OUR FATHERS SAW VII:

TABLE OF CONTENTS

ACROSS THE RHINE

AUTHOR'S NOTE	93
PART ONE	99
THE ROAD TO THE REICH	99
TO LIBERATE A CONTINENT	101
THE RANGER	103
A BRIDGE TOO FAR	139
THE PARATROOPER I	143
THE RECON MAN I	169
PART TWO	187
SETBACKS	187
THE CAVALRYMAN I	189
THE PARATROOPER II	199

PART THREE	**215**
CROSSING OVER	**215**
'THE WAY IT WAS'	**217**
THE INFANTRY SERGEANT	**219**
THE GIVER	**235**
THE FORWARD OBSERVER	**251**
THE ROCKET MAN	**265**
THE PARATROOPER III	**275**
THE CAVALRYMAN II	**295**
THE RECON MAN II	**307**
THE MEDIC	**321**
THE FALL OF BERLIN	**335**
THE PARATROOPER IV	**337**
JUDGMENT AT NUREMBERG	**343**
THE JEWISH GUARD KEEPER	**347**
THE COURTROOM SENTINEL	**363**

PART FOUR   387

LAST THOUGHTS   387

THE PARATROOPER V   389

DACHAU AND THE QUESTION   395

WAR STORIES   405

AMERICANS CAME TO LIBERATE   423

"Soldiers of the 55th Armored Infantry Battalion and a tank of the 22nd Tank Battalion move through a smoke-filled street. Wernberg, Germany."-Pvt. Joseph Scrippens, April 22, 1945. Source: National Archives, public domain.

Author's Note

I sat in the living room of the family of the eighty-year-old retired judge and former New York State Supreme Court justice, a reluctant but willing soldier who began his military career with the familiar letter from Uncle Sam, a ticket to picking up cigarette butts as a private at Fort Knox, then training in M4 Sherman tanks for what would become the invasion of France. He rocked in the chair and recounted hours of war stories, some funny, others that brought out the fluctuations between boredom and terror as his tank battalion moved from the beaches at Normandy to the Siegfried Line, the fortified dragon's teeth that demarked and viciously forbade entry upon German soil.

Some of his remarks at that conversation in the summer of 2001 struck me, and will be familiar to my longtime readers, as Judge Walsh became my friend—and my hero—in how he navigated his life with humility and concern for others, qualities that predisposed him to excel in his future occupation. As it was, in the summer and fall of 1944 he was just 23 years old.

> Now actually I was kind of an old guy for the time; a lot of the infantry guys were eighteen, nineteen years old. Oh yeah, I was considered an old guy. Now let me tell you about the combat I was in. Like I said before, you couldn't remember what your mother looked like; you thought you had been there forever. I was in combat ten months straight. You have to realize that was a long time to be in combat and still be

alive or not wounded! You just give up; you know there is no use to hoping that maybe you will get out tomorrow, you just are going to go on. You have that feeling and you just trot along; that's why we did [some] crazy stuff... Once we got to the Siegfried Line, then the Germans would tighten up. From October into December, it was bad. We were in Germany, the 743rd Tank Battalion and 30th Division, north of Aachen, we even fought at Aachen. That was tough going—to survive ten months was to survive a hundred years! I could not even remember my former life. I was a fugitive from the law of averages, as it was.

A few years before our talk, as a high school history teacher I had begun inviting veterans into the classroom to share their experiences. As word got out and other students wished to join us, I began organizing morning, afternoon, and sometimes all-day symposiums on various topics related to World War II and the Holocaust. We began in the late nineties with local Pacific veterans. Near the 45th anniversary of the liberation of Dachau concentration camp, April 2000, and a year or so before my talk with Judge Walsh that would go on to change thousands of lives, three members of the local chapter of Veterans of the Battle of the Bulge made one of their first of many appearances at my high school, before a student audience of over 100 polite and respectful kids. Two of the three were Jewish; one had been present at the liberation of Dachau forty-five years to the day, and the other, a guard at the Nuremberg War Trials after the war. Said one, in a later interview,

> There's three of us that have been going around to schools and churches and synagogues and so forth, talking to kids. They've got us running. That's been phenomenal. We each do about seven, eight minutes, a little bit of background of

who we are and what we did in the Army and whatever. We ask for questions. We now book no less than two hours, and we go over time. The kids, the hands never go down, unbelievable.

We did Hudson Falls High School. This was early on. We were only booking an hour and a half. We were supposed to talk from 1:00 to 2:30, and never got out until 4:00. Unbelievable. They're hungry. And the phenomenal part of the whole thing, the teacher wasn't even born yet.

That teacher was me. I was born sixteen years after the killing stopped; when I began my teaching career in the late 1980s, just forty years after the war, many veterans were still with us and newly retired—about the age I am now. Some felt ready to share their stories, and all who visited the classrooms across America were refreshed, energized, with a renewed sense of purpose after engaging with the future generations. As most of my readers with parents who lived through World War II can attest, most did not talk about it after the war. For many, it was only when they realized that people did not know about World War II, or worse, denied that the Holocaust had taken place, that they felt another duty to speak out. Teachers like me gave them the space and time to do that; I went on to create my own oral history project, and we were honored to ask the questions, listen to the answers, and provide the platform for a forum, a bridge between generations of Americans. The New York State Military Museum's Veterans Oral History Project came into being shortly after that; we gave our 200+ interviews to them and gleaned more from the interviews found there that were conducted at the same time we were doing our work. I knew I was doing something important, but it started with the spark of wonderment forty plus years ago, as the veterans of the European campaign returned to Normandy for the 40th anniversary of D-Day in 1984.

A lot of these guys lived with the trauma of war and witnessing the Holocaust for the rest of their lives. And because of Judge Walsh's interview, I went on to become a Holocaust educator as well (as detailed in my 2016 book and teacher memoir, *A Train Near Magdeburg*).

Our Dachau liberator told the kids,

> It was [the concentration camp] Dachau that we had smelled miles before we got there. And yet, people in the village who were right next to the camps said they didn't know what was going on; people in Munich, which was actually only nine miles from Dachau, didn't know what was going on. Now if you want to believe that, the Brooklyn Bridge is still for sale. But when you looked around some of these tough soldiers were throwing up and crying all over the place. It is not possible to really describe the number of feelings you get when you walk into something like that, because, well, first of all, nobody told us about the camp! We had no idea what a concentration camp was! We were going to Dachau, period. It was just another village as far as we were concerned. That's kind of a shock to get all at one time.

He continued, to his later interviewer,

> Every now and then they go, 'Gee, this stuff is not in the books.' I said to the kids, 'Now look at what you've learned today. You'll never find it in a book anyplace.'

Until now. The book you are reading is the seventh volume of my oral history series, with several more projected. Thank you for reading, and for remembering with me.

Matthew Rozell, November 11, 2021
Washington County, NY

PART ONE

THE ROAD TO THE REICH

'We're sitting there, and we're just bullshitting—there was really nothing in the town—and this command car comes up and it's his car! The command cars are wide, you know, because it has the flag and the three stars there, and he went right past us, and [the driver] squeezed the brakes and stopped, and he had the driver back up. We were sitting there; we weren't getting up for shit—we were still sitting there. General Patton looked down on us and then we realized who he was, but we still didn't get up, and he saluted us and he left; he never said a word. He must have seen the patches on our shoulders. He didn't say a word!'

—US Army Ranger, somewhere in Europe

Gen. Dwight D. Eisenhower speaks with men of Company E of the 502nd Parachute Infantry Regiment, 101st Airborne Division in England on the evening of June 5, 1944, as they prepare for the Battle of Normandy.
Credit: U.S. Army photograph, public domain.

CHAPTER ONE

To Liberate a Continent

The first Allied troops to land in occupied Europe in 1944 were tasked with the final push to free the continent from under the heel of the Nazi jackboot, an undertaking that would not be completed in that long year. While optimistic, no military planner had a crystal ball; no one could foresee the setbacks and brutality of almost an entire year before finally crossing the Rhine River for good in the spring of 1945. Suffering through cold, fatigue, hunger, and other punishing conditions, many a soldier wondered just what it was all about, and would question just what they were fighting for.

Later, almost every GI who finally set foot on German soil would get the opportunity to witness for themselves the things that would never leave them, and, in some cases, haunt and hound them for the rest of their lives.

They would have the answer to their question.

Nicholas Butrico holds up a copy of his famous D-Day letter as reprinted in a magazine. Source: NYS Military Museum.

CHAPTER TWO

The Ranger

Comfortable on his couch in his New York home, Nick Butrico gives a lively talk about his time in the 5th Ranger Battalion in Europe, from the D-Day landings and participation in the assault on the German fortified gun position at the formidable cliffs of Pointe Du Hoc, to spearheading into German territory at night, using, as he called it, rope boats to pull themselves across. To the astonishment of later D-Day historians, he even wrote a description of the scenes he encountered on June 6, 1944, a few days after D-Day, on the back of Eisenhower's famous Order of the Day letter to invasion servicemen, ending it with a supplication to God to keep him safe thereafter, his first dramatic day of combat.

Speaking quickly and gesturing emphatically, he has a lot to say about his experiences in the war, even to the point of turning the military acronym SNAFU into a verb.[14] He sat for this interview in February 2003 when he had just turned 81; he entered the service

---

[14] *military acronym SNAFU-*"Sarcastic expression 'Situation Normal: All Fucked Up.' The original military acronym stood for 'Status Nominal: All Fucked Up,' but also bowdlerized to 'all fouled up.' It means that the situation is bad, but that this is a normal state of affairs. The acronym is believed to have originated in the United States Marine Corps during World War II." Source: Wikipedia.

as a twenty-year-old Italian kid from New York. Like many of our World War II veterans, he had his medals and citations in a shadowbox display, which he described to his interviewers.

'This is the original dog tag that we first got when we first went in the service, but they were taken away when we went overseas. But I kept mine because your address is on here—where you lived, and they didn't want that to get in German hands. Now we come over here—This is the Bronze Star. That's for gallantry, I don't know how I got it.

Now this is the Purple Heart, and that little thing in there is the oak leaf cluster, which means you were hit twice. They don't give you a medal every time you get hit; they gave you a cluster. And this right down here is the Presidential Citation with an oak leaf cluster. It's equivalent to the Medal of Honor, only in a unit. We got a cluster—one was for Normandy, the other cluster was for Zeef [my last mission, in Germany].

I'll tell you about the guy that jumped off the boat in Normandy; he held on then, his name was Sergeant Walters, he was the nicest guy, he had two kids, I don't know what the hell he was doing in the Rangers with two kids! Well, another sergeant, he wanted a cup of coffee, but somebody had to stay in this foxhole.

Walters said, 'Go ahead, I'll go in your hole. You go for the coffee.' Now while he went for the coffee, the Germans were throwing artillery and one goes right into the foxhole and killed Walters. And I always said to the guys when I got back, 'He could have just as well died on the beach.'

The war was almost over; this was March. He went through all this, and he had to die that way! The guy that he covered the hole for went berserk. They put him in the bunker. He went berserk, you know.'

Nicholas F. Butrico

I was born in New York. I was born January 29, 1922. I only went to high school, that's all. In those days, not many people went to college.

[When I heard the news of Pearl Harbor], I was upstairs. I'm not sure about the time; it might have been the afternoon, I don't remember. I was [listening to] the football game, the Giants were playing, and they interrupted, 'Pearl Harbor was bombed.' I don't remember who was there with me, but I said, 'Where the hell is Pearl Harbor?' Hell, I never heard of it. I didn't realize it was our country being bombed. Then I went downstairs, and I met the rest of the fellas and they're talking, 'You know the United States is bombed and we're going to go to war.' I didn't realize at that time. So that's how I really found out that Pearl Harbor belonged to America.

'Look in the Dead Files'

I was drafted, but then again, maybe I enlisted. While I was home, all my buddies were gone. I had a few of the younger fellas [I was hanging around with]; I was considered 1A, [fit for military service]. I still have that stuff hanging around. And I went back to the local board, and I asked them, 'How come I didn't get called?'

He said, 'What's your name?' and then he said, 'We have no record of you.'

So I said, 'Look in the dead files.'

So he looked in the dead files, and my name comes up in the dead files! Now if I hadn't gone back there, I probably wouldn't have gone through the whole war! Then two weeks later I got the notice, went to Governors Island, and that's where I went for my physical. That's the preliminary—they want to see if you have two arms, two legs, you don't have a heart condition. That's not a real physical; the real physical came later on.

In October '42, I was drafted, and I remember going to Fort Dix, and Fort Dix shipped me out to Breckenridge, Kentucky. I was with the 98th Infantry Division. A funny story about that is, the 98th Infantry Division was a New York division—Iroquois. Every time I went out on [patrols with them], we used to get lost! So, I had another buddy—he passed away a few years ago—I said to him, 'You know, if we go out to combat with these guys, we're going to get ourselves killed.'

He said, 'Yes, I know. Every time we go out, we get lost.'

Well, we couldn't get out. I tried to get in the Air Corps, but they wouldn't take me because I'm colorblind. Later on, they were looking for guys [regardless of if you were colorblind], but they wouldn't take me. Then a general order came down—it was on the bulletin board. They were looking for volunteers for the Rangers. So, I said to my friend, 'What can we lose? At least maybe we get a better outfit. And it's not a big outfit.'

'Okay!'

Twenty-five-hundred men took the physical right there at Camp Breckenridge and only about two hundred passed. I was one of them. All these guys failed—either they were colorblind or something—and I was colorblind, but I was a little smarter. I was in the line and when I got up there, I had been to the back guy where they had [colored] cotton on the floor and they'd tell you, 'Pick the red one out,' and I was memorizing. So, when I got up there and the guy says, 'Pick the red one out...' They could have changed it and I wouldn't have known. [*Laughs*]

And then the 98th Division was going on maneuvers in Tennessee, and me and my buddy and a few other guys were pulled out and we were sent to the 5th Ranger Battalion in Camp Forest, Tennessee, with the 2nd Ranger Battalion. Both battalions were there. We trained there for a while and then from there we went to Fort Pierce, Florida, and we did a little amphibious training. I said, 'Hey, we're going to go to Japan, you know, they're teaching us how to use the rubber boats and stuff. Okay, we're going to Japan.'

But from there I came up to Fort Dix for about two months, just training and all this. The next thing I know, we're in Camp Kilmer, that's an embarkation point, and of course Camp Shanks is right down the corner from here. The 2nd Ranger came out of Camp Shanks, but we came out of Kilmer.

Shipping Out

We got on this ship, the *Mauritania*. We were going unescorted because the *Mauritania* was a big ship and it was fast; some probably couldn't catch up to it. Right out of the harbor, a tanker hit us in the front! Our boat didn't sink, but it shook it, and I said, 'Are we getting bombed already—torpedoes?' Then we found out we were going back to port, to 42nd Street to one of those piers, and pulling in there. Right away all the GIs—you know there were a lot of GIs on the ship—the rumors started. 'The war was over, that's why they brought us back to 42nd Street!' Then we got the news they were repairing that cut and they probably could have made the trip, but to play it safe they worked all day, and the next day when I woke up all I saw was water; we had pulled out.

Commando Training

I ended up in Liverpool. It only took us six days. We went to Liverpool and from there we were shipped to Wales. We only stayed there to do little problems, then they shipped us up to Dundee, Scotland—British Commando School. Most of our teachers were British commandos, and the training was tough there. A lot of guys were pulled out—couldn't make it—they'd fall out of marches. Every time we'd do anything it was live ammunition, no simulation, everything was live ammunition, and we had to climb cliffs up and down—from the top down and climb up. They showed us how to do it. I remember, we used to put [the line] through our legs, and you could do good down, but it was up that bothered us. We had a lot of forced marches; we had a march—I think nine miles—and we had to do it in at least an hour. You try force marching with your feet starting to get you and if you didn't stay in, out you went—in other words, they'd ship you back to the infantry outfit or wherever.

We made it all through and after we got through with Dundee, I ended up down in the Isle of Wight, right down in the southern part of England, and then we did a little more training with boats coming in and we ended up on Weymouth. And we got on the ship on Weymouth and that's where we got this letter that I showed you inside. But you know, I didn't think anything of it. But we knew now—this was June 4—we knew where the invasion was coming, but we didn't know exactly what day. We knew where it was because we were getting maps from the Air Corps every time they'd come back from a bomb run, they'd come back [to us]—Pointe du Hoc, that's what our objective was. They'd take pictures; no sooner than they landed, we'd have them in less than an hour on our tables—where this was, and where that was, and where the guns were supposed to be. While we were doing this, we weren't allowed out. They had us guarded—here we were, barbed wire all around, British soldiers guarding us, and then they had another [perimeter] rim—American soldiers guarding the British soldiers, and if anybody in our outfit tried to get through the barbed wire, they'd shoot to kill them, because we knew too much, even though we didn't know the date, but we knew too much—we knew where it was coming. I'm on the ship there; the next thing you know, through the night—the boat—they'd pull out. This is about June 5. I don't know, they'd stayed in the harbor—we lay in that Weymouth Harbor for two, three days eating British food. All they'd ever give you was greasy lamb and stuff like that. We used to have to eat that.

The Day of Days

We landed in Normandy with the British LCAs they called them—very low in the water. You've heard of the Higgins boat? You've seen the movies where they'd come down—the doors opened in the front? We were on this ship and the next thing I know it was the 5th and they told us it wasn't going to happen because the weather was bad. Then on June 6, as far as we knew—I found out after—June 6 was better, but it wasn't any better because I was seasick. You know we didn't have to climb down the ropes like you see in the movies to get on the [landing craft], we just stepped right on as if we were going on a lifeboat. See, they used to lie right along the ship and used to drag us down into the water. We'd get on there, about five or six boats for the whole battalion, and then we'd circle around the ship and the *USS Texas*—big cruiser out there, big warship out there—was firing, 'Boom, boom.' Every time they fired the whole boat shook, you know, the little boat we were on shook! And as we were going into shore, the water was so rough, we started to sink. So, the limey there, the British coxswain, said, 'Hey you Yanks, you better start bailing out or we're not going to make it!'

Okay, so now everybody took their helmets off. And me, I was so sick my rifle was lying on the bottom of the water. I wasn't worried about bailing out so we could get the ship out, but we finally got it out because a couple of them did go down. And we made it to shore, but this is where I really found out what war was like.

As soon as we got there, there was this Chester—he came from Brooklyn—he said to me, 'Nick,' you know, he was one of my buddies, he said, 'Nick, I don't know how to swim.' I figured, well, you have a life jacket; it's got to be a piece of cake. Well, as soon as we got in, the coxswain opened the doors. My friend and Sergeant Walters were the first two off. Now when they went off, they went right down. There was a shell hole there from the Air Corps, and it was deep. The sergeant held onto the door, but the kid, he was only seventeen or eighteen, didn't hold onto the door so he just jumped out, and a big wave—the water was so rough—just came over right on top of him. And I found out a few days later from headquarters that they found him on the beach. He died and I felt bad, and then I knew what war was like.

*

Once I hit the land, I didn't even know I was seasick anymore, I was worried about my ass. I hit this dune. I stood there a while and I saw what was going on, and I saw the 29th Division and the 1st Division coming in, and some of these shells that the Germans were throwing out—88s or mortars, one of them hit. They had these big ships, these LSTs, with ramps on the side that you walked down. Well one of those shells—while the guys were coming down—hit that ramp. Everybody flying all over the place and I said, 'Jesus Christ, what the hell am I doing here?'

Pointe du Hoc

Now our objective that day, we landed on Omaha, but our objective was to go into the Pointe. Now we had three companies and the 2nd Rangers went right into the Pointe—the 5th Ranger Battalion and three companies of 2nd Rangers landed with us. We were attached to the 29th Division. Now our job was to get up to the road and head to Pointe du Hoc, which was about five miles away, and capture these guns from the rear. Everything was so snafued that the original guys who were going to Pointe du Hoc were about three miles off course, so they had to bypass along the shore to get to the Pointe, and the Germans were shooting at them as they went by. Well, they made it to the Pointe, and we had Colonel Snyder go into Omaha with the 29th, get up to the draw and meet on the top—get to the Pointe. That was his job. Get to the Pointe, Pointe du Hoc.

Okay, so when I hit that sand dune, I looked out there and said, 'Jesus Christ, what the hell am I doing here?' There were a few other guys and we turned around and the whole countryside was burning. So, we had to put on the gas masks to get up to the top. I finally got up to the top; everything was disorganized. I finally happened to see my captain and he said, 'Nick, what are you doing?'

I said, 'I don't know, there are only three of us here!' We picked up a few more Rangers; we ended up picking up twenty-three [in total], because they were scattered all over the place. So, twenty-three Rangers—and the captain, he got a DSC for this—he said, 'Let's go to the Pointe.' Actually, we were supposed to meet the whole battalion and then go to it, but we went to the Pointe. Twenty-three men and the captain were the only ones on D-Day that got to the Pointe Du Hoc on June 6—it's in all the books—the rest of the battalion got there three days later, because the 29th was taking a hell of a beating; they were getting counterattacked. Pointe du Hoc was a big thing—in fact, we had artillery support. The *USS Texas* and the *Arizona* were our personal artillery support because they bombed the shit out of that place.[15] In fact, they even saved the guys [going up]. They threw so many shells into that cliff, it was practically going up this way! [*Moves left arm to indicate steep upward*

---

[15] *The Arizona*- Mr. Butrico probably refers to *USS Arkansas* (BB-33), which provided support at Omaha Beach with the *USS Texas* on D-Day.

slope, instead of vertical climb] But when the 2nd Ranger Battalion got to the top, there were no guns there—the Germans had moved them. They had like telephone poles for guns, but they moved them back about a mile.

And it just happened—Len would know, I see him so often—he and Sergeant Coon—who just passed away—were going with a few men up to this road, because they see heavy tracks, and there were the guns all ready to shoot ammunition all over the place, but there was nobody there![16] About a hundred yards away, there were about

---

[16] *Len would know*- Mr. Butrico almost certainly refers to 24-year-old Sgt. Len 'Bud' Lomell (1920-2011), a fellow Ranger of the 2nd Battalion born in New York and raised in New Jersey, not far from Mr. Butrico. Praised by historian Stephen Ambrose as only second to Eisenhower for the critical success of D-Day, Mr. Lomell was already wounded before reaching the beach and scaling the cliffs.
'I was the first one wounded,' he recalled in a 2009 interview with Charlie Rose. He stepped off the ramp at the front and immediately found himself in water over his head. 'When I bopped up, my guys grabbed me and pulled me up,' he remembered. 'And then we hit the beach.'
Lomell said the wound burned a little, but hadn't hit anything vital, and they rushed to the cliffs, where the rocket-propped grappling hooks were launched, trailing long lengths of climbing ropes. Loaded with gear and explosives, they began scaling the sheer wall, hand-over-hand, while the Germans on top were desperately trying to cut the ropes or shoot them.
Those on the ropes couldn't shoot back because they were climbing, hoping only for covering fire from the ground. Many were hit and killed or wounded. Others fell to their deaths. Those who finally were able to reach the top overwhelmed the Germans and found a surprise waiting. The guns had secretly been moved. The artillery barrels that appeared so clearly on U.S. reconnaissance photos were nothing more than telephone poles set at an angle to disguise the real location of the weapons.
Lomell said it was critical to find the missing guns. As the battle raged below on the beaches, he and two other Rangers followed a set of tracks leading inland from the cliff, where they found all five carefully hidden in an apple orchard, left unguarded. Using grenades and other explosives, Lomell and the others managed to disable them, eluding discovery and rendering the coastal defense guns useless. It's a story that's been well documented in books and films. Historians recount it as one of the most important keys to

one hundred Germans. They were talking and eating, and they were getting ready to do something, so what he did was, he got in there and he had a thermite grenade and threw it into the breach, into the barrel, and you know what that did—it melted everything. He only had two, but there were six guns there, so he had to knock out the other four, so he came back. He got a couple from the other guys in the back, and they knocked out all the guns, because these guns were facing Utah Beach. They could have been traversed to Omaha; that's why they wanted Pointe du Hoc captured, because those guns could fire on the *Texas*, they could fire on the *Arizona*, they could fire on the whole damn front. General Bradley had said, and it's in most of your books, 'The Rangers had the worst objective in the whole Normandy invasion—those guns,' but they didn't realize they weren't there. The French did find that they weren't there, but it was too late to get us because we were on our way. But the guns had been moved.

When we got there, they still had to hold on to a crossroad there so the Germans would not [counterattack]. But Pointe du Hoc was between Utah and Omaha, and they wanted a linkup and we were in the middle—Pointe du Hoc was in the middle there. They wanted us to protect the road, so the Germans wouldn't come in there. They wanted to keep us separated. But it never happened, they held on, so that's the story.

Allied success that day. But for Lomell, it was less a day of heroics than one of loss.
'There was a lot of death,' he said in a 2007 interview with *The Star-Ledger*. 'I lost half my guys. What more is there to know?' Source: Spoto, Mary Ann. *Leonard Lomell, World War II hero from Toms River, dies at 91*. March 2, 2011. NJ.com. www.nj.com/news/2011/03/leonard_lomell_d-day_hero_from.
Mr. Lomell was also featured in Tom Brokaw's 1998 book, *The Greatest Generation*.

When they knew we had the Pointe secured, [we were told], 'Stay with the 29th Division and give them a hand,' so they were supposed to come to the Pointe too; that's what happened.

And from there I was okay—I didn't get a scratch, not a scratch. I was pretty lucky—I could see what was going on. We stood at about D+10, maybe 13—I don't remember the date—that's when I wrote the letter, and they took us off the line.

'Not Made to Take Care of Prisoners'

Cherbourg had fallen. They made us take care of prisoners, prisoners of war—take them down to the beach. We were about three or four miles out, and they had the thing lit up like Times Square. I suppose the Germans knew that it was a prisoner of war camp, so they didn't strafe it or bomb it, and there was another one right down on the beach. But this was about D+15 or somewhere around there, and we used to get one hundred prisoners and we got Italian prisoners, German prisoners, Polacks, everything, and we'd take them down to the stockade right on the beach, and then they would put them on ships to England or America or wherever they were going. And we did that for—I think we only lasted two days on the job. We weren't made to take care of prisoners.

We used to take the one hundred prisoners, and there were a lot of ships—we had a big storm there, and it blew a lot of these big ships right onto the beach, and every time we'd take them down to the beach, we'd run them along the [ship]. The five of us, we'd line them up; that's where they got us, because when they were in the stockade they were interrogated, they would leave them with their watches and stuff like that. [So before they would go in], we used to line them up and we used to clean them out, in other words, the Germans have watches—there was one German who didn't want to give up his watch. I'm struggling with this guy, and so I just took the bayonet out, and he got an idea of what I was talking about. 'Okay, you can have it.' So, [he took something else out of his pocket], and I thought it was going to be the valuable watch he was [holding back on]—it was a glass eye! I was so mad I felt like shooting him! I took the eye, and I threw it right in the ocean. I said, 'You made me do all this for a glass eye? Don't worry about it, when you go to America, they'll probably give you another one.'

When you get to the beach, the Navy's in charge. The Navy put in a complaint that the Rangers weren't following the Geneva rules because we had one hundred prisoners, but when we got to the stockade we had ninety-eight or ninety-six. What happened to the rest, well, we know they didn't run away; we had a lot of nuts in the outfit. But one incident—and nobody ever believes me, but this is the God's honest truth; whenever I say this story people just laugh—they don't believe it. Going down to the beach—now you try to walk in sand, it's tough, and we used to speed march, because the quicker we got to the other stockade, we'd go get a truck, a lot of trucks were going by—and we'd get a break. We didn't have to dig a foxhole because it was light, and the Germans knew it was there. Anyway, we were walking down to the beach, and we had a couple of older Germans, and so my sergeant came to me and said, 'Nick, these guys are holding us up. Take these two guys, with the medics, tell them to walk slowly and we'll meet you at the stockade.'

I said, 'Okay,' and it was dark because this was at nighttime. We were walking and I fell in a shell hole; there were a lot of shell holes there and when I fell, I lost the rifle. I had the rifle and it fell out of my hand—right into the sand it went!—and these two Germans and the medics jumped in the same hole with me and right away something went through my head, and I thought, 'This is it. [I'm dead.]'

The Germans grabbed me, they picked me up, they started wiping all the sand off my clothes. They picked the rifle up, they cleaned it, and they handed it back to me. Every time I tell that story, nobody believes me, but that is the truth! Then I figured, maybe they thought they were through, where were they going to go? The front line was maybe six, seven miles away. What were they going to do—escape so they could go fight again? They were smart, they didn't want to fight. In fact, most of the Germans didn't want to fight. They thought, 'What the hell are we going to fight for?'

From there, they threw us off that detail, I think we lasted two or three days. Those were some of the reasons why we weren't made to take care of prisoners.

'It Went Right Through My Legs'

I ended up in Brest. We had to get new men, or sometimes [guys were] coming back who had been wounded, and we had to train them again—they didn't get the same training we got, but they got some of it. Now in Brest, I got stuck with the 29th Division again. The 29th Division, the 8th Division—now people don't know this, I don't know if I should say this—but the 8th Division ran. They had sent us up there to Brest with the 2nd Ranger Battalion and the 5th for support to protect their flanks, because the flanks are the weakest part of anything. The Germans come in on the flanks—they wouldn't come this way [*motions towards himself with two arms directly in front*], they'd come this way. [*Motions towards himself with two arms spread to the sides*] The 29th Division used to go up about three miles and we used to just wait behind there to go right up there—we didn't have any firing to do or anything. We stopped right alongside the division. The Germans made a counterattack, and they pulled back, but they didn't tell us. We were stuck out there by ourselves. We had a colonel—an Irishman, his name was Sullivan—because the other one we had went back to the States. He said, 'I'm not giving up. I got here and I'm not going to [go back].'

We stay until they come back!' And then a couple of days later [the 29th], they counterattacked and they came back again.

Now in Brest, there were twenty-six objectives. Now, mind you, there were two divisions there, I think three, the 8th Division, the 29th Division, which we were attached to—I think the 2nd Ranger Battalion was attached to the 8th—and we had a couple of armored divisions there, and there were other personnel. There were twenty-six objectives in the whole battalion, and we weren't supposed to do any fighting. Out of twenty-six objectives, we took twenty-four. And we were only four hundred fifty men, that's all. We weren't a big unit. You know a division has eighteen thousand men, and we took twenty-four objectives, which they were supposed to take. They only took two.

Brest was submarine base for the Germans. [The brass] wanted Brest very badly because it was a big port, but the Germans wrecked it; when we got there, they had wrecked it. And then we had this guy—I'll show you the book inside—this Sergeant Elms with eight guys went in there. He talked to the [German] colonel and he had the colonel believing that they were surrounded—he had eight men—so he told everybody to throw their arms down and go out the front door. Eight hundred, there were just eight guys who captured them. He got a DSC and I think he got the Silver; he got two awards for that.

While I was in Brest, I lost my hearing. We were making one of the objectives that we were going after for the 29th. We were running across this field—now this was July, and it was hot—and the Germans opened up. I was with two other guys, and we hit the dirt—there was a dead cow and the cow blows up like a balloon, you know lying dead in the hot sun, and they stink. So at least it was cover, but I said to the others, 'If we stay here, we're going to die. Either we're going to get shot or we'll die of the stink.' The smell was terrific. We got up and we started to run through a little hedge there, and as we were running the Germans threw up—they had forty-millimeter mortars—and I could see it coming right at me and I just froze. It went right through my legs and didn't even touch me, and exploded in back of me and killed the two guys behind me. All I got was a concussion, I was on the ground. The next thing I know I found myself at an aid station. I said, 'What am I doing here?'

They said, 'You have a concussion. You didn't realize it—that the shell had knocked you out.'

But I didn't get anything on me. Pretty lucky, but right after that I started having problems with my hearing. The guys said, 'Hey Nick, can't you hear what we're talking about?' And they always had to holler, and as the years went by, it got worse and worse. If I took this hearing aid off, I'm dead; I'm so bad—the hearing is so bad—but then the old age too, that doesn't help.

'Let's Go to Paris'

From there, I remember I came back to the outfit a couple of days later; they sent me back. They put us on a train—just a company, one section, the guard train. The French—the 'frogs,' we used to call them—were stealing the rations off the trains. Every time the train stopped, they'd steal the rations. We had this train, maybe one hundred cars, we were the last in the caboose in the back, and every time the train stopped, we had to jump off, some on this side, look up the line and see the French stealing the B-rations. The guys driving the trains, they probably were in cahoots, that was why they stopped. The Americans were losing a lot of stuff that way. But we took some of the B-rations, which was good stuff, like peaches and stuff like that; it was all good rations. What the hell, we always [got stuck] with K-rations, you know, a box of crackers. That's what we had. When we got to one of these boxcars there and took a box and there were peaches in a can—a big can—and other good food, eggs, powdered eggs, we took that to a town called Chars, but when we got there, the town was flattened. There was nothing there but just a train depot. We turned the train over to some outfit waiting for us; they took over. Now we were about six guys, so what do we do now? Our colonel was supposed to pick us up there. The rest of the battalion went on to Arlon, Belgium; Paris had fallen by then.

I said, 'What do we do now?'

The Irish sergeant said, 'Let's go to Paris.'

We weren't that far from Paris. We knew Paris was off limits at that time, but we got to Paris, we got in. There were a few Air Corps men there—they put us up in the Grand Hotel, a beautiful hotel in France. We stayed there, but we had a lot of trouble—the MPs grabbed us—we had our sergeant and another guy fighting with the MPs. They wanted to go out [on the town] and scout around and see what they could find. The captain from the MPs came up to this sergeant and ordered something. We happened to be upstairs—the MPs had locked the doors on us, they didn't want us to go downstairs. But these two guys—they both were sergeants—this captain from the MPs comes over and he must have said something, and this guy just hauls off and flattened the captain, right on the floor! That's a court-martial-able offense. They arrested him. Now finally our colonel comes to Paris: 'Weren't we supposed to be in Chars? What are you doing here in Paris?'

'Well, there's nothing there, so we decided to come here.'

He said, 'Where's the two sergeants?' We told him. He went down to the MPs.

'They're in the stockade there.' He got them out of the stockade, but they never were court-martialed. He just took them right out—I don't know, maybe he threatened them—and we went to Arlon, Belgium. We stayed there—a little training there—we got some new men.

The Last Mission

There are some parts [of the war] that I just don't remember, but the last mission we were on was Zeef, it was called Zeef. Patton had gone to the Bulge, left us down at the Bulge... [*claps hands together*] We were told they wanted the battalion to go over the Sauer River; we had to go by rope boats because the 94th Division had a piece of it on the other side. [*Gestures with hand-over-hand horizontal pulling motion*] We would go through them, eleven miles into enemy territory, and sit in secret—at the Zeef crossroads—and all they wanted us to do was to stop anything that came through there, tanks, anything. Well, I got a break on there; maybe I wouldn't have made it out of there.

The battalion was spread out, a company here, a company there. So, we were going to get all together at night—was about twelve o'clock at night, pitch black—and we were going to go eleven miles behind enemy lines. As we were going in, the Germans just happened to throw up harassing fire, which just happened to land right in the middle of us. [*Gestures to indicate artillery or mortar fire*] A lot of guys got killed; a lot of guys got wounded. I helped one guy up—he was hit in the stomach. I remember his name; it was Anderson. An ambulance pulled up and I put him in the ambulance. He was, 'Oh, oh.' He finally died. And then when I got out, the doctor in the ambulance or the medic said, 'Where are you going?'

I said, 'I'm going back to the outfit before they go over there.'

He said, 'You're not going anywhere. Don't you know you're hit?' I didn't know I was hit. I was hit right above the eye.

'You're lucky it didn't come down an inch. You'd have lost an eye!'

I was hit right about here. [*Points above right eye*] A small piece of shrapnel, but I didn't even know it. And it was bleeding, but I thought it was from the guy I was helping. And I kept... [*wipes eye repeatedly with back of his hand*] I must have felt relieved I didn't have to go. They took me back and checked it out and they said, 'You're all right, it didn't affect your eyes.'

Now, I couldn't get back to the battalion anymore; they had gone eleven miles into German territory and sat there. They were supposed to be relieved in three days—the 94th Division and Patton made this big push to the Rhine. We were supposed to see that the Germans didn't bring up tanks or anything. Well, I heard this from the other guys, because I wasn't there. A car pulls up, a German car; it's got the little lights in the headlight. They stop him. A funny story. A major of the German army and two medics, and our guys said, 'You are our prisoners.'

And he said, 'It can't be—the frontlines are about ten miles away!' He said, 'What are you doing here?' The Germans didn't even know we were there yet. And we took them prisoners. We captured a bunker, and we were kind of using it for headquarters. When the Germans found out we were there, oh, Jesus Christ, they kept making counterattacks. They'd go through our lines; we'd send in our own artillery on our positions to get rid of them. They were calling, 'Goddamn Yankees, Yankee bums go home.' But the thing is, I wasn't there—I missed all this, but then again, I could have gotten killed too, because we lost a lot of men there. I'll tell you about the guy that jumped off the boat in Normandy; he held on, his name was Sergeant Walters, he was the nicest guy, he had two kids, I don't know what the hell he was doing in the Rangers with two kids! Well, another sergeant—and he just passed away—he wanted a cup of coffee, but somebody had to stay in this foxhole. Walters said, 'Go ahead, I'll go in your hole. You go for the coffee.' Now while he went for the coffee, the Germans were throwing artillery and one goes right into the foxhole and killed Walters. And I always said to the guys when I got back, 'He could have just as well died on the beach.'

The war was almost over; this was March. He went through all this, and he had to die that way! The guy that he covered the hole for went berserk. They put him in the bunker. He went berserk, you know. He passed away a few years back; he was an alcoholic; I don't know if that caused it, or what.

The Germans were dead all over the place. We had so many Germans dead that we had the German prisoners stack them in a barn. You could barely close the door—they had them all stacked in there. Every time they came up the road, we'd blast at them, kill them. They were all over the place; the place looked like west Normandy, only they were Germans. The German wounded—and we had a lot of German wounded—they were brought back to the bunker. Now our colonel turned around to the major, the German doctor, and he said, 'We have our medics and a doctor taking care of ours; you have free [rein] in the bunker, take care of your men with your two guys.'

The doctor said, 'Yes.' Well one thing about it, it turned out our colonel shook his hand when he left. The German worked on Americans and Germans—the ones who were wounded. He was a doctor even in Germany. Not all Germans were Nazis; not all Germans even wanted to fight—they would rather give up.

And from there we stayed eleven days—it was supposed to be three days—before they got to us, running out of ammunition, and I wasn't there all this time. I'm telling you the story of what's happening—the guys told me when I finally got back. Eleven days, the ammunition was low, the food was practically gone, they were eating German stuff! Our colonel was going to throw in the towel, there were only three other Ranger battalions that gave up to the Germans because they were surrounded, and that was at Anzio, and he said, 'We'll be the fourth.' But as it turned out, he said, 'We'll hold on.' They held on. They said, 'We'll send in some Piper Cubs and send you in supplies.' Just like the Army, they snafued it anyway. They sent in the Piper Cubs and threw ammunition and food down; most of it, the Germans got. All our buddies got was the ammunition; but most of the ammunition—you know, machine gun ammunition comes in belts; they were sending it down and it came in clips! So, we had to do it by hand. You ever try putting it in by hand? We didn't have a machine. We were putting these bullets in, then they started giving us belts. Finally, after eleven days, they held out, the 94th and I think the 10th Armored finally got to us. And they passed us up, and then we were pulled back.

*

I went back to the outfit and the doctor called me in the office and he said, 'Nick,'—everybody was 'Nick,' none of this… [*makes a saluting motion*]. We didn't salute—none of this saluting—nobody saluted anybody. Our captain—you never saluted him. We used to call him Ace; he never carried bars on his shoulder because the Germans would shoot [for the] bars. 'Don't salute; I don't want you to salute me.' Well this captain, he came back, and he called me in the office, and he said, 'Nick, we've reclassified you.'

I said, 'What does that mean?' I thought maybe they were going to send me home.

'No, you are going on limited service.' The war was almost over, it ended about a month later. This was March, and it ended in April. He said, 'We're going to send you back to another outfit.'

They sent me back to Compiègne. I was in limited service—Compiègne, France. That's where in the First World War they signed the [armistice ending the fighting with Germany] and Hitler took the train back out of there.[17] I went there. There were six of us. Pretty quiet—there was no war going on. We took care of Italian prisoners. They had their own kitchen. We didn't have a kitchen. We used to eat with some platoon outfit there; their food stunk.

---

[17] *Hitler took the train back out of there*-Hitler insisted that the defeated French sign the Armistice of June 22, 1940, in the same rail carriage at Compiègne that German forces had capitulated to the victors in World War I.

We had a captain—he was reclassified—so he said, 'Let's go to the Italians.' Now, they were prisoners, and they were eating better than we were! He set it up where they would feed us, we would give them the stuff. They made spaghetti. We couldn't eat that other stuff those guys were giving us! We were only six guys; they would serve us; they had a table all set; we had a tablecloth. We ate like kings! I was there until the war—I would have come home—they had a [point] system; I was going to come home under the [point] system. Even though the war was going on, I was going to get discharged, but I had no priority. The war was still going on with Japan—even when the Germans surrendered, I still had no status to go home, so I stuck with the [prisoner detail]. They finally repatriated all the Italians back to Italy.

The Accident

Now I remember a couple of days before we were going; I had a big GMC. We were driving. It was about seven o'clock in the morning. I had two Italian prisoners and myself; they did the driving. I said, 'Come on, pull over.' The roads are narrow in France. So, they pulled over because the roads are narrow.

We went in this café and had a cup of coffee; even though the coffee stunk, it was coffee. While we were inside, some dopey frog, you know what a frog is; he was on a motorcycle coming up that road. I don't know if he saw the truck—he hit the truck right in the middle and went right through the windshield and he got killed; he died. The MPs came and asked, 'What are you parked here for?'

We told them, 'We got a cup of coffee.'

Okay, we drove back—the two Italians and me. The two Italians couldn't go back to Italy; they had to get charged and I was charged with manslaughter, and they were charged with manslaughter. But the captain says to me, 'Oh, don't worry, this is a technicality. The reason that they do this is if you or these two prisoners decided to stay in France after the war, their family might sue you, press charges against you. We don't want that. And if we put you on trial, whatever comes out—you won't get anything.'

I was busted down to a private, and what did I care—I was going home, and a carton of cigarettes, that was the fine. And the Italians too—they finally went home. I got on the ship. I remember I was at Camp Lucky Strike.

*

I got on a Liberty ship to come home. This is from Le Havre. The name of the Liberty ship was the *Colonel Darby*.[18] You know who Colonel Darby was? He started the 1st Ranger Battalion, and all the 5th Rangers were under his command. That ship took eleven days to go from Le Havre to Brooklyn. Eleven days, and that ship bounced all over the place! It was November. Bouncing up and down; bouncing up and down—I thought the ship was going to split in half, it was so bad! I remember we took it out when it was a blue, calm day. I looked out—the *Rex*—the Italians had a big ship named the *Rex*. It wasn't as big as the *Queen Mary*, but it was named the *Rex*. We passed it while it was docked in England. We had been out in the water maybe three or four days and it passed us; you could see it passing us. I said, 'Why don't they put us on that ship?' They put us on this thing even though it is called the *Darby*. Well that ship, every time it went up it came down, boom, it hit the water, and the whole ship [*makes a shuddering motion*]—Jesus Christ! 'I hope this thing holds up!' We finally got home, and then I got discharged. And while I was getting discharged—they give you a physical—the doctor said to me, 'You're losing your hearing, you know.'

---

[18] *Colonel Darby*-William O. Darby (1911-1945) was regarded as 'the father of the modern Army Rangers,' leading his men in battles in North Africa, Sicily, and Italy. He was killed a week before the war in Europe ended. See more about him in Vol. 4 of this series, *Up The Bloody Boot*.

I said, 'Yes, I noticed that. The guys were talking to me.'

'That's probably because you were shot, the firepower—that's what could cause it.' He said, 'I'm just letting you know; tell them to put it down.'

Later on, I went back and said, 'I want this put on the records that I'm losing my hearing,' because if I hadn't done it, I wouldn't be compensated for my hearing because I get a pension for this. I wouldn't be getting compensation and I wouldn't be getting hearing aids for free or anything because it's not service connected. But today they do give it to you even if it's not service connected. But they wouldn't give it to me. These two hearing aids I have, this one is broken [*points to left ear*]–you know how much these cost? Six thousand dollars. You're paying for it, and you're paying for it. Three thousand each, and I'm getting new ones tomorrow and I don't know what they cost. Because I got these—every two years they give me new ones, these are two years old and then they take them back and they give you another two.

[*Phone rings in background*] That woman's husband [*points to phone*]—4th Ranger Battalion—we get together every so often. The funny part of it is I picked him up—we always go to the reunions and that's where I made friends with him, but I picked up something on the internet on Ben, he lives right in Queens. He was from the 4th Ranger Battalion; this guy's name is Black, his second name. His son put on there, 'My father was a 4th Ranger and he's looking for so and so. Fifty years ago, they were in a hospital together in Anzio and they came home together during the war and he's looking for this guy.' Right away [*points to head*], [I knew]. So, I wrote his son, 'Yeah, he lives in Clifton. Yeah, I know the guy.' I wrote back and I gave him the [information]. He finally came to the Ranger reunion in Atlantic City and they met after fifty-six years, and I was responsible for that. That's his wife that just called, because they call us every so often.

Looter Nick

Now I am going to tell you this—I was known as 'Looter Nick.' Every place I went—I don't care if it was a French house, Norwegian house, I don't care—I looked for loot. They used to call me Looter Nick. One time I went into a German house, and I always wanted a grandfather clock. I took it out of there, but the thing is, how would I get it home—how do I get this thing home? When I go up on the front line, what do I do? I knew a lot of guys in the kitchen because wherever we went, the kitchen went. It wasn't like the infantry where the kitchen was way back somewhere. But our kitchen—always when we moved, they moved. In other words, if we needed them, they'd tell them, 'Drop your aprons,' and they'd give them a rifle and they'd get out there because they were trained like we were. I said, 'Do me a favor. I have a grandfather clock and I've got to get it home some way or other.' I said, 'Would you put it on the truck?'

He said, 'Yes, I'll leave it on the back of the truck, and we'll move. But [moving it] on and off—it finally got damaged, and I told the guy to forget about it, leave it somewhere. But I did take a cuckoo clock; the Germans are good for cuckoo clocks. The cuckoo clock I got home because, you see, it wasn't as big. I put it in a box, and I shipped it home, but one of the weights was lost through the mail. My mother treasured that clock so much she finally went down and got a weight to keep time. I had that clock for years but I finally gave it to some guy because the cuckoo didn't cuckoo anymore because the lambskin inside dried up, but it kept pretty good time. I finally gave it away to somebody. I don't remember what I did with it.

That's why they called me Looter Nick. Every time I went into a German house, I opened all the drawers. I used to curse them because they must have taken all the good stuff with them; they left the sheets—who the hell wants sheets? A lot of things I didn't do—what I know now if I knew then, I'd be in a lot of money.

I remember I was in a repple depple, you know what a repple depple is?[19] I got into a repple depple after coming out of the hospital—they could not send me out as a replacement to the infantry like the 3rd or whoever they needed. They had to keep me there until our colonel picked us up because they weren't going to send me to the regular infantry. So, the guy that was in charge said, 'Listen, you guys are going to be here a while.' We were in a German camp. He said, 'Look around the camp and see if you can find some stuff.' The troops that were coming through had a day room where they could play. So, okay, so we went down there, and we went into one of these empty buildings. I go into the cellar and what do you think I find down there? German loot! Pictures, big, framed pictures, and I looked at the date—1600.

I said to the other guys, 'What the hell? Who wants these old pictures?' What the hell did I know? If I knew, I'd have cut them out, rolled them up, and taken them home. But I didn't know. There were so many pictures there, I said, 'Who the hell would want these here?' And we went back, and I told him, 'There's a lot of pictures.'

He said, 'Where?' So, he went down there and the next thing I know, there's a couple of trucks backing in and taking it all out! But I didn't know. Like I said, if I knew then what I know now, I probably would have taken a couple, but I didn't. I said, 'What the hell am I going to do with these pictures—they're too old.'

A Chance Meeting with Gen. Patton

I saw Patton one time. I don't remember exactly where—it was someplace in Germany or in France. Three of us were sitting on the

---

[19] *repple depple*-replacement depot

curb. We're sitting there, and we're just bullshitting—there was really nothing in the town—and this command car comes up and it's his car! The command cars are wide, you know, because it has the flag and the three stars there, and he went right past us, and [the driver] squeezed the brakes and stopped, and he had the driver back up. We were sitting there; we weren't getting up for shit—we were still sitting there. General Patton looked down on us and then we realized who he was, but we still didn't get up, and he went like this [*salutes with right hand*] and he left; he never said a word. He must have seen the patches on our shoulders. He didn't say a word! He figured the infantry, you know, he was more infantry than—he respected the infantry more than he did the army [brass]. That's the only time I really saw Patton. Other times, I read in the papers where he slapped this guy in the face. I read that in *Stars and Stripes*.

*

I don't remember too well when President Roosevelt died. I might have said, 'Gee, the President died,' and then it got around to everybody—the president is dead. And I think I said, 'Who's this Truman? Who is this guy—I never heard of him.' Personally, I think he was the best president we ever had; we need more like him, because I worked in the post office, and he was a man that came up from haberdashery—worked his way up. Whenever the post office was looking for a raise—in those days the post office could never get anything until now, recently it's not so bad—but in those days, you couldn't get anything. Every time they gave us a raise, they gave us a big two percent, maybe about three bucks a year. Well, Truman came out with something different. We got two raises under him—four hundred dollars across the board a year for all government workers! And the big guys up there, they didn't like that because if it was a percentage raise, they'd get more. So, we all got four hundred. We loved this guy!

And then we had Eisenhower; he was another one—he vetoed everything. Then we had Nixon—that's when we went on strike. After that, the pay in the post office today is good. But I can't see these post offices—the kids today don't want to work anymore! You know how much you start at in the post office? We have a letter carrier, a nice guy, he's an Indian—he took the job. Americans don't want to work! You know how Americans are—they want to start at the top, but that's an unskilled job. Sixteen dollars an hour, twenty-four days' vacation, you get paid all holidays and you get hospitalization—now you pay a little, but it's cheap. I'm still paying it today.

When I retired from the post office in '77, I got a job right here in town. It was a pretty good job, pretty good salary I was getting there. I was in charge of the shipping. We used to make machines to make the chips for the computers we have today, and I worked there for ten years. I had no Social Security. When I got out in '77 we never paid Social Security. Now they do. You had Reagan calling us people who were getting two pensions double-dippers. You son of a bitch—he was triple-dipping! He was collecting Social Security, he was collecting from the theater guild's pension, and he was collecting, I think, for the presidency, and he's calling me a double-dipper? I might be a double-dipper, but he's a triple-dipper! Well, that's Reagan.

I worked there for nine years, and I finally built up my Social Security. I don't get much, but it's better than nothing. I retired from there at 64, going on 65; they gave me a buyout and I took it. That was a good company to work for. Boy, I wish I had that now, I was 100 percent dental. You see all this bridge here [*points in mouth*], they paid for everything, and they paid the hospitals, I was getting hospitalization free, it didn't cost me anything. The company finally went under. They sold it to the Japs—Sony—and then, I had to get out after that. They gave us a buyout and I took it.

I used the GI Bill when I got out of the service—at that time I wasn't married. I said, 'I'm not going to work.' I was one of the record holders [for the '52-20 Club']—a whole year.[20] I was getting twenty dollars a week and that was a lot of money. I was keeping it and I was getting a pension for my hearing and my mother used to keep that. But the funny thing about it was we used to have to report—today you don't, you send a letter that you're not working, and they send you a check. In those days, you had to report once a week, and they had a special line for veterans. So, the other line was for people who had worked and had gotten laid off. And every time you went there, there was always a line. I had to be there at 1:00 in the afternoon, but I used to go at maybe 9:00, because the guys got together—we had an old, beat-up car and we went to Jones Beach, swimming, [in the afternoon].

Mr. Butrico brings out and displays a magazine on the opening of the National D-Day Museum New Orleans and commences to read from it.

'Nicholas Butrico, a Private in the 5th Ranger Battalion, received the Order of the Day issued by General Eisenhower to all the troops heading into France; he scribbled a brief prayer at the top. Shortly after D-Day he wrote his memories of landing on the back. Years later, he talked about what had happened to the 'buddy' he mentioned. "We were on the landing craft. His name was Chester, and he was standing next to me, and he says, 'Nick, I'm afraid I can't swim.'

I said, 'Don't worry about it; this boat will go right up to the land.' But a sailor dropped the ramp too early, and my buddy happened to be the first one out, and as soon as he

---

[20] *the '52-20 Club'*-The Servicemen's Readjustment Act of 1944, or the G.I. Bill, included a provision for servicemen to apply for a twenty-dollar payment a week for up to a year as they re-integrated into the workforce seeking employment.

132 | WORLD WAR II GENERATION SPEAKS III

went out, a big wave caught the craft and pushed it right over his body. A few days later I heard from headquarters that he was found on the beach."

The Letter

I think this is from when they opened the D-Day Museum down in New Orleans a couple of years ago, I don't remember the date.[21] When you go into the museum, they have a Higgins boat, they have a P-51 hanging up, and if you go, they have a lot of things about D-Day, and on the third floor, it was more dedicated to the Rangers. Now, I never knew I had this [on display]. I didn't know they did this. But when you go on the third floor—they had this letter copied; you could see this picture [*shows the picture of young Nicholas Butrico in uniform*]. The picture was taken in Camp Breckenridge, Kentucky, in 1942, around there. There are a lot of [copies of Eisenhower's D-Day Order of the Day] around—but this is the only one that has a letter written on the back. Nobody else had it; see, I had it in my pocket. I didn't realize it—if you notice it on the top, June 4—now that's two days before the invasion, and if you'll notice on the back of the letter, June 6, but I didn't write the letter on June 6. I just put down what I saw on June 6, and I mention that on the bottom.

Would you like me to read it? It's a prayer, more or less. [*Begins reading*]

---

[21] *D-Day Museum in New Orleans*-The brainchild of author Stephen Ambrose, the D-Day Museum opened its doors on June 6, 2000. Three years later, Congress officially designated it as the United States' official National WWII Museum, changing the name to reflect that. New Orleans had been the home of the Higgins boat, the shallow draft invasion LCVP made famous on many D-Days that was based on boats made for operating in the area's marshes and swamps.

'June 6. Landed one hour before D-Day, H-Hour. It was my first combat. As I turned around, I could see hundreds of bodies lying on the beach, not one moving. Some tried to move, and some were drowning. I'd never prayed before, but I really prayed that day. I lost somebody but I made it and we took our objective.

'That day I'll never forget—we landed on the worst beach of the invasion—Omaha. At night Jerry planes would come and try to knock us out and we held out. We had to or all the plans would go haywire. All I thought of was, if anything happened to me, [I hope] my family wouldn't take it too bad, but I'm glad I made it for my family's sake. I thought of the boys that didn't make it, and how their families would feel. I lost my best buddy on the beach. He never got to shore—just a kid of eighteen. He came from Brooklyn, and he was Italian. All I can say is I am thankful that I made it. Please protect me for whatever lies ahead for me! I thank you, Lord.'

Now this is the only one; there is no other one. This is what they were interested in, asking me if they could copy that. The next thing you know I got a phone call from somebody from Virginia telling me they would like to have it. I said, 'Well, I don't know—my kids don't want me to give it up.'

They said, 'No, you send it to us. The copy that you sent to the Eisenhower Museum is just a copy. We want to make a copy the way we want to copy it.' They sent me a box, Federal Express, prepaid. They said, 'Put the letter inside, seal it, and if you notice it's insured for $1500.' So I sent it. I think a week later I got it back, then a couple of days later I got a call from California. A woman got on and she said, 'We saw your letter.' I don't know how they saw it, they must have seen it somewhere; it was in a *Forbes* magazine—I remember getting that, I was sitting in here. My wife says, 'Here—

brown envelope,' and I open it up and see the magazine. So, I opened it up, in the first few pages, there is the letter, big—and it tells the story. And I call my wife, and my daughter-in-law got all excited, and the next thing you know, she's in the store buying all these magazines. Then a few days later, I get this call from California. They'd like to interview me for the D-Day Museum opening. I said sure, why not. I was on Channel 7; I was on Channel 2; I've been on all these channels. I've got a lot of newspapers I've been on around in this neighborhood. In fact, some friends of mine just went to New Orleans, they went on a senior citizens tour, and they asked me, 'Nick, tell us where it is!'

I said, 'It's on the third floor,' but they couldn't find it, and they finally did find it, and then they're telling these people—this was only a couple of weeks ago—'This fellow comes from our own hometown, Congers!'

[When I got that call], they said, 'You just sit still. We'll send a limousine to your house, pick you up and take you to 52nd Street and 5th Avenue, up in a big studio. We want to tape.' Big cameras there and they put a wire on my neck.

The limousine picked us up and I talked to the guy. I said, 'Is this limousine you are using only for celebrities?'

He was telling me, 'I've taken President Nixon in this limousine, and I've taken big movie stars. We don't cater to college proms.' He said, 'It costs you a lot of money to use it.'

So, I asked him how much would it cost because my nephew is Jewish and he's getting barmitzvahed at Tavern on the Green and we're all invited, so I asked, 'How much would it cost us to rent this to take us one way and then back—that would be 57th Street right off Central Park?'

He said, '$1800.' One trip! That's what they charge.

I said, 'Forget about it.'

He took us to the city, and they took me to this room, and they asked me all kinds of questions. I must have been up there for two hours, and the guy said to me, 'I'm talking to you, and you will not hear it. We'll just hear your voice.' Now when it came onto the History Channel, they cut it, they just took the parts that fit into the [narrative] because there were other people on there.

When I was in New Orleans, I was treated like a king, and then I was on the podium—I was sitting there, and guess who's sitting next to me, on both sides? Tom Hanks and Stephen Spielberg. Because Stephen Spielberg made *Private Ryan*. [I saw it, but] even the beginning—it's ridiculous—the guy running around with his [severed] arm [*raises left arm overhead*]—that's overdoing it—and another guy running around with his guts hanging out. That's overdoing it. He's hollering, 'Mama, Mama.' Well, I heard guys hollering, 'Mama,' but this guy has his guts out; he's not going to be living. A lot of the Rangers—we go to reunions, and we talk about [that film]. Well, the Army would never have taken one section out of the Rangers to go look for one guy to get him home because the Rangers, when we landed in Omaha, we had one objective, Pointe du Hoc.

*

Now I will tell you a story about Dinah Shore, which I never told. We were just outside Saint-Lô. I tell you the truth, in all the time I was in the service, in combat, overseas, I never saw a USO show. We always said, 'If you are in the Air Corps, you see it.' You don't see it, maybe if you're in the hospital. The rear echelon always saw it. But it just happened this jeep pulled up, and Dinah Shore was in it with two captains or something and she was going to entertain us. This was just before we were going into Saint-Lô and they were pushing towards Paris. So, we got there and that's just before we went to Brest; she got on the jeep and no sooner had she sat on the jeep, [we were told], 'All right, get your stuff ready, we're pulling out!' But she's sitting on the jeep and the two captains are mushing her up like mad, [acting a bit randy]. She said, 'Now behave yourselves, boys!' [*Laughs*] You know how she was.

Jesus Christ, that's the only time I ever got close to [a show]. John Garfield came to the USO—I heard this from a guy up in the 4th because he was there—so he went there to entertain the troops.[22] Just to show you how this government of ours works, when he got out [on stage], he said, 'First of all, ladies and gentlemen, before I start, all you people in the front, colonels, generals, you know, all brass, I will not entertain while you people are sitting there up front, and all the GIs and wounded veterans are all back there! Have them come up here, and you go back there.' The next day they shipped him back to the States. [*Laughs*]

Well, that's the story. I hope it was interesting.

In 2005, Nicholas Butrico got to attend the 50th year anniversary of D-Day ceremony in Normandy along with his comrades in arms. He passed the following year on August 6 at the age of 77. Today, a memorial plaque in his honor is displayed at the WWII Museum in New Orleans, a testament and tribute to the twenty-two-year-old Italian kid from New York

---

[22] John Garfield (1913-1952), remembered as the 'Jewish Brando' after his death, was an American actor who played tough, working-class characters who didn't mince words, preceding the likes of Brando, James Dean, and others. From *Body and Soul*, a 1947 film noir sports drama, in which he played an up-and-coming Jewish boxer facing bad choices and moral dilemmas: *"In Europe, the Nazis are killing people like us just because of their religion. But here, Charlie Davis is champion, and we are proud."* Garfield was attacked by the House Committee on Un-American Activities and denied communist affiliation and refused to give the committee 'names,' for which he was blacklisted, ending his career. Hounded by investigators, he died at age 39 from a heart attack. The HUAC then closed its investigation without charges, which cleared his name.

who prayed to God to keep him safe, and for the friends whom he lost on the beach, and their families.

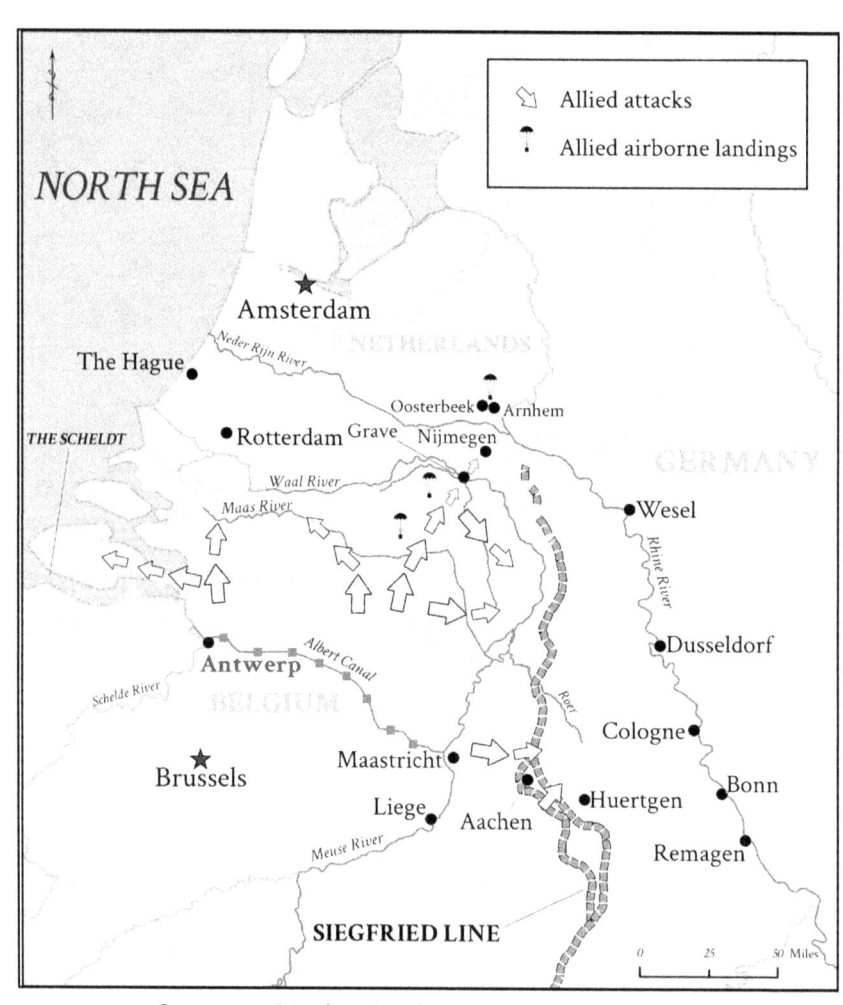

Operation Market Garden. Map by Susan Winchell.

CHAPTER THREE

A Bridge Too Far

Following the success of the Normandy landings and the breakout in France and across Belgium, the Allied armies were moving so quickly that the supply lines simply could not keep up as the reconstruction and further expansion of the significant coastal ports could not happen overnight. The Red Ball Express, manned by mostly African-American servicemen and operating literally around the clock, moved about 12,500 tons of supplies a day at its peak, but more ports had to be opened, including the port of Antwerp in Belgium, which in the near future would also be the coveted objective of Hitler's push through the Ardennes Forest in December 1944.[2]

Two different proposals competed for the attention of Allied logistics planning and supplies in the drive to cross the Siegfried Line and Rhine River in the push to Berlin. Omar Bradley, Commanding General of the 12th U.S. Army Group (including the First, Third, Ninth, and Fifteenth Armies, 1.3 million men strong) and British Field Marshal Bernard Law Montgomery had different ideas. In simple terms, the Eisenhower and Bradley camp advocated for keeping the pressure on Germany in a 'broad front' approach, while Montgomery was convinced of his 'single thrust' strategy that would concentrate resources specifically targeting the industrial

Ruhr Valley and the Rhine River, driving a dagger into the heart of the Reich.

Antwerp had fallen on September 4 to the British 11th Armored (the same outfit that would be stunned to the core at the capture of the Bergen-Belsen concentration camp the following spring, with its 60,000 sick, emaciated, and dying prisoners), but with the Germans controlling 60 miles of the Scheldt River's tidal estuary, it could be of no use until the waterway was opened.

Given that roadblock, and the fact that the Germans were still launching hundreds of V-1 and V-2 buzz bombs a week toward England and elsewhere from the occupied Netherlands, Monty proposed crossing the Rhine in the north, in the Netherlands, and outflanking much of the fortified Siegfried Line. The way to do it, he argued, was to allow him command of the First Allied Airborne Army (which included the British 1st Airborne Division, the Polish 1st Independent Parachute Brigade, and the United States' 101st and 82nd Airborne Divisions), pairing it with the ground operation of the British Second Army. In order to reach the lower Rhine at Arnhem, four rivers and three canals would have to be breached. It was imperative that the airborne troops capture the bridges intact, if possible (as it would be equally important to the 9th and 10th SS Panzer Division to hold the bridges at all costs to facilitate control and counteroffensive measures, once the attack began). The bridges would be seized and defended at key locations while awaiting ground reinforcements; the last bridge to be taken by the British Red Devils in Arnhem was a daunting 65 miles distant from the start of the British Second Army ground offensive. It was a bold plan, and one that Eisenhower had his misgivings about, but something had to be done; it was approved in early August in a concession to circumstances, to the dismay of General Patton and other American commanders, as it would siphon men and materiel from their own drives.[3] Still, Ike may have seen Operation Market

Garden as a side 'theater' of the broad thrust into Germany plan. It would go on as planned, but plans, especially military ones, don't always come off the way they are expected to.

Sgt. Albert Tarbell, 504th Parachute Infantry Regiment, 82nd Airborne Division, World War II.
Source: Albert Tarbell.

CHAPTER FOUR

The Paratrooper I

On the morning of September 17, 1944, 4,700 aircraft carrying more than 35,000 men began leaving England in the largest airborne operation in the history of the world.[4] *Between 1 and 1:30 in the afternoon, the C-47s began the approaches to the drop zone; the first hours were considered a success, with the majority of men landing near their assigned targets. Not every paratrooper, however, was that fortunate, although twenty-one-year-old Albert Tarbell hit the Dutch drop zone successfully.*

Albert L. Tarbell was of Mohawk descent, born at St. Regis Reservation in northern New York in the late summer of 1923. The Mohawk people were traditionally the 'Keepers of the Eastern Door,' the most easterly of the five original nations of the Iroquois, the fierce guardians on the eastern frontier of the indigenous confederation, a power to be reckoned with by European interlopers for over 200 years. In the early 20th century, many of the Mohawk established a reputation for bridge and high-rise building construction, particularly in a burgeoning New York City, over 300 miles down the Hudson from their traditional settlement area along the border with Canada. Colloquially called 'skywalkers' for their prowess and fearlessness in working at dizzying heights, and renowned for their ironworking abilities, these Mohawk men took pride in doing jobs that most would shy away from; in 1931, they helped complete a project that became emblematic of the Empire State, an eminence that would be, like the Statue of Liberty, one to welcome home returning soldiers in 1945—New York's iconic Empire State Building. At 1,454 feet tall, it would be the tallest building in the world until 1970, when the twin towers of the World Trade Center were completed. Following the horrific attacks in 2001, it reassumed its title, only to be surpassed once more in 2012 with the completion of New York's Freedom Tower at One World Trade Center in Lower Manhattan. Notably, fully ten percent of the iron workers on that deliberate, painstaking—and defiantly proud—rebirth of sorts were Mohawk.

Imbued with this incredible Mohawk work ethic, Albert spent his life creating and building, bringing good into the world and retiring after 34 years in ironworking and related work. Like many of his peers witnessing Pearl Harbor unfolding, the young man of eighteen was anxious to join up and defend his nation—but like several northern New Yorkers, he was already serving a hitch in the Canadian army. Released from that obligation, he would meet up with Canadian armed forces again, in a land he probably never dreamed of going to, thousands of miles away and years on the horizon.

In 2003, Mr. Tarbell sat for this interview in Syracuse, New York, recalling his participation in the war as the very first Mohawk Indian paratrooper to qualify and be accepted into the legendary 82nd Airborne Division. Now eighty years old, spry, and with a twinkle in his eye and a subtle self-effacing chuckle punctuating some of his humorous incidents, he also grew serious in recounting the harrowing nature of his combat experience and remembering the friends he lost, buddies sometimes right next to him, or worse—someone who had momentarily taken his place on the line.

In this first part of his nearly three-hour-long epic storytelling, he recalled his paratrooper training, his first combat experience in Italy at Anzio, and his part in the largest airborne operation in the history of the world with the 82nd Airborne's 504th Parachute Infantry Regiment, soon to acquire the enemy nickname the 'Devils in Baggy Pants.'

In 1977, the film epic based on Cornelius Ryan's book *A Bridge Too Far* was released to great fanfare. In a memorable scene, actor Robert Redford, portraying the 504th Parachute Infantry Regiment's 3rd Battalion commander Col. Julius Cook, leads a daring daylight river crossing to assault the northern end of a bridge over the Waal River in the Netherlands; in real life, Mr. Tarbell was right there with Julius Cook.

'We got out in the river just a little way, and it was just like [it was starting to] rain! The Germans opened up with machine guns on us and the water was rippled just like rain was falling on it! They threw machine gun [fire]. They threw mortars. They threw 88s. You name it, they [threw it at us].

Out of the twenty-six assault boats we had, there were only eleven that were still in service when we got to the other side. Most of them were either sunk or the guys were all killed; we lost half our company there. The boat right next to me took a direct hit; I could still see the guys [who were in it] as I was turning and paddling, I was trying to call cadence with these guys [for the paddling] ... trying to keep it together at the same time.

About midway across there, I looked [to] the side, and I see my buddy stand up. Then he just looked at me like as if he'd given up... I turned, and he was gone. I can still see that look on his face, you know—his eyes, his eye contact with me. They never found his body until, I think, after the war. They found it up alongside the bank further down the Waal River.'

Albert L. Tarbell

I was born on the St. Regis Indian Mohawk Reservation in Hogansburg, New York, August the 24th, 1923. When I went in the service, I had two and a half years of high school, and it was not until after the war that I got a full high school diploma from the Fort Covington High School.

[In late 1941], I was attached to the Stormont, Dundas, and Glengarry Highlanders in the Canadian Army, and when we heard about Pearl Harbor, we knew that the United States was going to war. There were quite a few of us in that area there that were from the American side that were in the Canadian Army. [I joined the Canadian Army] after I dropped out of high school. I see all these parades in Cornwall and this and that, and I guess, next thing you know, my cousin and I joined, and then we were really too young to go overseas, and so I ended up being a corporal in the training staff—but when I heard about Pearl Harbor, I knew then that eventually I would probably be going back to the States. I left Ottawa, I think it was around March. It was a bitter cold winter, and I had a slight cold. I got home and I caught pneumonia when I was home on furlough, and my father and mother discouraged me from going back. They said, 'If they can't take care of you, you should not go back.' So I stayed home, and I worked on a farm, and then I went to work in the spring in Massena; I ended up working as an apprentice lineman. To make a long story short, I ended up in Syracuse, New York, and then this is where our union hall was and I worked around the States for a while, in New York State, Buffalo and mostly in Syracuse, doing repair work for Niagara Mohawk. That was all through the union, Local 1249 of the International Brotherhood of Electrical Workers.

I was drafted and I got my call to report in February of 1943; I entered the service in March 1943. We went for induction through Utica, New York, and then from Utica went to Fort Niagara. From Fort Niagara, they took us by train to Camp Swift, Texas, which was a new camp outside of Bastrop, Texas; I think it's northeast of Austin, Texas. There was a new camp there. The 97th Infantry Division was being formed there and mostly all us guys from the north were sent down there. We had eight to 12 weeks of training there, basic training. I ended up in the communications section. Being out of the union, they figured I had something to do with linework, so I ended up doing my basic training in that. They were much more strict in the Canadian Army. Our corporal was just as high as a master sergeant there. He had a lot of authority. And in the States, it was a little more lenient. It wasn't as strict. I found the training not as hard at all.

Into the Paratroopers

Before I was drafted, I had gotten married, and my wife came down to visit me for a while in Texas. And then when my furlough came, I came back to Syracuse, and then after my furlough, I noticed this guy prancing up and down on the train here, with some outfit he was in, and we couldn't figure out what outfit he was with. He had a cocked hat on, you know, and he had boots on with a blouse. Man, he looked terrific! When he told me he was getting $50 a month more than me as a private, I said, 'Well, I think I'm going to look into that.' So when I got back to Texas, I put in for my transfer.

And in the outfit that I was in, being in communications, I could only go into the Air Force or the paratroops, so the paratroops like that, so I joined the paratroops. About a month later, around August the 13th, at 1300 hours, 13 of us left Camp Swift, Texas, for Fort Benning, Georgia, and then I had to start training all over again. And this was basic communication training, airborne. And it was not until around November that we got into jump school, and all that summer, we trained, physical training, airborne infantry training, shooting different weapons and stuff like that.

It had taken four weeks to go through jump school and we received our wings, I think it was around December 2. We were given 14-day furloughs to come home after our graduation. We had had a little baby born while I was in jump school. I couldn't come home because I couldn't interrupt my training there; they wouldn't let me go. So, I met my baby, and we went up north to visit for a few days and then we came back home. Meanwhile, this buddy of mine from Rochester who rode back with me asked me, 'Did you get a notice to come back to camp?'

'No,' I said, 'did you?'

He said, 'Yeah, I got a telegram, but I was only home a couple of days.' So I thought he was just kidding. When we did get back to camp, there was nobody there! They had moved out to the Alabama area and were getting ready to ship away from Fort Benning! And the first thing my company commander said when he saw me, when I reported back to the camp, was, 'Did you get the telegram to come home to report?'

I said, 'No.'

He just smiled a little bit, you know, and said, 'You sure?'

I said, 'Well, sure!' It wasn't until years later, when I got out of the service, I asked my dad, 'Did I ever get a telegram?'

'Yeah,' he said, 'the telegram came in about two days after you were home.' He said, 'Heck, I tore it up. You just got here, and they wanted you to report back to camp!' So right after New Year's we moved out of Fort Benning to Fort Meade, Maryland. Meanwhile, my wife came to Baltimore. My mother was living there at that time, and I was able to get a pass every night while I was in Meade. And then, around about the 15th of January, I could not go out on pass anymore and I was told that we were going to be getting ready to move out. [The commander] said, 'Tell your wife that you won't be seeing her for a while.' So, we ended up at Hampton Roads, Norfolk, Virginia, and I ended up on the Victory ship *John Hart Benton*. Two hundred and fifty of us got on that ship in the afternoon and we heard this band playing music. We looked down the street and we could see some soldiers marching up there, and we saw these guards on the side with shotguns and we ended up with 250 'shotgun volunteers' with us on that ship to go ship overseas. These guys were out of the stockade, and they marched them right out to the Victory ship. They posted those guards on there until we got ready to pull out, but we got along great with the prisoners. I was made acting corporal, I had charge of the KP on the ship, and I made sure that the guys all reported for work duty on the KP work roster, and we just had no problems with them. Three miles out, I never saw so many pistols show up on these guys, I don't know where they got them from, but they had them in underarm holsters! And one of them was Rita Hayworth's brother, and he said that he was not part of those guys, but he got on the ship with them, though he said he had nothing to do with those guys. [*Laughs*] We lost track of them when we got to Casablanca.

Italy

We had joined the convoy, and about three days later, we woke up one morning and we were all alone—the convoy had left us, and we had gone in a different area, different direction. And it took us eighteen days, and we ended up in Casablanca, French Morocco, where we stayed a couple weeks, and then we went by train from there to Algiers, Algeria. There was a camp outside there near an airbase. About a week or so later, we went by plane to Naples, Italy, and then from there I ended up in Venafro. I was attached to the H

Company, [3rd Battalion], 504th Parachute Infantry Regiment, 82nd Airborne Division. When we joined the outfit, we came back to Naples Harbor, and we got on LCIs and went to Anzio beachhead as replacements for the 504th Parachute Infantry Regiment.

It was in the latter part of February when we got there, and we stayed there until the latter part of April. We left Easter Sunday on the *Capetown Castle* to go to England. We left Naples on April 11, 1944, and we arrived in Liverpool, England, on April 22.

We did extensive training there in England for the Normandy invasion. We did all their problem jumping, and we did anything to do with dispersal areas and flight formations for the planes and this and that. We usually jumped in mass jumps, we jumped two men to a plane, and all different things like that; we had to [try to experiment] for all those problems they figured they would encounter in the Normandy invasion. We did not make Normandy, because the big boss figured that our men were all so new—they had lost most of their men in [the fight at] Anzio. So the two other outfits took our place, the 507th and the 508th Parachute Infantry Regiments took our place, and they went into the 82nd for the Normandy deal. So we stayed in England training, and then we started training for more missions; there was always training, airborne training, jumping. I did a lot of jumps in England, practice jumps. We had about four or five different alarms to go on a mission, and they were canceled each time, because the army was moving so fast in France.

Market Garden

Around about the 15th of September, we went back to [RAF] Spanhoe Airfield and we were closeted in, and we couldn't leave or nothing, you know. And we were just stuck in that camp, and we knew something was coming up; we were getting lectures from intelligence and stuff like that, [so] we definitely knew we were going on a mission, we were going in the Netherlands, Holland. We started getting our equipment ready, more or less honing up for our mission.

We left Spanhoe Airfield Sunday morning, September 17, about ten o'clock, and jumped about sixty-five miles behind the German lines around 1:15. We landed in Grave, Holland. On our way over, it was quite a sight to see all those planes—in fact, this was the first daylight mission in American airborne history. We had planes like, my God, when we were jumping in Holland, they were still leaving the airfield in England! And it seemed like you could just walk on the planes, you're glad you saw so many planes in the air, and we had fighter escorts. As we hit the mainland, we got some artillery flak from flak stations. And the fighter planes went right to work on them, knocked them right out.

As we were going in, you could see the people sitting on the roofs, they're waving to us, they knew something big was coming on. Being Sunday, everybody was home, and not working. And then when we got near, oh, just two miles inland, my company commander and I looked out the window, I was sitting next to him by the door.

I said, 'Jeepers!' I said, 'We're not at the DZ yet, these guys are starting to jump!' We noticed the plane next to us was on fire, the bottom was all on fire; guys were jumping through it! And they had shot another one of the planes down, and we could see it go down, but we lost track of it—it was right next to ours.

All of my buddies were in that plane [with the hole in the floor]. One that I chummed around with quite a while [was also in it], and I met him again 34 years later, [after] he had retired from the CIA. He verified what happened; it was that they had taken [flak] fire, and underneath the plane, these equipment bundles which contained Composition C-4 [plastic explosives] caught on fire, and it melted the bottom of the plane, so they just fell right through; they hooked on their static lines and fell right through. Most of them were captured, I think an exception of two guys showed up about a month later; they rejoined our outfit, they hid in with the Dutch underground.

Now we were still going in, and a little while later we were talking to first sergeant about the plane, what happened. And we were leaning in, talking to each other, and all at once, he flew up in the air and landed right in the middle of the C-47, middle of the aisle. I looked around, and I said, 'What the heck's going on here,' you know. One of the guys looked at where [Sergeant McHogan] had been sitting; there was a bullet hole right where he was sitting. It missed him, and the bullet went right up his shoe—the impact sent him flying right up to the middle of the floor! So it wasn't long after that that we got to our [drop zone], and we were starting to get flak from the bridges there, Grave Bridge. And when we got up to get ready to check our equipment and hook up, the company commander told him, he said, 'First Sergeant McHogan.' He said, 'Mike, you don't have to jump that chute. You can go back to England.'

The first sergeant said, 'Like hell I am. I'm getting the hell off this plane right now!' [*Chuckles*] We made our jump; so he jumped the chute, and he was all right.

Out the Door

I had a radar bag with a radio in it and rope. When we left the plane, I let loose of the static line, you know, and it broke. I think shrapnel cut it, because we were getting shrapnel from the bridge, flak shrapnel. They were aiming for the door; I think it cut my line. Anyway the radio went one way, and I went the other. Coming down, the first sergeant hollered over and I could hear him, you know. I was looking around for a few seconds. He said, 'There's a guy behind that barn, that building, watch out!' So when I come in, I come in backwards and I landed on an apple tree. I had all my weight and the weight of all my gear, and it just put me right to the ground nice and easy, no problem. I took my chute off, grabbed my Tommy gun, and I got ahold of this guy, he was just a young kid standing there. He was watching us jumping, wondering what was going on, you know.

So I motioned to him, there was a wheelbarrow near the barn door, and I said, 'Bring her over.' We loaded our gear on there, and he took it up to the main road for us. The first sergeant and I, we brought our stuff, and [the kid] wheeled it out for us. First thing I saw when I got there was a priest was there, and there were a lot of kids and parents in the road, and every one of them had orange on—the girls had orange ribbons, the men had orange lapels or something orange in their suit jacket there, to show that meant that they were going to help us. They would be our friends. They were always Queen Wilhelmina's colors, orange. We were told by the intelligence then that whoever had that on would be helpers, be willing to help the Allies. So that was about the first day of the jump.

We didn't receive too much opposition on the ground. We more or less saw we had part of our regiment there. One company jumped on the south side of the bridge; the rest of the battalion came in from the north side. We had our mission accomplished before five o'clock that night! From then on, it was mostly going from village to village, town to town, and capturing other small bridges. We had to take these bridges for the British armor to go through, to go into Arnhem, where the main British force jumped the bridge in Arnhem. Ten thousand men jumped there; the 101st jumped in Eindhoven. We jumped next. We jumped in Nijmegen area. Our area was the Grave Bridge outside of Nijmegen. We had to get all of those bridges to make a direct link to Arnhem and then the 30th Armored could go right through into Germany or the Ruhr River

Valley, or wherever they were going to go. That was the idea. [But] I think that if the British had gone through like they were supposed to do, we could have had that problem, [but the British armor was slowing down]. As it was, we ended up, on the 18th, we got resupplied; the gliders come in and I was there on the ground. I had to meet our company driver, he came in, and I had to lead him back to our area. So that was quite an experience there, being in the field when the gliders came in. They didn't have no brakes, you know. They just plowed right along the field until they stopped, they stopped—and I never wanted [to be in] one, either. [When my driver got me there], I found out from the, I guess it would be the landing officer in the field there, he said, 'Stand right here. Your friend will be somewhere here in this area.'

And sure enough, just a few feet away from where this glider came in, he was on that. They opened a side up, and when he got off that glider, the front opened up and he drove his jeep out and he hollered over, said, 'Tarbell, run over here!', and I run over there and he threw his hat on the ground and said, 'Tarbell, that was the last damn time I'm ever going to ride in them things!' I guess he had quite a ride coming over. [*Chuckles*] But anyway, then we got supplied by B-24s, and years later I found out one of the guys resupplying us was a rear gunner on a B-24, a guy from up home that I knew very well, John Cook was his name. It was a small world. Here I'm on the ground helping [in retrieving and] receiving the supplies, and he's up there in a plane delivering them, you know. We never found that out until about forty years later.

The Dutch Underground

We got all our mission pretty well done. Mostly we worked with the Dutch Underground for a while here and there, from village to village and this and that. We were accepted with everybody, all the

Dutch people; the Underground cooperated one hundred percent. Everybody was just so happy to see us, willing to help! First mission, we went out on this little town. We went out with one truck, we came back with [German] motorcycles. We came back with a [captured] truck, another car, you name it—and we even met the Dutch Underground there, they drove us around looking for pockets of Germans! Just unbelievable, you know. We'd never seen anybody help us like that, you know, [in] the other places that we've been. We never got that cooperation from any other country as we did in Holland.

Around about the 18th, the 19th, the British showed up at the bridge; we heard early in the morning that they were coming in, so I went out early in the morning with some of the other guys. We sat on the bridge waiting for them to come in. We're just sitting there, waiting and [walking] around, smoking and talking. One of the civilians comes up and he said, 'You know they had an office down there.' He pointed down at the valley below the bridge. Three of the guys run down to it, and I went down with them. By the time I got down there, they had everything all cleared off, they had taken the mementos off the table. All there was left was a flag behind the desk, so I took that and I folded that up and put it aside; I still have that flag from that bridge. It was from the guard staff who had their office there.

We stayed there for I think it was that afternoon, that was the 19th, and we got back to the area where we were staying. We had to move out towards the city of Nijmegen, which was just a few miles, but we moved on and I don't remember if we got trucked out there or not. Of course, at that time, we didn't know that they were having such a hard time at the Nijmegen Bridge on the Waal River. They were trying to get the assault in, [the bridge was] heavily fortified. They were able to get part of the railroad bridge, but on the main bridge, they were having a fierce fight at both ends. The SS were there, you know—the 9th and the 10th SS Panzer Divisions were stationed there. Bittrich was the commanding general there, General Bittrich of the SS, and they said that they'd have to make a river crossing and get in the north end of the bridges in order to take over the bridge. So they told us finally the following day, the 20th early in the morning, we found out we were going to make a river crossing. We were told there was an assault boat coming up that we're going to use, so we got ready for the river crossing. I was on the first wave of H Company; H and I Company were to be ready to make the first wave.

Crossing the Waal

We kept waiting all morning for those boats, and finally round about three o'clock, they showed up. They were the [portable] canvas boats with plywood bottoms, and they had sticks that you turned counterclockwise to spread them out like an accordion, to open them up to make it stable. God, they were just nothing but canvas, I don't know how many paddles they were supposed to have had, but we ended up with sixteen men; thirteen men to each boat, and then three engineers to help navigate the boat. They had little bitty motors on them, they weren't worth a crap! You know, you're getting sixteen people on that boat, and you've got over ten-mile-an-hour currents, and they didn't figure on that.

Anyway, when we started down, I was right behind my company commander, and we grabbed the boat; we took it on each side, and we ran down the bank. All at once, the CO took all his gear off, and he dove right into the river! One of the guys on the other side had fallen in and he was drowning with all his equipment on. Our company commander just threw his gear off, dove in, and got him up to shore, and then we helped him back up! Then we jumped in whatever boats we could; it was just a fiasco. When we first started out, the boat was going one way and then the other, the guys were not used to paddling the boat—I don't think that some of them had ever even been on a river or something like that, you know, with a boat! We had quite a time navigating. Finally, we got somewhere near a decent [stroke]; we got out in the river just a little way, and it was just like [it was starting to] rain! The Germans opened up with machine guns on us and the water was rippled just like rain was falling on it! They threw machine gun [fire]. They threw mortars. They threw 88s. You name it, they [threw it at us].

Out of the twenty-six assault boats we had, there were only eleven that were still in service when we got to the other side. Most of them were either sunk or the guys were all killed, and this and that. We lost half our company there. The boat right next to me took a direct hit; I could still see the guys [who were in it] as I was turning and paddling, I was trying to call cadence with these guys [for the paddling]... trying to keep it together at the same time. About midway across there, I looked on the side, and I see my buddy stand up. Then he just looked at me like as if he'd given up... I turned, and he was gone. I can still see that look on his face, you know—his eyes, his eye contact with me. They never found his body until, I think, after the war. They found it up alongside the bank further down the Waal River.

We finally did get to the other side, and we fought our way up to the canal. At one time I ended up with the colonel, Colonel Cook, and Captain Kep. We were fighting wherever we could; we were all kind of mixed up, you know; there were so many casualties and things that went on. We tried to regroup as we went inland towards the bridges. One of my buddies came by and he said, 'Hey, look, I got another Purple Heart!' He had his thumb shot off. Just a few minutes later there I see his body on the other side of the building. He was killed, so he got two Purple Hearts that day.

The Railroad Bridge

We ended up on a railroad bridge. My company commander was there, and the executive officer was there; at each port hole, they were there, and we were passing grenades to them. We had a lot of Germans trapped in the middle of the bridge; the guys that were shooting at us as we were crossing the river. [We were using] Gammon grenades, composition C2, C4, C2. We made them up ourselves; pound and a half pound, whatever. They're concussion grenades. When you would throw that, it's got a little metal belt on it. You throw that and it had a lead weight on the end. When it's in the air, that belt comes off, and it pulls that pin out and that's going to go off. We did quite a job with that. We used up all that with our Gammon grenades because they would rush us. As they would rush us, we would throw the Gammon grenades at them. They had quite a few casualties there on that bridge; the Germans did. They had over 264 on the bridge and I don't know how many jumped over on the side.

They had those bridges loaded on the girders [*glances upward to indicate explosives above*] and every place else. They really ambushed us coming across [the river], but we caught them when we got to the bridge, because we sealed the north end off. By that time, the south end was sealed off by the 505th Parachute Infantry Regiment. Then finally, towards evening, we ended up to the north end of the main bridge; the railroad bridge was where we fought at first. The main bridge, where the tanks would come across, was where we ended up that evening. Then, when the British took over that area there, the I Company was there, the I Company commander and some of our platoons took it over. We ended up all up there and the rest of H Company. We seen the tanks come across and they didn't go any further than just to the end of the bridge. One of the tanks got hit, so they said, 'Well, that's all right. Keep on going.' One of the officers said, 'We'll knock that tank gun out for you. Keep on going to Arnhem.'

The reason that we were doing this was that the British Airborne was being annihilated in Arnhem. There were 10,000 of them there, and they had run right on top of a nest of panzers; they came and they were fighting for that bridge but the rest of them were being isolated on the other side of the river.

The tanks that they had to get there to help them to fight to get that bridge, and to relieve those guys there, [but] they stopped right at Nijmegen. They didn't go any further than there.

'They're Zeroing In!'

The next morning, we fanned out. We set up a CP; I think it was the 21st or the 22nd. I had my SCR300 radio.[23] That was my job, I was an SCR300 communication man. As a sergeant, my job was to make sure that we had company communications from company to platoons and to outposts. I'd make sure that we had that. We had the SCR300 for battalion communication. The following morning there, we were trying to see how many casualties we had at the CP we were at. The company clerk and I were on a call with a bunch of others. When the battalion called, I would [set up] contact with my radio and then I was using the phone line to contact the different platoons and see what their casualties were. We were writing the guys' names on the list; Sheldon, the company clerk, was writing the names of the guys. Then we started getting shells, which were getting closer and closer to our CP. The first sergeant was downstairs in this building. He said, 'Tarbell, they better bring that radio down here. I think they're zeroing in on your radio set! They're getting closer and closer to us!' We bent over to pick up the radio,

---

[23] *SCR300 radio*- backpack-mounted radio transceiver used in World War II, the first radio unit to be nicknamed a 'walkie-talkie.'

Sheldon and I, and our heads were together and a shell came into the courtyard, right behind us. Shrapnel came through the window, missed me, hit Sheldon in the forehead and killed him instantly; blew his head off and the back of his head out.

We had three other guys on the other end of the building. There was Rosser, I think it was Keith, and Zimmerman. They all got just slightly wounded. It never touched me. I mean, I don't know how it missed me. [*Shrugs slightly, looks down, shakes head*] Then first sergeant came up. The worst part of that deal was having to put Sheldon's name on that list that he was making out. We had fifty-four men down; when we ended up, it was a fifty-fifty casualty [rate] from our company for those two days. The hardest part was putting Sheldon's name on that list that he had started… [*Pauses reflectively*]

I got downstairs and company commander said, 'Call the medic over. Give him something to calm him down,' because I was just about ready to do… [*shakes head*] … something. I went right to sleep. The medic said, 'Lay down here and rest.' I went right to sleep. I slept finally. I slept until it was just about getting dark and the company commander woke me up and said, 'Grab your Tommy gun. Let's go and check the positions.' So, that felt good. I felt better then, you know.

We stayed there a couple days. A day or so later, we pulled back out and those tanks and those guys were still in the same area north of the bridge. They had never moved. We didn't [accept] that too well. We figured they'd be all the way over in Arnhem or some place, but we lost all those men for nothing, really.

So we came back and walked across the bridge and then we got on to some ducks over there, amphibious trucks, and they trucked us back to division reserve, and then after that we had a lot of fighting in different defensive setups.[24] For what was supposed to have been a two-day mission, we fought [for almost two months]; we ended up getting relieved on the 12th of November. We were there from September 17 to the 12th of November until we were relieved by the Canadian army. You know, between that time, we lost a lot of men from shrapnel, or from mines and from artillery barrages, mortars, being out on patrols.

A lot of things happened in that time there. One time we had an outpost way out in the Den Heuvel Woods, and we had a fierce SS counterattack there against us; there was a lot of fighting there. Because we had the outpost way out there and we had lost our communications, I had to go out that night, and I had to feel the line. I didn't know where [the outpost] was; I had to find my way out there by following the lines. As I got near this building, a barn, I found the break in the line, and every time I tried to fix it, I would get shocked, if you know what trying to fix a communication wire is like.

It was thirty years later, when I found my buddy [who had been back at the CP], and he said, 'Lieutenant was on the floor there, just grinding away at that crank!' I was getting shocked...[*Chuckles*] Finally, I was able to repair it, but meanwhile the Germans crossed the side of the road and started shooting at me, and some of our men started shooting back, and here I'm between the devil and the deep blue sea. Finally I got the line fixed, and the sergeant came out—Rosencrantz was his name—and he said, 'Tarbell, come on in, it's all right now!' They quit shooting, our guys quit shooting, so the Germans stopped, too.

I went in, he said, 'Come on in, have a cup of coffee.'

---

[24] *ducks*- six-wheel-drive amphibious modification of the 2 1/2-ton CCKW trucks used by the U.S. military during World War II and the Korean War; the DUKW was colloquially known as the Duck. Source: Wikipedia

I said, 'I'm getting the hell out of here!' So that's the last time I saw Rosie. He got killed the following day. We lost a few guys there.

'Let's Have the Indian Work on Him'

I think it was the following night, they sent a patrol out, and they wanted to get a prisoner. They went up to this one building there, in a barn, or some building, this lieutenant was coming out to take a leak, and they grabbed him, German lieutenant or captain. I think he was a first lieutenant.

Now that time in our area there was a grenade fight in one of the buildings, and one of the guys got killed. Rice was his name, Sergeant Rice, and I think it was Private Byer. They would throw hand grenades in there and watch for each other's back. The Germans would throw them back out. Finally somebody threw one grenade, it landed behind Rice's back, and it blew up and killed them. So we heard about it, and the commander went out there, and we saw him, his body right there on a stretcher beside the building. He was pretty broken up about it, the commander, because [Rice] was a well-liked kid, a well-liked guy.

Just then, who comes in? The patrol came in with this German lieutenant, and the commander said, 'Tarbell, let's get this guy out of here before he gets killed here!' We needed [this prisoner] for interrogation. So we took him back to battalion, and there was an interpreter there, he was with the intelligence, interrogated him, kept him. Colonel Cook was there, and Captain Kep and myself, and the guy couldn't speak English. He couldn't understand nothing, he couldn't understand nothing.

So Captain Kep said, 'Colonel, let's all go in the other room, and let's have the Indian work on him!' He then turns around to me, loud so everyone could hear, and he said, 'Tarbell, get him in the guts! Work on him in the guts!'

God, he was surprised by how that guy spoke such good English right after that, and let me tell you, I was too. [*Laughter*] He said, 'Let the Indian work on him,' but I was one happy Indian myself, that he could speak English. I would have had to do it, but oh my God, that would have been awful if I had to, so I was sure happy he spoke good English. He gave up some machine gun positions and stuff like that. Years later, he met Lieutenant Carmichael, and he said, 'You guys accused me and my men of killing that sergeant, that was not my patrol. That was an entirely different patrol that had the fight there,' but they were going to kill him. Rice's men would have killed him if we had left him.

The Rosary Beads

So anyway, it's like that, you know, you go out on combat patrol, and you get guys wounded, and you get guys killed. It was just trench warfare. There was another funny instance that happened one time [when we were on patrol duty there]. There was a Dutch family that was supposed to be moved to Belgium, but instead of moving them to Belgium, they moved them up towards [what would become] the front lines where we were fighting. So this family was staying in a barn, and whenever we came off the front line to come back to the rear, I used to stop in and visit these people; there was a bunch of kids, and we got to be very friendly with them. They were the Smollers family—in fact, I'm still in contact with them right to this day—but anyway, one day I didn't come in there, and they said, 'Where's Tarbell? Where's Tarbell?'

One of the guys from another company, I guess, said, 'Albert? He got killed last night on patrol,' but there was another Albert, you know. [*Laughs*] So I went there the following day to say hello to the kids—they were just little kids. There were two boys grown up, there were [a couple] 14 or 15-year-old girls, and then the little kids. There were about five or six of them at the end, and they were saying a rosary for my demise, but I walked in and all hell broke loose! [*Laughs harder*] Oh, they were so happy to see me that they gave me silver rosary beads! I still got those rosary beads; I carried them all the way through.

The Old Cat

Then another time we were in a bivouac area in a big circle, and we went to the center of that circle because we had troops all the way around; in an airborne operation, that's how you do it. We were getting shot at by these nebelwerfers, God, and they would call them 'screaming mimis.' I think they're light barrel mortars and they would fall over the place, here, there, and everywhere, but they made the weirdest sounds coming in. Well, I noticed this old cat that came around. I love strays. I would give them milk or whatever I could find, I would give them bits of my food. He was always sitting inside our dugout; we had a good dugout where we were staying. He was inside there, and finally one day Clark Fuller said, 'Let's watch that cat. I think he knows something about them nebelwerfers.' The cat's ears were all ripped up and he was deaf, yet he could hear those nebelwerfers before they'd [start screaming], before they landed! All at once, his tail went straight up, and he made a beeline for a foxhole and we followed him! After that, I'd holler, 'Incoming mail, let's go!', and everybody would scatter. [*Laughter*] The nebelwerfers came in after we were [safe] inside; that was a comical thing. [*Chuckles*] I don't know what happened to that cat, but we sure took good care of him there. The nice thing is you think about it afterwards, you live to talk about that happening, and that's just one of those experiences you talk about afterward that makes you feel good.

*

We were supposed to be relieved the 11th of November by the Canadians. And at 11:00, the company commander said, 'Let's shoot all that extra ammo out. Let's shoot it towards the German line.' We were shooting it towards the German line, and I asked the captain, 'What if they decide not to relieve us tonight?'

'Yeah,' he said, 'that's a possibility. Call them back, tell them to cut it out.' So we got hold of the platoon and they stopped, but we ended up getting relieved the following day.

The Outpost

We got relieved on the 12th. We headed right through Belgium, right into France on the trucks to a French army barracks, licking our wounds, getting replacements and stuff. We had a lot of replacements to do. Most of our company was wiped out and we had different activities to do, and they were sending some guys, the old guys on leave to Paris, some of the older men. They were going to Paris. See, I was their replacement; there were guys older than me from Sicily [invasion jumps]. I had nice duty, though. You see, in combat, I was a communications sergeant. Three of us sergeants in the company, we manned the switchboards, and we did any line communication and voice communication by radio, and we [escorted] the company commander, when we were not on [switchboard] duty; he worked us like bodyguards—wherever he went, you went.

That's what our job consisted of. It was Sergeant Brick, myself, and Sergeant Photowell. He had a rank of buck sergeant, and Clackford was our media sergeant, he was a staff sergeant. When I went to the outpost, they were having a cover attack on those Den Heuvel Woods, and everybody was on edge because there was such fierce fighting that everybody was involved. There was, during the day, an AT [rocket] gun that got set up just across the road from us.

It was, I think, [manned by] five guys, and it was a 57-millimeter. The first sergeant watched them set up across the road from our CP. And all at once we saw, they got one shot off and a few seconds later they had a direct hit from a German self-propelled gun. We went over there to check the guys, and all five of them were dead. It was just a direct hit, killed all of them. We figured, well, they're gone, let's see if we can at least get the wristwatches. Even the wristwatches—the glass was all busted in that, too. It's just no good. So, we started back and between the gun position and our CP there was a haystack. And meanwhile, with all of this fighting going on, we had foxholes dug around in case we got overran. We could fight from there. Well, that self-propelled gun [crew] saw us walk away from that gun position and go towards the haystack. They must have figured we had another gun set up near there. And all at once, we could hear that shot coming and we dove behind that haystack, right into that. And we had about seven or eight shots fired at us—and you're talking about being shot at point blank by an 88. That's an awful weird feeling. You could hear that shot and then you could hear that crack when it sort of hit—just like a rifle. Man, I'm telling you, I never hugged that ground so fast. I dove down to that ground, and who the hell did I find underneath there but my first sergeant, all six foot four of him, underneath me already. We stayed there and they just tore it up. They just abrogated that haystack.

When I came back that night, from the outpost, I got into my sleeping bag, and after I reported to my sergeant what happened, about being at the outpost, and a guy shooting at me and Germans shooting back. So, I was just falling asleep in a sleeping bag, and I heard the first sergeant say, 'Lieutenant, don't go out there. You'll get shot! Don't go out there. Leave those guys alone. They're okay.' This little lieutenant, a new lieutenant who joined not too long before we were coming from Holland, he wanted to check the guard outside, and the first sergeant kept telling him, 'Lieutenant, you're going to get shot!' Sure enough, he had to go check the guard. Sure enough, he went out there and he got shot and he died about three days later. He got shot by one of the guards. Just very on edge.

Unfortunately, history would record over 15,000 Allied troops as being killed, wounded, and captured during Operation Market Garden, while German loss estimates range between a half to two-thirds of that figure. In not accomplishing the taking of the bridge at Arnhem, the operation failed to achieve the intended mission.

The Rhine would not be crossed in 1944.

The war would not be over by Christmas.

Mr. Tarbell's story will continue.

Nineteen-year-old Richard Marowitz (behind driver's left shoulder) and men of his Intelligence & Reconnaissance platoon.
Source: Richard Marowitz

CHAPTER FIVE

The Recon Man I

I met Richard Marowitz when I invited a trio from the Hudson Valley (NY) Chapter of the Veterans of the Battle of the Bulge to come up to the high school for a presentation on April 28, 2000. Now retired, he was busier than ever, and with a quick sense of humor that served him all of his life, he was quick to point out the funny things of his World War II experience.

'There's three of us that have been going around to schools and churches and synagogues and so forth talking to kids. They've got us running. That's been phenomenal. The kids, we each do about seven, eight minutes, a little bit of background of who we are and what we did in the Army and whatever. We ask for questions. We now book no less than two hours, and we go over time. The kids, the hands never go down, unbelievable. We did Hudson Falls High School; we were only booking an hour and a half. We were supposed to talk from 1:00 to 2:30, and never got out until 4:00. Unbelievable. They're hungry. And the phenomenal part of the whole thing, the teachers weren't born yet. Every now and then they go, 'Gee, this stuff is not in the books.' I said, 'Of course not. What you have in the books came off of the front page of The New York Times back in 1944.'

He took a more serious tone when discussing a traumatic experience that happened to him on a spring afternoon like the day he was speaking to students—in fact, just one day shy of the 55th anniversary of the notorious event. As part of a well-oiled intelligence and reconnaissance task force, Rich and his friends were frequently the first Americans into enemy territory. Now only twelve miles away from the objective of the German city of Munich on that sunny spring day, they were assaulted by the overpowering stench of death—but while not uncommon in wartime, something even more sinister lay ahead, something that would register shock in soldiers not even out of their teenage years.

'We all thought the same thing. We never talked about it, but later on afterwards, after the fact, we realized that we all thought the same thing—we figured we're coming to another bombed-out farm with a bunch of dead animals. That's what we thought! Nobody ever told us it was a concentration camp! There is a village of Dachau. So, on the map, we saw a village of Dachau.

We were going to take the village. That's all we knew.'

Richard M. Marowitz

I was born in Middletown, New York, February 6, 1926. I grew up in Middletown. I went to public school and junior high, and then we moved to Brooklyn, the home of the Brooklyn Dodgers, and I was walking distance from Ebbets Field. I went to one game, and the team was great, but the fans were the worst fans I ever saw in my life, throwing bottles on the field. I said, 'Well to hell with this. I'm taking the subway to The Bronx and I'm going to go to Yankee Stadium,' and I became a Yankee fan. When the war broke out, I was on Broadway with my father, and the Times Square [scrolling news bulletin ticker] that was going around, that's the first place I saw it. I couldn't believe it. I didn't know; then, of course, I was [just fifteen].

[At that time, in high school], I actually played the trumpet. I was a little ahead of my time with that too; I joined the union when I was sixteen, doing club dates around New York, and if they had known how old I was, I never would have made it. I went on the road with a band actually, a couple of bands, and I turned eighteen in Dallas, Texas; I was playing at a club in Dallas, Texas. I went into a draft board in Dallas and signed up for the draft. I knew it was going to happen, so I had the address of the Brooklyn draft board, and I had him transfer it there. They finally caught up with me. I got a call from my sister to come home for the physical, and I was in so fast. I weighed 124 pounds. I was dead white from working all night and sleeping all day, and these big guys were stamping them rejected, rejected, rejected, and this skinny bag of bones walks up there, and was accepted. I said, 'What are you, blind?' But I don't really regret it.

I went to Camp Croft, South Carolina. At that point in time, it had slipped to third place. What I mean is, it's a gorgeous little camp in Spartanburg, South Carolina, but it had the reputation for years of being the toughest infantry camp in the country, believe it or not. They got a new commander in there that wanted to bring it back up to first place. The training was so tough he was burning guys out, guys were going to the hospital. It was awful. They finally got a new commander in. It was tough. My problem was that I was going to a specialist side of camp, so seventeen weeks of basic. So, the first seven weeks, I was supposed to do everything that the other regular straight rifle guys were getting in fourteen weeks, so they had us go night and day.

I couldn't get into a band, so they said, 'How about being a bugler?' I said, 'Great.' Well, I didn't know a bugler in the Army at that time was the scout and message runner. So, I didn't make out too well with that. I was getting all this special training, for the next seven weeks, we're supposed to go to school, learn the code converter [for the bugle]. About a week into school, they said, 'Well, they need the straight riflemen overseas. We don't know what to do with you so we're going to run the first seven weeks over again.' So, we did the first seven weeks over again, and two weeks of maneuvers and testing, and we were out of there. But I don't regret it. That training paid off later on.

South Carolina, Spartanburg, was a village, and it was all bars. The Army took over the town. It was ridiculous. It was totally ridiculous. I wasn't used to the black and white. Everything was marked black and white. That really teed me off, discrimination, oh yeah. You couldn't avoid it back in those days. I got on the bus one day—I always liked to ride in the back of the bus. I went right straight to the back of the bus, and the bus stops. Everybody is looking at me, and the bus driver said, 'Get up in front of that white line.' There's a white line on the aisle floor.

I said, 'Why?'

He said, 'You can't sit back there.'

I said, 'Did I give you my dime?'

He said, 'Yeah.'

I said, 'I'll sit where I want.'

The bus ain't moving. Now, I see all of these rednecks looking at me.

I said, 'Open the door.' I got off of the bus. I'm not dealing with these idiots.

So basic ends, and I had an 11-day delay en route to go to Camp Gruber, Oklahoma, to join the Rainbow Division. The first thing that happened to me walking down the street after I checked in, they put me right into Headquarters Company, 222. Great regiment. They put me in there, and I didn't know what I was there for.

I didn't know what I was supposed to do, but I was still listed as bugler. So, every day, I went over to the rec hall because Corporal Stipple was in charge of the drum and bugle call. They gave me this plastic bugle. I'm double tugging and triple tugging, and doing all this crazy stuff on the bugle, and it blew his mind. I had brought my own mouthpiece; I had my horn with me. It just blew his mind. So, he said, 'How did you learn how to play a bugle like this?' Used to go to the rec hall and jam with the guys, and then I found out what I was doing there. The bugler that the Headquarters Company had was unfit for his duty, so I was taking his place. That's what I was doing there.

Then I helped them pack to go overseas. I didn't really know a heck of a lot; I was busy. I'm a workaholic kind of a nut anyway. The captain took me up to the motor pool and he gave me the clipboard. He said, 'These are the numbers that go on those crates, and you supervise.' He told me what to do. He said, 'Somebody will be here in eight hours to relieve you,' and nobody showed up.

I went to this lieutenant, and I said, 'Somebody is supposed to take my place.'

He said, 'Well, just keep doing it and I'll find out about it.' I never saw him again. Another eight hours went by, and the same thing happened.

So, the following morning, Captain McLaughlin, my company commander, walked in. He said, 'What are you doing?'

I said, 'I never left.'

'You've been here 24 hours?'

I said, 'You see all those crates? I could have my name on them.'

'Get in my jeep.'

We went over, and he balled the hell out of one of his second lieutenants. He took me back into his office, and he told the first sergeant, 'This guy is going to sleep. When he wakes up and when he feels like it, you just tell the mess sergeant to give him whatever he wants. And after that, forget the quarantine crap.'

He said, 'Give him a pass and let him go to town for two, three days. Doesn't make any difference.'

I said, 'Gee, that's pretty good, Captain.'

He said, 'You earned it.' That was it.

Captain McLaughlin probably turned out to be one of the nicest and best officers I ever had. This followed through in everything. His wife lived in town. He would go over and say, 'You going to town?'

'Yeah.'

'Take my car.' He gave me his wife's address, where his wife was living.

'Drop it off at the house, would you?' No problem. Then he'd take us all home, drunk or sober. It didn't make any difference when he found us, but he was a great guy. He didn't have to holler, and he didn't have to scream, although he could have. He was a big, tall, very handsome Irishman from Los Angeles. He was kind of a guy you just had to like. He liked action, but he wasn't getting it because theoretically one of his jobs was to find the next CP. If we were in this little village, and the regiment moved up, then he would find a suitable CP in the next village or whatever. But that wasn't good enough. He wanted action. To give an example of what kind of a guy he was, they used to get a liquor ration every month. His liquor ration came in, because we didn't know what he was getting and what he liked. He said, 'You guys come and see.' So, we went in, and he went into his little room that he had for an office, and the desk or the table, whatever it was at the time, was loaded with booze. He said, 'Okay, you guys, take whatever you want.'

'Captain, what did you say?'

'Take whatever you want.'

I said, 'And what is this for?'

He said, 'I have your necks out where they're not supposed to be.' We split the whiskey ration every month. I don't know if you know any officers like that, but I never met another one like that. That's the kind of a guy he was.

Shipping Overseas

I don't remember the exact day [we left to go overseas], but we left in November of '44. We landed in Marseille, France, at the end of November, around Thanksgiving, the hellhole of the world. Three infantry regiments went over, and it was called Task Force Linden because General Linden was in charge. This is what screws up the records. Actually, the rest of the 42nd Division didn't come over until February of 1945. So, we didn't have any support. So, we were being attached to the 86th or the 101st. There's a list. One of my buddies, Al Cohen, who was one of our [later classroom visiting veteran] trio, he got this list from somewhere, it lists every division, and how many days they were in combat, how many were killed, how many were wounded, percentages, and all that stuff. The Rainbow is listed as coming over on February 17, 1945—only a little bit of combat and not much action. It's totally wrong! I'm now a past president of the Veterans of the Battle of the Bulge. Now, the Battle of the Bulge people do not have the 42nd Division as having been in the Battle of the Bulge because it wasn't, but Task Force Linden was in the Battle of the Bulge for a short time, [because] they needed bodies as fast as they could get them. So, they sent over the three infantry regiments to get the bodies over as fast as possible, then everybody else dragged in later when all the fun was over.

[The first camp area we set up] was a big, huge, windswept, ice-cold sea of mud in the middle of the night. You found a buddy. If he was alive, he got to have a tent. We pitched tents. We went to sleep. In the morning, we got up, and naturally the tents were everywhere. The officers were as green as we were, and they were still going by the book. The book was never ready for wartime. It was written for peacetime. The first thing they did was get these tents [re-set up] in a line. They wanted them perfect, holding the snap string. After that happened, that night, Bedcheck Charlie came over. I mean, what a target that camp was! Straight up one side, and come back down the other; it's just models for them. Did anybody ever explain Bedcheck Charlie to you?

The Germans, what they did is they usually sent over a small plane, like a two-engine job, and they had the motors a little bit out of sync, so when they came over, you knew it was Bedcheck right away because you heard it, recognized they were out of sync. You knew he was here. That's to throw the fear of God into you right away, and they would drop a 25-pound bomb or something just to keep you from sleeping, just to get you edgy. They never really did much damage that I saw. Once I was in a house and they took a piece of the roof off. Scared the hell out of you, but it hurt the house, it didn't hurt anybody in it. So, that was Bedcheck Charlie. Of course, after Bedcheck started coming over, they put the tents back where they were in the first place, then they moved us up to a quiet front to learn—you go to college to learn how to become a doctor, but you don't really know how to become a doctor until you go into a hospital and learn how to become a doctor. Well, the same thing happens in the Army. You've heard that before. So, we went in for our baptism of fire. It was supposed to be a quiet front. They spread us out so thin… for a short time, it was okay, until the Germans got frisky. The Battle of the Bulge started on December 16, and then they started getting frisky down at our end too. Then we started to lose people. The guys learned what war is about.

I&R Men

My job at that point was taking care of the officers. I was in charge of the mess for the officers and the staff. How I got that job, I don't remember, but Captain McLaughlin gave it to me. Colonel Longo, we later got along very well, but in the beginning, he had an asbestos mouth. The coffee could be boiling, and he'd say, 'The coffee isn't hot.' I would feed the officers, and they were aggravated. They were prima donnas, and there was a big ego trip at that time. I went to the mess sergeant, and I picked up the food and cans, and I brought it to the room where the officers are going to eat. They had their own plates and stuff like that. I would give them what the GIs were eating. So, I would say to Sergeant Sedowski, 'What are the guys eating today?'

'Well, they can only have one piece of bread, because we're short on bread, or they could only have this, they could only have that. This is what they're going to get.'

I said, 'Fine,' and I would bring enough so each of the officers would get the same thing.

And then the first time the colonel said to me, 'Got any more bread?' I said, 'No, the men are only having one piece today. You know what the book said. The officers eat what the men eat.' Actually, the officers are supposed to eat after the men eat, but I didn't go that far. But this is what I started to do. I started to become unpopular, but not unpopular enough, and one day I said to the captain, 'Captain, you have to get me out of here. I can't stand these guys anymore.'

So he said, 'You come with me,' and that's when I got to be with Flatt and the captain. We became the Three Musketeers. Theoretically I was still the bugler, but I was kind of hanging out with the captain. So, his driver's name was Flatt, F-L-A-T-T it was. Captain said to me one day, 'You know anything about a .50 caliber machine gun?'

I said, 'I can take it apart and put it together blindfolded,' which was a lie. I'm sure he knew it.

He said, 'Get in the jeep,' because he had a .50 mounted on his jeep. He said to Flatt, 'Get in,' and we went out into the woods. He was pointing at trees and I was [shooting], chopping them down. He said, 'That's good.'

So, the three of us were always where we weren't supposed to be. His dodge was, 'I'm looking for another CP.' But when you meet the I&R [Intelligence and Reconnaissance] platoon out in no-man's land, you know you're too far out.

*

We never knew what we were in because they kept bouncing us from the Third Army to the Seventh Army, from the Seventh Army to the Third Army, and did you ever hear of the other Battle of the Bulge, Operation Northwind, which came on the heels of the first Battle of the Bulge? This was another thing that you don't hear about much. Just in the last couple of years you start to hear about it, and they're starting to write about it. It was a hush-hush, not popular thing, mainly because some officers way up there made some mistakes; we lost more people than we should have. Anyway, this was considered as bad as the first Battle of the Bulge. The 101st by that time had come down. We were more or less on the bottom of the bulge. Everybody thinks of Bastogne. They don't realize that the bulge, the front, was over 80 miles, the bulge front. We were on the southern tip of it, which was also close to Alsace-Lorraine. During this Operation Northwind, Hitler's baby, even the 101st took a bath. We were attached to the 101st at that time. We never knew from day to day what we were in. It got to the point we didn't even ask because it didn't make any difference. Wherever we went, they were shooting at us anyway.

We were maintaining a line. Of course, we kept moving and the line kept changing, naturally. Sometimes, it went back, and sometimes it didn't, and we were taking the bad stuff. A lot of guys were getting hit because we just didn't [have the manpower]. The problem there was that they started bringing everything up in the main body up towards [the relief of] Bastogne, and they were taking people from us down below. We were spread out pretty thin, and we couldn't fill in because they were still taking people away from us. So, it got to be a little bit hairy because we were always understaffed, and we didn't have the support we should have had.

[Our biggest concern was] Tiger tanks. Did you ever see a German Tiger tank? Well, at one point, a little later on, the I&R platoon ran into an ambush. We're still trying to figure out who gave the order that caused this, because you don't send an intelligence and reconnaissance platoon out on a night reconnaissance. That's like committing murder. They sent the I&R platoon out on the night reconnaissance, traveling down the road in jeeps. You can't see a foot off the sides of the road, but everybody off the sides of the road can see you like daylight, especially when the moon is out. There was a lot of reflection because there was a lot of snow, so you're a sore thumb going down the middle of the road, so you're going to get killed. But you can't see anything. So, how can you have a night reconnaissance when you can't see anything? That's the name of that game.

Well, the next day, I volunteered for the I&R platoon. The captain said to me, 'Do you know that's a dangerous operation? You can get killed in that operation.'

I said, 'I'm playing the odds, Captain.'

He said, 'What do you mean by that?'

I said, 'Well, right now, as it stands, it's three to one. With them it's 28 to one. I'm going with them, if it's okay with you.'

He said, 'Okay.' He said, 'Pack your bag. Go over to join them right now. But if you change your mind, I'll take you back.'

So, I said, 'Okay.' He was a hell of a guy. He really was one hell of a guy, and we got in a lot of trouble.

On The Road

[The primary mission of an I&R platoon] is to find the enemy and report back. Take prisoners, interrogate. You have no choice but to engage. Generally, when you find them, they find you. Sometimes, they find you before you find them because your neck is out. There's hardly ever a day when you're not engaged, sometimes more than once. If we're that close, sometimes we just engage them because you really can hardly get away from them without it. Most of the time, they see you first. But you know, you're coming around the bend. We came around the bend in the road. There was a bank over here. We came around the bend, and then boom, we almost ran into a bunch of Germans with a horse and a wagon. There were like 40 or 50 of them. We split up into squads, two squads, 12 men in each squad. We almost ran into them. Of course, they got more scared than we did. So, we just started popping.

That day, I'll never forget that day. I might be a wise guy. Came across a carbine, and I said, 'Gee, why carry the heavy end one when I could carry this little carbine?' We had the little skirmish, and it was close. This German was in the ditch, and I came down on him, and he was coming up with his rifle. I [pulled the trigger of the carbine, it didn't work] and my buddy in back of me took care of the German, and I threw that carbine so far. You could tell me it was a good weapon, but it didn't work for me, so I just got rid of it.

We were always in jeeps. It was seven jeeps, four men in a jeep, 28 men. We were assigned our own medic, because there was an aid station back at headquarters company anyway, so they gave us a medic. We had two squads, and we split most of the time. We took parallel roads. The medic, the lieutenant, the driver, and the platoon sergeant were in the seventh jeep. He had the big 694 radio, so he could call the artillery if a Cub came over or something, have a little conversation if we needed help. [Standard issue] for an I&R platoon was two radios, one for the platoon leader and one for the rest of the platoon. We ended up with one in every jeep. We stole everything we saw. [*Laughs*] You've got two squads. One radio between the two of them, that's not possible even. How do you keep in touch with anybody? Some dingbat with a glass eye wrote the book.

[We improvised a lot]; there was a .50 caliber machine gun on the lieutenant's jeep. We were supposed to have one .30 caliber machine gun. We had a .30 caliber machine gun, every jeep. We had a couple of bazookas that we acquired. We had grenades. We had a couple of 60-millimeter mortars, and we had grease guns and more BARs than we were supposed to have. We were fired on. On the way to Dachau, we were fired on coming out of the woods. There was a little knoll to the side. This almost sounds comical, I know. We laugh about it all the time. There's a little village right in front of us. We dragged all our crap up on the hill. Those Germans in that village probably thought they hit the point of a division, because we unloaded on them. We hit them with bazookas and mortars and everything you could think of. Made a lot of noise. We were great bluffers.

Lieutenant Short used the three-man assault at the time; he had an order, I don't know why. The two point scouts, myself and Larry Hancock, and Howard Hughes, who was a great BAR man, went in and we cleared the first few houses, and then we waved the rest of the guys in. We took close to 200 prisoners! We broke up their weapons, told them to put their hands on their heads and walk back up the road. The reason we were in a big rush to get to Dachau was that we were being pushed like crazy. What are you going to do with these guys? So, that's what we did, and then we took off, but we needed that stuff. A bluff works, it really does. We were great poker players.

Lieutenant Short was a great guy. His father was General Short. This guy, he's a bag of bones, nervous as a cat, came up from private right up into lieutenant, all in the field. I guess he was in Africa, he was in Italy—I know he was in Italy. It was nerve-wracking with him. I mean, he would get up [during a firefight]. I said to him one day, 'What do you think you are, George Washington crossing the Delaware?' He'd stand up. Things are going on.

'You guys go over there! Watch that over there!'

I said, 'Get down.' He was a pip. He was an absolute pip, but he watched out for us.

This captain came out with us one day. He wanted to see me. He was new. He was put in charge of us too. He messed up cannon company, so they put him in charge of intelligence. Yeah, it's the truth, and he came out with us one day to see how we operated. We got into a little skirmish. He had this Italian Mauser, I guess it was, this 'blunderbuss,' and he flopped down next to me, right over here, and he let go of that thing, and I thought my head was coming off. When we got finished, I stood up and I went right into his face and I started… I called him everything you could think of. I was really mad. My whole head was ringing. I had a problem from that time on, and he… 'Your fanny is court-martialed. When we get back, you're dead.' Lieutenant Short walked over to him, and he said, 'You're not going to do a thing. I saw what you did!' I'm cleaning this up a little for you. He said, 'You better not come out with this again, not if you want to go home,' and that was the end of that. That officer never looked at me again.

This is probably the best bunch of guys I ever worked with in my life. I mean, Larry and I, we worked point together a lot, most of the time. As a matter of fact, they took us out of point one day, and we got nervous because the guys up front hadn't worked much. So, every time they saw a bush, they stopped. We weren't getting anywhere. So, the lieutenant finally came back and said, 'Would you guys mind going back up to point?' Because you know I'd be happy to do it.' We trusted ourselves. We didn't trust anybody else. We worked point most of the time. It wasn't that bad.

*

Larry and I almost didn't ever talk when we were out. I mean, we'd be on opposite sides on the road. We never walked the shoulders. That's where the mines are. We'd look at each other, throw a signal, and I knew what he was going to do, and he knew what I was going to do. We worked together so much. We'd go in. You're running across a lot of little villages. You don't do this in a big city, but you're running through one village after the other. They're all farm villages and so forth. So we cleared the first few houses, and then wave the rest of the guys in. It isn't like we had a lot of men to work with. We did a lot of things like that; we threw the book away. For example, for the I&R platoon, I think in the book it said when you're coming down the road and you stop for any reason, this jeep backs on like this, this jeep goes like this, the next jeep goes like that [*gestures with hands indicating vehicles turning, reversing, lining up parallel*]. Theoretically, that's good. You can go in any direction if something happens, right? Well that's good if you're still alive, because all the mines are on the shoulders of the road, so you back up onto the mines, and you blow up. We never hit a mine. We never hit a mine. You look at any film of troops moving down the road. They're walking on the shoulders on the road, so that the tanks and the jeeps and the armored guards can go through. They're the ones that are stepping on the mines and blowing up. So we ignored the book. We did what was expedient; we just really never thought about it. We knew what we were going to do. We just stayed away from shoulders of the road, period. Said there was nothing to worry about, as far as we were concerned. As far as the middle of the road is concerned, most of the time, if somebody is putting something in the road, you can see where the road had been disturbed. Well, you go around those things. These become second nature, so we never had a problem. But if we came upon tank tracks, and if we saw tracks in the snow, well, we just turned around and went the other way. What are you going to do with a Tiger tank? The armament is that thick [*moves fingers several inches apart*]. Everything we had would bounce off of it. So, there's no point in it. If you happen to be in the Fort Knox area, which is outside of St. Louis, right next to Fort Knox is Patton's Armor Museum, and it's the most marvelous thing you ever saw in your life. There were a bunch of us together, it was a Rainbow reunion, so we were all together. Here's this Tiger tank, and you know it scared us. You get scared just looking at it. They had cut away one side and put plexiglass over it. They had three full-sized dummies sitting around a table playing cards in the tank. You saw the steel on this thing, and it's still a scary thing. Of course, now we have bigger than that, but that was just a scary piece of work. [And the German] burp gun, nothing could shoot faster than that. Did you ever hear one? It's just unbelievable. That's another thing. It seemed like almost every German had a machine gun. It's just that later on, as our stuff started to come over, we had so much stuff. Even though they were destroying it, we replaced it so fast, where they couldn't replace theirs. The Tiger tank actually I think had a problem moving their turns. Did you know that? But it really didn't make any difference if it was a little slower because things were bouncing off of it anyway.

The I&R man's adventures were just beginning. The men soon found themselves at the gates of Dachau, and the next day, burst into Hitler's Munich home.

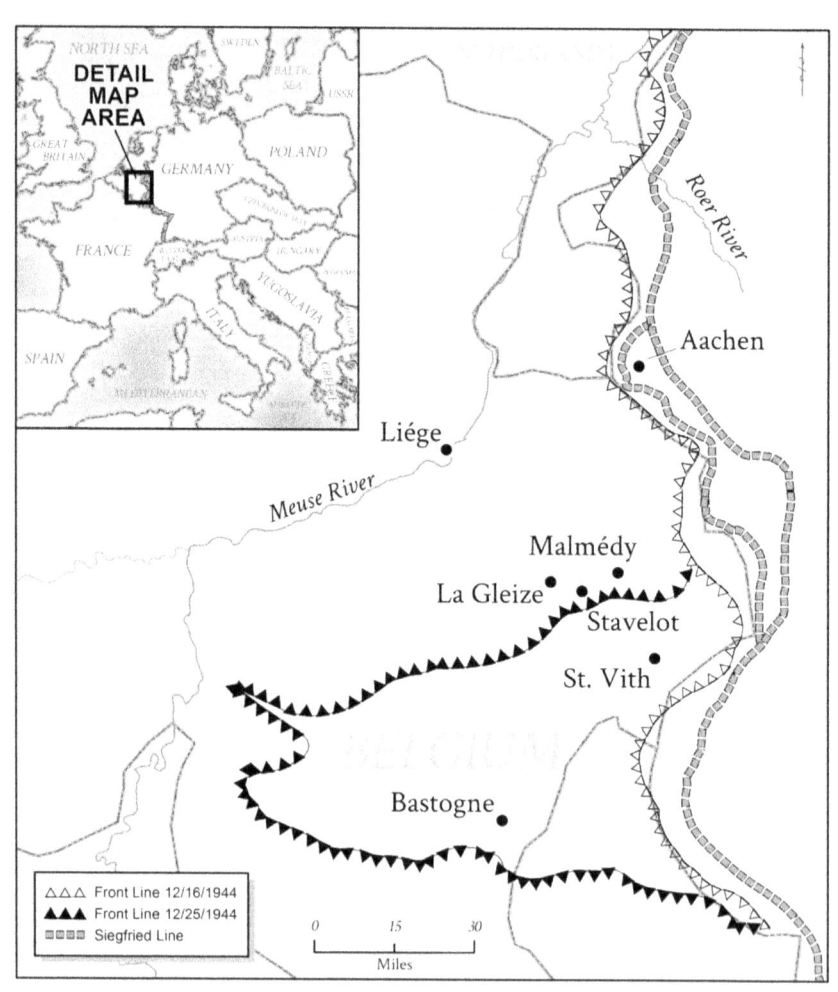

The Battle of the Bulge. Simplified map by Susan Winchell.

PART TWO

SETBACKS

'I woke up early in the morning, and I heard a lot of commotion. I looked over from the haymow, and God, there was a line of stretchers, stretcher bearers, and all at the barn. In the passageway, the guy looked just like my company commander on one of the stretchers there! So I hurried down the ladder on the side; by that time they had him in a van.

[A few hours before], he had said, 'Foley's back, let him take your place for tonight.' He said, 'You're all set, report to the medics.' Foley was going to take my place, cover for me.

So when I saw that company commander in a stretcher, in the ambulance, I said, 'Captain, what happened?' He started crying, he was hurt pretty bad, he said, 'Foley got killed.'

[My friend] that took my place got killed. And then the captain said, 'Your [new] company commander—be good to him, like you were to me.' He said, 'I don't know when I'll see you again.' We had a little talk there, and then they took him away.'

—Paratrooper, Battle of the Bulge

Timothy Horgan in uniform, World War II.
Source. Tim Horgan.

CHAPTER SIX

The Cavalryman I

Sitting comfortably in his office at his home in Glens Falls, New York, 'Hometown, USA,' Tim Horgan affects a relaxed and friendly demeanor when speaking with a high school senior [sixteen years later, now an Air Force doctor] for our school project. Like his young interviewer, Mr. Horgan had just turned eighteen during his senior year. He was drafted two weeks after graduating high school in 1943, and was trained to be part of a tank destroyer outfit and then sent to Europe, where he wound up eventually assigned to the 2nd Cavalry Reconnaissance with Patton's Third Army. In his 19-month tour of duty, Mr. Horgan participated in the Battle of the Bulge, where he was awarded the Purple Heart after one of his friends tripped one of their own boobytraps, forgetting it had been set up.

'That's how I got my Purple Heart—I was watching a guy on fire right in front of me, trying to pull off his clothes. A hell of a sight, that poor guy, well, he's just gone. He burned right up in front of me, went right down; I was trying to pull off gasoline-soaked clothes from my buddy who just went up in flames. It was a hell of a sight, and just in two or three minutes, it was all over with, boy.... but I got my hands burnt up.'

Near the end of the war, after crossing the Rhine, Mr. Horgan was part of the liberation of the Flossenburg concentration camp and the famous rescue of the highly prized Lipizzaner dancing stallions. After traveling back to Europe in 1994 around the 50th anniversary of D-Day, like many of our veterans, nearly 50 years after the end of the war, Tim began to share his World War II stories.

Timothy J. Horgan

I was born in 1925 in Brooklyn, New York. I went to St. Francis Prep. That was when they were in Brooklyn at the time, now they are out in Queens. And they are greatly increased, up to 4,000 students. When I went there, they only had 400. On December 7, 1941, I was not quite seventeen. And I went to the movies, every Sunday afternoon, I'd go to a movie. We stopped at a candy store and found out everybody was crying in there, so we asked why. We found out it was the bombing of Pearl Harbor. Well, I was young and didn't quite realize exactly what was going on, not until I could absorb it more.

I turned eighteen on January 18, 1943. I had to go up to register with the draft board and they said, 'Fine. What are you doing?'

I said, 'I'm going to school.'

'When are you going to graduate?'

I said, 'June.'

They said, 'Fine, we will see you then.' And sure enough, the second week of June I get a postcard in the mail; come over to the Grand Central Palace in New York for my physical. So I went through my physical there. When you have finished your physical, then they say 'there are tables over there and go pick your table': Army, Navy, Coast Guard, whatever. [*Gestures to imply tables in a row*] So I picked the Army. And then I got sworn in on July 14, three weeks after I graduated high school, and they gave me two weeks to clear up all my business. August 4, I had to go back to the draft board. That morning they took me on a subway, the Long Island Railroad, out to Long Island to Camp Upton, which was the indoctrination camp out there at the time. I stayed there a week or so and then I got on a train again for two days and wound up down in Waco, Texas, Fort Hood. We got down there in 130-degree heat. Well, all of us New York boys had to go ahead and get acclimated to the weather. So we didn't do anything for about four or five days so we could get our bodies adjusted. That was tank destroyer training I went through; that lasted until the day after Christmas, when they gave me a ten-day furlough to go to Fort Meade in Maryland. So I come home, and I was home for New Year's, then I had to go back to Maryland. We stayed there a couple of weeks and then we got out of training again, went on up to Massachusetts to Camp Miles Standish, which was a debarkation camp, which means you assemble all of your troops together from the camp right outside of Boston, go down to the harbor, get on the boats, and go in the convoys over to Europe.

Replacement

I had just turned nineteen and I landed in Liverpool, England. It took us fifteen days to get over, which is a different story. In Liverpool we got out and went over up in the hills of Wales for a couple of weeks of training. Now this was in February or March of '44, and we knew the invasion was going to come, but we didn't know when. In May I was still a replacement. See, back in '43, the whole graduating class of young fellas was destined to be replacements, because once you get into combat, well, you got to keep feeding the troops in. So anyway, they started setting up replacement depots, which were to take the troops that are landing in the Liverpool salient, put them on a train and bring them down to our camp set up temporarily outside of the town of Taunton; this is southern England. And we would process all of the GIs over 36 hours and we would let all of the goodies they would bring stay. A lot of guys would come over with dress shirts with all tailored or whatever, but [we'd say], 'Buddy, throw it in the pile in the corner.' And we told them, 'Two of this, and one of this, and three of these or four of these, over there…' Get them out in 36 hours, get them on the train, and ship them over. And this was right after D-Day, June 6. Luckily, I was there. My buddies whom I went overseas with, they hit [Normandy] on D-Day D+3. But if I didn't take this job, temporary job, I would have been with them. But I stayed there all summer long because we didn't have the facilities in France yet, through June, July, August, the end of September.

Then they opened up Le Havre in France, so that the ships went right over to Le Havre to unload the soldiers coming over; so then I got into the replacement pool and then I got assigned to the 2nd Cavalry Reconnaissance, with Patton's Third Army. There was a history, big history of the 2nd Cavalry Reconnaissance, they go back 150 years; my Colonel Reed was a graduate of West Point, 1922. His first assignment was Fort Riley in Kansas, which was a cavalry [camp]. So he started in the cavalry with General George S. Patton; he too was a West Pointer, and he too was a cavalryman from way back; in fact he was in the Olympics—well, that's part of another story. Both were cavalrymen in a very aggressive organization. And you learned a lot between Colonel Reed and Patton. Patton didn't take any guff at all and Patton, he was a military general—not a politician—a military general. He'd get his assignment and go, he wouldn't take any malarkey, he would just go. I never met him, but I saw him, moving into some town, I don't know, I can't [remember]—when you go into combat, you don't know what day of the week it is. You don't get any daily newspapers and you don't get the news on the radio. [*Chuckles*] So you just go from day to day to day.

So in this one town, he came on through, in his jeep, his escort, and there are his pearl-handled guns; he was noted for his pearl-handled guns. And also an Eisenhower-cut jacket, and his riding britches, because he's a cavalryman, riding britches and high riding boots, that was his thing. So I saw him once coming on through, it was in France and [maybe early] November. Again, you don't know what day of the week it is, or the month. But I got over there and it was about then that I was assigned to the cavalry—when the Third Army was running across France, and the only way you could stop General Patton was to stop his gasoline supply. [*Laughs*]

The Battle of the Bulge

We actually were in Germany when the Battle of the Bulge was beginning. The 2nd Cavalry was in Germany, down in Saarbrücken in the Alsace-Lorraine Saar region of Germany. We were on our way, going through Germany, but all of a sudden Hitler pulled this invasion up there in the north of Belgium and Luxembourg; that was the weakest part of our line up there at the time. When they came on December 16, I was down in Saarbrücken, and two or three days later, I think it was, when Patton got his orders to make a 180-degree turn, go due north, we went up into the Battle of the Bulge. I was in Luxembourg at the time, at the southern end of the bulge on the Moselle River; that was a good barrier for the front line. I stayed there, January or December; oh about the 20th or 21st or whatever day it was that we landed up there. And that was a feat in itself taking a whole army and moving it in two days right up north! But I stayed in Luxembourg for the Bulge, and by the way that winter was the coldest winter in fifty years, and I mean cold! All of us GIs, we didn't have winter clothes, and we tried to layer up: two pair of pants, two jackets on. I had three pairs of socks on, one on top of the other, and every day I'd get up and rotate them,

1-2-3, 2-3-1, so that the sock which was next to my skin and took all of the perspiration would then be moved to the outermost layer, and the other two socks were on the inside.

Patrol Duty

A lot of the GIs got trench foot. Our boots weren't waterproof and the snow and cold; that was a rough, rough winter. In fact, see, we weren't equipped for it; we didn't have our winter clothes. It was all light, light stuff, and in the Battle of the Bulge we had these white parkas like a sheet so that we'll go on patrols, and most of the patrols were at nighttime. So when you went on patrols at night you blend right in with the terrain; it's all snow on the ground, and I mean a couple of feet of snow. Finally, that came until about the middle of January. The army was really relaxed in the equipping of the GIs over there. I really felt sorry for the infantrymen because they were in the foxholes all the time; they had no place to get warm. At least I could go ahead, get into a house, on the first floor, always on the first floor for security reasons—the back door was our escape route, but never the front.

We were right there on the Moselle River in a small little town called Ahn. It was in wine grove country, and the wine grove country has the mountains and the hills that come down to the river. So at daytime, you couldn't walk around because the Germans were on the east side of the river watching you; if you go walking around in the town, they will take potshots at you, and conversely if we saw them walking around, we would take potshots at them—I mean, you know, you had to break up the monotony somehow or other. [*Laughs*] That's how it was, so you had to be careful, and we had our patrols that'd go back and forth; at nighttime, walking up and down that road, to see if the Germans had come across the river and come in on their patrols—they'll come in and play havoc with us, so we would have to go ahead. We had to go out every night, always had guard duty into the wine groves. Your eyes and mind wander a little bit when you are out on guard duty. Two hours on, four hours off, two hours on, four hours off. So when you are out there for two hours, it is cold, but you just have to look and listen, see if you see any enemy patrols going up and down this road; I can remember in January, when it was clear, cold, blue sky, and now and then you would have clouds going by, you know, partly cloudy, but you would see those wine groves [seemingly] moving up and down. You know how a wine grove is, with the poles sticking up to keep the vines of the grapes? And every now and then, when it was so clear, and then a cloud would come across and it would change your opinion because you would look out again and your eyes would play tricks on you, and you would think that they were marching on you. [*Laughs*] Oh yes, and you are out there, and you just look and listen, you don't talk, a cold two hours. You come on in from guard duty, come back into the house again, and it was no warmer in the house because there was no central heating in those homes over there, it was all in the fireplaces. And you couldn't start a fire in the fireplace because the smoke would go through the chimney, the Germans would see the smoke coming up, throw a couple of mortars over on you. So what we actually did is, in the back of the house, we would go ahead and break through a pane of glass, you know there were nine panes of glass in their window, break out one of those, get the stove pipes, rearrange it to put it out that window on the first floor, so by the time the smoke got to the top of the roof, it had dissipated. But then that wasn't that warm either, so you had to be in sleeping bags and it was cold, really cold.

That was rough, Battle of the Bulge. You had guys losing feet with the trench foot, we weren't clothed. When you had to go on patrol, even the infantry, they would get shot and fall on the ground in a field. You couldn't go out and get them because then you would be subject to being shot, so you would have to wait until the nighttime to go out and get them. So you got out there at night and that's after five, six, eight, ten hours, and the guy's frozen. It was below zero; the guy's all frozen on you. But the Battle of the Bulge was a rough affair. That was a rough affair.

I had been promoted to corporal and that there is the jacket that I had when I was 160 pounds, a few pounds ago. [*Chuckles, rubs his stomach*] I can't get into that thing today. But I have it and I have my ribbons on it and my battle stars and whatnot. This patch over on this right shoulder there is the 2nd Cavalry patch, and on the other side is the outfit I came home with, which is the 90th Infantry. We were spearheading a lot for the 90th Infantry. See, what cavalry reconnaissance does is goes out on the drive, on the point, or come in between the two drives, between two divisions going through. We'd have to flush out in between; be sure that there were no enemy pockets in there that would come around and cut off the drive, so we are cut off. So we were either on the point or flushing out in between the drives in the towns and back countries, dirt roads, two-lane roads, make sure there were no enemies around. But we'd draw the fire first.

The Booby Trap

I was wounded during the Battle of the Bulge. And in this town we stayed in, we had to have security, so we set booby traps in certain areas. So when you come out of the house that you are staying in, you would go 20 steps this way, take a left, 15 steps, take a right or whatever because the booby traps were set with wires. So if anybody's walking around there, they'd trip a wire [whistles], and the booby trap would go off, so that is how we kept our security. This is right after what they declared to be the end of the Battle of the Bulge, the 25th of January, but that still lingered on into February.

But at any rate, you never drank the water over there, because you didn't know if it was contaminated, you never had milk, forget it! Even in England you don't drink milk. So what you did is, you drank wine, not powerful wine, but just wine; everybody over there drinks wine. You always had a bottle of wine, you'd take a sip of wine a couple of times a day and that's like drinking water.

So one of my buddies there—see, around a platoon, there were thirty of us in a platoon, three teams of ten. He went ahead and he was looking to get a couple of bottles of wine, so he went down, a couple of houses down there, and into the basements. You always had a wine cellar in the basement over there. So he went in, and he picked up a couple of bottles of wine, but in the corner of the building we had a booby trap set up, a couple of sticks of dynamite with buckshot shells taped around it, sitting on a five-gallon can of gasoline. He came out, he ducked under the wire, but he had his gun on his shoulder, and the point of his gun was still up and he came right on through; he didn't duck down far enough, and he tripped the wire. When it exploded, the gasoline came all over his clothing.

We heard the explosion, I came out of the house, I was the second guy out to go down and see what happened to him, and here he is all up in flames! So my first instinct is to get rid of his clothes. I went at him, and I was literally trying to pull his clothes off, and I got quite a bit of his clothes off, but he was still on fire and after a minute or two he just fell right down in front of me, dead. And we take a look at him; he was already dead from the buckshot; you could see all of those little holes all over his body. But his skin and his upper chest here [*gestures to chest*], was just like a stuffed pig when you spick the pig on an open fire, and the smell of skin is something you don't want to smell.

My both hands were all burnt, enough that I had to go back to the medics, and they put balsam on me, and they bound me up with mittens—I called them the white mittens—but they were gauze;

that's what I had for about a week. It wasn't enough to send me back to the hospital or keep me back out of the outfit—no, no, they put me back in the front line again! So I had mittens on there for about a week. I had no duty; the only duty they gave me was to get on the telephone in wherever we were set up for command, and I was working the telephones so I could go ahead and get a telephone up this way [*gestures holding a phone up to his face*], but nothing else.

That's how I got my Purple Heart—I was watching a guy on fire right in front of me, trying to pull off his clothes. A hell of a sight, that poor guy, well, he's just gone. He burned right up in front of me, went right down; I was trying to pull off gasoline-soaked clothes from my buddy who just went up in flames [*lets out sigh, pauses to compose himself*]. It was a hell of a sight, and just in two or three minutes, it was all over with, boy. I pulled off most of his clothes; the only thing I couldn't get off was his collar, his belt. I could get the other clothes off, and see, it was a double stitch, double layer of the clothes, but I got all this off [*gestures to chest region and leg region*], and pants off, and everything else...but I got my hands burnt up. So that's my Purple Heart story. And I understand they put me in for a Bronze Star, you know for bravery of doing that, and somebody came on back and said, 'Well, our quota for the month is up, so we can't issue another Bronze Star.' [*Laughs*] I said fine, whatever, whatever. Let it go. [*Laughs again*] But I suppose I was thankful nothing else happened [to me], and after a couple of weeks, I was back to normal again—well, I still had sensitivity in my hand, my skin, but I could still move around.

Mr. Horgan recovered from his physical injuries. The other scars would take years.

CHAPTER SEVEN

The Paratrooper II

Fresh from the failed Market Garden operation, Albert Tarbell continues his story with the 504th's unexpected insertion into the heavy fighting in the Battle of the Bulge.

Albert A. Tarbell

So, we're back to France, doing parachute patrol. This was right about the 17th of December, and we went off to Reims, France, where I was supposed to be doing the chute patrol; we had two non-coms from each company working with the MPs. We would get ahold of the paratroopers before they would be arrested by the MPs—they would fight the MPs instead of giving up to them, whereas we could talk to them, and they'd listen to us, because the paratroopers, they were just like that; they didn't want nobody bossing them around. But they would listen to us, especially a non-com paratrooper, talking to another paratrooper.

On the night of, I think it was the [16th of December], we were bringing these guys in, and all these guys were singing and raising hell and all drunk; [we were] taking them back to camp. Well, we didn't know what was going on; when we got back to camp that morning, we're already at warning. I was going by the CP, and I've gone up to my room and I heard this one guy say, 'Well, jeez, Sergeant, I've never fired an M-1!'

He said, 'That's all right, son. You'll learn. You can learn fast. Where we're going, you'll learn fast!'

When I got back to the barracks room there, my bags were all packed—my sergeant packed all my gear and everything. I said, 'We're going out on range to fire today?'

He said, 'Yeah. We're going on the range, all right. We're going back on the front line! The Germans broke through!' The Germans went over, right into the 'bulge.'

The rest of the night, we helped the orderly room distribute clothes, equipment, and I got some of the [new] guys who were just coming in from England, replacements, assigned.

Moving Out

About 8 o'clock in the morning, the trucks started coming in. Open-top trucks, Air Force trucks, semi-tractor trailer trucks. We loaded on there and took off. We didn't know where the hell we were going. We drove all that day. We got to the end of the day there; we got up towards Bastogne. Then from Bastogne, they rerouted us. They said there's another outfit coming in to go there, the 105th's going to go there. So we went on, going towards Roeselare, Belgium, but nobody knew what was going on; we didn't know what was going on!

We saw one guy coming out through the woods, and we asked him what's going on around there. He just threw his helmet on the ground and kept on going—he would not talk to us! So that was quite an [eyeopener], seeing [that]... The Germans had broken through and there was a lot of heavy fighting, from St. Vith and all through those areas there.

The 504th was about to angle with the notorious Waffen-SS Kampfgruppe Peiper, led by Joachim Peiper. With their seventy-ton Tiger II tanks and a penchant for war crimes in the east and now in the west, they were determined to take the crossroads and bridges that would get them to Liège. Just hours before, Kampfgruppe Peiper had murdered 84 unarmed GIs who had surrendered.[25]

'They Turned the Flak Guns on Us'

Well, I believe the name of the first area where we stayed was in Rahier, and we were there, I think, a day. Meanwhile, Colonel Peiper's panzer outfit was trying to cross a bridge near there, and they sent the 1st Battalion in there, and they had a fierce fight there, and they stopped them. G Company, and our 3rd Battalion went in and helped them also, just across the valley from us; I think the name of the place was Monceau. And as we got up on the top of this hill there, the knoll, we looked out on the side to our right, you could see three [enemy] flak wagons out there. We didn't pay much attention to it; we thought they were disabled flak wagons, but Lieutenant Rivers said, 'Get those guys before they get back to those flak wagons!' They weren't [abandoned]; the Germans had left them and gone some place, and now they were running back there when they found out we were coming up this knoll.

---

[25] Joachim Peiper (1915-1976), notorious commander in 1st SS Panzer Division Leibstandarte SS Adolf Hitler, responsible for tolerating, condoning, and ordering the abuse and murder of civilians and GIs who had surrendered, particularly the Malmedy Massacre, where 84 GIs were murdered by his men on Dec. 17. At his war crimes trial after the war, it was alleged that his unit, Waffen-SS Kampfgruppe Peiper, was responsible for killing a total of 350 unarmed American soldiers and about 100 Belgian civilians over a one-month period, as well as other atrocities when they were dispatched to the eastern front. Source: USHMM, Holocaust Encyclopedia. *The Malmedy Massacre.* encyclopedia.ushmm.org/content/en/article/the-malmedy-massacre

Well, we started shooting at them and we couldn't reach them. And they turned the flak guns on us, and they hit the trees above us, and oh, man, they peppered our company! [*Shakes head*] We must have lost over half of our company; we lost all the new officers we had, but it was all shrapnel wounds. I think there's only one guy that got killed, and he took a direct hit—it was a captain from a service company. Another guy got hit in the leg, a direct hit. Other than that, they were mostly all shrapnel wounds and flak wounds from the flak gun.

We had quite a battle there, most of the day, and we did finally end up getting into Monceau, and we went into fighting all day, and oh, yes, I ended up helping carry the wounded back into the trucks. We had some trucks back there, and we took three truckloads of wounded. And those trucks couldn't get out, either; they were more or less bottled up in there.

We could move around on that knoll—we took over the knoll; we had all that knoll, and on the sides there. Anyways, we headed out, and towards dark, we fought on, and that evening everybody was so tired out.

I went over to check the trucks later. It was dark, and those guys were still there. And I especially remember one of my buddies, he had gotten hit in both legs and both arms, but they were flesh wounds, didn't break any bones. I remembered I wanted to check on him and see how he was. By that time, he couldn't move his arms and he couldn't move his legs, and he just stiffened all right up. But I guess they did finally move the trucks later on, but at dark they still hadn't moved, they couldn't get them back to the medics.

Anyway, we ended up in one building there after fighting, early in the evening. And we fell right asleep, and we always just slept wherever we could in the building. I woke up early in the morning and I went snooping around. I went in the other room, in the living room in this building, and there was this [dead] guy laid out on the table! God, I thought, we're in a funeral home! Here's a guy all laid out, funeral-like, so I told the guys, 'Let's get the hell out of here, we're in a funeral home!' And everybody got up and we got the heck out of there. You know, forty years later when I was back there, I asked one of the [locals], 'Where's the funeral parlor here? I want to show my wife where I slept that night and woke up and I found that guy laid out on the table.'

He said, 'We don't have no funeral parlors here, the nearest one is in Reims.' So then I told him about what happened, but he knew who that [dead] guy was. He said that so-and-so had died at that time of natural causes, and he was laid out in his home. This is where we were, see. So that kind of made me feel a bit better. But okay, I'm getting ahead of myself, forty years ahead.

'An 82nd anti-armor bazooka team covers a road near Cheneux on December 20, 1944.' Source: National Archives, public domain.

The Priest

The 6th SS Panzer Army's mission, which included Kampfgruppe Peiper, was to break through the American lines between Aachen and the Schnee Eifel and secure the bridges over the Meuse, working up to the city of Liège.

After our Monceau battle, we ended up in another CP, where our lines were very fluid; [we were constantly] sending out patrols. Nobody knew where everybody was, but we knew that we had to stop Colonel Peiper's group from making it, from getting through Cheneux, in that area. And at the CP that we were at, there was a priest there, and there was a hired man, and supposedly the farmer that owned it. I was kind of happy. 'God,' I said to the priest, 'I'm glad to see you! You're a priest! You'll be able to say Mass for us at Christmas while we're here!' This was a couple days before Christmastime, right?

He said, 'I can't do that. I can't do that.' You know what he said? 'I have to have an altar. I should be in a church to say Mass.' I thought, my God, my chaplain said Mass with a couple of beer barrels [for an altar], K rations [for the wafer host], on the top of a jeep, you name it, wherever he could, you know, whatever he could use for a [makeshift altar].

I told the commander and the first sergeant, 'I don't think those guys are what they are saying.' I said, 'I think they're darn German soldiers!' And just then over the radio they said, spread the word, pass the word along—they're dropping German paratroopers behind our lines! I don't know what became of those guys, but I had to notify the company to watch out for German paratroopers. And some forty years later, I met the priest at Cheneux. I said, 'Were there any priests here, how many priests were here [during that period]?'

He said, 'Two of us. Me and a younger priest were here, and we stayed in the cellar with the women and kids all during your fighting days here!' So those guys were not what they were. Forty years later, we found out that they were not.

But anyway, we moved out. Our lines were very fluid here, and they were moving around, and this and that. You really didn't know who to make [contact with]; we were trying to contact the American soldiers, the American divisions there, and trying to contact our own 3-2-5.[26] There were two divisions near there. And we made our way towards, I guess it would be toward Saint Vith, or in that general area, La Gleize, Werbomont, and through there. And on the 23rd, it was a sunny day, the first sunny day there was, the P-38s came out. They were raising Cain, and at this area where we had moved to, you could see way out, you could look down into the valley. You could see these German vehicles moving. I didn't know which way they were going, but there was a lot of troop movement, and the P-38s were bombing them and strafing them, and then you had a lot of air activity that day.

Christmas Is Here

And then we ended up in some area there, oh my God, after all day walking, it seemed like. And we just got settled in, and word came down that we had to move back out. And we had to go back all the way, it seemed like about ten, twelve miles. I took cross

---

[26] *our own 3-2-5-* Mr. Tarbell refers to the 325th Glider Infantry Regiment. "Originally, the 82nd Airborne was to defend Bastogne but the 101st Airborne drew that assignment and the 82nd was sent north to Werbomont. The 325th dug in around the crossroads at Baraque de Fraiture and held. During the intense fight in December 1944 the 325th decimated two German divisions." Source: The 325th Glider Infantry Regiment-Unit History. The 82nd Airborne, World War II. www.ww2-airborne.us/units/325/325.html

country in school, and you could hear the tracks of the tanks, or they were ours, or Germans, I don't know. And you could hear the trees being knocked down. Our engineers were knocking the trees as we were going through. They would knock the trees down, you know, blocking the roads. Every now and then I had a pair of pliers on me, PL29s, and I would get called to the front; we would come across a field fence. I'd cut the wires, cut the wire fence off so that we could come on through. We seemed like we walked most of that night, Christmas Eve. All that Christmas Eve we walked. We got into Bra, and then we set up a defensive position.

They said that it was a strategic withdrawal to consolidate our positions, more or less. That's what we were told, because they said that they had panzers, but our tanks were coming in from the south, and they were bottling in the Germans. And that was the way for them to get out, so [our line had] to come out, so that we can really hold them in.

We set up Christmas Day, it was so damn cold Christmas Day! And we didn't have no water for coffee or nothing; pumps were all frozen up. Well, we soon got set up, we had one hell of a gunfight there. The SS are right on our ass as we got there at Bra, and we were just there at the outside of town. We got hit pretty hard a few times. I think it was that same day, I took three prisoners into battalion, SS guys. That's why we knew they were SS hitting us. And I turned them over.

Just as I got to the CP, Colonel Cook was there and he said, 'Get them over here!' I took them over to him and he took his .45 out—they're prisoners but they were still pretty belligerent. He took his .45 out and he shoved it right in that first SS guy's mouth! All three of them landed right on their knees. I thought he was going to blow that guy's—'I'm blowing your effing head off!' he said. Boy, they got down to their knees and all that bravado went right out of them fast. [*Chuckles*]

And I was glad that he didn't do that, because you hate to see anything like that, I don't care who it was. It took me off guard—here was my colonel, and he was going to kill these guys—but anyway, they were prisoners and we turned them over to the MPs. And that night, I think it's the same night, we heard some guy moaning and crying and moaning outside, he couldn't talk. And somebody said, 'Let him walk through, let him come in.' We let him in, and he comes into the CP, he had a grenade in his belt, and he had a hole you could put your thumb right through his forehead right in here, the side of his head where the bullet had gone through. [*Points to above left eye*] You could put your thumb right in that hole there.

He was incoherent. One of the lieutenants said, 'You better take him to the back and shoot him. He's going to die anyway.' And you could see the look on the guy's face, you could tell that he understood that, but he couldn't talk, that they had to kill him just to get him over his suffering. I said, 'Aww, better still, I'll take him back to the medics!' Me and another guy took him back to the aid station, and they said, 'We'll let him sit there. If he's alive in the morning, we'll send him to the hospital.'

I check back in the morning and then one of the lieutenants checked back too. I didn't know this until later; he checked back to see if that guy was alive. He was alive yet; he said, 'He's alive; he's on his way to the hospital, he's already gone.' So they shipped him back. But if he's still alive, he's had a headache ever since, I guess.

Airstrikes and artillery destroyed many German vehicles trying desperately to retreat. Kampfgruppe Peiper was in shambles, units separated from one another and hindered by the terrain and the dark; having advanced to Stoumont by the 19th, Peiper now was cut off. On Christmas Eve, he abandoned his heavy armor and fled with his men, leaving behind his wounded and some American prisoners. Some historians place the victims of his murderous campaign at 362 prisoners of war and 111 civilians; he reported that out of a force of 3,000, only 717 of his men returned to the lines with him.[5]

*

'You're Going To Freeze to Death'

But anyway, we had a lot of fighting there. And winter fighting I think is about the worst you can do. You freeze. One time, we went on this area here and we stayed overnight; we marched during the day, and we got to this area, and we stayed overnight. We got in our sleeping bag, and I woke up early in the morning, I felt so good. I was so warm, so nice and warm sleeping. It had snowed during the night; we were sleeping underneath these pine trees and the snow had covered us just enough for insulation. Our boots had dried out and everything was all wet when we had gotten in there. We got up and they had a hot meal for us there! Whenever they could have turkey. We never got no Christmas turkey; I think it was days later before we got a warm meal—I think that was one of the first warm meals we had; even rations heated up in hot water was good, though. And coffee, hot coffee! After that, we got ready and then we started marching down the road. It was such a beautiful sight! It was bitter cold, but was such a beautiful sight to see. You're in this mountainous area, there's snow on the trees and it was just like you could have been on vacation someplace. Except for when you got tired, you know, you had to take a break. Take ten and have a cigarette.

That's where your training comes in. Just when you think you can't take another step, you take a ten-minute break and in ten minutes' time, you're right back up there. Ready to go. That's where your hard training comes in later to pay off, that gives you good physical condition. And we were always in good physical condition.

We got to this area here and they said, 'Put all your gear down here.' There's a big hill right near the mountain lake. So we put all our gear there and just sit down. We're going up here to attack, and they'll bring our supplies, bring our equipment up to us.

So we got up this hill here, and between the adrenaline and the climbing of that hill, we were soaking wet when we got to the top. And when we got to the top, we didn't know where we were. Half the time you didn't know who the heck was the enemy, the cold or the Germans. We started to get cold, and we had a few skirmishes there, and a few guys got wounded. But we didn't have no warm clothes or nothing. Nobody brought up our equipment from down the foot of the hill!

We had one blanket in our company, so we spread that out and we had six guys under there, trying to keep warm. Wounded guys, we covered them up with that. There was a tree right nearby. I grabbed that tree and I started walking around it, and I told some of the other guys, too, I said, 'Don't you go to sleep!'

I said, 'It's going to be awful cold tonight. If you go to sleep, you're going to freeze. You're going to freeze your feet. You're going to freeze your hands. You might even freeze to death.'

I said, 'If you feel like it's getting warm and cozy, get the heck out of there and start walking around.'

I started walking and holding on to that tree. And I would doze off and hold on to it; the next thing you know, there's about three other guys all doing the same thing I was doing. You can do that, walk and sleep. I just hung right on to that tree, and in the morning, those guys, some of whom had went to sleep, they were walking on their knees. They had frozen their feet and their hands—it was that cold; how cold it was! It was very cold.

*

We had penetrated behind the German lines. We didn't know we had walked so far back and over that mountain there! The colonel walked by, he was laughing, and he said, 'I had this guy follow me.' He was now a prisoner, a German soldier who had surrendered to him. The colonel was relieving himself when this guy surrendered to him! Guess we're all behind the line then, they didn't realize. I guess it was some artillery outfit that had gotten behind him.

We ended up, that afternoon, looking out down the valley and there was a German motorcade. We put all the fire we could in our artillery, everything into it. We did get one of the last vehicles; some of them were Rundstedt's headquarters people in that van.[27] There was a colonel in there; they were killed. And later on that afternoon there were some horse-drawn caissons moving out in the field way beyond. We could see them, and we called in artillery on them. And God, they just tried to pepper them there. That's the first time I'd seen horse-drawn caissons—there were sleighs, on sleighs and horses. They used a lot of horses in World War II. But from the distance that they were, we couldn't do nothing, all we could do was watch.

Anyway, we ended up moving again and attacking and this and that and oh, God, it was just hard to tell where you were; us being lowly GIs, down at the bottom of the pole, we didn't know what really was going on. All we knew was, well, there's another air raid, we got hit again. Another battle. And you never had no places for names, you only had coordinates—our orders, they were only in coordinates. You weren't given no name, like, 'Well you're going to go to Manlius today,' or 'You're going to go into East Syracuse.' All you were given was certain coordinates where you're going to go, and this and that, so that's where we went, [maybe why it's hard to remember exactly now]. We ended up in a lot of bitter fighting.

---

[27]*Rundstedt's headquarters people*- Gerd von Rundstedt (1875-1953), German field marshal during World War II.

'Be Good to Your New Commander'

A short while after that, I think it was around about the 7th of January, I was supposed to go back to report to the medics—they said, 'Go back to the medics and have your foot inspected.' For trench foot, for frozen foot, to make sure I was okay, make sure I could get some sleep.

So I went back there, and I saw Doc Ketchen, and Doctor Shapiro, but first we had a nice bath, and got all clean, dry clothes—had a nice hot meal, coffee, and then we went to see the doctors. They checked us over.

Doc Ketchen said, 'Well, about time you got back here, Tarbell! About time you come and visit us.' We were laughing, kidding around. He gave us some 'blue heavens,' they called it, pills. They said, 'Drink your coffee, get a hot cup of coffee, take this and grab some blankets.' They issued us some blankets, said, 'Go to the haymow.' The aid station was in the [barn]. The barns, in Europe, the way they were built was one area is like a house, then you had like an area way, and then the barn, it's attached to it. We were in the upper barn, up in the haymow.

Four of us from the company were there, and just as we took that blue heaven and coffee, we went in the haymow with our blankets—there was an artillery outfit nearby us, we didn't know that, and they started blasting away! I was saying to myself, 'How in the heck am I ever going to get any sleep, with them guys blasting away?' That was the last thing that I remember—I zonked right out!

I woke up early in the morning, and I heard a lot of commotion. I looked over from the haymow, and God, there was a line of stretchers, stretcher bearers, and all at the barn. In the passageway, they had stretchers and stuff like that, so I looked over, the guy looked just like my company commander on one of the stretchers there! So I hurried down the ladder on the side; by that time they had him in a van. See, now I get ahead of myself again.

I was telling you about going to Paris on furlough; my buddy, Phil Foley, had come in from the 505th Parachute Infantry and he joined our outfit. He was with company headquarters and carried the radio and stuff like that, but he [had] had three court martials! And he was a holder of the Silver Star, and he also had a Purple Heart, and he was always after his third medal. So when he rejoined us around the 6th of [January], he came back and he brought me a nice present, a pipe to smoke; I liked to smoke pipes when I could. We had his Christmas packages, and we ate cookies together. He was telling me about his trip, this and that. That's when the company commander said, 'Foley's back, let him take your place for tonight.' He said, 'You're all set, go to the medics, report to the medics.' That's when I went to the medics. Foley was going to take my place, cover for me.

So when I saw that company commander in a stretcher, in the ambulance, I said, 'Captain, what happened?' He said—he started crying, he was hurt pretty bad, he had been hit through the back to the rectum, stuff like that—he said, 'Foley got killed.'

[My friend] that took my place got killed. And then the captain said, 'Your [new] company commander—be good to him, like you were to me.' He said, 'I don't know when I'll see you again.' We had a little talk there, and then they took him away.

Annihilated

We were waiting for our ride back to re-join our outfit, and I noticed there was a stretcher there, a person lying there, all covered up, and he had hobnail boots on. I figured him to be a German. I just went over there, and I uncovered him, to see who it was. It was the colonel; it was a United States colonel. It was Colonel Jurak from 555th Parachute Infantry; he had been killed that day, the same time that my company commander got hit, and Foley got killed. He had been killed that day. Jurak was a commander of the 555 and they were, in fact, annihilated in the Bulge, and they broke up the regiment, or the battalion, or whatever they were.

The 82nd Airborne got cleaned up and billeted. On February 2, they would jump off through the dragon's teeth on the Siegfried Line.

Private Leroy Johnson, 32nd Cavalry Recon Squadron, 1st US Army of Lakewood, NY, operates a traffic control telephone for the pontoon bridge from Remagen to Erpel, Germany, March 17, 1945. Source: National Archives.

PART THREE

CROSSING OVER

"The Rhine was more than a river. It was a sacred waterway to the Germans, the source of most of their legends and myths. And at this stage in the war, crossing the Rhine was the last barrier between the advancing Allied armies and the conquest of Germany. If the Germans could hold their beloved river, they might be able to stand off the Allies."[6]

*

'I got back to the boat and Fred was nowhere around, he was nowhere to be found. We think to this day that the machine gun burst got him, and you know the force of the shot pushed him right into the Rhine River, and the current was very strong. We never found him, never found his body.

We made it to the river. I started to get back on the radio to call back our situation, and I started to talk, and somebody said, 'Shut that goddamn thing off!' because, you know, as we're going down the river, everything's quiet and you could hear all over for miles.

The CP is saying, 'How come you don't talk? Give us your status report, give a status report!'

—PARATROOPER, RHINE RIVER NIGHT PATROL

Ludendorff Bridge over the Rhine between Erpel (foreground, east side) and Remagen (background, west side) after it was captured by US troops on March 7, 1945. Source: US Signal Corps, National Archives, public domain.

CHAPTER EIGHT

'The Way It Was'

Measuring in at over 750 miles long and averaging a quarter mile wide, Germany's formidable Rhine River was the most effective barrier against Western invasion for thousands of years. So can you imagine being the first American GI to cross the famed Ludendorff Bridge at Remagen, Germany, on March 7, 1945?

As the 8th Infantry Division and the 9th Armored Division approached the vicinity of the bridge on the west bank of the Rhine, scouts were shocked to observe what looked from a distance like an actual intact structure still spanning the 1,300 feet of river when so many other Rhine crossings before it had been destroyed. Postponing a 'Destroy-the-bridge-NOW' order from above, the German commander on the west side was still ferrying men and materiel over the structure when the Americans appeared. Sergeant Alexander A. Drabik of the 27th Armored Infantry Battalion, a 34-year-old son of Polish immigrants, was tasked with leading his men over to the east bank to establish a foothold before it could be blown by frantic German engineers desperately trying to complete their charges. He turned to his men and said, 'Okay, who's going with me? I'm going across!'

The men moved quickly, literally running the equivalent of three football fields single file under heavy machine gun fire.

'We ran down the middle of the bridge, shouting as we went. I didn't stop because I knew that if I kept moving, they couldn't hit me. My men were in squad column and not one of them was hit. We took cover in some bomb craters. Then we just sat and waited for others to come. That's the way it was.'

In the next twenty-four hours, 8,000 Allied troops had crossed. Many thousands more crossed before the debilitated span collapsed ten days later, taking twenty-eight Army engineers to their deaths.

Ike was said to have claimed that the capture of the bridge at Remagen shortened the war in Europe by six months.

When Sergeant Drabik made it to the other side, he was confronted by a teenage soldier with a rifle. The boy lowered the gun and surrendered at the sight of the rest of the squad and company pouring across.[7]

'It wasn't a historical moment for me; I was too busy running. I didn't think about the bridge blowing or anything. I just wanted to get to the other side.'

That's the way it was.

CHAPTER NINE

The Infantry Sergeant

Larry Bennett wears a suitcoat over his sweater and shirt, sitting for this interview in Newburgh on the Hudson, his hometown. At 79 years old, he gives the air of optimism; he is a confident, well-spoken man who has done some remarkable things with his life. As a sergeant in the 86th Blackhawk Infantry Division, he served in both the European and Pacific theaters in World War II. He was awarded the Bronze Star with First Oak Leaf Cluster for heroic action in Vohberg, Germany, in April 1945, when he carried a wounded officer to safety under enemy fire after his company's medic was mortally wounded while attempting to treat the officer. He didn't go to college but worked in the chemical industry all his life. A lifelong Democrat, he was elected in a primarily Republican district to four terms in the New York State Assembly, guiding several veterans-related bills through the legislature to fruition.

'We crossed the Rhine on a bridgehead that had already been established. The Remagen Bridge had collapsed, but they had built a pontoon bridge just north of that. We knew we were getting close [to combat]. That afternoon we had passed through this town, and we saw dead Germans there and something that really amazed me, German horses that had been killed. They were lying alongside the road because the Germans had used a lot of horse-drawn artillery throughout the war. And then that night, we were near a town where there were some snipers, and I'll never forget this [sight]: there were several GIs lying along the road, and they were covered

with blankets, and all you could see were their combat boots, and the guy next to me said, 'Sergeant, that's going to be us before tomorrow morning.'

I said, 'It's not going to be me.' I tried to be optimistic [to the point of] where I think I was saying something I couldn't really be that sure of. I just figured, I'm not going to get cowered this early in the campaign.'

Lawrence E. Bennett

I was born in the town of Newburgh, New York, on September 15, 1923. I was only sixteen or seventeen, and it was on a Sunday afternoon and a group of us were playing touch football. I got home around five o'clock for dinner and that's when I first heard that Pearl Harbor had been attacked. I had an Irish grandmother who was very optimistic, and never wanted to give you bad news and her reaction was, in her Irish brogue, 'Sure, and you'll hear nothing about that tomorrow,' which did not prove to be true.

[Later], I took what was called the voluntary induction. I was working for the Glenn L. Martin aircraft company in Baltimore, Maryland, at that time, although I lived in the town of Newburgh, and I was eligible for a deferment—they used to give six-month deferment, but I wanted to get in the Navy. I wanted to get into service, and in December of 1942, they stopped enlistments because they claimed the Navy and the Marine Corps were getting a disproportionate number of people, so they had what they call a voluntary induction—if you volunteered to be inducted, they would see that you got the branch of service you wanted. It sounded pretty good to me.

My draft board was in Baltimore, and I went down about seven in the morning to start the induction process, and ended up about 11:30, and at that point I thought, well, my physical examination was for general service, so I need a branch. I said, 'I want to go in the Navy.' And the gentleman said, 'I'm sorry, the Navy took thirty-four [men] and they were out of here by 9:30 this morning, and the Marines took ten [men], and the rest of you will go with the Army.' That was my first example of 'be careful before you volunteer for anything.' [*Chuckles*]

In February 1943, I went to Fort Meade, Maryland, after I was inducted, and about two days after that I got on a troop train. Of course, everything was secret then, you didn't know where you were going, but I knew we were heading in the general direction of south. We had gone to Cincinnati, Ohio, and places I forget. I said, 'This is great, I'm going to go to Texas where they have a lot of Army Air Corps bases, and I'm going to get into the Army Air Corps. That didn't happen to be true. They also had a lot of other camps there that were training infantry, so at about four o'clock in the morning, the train station pulled into this railhead and there was a very huge sign that said, 'Welcome to the 86th Blackhawk Infantry Division.' And I said maybe I'll get in the ordnance, because I worked as a machinist for Martin, but I lined up and they said, 'Company D, 341st Infantry over here.' That's how I started out. Our division took basic [replacement troop] training at Camp Howze, Texas.

In the fall of 1943, [we] went into the Louisiana Maneuvers area, which was the worst living conditions I had ever been under. It was winter, and don't let anyone tell you it doesn't get cold and damp in Louisiana. We finished our advanced infantry training, we were sent to Camp Livingston, Louisiana, following the Louisiana Maneuvers. We went onto short maneuvers again and were sent to the west coast to take amphibious training, so all the indications were that we would be sent to the Pacific Theater of Operations; however, the Battle of the Bulge occurred, and that changed those plans. Some of our equipment was already loaded on ships in San Francisco, but we were shipped to Camp Myles Standish, Massachusetts, and were sent to Europe and landed at Le Havre, France.

*

We were in a convoy, a very large convoy. I can't estimate the number of ships, but we were on a troop ship that carried 6,000 soldiers. And the division artillery commander was with us and his flag was flying before we left the port, and we figured maybe we would get a better escort than some of the rest. The voyage was fairly uneventful, except it was the wintertime in the North Atlantic, very rough in the winter, and when we [got] into the English Channel you could hear depth charges being dropped, because German U-boats were still very active at that time; in fact, they were sinking ships all the way up to the last day of the war. None of the ships in our convoy were hit.

We land at Le Havre [at] about midnight and the harbor area was almost completely destroyed. It had been destroyed by the Germans before they left, before they evacuated. We had to go down in landing nets, just as you would in an invasion. We got into small landing craft and went ashore and were put on these trucks, [which were] more like something you would carry cattle in, a trailer towed by a tractor, and there was some straw in it, and you lay in it until you got to a camp. We went to Camp Old Gold—they had a number of camps there named after cigarettes—and had a brief training period there before we went up to the front [lines], which was just west of the Rhine River at that time.

'They Had a Lot of Fight Left in Them'

We entered combat in early March of 1945 in the Cologne/Bonn area. [It] was actually a defensive position on the west bank of the Rhine, in the little likelihood that the Germans could come back across the Rhine, but they were sending extensive patrols, you know, to try and keep the American army off balance. We suffered some casualties there, but not heavy casualties. Then our next phase of combat we went across the Rhine River and into the general area of Siegen, Germany. At that time, they were attempting to seal off the Ruhr Pocket and to make sure the Germans who were in the Ruhr Valley could not break out and possibly cut off the spearheads, which were further advanced into Germany at that time.

The first night when we were moving up, as we sat up on the Rhine, we were subjected to some artillery or mortar fire, but we had the river between the German army and us. Then we were moving up, and you could tell we were getting near a battle zone because you could hear artillery firing and see the firing in the distance. We crossed the Rhine on one of the bridges, a bridgehead that had already been established. The Remagen Bridge had collapsed, but they had built a pontoon bridge just north of that. As I said before, we knew we were getting close [to combat]. That afternoon we had passed through this town, and we saw dead Germans there and something that really amazed me, German horses that had been killed. They were lying alongside the road because the Germans had used a lot of horse-drawn artillery throughout the war to save on gasoline and so forth. And then that night, we were near a town where there were some snipers, and I'll never forget this [sight]: there were several GIs lying along the road, and they were covered with blankets, and all you could see were their combat boots, and the guy next to me said, 'Sergeant, that's going to be us before tomorrow morning.'

I said, 'It's not going to be me.' I tried to be optimistic [to the point of] where I think I was saying something I couldn't really be that sure of. I just figured, I'm not going to get cowered this early in the campaign.

Our objective was a town called Hagen, a large industrial town in the Ruhr Valley, and we moved up into an attack position. The next morning, we attacked that town and maybe about two days later, the Germans finally capitulated there. There were more anti-aircraft guns in the Ruhr Valley than anywhere in the world, because they used them to protect their industrial area, and they were using them as regular field artillery pieces, and they had a lot of ammunition. I'll never forget that one of our guys in the 86th [Infantry Division] later wrote a book about it. They later asked him, 'What do you remember about the Ruhr Valley?'

He said, '88s, 88s, and more 88s!' The Germans, even at that stage of the war, had a lot of fight left in them. [They] were still counter-attacking; you'd take a town and maybe lose it the next day. Finally, after about ten days in there, the German army surrendered. There were just thousands and thousands of German troops coming down the road with their vehicles, their field hospitals, surrendering en masse; I remember that very well.

The German Soldier

Even though we had met the German soldier and German army when they were on the decline, I would say they were good. They were well trained, their officers led them well. At the very end in Bavaria we noticed younger solders, maybe fifteen or sixteen years old, but in the Ruhr, German Army Group B was the largest army they had still intact. I did not particularly see a lot of young people, maybe nineteen or twenty, the age of some of us. As the war got near the end, as the Germans had done in Berlin, they put kids in. They were young. Having said that, some people fail to realize these kids, they had trained since ten years of age. They knew how to handle weapons even though they were only fifteen or sixteen years of age. I remember saying to a German major who had surrendered, I said jokingly, 'You have kids in your army now.'

He said, 'Yeah, we have kids, but those that you call kids'—and he could speak English—'are better trained than many of your soldiers, because what we hear of your army, you take your people in and train them for 17 weeks in infantry training camps and then you send them to a division.' He said, 'These kids you're calling have been training since they were ten!' And they were particularly good with the panzerfaust, which was a German [anti-tank] bazooka. We met some of them in the Ruhr, they would be in the wooded area. They would attack a convoy and some of them would seem to disappear; that was a very lethal weapon. They could knock a tank out with that [or] a truck full of GIs. One of the regiments in our division was going to a town in the Ruhr Valley which they thought had been secured. Just before they got in there, they passed a wooded area, and they were attacked. About fifteen or twenty GIs were killed in this truck—the panzerfaust just hit it and blew it to smithereens.

I would say the [German] leadership was good. They knew how to take advantage of hilly terrain; they knew how to defend rivers. That continued right through the war. They were first-rate soldiers. The fact they were able to carry on a war against major allies like England, the United States, France, Russia, and survive proved they were good soldiers. I didn't agree with their ideologies, but they were good soldiers.

German Prisoners

General [Walter] Model was the German commander in charge of that and had a tremendous reputation as a defensive general. He had bled the Americans white in the Hürtgen Forest just previous to that [*shakes head*] and didn't give up very easily. General Ridgeway had sent him a note days before this asking that, on a humanitarian basis, that he surrender his forces now to save Germany from the further destruction of their infrastructure, their industrial buildings that were left and so forth, but he refused, saying that a

General Field Marshal does not surrender. So, in the last two or three days of the war, [that German army] started discharging their soldiers. He wasn't surrendering himself, but they would come down the road with a discharge pass, and they still had to be taken in as prisoners of war.

One of the worst sights I saw was right near the end. [The Germans] were surrendering at such a rate that [we] didn't have facilities for them. It was raining very hard, and I was cold, and to see them in these large enclosures, huddled next to each other trying to keep warm, and no sanitary facilities, and very hard to get food to them—even though they were the enemy, I thought of myself in that same situation. They were just helpless. There was nothing they could do, [though] they'd have their own Red Cross representatives trying to help them, they'd have some of their officers trying to organize them, but it was a very pathetic sight. It shows you what happens when you are not successful in a military operation, when somebody else has your fate in their hands.

[By that time, we were aware of the concentration camps]; we went into none of the large ones, but we saw some small concentration camps in the Ruhr. We also saw a field hospital where they had German and American wounded, and I would say at that point the Germans were doing the best they could for both their own wounded and the Americans who were being liberated. They were short of supplies, short of medicines, but some of the people we liberated were in pretty bad shape. We also saw a large number of slave labor camps where these people worked in these various factories in the Ruhr. [These people] were from Russia, from Poland, from anywhere, thousands and thousands of them—I guess it was that source of manpower that kept the German armament [factories] going, because they had drafted so many of their own people that they depended on this slave labor. Some of the factories were underground, and the [slave laborers] had come out of these shafts. It was pretty pathetic.

After the fighting in the Ruhr Valley, we were transferred to the Third Army, and we joined the Third Army just before they went into Nuremberg in about the last fifteen days of the war. When you're with Patton's army, you move pretty quickly. In that operation we were involved in four river crossings. The Altmühl, which is a fairly large German river, the Inn, and the other one that I remember most is the Danube, because by that stage of the war we had lost quite a few men. The medical aid man that was with our platoon was a very, very good friend of mine, and he lost his life about ten days before the war ended.

'A Hornet's Nest of SS'

The most street fighting we were involved in was in two towns, Ludenscheid [and] Hagen, which was a large industrial city. Street fighting in Vohberg, and the 342nd was heavily in Ingolstadt; that was house-to-house fighting there, mostly against SS troops. SS troops were very fanatical about defending, they just didn't give up easily. I don't recall seeing a large group of SS give up, where with the German army, the Wehrmacht would. The [Wehrmacht] would hide in basements, attics, and so forth, and the first chance they got, when things quieted down, you would see them come out, throw their weapons down or put a white flag in the window.

We had crossed the Danube River and there [was] a place called Vohberg, and we were told earlier that the German garrison may have pulled out, but it was a hornet's nest of SS troops who made up their mind that they were not going to surrender. In the initial assault, our battalion was hit pretty heavy, and we were very surprised—we just thought all we were going to see was white flags, but it was just the opposite! I was in the second story of a building with my machine gun squad, and the medical aid man was in that building, and we looked out on this field where the Germans were dug in, after we had cleared the village. At that point an officer of B Company, the rifle company we were supporting, walked right in front of the window—I can see it like it was happening today. He raised his arm like that [*gestures, in the air*], and a bullet went right through his sleeve, and he said, 'Look at that, a souvenir!' He said, 'I'm going to keep this shirt!' In two minutes, he was down.

The medical aid man left that covered position and went out to assist him. There were several wounded at the time and several people yelled, 'Medic, medic, medic, over here!' but there weren't enough medics to administer first aid to each one of them. So, our medic got about halfway between the house and where this officer lay, and he got hit, but he tried to get up. When the officer had gotten hit, he just lay there like he was dead, but the [medic] got [up and was] hit again. So, me and one other fellow left the building, went out and brought him back. When we got him back behind the building, a [new] medical aid man who had arrived by that time said, 'You guys wasted your breath, this man's already dead.'

We didn't know, but we also went back out and got the officer, and he survived. I remember this so clearly, because as we got him behind the building, and they administered blood plasma—and he was as white as a sheet—as he started taking that plasma, you could see his color start to change a little bit. He survived, [but] I never saw him again after that. He had gotten hit here [*points to the right side of torso*] and his thumb was almost shot off, and the last I saw of him was when they were taking him back down towards the river to evacuate him. The Germans had a lot of these wagons, particularly in the Ruhr, that they hauled wood and things on, and they had steel wheels and so they had him lying on this. I heard since he had survived the war.

I received the Bronze Star for that with the oak leaf cluster because my Bronze Star was not just for meritorious but was also for what they called 'heroic.' I don't want to try to appear to be a hero, but I was there, and I'm lucky I'm here. That same day I could've lost my life. Our battalion lost about 25 or 26 [men] killed and 40 wounded in practically one day, which is a large loss for that period of the war, when you think, 'Hey, these guys are done, we're going to see a white flag.' The Wehrmacht regular German army were more ready to surrender, these SS were not. I could never understand what was in their minds. They thought, 'We're going to turn this thing around?' You know, like a football game. 'We're behind, but we're going to win!' I could not understand their psychology, but I guess it was part of their indoctrination.

The General

I didn't get to see General Patton, but some of our people did. The 342nd Infantry Regiment of our division approached a city called Ingolstadt, which was a fairly large city in Bavaria around the Danube River. Again [there was] unexpected resistance, and Patton came up and asked the regimental commander how things were going, and he said, 'We're not making as much progress as we thought, and our casualties are fairly heavy. I don't know if we'll get to cross the river.'

And it's reported, I wasn't there, Patton said, 'Listen, I want you to cross the Danube River by 7 o'clock tomorrow morning. I don't give a damn if you have to swim across.' I guess all Army commanders are a little egotistical. He wanted the Third Army to be the first army across the Danube River. You know, all blood and guts. His guts and my blood.

War's End

When the war ended, we were in Austria. We could have stayed there, but after about ten days in Austria, we moved back to Mannheim, Germany, and I guess it would be called the army of occupation. Very good duty, very light duty. Within a short period of time we were given orders, our division would return to the United States to prepare for service in the Pacific, which would have been, if the war continued, the invasion of Japan. So, we got back to the States and had furloughs, rest and recuperation, whatever that meant, and then we were sent to Oklahoma for a brief period of time and then shipped to the west coast at Camp Stoneman and proceeded to the Philippine Islands. So, we were in the Philippine Islands just as the war ended.

I was very happy [when we heard about the dropping of the bombs on Hiroshima and Nagasaki] because [coming back to the States] on the ship, we were briefed on what possibly could happen, and when they started to give the casualty estimates for our division, and any division that would have invaded Japan. I wouldn't be here talking to you today if that invasion had taken place, because based on what had happened at Okinawa, when the casualties were horrendous, it would have been Okinawa ten times that scale. The Japanese had five to seven thousand aircraft hidden in caves, they had, I think, still five million men in the whole army in Japan, and they had equipped civilians with spears. They were not going to surrender if the atomic bomb had not been dropped. That would have been a horrendous campaign that could have gone on until 1946. The casualties had been horrendous. Thanks to Harry Truman, who I've always admired, I'm here today, and many GIs that were scheduled to be in that operation will say that. I arrived in the

Philippines at that time in August 1945, and I left late January 1946; I was discharged at Fort Dix.

After the war, I was in the National Guard for two years, the 170th Field Artillery of the 27th Infantry Division. I enlisted for a year, and I was extended for a year, but our division was not called up [for Korea]. Some Guard divisions were, but the 27th was not.

I did not [make use of the GI Bill]. I should have, but I did not. I came back and went to work for the Dupont Company in Newburgh, which was one of the largest employers we had. I worked with them for a good number of years, and they were purchased by another company called the Stauffer Chemical Company, so between the two companies, I had 31 years of service. While I was working there, I was elected as a member of the town board. Sort of a miracle in this Republican town to have a Democrat elected, but I was, and I went on to become supervisor and later on elected to the New York State Assembly and served there for 12 years. I served on the veterans committee, and I was very proud that I was able to pass the first bill to get long-term veterans care for New York State. It just seemed the language, [the way it had been written], nothing was happening. But since then, we've had several opened, [most recently] one in Queens, one in Batavia. That was one of the things I was pleased I could be in a position, as a GI, [as a veteran], to have some influence on legislation later on in Albany.

'The Spirit Is There'

I joined the American Legion, the Veterans of Foreign Wars, the Catholic War Veterans, and I'm a member of the Combat Infantrymen's Association as well. Now also, in 1985 our division formed an 86th Blackhawk Division Association; I joined that immediately. For six years I was the treasurer, and at that time we had over 2,000 members, so that six years was like a full-time job. There was something coming across my desk at home every day. I enjoyed it, and we had reunions every year. In the beginning, it was every three or four years a group of us got together. Then, starting in the early '80s, we started meeting every two years in Indianapolis. The last one we had was three years ago. Our numbers are really dwindling. We're talking about having another one, but it's hard. When we have our division reunions, some of the fellows do attend. We've had as many as eighteen; the last reunion in Cincinnati last September we had [just] seven. With the age and so forth, it's hard to get guys together. The spirit is there.

Our casualties were not as heavy as some other divisions, since we arrived later in the war, [but I remember two replacements in particular who came up with us]. One who came in came up at night, and he was obviously very nervous, as anyone would be. He said to me, 'I don't think I'm going to be alive by tomorrow morning.'

I said, 'You have to stop that talk. Just worry about getting through the next hour.' I remember he survived. Another member of my company, fellow by the name of Jim Kelly from Pittsfield, Massachusetts, he came over as a replacement and joined a division in the Ruhr Valley. He trained with a guy named Paul Holland. Paul Holland died on his very first day in combat. [Kelly and Holland] had struck up a real friendship on the troop ship coming over, and of course we're assigned to the same division, and Paul only lasted a day.

Reflections

Going in as a teenager, it made me suddenly a more serious person. One thing it made me value is, every day I live because I could have been in one of those military cemeteries overseas, or in a local cemetery here. I have a different attitude about life. Doing the best

I can every day, and not looking too far into the future, or worrying about what happens. I think that experience of being in combat and possibly being killed does leave you with a different perspective on things. You seem to be able to put things in their place. I think GIs who have been exposed to that can do it better than many other people. Don't look too far down the road, don't worry about every little thing that happens. Just thinking how lucky I am, at seventy-nine years of age, to have gone through the Second World War as an infantryman, seen some combat, and be still alive and in good health to talk about it.

It's a blessing.

Larry Bennett lived until the age of 92. He passed away on March 9, 2016.

Mr. DiFiore at the time of the interview. NYSMM screenshot.

CHAPTER TEN

The Giver

He sits in a hotel room with his interviewers, all decked out: red, white, and blue flag tie, a vest covered in ornamentation, military patches and regalia. He speaks quickly, almost as if he is in the present as he recounts his past as a 19-year-old replacement combat engineer. He does a good job of downplaying the pain of not being fully accepted into his new unit, even after weeks of combat, but he can't hide the fact that he is a sensitive man, formed in hard times, even to the extent of attempting to save an enemy soldier from a vengeful mob two days after the war was over—to the disdain of his own buddies and officers.

"My two friends and I were walking around, just looking around, and I heard a lot of noise—talking, yelling, and screaming. I walked into the woods a little bit, there's about twenty people in there or so, grown-ups yelling and screaming. I then saw this young German kid about sixteen or seventeen years old. They had him stripped down to his jockey pants, just jockey shorts, and they had a rope around his neck. [Pauses] They were going to hang him.

So remember, the war had been over with now for a couple of days. Something told me, 'Don't let them do it!'

I went over there, and they were pushing me away. I said, 'You can't do that to him!'"

'Johnny D' DiFiore stepped up in the face of enormous social pressure to 'do the right thing'; this event exemplified his entire life. This interview was recorded in 2003 when he was seventy-eight.

'People who know me say that I'm happiest when I'm at the VA hospital; I am happiest helping our veterans—I just love going there and being with them. I have been doing it for well over thirty years because they need help. I'm a giver. I'm not a taker.'

Augustine John DiFiore

I was born in Yonkers, New York, on June 1, 1924. I was one of eight children, the fifth one. I came from a very poor family. We lived in a cold-water flat. At that time, with eight children, my father was working for the state in a WPA project, and his earnings were $25 a week. With that, we had to survive.

My two sisters dropped out of high school to go to work. They were the oldest, and I had an older brother. He dropped out of high school when he was about seventeen or eighteen years old, and he joined the army, the 1st Division, 16th Infantry, 1939. My other brother joined the Civilian Conservation Corps (CCC). He was 16 years old, and was sent out to work in the forest in Montana. When I graduated high school at eighteen years old, I tried to join the Coast Guard or the Air Force, but I was rejected because of my eyesight. So I found a job in a factory that made Army Signal Corps wire. It's two wires that are twisted and it's laid on the ground or trees or poles; the army then communicated on telephones. I worked there until they drafted me on March 11, 1943, when I was about eighteen and a half years old.

When I heard about Pearl Harbor, I was in my house. I remember it was a nice sunny day, and I heard it on the radio; it didn't weigh on me that much, because maybe I was ignorant of something about all this. But then as the days went by, I see everybody's getting excited. Most of the guys were joining the service. They were joining the Army, the Navy, the Marine Corps, young guys, they all wanted to go.

I had a very close friend and I said, 'Come on. Let's go. Let's join.' Then, we went down to Whitehall Street, New York City, to join the Coast Guard, the Air Force, and we got rejected by both of them. My friend was accepted, but I was rejected because of my eyes.

So he says, 'I'm not going in if you're not going.' So we waited until we got drafted. From Yonkers, we were shipped out to Long Island, Camp Upton. It's way out in Long Island. Over there, they gave us different tests, a lot of needles, and they gave us our uniform and an old 1917 Enfield rifle with a bayonet and everything. That's when I started to realize that I was in the army.

We were there a few days and then we boarded a locomotive train, that's what it was in those days. We traveled north and then after an hour to two hours of traveling, one of the officers, we can see from his lapel that he had an engineer insignia on it. They talked to us, and they told us that we were in the 204th Combat Engineer Battalion, and we were going up to Fort Devens, Massachusetts, for our basic training.

We did three months of basic training there. I was a squad leader. I really loved it. I was a kid, I was very strong. I could run. I was up in the front with a captain all the time, on the hikes and all that. I ate it all up, especially the food, because there wasn't much food in my house. We only got one dish of food, and that was it. Most of the time, we went to bed, we were hungry. So I really enjoyed what I was doing in the army, and I did well. I was squad sergeant for the three months, and then after, we were inspected and they said that the battalion needed another three months of training, so we stayed there for another three months.

When I finished the six months of basic training, my platoon officer, my lieutenant, came to me. He said, 'Johnny, we see by your records that you have a 120 or something IQ.' The army has a special name for it.

Harvard Man

He says, 'You want to go to officers candidate school, or do you want to go to ASTP?'

So I said, 'What is ASTP?'

He says, 'It's a college course, an engineering course, a two-and-a-half-year course. We'll send you to Harvard.'[28]

So I said, 'My God.' I heard of Harvard, but I was a poor guy, I couldn't afford to go to college. So I jumped on it, and said, 'I'll go.'

I went there and I met all these young fellas; a lot of guys were older than me and much smarter than me. So, we had a great time at Harvard; we lived in a suite like three or four bedrooms, with two guys in a bedroom, and then we had our study room in the center. One of our roommates was a guy named Hal Holbrook, a kid. He was nineteen years old. Ever heard of him? The actor? He walked straight as a pole and he was like… It was like you couldn't touch him, but I got to be good friends with him. I think I was the only guy that was his friend.

---

[28] 'The Army Specialized Training Program was a military training program instituted by the United States Army during World War II to meet wartime demands both for junior officers and soldiers with technical skills. Conducted at 227 American universities, it offered training in such fields as engineering, foreign languages, and medicine.' Source: *The Army Specialized Training Program. Shared Sacrifice: Scholars, Soldiers and World War II.* Ball State University. Wikipedia.

He came from Ohio, his parents were divorced, and he had a grandmother that lived near Boston. We were always broke because we used to go out with the girls from Radcliffe, or Wellesley, or Sergeants Teachers College on Friday or Saturday night. We danced around a little bit like that. We couldn't go for much money; we didn't have much money. We'd only make $50 a month, and we had to pay the cleaning bill, there were cleaners there; the uniforms had to be clean and neat all the time.

We did good. He used to call up his grandmother and we used to meet her in Boston. She would take us out to dinner. I don't know, but she must have given him a few dollars. I remember one time we went to the Boston Symphony Hall, and I thought it was boring, but I guess we made it through. There were things like that.

*

The invasion of France was on the planning board. They needed replacements. So after nine months, they took me and a lot of guys out [of the ASTP program][29]. We went to the camp. We wound up in Camp Shanks, the embarkation camp in New Jersey. From there, you get all your equipment and everything like that. They put you on a train and take you down to Jersey City and get on the ferry, cross the river, and you get on the boat. The troopship was the *USS George Washington*. We left and we were in a 75-ship convoy. It took us fourteen days to get to Liverpool.

Now when we got to Liverpool, we took a train to Chester, it's a little north. We trained up there, marched around, and stuff like that. Then, we got shipped down to Winchester when they had the invasion, where all our power troopers were. After they moved out, we moved in.

---

[29] The ASTP program was terminated due to infantry manpower shortages coupled with the growing feeling by some top brass that stripping men away for college undermined regular troop morale.

Then from Winchester, they shipped us down to Southampton and we waited a day or two to get on the ship. It wasn't a big ship, it was an English infantry ship that could carry maybe a thousand or so men. It took us a couple of days to cross the channel, which was full of mines. The next day, August 1, they loaded us into the landing craft boat and led us into the water. We went to Omaha Beach; we tried to get off the beach as fast as possible, but we were loaded down with all the equipment, ammo and everything. We even had impregnated clothes on for gas, we had gas masks, everything. We finally made it to the top of the hill where the trucks were waiting for us.

I went over as a replacement to the 19th Replacement Depot in the hedgerow country. That's where we were organized. We had to dig long slit trenches, or fox holes, and we put our pup tents, with raincoats or whatever, on the bottom. We slept two or three guys together. We had our shelter at the top, but we slept in the hedgerows. There were only one or two cows there. A young French girl used to come in the morning, and she had a little horse and wagon, a two-wheeled cart, and she used to milk the cows, but most of the cows around were dead; when we got there, there were a lot of dead animals, a lot of debris.

We stayed there until I was assigned to the 166th Combat Engineer Battalion. The man that I replaced was a young kid, 19 years old. He had drowned coming back from a river crossing; my battalion made a lot of river crossings; they were always up in the front. There was a captain or the major, whoever was in charge, he always wanted to see who's up in the front. We were always up in the front.

'A Little Lost Puppy'

I told my kids [about my experience as a replacement soldier]. I was like, forget about it, like a little lost puppy. They didn't bother with me. They wouldn't extend their hand like a buddy. They were a very close clique; they had trained in the States down in Mississippi, Missouri. Half of the guys were from New England, half of the guys were from around Mississippi, and I guess they cliqued up and they don't know me, they didn't put too much faith in me.

I got all the dirty details. For instance, when it was guard duty time, I always got the 12:00 to 4:00 shift. There was another guy in my squad, they called him the 'Sad Sack.' I got a picture of him. They would put us two guys together. What was good about him was that he knew his weapons, his bazooka, and his machine gun, .30 caliber water-cooled. Everybody called me DiFiore or Brains; because they found out I went to Harvard, they used to call me Brains. They said, 'Okay, you and...' I forgot the other guy's name. 'You've got twelve to four.' Okay. I would just sit down and try to snooze a little bit; about maybe a quarter to twelve or something, the corporal and somebody else would take us out. We walked in the dark. [One time], we walked for I don't know how long until we came to these two guys that were lying on the grass with a machine gun. They said, 'Okay, we'll be back. We'll be back to see you in a couple of hours.'

At about 2:30 in the morning, I hear footsteps coming. We were on the grass, but they sounded like on a dirt road. So I thought it was the guys, right? So we kept walking and something. So, I yelled, 'Halt, who goes there?' Then all of a sudden, they started running. Meanwhile, I was lying on the ground with my rifle. After I yelled, 'Who goes there?' the third time and they kept running, I just let out three shots. I couldn't see anything and my friend there was at the machine gun. I said, 'Hold it, let's move out of here.' So I helped him with the machine gun, and we moved maybe about a hundred feet away. We waited and nobody came.

At about 4:30 in the morning, we hear the guys coming. I told the guys, 'Where the hell have you been? You didn't hear the shooting? Was that you guys?' They came a half-hour late, and I thought that's the way it was. You know, no concern [*shakes head*].

We went back, and the sergeant said, 'What happened, DiFiore?' I told him the story.

'The captain wants to see you in the morning, he wants to get the story.'

I told him, 'Usually we go on guard duty in the daytime, and we know where we are. I didn't know where anything was.'

He said, 'Well, go see.'

I walked out there now in the light, and we were on the grassy plain. About ten feet below us was like a wagon road, and to the left of that was the whole battalion! All the way, all our trucks and vehicles. I happened to be shooting almost straight but at a little angle. I didn't hit the trucks.

Captain said, 'Good thing you didn't hit the trucks, DiFiore.'

I said, 'Everybody heard me shoot, but nobody came out to see what was going on!'

'We Ain't Taking No Prisoners'

Now we had come to Frankfurt, that's the ninth largest city in Germany, and they surround the Main River. We parked our trucks and our platoon walked down this wide cobblestone boulevard to the bridge; it looked like the main bridge going into Frankfurt. It was a stone macadam pavement bridge, we had shovels and picks with us. They told us we're going down there to fill in the pavement because it was blown up. We got down there and it was a mess. You can never fill those right. It was getting dark, they really blew up the bridge, it was so bad. I was on the left side walking down. No sooner than we got on the bridge, I'd say about 8:30, a couple of mortars start falling on the bridge. So I hit the ground; I think about maybe three or four mortars hit.

I looked around and I saw nobody. I got up late and saw nobody. My rifle was there. I picked up my Garand rifle and started running back the way we came. I ran across the opening of the bridge until I came to the sidewalk. Meanwhile, the Germans must have somebody cornered; there was a big apartment house on the block on the corner, they must have had somebody there. The Germans started shooting 88 artillery, armor-piercing rounds, and as I was running on the sidewalk, these rounds were just ricocheting, skimming off the cobblestone streets and slamming into the buildings.

You can't believe it and I didn't count them. It must have been at least a dozen of them, but I just kept running. Something told me to keep running. I got halfway down the block, and I heard heavy footsteps behind me. I turned around, there were two German soldiers that had their hands up in the air right away! I saw that they didn't have their steel helmets on. Usually, when a German gives up, they take off their steel helmet and everything else. They were yelling, 'Bitte! Bitte!' 'Please! Please!'

I just turned around and something told me just keep running. So I ran for maybe a hundred and something feet. That was the corner of the big apartment house. I ran around the end and ran another hundred feet to the end of the building. There was a driveway, my platoon sergeant was there.

He said, 'DiFiore, where the hell have you been?' What can I say?

I said, 'Nobody told me to get out, you know, let's go.'

So he said, 'Okay. The guys, they're down in the basement. Go down the driveway and get down in the basement.' Then these two Germans come right up behind me.

He said, 'Where the hell did you get them?'

I said, 'They followed me!'

He said, 'We ain't taking no prisoners.'

With that, I said, 'F you.'

I ran down the driveway and the Germans, I guess they must have sensed that. The Germans were at least 40 to 45 years old; they weren't kids. They followed me and I ran down the steps into the basement and all the guys were there. It was a dark basement; there was maybe a couple of flashlights and some candles.

As soon as they saw the two German soldiers, they got around them and started to search them. I just walked away because they seem to like to take control, these were the kind of guys who you could never tell to stop or whatever. I just walked away, and my friend came to me and he says, 'What happened?' I said, 'What's the matter [with them]? Nobody told me to get out of there; I didn't know what the hell to do!'

We walked out of the basement, and we rounded a corner. As we round the corner, I saw a steel door. Nonchalantly, I just opened the door, looked, and it was a big room, at least 30 feet wide by about 40 to 50 feet long. It was all mattresses with people in there, mostly women and children or old people, because I heard a lot of whimpering and crying. Candles, here and there. So right away, I closed the door. I didn't even enter it, I just closed the door and told my friend, 'Don't tell the guys.' I don't want to expand on that, because... [*pauses*].

We stood there for about another hour or so, then the sergeant said, 'Let's go.' We walked a couple of miles up the road, either way. Meanwhile, these armor-piercing 88s were landing, they were really something. I don't know how [we got out of there]; I still say it's a miracle. We went about a mile up the road and we slept in another house.

'We Were Supposed to Draw Fire'

The next day, they drove us back to the bridge again. It was a nice sunny day. They said, 'Okay. Go back to work.'

We didn't even get to the bridge when they started shelling us again. Right on the left corner was a three-story old brick building which was an old pharmacy, and on the side of it was like a concrete grease pit. I don't know if you have seen it around, like, a car would go over it and the mechanics would work underneath the ground, a little room underneath; so about half a dozen of us, we ran down there. The shelling lasted about an hour and 45 minutes. I timed it on my wristwatch. My mother gave me that when I graduated high school.

After it ended, we went outside and there was our squad truck and the kitchen truck all blown up. So we waited while the sergeant went to get a couple more trucks to take us out. When we got into the trucks, we went up the road a couple of miles, and then we saw what the whole story was. A couple of miles up the road, A Company was put to work the previous night and was putting up a Bailey bridge across the Main River. The sergeant said we—I was in B Company—were supposed to draw the fire while they put up the bridge! So we crossed that bridge into Frankfurt. We went into where the railroad station was, and they told us to unload again. We're going to fix the streets, but the cobblestones were piled up as high as the gutters. We were there for maybe an hour or so. He said, 'Okay, load up again. We're moving out.' That's the way it was with Patton—he didn't let you rest, and we moved out.

Mostly, we made river crossings, we took the infantry across the rivers. We had plywood boats, two engineers, one in the front and one in the back; you get about 10 or 12 infantrymen. They get in the boat and put their weapons down on the bottom of the boat. You give them a paddle and tell them to paddle. No picking up your weapons when you go across—you paddle across [to get to the other side as fast as you possibly can]. So what happened one time as we cross this river, there was a nice sandy beach, they got off and start running. The first thing you know, the beach was loaded with booby-traps, teller mines and bouncing betties; it bounces up about three or four feet and then explodes. Sometimes it's full of ball bearings, or nails, anything. A lot of infantry guys were wounded. We were now on the other side, we heard them yelling for the medics. My lieutenant, Fred K. Lawson, said, 'Come on. I need some volunteers.' I was in the 3rd Squad. The 1st Squad sergeant said, 'We'll go with you.' They took about three or four boats and went across. Now, the lieutenant, when he got on the beach, the poor guy hit a tripwire and it went off. He was killed right there. The squad sergeant and the corporal were wounded. Another guy was wounded. It was a pretty bad mess. They let the guys stay there until everything calmed down a little bit, before we all went over there to help out.

Seeing General Patton

Another time we helped put a heavy pontoon bridge across the Rhine River, that's when Patton came. He pulled down his zipper and he pissed in the river; we were all clapping. [*Laughs*]

I saw him again. One time, I was with another friend. We're running outside of this town and there was a tank staying with us. We had our bazooka; they give us a bazooka instead of a machine gun. Patton came by in a staff car. He said, 'How are you doing?'

I said, 'Okay.'

He said, 'What were you guys doing? A big Tiger tank came down here.'

So, my friend was the bazooka commando, all I did is put in the rocket. He said, 'I would shoot and then run like hell.'

Patton said, 'I would do the same thing,' and then he took off. You're supposed to salute, give your name and outfit.

We wound up in Czechoslovakia, just before Prague. That's how far we advanced and because Patton just wanted to keep going. He got word to pull out. We pulled out of Czechoslovakia, came down into Austria. We followed the Rhine River up into Regensburg. Then on the banks of the Danube River, in Regensburg, we put our pup tents. That's where we slept for so many weeks.

We finally move into German cavalry artillery buildings. They were nice two-story buildings with stables underneath. Stone and brick. We lived there when the war was over. Patton had his headquarters right across the street from it. One guy I knew was a surveyor in our company. We had to build an airfield for the Piper Cubs; it was a big farm area. We had to flatten out the area so the Piper Cubs could land. That was the only way of getting messages to and from different cities and different outfits, through a Piper Cub. That's what we did for Patton.

'They Were Going to Hang That Kid'

There was another story I wanted to tell you. This was in Czechoslovakia, two days after the war ended. We were in this little neighborhood, half a dozen houses; that's how small this whole neighborhood was, but there was a work camp. When they had these displaced persons, like Polish or whoever they were, they lived in the stockaded work camp, in the factories or fields. My two friends and I were walking around, just looking around, and I heard a lot of noise—talking, yelling, and screaming. I walked into the woods a little bit, there's about twenty people in there or so, grown-ups yelling and screaming. I then saw this young German kid about sixteen or seventeen years old. They had him stripped down to his jockey pants, shorts, just jockey shorts, and they had a rope around his neck. [*Pauses*] They were going to hang him. [*Pauses again; looks down*]

So remember, the war had been over with now for a couple of days. Something told me, 'Don't let them do it!' So, I went over there, and I told them, 'Nix, nix, nix,' and they were pushing me away. I said, 'You can't do that to him!'

I tried to explain to them that the war was over. They said, 'No.' They must have said something, and I couldn't understand them. So I called to my friends; they didn't want me to interfere. My friends came over and I said, 'Well, look, they are trying to hang the kid here.'

They said, 'Let them hang the Nazi bastard!'

You know, the war was over. The people were pushing me, the kid screamed, 'Help me!'

I said, 'Okay!' I grabbed the kid's arm and took the rope off his neck and dragged him with me… [*Pauses*]. He was crying. The kid was crying.

I took him to where my lieutenant and sergeant were. I said, 'Here, they were trying to hang the kid in the woods.'

They said, 'What the hell did you stop them for?'

I said, 'The war's over!' I wasn't a killer.

*

After the war, we were in Regensburg. When the war was coming nearer to an end, the Germans were giving up themselves, just hundreds of thousands of them. They were in their vehicles, in our vehicles, [on foot], maybe hundreds of thousands of prisoners. We were told to build a stockade, a prison camp for ten thousand prisoners there, because after the war, a German soldier couldn't walk the streets unless he had his discharge papers. I guess they had figured everything out.

Our job was to build this camp and we used a lot of German prisoner [labor]; there were German and Hungarian prisoners. My job, I had a truck, I usually drove about 30 miles outside of Regensburg; [there was] a big lumber camp there, and I used to bring the lumber orders, what kind of lumber they wanted, and give it to the manager of the lumber camp. I used to hang around, and the twenty to twenty-five German prisoners that I used to bring, they used to help cut the lumber down into whatever we needed, then loaded it up on the truck and then I would drive them all back to the stockade. That was my duty after the war, until the end of August.

From the end of August, I think it was a Sunday. Bob Hope came to Regensburg with his troupe and performed at the airfield there. He put on a big show, there were ten to fifteen thousand GIs there. The next day, Monday, we were shipped out. They had the trains, they had the boxcars, the 40 and 8s, the same box cars that [probably] would carry the Holocaust victims. There was hardly any straw on the floor, nothing. They put us in there, and for four days and three nights, it took us to Camp Lucky Strike, where we got on a boat and came to Boston.

'I'm A Giver'

I was 19 years old, and I tell you one thing, we had a lot of faith in General Patton. We thought very highly of Patton, especially when he went up to the Bulge, because they were hurting up there bad. We weren't afraid of nothing with him. I just cried [when I learned of his death]. I didn't think it was an accident. He was too good of a man. He believed that we should have gone to... he wanted to go to Russia. When we were in Germany, deep into Germany, the people used to come and tell us—the soldiers too, when we were taking prisoners— 'Let's go fight the Russians now!' I mean, what the heck do I know? I was only a kid. I was just trying to stay alive, and I followed orders. I did whatever my sergeant told me. I was very obedient and disciplined, I never strayed. These guys were really veterans, the guys that I was with. I just toed the line and I tried to do the best I could.

I used to write to [my former comrades-in-arms]. They were mostly from New England or Mississippi or Missouri. They sent me an invitation one time that they were having a 45th reunion up in Warwick, Rhode Island. At that time, I had a problem, an anxiety problem. I couldn't drive and I love to drive. So my kids said, 'Okay. We'll drive you up to Grand Central Station, put you on the Amtrak train. You take the train up there and then you take a cab to the hotel.' That's what I did, I went to the 45th anniversary, me and my wife. It was very, very nice, but even up there, nobody put their arms around me. Nothing like that, you know. They just shook hands, and they didn't even talk to me, maybe because I was a replacement and these guys, they started from the beginning. They had a lot of reunions which I didn't go to. I could see [they had] a thing. They kept to themselves, it was their own clique. That's okay, I know life is like that.

I'm very happy with my family and my church. That's my life, my family and church. [I think my military service] was the best thing that ever happened to me. Of course, I was alive! But the experience gave me so much confidence in myself and making me independent; I'm an independent guy and I don't go looking for help from anybody, but I do give. People who know me say that I'm happiest when I'm at the VA hospital; I am happiest helping our veterans—I just love going there and being with them. I have been doing it for well over thirty years because they need help. I'm a giver. I'm not a taker.

Augustine J. 'Johnny' D'DiFiore passed away on March 31, 2016, a couple months shy of his 92nd birthday.

CHAPTER ELEVEN

The Forward Observer

Robert C. Baldridge was a forward observer and frontline artilleryman with the 9th Division. Born on November 9, 1924, in Omaha, Nebraska, he attended school in the east and was able to get into Yale and then joined up via the Enlisted Reserve Corps. In this 2004 interview, he recalled nearly constant combat, punctuated by moments like witnessing the collapse of the famous bridge at Remagen spanning the Rhine.

'Me and my crew at the time went up to a big hill and set the OP post up there, and stayed there for about ten days, firing into Germany, firing at targets that we could see. It was a wonderful OP post for visibility. Seven or eight days after we'd gone over, I saw that bridge collapse all of a sudden, from the bombing that had weakened it, and kept weakening it further. By that time, we had a lot of pontoon bridges that troops could go over on, but there were Army engineers working on trying to shore up that bridge, and all of a sudden, that bridge collapsed, and about as I recall, [twenty]-eight engineers died and drowned as it collapsed, and I saw that happen from the top of this hill. They were maybe eight hundred, maybe a thousand yards at the most, away. I heard the noise and saw all of this dust coming up. That was the end of the bridge.'

Robert C. Baldridge

I read [about the attack on Pearl Harbor at school], in the *New York Times*, and of course heard what was going on, on the radio. It just enthused all of us to get through, get out and get moving and get into the service. Actually, I was not a senior yet, I was upper-mid or junior year there. I was just seventeen and I was able to get into Yale for two or three terms and then enlisted in the Enlisted Reserve Corps.

Like many boys or young men, my father was a battery commander in the artillery in World War I and he was back in service in an administrative job as a major at the time in the Air Corps, so I wanted to go into the army because of his army service in World War I, and I wanted to go into the artillery because he was artillery all the way and had been in Artillery ROTC in World War I. I wanted to follow in his footsteps.

I was in a 155mm Howitzer battalion under then Lt. Col. William C. Westmoreland. He was absolutely superior, the best. Some people outside our 9th Division thought he was like a Boy Scout, but he wasn't any Boy Scout. We respected him because of his knowledge and his ability to command the battalion. You didn't call him 'Westy' except behind his back; he was most admired. It was ridiculous, in our opinion, whether you were an officer or a private, this baloney that he took from Mike Wallace as a result of the problem in Vietnam. I am sure if he had to do it all over again, he would have made some adjustments in there, but I'm telling you we honored and respected that man up to the limit.

He knew that I'd been to college and that set me somewhat apart from most of the guys in the division. It turned out that he had an eye on me. I didn't know it at the time, but I ended up getting a battlefield commission during combat towards the end of the war.

Mr. Baldridge and the 9th Division waded onto the Continent at Utah Beach on June 10, 1944, D+4. They then went up near Cherbourg and were near Aachen when the Battle of the Bulge began.

The Fire Direction Center

I had a lot of experience being a forward observer and all of a sudden I am put into the Fire Direction Center at battalion headquarters. That's where the mathematics are done and the commands over wires—the telephone wires and radios are sent to the guns for firing. I did that for about three months, then I got a promotion. I was a gunner corporal—a guy that ran a gun underneath a sergeant who was head of the gun section. Being the gunner corporal, I was second and I was the guy who looked through the panoramic telescope and made the adjustments to sight in on the aiming stakes and so forth. I did that for a number of months. That's what I was doing during the Battle of the Bulge in Belgium in the winter, which was cold.

You had to be careful not to touch the barrels of the guns, or your fingers would stick to them. The only way you could get them off was to tear the skin off your hands. We learned about that, but we were acclimatized. Nobody caught cold or anything like that. The worst part of it was not to let the snow—we were in three to four feet of snow all the time—not to let the snow get into your socks. We didn't get the shoe packs—the rubber boots—until later on; all the guys in the rear were getting them. We had to be careful—we were advised to do this and knew it—we just had extra socks that we would carry around in our hip pockets. We'd try to dry them overnight and keep the socks, keep your feet, as dry as possible so that you didn't get trench foot.

We had plenty of food; we never went hungry, but several times we were under severe limitations on shells, the shortage of ammunition for the howitzers. We were told how many rounds we could fire from the experts in the Fire Direction Center knowing from headquarters further on up how many rounds we could expend depending upon the targets and the problems at that time. The shortage of ammunition at times was as serious as the shortage of gasoline, which everybody knows about. But that finally got changed and we had plenty of ammunition by the time we hit the Rhine River.

The Guns

I was in combat the entire time until V-E Day, which was close to a year, with the exception of a rest period of just three to five days after the Normandy Peninsula was cut and solidified. Otherwise, we were on the line continually until the end. To give some rest, you'd get pulled back from the front line maybe a mile or a few miles, but you were still in combat ready [status] under the possibility and probability of being shelled by enemy fire plus the V-1s and the V-2s, and all of that. Then you'd go back into the front lines. Then another one of your regiments or another division would get some period of rest where you just weren't under direct fire attack constantly.

We suffered thousands of casualties; only two divisions suffered more casualties than the 9th. If you're in the battery and not a forward observer, the guns could shoot as far as sixteen or seventeen thousand yards—they would usually be going over the front line as opposed to trying to hit the front line. But, if we could hit the enemy, they could hit us, so we are talking about [a range of] from a few thousand yards to maybe ten thousand on the average. Now a forward observer would be up close in the range of yards or a few hundred yards; occasionally, you'd be on the point. Sometimes when I was a forward observer—depending on the geography and the position of the enemy—you might be out in front of the front line. The German 88 was a wonderful weapon, absolutely fabulous. The weapon was an anti-aircraft weapon and a direct firing artillery weapon, just by lowering the barrel. It could hit a plane up at twenty thousand feet! We were under fire of the 88s quite a few times, and if you heard them, you were all right because you didn't hear the one that got you.

Crossing the Rhine

A critical discovery and subsequent capture of the Ludendorff Bridge during the Battle of Remagen in early March 1945 by the US First Army helped to shorten the war. The bridge and supplemental pontoon bridges ferried Allied forces to the German town of Remagen on the west bank south of Cologne, one of the few bridges over the Rhine that remained intact, although the Germans tried to destroy it multiple times before it finally collapsed on March 17, 1945, taking twenty-eight Army engineers to their deaths in the swift current of the river.[8]

The next real target area was the Rhine River. Of course, there was a lot of feeling about getting a bridge safe without it having been blow up by the Germans across the Rhine. The 9th Armored Division accomplished that, and my division happened to be right close to them—we were the second division over the Rhine, with the 9th Armored being the first division over the Rhine. The 9th Armored Division's assignment was to stay on this side of the Rhine to contest and continue battling on the Germans that were in that area; there was a whole German army down there on our side of the Rhine.

I went over the very second day, something like March 8, after the Remagen Bridge was actually captured.[30] We were the first division after the 9th Armored to get over. Me and my crew at the time went up to a big hill and set the OP post up there and stayed there for about ten days, firing into Germany, firing at targets that we could see. It was a wonderful OP post for visibility. Seven or eight days after we'd gone over, I saw that bridge collapse all of a sudden, from the bombing that had weakened it, and kept weakening it further. By that time, we had a lot of pontoon bridges that troops could go over on, but there were Army engineers working on trying to shore up that bridge, and all of a sudden, that bridge collapsed, and about as I recall, [twenty]-eight engineers died and drowned as it collapsed, and I saw that happen from the top of this hill. They were maybe eight hundred, maybe a thousand yards at the most, away. I heard the noise and saw all of this dust coming up. That was the end of the bridge. But we didn't need the bridge anymore and, in fact, weren't using the bridge because everybody knew it was unsafe at the time.

The New Jet Planes

We lost three of our casualties who were nearby at that time from the strafing that the German planes had been doing on that bridge since we had first taken it. That strafing included the new planes, the new jet planes that the Germans had.

When you saw those, 'oh boy,' [I thought], another super weapon like the 88 that they had; one of Hitler's secret weapons. We didn't know what the hell they were! We had earlier been

---

[30] Remagen Bridge-sometimes termed 'the Bridge at Remagen,' the Ludendorff Bridge was constructed during World War I for war use on the Western Front by Russian prisoner slave labor. American GIs commonly referred to it as the Remagen Bridge.

subjected to the V-1s. The 'V' in the German language stood for the 'vengeance' weapon—the V-1s and the V-2s. So, those were the ramjet pulsing engines. The pure jets, of course, were not pulse jets, and you could see how fast they went. Our pilots at the time, they learned how to avoid them, and hopefully come down on them from the top. Our own pilots learned how to down these jet planes, if they were able to get up high enough above them to come down on top and figure out where they were headed for and before the jet pilot could really see them.

*

After Remagen, we headed due west into Germany and participated, along with many other divisions, in encircling the Ruhr River Valley, which was a big industrial area of Germany, encircling and then cutting it up. That's where the German commander Model, he didn't surrender, he killed himself because a German field marshal doesn't surrender; he wasn't going to surrender his army. This is quite a story, that we found out later. He knew that he was completely surrounded and that to stay fighting, just everybody would be killed. He wanted to surrender, but he couldn't, so he issued an order to his army dissolving the army and saying to everybody in the army, whether officer or private, that the army is dissolved so you can, in effect, go home, if you can escape. Then he went out with his jeep driver into the woods somewhere and shot himself and was buried right there. He was found about twenty years later and was properly removed and buried wherever his family was buried. That was Model. He saved a lot of German lives by dissolving his army, which had never been done before, but he didn't surrender. As a result, his family and he and the army weren't in disrepute.

Nordhausen

On March 30, 1945, the men of the 3rd Armored Division overran the notorious Dora-Mittelbau concentration camp complex near the town of Nordhausen, which gave it its common name. It was a subcamp of Buchenwald, established after V-2 missile sites were being heavily targeted by the Allies. It became independently run by the SS and grew to over three dozen subcamps including dark, unventilated tunnels mined out of solid rock, where prisoners suffered brutal conditions, neglect, and abuse. Sickened slaves died by the thousands, and near the end, were selected for 'extermination.' SS Major Wernher von Braun was the lead scientist for the project. [31] [9]

From there we went on through to a mountainous area that wasn't too far from the Elbe River. That's where we went through and visited that terrible Nordhausen concentration camp, where the V-2s were being made. Wernher von Braun was the genius of that camp—the technical genius. I know that Wernher von Braun and a hundred of his guys came over to help start our [rocket] program, [but] he knew what was going on in Nordhausen. He was

---

[31] Wernher von Braun-(1912-1977) The 'father' of the United States space program, von Braun's Nazi past became more evident after his death in 1977 at the age of 65, and he remains a controversial figure. His contribution to American rocket science is unquestioned, leading to the development of intercontinental ballistic missiles but also allowing President Kennedy's wish of seeing a man on the moon by the end of the 1960s to come true. Still, his official NASA biography skates rather lightly over his Nazi ties: "The V-2 assembly plant near the Mittelbau-Dora concentration camp used slave labor, as did a number of other production sites. Von Braun was a member of the Nazi Party, and an SS officer yet was also arrested by the Gestapo in 1944 for careless remarks he made about the war and the rocket. His responsibility for the crimes connected to rocket production is controversial." Source: *Biography of Wernher Von Braun*. National Aeronautics and Space Administration, August 3, 2017. www.nasa.gov/centers/marshall/history/vonbraun/bio.html

down there all the time! True, he wasn't in command of the SS guys who ran Nordhausen, he wasn't giving any orders to work these poor guys to death, which is what they did. But he knew about and, I guess, he couldn't or felt he couldn't do anything about it, and so he didn't. So, I don't want to hear anything about Wernher von Braun [not] knowing and seeing what he, in effect, allowed to continue on. I have been down to our three centers where they make the stuff, and where they shoot it off, and where the command center is. I've got books on Wernher von Braun's history, and I always felt that America closed its eyes to what von Braun had been doing, merely to get a hundred experts over to save a few months' time in building our space program and allowed him and everybody else to become American heroes.

General Eisenhower, when he saw some camps in the Nordhausen area, he describes it in his book, and he had Patton with him. They got sick in their stomachs, and he sent out an order to all combat divisions: when they captured in any of these areas like the Nordhausen area—Nordhausen was the name of the city there—to parade every single person, German civilians, through the camps. Every person, including children over something like ten years old. If you were a child under ten years old, you didn't have to go, but ten-year-old children and up, everybody was paraded through those camps. They all said, 'Well, we didn't know'—the standard expression. 'We didn't know what was going on!' We saw that!

Nordhausen was a huge camp, and there were many other camps, of course. Here are these huge camps that were run by the SS troops, and they needed civilians, technicians, civilians to come in to lay wire, do technical work, and do things like that and those civilians would go back. What do you mean they didn't know what was going on? What a bunch of... we felt pretty strongly, I felt pretty strongly about that. 'We didn't know'—that was a hell of an answer! They got the answer to that as a result of the trials.

'No Hero To Me'

All I know is that I don't think von Braun should have been glorified and sent back to America with a hundred guys right away to help our space program get developed a few months earlier than it would have been. We had plenty of guys like Goddard, the Space Center. We knew a lot about it. Not as much as he did, and the Germans did, but how long would it have taken? I say a couple of months to have developed a V-2 type of program. So, I don't know that he should have been jailed or anything like that, but in answer to that question, I think he should have been tried in some way and let off—tried in some way with his sentence a small sentence or let off instead of bringing him back to make him a hero. He's no hero to me.

The Russians

We were right on the Elbe River. All of the divisions were on it.

We [were halted, and] we got bored, we wanted to go on. Actually, we didn't want to go on, we'd been through a lot. We knew that we and the other divisions could have gone on and taken Berlin ahead of the Russians, timewise, but Bradley told Eisenhower it would be at the cost of one hundred thousand lives, that's in Bradley's book. By that time, we were just sitting there waiting for the Russians; we knew that we couldn't go over the Elbe. Everybody knew this, that the Russians would be at the Elbe soon, and we weren't to go over the Elbe. So, we didn't care. It just got boring. The 9th Infantry Division was right alongside just to the left, just to the north of the division that first met the Russians, which was the

69th Division. All of our divisions were just along the Elbe in a stream. Actually, our officers met the Russians the day after the 69th first met them. I think it was at that place called Torgau. Me and my battalion were probably maybe three miles north of Torgau when we contacted the Russians for the first time.

The Barter System

Then, amazing as it was to us, but obviously it had all been worked out and planned before, the day after V-E Day, which was May 8 or May 9, we packed up and moved back to the autobahn and went right down to the Munich area where my division, the 9th, was assigned to occupy in a big circular area around Munich. That was a nice assignment. I was in that area for six months until I left to go back home on points. Now, the orders from Army headquarters to everybody was no fraternization, absolutely no fraternization. That order turned out to be impossible. Consequently, it only lasted maybe two or three weeks. Then you could do whatever fraternization you wanted to because the Germans, they were so glad that we, and not the Russians, were occupying them, they couldn't have been more friendly.

Munich, as I mentioned, we were stationed at a little town called Pfaffenhofen, which is a suburb of Munich maybe ten miles away, fifteen miles away. Most of Munich had just been flattened, not by fighting but by bombs over the years. There was nothing there and in many other towns. Dresden's the famous one. Cologne, any big city like that, had been flattened by bombs for years and there was nothing working. There were no post offices. No shops open. No banks. Nothing was operating. The people that lived out in the farms, they were [the basis of the economy]—money and our pay and German marks didn't mean anything. You couldn't go into a store and buy anything. Currency of any kind was useless. It was a barter system that allowed the Germans to survive. You should have seen the kids that would line up at the end of meals, would line up to get whatever you had that they could eat. Somehow or other, food got into the city dwellers.

We had these little packs of cigarettes that came in the C-ration cans. They were all over the place, there would maybe be ten or twelve [in a pack]. The currency used for bartering, three or four cigarettes, the money was cigarettes—worth more than gold! I don't know. I never smoked, so I gave my cigarettes away. That got straightened out, of course, in due time, but you were talking due time, in six or eight weeks.

'I Can't Get Home!'

General Marshall set that [point system] plan up. As I recall, my point score was, I think, ninety. You could go home first at something like eighty-five for an enlisted man, or for the officers, maybe the score was ninety-five. Here I was ninety, I had more points and often thought why did I accept that battlefield commission? I should have said no! Here because I accepted it, I got more dangerous time as a forward observer, but yet here I was still sitting, I could have been home by now! So, then my point score came up where I was eligible to go home, and I didn't have to take so much baloney anymore because I was on the eligibility list to go home, but I couldn't get home because there was no transportation! The ships were all used. All the ships to take you back were returning with divisions—whole divisions!—that were scheduled to go to the Pacific, and any other ship was on its way to the Pacific to carry our troops from the west coast to the Pacific. There wasn't any shipping, so you just had to stay there.

I remember my father, who by that time was home—he'd spent two years in the Balkans, and he finally wrote me a letter telling me to stop complaining. I am eligible to go home, and I can't get home—'Stop complaining, that's all you write about.'

I wrote him a letter back and said, 'Dad, it's okay for you to write me to stop complaining about not being able to get home, but you're home!' So, he laid off any more such letters and I finally got home in January, after spending three Christmases overseas. I should have been home the previous September.

*

Using the GI Bill, it took two and a half years to finish up at Yale. I don't think it cost anything. I joined the 9th Division Association early and have been to six or seven reunions. They have a reunion every year and I've been to maybe six of them, after the fifty years. I am a member and former director of what's called the National Order of Battlefield Commissions. We have reunions every year. It's a smaller group, and all I can say is that I am on the young side, all of the members of my division having been through North Africa and Sicily, as I mentioned. They were all, on the average, six years older. They're dying off pretty fast now. Same thing with the National Order of Battlefield Commissions. I think I was the second youngest guy that I knew of to have been awarded a battlefield commission.

I am seventy-nine now, but all of these guys, all my friends and everything else, are eighty-six and eighty-eight.

It's sad.

Mr. Baldridge died a year after this interview took place, on February 19, 2005.

CHAPTER TWELVE

The Rocket Man

He speaks with an accent, an obviously well-educated man with an affable manner and a twinkle in his eye. Born in Vienna on the eve of World War I, twenty-five-year-old Rudolf Drenick immigrated to the United States just as World War II began. He wanted to fight the Germans so badly, he was upset when his superiors saw what they perceived as a higher value for the war effort in putting his intellect to work on a top-secret job—sorting through captured German scientific papers that laid out the birth of the rocketry age.

'I had a grudge against Germany, and I was itching to get into the act! I had been active in the anti-Nazi movement in Austria for several years before the Germans moved in, very much at the urgings of my father, and maybe this is part of the story. He was paralyzed from the waist down and he knew that we would never leave the country without him. So in the fall of 1938, he committed suicide, and that clinched the situation for us.

I was drafted. I was told that I couldn't enlist, not being a citizen. Oh, I really wanted to be in the infantry! But then the president of Villanova College had all kinds of strings he could pull in Washington, and I was yanked out of the infantry, to the dismay of my buddies, and to me, too, because I never got [to do what I wanted, which was] practice firing on the machine gun.'

Rudolf F. Drenick

I was born in Vienna, Austria, on August 20, 1914. I came to the United States in April 1939, just before World War II started. I came here with my brother, who was a year and a half younger than I. And we were welcomed by my uncle and his wife, who had come earlier.

I had gotten my PhD in theoretical physics on March 5 at the University of Vienna. I left Vienna on March 8 and crossed the border in Yugoslavia on March 13, so it was a quick action.

I had to learn English pretty fast. I think the attitude among the people who came here in '39 was different from the immigrants now. We tried to learn English as quickly and as well as possible.

First job I had was as a camp counselor for the summer of that year, '39, and in the fall of '39, I got a job as an instructor at Villanova College. Just before the summer, somebody advised me to send my resume to Catholic colleges in this country. And I got three types of replies. One was we have no openings, the other one was we'll pray for you, and one was well if we have nothing by September, come and see us, and that was Villanova College. [*Laughs*]

[When Pearl Harbor happened], I was at Villanova College, listening to a symphony broadcast in my radio when there was an interruption that said there has been an attack on Pearl Harbor. Except for being very excited, I don't remember any other reaction. But if anybody had asked me, I don't think I would have expected Germany to be the one to declare war on us rather than the other way around.

I was drafted. I was told that I couldn't enlist, not being a citizen. So I taught Navy V-12 programs at Villanova College, the special program in which we instructed sailors in the US Navy in mathematics, physics, and navigation. And that was my job, including navigation, which was a little bit odd for me, coming from the center of Europe, never having seen the ocean until I was already 20 or some years old.

'I Had a Grudge'

I was drafted into the U.S. Army. At first, I went to the infantry, which is what I really wanted, you know. I had a grudge against Germany, and I was itching to get into the act! I had been active in the anti-Nazi movement in Austria for several years before the Germans moved in, very much at the urgings of my father, and maybe this is part of the story. He was paralyzed from the waist down and he knew that we would never leave the country without him. On the other hand, he also knew he couldn't leave with his disability. So in the fall of 1938, he committed suicide, and that clinched the situation for us.

But then the president of Villanova College, who had all kinds of strings he could pull in Washington, pulled some of them, and I was yanked out of the infantry, to the dismay of my buddies, and to me, too, because I never got [to do what I wanted, which was] practice firing on the machine gun. Oh, I really wanted to be in the infantry!

I was first put in an outfit called a technical attachment to the War Department and was stationed in Fort Myer just outside the Pentagon. And there, I was used to translate and evaluate captured German documents, technical documents. And from there I was moved to the Ordnance Department, the first citizen member of the technical detachment, and there I got into the evaluation of the documents captured at the German proving grounds for the V-2 rockets. And I was with that, finally as a member of the Ordnance Department, until I was discharged in '46.

When I was drafted, I was drafted as a private. As I remember it, they did an IQ test on everybody, and I must have done really well on it, because I remember being interviewed with a sort of awe by the interviewer. I don't know how well I did, but at any rate I still was a private. [*Laughs*] [I could not be an officer], because I was not a citizen, and I was quite happy being a private, [even with a Ph.D. degree]. And I think to some extent in my early 'private' career they showed me that there was not going to be any honor scheme for Ph.D.s; I got KP of the worst kind. [*Laughs*]

The Secret Documents

[A lot of the documents were] from Peenemunde.[32] The way it happened is three enlisted men, all of whom were technical people with the knowledge of German, were all of a sudden shipped from Washington to Aberdeen Proving Grounds. And on the next morning, a major appeared with a staff car at our barracks and picked the three of us up. Now I don't know whether you have any notion of what it's like, to be a private and be picked up in a staff car and taken away, but I was. And the three of us were taken down to the firing line where there was a huge unused garage. There was a soldier there with a side arm guarding the entrance and the major unlocked the garage and we were taken in.

---

[32] *Peenemunde-* Peenemunde, on the Baltic Coast, had nearly 5,000 personnel halfway through the war. It utilized slave labor to construct and test the V-1 and V-2 rocket missiles.

Operation Paperclip

By war's end, operations had moved to Nordhausen, where slave labor was utilized to the extreme to produce the Vengeance weapons. With the liberation of the Dora-Mittelbau slave labor tunnel factory complex, documents and as many as a hundred intact forty-foot-tall V-2 rockets were put under secure control, crated up, and shipped to the United States, along with some of the scientists and technicians involved under the top-secret Operation Paperclip.[10]

There was what looked like an acre of huge crates, the documents from the Peenemunde Proving Grounds, and they were marked 'rechecked fuses.' Because as we learned later on, the Ordnance Department didn't want the Air Force to know that they found them in the mine in Germany and quickly shipped them to the Aberdeen Proving Grounds, and that's where we met up with them.

[Our job was to basically translate and then analyze] them. The major said, 'Here, evaluate.' So we got a crowbar, opened up the boxes, and started going through them. One of the problems was they were coded, full of code names, and we had no idea what they meant. So what we did is, we wrote the code names on the floor of the garage in chalk, and then piled the documents on them and gradually we began to gather what they meant. And then we also found a sheet in which one of the people at the Peenemunde complained about the misuse of the code names and there he gave away part of the secret. So gradually things began to fill in their place, but progress was very poor. We finally realized that we needed help.

Some help came from the Peenemunde scientists themselves. Five of them arrived at the Aberdeen Proving Grounds. The war was still not over. Germany had collapsed, but the war with Japan was still in full force. So here landed these five German scientists, and the people in the Aberdeen Proving Grounds obviously didn't know quite what to do with the enemy aliens at the time, so they put them in the bunch of barracks way out on the spit sticking out into the frozen Chesapeake Bay, and there were about three or four GIs, me included, who had to shepherd them around. We had to stoke the stoves in the barracks and take them to their meals in the limo, and of course, to the garage where the documents were.

They were very cooperative. At first, there was a, how should I say, distance between them and us, and sort of a wry anger to it, but working with them, we gradually warmed up. One of the Germans had lost his whole family in an Allied air raid, and he became friendly with a General Electric man who had been delegated to work with us who was Jewish, and who had lost his parents to the Holocaust. These two men became especially friendly.

[When we realized what these documents were telling us], we were fascinated. Fascinated. In fact, they changed the course of my life, and that's really what I think. I became interested in the application of mathematics to technology for the rest of my life.

*

I just missed meeting von Braun. One of the five Germans with whom I did work was his deputy, but I forget his name, sorry to say. [These German scientists helped with the code], but still it was a labor without end, but then somebody had the idea of inquiring among German prisoners of war as to whether anybody would be willing to help with the work, and about 150 or 200 did volunteer. They were set up in a special compound in Fort Eustis in Virginia. I remember going down there with an American major and we interviewed them. Most of them spoke English, some of them better than I. All of them quite interesting people and anxious to help the Allied cause. Their compound, which was a low security compound, was next to a high security compound. The German PWs from that came charging across the barbed wires, threats of what they would do to our volunteers when they got back to Germany. Our volunteers were quite worried. As it turned out, they were unnecessarily worried; when [the German PWs] got back they had worries other than revenge—their worries were how to live with what they did [during the war].

[The German prisoners] evaluated the documents, which were shipped down there by the ton and worked on by the Germans, who were as fascinated with the stuff as we were. A few of the documents pertained to Germany's nuclear program. Since I was a physicist, I was especially interested in them, even though I was not well-informed—in fact knew nothing about the American program—but my impression was that the German [nuclear] program was a low priority program.

[They were not close to developing an atomic bomb], I don't think so; the facility was in Norway. It was a heavy water facility, and it was a much smaller enterprise than it turned out later than the American enterprise. The American [one was] really drawn up in a very far-sighted and imaginative way.

The End of the War

I was delighted [when I heard about the dropping of the atomic bombs on Japan]. I mean, I was like most Americans, I really hated the Japanese and I felt they had it coming. I know there was some talk we heard that some of the German people thought that we would, when the war ended, join forces with the Germans and go against the Russians. I think that's probably right. My favorite story about the post-war Germans doesn't bear on this terribly, but I'll tell it anyway. One of the Germans among those who helped us with whom I got friendly was an ex-judge who spoke seven languages or something like that. And he wrote me a few times after he got back to Germany. And one of his letters said, 'Mr. Drenick, please tell me the truth. The Americans are making us eat peanut butter. The rumor is that they are stuck with warehouses full of peanut butter, they don't know what to do with them, and they now make us eat it. And we Germans feel it was bad enough to lose the war, but to have to eat peanut butter afterwards, that was going too far.' [*Laughs*]

During my stay early on in Washington at the Pentagon, I was at the south post of Fort Myer, which was a really grubby set of barracks, but they brought in a number of extremely interesting people. A Russian sea captain was one of them, and I remember two American [former] prisoners of war in Germany who had escaped from the German prison by axing to death the guards, and they escaped that way. I was glad I was on their side at that point. Another fellow who turned up came from New Guinea, and his reason for being there was he was infected with molds, and they were completely new to the medical profession here. They brought him back [to study] for that reason.

[I was discharged in] September '46, [but I had contact with many of the men I served with] for quite some time. Because of the work with the German material, I was hired by General Electric and their guided missiles program. And another fellow who had worked with me in the army had gone to General Electric about the same time, so for a couple of years we were quite close. I left GE about two and a half years after I got there and went to RCA, and then I lost track of this one buddy with whom I was in contact. The others I don't remember being in touch with very much.

[Working with these documents changed my life], yes it did, yes it did. I was a theoretical physicist; I had met Einstein because of my thesis. I think he took pity on me, truth be told. [*Laughs*] I was in a seminar with another Nobelist, [Linus] Pauling, because of the work I was doing. But after I went into the Army, I dropped physics until now, really. Now I am toying around with it again.

Professor Emeritus Drenick passed away on September 24, 2010.

CHAPTER THIRTEEN

The Paratrooper III

Welcome to 1945. The 3rd Battalion of the 504th Parachute Infantry Division had just come off the line after weeks of non-stop brutal cold and combat. Albert had nearly frozen to death and had just lost a friend who was instructed to take his place on the line, so that he might pay a visit to the medical aid station to have his feet looked at. In the shelling that followed, his friend was killed in his place, and he lost his company commander. The men were exhausted and were granted a temporary reprieve.

Albert A. Tarbell

At Rest

We [left the aid station] and there was some more fighting, and oh, God, always the cold weather, you know. You just get settled in one place, and you've got to move again! And then word came down we were being relieved. We're going to go for some R&R, some rest camp. And they sent us back to Reims, and we were there, I think it was a week or two weeks, and God that was so nice there! It was so nice. We stayed with an old couple, and they had two daughters. There was one that had just gotten out of a German jail, or whatever it was; it was run by the Germans anyway. She had been feeding Allied airmen in the woods, sneaking food out there, and somebody squealed on her. Anyway, they had her in jail for a while.

This other woman, her husband was doing forced labor in Germany, and they had a little three-year-old girl. Oh, they were so happy to receive us. Everybody was just open arms, you know. And the first night we got there, she gave us the top floor, their master bedroom. Down blankets, pillows, even the mattresses, you know, feathers, all goose down they have there in Europe. Just as we were falling asleep that first night, I could feel somebody poking around at the foot of my bed, raising the blanket up. It was the old lady. She had hot irons, wrapped in blankets, and she put one under my foot, and one under Brit's foot, to keep us warm. Oh, I said, I couldn't believe this; God, this is living!

And just as they went downstairs—they stayed in the cellar—the buzz bomb went over. You could hear the 'Rrr, rrr, rrr.' Everybody's saying, 'Keep going, keep going, keep going!' Because if [the sound] stops, you know it's going to come zooming right down. They were going into Reims, about 15 miles away, you could feel it when they hit, you could feel that jar. But that was heaven. They were so nice to us.

Later, the older girl said, 'Can you get me an extra sleeping bag?'

I said, 'Yeah. Okay.' I got it from the supply sergeant, he was a friend of mine. I gave it to her and then that was it. Word came down we were moving out, and we moved to outside of Saint Vith, and we went on an attack. That would be on the 28th of January, and it was snowing. We left early in the morning.

*

Our 3rd Battalion was leading in our area. J Company led first and we, H Company, would jump ahead, J Company would fall back, we kept [leapfrogging] like that. I Company would be next. The snow kept getting heavier and heavier and deeper and deeper. We were walking parallel, I looked down and I said, 'Look, we got company!' There was a bunch of Germans walking just below us. They were going the same way we were, and I don't think they ever saw us. We didn't see them [at first], either. So I said, 'Lieutenant Megellas,' I said, 'We got a lot of company here.' And boy he turned right around, just like a tomcat. Boy, it's just like we had rats cornered. They didn't want to fight, they surrendered. But he spaced our men right on them, we just closed right in on them, turned them over to the MPs. They picked them up, we left them there as prisoners.

We kept on going all that day. That's a long haul. I don't know how far we went. It was just knee-deep in snow, sometimes waist-deep. You didn't know where the heck you were, or how good it was, or whether there were [enemy] troops looking at you or waiting to ambush you. And then we heard them. When we stopped, Colonel Tucker got on my radio for a while there and he was talking to one of the other battalions. And a lot of the other officers had been saying, 'Oh, that colonel never knows what he's up to.' I verified it because he used my phone, my SCR300. The reason I remember it so well was that he had such poor procedure to talk on the radio. You would think he would have good radio procedure, you know, to talk and all. He just talked any old way he wanted, as long as he got his messages through.

At 4:30 p.m., as darkness began to blanket the knee-deep snow, it was decided that the battalion should stop for the night. Colonel Tucker had tried to get their bedrolls and packs, which had to be left hastily behind, brought up, but it wasn't going to happen. As a patrol returned and reported that the Germans seemed to be preparing a counterattack, Lt. Colonel Cook came up with the idea to attack first, with the hope of capturing the town for warm billets for the night.[11]

We learned that there were some [enemy] troops on the way to come attack us. One of the other guys said, 'I'll take the radio now.' We changed up. He took the radio, and I grabbed my tommy gun; I would be trying to patrol if I'm not with the captain or if I could get away from the captain, I would join a patrol. It was just something to do, you know, instead of just standing by idly.

The Mark V

I went on a patrol, and we took two [tank destroyers] with us, following us. We hit these guys head-on, it must've been a company of them, over 200, maybe about 300, [outside of Herresbach, Belgium.] Their tank didn't show up right away. We killed every one of them, it's hard to believe.

We went and got into Herresbach. Their tank came around the corner and he would have really done the business on us. But Megellas threw a hand grenade on the tracks and disabled it. He took a fragmentation grenade and he jumped up on the top, and he threw one down the hatch and disabled this Mark V tank all by himself, two grenades! That had never been done in World War II, which is one man with two Gammon grenades disabling a Mark V.

Now, they had around pretty close to two hundred guys killed. We never got one casualty in our company. They were going to put Megellas in for the Congressional Medal of Honor for knocking out the tank single-handedly, because he saved our company. That tank would have just really done a number on us because at that time, one of the TDs had gotten into the ditch and he was not in the position to fight them.

When we went into Herresbach, I was standing there at this burning building across the road and there was a tank right there, this knocked-out tank. I see this guy coming behind in the dark with his hands up. I said, 'Hey,' I said, 'we got a guy coming with his hands up.'

One of the guys said, 'Let's shoot him.'

I said, 'No, no.' I said, 'Let him come in. He wants to surrender. Let him come on in, there may be more out there.'

He came in, and he has his hands up in the air. And I could see the [Luger at his belt] right there. I said, 'Oh, there's my prize right there. I'm not shooting him.' He came right up, and just then this young whippersnapper, George Height, went right up, grabbed that Luger from his waist, and he surrendered. There was about seven others who then came out of the darkness to surrender. Now, you see, they waited. Had we shot that guy, they would have probably shot at us. They surrendered instead.

Height, he stayed in the army. He retired as a colonel, you know. And to this day I still rip him about that. He still gives me presents and favors. He said, 'I'm still beholden to you for that Luger.' [*Chuckles*] But you know, that was just one of those things. He was new, always following us around, when he joined the outfit during the Bulge. Lieutenant Megellas, we're still working on that Congressional Medal of Honor for him. At that time, General Gavin said he would get the Silver Star, but he said, 'We can't put him in for the Medal of Honor because there were no casualties.' At that time, now, you would think that would work in reverse. The first award never mentioned about him knocking off the tank, and then we had the award updated. We're still working on it, it's worded different now, and hopefully he'll get [the MOH] before he dies. He's 85 now. He's had one heart operation.

*

Anyway, we got out of that, but there was a lot of heavy fighting that following day. We spent that night clearing a lot of buildings of Jerries; we got a lot of prisoners, put them all in a big barn, put guys around them. Right after that incident about the seven guys that came out of the dark to give up, I went up to the farmhouse where they had come from, and here were all these tables, all filled with food. They were just getting ready to eat when [we caused] all this commotion. There was fried potatoes, there was brown bread. Of course, nobody likes brown bread. There's bacon there, I think there was eggs there, too. Anyway, boy, I sat right down there, we started eating just as the company commander and the first sergeant walk in and said, 'Tarbell, you're a hell of a man. You're a hell of a guy. You got all this food, and you don't tell us.' [*Laughs*] They sat down, and we ate. We got through eating, and this first sergeant said, 'Well, I hope the food wasn't poisoned!' [*Chuckles*]

Anyway, there was quite a bit of battle that day, and the following day, we had a lot of fighting, too. We were held up at one time by a bunker, they held up our whole outfit, machine guns, you know. They were traversing fire, but finally they ran out of ammunition. I was standing right by the bunker when they started coming out, had their hands raised up. They all wanted to surrender at a distance, and God, they were all older men. They showed us their wedding rings, they were giving us their wedding rings, and showing us their children's pictures and wives' pictures, you know. They thought we were going to kill them all, but we didn't, we just took them all prisoners, put them with the rest down there.

'It's Not My Time Yet'

Then we had some fierce fighting the following day, real bad fighting. I was all excited at the CP there, a couple of soldiers brought up a sleigh with two wounded German soldiers, and two German prisoners were pulling it. They were turned over to us. First sergeant said, 'Tarbell, grab somebody and take them to the medics.' I couldn't find anybody. He found a guy, said, 'Give Sergeant Tarbell a hand here, take these guys to the medics.' Okay, he walked over. First sergeant said, 'You go to the church, that's where the medics are located.' We went to the medics, and just as we got there a shell came in. It landed right in a snowbank. That's the last thing I remember because I was flying in the air. This other soldier that's helping me, guarding, he was between me and the church door. It blew us through the church door, and I come to.

I was lying on my back, and I could hear somebody say, 'Ugh,' like that.

This voice said, 'Well, he's gone, he's done.' I fell on my face. Somebody slapped me, said, 'Oh he's coming to, he'll be okay.'

I know they're talking about me, and I said, 'Oh my God, what the heck happened?' I checked to see if I have my limbs; I sat up and I looked at the guy who's next to me, obviously he's dead. He took the shot for me, you know. The concussion threw me right against him and through the door, we went through the door together. I was just thrown in the air, and he took all the pressure and it killed him. Do you know that I got up from there and I went right back to the first sergeant, I said, 'Who was that guy that just sat with me?'

He said, 'I don't know, I just grabbed him outside, because he was standing out there!' To this day, I still don't know who that guy was! There was no way I could find out because we were moving all the time, on the move. I think I had it narrowed down to one guy, I think was in G Company there, who died on that day, you know that one particular day.

Things like that, you know, happened. You wonder how the heck... to this day, I don't know what happened to my four prisoners, the two wounded journalists and the two guys, the two German prisoners who pulled the sleigh. For all I know, they might have got killed right there or they might have taken right off, I don't know. I never found out. That's what happened that one day there, it's just hard to figure out why the guy upstairs [decided] it's not my time yet.

The Siegfried Line

[In February], we ended up at Siegfried Line, and we had the bunkers to contend with.

One of the guys was very instrumental in getting [Germans in the bunkers to give up]. About the only way you could get those guys to surrender was if they ran out of ammunition, or if you could just coax them out of it. Fritz Toenjoest was one guy that was always instrumental in getting a lot of those guys out of there; one night, I think we had around ten or twelve bunkers surrounded, and he talked out the guys. He was German, born in St. Louis but of German descent, and he could speak German; I guess he told them there was no sense in fighting anymore. He was a good friend of mine, passed away a long time ago.

They say, 'Well, these German troops are inferior.' There is nobody inferior when you put him behind a loaded gun, I don't care who he is, there's no such thing as 'inferior troops.' That guy will shoot at you, and he will kill you. You go and you're still fighting him, you're still fighting a soldier.

We ended up fighting small skirmishes here and there, and we ended up near Aachen, Germany. In the latter part of February, we were supposed to make a river crossing there again, boy, nobody looked forward to that. We were practicing how to do that, and then we got [suddenly] relieved. That was unusual; we were going to make this mission and then they relieved us. We came by train back to France.

We went back to France, and we went to Lyon, France, this time. We started jumping in all of this and that. The new planes were coming out, we had to make a jump in this field here, and it was a beautiful jump. Everybody jumped, nobody got hurt except for the company commander, but the 508th, I think it was Headquarters Company, had a runaway plane, a runaway propeller, and it ran into a stick of guys and killed, I think, about six or seven guys. There were a bunch of dignitaries there watching that jump—I think Marlene Dietrich was there at that time.

The company commander broke his ankle, and everybody else came back saying, 'Wow, that guy refused to jump!' One of the guys wouldn't jump, he was endangering the whole plane, you know; he was going to face a court martial and ten years. Other than that, it was a very good jump. That evening, we were all back in Lyon in barracks. The captain was walking around with a homemade crutch. He said, 'Anybody want to jump tomorrow?'

I said, 'What are we going to jump for? We just got through jumping today.'

He said, 'The Army Air Force is here. They've got a new plane, and they want combat veterans to try it out, a C-46, it's got twin doors, one on each side. You can use both doors going out the same time, carry twice as many men.' First sergeant said, 'I'll volunteer to jump. Sergeant Shields will too.' He said, 'Give us a two-day pass [outside the zone], we'll take Fredericks with us.' He was the one who refused to jump, he was probably facing ten years.

'I'll think about it, but you can't go [outside the zone]. It's off limits.'

'We want to go there, nobody will bother us.'

'All right, but you stay out of trouble!' [*Chuckles*]

The next day, we jumped. I followed the jumpmaster, the lieutenant; Fredericks followed me, Shields followed him. Beautiful jump, I could have landed standing up. I asked Fredericks, 'Why the hell didn't you jump?'

'Bah,' he said, 'I didn't feel like it yesterday!' [*Laughs*] He was one of those guys, you know, a little unpredictable. But he was a good soldier, in his own way.

Anyway, those are some of the things that happened there. I think we had Easter Sunday. We left right after that, I think around the fourth of April. We went back on the line, north of Cologne and the Rhine River, on the west side of the Rhine River. Of course, we didn't know what was happening at that time, but afterwards we found out that the 97th Infantry Division was coming down through the south, and that was always known as the Ruhr Pocket. Now, as they were working their way down south, our position was to hold the Germans from coming across the Rhine River, stay in that north pocket.

There were quite a few skirmishes there, and we had a funny thing happen there. We got word that there's a boatload of Germans coming over the Rhine River under a flag of truce. There was a colonel, and a captain, and some enlisted men that crossed the river. They brought them over to our CP, the colonel to our CP, they sat down, we had their captain as an interpreter. He spoke beautiful English; he spoke better English than I did.

'We're here under flag, a truce, and we're protesting your forces shelling our hospital. We have a lot of wounded there!'

The company commander said, 'Well, that's not our department, but we got higher-ups coming.'

The guy from battalion showed up, and he said to the German colonel, 'Well, your fighting days are over!' They took him away, interrogated him at battalion or regiment, I don't know which, but they took him away from there.

Anyway, I ended up with the German captain interpreter. At that time, there was a *Yank* magazine on the table, with our General Gavin's picture on the front cover. I said, 'Read this, it's very interesting.'[33]

---

[33] *General Gavin*- James M. Gavin (1907-1990), third commander of the 82nd Airborne Division, was, at 37, the youngest major general to lead an

And all this captain would say is, [*imitates pensiveness*] 'Very interesting. Very interesting.'

I said, 'Where did you learn such good English?'

'Oh,' he said, 'I used to be an editor of the English-speaking newspaper in Paris. 'That was my job,' he said, 'before the war.' I really loved talking to him.

So I noticed that when I first saw this colonel, the doctor, he had all kinds of decorations on him. Oh man. Oh man. And they said, 'Where are we going to put them for the night?'

I said, 'Well, you can sleep on my bunk.' I had my switchboard there and the radio there and my room was right next to it. I said, 'They can sleep in there.' I had my eye on that jacket; he's going to take his jacket off when he goes to sleep and hang it on that chair. He's going to end up without a jacket the next morning. Those decorations! [*Laughs*]

The Last Rhine Combat Patrol

That night we had to go to combat patrol, of all the times, we had to go on a combat patrol. They said, 'You're running combat patrol tonight with Lieutenant Broadway.' Rufus Broadway, he was a new officer in the outfit. They said, 'They're going to put out the combat patrol and you're going to take your radio.'

I said, 'Okay.' So we went over the river in a boat, nice and quiet, nobody shot at us crossing the river—come to think of it, they must have thought that it was those Germans coming back, that boat, you know. When we got over there, even their foxholes were empty. We went onto the Bayer Aspirin plant; I think there was a Bayer plant right across from us.

American division in World War II. 'Jumpin' Jim' was known for taking part in combat jumps with his men, and the only general officer to do so four times.

There was a big viaduct there, we went on through, and then we got into a firefight further up, and they told us to hold tight right there; a little while later word came down, 'Head back for the boats.' But when we headed back for the boats, all those foxholes that were empty had soldiers in it this time; the Germans were in them and they were peppering us, you know shooting here and there. Just as I ran through the viaduct, the guy that was guarding me, his name was Fred Hoffman—on a patrol like that, all I could carry was the radio and my .45, no other weapon, so I'd have somebody guarding me, you know, in case I needed somebody to protect me—the fire came on through that viaduct; I just heard it and you could tell it was a machine gun burst. I got back to the boat and Fred was nowhere around, Hoffman was nowhere to be found. We think to this day that the machine gun burst got him, and you know the force of the shot pushed him right into the Rhine River, and the current was very strong. We never found him, never found his body.

We made it to the river. I started to get back on the radio to call back our situation, and I started to talk, and somebody said, 'Shut that goddamn thing off!' because, you know, as we're going down the river, everything's quiet and you could hear all over for miles.

'Stop that damn talking and keep quiet.'

The CP is saying, 'How come you don't talk? Give us your status report, give a status report!'

We had to sweat out getting shot by our own men when we finally got back to the other side, but we made it back all right.

I finally got back to my CP. I'm ringing wet from the Rhine River, the adrenaline. I lost my guard, he got killed, and there was the German colonel sleeping in my bunk, he's got his jacket on, he's got his arms folded right over it, like as if he was protecting everything he had on his chest. That was a hell of a night for me!

That was the last combat patrol of the Rhine River that we had. Two years ago, in Highlands, North Carolina, they brought that up. This Rufus Broadway is a retired doctor and he had us to his place in Highlands, North Carolina, and we had a nice get-together there. We had a beautiful get-together and we had a beautiful time.

Another thing that happened that I'll never forget, President Roosevelt died and we were in that holding position when he died. Everybody was so depressed. You know, what are you going to do? We didn't know who this Truman was, we never heard of him. How many of us are politicians? At 18, 19, 20 years old, you were right off the farm, or right off of high school and right into the Army, you're not into politics that much. We didn't know who the heck Truman was! That was one of the bad times, nothing you could do about it. We just stayed right in that area there, holding position.

Finally we got orders to move out, and we went by train from there to Hamburg, Germany. And from Hamburg we were trucked down to a small town on the Alt River, and we had a river crossing there, the pontoons were already in place. The 505th made the river crossing first, and when we got there, just as we got off the pontoon onto the dry land, we see this tank hit a mine on the road, and took this 40-ton tank and it just flipped it right over! That's how powerful the mine was. The Germans had planted sea mines and they had put detonators in there so that after maybe the 10th of each vehicle went over, it would set it off, so you didn't know when it was going to blow up, or where it was.

And so they said, 'Go over on the side, go over around it, and go alongside the road.' We had no sooner gone about 20 feet up ahead when a truck hit another mine and it blew the guys right out. I could see one guy, he looked like he must have been sitting in the back of the truck, it looked like if you threw a hat up in the air, you know, just flopping up in the air, and the truck went way up in the air! Boy that was [awful].

Now, we kind of had an idea that the war was going to end pretty soon, because we would hear Churchill's speeches on the radio every now and then, and he was pretty accurate. Usually what he told was the truth and it usually happened, so we knew the Russians were pushing hard on the Eastern front. Now, we really were [moving fast], and we started getting more prisoners giving up to us; groups, maybe platoon-sized.

We started getting jeeps up there to ride in. I said, 'God, this is the way to fight a war.' It was walking and running, and we were riding in jeeps across this open field; there was a whole line of us, we got to the end of this open field and there was a little bit of woods, and behind the woods there was three Tiger tanks sitting there! That's when I knew, I said, 'Hey, this war's winding down.' Those guys could have had a field day with us. They could have just wiped us right out.

So we went from one town to the other. One place there was a whole company, their platoon all lined up, ready to surrender to us. And then another time we kept on going, the truck traffic kept getting heavier, and heavier, and heavier. At one point, I don't know whether it was that same day, I think it was, or it might have been the day after, we got to this one point where it got so bad, we put outposts out to direct traffic. Zimmerman, myself, and George Height was with me again, it seems like everywhere I went he was with me, following me, so we directed traffic. 'Vehicles to your right, walk on foot to your left.' Those German guys were throwing their weapons away, and this and that, and oh man. And they even had a calvary ride through [to surrender], God, beautiful horses. But some of these solders were pathetic, you know, worn out, clothes worn and torn, beat up, you know, tired, battle worn.

Towards about dark, a staff car pulled up and out got, you know how you see in movies, German officers, got shiny boots on, got shiny long leather jackets on, the whole nine yards of it—that's the way these guys were dressed. One said, in perfect English, he said, 'Where is your general's command post? This is the commanding general here!'

From what I gathered after, it must've been the commanding general of that 21st German Army that surrendered to us. They wanted to surrender to us instead of to the Russians, to get out of the path of the Russians as they were coming in.

So I said, 'What do you want to see our general for?'

He said, 'This is the commanding general here, we're going back there with your general, and we're going to regroup and fight the Russians!'

I looked at Zimmerman [*turns head, makes incredulous expression*]. I looked at Height, and I said, 'Well, I'll tell you what you do, you just go right down this road here, to my right,' I said, 'there's some MPs down the road, they'll show you right where to go.' And I think that was the commanding general of the 21st German Army. They looked like they were in pretty good shape. We laughed, but they were serious. They probably were put in prison; our general wouldn't have had anything to do with them.

General Gavin commented on the incident, and what would follow, in his 1978 war memoir.

By midafternoon, I arrived at the charming German village of Ludwigslust in Mecklenburg. The streets were jammed with retreating German soldiers and their camp followers. Young and old, crippled and wounded, robust and ailing, men and women, but mostly men, were trying to get through the town to go to our rear.

Adding to the confusion were civilians and shopkeepers, piling whatever they owned in wagons and small handcarts, their faces stricken with fear for what would happen if the Russians were to capture them. Our troopers were attacking just beyond the town, and more were coming up. I was standing near the curb of a main street intersection, wearing a parachute jumpsuit faded from three years of war, carrying an M-1 rifle over my shoulder, looking like any other GI in the 82nd, except for the two stars on my collar and on my helmet.

An American GI came up to me and said that there was a German general looking for the American general who was in charge. I told him to send him over. He arrived, rather haughtily, I thought, and a bit threadbare, but otherwise impeccably attired in the field gray uniform of the Wehrmacht. It was set off by the red collar tabs and insignia of a general, and an Iron Cross dangled at his throat. When told that I was the American general, he looked at me with some disdain, saying that I couldn't be; I was too young and did not look like a general to him. It took only a moment to change his mind.

In the meantime, Von Tippelskirch came to my Command Post in the Palace, which, as it turned out, was a resplendent building, the like of which we had not seen at any time during the war. Von Tippelskirch offered to surrender his army group to us, making a specific point that he would surrender to me and that I was to tell the Russians to cease their attacks. Of course, I had no control over what the Russians would do, although I had already established contact with them, so I told him he would either surrender unconditionally or I would continue to attack until I joined the Russians. The surrender document was typed while he and his staff stood about. When he signed it, he added in longhand, in very soldierly fashion, I thought, that it was to be effective upon entry into the American lines. The meeting had been cold and very proper.

By the time we reached Germany, there was much ill feeling on the part of the troopers toward the German military establishment. On that eventful day, a complete army group surrendered to the 82nd Airborne Division, more than 150,000 troops with all of their impedimenta. At dawn the next day I learned that the Mayor of Ludwigslust and his wife and daughter had committed suicide. I was shocked and puzzled. I could think of no reason for their suicide. From the day we crossed the German frontier, we had been anxious that our troopers behave properly and that they be in no way abusive to non-combatants. It was difficult to understand why, when the war came to an end, these three would commit suicide. It was two days later that we discovered the reason.

One could smell the Wöbbelin Concentration Camp before seeing it. And seeing it was more than a human being could stand. Even after three years of war it brought tears to my eyes. Living skeletons were scattered about, the dead distinguishable from the living only by the blue- black color of their skin compared to the somewhat greenish skin, taut over the bony frames of the living. There were hundreds of dead about the grounds and in the tarpaper shacks. In the corner of the stockade area was an abandoned quarry into which the daily stacks of cadavers were bulldozed. It was obvious they could not tell many of the dead from the living.[12]

On May 2, 1945, the 82nd Airborne Division and the 8th Infantry Division stumbled across the Wöbbelin concentration camp, a subcamp hastily established in 1945 to house prisoners being evacuated from other camps as the Red Army advanced in the east and the other Allies in the west. Living conditions were unfathomable; the GIs found nearly a thousand dead inside the gates.[13]

Mr. Tarbell and the 504th were some of the first soldiers on the scene.

The next day, near V-E Day, we started exploring around the city of Ludwigslust, and our company ran into a German concentration camp. It was not a concentration camp in the word, say, it was a starvation camp. It was called Wöbbelin, and my buddy, Shields, shot the lock off [on the gate]; we went in.

There were no ovens there—it was a starvation camp, where they brought the slave labors, a lot of political prisoners, and what have you. Germans, different nationalities, there were a lot of French Jews; I don't think there were any Russians in there, but there were Polish. Some Dutch people in there. They just starved their people there; we walked in there—it was, oh God, pathetic; you could just see… [*pauses*]; just bones, you know. You couldn't feed them. Somebody gave somebody something to eat, and they died. It killed them because they're not used to food.

I went into one building there, and you couldn't tell the living from the dead, because when they died, they had their eyes wide open. The starving guys are the same way, they look the same way. Couldn't tell them apart.

In the latrine, they had an open latrine there, guys were floating in there, so they must've gone to the bathroom and probably fell in there, and drowned in there, what have you. There'd be a pile of seven or eight deep, dead, and they hadn't got a chance to get rid of them, in mass graves or whatever.

It was just one of those things that the general would say, 'Hey, my God, I guess that's what we're fighting this war for.' It's an awful thing. Never forgot it.

We got back to the States, and you know I mentioned it and nobody believed me. They just said, 'Ahh, you're probably making it up,' you know. That's the way it used to be, you know. 'Oh, you're making it up,' probably. It wasn't until the Jewish people talked about the Holocaust that they said, 'Oh my God, they really had that?'

I said, 'They sure did!' Never left me! I always remember right to this day what I saw there. It's just unbelievable! You can't—their bodies, they weren't burnt. There weren't any ashes. There were bodies, they were alive maybe a day ago, maybe a few hours ago. They're starved to death! They died of starvation; you know how bad we feel when we miss one or two meals. Three meals, how bad we feel. These guys were worked and then starved.

The mayor there said that they [did their best], that the people there didn't know nothing about this. I understood in later years, that they were supposed to make sure that those people had food there, the mayor of that town, because it was in his district. They had plenty of food there, but the prisoners were never given none. [General Gavin] made all the people walk through there, through this place, and then right in the center square of the town of Ludwigslust, they buried a lot of these people right there. They would see, all the civilians, everybody, all of Ludwigslust, what happened there. They made all the people go through there.

The mayor killed his wife, his daughter, and then committed suicide. Killed his family, then himself.

You can't explain it, you know what I mean? Unless you've seen it, how bad it is. It's very, very bad. It was very bad. We felt bad. What are you going to do? All you can do is just go and get loaded. A lot of us did that. [*Raises eyebrows slightly, slowly nods head, knowingly*] We did that for years and years later, too, because nobody listened to you anyway if you told them, after the war was over, it was entirely a different thing, you know. They forget that very fast.

Then when Holocaust [awareness] came along, then the people realize that that actually happened, and that you were part of it.

On May 7, 1945, funeral services were authorized and conducted by the 82nd in the center of the town of Ludwigslust, in accordance with Eisenhower's directive that 'all atrocity victims be buried in a public place,' with appropriate grave markers and a stone monument to memorialize the dead. Captured German officers, town citizens, and hundreds of paratroopers were in attendance. The US Army chaplain's eulogy stated,

> The crimes committed here in the name of the German people and by their acquiescence were minor compared to those to be found in concentration camps elsewhere in Germany. Here there were no gas chambers, no crematoria; these men of Holland, Russia, Poland, Czechoslovakia, and France were simply allowed to starve to death. Within four miles of your comfortable homes, 4,000 men were forced to live like animals, deprived even of the food you would give to your dogs. In three weeks 1,000 of these men were starved to death; 800 of them were buried in pits in the nearby woods. These 200 who lie before us in these graves were found piled four and five feet high in one building and lying with the sick and dying in other buildings.[14]

It would be years before the unimaginable extent of the Holocaust would be known, and to some measure, our knowledge of the greatest crime in the history of the world is still unfolding. The GIs were now sudden witnesses, without an audience who would believe them later on back home. There would be consequences, and trauma would be passed down.

CHAPTER FOURTEEN

The Cavalryman II

After recovering from trying to save his burning friend, young Tim Horgan made it across the Rhine, which he would revisit later in life. He also became involved in a famous rescue mission.

Timothy J. Horgan

Hitting the Rhine

Right after the Battle of the Bulge, we started going fast across Germany on the south side, because the First Army was up north, and we were in the middle, the Third Army, and the Seventh Army was on the south side of us. [The weather had cleared], the skies opened up [from being] all cloudy, snowy, and miserable, and then you had the P-47 planes come around strafing. What they would do is come down and take a look at the troops moving, come down and strafe them, the enemy troops, hopefully. [*Chuckles*] So to distinguish between us and the enemy, they issued us linoleum cloth, maybe about eight foot wide by three feet. And it had straps on the end, and we put those on our vehicles, and every day it was a different color. It was the color of the rainbow—there was a red one, there was an orange one, there was a blue one, there was a white one. We had to strap them on our vehicles so when the planes would come in and try to look for the enemy and strafe the enemy, they would spot us and then they wouldn't spray us; we had that for maybe about two months, because every day we were out in front doing the spearheading, reconnaissance—you know, go out and find out what's out there and draw the fire first, thank you. [*Laughs*] So, a little hairy, but remember I'm only 19 years old, so I can handle something like that, thank God.

Then we hit the Rhine, I crossed the Rhine in Frankfurt. When we entered Frankfurt, I can remember that was the first time I had a shower in three or four months. The outfit come on in and set up a great big tent that had showers all along it, so you go ahead and take your clothes off in the pile, get your shower, come out the other end and pick up clean clothes, look for your sizes and so on. [*Laughs*] But we crossed the Rhine in Frankfurt, and then we kept going through Germany and actually we were on our way to Prague in Czechoslovakia; I was about forty, fifty miles inside Czechoslovakia when the war ended.

The Concentration Camp

At the end of April, I was sent to the Czech border, and all of a sudden, this one day we are going through and come into this town, and come across this concentration camp, Flossenburg. I don't know if you are familiar with all of the concentration camps there, but that was one of the ones. We liberated it. That, my boys, is a sight you [don't] want to see, really. Did you ever see the movie *Schindler's List*, by Stephen Spielberg? He did a very good portrayal of it. Remember the *Band of Brothers* series? On one of those tapes in there is the concentration camps, and that's a true story. I don't know how anybody can say that that was false, it was all made up. I saw it! [*Points to his own eyes*] Well, we got in there and I'll elaborate on that.

I drove the M-8—it's like a scout car—and there were ten of us in the team. We had a lead jeep with three guys and a mounted 30 caliber machine gun, then the scout car, which was four of us—my commander, the gunner, radioman, and me as the driver—and then a third vehicle behind us was a mortar jeep. That's how we patrolled the roads, highway, back roads, two-lane roads, whatever. We got in the town and then we saw the concentration camp; the Germans from the camp were going out the other side of town from where we came in. But we got up there and [the prisoners] were so excited to see us, they wanted to get out, naturally, because they [knew they were now] liberated. But my sergeant was of Polish descent, and he grew up in the Detroit, Michigan, area, and he could talk conversational Polish. These people always had a couple of languages they could talk, and one of them was Polish. And he tells them, 'Okay, you are safe, you are liberated, but we can't let you out.' Because really if we had let them out, they would have run down the street, and after a hundred yards they would have fallen right on their faces, dead, because they were so weak and so excited.

So we kept them in there and I [took] my canteen of water and just give them, each one a little sip of that water, unscrewed that little cap you had on it, just give them a little sip of water. We broke our rations and gave them a little bit because they were so hungry, and they couldn't eat or drink that much. So they ate, and we told them the [MPs] were going to come the next day and let them out and take care of them. But it was my sergeant, he could talk the language, and he calmed them down a little bit. That was Flossenburg, the concentration camp, and right after that we got into Czechoslovakia on our way to Prague.

The Russians

All of a sudden, we get orders to stop—we can't advance anymore—which now I know from history, it was the Yalta Conference that Roosevelt, Churchill, and Stalin had divided up Europe. The Soviets were going to get Austria, Czechoslovakia, and then eastern Germany. The United States was going to get the southern part of western Germany, the British were going to be the north part of Germany, and Berlin was going to be split in three zones: the Russians, the British, and the Americans. Now you always know the Berlin Wall and all of that story, but that's the reason why we couldn't, that we had to stop. I was in the town of Klatovy in Czechoslovakia, and we couldn't go any further. So our colonel went ahead and got our F troop, which is a tank troop, and he put them on the outskirts of town, and he said, 'Don't let any Russian come in here.'

We couldn't advance, and it was only a day and a half, and we could have been in Prague; we would have liberated Prague. We couldn't go, so we had to wait until the Russians came to us. The next morning we look up and there are all these American flags. Now all of the European cities have a town square and there we are in that town square, and on all the buildings on the town square were American flags because we liberated the town. After a day or two, the Russians come into Prague and liberated Prague, we wake up the next morning we see all the American flags are down and all the [Soviet] flags are up, because the Russians liberated their capital.

After a couple more days the refugees didn't want to stay under Russian rule; they were migrating west to come over to Germany to come under United States rule, and they started bringing some stories with them, how the Russians treated them when they went into Prague. They trashed the place! The Russian soldier himself is a different breed; they didn't have any food, and they were really rough, tough. So they started coming across the border with these stories of what the Russians are doing; the next morning we wake up, the Russian flags are down, the American flags are back up because they liked how we treated them, and the stories changed [the locals'] minds. [*Laughs*] But then we had to pull back, we had been about forty miles into Czechoslovakia. That is where we stayed for the rest of the summer, on border patrol between Germany and Czechoslovakia; control the movement of refugees going back and forth. So that's where I wound up, in Czechoslovakia on May 8 when the war was over. You don't know what day of the week it is, you don't even hardly know what month it is. And all they do is we had to have, well, there was movement going on. The actual story, which I have now in my book, my history book when I go back, it was our sister squadron in the cavalry, and it only made up maybe about three to four hundred in each squadron. That makes up the group, so there was only about 800 of us and it was our sister squadron there under Captain Steward. He led this task force in there to, well, we... let me track it back.

Rescuing the Lipizzaners

[Shortly before the war ended], we captured a German general, and through his interrogation, he told us about a prisoner of war camp in Czechoslovakia in Hostau, Czechoslovakia. It was made up of American, British, French, and Polish prisoners of war. There were also a thousand horses in there, too, and about two hundred of them Lipizzaners. So as soon as he had mentioned the Lipizzaner breed, my colonel's ears popped up. He immediately called Patton, who said, out of spite, 'Get them, go!'

So Captain Stewart in our sister squadron led this task force of three to four hundred men, and he went into Hostau to go ahead and liberate the prisoner of war camp, and we did. Then we went ahead and got those horses out of there and we brought them into Schwarzburg, Germany, where there was a German horse breeding camp. The Germans knew the value of the Lipizzaners; the Russians, forget it! [Most would have just] cut the horses up for horsemeat. So we went ahead and got them into Schwarzburg; I was just giving support, I know that we got orders to clear this road, secure that town, so that there were no pockets of Germans around at all and be sure there were no land mines on the roads, there are no trees dropped across the road.

The biggest trick that the Germans had was stringing wire across a road, from one tree to the other tree, and if you remember your World War II pictures of the vehicles, you see that L-iron that they had in the front of the bumpers. Well, there was a reason for it, because most of the guys driving the jeeps would have their windshields folded down, so going down a road, you wouldn't see a wire, and all of a sudden, you'd catch it right there and be decapitated. [*Whistles and gestures at neck*] So that is why all of those vehicles had that L-iron with a little hook on the top, so if they did catch the wire, it would break the wire. So that was our job: be sure the roads are clear, that all the tunnels are cleared.

We did have one segment up there, our task force went in, where there was a little pocket of SS troops and they gave a little resistance, but thankfully we had more firepower than they did, so it didn't last too long, and they gave up. So that was our one little discovery, [their major concern being] these little pockets of Germans, that if you bring the convoy out, it would get ambushed. So that's my involvement of the Lipizzaner rescue, giving them support to be sure that they could get out of Czechoslovakia and into Germany. And then about the third week of May, the war had ended, and we had the horses up there, had a couple of veterinarians come in, and we transported them back into the Spanish Riding School in Vienna. We saved that breed.

I didn't realize it at the time. All I knew is we had a job to do, go out and clear this road, so that was my own involvement, but I didn't realize exactly what was going on until I could get into the history. But here in my [division history] book, in July of '45, when the war was over, we had the Russian Cossacks come in and put on a show for us. We are cavalry, and the Russian Cossacks are cavalry, and so there is a relationship between horse lovers. The pictures here aren't clear because they are too far away, but they were out there doing all of their tricks, horses go jumping to one side, the other side, and riding them and all that stuff, so I saw that in July, see, but I didn't realize what we were doing until after I could start reading some history. Then I put it all together.

All that rest of the summer, we were on border patrol between Germany and Czechoslovakia, regulating any movement of the refugees coming across the border; we were one week out on the border, there was a small little town in that area where we were billeting. So we'd go out a week, [come back] in a week, go out a week, and [then back] a week. Then in October, I finagled a five-day pass, but instead of going to Berchtesgaden in the Alps to go skiing—hell, I'm a Brooklyn boy, I don't know skiing—I elected to go to Paris. So I got on a train and went into Paris; I was in Paris for three days, and I had a cousin who was in Munich. So I said, 'Hey, I'll go from Paris to Munich.' I went on down to Munich and I looked him up and he was an officer, and he was in charge of the movie theatres in Munich for the GIs there, it was his job after the war was over. In Munich, you had town squares and there is an opera house in Munich that Hitler used to come on down to, the famous [Munich] Opera. So he would come into the opera a lot of times, and a lot of the time he would stay in this apartment right across the square from the opera house; it's this restaurant [at that time]. I asked a couple of GIs and they directed me on over to this restaurant. I asked the GI at the desk at the front, I said, 'Where's Lieutenant Malave?'

'Oh, he's down there.'

So I come in, it was a great big banquet hall type room, and it was at mealtime, dinner, so I went down there, and I surprised him. He was staying up—I think it was on the third floor or whatever—in this apartment. That was the apartment that Hitler used to rent out and stay! And it was only one bedroom and a living room and a galley kitchen. They set up a cot for me in the galley kitchen, and that's where I slept that night. My cousin had just got back from Ireland a week or two before that, and he brought back an Irish quart of whiskey. He intended to bring it home with him as a souvenir from Ireland; he told me about all the cousins over in Ireland—the word spread so fast he was there, he said, that they were coming over hills and dales, a ton of them he had never met, 50, 75 of our cousins came right out to greet him! So at any rate, he said to me, 'I can't keep this bottle, we're Irish.' We opened it up, and him and his two buddies who lived with him, the four of us, polished off the quart of Irish whiskey that night. [*Laughs*]

From Munich, I went back up to my outfit up at the Czech border. That was in October, and then about the middle of November I had the points. See at that time in order to come on home there was a point system; there was the high, medium, and low. If you had high points, which was all governed on the number of months that you are over in Europe, and number of months you were in combat or whatever, they made up the points. If you had high points, you come on back to the States in May, June, and get discharged. The low points, they took and transferred them back through the States and were going to send them down to Japan and the South Pacific to fight that war. The middle group was just in limbo waiting for these two groups to be processed to the States. So that is why it took me up until the end of November, when they assigned me to the 90th Infantry Division, on their way to come home. You have to go into a division group.

I left Marseilles, France, on December 8. I landed in New York the 26th of December, one day after Christmas! It took us so long because of this hurricane out in the Atlantic, and it's only a little Liberty ship, about 400 guys on it, and we had to skirt around the hurricane, so it took us four or five days longer to get around. So I come into New York harbor, the 26th of December. We were coming in—I was born down in Brooklyn, as I told you, also [lived] down in Rockaway—I don't know if you are familiar at all with the city, but that's right on the ocean. All the ships coming and going in New York harbor [would go by], you could look out because between there and Jersey is twenty miles, and the ships would come in from the Atlantic there—you could see the ships coming in from a far-off distance, maybe ten, twelve miles away. Here I came in on the ship, and could see where I was brought up down there, right on the beach of Rockaway. Came around the end, and there's Shore Road, Brooklyn, that's where I lived, that was only three blocks off the bay! And here I am and... [*sighs*]. But I'm home anyway. So we go and dock up in Jersey, go on down to Fort Dix to get processed and get discharged. By then it was all over with. It was the middle of August that the atomic bomb was being dropped, the two of them were being dropped then, and that saved a good million GI lives. Oh yes, that ended that war real fast. Real fast. So you know the war was over, so I had no fear there. I was thinking, now what am I going to do after service?

As I told you, I had gone to Saint Francis Prep, in Brooklyn at the time, so I went back to them and I asked them, you know I'd like to go to college, but I can't go in the city because I don't think I'd ever be able to make it living at home because I had to change my environment. So they said [to consider] Saint Bonaventure, our sister college up there, it's another Franciscan college, in western New York, or we have this other new one that just opened up a couple of years ago in '39, Siena outside of Albany.

So I had the GI Bill and went on up, applied for Siena, and I got into Siena in January of '47. I graduated in August of '50, three and a half years; I didn't want to spend too much time in college [because] when I was a junior, going to be my senior year, I got married on August 27 of '49; so when I was a senior I was married and graduated in August of '50. I came up here and I've lived here since. My wife had gone to nursing school at Saint Vincent's Hospital in New York City, so I met her down there, and she was up here when I was going to school. I would come up here on the weekends and, boy, they didn't have dorms in Siena at the time, just boarding in private homes, so I had a room in a private home. But on the weekends, I would come up to Glens Falls and stay over here in my wife's family home and things took off. We got married, had three boys [*Describes his family, with pride*]. Yeah, it keeps me going, glad to have them. [*Chuckles*]

Return to the Rhine

My second son and I went over to Europe in '94 to celebrate the 50th anniversary of World War II. We went to London, Paris, Luxembourg City, Munich, and Frankfurt on a ten-day whirl. That was quite an experience because I always wanted to go back over and see Germany; Germany is a beautiful country. In fact, I had one memory [from my time in Germany in World War II] which I had on my mind. Now when we hit the Rhine River, there was a road going along the west side of the river. A couple of buddies and I got up in this hotel, went up to the seventh floor, and they all had these little balconies outside of the windows. Now this is about the beginning of March, I guess. Now we go on up, we get out there and stand on the balcony, and here it is, a beautiful spring morning [in the middle of a war]. It was early—seven, eight o'clock—and you could just smell the spring air, and I looked up. Look to the right and there, down south of the Rhine River, or go to the left and look up to the north of the Rhine River, and I said, 'This is a beautiful country!' And I always wanted to go back and see it, and sure enough, I did.

Tim Horgan passed away on February 20, 2013, at the age of 88.

Nineteen-year-old Richard Marowitz hamming it up with Hitler's dress hat, 1945. Source: Richard Marowitz.

CHAPTER FIFTEEN

The Recon Man II

Rich Marowitz, with a flair for humor and magic tricks, invokes a more serious tone discussing a transformative event shared by many GIs—the liberation of the concentration camp at Dachau. Set up in 1933 as one of the first concentration camps for perceived enemies of the Reich, it now burst at the gates with over 30,000 inmates and freight cars full of dead.

Richard M. Marowitz

The First Ones in Dachau

I'll tell you, we were the first ones in Dachau. Dachau was the only camp that had to be fought for. I don't know if you know that. The other, Buchenwald, and all these other camps, were walkovers. The Germans just left. The Germans didn't want to just leave Dachau, maybe because it was the oldest camp in Germany. It was in Germany. But they were giving us a pretty hard time, even dropped some 88s on us. We were pinned in the ditch. Of course, we got there a long time before anybody else did. So, we were waiting for the troops to come up to us. [Dachau was the objective], but of course, they never told us anything. They got us up in the morning, and they said, 'Here's your new map. There's Dachau. Go. You have to make contact with the tail end of the 20th Armored and be liaison between the 20th Armored and the infantry who are coming down.' Two-and-a-half-ton trucks were having a race, with the 3rd Division on the left, and the 45th Division on the right, and we [the 42nd] have to win. Every five minutes, they called us on the radio and said, 'Where are you? What are your grid coordinates?' They said, 'What's taking you so long?'

So, we finally stopped, and lieutenant said, 'This is the way it is, guys. If we're going to be tactful about this thing, we're going to lose the race, and they're going to kill us. Our own officers are going to kill us.' He said, 'Or, we can just step on the gas and go like hell.'

So, we said, 'Let's step on the gas and go like hell.' The rest of it was like a bad movie. It really was. I mean, we went through one village and the Germans fired a panzerfaust over our head and blew us right out of the jeep. We dispatched them quickly and we got back in the jeep and took off again. These are the kinds of things that happened on the way to Dachau. That little town where we got the 200 prisoners, that's why we told them to walk back. We didn't have time for those guys. We had to get on the road.

Now, it's not uncommon to smell death. Different areas, you smell different things depending on what's going on; usually, it was farm animals that were killed, who had been strafed, they were bombed, or whatever, and they're bloated and they're rotting in the fields, and it stinks terrible. It just smells like hell. As we got closer to Dachau, we didn't discuss it. We were used to that. We all thought the same thing. We never talked about it, but later on afterwards, after the fact, we realized that we all thought the same thing—we figured we're coming to another bombed-out farm with a bunch of dead animals. That's what we thought! Nobody ever told us it was a concentration camp! There is a village of Dachau. So, on the map, we saw a village of Dachau. We were going to take the village. That's all we knew.

*

We cut one German convoy right in half. It was on a crossroad. We went through it, firing as we went, and they just went off the road. They didn't know what the... We weren't supposed to be there! So, what happened, they were fighting to get up to us because we raised so much sand on the way to Dachau that they had trouble getting to us. All of a sudden, we're pinned in this ditch, and an M4 tank comes out of Dachau. We jumped up out of the ditch, and the tank gun came down on us. It was a captured tank! Fortunately, one of our tank destroyers came up behind us and blew it away just in the nick of time. That day was the first time I kissed the tank destroyer, but that was a scary moment.

The Rainbow took Dachau. You can take my word for it, because we went in the main gate. The 45th came in the back end. They still think that they took Dachau. It has been proven, and it's been certified, that Rainbow did take Dachau. I can vouch for that. I saw a film on the History Channel, one of those channels, Discovery, and it was all 45th Division and how they went into Dachau from the back and the railroad side, and you get all the other jazz. Their officers all remarked, 'It was so quiet when we entered.' Well, sure, it was quiet when they went in because we got finished fighting before they got there.

So lieutenant colonel, the commander of the 2nd Battalion—great guy, tough as nails—he was sitting on the top of that tank destroyer, took a ride in on the tank destroyer. We're next to this farmhouse. He said, 'Did you clear the house?'

We said, 'No, sir.'

'Clear the house!' Well, snipers were all over the place. So, our job initially was to clear out the snipers, so we knocked off a number of snipers and took 25 prisoners out of the basement of that house who were more scared than we were, and we took three SS prisoners. One of them was really driving us crazy. He was in another house just up the street a little bit, and he was really giving us a hard time, so we finally did away with him, and when we got up into the house, he couldn't have been more than eleven or twelve years old, a squirt. Hitler Youth. They were just so brainwashed; we ran into a lot of those kids in their short pants.

On the siding, you saw pictures of it in the slides, outside of the camp, adjacent to the camp, there were actually forty boxcars of bodies and we found one man alive in that forty…there are some pictures of that one man, I don't know whether he survived or not. The prisoners were just walking skeletons, and they just dropped where they were and died. There were piles of bodies, of bodies that had been gassed and readied for the ovens. Some of them still lived because those boxcars were brought to Dachau to burn those bodies. It was a total mess. And the smell was not a farm; it was Dachau that we had smelled miles before we got there.

Well, as soon as I saw what the camp was… you really can't describe it. You really can't. It's not possible, it's not possible to describe it at all. But I'll never forget the 29th of April, 1945, I can tell you that. We didn't know anything about a concentration camp, and on the siding before you even get into the camp, there were forty boxcars of bodies.

[We also picked up] these two little Greek Jewish boys who were with us for a while, doing chores, washing, et cetera. Eventually, both got to Canada. Then one of them died, and the other I lost track of, and he ended up in Israel. At a Rainbow reunion in Seattle in 1995, one of my guys had gone over to Israel for a wedding and looked up Marcel. He had just retired himself; he had a wonderful family, did well in business, and Marcel treated them to dinner at his house. He then went into another room and came out with our Rainbow map with all our names on it! So I said, 'Did you get a copy of it?' We had all lost our maps.

He said, 'No!'

I said, 'You may have done well in real estate, but you're too stupid to try to get a copy?'

So Sid said, 'I'll call him up.' So eventually, I got a copy of the map, which you can hardly read. It's a terrible copy, but I have it.

'I'm Throwing Her Down the Stairs!'

I'll also not forget the next day, the 30th of April, 1945, because twelve of us went into Munich before the rest took the town. A couple of our spies, or whatever the hell they were—I really don't know what they were—knew where Hitler's house was. We went to Hitler's house hoping, though we knew he wouldn't be there, but we were hoping... The town was ready to give up. Actually, in the afternoon, we just rolled in, we had no problem with it. These guys said, 'Don't worry about it. The town is not taken yet, but there's SS snipers in there.'

We went in there. We really didn't have much trouble, got to Hitler's house and banged on the door, and he had an English housekeeper who called us ruffians. 'Why is everybody so mad at Mr. Hitler, he's such a fine man.' My buddy Herb Herman said, 'I'm throwing her down the stairs!' He had a couple of other little words in there besides. [*Chuckles*]

I said, 'Forget it. Let's check out this joint and get the hell out of here.' You know, you're not comfortable when you're the only ones in town. So, we went through the place.

I ran into a bedroom. I didn't know whose bedroom it was, but it was gorgeous. Well, the whole place was nice. The furniture was all intact and the pictures were on the wall and the stuff was on the desks and everything was there. I went in and I opened up all the drawers, and they were empty, and the closet was empty, but I saw something dark in an upper shelf. I dragged over a chair and reached up and got it. It was the most gorgeous top hat I ever saw. I pulled it from the shelf and when I looked inside, in big, bold gold letters were the initials **A. H.** I could put two and two together.

It also stands for something else. [*Laughs*] I could picture his head in the hat, and I remember leaping from the chair where I stood, onto the hat, and jumped up and down upon it, repeatedly. I stomped it. It wasn't a collapsible hat, but it is now; as a matter of fact, I have it in the case, I thought you might be interested in seeing it.

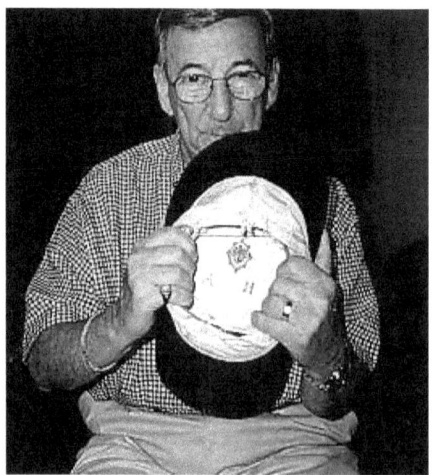

**Richard Marowitz and the inside of Adolf Hitler's hat.
Source: Richard Marowitz.**

Now Herb tells me I walked out of his bedroom with the hat on my head and the comb under my nose and then walking around like Hitler, and the hat now has a life of its own. Shortly after, I heard Hitler committed suicide [that day]. Herb said that it was because he pictured a skinny Jewish kid from Brooklyn walking around with his hat on. [*Laughs*] It was a good day.

'These Things Come Naturally'

And then we were out of there. See, I&R is a peculiar situation. The war wasn't quite over. It was almost over, but it wasn't quite over. You get into a place and you take it, and right away, you got new orders. 'Go check out the road to…', and you're off again. They never even saved billets for us when we would get back. Well, first of all, they never knew if we were getting back, because we had a 75% turnover rate in our platoon. We would get back and report in, and they'd pick our brains and would ask a lot of questions, and then we would go out and liberate a house somewhere, kick some family out, and take over the house, and go to sleep, but we always left a man on guard with a radio.

[The replacements] have to depend on us more than we're going to depend on them. We want to be able to depend on them because we don't have a hell of a lot of guys. So, you bring them in and you do what you can with them right away. I'll never forget the day I went back to headquarters to pick up a replacement. I look at this guy. I have his name, Fritz Krinkler, and I look at this guy, and this guy is German. He still had a German accent. I'm bringing him. I said to him, 'Did you get tangled into the wrong outfit here?'

'No.'

So, I dumped him in a jeep, and I'm taking him back to the platoon. He said, 'Rich, I don't know what to do.'

'What's your problem?'

He said, 'Well, I'm from here.' His father got the family out just before Hitler slammed the door. He was able to get them out because he was German. He somehow got the family out just before it was not possible to get out anymore, and they got to the States. Fritz went to school for a few years, got drafted, came back over. He said, 'I have relatives here, Rich. I have relatives. I have friends. I have family here. I can't shoot at these people. How am I supposed to do it?'

'Don't even think about it.'

'Why not?'

I said, 'Because these things come naturally.' Of course, the next day, it came naturally because we ran into a situation. The Germans were hollering for us to give up. One of the guys, little Jackie Walker, was stuck in the ditch by one of the jeeps, and he couldn't move. They had him zeroed in. We got into a little clump of woods, and Fritz followed me. I'm the one that picked him up. He knew me the best. So, he followed me up into the woods, and he said, 'Hey, I dropped my gun. I don't have a weapon.' So, I had a .45 that I was dying to give to somebody anyway, because that is the worst thing that was ever invented.

I said, 'Here, take this. Keep it.'

So, he's sticking the cigarettes out. I said, 'Don't smoke!'

He said, 'What's the matter?'

'The smell of smoke carries. There's a little breeze. You can see the smoke. Just sit with your back against that tree, and I'll sit with my back against this tree. You'll check me out and I'll check out.'

'Why? Where?'

'You hear them hollering up there, but that doesn't mean there aren't some people coming down around in the woods here. Just keep your eyes open and listen.'

'Okay.' He said, 'Well why are we here? We can get to the couple of jeeps that haven't come out of the woods yet. We can get out of here.'

'No, we can't.'

'What do you mean we can't?'

'Because we never leave anybody.' I said, 'Jackie is stuck in the ditch.'

'But we can get out.'

I said, 'Let me say it another way. If you were stuck in the ditch, would you want us to leave you?'

'Forget I said anything.'

He said, 'So what are we going to do?'

I said, 'Well, the getaway jeep took off.' The last jeep in line, we always called the getaway jeep. Something happens, that jeep takes off to get some help. So, about a half hour later, they came back with some of the Rainbow rangers, and then together we cleaned up the mess, and that was all over with, and we got Jackie. Nobody got hurt, and everything was fine. But Fritz, we went through another village that same day, and he was looking to kill Germans! He was a totally different man. I said, 'Fritz, you see how quick you learn? Nothing to it,' and he was a good guy. He was really good.

*

That's pretty much the end of the war. I mean, we're talking about April 30 was Munich. The war was over, what, May 6 or something? You just saw lines of Germans. The roads were just crowded with lines and thousands of Germans with their hands up on their heads, just giving up. The only action, or almost action, we saw was I think about two weeks after the war was over. They called the guys in our platoon out again. If there was a problem, get the I&R. They brought us into the CP, and they said, 'Well, there's German SS up in the mountains.' Now, we're in the Bavarian Alps. They either don't know the war was over, or they don't care if the war was over. There's some shacks up there, I'm told, [and we were to] break up their weapons, their radios, or whatever. So, you've got to climb about six peaks, which is another stupid thing. I mean, think about it. We've got to climb all these mountains. The idiot that's up there looking down is probably laughing like hell. We're going to be dead when we get up there, and that's going to be hours away. By that time, this guy is in another state. Insane. Anyway, officers have bad dreams I guess sometimes.

We found some shacks. We broke up some radios and stuff like that, but we didn't find anybody. Who's going to wait for us? You're going to sit up there and wait for us?

[I didn't have enough points to get out] until June '46, but I'm a pretty flexible kind of a guy. They pulled my record. Of course, most of them knew anyway what my experience prior to the Army was. So, they gave me a two-and-a-half-ton truck, and they told me to put together a van, some music, a group or something, and get some guys together and go around to the outlying companies that were spread all over the place to occupy and provide a little entertainment. So that's what we did, and little by little it expanded and expanded, and then we moved to Vienna, and then we took over a beautiful coffeehouse on the main drag with crystal chandeliers, and we had German waiters in tuxedos, and by that time we had a 12-piece orchestra. It was picked by General Mark Clark to broadcast in the States as a Christmas in Vienna. My brother was sending me special arrangements; he was with Woody Herman at the time. We were having shows and all this other stuff. We had a hell of a time going there.

The first sergeant kept calling me. 'I got three stripes for you. I got two stripes and a diamond, a couple of rockers.' He used to give me all these things.

I said, 'I don't want that.'

He said, 'Well, you can take my job pretty soon. I'm going to go home if you would accept it.'

I said, 'I don't want your job either. I don't need it. I make more money than you do.'

He said, 'What are you talking about?'

I said, 'Well, we finish at the art club, then there's a truck outside from the Air Force, the airbase outside of town, and they load us up and they take us out to the airbase. We play all night for them. They feed us steak dinners and everything. They give us booze and broads and everything else and they pay us well.' When we moved to Linz, Austria, we were playing the showboat up and down the Danube. I said, 'You know, we're doing fine. I don't need your stripes.' So, I left still a PFC, but I made out very well.

*

[In 1946] I came home, and my father had just sold out his business. He manufactured ladies' coats. I went back to see my professor, my trumpet teacher, Charlie Colin, who was the best in New York, for some brush-ups. He was good. Dizzy Gillespie and all these pros used to drop in for a brush-up. Charlie straightened me out a little bit, and the big bands were breaking up at that time. The rumba bands got popular. You remember the Spanish craze? You're too young for that. So, I walked into Charlie's one day, and he said, 'Go up there to the studio. There's a new Spanish band auditioning trumpet players.' I went up there, and I could always read anything. If a fly walked across the page of a manuscript paper, I would read his footprints. So, it must have been forty trumpet players up there. I went and sat down. The guy said, 'Two more.' So, I went up and sat in the first chair, and he beat it off, and I played it, period, no mistakes. He called off another arrangement, and I played that. He said, 'Everybody else go home.'

I said, 'Wait a minute. Before you send those guys home, what's the deal?'

He said, 'Well, will you give me a few rehearsals?' Of course, I was the union, Local 802 New York.

I said, 'The union said you've got to get paid for rehearsals. I'll give you some rehearsals. But I only get Class A money. I don't accept anything less than Class A money.' At that time, it was 20 bucks an hour. Do you know what 20 bucks an hour was in 1946? Anyway, so that was a world off. I started to write.

He said, 'Okay, you got it.' So, I played. Everybody thought I was Spanish. I grew a thinner mustache than this. Little girls were talking. We were playing Spanish clubs in Spanish Harlem. These little girls were yakking, yakking, yakking. I turned around to the guy next to me who could hardly speak English, and I said, 'What'd she say?'

'She's after you, man.'

I said, 'I'm not after her, pal. I can't talk her language.' Anyway, it was fun for a while, and then my father decided to go back into business. So, I went with him, and we moved up to Albany, found a shop in Albany, and that was it. Since then, I ran two shops, and I sold out in '91, but I'm busy as ever.

*

In [World War II], I got away with murder. I really did—I [felt like] I was a civilian through the whole damned thing. The guys used to say, 'How do you get away with it? How do you get away?'

I would say, 'Get away with what?'

They said, 'You horse around with these officers. They ask you dumb questions and you give them dumb answers and they laugh at everything.'

I said, 'Yeah, what the hell?' They like to laugh, too. I was always a little bit off the wall myself.

I use this [Hitler top hat as a prop] when I go to the schools and talk to the kids. It gets their attention. Somebody said to me the other day, 'You're going to destroy the hat.'

I said, 'Look, I really don't care. It's a great teaching tool, and people will remember it. The kids will remember it because kids don't know anything about World War II.' If Hitler knew what I was doing with his hat... I'm getting the last laugh. PFC Marowitz gets the last laugh...

I never went back, and I don't intend to, I don't feel like I want to. But it is almost impossible to describe the feelings, so I'm not going to try. But when you looked around, some of these tough soldiers were throwing up and crying all over the place. It is not possible to really describe the number of feelings you get when you walk into something like [Dachau]. Because that's a scene that—well, first of all, nobody told us about the camp! We had no idea what a concentration camp did! We were going to Dachau, period. It was another village as far as we were concerned. That's kind of a shock to get all at one time. And yet, people in the village who were right next to the camps said they didn't know what was going on. People in Munich, which was actually only nine miles from Dachau, didn't know what was going on. Now if you want to believe that, the Brooklyn Bridge is still for sale.

Richard Marowitz passed away at the age of 88 on August 6, 2014. 'Hitler's Hat' currently resides where it belongs—the National Museum of American Jewish Military History in Washington, DC.

**Nineteen-year-old Charles Zappo, World War II.
Source: Charles Zappo.**

CHAPTER SIXTEEN

The Medic

I found this photograph as I conducted my research for this book. Look at his face. A boy, really.

At nineteen, a baby-faced combat medic. And as a member of the 42nd Infantry 'Rainbow' Division, one of the first soldiers into the gates of hell, otherwise known as Dachau. What did those young eyes witness? What business did he have being in these circumstances? And what did it mean for the rest of his life?

Of course, we can ask this of any combat veteran, yet unless we were there with him, we will never truly know.

But this tiny, wallet-sized photo is haunting to me.

Charles J. Zappo

I was born in Buffalo, New York, on December 9, 1917. I only went up to the 8th grade, I had to quit school because my father got sick. I graduated from 8th grade and that's where it all started, I had so many jobs, it wasn't even funny [*Laughs*]. I'll give you just one basic job. I worked at the Curtiss-Wright plant making warplanes; in 1943, I worked there two years as an assembler before I left for the service. Before that I was in the CCC camp, if you ever remember one of those camps, I was out in the state of Washington for six months at a CCC camp. We helped the farmers, and my main job was soil conservation where you go along the rivers and planted little trees.[34]

I got one deferment for working at Curtiss-Wright because I was a sole worker in the family. Now, well before then I had volunteered for the Navy. I really volunteered because I knew I was going to get drafted anyway, and so I had passed the Navy test. Then, I was scheduled to go, say on a Monday, then on a Saturday, my mother, who always opened up my mail [*chuckles*], she saw I got another deferment and I stayed. Then later on, I went to join the Navy again, but I failed the eye test. They gave you these circles with numbers in it, and you had to pick it out, but I was colorblind at that time with certain colors. [*Laughs*] I couldn't pass the test, so they put me in the infantry in August of '43; went to Camp Gruber, Oklahoma, I had basic training there, stayed at Camp Gruber probably ten months or so before we went overseas; before the army, I had gotten married. What happened is, after basic training my wife came over and stayed near the camp and I would go and visit her all the time on a fake pass. [*Laughs*] After basic training, they put us on a train and went to another camp; we left from New York City, I think it was Camp Dix, and we went and landed in Marseilles, France, right around my birthday in December 1944. In the meantime, my wife had a child I had never seen. I didn't know I had a child until I went into combat.

'A Horrible, Horrible Battle'

[I was sent over with the 42nd Infantry Division, the 'Rainbow' Division]. However, we went over there without any backing, we didn't have any artillery. Just the infantry fellas were over there, and

---

[34] *CCC camp*-Civilian Conservation Corps, a New Deal public work relief program (1933-1942) offering jobs for unemployed young men aged 18 to 25.

we were waiting for the remainder of our division to come over. In the meantime, the Germans rolled through in the Battle of the Bulge. So they sent all of us green troops up there and on Christmas Eve, and there we lost quite a few people.

The first combat experience was really awful. [*Pauses in reflection*] When we went over there, it was the worst winter that Europe really had. And I just lay there when the Germans broke through, I remember that I was scared; I was in a foxhole and these German 88s were upon us, landing all around us, then our fellas were all around, the ground littered with our dead soldiers, they just lay there frozen. We lost probably fifty percent of our men; just green troops up there.

I didn't carry a weapon because I was considered a medical technician—I was a combat medic. And all we had was the big Red Cross stripe on our helmets and we had the armband with a cross on it. We weren't supposed to carry any weapons. We just carried medical supplies on us, we took care of a few wounded people there, but a lot of them were dead. I mean, after all, we administered first aid, and then of course the aid station was behind us, and they would cart out the aid station and then they went over to the medical battalion.

We really got hit pretty bad because the German tanks came right through. Gosh, the guys were all green troops, they hadn't seen any combat. We didn't have any artillery with us—they had just thrown us into battle. It was a horrible, horrible battle. That was the beginning. We were in Marseilles three weeks, and within three weeks we were thrown into battle! They didn't expect to see the Germans come through, but they had a huge offensive, really, and the Tiger tanks that came down through there… you'd be surprised. A couple of my friends, they were medics, they came out of that, they received the Silver Star for being medics. My experience was to be a combat veteran and you get a combat medical badge; I got the Bronze Star that came along with it. We had painkillers; our main pill was the sulfur pill. The sulfur pill then was just like penicillin, and you use that for, my God, they gave penicillin all over the place, but actually, we were there just to give first aid. Then, people in the back took over.

During Battle of the Bulge, I landed there at the front on my birthday, on Christmas Eve, and I was there probably about a couple months. And then when they stopped the attack, they sent us to an area there for a while.

Matter of fact, a lot of our replacements were from the Air Corps, because they took a lot of people from the Air Corps and put them in the infantry, and boy, you should have seen them. And we got a lot of replacements over there; I don't know, I think a division is around 15,000 men, and without the artillery and all those attachments, I figure I bet we probably lost six, seven hundred men there; it was a big loss—the fellas are just lying all over the frozen [ground] and it's so sad to see young fellas, you know, they just lay there. It was a bad, bad start. Believe me.

*

You talk about offensives. In March 1945, during our great offensive, we were the first troops to march into Germany, first to hit the Siegfried Line, and the first to cross the Danube. We crossed the Danube on little boats, and it was pretty dark, must have been early in the morning, probably three or four o'clock, and we were crossing when somebody lit up a cigarette and before you knew it, we were getting machine-gunned down there.

We captured cities like Wurzburg, about the size of Buffalo. We started from Alsace-Lorraine, we crossed the Rhine, we ended up in Munich. On the way to Munich, we came across a concentration camp. We captured Schweinfurt, the big ball-bearing city that the Air Corps really, really leveled. We had to fight from door to door in Wurzburg, Germany. I remember distinctly that we went into this store and found all of this champagne that the Germans brought over from France, you know? And the fellas didn't have any water or anything like that and they were emptying the bottles of champagne and were washing their feet with champagne. [*Laughs*] But an awful lot of fighting in Wurzburg; the ironic part about Wurzburg is, I have a nephew that works the *Buffalo News* and they had all of these new printing presses put in. You know where they came from? Wurzburg! Over 40 million dollars' worth of presses, and they had Germans over there teaching them all to run it from the city that was completely leveled! [*Chuckles*]

Then we went on and captured Furth, that's near Schweinfurt, and Nuremberg. Nuremberg was another place that was on the way to Munich.

'A Horrible, Horrible Sight'

American soldiers view the bodies in one of the open railcars of the Dachau death train. Source: National Archives, public domain. United States Holocaust Memorial Museum.

And then we came across Dachau; actually we didn't go over there to 'liberate' Dachau. We were out there to capture Munich, but we came across Dachau. You probably know all about Dachau. Well, I went there, first thing we saw was [like] fifty freight cars filled with bodies before you enter the camp, men, women, and children.[35] The freight cars were surrounding the camp—the [bodies] were carted in from other concentration camps, and they were going to be cremated in the ovens at Dachau. They lay out there, and we saw the boxcars and all the bodies. They did find one guy alive; it was a horrible, horrible sight.

Of course, you got to remember that at that time we were going through a lot of deaths in the army. We were pretty hardened at that time, so we realized how bad it was. You knew it was bad. And as we were going through the camp, they had just us troopers and they were lined. Like my great-grandson says, 'Did you capture any of the Germans in the camp?' I says, 'No, Charlie.' They were shot. They were killed. A lot of them took over the striped uniforms that the prisoners were wearing, and they tried to escape, and the prisoners knew who they were, so they went out there and they clubbed them, and they shot them, and threw them in the moat, you know. So, as we walked through the camp, it was just a horrible sight. You saw the ovens and you saw the bodies piled up, piled up like sacks of flour. It was really the most horrible sight I have ever seen. And then they had about 33,000 prisoners here, I guess.

[*Reads from his narrative*] "The German lieutenants surrendered the prison camp to our General Linden, commander of our unit. However, German SS troopers, they were the elite troops, refused

---

[35] *fifty freight cars filled with bodies-* 'The train consisted of 30 rail cars with nearly 5,000 prisoners who had been evacuated from Buchenwald in the last days of the war.' You can see a short silent film of this at bit.ly/BOXCARS-DA-CHAU.

to surrender the camp, [so] inside the camp, I saw many dead SS troopers lying on the ground; they had made a futile attempt to defend the camp. Just prior to the liberation, they tried to kill as many prisoners as possible. I think they shot approximately 200 prisoners with machine guns. The bodies were stacked like cordwood; I saw bodies of women and children also. I saw the gas chambers where thousands of prisoners were led to believe they were showers, then they were gassed. We saw the bodies in the adjoining rooms. Bodies ready to be cremated, they were piled up all over the place like sacks of potatoes. And the stench in the camp was horrible. The prisoners had become like animals. As they moved the camp, many were dying even though they were being liberated. So Dachau was really a nightmare to all of the men in the division. Man after man was saying, 'Now I know why we are fighting. These Nazis are mad. People who operated the camps were insane.'"

[*Looks up from a narrative he was reading from*] Now in the nearby town, a few miles away over there from Dachau, I asked a few of the townspeople, 'Did you know what was going on in the camp?'

They said, 'No, we just hear the freight cars pulling in and out of the camp.' And nobody knew what was going on? Then I said, 'Well, couldn't you smell the fumes? Couldn't you smell the fumes coming out of the smokestacks?'

They didn't say anything.

[Now], as a medic, you see, we were there just in the camp as soldiers; I don't think we were there more than just a couple of days. We were marching on; we were marching on to Munich. What happens is, you have the medical battalion, and then they come in, and they're supposed to take care of all the men. Imagine taking care of 33,000 prisoners? They were all skin and bones, you know? And so, it was really a horrible, horrible sight. Just like I say, people in that town 'never even knew what was going on.' It's hard to believe they didn't know!

After that, what they did is, they went out and got all the people from the town, had them all come into the camp, and they had to bury all the dead prisoners. And carry them—you should have seen [that], they were carrying them on their backs, and dragging them, and putting them in trenches, and then they would bury them in the trenches. You can't imagine how terrible that [camp] was! So that's what happened, I mean, we weren't there [at that time]. We just liberated the camp, then we got to Munich, and we liberated [some people], there were about a quarter of a million slave laborers there. When they were liberated, they went wild; they went and looted the whole city and it was really unbelievable. [*Chuckles*] So, [it was more than] just the Dachau concentration camp.

Russians

We became an army of occupation and we ended up in Salzburg, Austria. [We had some contact with the Soviet troops]; I'll tell you a little story. There were Russians all over the place and we went to this great, great concert, the Russian troops were all sitting up in the front and they were all over the place. All of a sudden in the middle of the concert, you see all of these small balloons floating down into the concert. You know what those balloons were? [*Laughs*] And I thought that was a terrible thing, you know, you're in a concert.

When we were stationed in Salzburg, my buddy and I heard all of this singing down in the valley. So, we went down to the valley, and saw a trainload of Hungarians and they were trying to get into the American section. They wanted to get away from the Russians because the Russians had a bad reputation. And this whole train, they were elderly people and young people, and I talked to a few of them, and they said they had women and children on the train, they didn't have much food and needed some blankets. At that time, I was stationed in some mansion in Austria. It was a beautiful place. So I asked a few of the fellas to come up with me during the day and gave them something to take back with them. I gave them blankets and food and gave them a lot of clothing. They didn't want any part of the Russians at all, to be under Russian occupation. Everybody wanted to come over to the American side. And of course the Germans, I remember being in Austria and I got acquainted with a German and his wife, she was a pianist, and you see, when the Germans were in Austria, they got better treatment. They had had about a six-month stay in Austria, and they wanted to get another six months, so I helped them get another six months. I told them that we needed some signed papers, and they gave them another pass. He was thrilled to get the pass and stay there, but I miss the nice German people.

*

In January of 1946, [I finally had enough points according to] the point system [they had], so I got transferred to the 84th Infantry, because they were going home. And, while I was in Heidelberg, we heard that General Patton died; he was in Heidelberg, he got killed in that car accident.[36] It was an ironic thing, this general like General Patton getting killed because he wasn't wearing his seatbelt.

So, we got on a ship in France, I think it was at Le Havre, and we sailed for home. It took us about seven days to get home. And when I got home, I saw my son, whom I had never seen. He was about fourteen months old and of course he starts screaming, you know, I don't know who the hell this guy is, and so we had a very bad start. [*Laughs*] You know, because here you are. You don't have

---

[36] *we heard that General Patton died-* On December 9, 1945, the car Patton was riding in collided with an American army truck, resulting in a broken neck and spinal injuries. The others traveling with him in the car had only minor injuries. He died twelve days later on December 21, at the age of 60. One of his final remarks was, 'This is a hell of a way to die.'

a job; you really have no place to live. And then one day I was working in a piano factory, and it laid me off. And here I am with two children now, and living in a really bad, bad flat on the west side. And I decided to go back to school. I used the GI Bill. And I didn't have any high school. So they had what they call an accelerated veterans high school over in Elmwood Avenue. So, I went to working part-time and I went through and completed 4 years of high school in one year and got a diploma from our regular high school. And that was really a struggle. Then I enrolled in business college over here, Bryant & Stratton, two years. I majored in accounting, and I became an accountant; I worked at a bakery where I had to be a cost accountant and we used to ship baked goods to about a hundred stores. After that, I figured I'd start taking some civil service tests, because I could see I wasn't getting anywhere. I took a chance for the Internal Revenue Service, and I passed that exam. It's like an exam for New York State auditors exam tax department and I became a became a New York State corporation tax auditor all from that. I could work pretty damn hard.

Imagine going through all that, these kids can't get through four years of high school; of course, I only took the basic courses. But I go way back, you know, way back when I was just a kid I used to go out and shine shoes downtown, six, seven years old—could you imagine a kid going out there in the city? I had so many jobs it wasn't even funny!

*

At the end of the war, people were coming down from all the hills. I even had a lot of Germans surrendering, even to me, coming down with white flags. I was put in charge of this German POW camp in Germany as a medic, and I helped some of the Germans over there that were really sick. One guy had pneumonia, and I wonder if he still remembers me. And then I remember when I was in Camp Gruber we had a prisoner camp there, a German prisoner camp at Camp Gruber, and you know they went out there striking for more cigarettes. Then I had a brother that was a POW. He was captured in the Battle of the Bulge. Do you know what they were doing to these American prisoners? They were segregating them. If they were Jewish, they were put into the terrible camps. They thought my brother was Jewish, and they put him in one of these camps and they were digging tunnels.[37] I guess he lost 70 pounds or something like that. He went through a terrible time in that. What a contrast. And now, he died last year, but they're giving him reparations, to these POWs. As a matter of fact, I was over to the VA administration office over here in Buffalo. And I took a lot of this stuff [*points to notes on the table*] over there and they were all interested in this stuff. One of the POWs, he had things to do with the POW prisoners and their activities, I was telling one guy that Germany has given reparations to some of these prisoners, our prisoners, and he didn't know about it, because they put these fellas, our prisoners, into minor concentration camps. My brother, gosh, he almost died in that camp. But people don't realize what the fellas went through.

'You Don't Realize How It Is Going to Affect You'

Well, I tell you, I realize [now] how this affected my life, this thing I saw here at Dachau, I didn't realize it, but my wife says at night I'd be twitching all over the bed. You go through all of this, and you don't realize how it's going to affect you, throughout your life. That thing is affecting me, I don't know why, but as a matter of fact, this is the first time I haven't really broken down [trying to talk

---

[37] *They thought my brother was Jewish*- the camp was likely Berga an der Elster, a subcamp of Buchenwald, detailed in Vol.6 of this series, *The Bulge and Beyond*.

about it]. Maybe it's because [I had] my last breakdown with my grandson. But it stays with you—this post-traumatic stress that all these young fellas are coming home with, it's real. It's a serious thing. I go to the VA Hospital, they treat me real good. Matter of fact, I got my hearing aids there, and my glasses. Of course, if I live to the end of the year, I'm going to be 90 years old. And there's 1,200 of us World War II veterans dying every day! There aren't too many of us left around here. So I've been all over, and they want people to remember this stuff. I don't like doing this stuff anymore, but I do it because I feel I should do it, [because] people don't realize that it's just like this right here [*points to paper on table*], 'Lies about the Holocaust.'

If you were to see what went on in Germany...Hitler, he was a madman.

Charles Zappo passed away on June 19, 2015, at the age of 97.

The Brandenburg Gate amid the ruins of Berlin, June 1945. Source: Bundsarchiv.

CHAPTER SEVENTEEN

The Fall of Berlin

By March 25, 1945, resistance on the west bank of the Rhine River had all but collapsed, with German troops surrendering by the hour, now trapped by the encircling Allies. Another 325,000 would be trapped in the Ruhr Pocket in the next few weeks; by April 11, the Ninth US Army had reached the Elbe, just 50 miles from Berlin.

The previous month at Yalta, the Big Three had planned for the division of Germany into zones of occupation, with Berlin lying squarely within the Soviet sector. Evaluating the situation, Eisenhower concluded that an assault on Berlin from the west would be too costly, given that Berlin would revert to the Russians anyway. He decided to wait. The Red Army launched its final assault on Berlin on April 16. In the two weeks that followed, it suffered over 350,000 casualties, more than the United States in the entire European Theater of the war. The Battle of Berlin was the Red Army's costliest battle in World War II.[15] Delusional and unrepentant, Hitler dictated his last testament to his secretary, lashing out at the German people for failing him and his National Socialist visions, killing himself in the Führerbunker in Berlin on April 30. The victors would enter the ruined Reich capital, twelve years into its 'thousand-year reign.'

CHAPTER EIGHTEEN

The Paratrooper IV

Albert A. Tarbell

On To Berlin

We were soon thereafter on occupation duty. Guys on high points were being shipped back to the States, I think it was 85 points or something like that, they could come back to the States. The war was over in August, when they dropped the bomb. That stopped us from going, because we figured we were going to Japan or going to the Orient.

[The atomic bombs] couldn't have happened at a better time. We wanted to come home. We didn't want to go over there, you know. I don't think anybody liked the idea of jumping into Japan, I think that would have been wholesale slaughter. We would have lost a lot of men there, because they were going to protect their country. I think they would have protected it very well, very hard.

We started having few leaves and then started regrouping. They said we were going to go to Berlin, occupation duty. I went from Charlottenburg to Berlin by jeep; the colonel put me in charge of battalion beer and liquor supply after the war. That was a good duty.

I got orders to report to the medics. Good old medics. I went to the medics, Captain Ketchen and Captain Shapiro over there. They said, 'Tarbell, we got something here for you and your guys.'

I said, 'What is it?' Here was a flask, five gallons of 180 proof alcohol. They had checked; they said, 'Oh, we checked it, inspected it, it's good for consumption.' I was dishing out this alcohol, vermouth and grape juice, and the guys didn't come around for seconds. [*Laughs*]

I finally got detached service with Colonel Cook at his battalion. I still was carried in the company, but I worked at the battalion. When I went to Berlin, I couldn't get anybody to drink that vermouth [we 'liberated' weeks back], because we didn't have nothing to cut it with. One of the guys from officers' mess said, 'Hey, Tarbell, I got about six cases of gin.' He said, 'I'll trade you for that barrel of vermouth.'

I said, 'You got a deal.' I took the colonel's jeep and his driver, I had about six cases of gin. I took it to Berlin with us with other stuff we got, like schnapps from Essen, Germany.

That was quite a jeep ride, on the autobahn, in and out, in and out; wherever the bridges were blown you had a detour, then you had to get back on. We got to Helmstedt, and from there we went into the Russian zone; from here to Berlin, it's all Russian zones. You're going to see Russian guards every so often. They said, 'When they salute you, return the salute. You know they're liable to shoot you if you don't.' Or do something, you know, get pissed off anyway.

We're driving and driving, and I got so sick of saluting. God, it seemed like every couple of hundred yards or something there's a guard. We stopped at one place, we had a piss call, a relief call. God, there were a bunch of women working in a potato field or some kind of a field, doing something. They all come running over to us! You ought to have seen how quick those guards moved, boy, they just held them right back. The women were going to come over, you know, they knew we were Americans.

Anyway, we got into Berlin, and it was quite a city. Oh, that city was so beat up, God. The subways there, they had artillery there. They used to fire artillery [from] the subways and everything else. In a lot of places, the whole street was crumbled, and they had blocks and blocks of buildings that were all demolished. Do you know when we got there, we relieved another outfit that was already there? The people were already cleaning bricks and this and that. The other unit had set up work details, already rebuilding, they're trying to rebuild.

I understood that in order to get a heating or food permit, you had to work. Whoever we hired, they got a ration card to go to this soup kitchen and they were fed meals. We had two restaurants that I took over, one for the enlisted men, and the non-com club. I took care of the non-com club; my buddy Fritz took over the enlisted men's club. We had beer there, and I was getting liquor supply from the States. I'd bring that down to the sergeants, first sergeant, mess sergeant, took care of them guys first, you know, then all the others, everybody got something. We tried to break it up even.

It was a good living. We had football games at the Templehof—not the Templehof, but where they had the Olympics, the Unter den Linden ran right into it. Brandenburg Gate was nearby there. I went a couple of times to the Russian zone, but I didn't want to fraternize with the Russians at all—they were not people to fraternize with. We didn't get along, but oh, they bought watches from you. They'd buy a Mickey Mouse watch; they'd pay you three or four hundred dollars for it! They had never been paid in about six years; they were going to spend it all right there when they got paid. They bought things like that, you know, that they had never seen before. They were taking everything apart; they were taking plumbing apart and everything else, furniture—it was all being shipped back to Russia.

In one of the areas there, my company commander was in charge. A friend of mine got word one night that the Russians were coming in there and raiding this woman's home, taking all the furniture and everything else. This woman was complaining. The commander, he took Renner with him. He told Renner, 'Don't let that guy out.' He sent another lieutenant with him.

The lieutenant told the Russians, "Guys, that's not right. You're out of your area. This is in the American zone. You shouldn't be taking this stuff out of here. Don't move that truck.'

He told Renner, 'If that truck moves, shoot that driver.'

You know, we never figured that the Russians would go back to try to move it. The lieutenant went in, and he tried to pacify the woman. So what do the Russians do? The guy jumps back in the truck and told the driver to take off. Renner straightened out and shot the driver and killed him. He was the first American to kill a Russian soldier. They questioned him later, they asked the colonel, 'Couldn't he have just wounded him?'

The colonel said, 'I didn't train my soldiers to wound people. I trained them to shoot to kill.' My company commander went there, and [met with] his Russian counterpart, and they did a lot of finagling, and Renner got out of that. But that's the way the Russians were.

When we first went in on leave in Berlin, they said, 'You cannot go out on pass unless you have a .45 or a tommy gun. You have to be armed. If you don't have that, take a rifle, but you got to be armed.' I got on a tram, running near Hofstrasse. I looked at the people. My God, everybody was either a cripple or they were old people! I said, 'My God, what's my sidearm for? Not for these people.' I found out that night what it was for. The Russians would come over in our zone and they would raise hell. It was to protect us from them! Why, they were an awful bunch. They just went hog wild there, in Berlin, because I guess, after six years of [being invaded, German occupation], fighting the war. But their values and ours were different; we valued human beings and they didn't seem to care too much. At least, that's my impression of them. I didn't care for the average Russian soldier. Maybe we're just brought up different. I don't know.

View of the defendants in the dock at the International Military Tribunal trial of war criminals in Nuremberg, Bavaria, Germany.
Source: National Archives, public domain. United States Holocaust Memorial Museum.

CHAPTER NINETEEN

Judgment at Nuremberg

Just before Thanksgiving in November 1945, Justice Robert Jackson opened the most spectacular set of trials in history. A man of unimpeachable credentials and integrity, Jackson was asked by President Truman to serve as chief prosecutor of the International Military Tribunal, as the court was formally known.

In the 1943 Moscow Declarations, the Soviet Union, Great Britain, and the United States published their joint statement that Nazi war criminals would be pursued 'to the uttermost ends of the earth ... so that justice may be done.' In late 1944, as it was becoming clear that the Allies would eventually prevail, high level discussions began to crystalize the process for the judicial accountability of the leadership of Nazi Germany responsible for the Holocaust and other crimes against humanity.

It was important to the Allied leadership that the trials be held on German soil. Jackson and others settled on Nuremberg as an appropriate choice, given that its Palace of Justice was intact, but symbolically, Nuremberg was the home of the early Nazi Party massive rallies, and the 1935 Nuremberg Race Laws, which set out to define 'Jewishness' and began specifically codifying acts to be considered criminal.

In the first and best-known trial (out of a total of thirteen, trying over 200 German defendants, lasting until 1949), twenty-one defendants stood trial. It lasted nearly a year, and one has to consider the gravity and general unprecedentedness of a war crimes trial; today, its significance for putting potential human rights violators on notice cannot be overestimated. Many of the GIs who were present at Nuremberg after the war understood on some level that they had a front row seat at a hugely historic moment, yet frankly, with the fighting over, it was a peripheral affair. Most were guys who had not collected enough points under the demobilization Adjusted Service Rating Score point system; they just wanted to get home.[38]

---

[38] *Adjusted Service Rating Score point system*-Witnessing the frustration incumbent with the Army's failed demobilization efforts at the end of World War I (where entire divisions were sent home at once, rather than individuals based on merit/time served) as General Pershing's Chief of Staff, General George C. Marshall ordered up a study for a more objective, timely methodology for getting the troops home in late 1943. It called for the following:
One point for each month of Army service
One point for each month in service abroad
Five points for each campaign
Five points for a medal for merit/valor
Five points for a Purple Heart
Twelve points for each dependent child (up to three)
Source: Bamford, Tyler. *The Points Were All That Mattered: The US Army's Demobilization After World War II.* National WWII Museum, August 27, 2020. www.nationalww2museum.org/war/articles/points-system-us-armys-demobilization

Alvin Cohen's Nuremberg International Military Tribunal ID card.
Source: Alvin Cohen.

CHAPTER TWENTY

The Jewish Guard Keeper

Al Cohen was another one of the trio of New York's Capital District ETO Army veterans who visited my high school every year for a while, beginning in 2000. He was very active in many veterans' organizations, co-founding the Hudson Valley (NY) Chapter of the Veterans of the Battle of the Bulge, where he even served as president. In tandem with my slides and mini-introductory lectures, they would speak in turn of their experiences in the battle, crossing the Siegfried Line, and fighting into Germany. I would usually ask the soft-spoken Al to present last to the students, as he had a very special task, though it was lost to him as a nineteen-year-old, impatient to get home after the war's end.

'This was my ID card to get into the cell block as a guard at the [International Military Tribunal's] Palace of Justice in Nuremberg. We were supposed to turn them in when we left the war trials, but I hung onto mine just for the heck of it. At first, I was guarding one of the criminals. I don't recall who it was at that time, but on the right side the first cell was Goering, the second one I believe was Hess, and then Jodl, and so on Ribbentrop, and so on down the line. Von Schirach was head of the Hitler Youth, and

he and Speer, they could speak very good English, and they would try and talk to us. We weren't supposed to, but we did. The first thing I say to any of them was, 'How do you like having a Jew guard?' Most of them, I think, understood English, but they wouldn't say a word. I've got a couple of their autographs, but nobody wants them. I try to get rid of them. Nobody wants them!'

This chapter is drawn from his testimony recorded in May 2000 and August 2001.

Alvin M. Cohen

I was born in Utica, New York, on October 1, 1925. [We lived there], I don't know, maybe for a couple of years, and then my father was transferred around. We ended up settling in Albany, where I went to the Albany public schools. Then I left school; I figured I was going in service, so I went to work at the American Locomotive in Schenectady. From there, I was drafted in '44. I got there in August, beginning of August, and it was very hot. September cooled off, and finally, when I left, it was December, and it was cold and damp. In fact, we're out in the field, and we've got a shipment of down sleeping bags out of the Schenectady depot.

We didn't like it down South. The people down there weren't too appreciative of servicemen. They like to take your money, but that was as far as it went.

[I had been in the New York State] National Guard, so I already had had some training. The Guard was now federalized, and some of the fellas from school were signing up because they got paid. I don't remember what it was, maybe seventy-five cents a drill. I figured, 'Oh, I'll go anyway, and I'll get some military training.' We had green, one-piece uniforms, leggings, and the old World War I helmet. We were drilling with shotguns. There were some rifles, shotguns, and Thompson submachine guns, etc., which I believe are still stored down in Peekskill. So, [basic training] was easier for me than some of the others. When we first started out, as an example, the sergeants were going to show us how to pack a full field pack, the old-style World War I. That's what we had here in Albany. He said, 'Does anybody know how to do it?'

I said, 'Yes,' and I raised my hand.

He said, 'Okay. Let's see if you can do it.' I did it, and then they gave me acting corporal. I got out of KP that way. After basic training, I came home. I had, I think, seven days' delay on the road. Travel time was about four days. I ended up with four days at home, and I had to report to Fort Meade, Maryland. They went over our clothes, gave us shots. After about a day and a half, they loaded us on the train, and we went over to Camp Kilmer, New Jersey, dropped our barracks bags in one of the empty buildings, and they marched us into a warehouse, gave us a brand new M1, new trench shovel, new web equipment. Out the other door, back to the barracks, we cleaned our weapons. They fed us. We got on a train over Jersey, crossed on a ferry boat, and up on the dock, it was a Queen Elizabeth tied up to the dock. That was the start of a four-day trip; there were about twenty-seven thousand troops packed in that thing. You couldn't move. We were lucky. We had about twelve of us in a compartment, and all our names started with C. Luckily, we all stuck together, right straight through until we were assigned to M Company, 359th Infantry, and it was the 90th Infantry Division.

Overseas

We landed in Gorx, Scotland, and they took us off. The ship was too big to tie up to the dock, so they took us off on a lighter, got us on a train, and we started down towards London. The transportation crew told us, 'If you get stuck, if you don't cross the Channel tonight'— this was on a Friday—'we'll give you a pass to London.' Everybody's all excited they're going to get a pass to London. We got down; we ended up at Plymouth, and we got right on the ship. The next morning, we were all going to Le Havre; that was what I saw of London. [*Chuckles*]

Everything at Le Havre was pretty well beat up. They started marching us up the hill; I think they called it Camp Philip Morris, one of those names after a cigarette. As we're marching up, we see these little kids alongside the road, looking for candy and cigarettes. You couldn't get over it; they spoke French. It was hard to visualize that you're in a different country and they're speaking French but not speaking our language.

When we got up to battalion, they needed volunteers for heavy weapons. As I said, the fifteen of us or so that were in the compartment, we were all together. A couple of the fellas said, 'We're getting the mortar platoon.' That was 81-millimeter mortars; well back of the line. They started volunteering, and the rest of us knew each other, so we stuck together, so we all volunteered. We get up to the company, and they signed us to a platoon, heavy weapons. Well, we all volunteered for the heavy weapons platoon, but we ended up in this machine gun platoon. That was the best thing we did because out of the whole group of us, some of us went back to the hospital, but we all came back—out of the fifteen of us, only one fell and got hurt bad enough to come back to the States.

The Siegfried Line

I started out carrying ammunition. I had two cans of ammunition, picked up a leather strap someplace. It's strapped over my shoulders. I had one can on my chest, one on my back, inside my pack. They took the M1 away from me, and I got a carbine, and eventually, I became the second gunner. I carried the water jacket receiver. We'd be assigned to a rifle company, a squad of us. They were moving us around a lot to change different sectors. That was just before we went through the Siegfried Line. We got through there, and through the dragon's teeth, and there was a road, a bombed-out farmhouse. We had our squad in there, we had our machine guns set up outside. It was pretty much a holding position. We were lucky that we got through. We were moving around quite a bit. Our regiment was always stuck out in the woods someplace; we didn't get to see anything of the cities or towns. In fact, at the end of this month, I'll get back to a division reunion. I'll see some of the fellows that were in our squad.

The Siegfried Line were rows of dragon's teeth. It's like a pyramid that's cut off on top, without the point, rows of them. In between the rows, they'd have booby traps or mines to keep the tanks from going through. Where we went through, we were lucky the engineers had cleared the path; there were no mines when we got through there. We were up in some woods, and it was a log dugout, about six or seven feet tall, but it was sunk in the ground, just a little was showing. We opened up the door, and it's covered with sawdust, just like someone took a rake and raked it out. Right in the center was a German element, so nobody would even walk in there, but the lieutenant went in, put a rope around it, and then dragged it out. Luckily, it wasn't booby-trapped or anything. That's the problem we ran into. The Germans were pretty cute. They'd like to booby trap a toilet seat, places you'd least expect something.

'I'll Blow Your Goddamn Head Off'

In basic training in Arkansas, I had a run-in [involving antisemitism] with one fellow. Then once overseas, after we made the river crossing, we got a building to get in out of the cold to sleep in. The building was in pretty good shape, so it wasn't bad, though there wasn't any furniture in it. They brought up copies of *Stars and Stripes*. We were sitting on the floor, and I got through cleaning my carbine, so I clipped in. As I'm doing that, this one fellow who came in a short time before, as a replacement, he was off of some farm up in Northern New York, and he was looking at the paper, and he said, 'We're over here, getting our rear ends shot off, and the Jews are back in the States, making all the money.'

I finished putting a clip in the carbine; I put a round in the chamber. I put the safety on, I walked over and stood over him, and I said, 'What did you say, fella?'

He repeated it.

I said to him, 'I'm Jewish.'

He said, 'No, you're not.'

I said, 'Well, what am I?'

He said, 'You're Italian.'

I said, 'With a name like Cohen?'

He said, 'No, you're kidding!'

I dropped the muzzle of the carbine right down in his chest, and I said to him, 'If I ever hear you say anything about the Jews in front of me, or at the back of me, I'll blow your goddamn head off.'

The lieutenant sitting there never said a word. After that, he wanted to be my buddy when we wouldn't have anything to do. Other than that, I've had no problems. A lot of fellas had it a lot worse.

Our platoon leader was a tech sergeant, and he made battlefield commission, and he was terrific. None of the non-coms wanted stripes because as soon as you got stripes, you got hit. When he was with us, nothing could happen. In fact, at the reunions, I see my old company commander, our mess sergeant. Our battalion commander retired recently, maybe eight or nine years ago, as a major general. He stayed in; he had the 1st Division in Vietnam for a while. Quite a few of them stayed in after the war.

We very seldom saw the other platoon; we never saw the mortar platoon. Even if we went back for a rest, they'd have one platoon in one building, another platoon maybe five miles down the road, in another building. Most of them were all bombed out. We never got to see them. In fact, at the first reunion I went to, there wasn't anyone there that I knew. They were all fellows out of our M Company, but they were either in the hospital, they were back someplace, and we never got to know each other; the only ones we really knew were the fellows in our own group. They tell us we're going back and getting off the line for three days. We get back to town, miles back, and they tell us, 'You're going to be here for three days.' The first thing you had to do, you had to clean crew-served weapons, then you cleaned your own weapons. If you had time, you try to get cleaned up. Usually, we didn't have time to do the latter. We'd be back for supposedly three days. Maybe four or five hours later, we're going back up, somebody's in trouble, so we'd come back and have to relieve someone. If we get in a town, the standing order was, if you're going to spend the night in the town, you had to take the civilians and lock them in the cellar. Sometimes, they give you a hard time about that. All you had to tell them was that the Russians are coming. They were very docile after that. They'd get down. We'd lock them in the cellar.

Pulling Guard Duty at Nuremberg

After the war was over, I didn't have enough points; most of the replacements didn't have enough points to come home. They shipped the low point men to the 1st Division at Nuremberg, pulling guard duty at the war trials. I start pulling guard at the war trials and the cell block.

This was my ID card to get into the cell block at the [International Military Tribunal's] Palace of Justice in Nuremberg. When I first got there, you didn't need a card to get in. Then, the FBI had a detachment there and they came out with this ID card. We were supposed to turn them in when we left the war trials, but I hung onto mine just for the heck of it. At first, I was guarding one of the criminals. I don't recall who it was at that time, but on the right side the first cell was Goering, the second one I believe was Hess, and then Jodl, and so on Ribbentrop, and so on down the line.

Alvin Cohen, second on left, watching sleeping prisoner at Nuremberg. Source: Life Magazine.

It was miserable. To stand in front of a door and look at Goering, or looking at Hess, we were looking at Speer, von Schirach, any of those twenty-two war criminals, they're just sleeping, and you're standing there [outside of the door, looking into the cell]. We have to watch them. I don't know, just, to me, it didn't sit right. Anyway, I suppose it was better than pulling guard out in the cold.

The doors were wooden, I can't say it was oak. The doors were about that thick. [*Gestures inches apart*] They cut squares in them. There's a metal grating, and light is hooked on it and shined into their cell. You had to make sure that they slept with their hands out, face exposed, and that they didn't try to commit suicide. This was right after one of them hung themselves. I did that for a while, and then I got so-called promoted to an escort guard. I used to take them up to see their lawyers in the courthouse. We pulled guard for two hours on, we stood in front of the cell during the day; they always had to be visible to you. They had a toilet there, a bed and a table with one chair. They used the toilet, and that was the only time they could be out of your vision, for how long it took.

'Fresh Air Fanatics'

There was one window in the back of the cell. In the spring and the summer it wasn't too bad, but in the winter, it was hot in the cell block where we were standing. It was freezing outside, the windows were wide open because all these German criminals were fresh air fanatics, and you had to stare at them continuously to make sure they didn't try and commit suicide. That cold air would flow in your face, and it was a rough job trying to stay awake. Two hours on, two hours off, and they had one room, which used to be a gymnasium, they had cots set up where we could lie down, rest, some of the fellas played cards or read. That same room was the room they cleaned out and then built the scaffolds to hang them.

[In this photograph], on the left side, I'm the third one, right there. It was in *Life Magazine* in January of '46. I didn't know anything about it; as it happened a friend of mine went to the dentist and sitting in the waiting room, she's reading through *Life Magazine* and found it.

They kept the most important ones on the first tier, that's the ground floor, like Julius Streicher, Jodl, Ribbentrop, I believe twenty or twenty-one of the most important ones. The second tier, there was a catwalk, and the flooring was like a piece of tin. Every time you would walk it would bounce up and down. They had four or five cells to watch. The less important criminals were kept there. The third tier held witnesses and some of the criminals.

One of the ones on the top floor was Ilse Koch. She was a notorious guard at one of the camps. She would take the skin off the prisoners when they were killed, if they had a tattoo or something, she would make lampshades out of them and all kinds of decorative ornaments. When you were on the third tier, which she was on, you had to watch them the same way by making sure they didn't kill themselves. She was a cute one; when she heard the guard coming, she would take all her clothes off and stand there naked. You had to look into the cells, so what happened—you had to look, she would write a letter to the commanding colonel or commanding officer of the prison. First thing you know, you were on the carpet for looking at her. After a while, I guess they got used to it, and that was the same with a few others.

At night, there is a grate with a light on the side of each cell. The light went over the cut-out of the door and that light shone into the cell continuously. I pulled that kind of guard for three or four months, and one day we got back to our barracks, and we fell out.

'How Do You Like Having a Jew Guard?'

Von Schirach was head of the Hitler Youth, and he and Speer, they could speak very good English, and they would try and talk to us. We weren't supposed to, but we did. They used to tell me that their parents used to bring them over to the Catskill Mountains [in New York state] in the summer. One thing I did when I pulled guard, the first thing I say to any of them was, 'How do you like having a Jew guard?' Most of them, I think, understood English, but they wouldn't say a word. At least they used to rotate us, they had a stone wall around a little courtyard between the prison and courthouse. It was like a garden, some grass and trees, for the use of the exercise of the prisoners, and they wanted somebody who had to be handcuffed to Hess when he was out in the yard with the other prisoners. I was elected for that. It wasn't too bad, but he had arms over twice as long as mine. At first, I was walking with one shoulder down, and then I got smart and made him hold his arm up. He didn't even speak to the other prisoners, but you could tell by the expression in their eyes. They acknowledged each other. I've got a couple of their autographs, but nobody wants them. I try to get rid of them. Nobody wants them!

*

One morning, the first sergeant read off the day's schedule and he wanted a volunteer; he needed a radioman, but nobody raised their hands—nobody ever volunteered for anything. Then the first sergeant grabbed me. He said, 'Do you know anything about a radio?'

I said, 'I know how to turn it on and off. That's about it.'

He said, 'Good, get cleaned up, get a jeep, get down to the [military] police station.' So I go down there, to the MP station, which was adjoining the courthouse where the war trials were, and I saw this lieutenant.

He said, 'What do you know about a radio?' I told him the same thing.

So he said, 'Good, you'll be the radioman here. From now on, you're on detached service. You have to go for twelve hours on, twenty-four off. If you want to, you can stay back with your company, but just be here to go on duty.' While policing Nuremberg, we had anywhere from twenty to thirty jeeps patrolling the town, day and night. So I became a radio operator for about four months.

The time that I had off, I could do whatever I want. I lived back with the fellas at the 1st Division. When it was time to go on duty to get on the radio, I would get picked up by one of the patrol jeeps on duty to take me to work. That was a good deal, but eventually it didn't work out because the division MPs weren't issuing enough citations for uniforms and being drunk and all that, so they brought in a special MP unit. That ended my job. I started pulling guard again in the cell block; I went back to guarding the prisoners for about a week, and after that I became, as they called them, an escort guard. I wore a white helmet and a white belt, and I would take the prisoners up to the summary court, where they had lawyers from Russia, France, and other countries, and they would interrogate some of these prisoners. It was amazing some of the stories you heard, one of them was how they provoked Poland into a situation. They sent over German troops dressed as civilians and they fired back across the border at German troops over there, and that's how they started the incident that started the war—it was things like that that were very interesting.

The Russian Delegation

Once in a while, we lived on the outskirts of Nuremberg, a town called Fürth. When I had time off, I'd go into Nuremberg, each company had their own beer joint. I'd go in with the PX sergeant, he ran it, and they had a bar set up in there. There were Russians in there, there were French, English, and everybody got along fine. No problem. Every Monday, you could look down at the Palace of Justice, and in the basement, there is a window. Every Monday morning, I'd see a two-and-a-half-ton truck back up with crates of bottles that looked like water. It was vodka. You can see that room was piled up high with cases of vodka. Next Monday morning, when they back up another truck, it was empty. That's how [fast the Russians at the trials] went through that stuff.

Finally in June, beginning of June of '46, they came around with a deal that if you wanted to sign up for six months to stay at the war trials, they'd fly you back to the States for thirty days, then you'd have to go back. The reason for that was that fellas that had decorations and combat badges were being shipped home and they wanted to put on a show for the other countries, so they wanted to keep their combat troops in to pull guard. But it didn't work, most of us went home.

*

I got out on July 3 of '46. A few years ago, my wife and I and twenty-five of the men from the division with their wives, we went back over to [follow our combat route and see Germany]. It brought back a lot of memories, especially when we went up to the place called Habscheid, where we went through the dragon's teeth. It brought back a lot of memories. Of course, I couldn't find the farmhouse that we slept in. That was long gone. And we toured the Flossenbürg concentration camp, which our regiment liberated, but at that time we were out in the woods someplace.

I was nineteen years old, the war was over, we were anxious to get home, [guard duty at the first Nuremberg trial] was just another job, really. But as we got older, those of us that were pulling guard there, it had a different meaning, it was part of history. Now when I look back, and I see all these programs about the war trials and everything, it's kind of like [a surreal experience]. [At the time], I couldn't wait to get home; I just didn't want any part of it.

Alvin Cohen was the recipient of the Bronze Star and many other awards and citations. He passed away on March 25, 2014, at the age of 88.

"Former Nazi Party ideologist Alfred Rosenberg in the witness box at the International Military Tribunal war crimes trial at Nuremberg. Emilio DiPalma is the military policeman standing guard next to him."

Source: National Archives, public domain.

United States Holocaust Memorial Museum

CHAPTER TWENTY-ONE

The Courtroom Sentinel

Leo DiPalma was the son of Italian immigrants who grew up in the western part of Massachusetts in the Great Depression. Like many young high schoolers at the time, he was shocked at the news of Pearl Harbor, and ready to serve when his number was called three years later at the age of eighteen. He gained combat experience as an infantryman with the 79th Division, crossing the Rhine in 1945 before being tasked with a new assignment in the 1st Division—standing guard, at the tender age of nineteen, over some of the most notorious war criminals of the 20th century.

'I pulled guard duty on the witness stand with von Schirach. He was head of the Hitler Youth. One day, there was quite a confrontation between him and Chief Justice Jackson. Of course, we could understand him. And he spoke decent English now, but most of his replies were in German. But through the interpreter, we could hear what was going on. They were arguing back and forth about the duties of the Hitler Youth. Well, they called a recess shortly after that, and he turned to me. I was on his left side. He turned to me, and he said, 'But the Hitler Youth is nothing more than your Boy Scouts.'

I said, 'Really?' He doesn't realize that I was a frontline soldier.

I said, 'I fought your Hitler Youth.' He never said a word [after that]. We found Hitler Youth that could take apart our BAR, our M1s, or any of our equipment. So they weren't Boy Scouts like he wanted to portray them.

I came back from the service, but I never thought about it. It's only been the past ten years I've had time to think about it. I'm kind of a low-key person, but I'll do anything to enlighten people that weren't even born at that time.'

Emilio Joseph 'Leo' DiPalma

I was born in Springfield, Massachusetts, June 3, 1926. I had a little job before I graduated. I was working nights at a defense plant, American Bosch. I, of course, graduated. Let's see, I graduated in February. I was a half class, you know. I worked there until September 15, 1944, when I went in the service. I was, let's see, eighteen and three months, I guess. [When Pearl Harbor occurred, I was still in high school]; actually, my dad had trouble with his car, and he was driving around with it, trying it out. I guess he'd had some work done. He stopped at my cousin's gas station. First thing my cousin said when he come out, he said, 'We're at war.' Of course, I didn't say anything. I wondered, with who? I got to thinking, I said, 'Geez, I probably won't go in, I'm really too young.' But turned out that I wasn't. The next day at lunch, we heard President Roosevelt say how we had gone to war, we had been attacked by Japan, gave all the details. Actually, as young as I was, it did make me angry, because it was an attack. It wasn't something that we had initiated or done wrong.

I was drafted September 15, that was '44. I went to Fort Devens, just to get squared away, I guess. Then they sent me to Camp

Blanding, Florida. I had infantry training. Well, that, as usual, in a way, you're kind of glad you were going. At that age, you really aren't afraid of anything, you know. It used to be kind of a drag, every day was a drag. You would learn about this, you would learn about that. And the next day, you got the same thing. And you really wanted to go; you wanted to go in combat, you wanted to do your duty.

Well, from there, after basic training, I believe I had 14 weeks of basic training. Of course, in the meantime, or just at the end of our training, the Germans broke through, the Battle of the Bulge, and we were headed for Fort Ord, to go to the Pacific. They re-routed us, and I went to Europe instead.

Well, we went overseas on the *Ile de France*. I never saw so many soldiers on one ship in my life. They said there was like 12,000 of us on that ship; it doesn't seem possible, but it was a big ship. We were stacked five high. And of course, landed in Greenock, Scotland, immediately hopped on a train, and we went down to Southampton, England, and got onto a small English ship, and went to France.

Le Havre Replacements

We landed in Le Havre, and they gave us a meal, and we walked immediately to a railroad station. Then we were put on the infamous 40 & 8s, you know what those are? Each car was marked in French, 'forty men or eight horses.' I mean, you were like mosquitoes in there, I'll tell you. And we ran up into Belgium a short ways, a two-way repo depot, replacement depot.

And here we are, we had carried all kinds of equipment over. When we got to the replacement depot, we were outside of a big, big building, it looked like some sort of a castle. We were told to put all of our stuff in piles, neat piles. Your gas mask, and any clothes you're not going to bring, and stuff like that. All you're allowed to take was what you could stuff in your pockets. That just meant socks, maybe a pair of underwear, and handkerchiefs, that's about it. Believe it or not, they burned some of the stuff. I never could believe what they did. The gas masks, that really bothered me. Just being a kid, you'd heard about being gassed in World War I. And I thought, gee, isn't this, might they be a necessity? So we went up on the front lines without a gas mask; thank God we didn't need them.

I was a replacement to the 79th Division, 314th Infantry. I believe it was just one over-nighter, we stayed in a building there. The next day, we went up on the front lines and got put into squads that were missing men. I happened to be in Company B, 324th Infantry. You met the guys in your squad, and not too many older people. They were all pretty young at that time. I think probably the oldest one in the squad was maybe 28 years old, something like that, my staff sergeant. We did have a first sergeant; he was a former coal miner. He was close to forty! There was a man that I still think about an awful lot, serious, serious. He was a good guy. When he expected you to do something, he didn't just send you. He went with you. We had this captain, Mack, who was our company commander. Same thing. He was always up front with you. Very nice. Very good soldiers. Very good soldiers.

We didn't have that good of equipment. In fact, when we could, when we took prisoners, we took some of their clothes. Gloves, especially. Sometimes a sweater or a jacket. They always wore the long coats, too, if you remember seeing Germans. The worst thing with us was, that was winter, February, our shoes were terrible. Terrible situation. We had those, well, even with the GI shoes, are the six-inch boot, and there's the little flat sole on the top. The leather was turned inside out. You've probably seen those, the rough outside. And there was no insulation whatsoever. They did issue us some snowpacks. You know, the rubber bottoms. Well those were good, as long as you were walking fine. You sweat in them. But at night when you're in the foxhole, man, did they get cold. One of the worst things, like I mentioned before, the gloves weren't that good. I think you still see some of these here, around, they were khaki, not patent leather, but an imitation leather on the front. You couldn't even fire a weapon or do anything with them. So most of the time, you didn't have anything. Or if you grabbed a prisoner, they had fine, leather gloves, with a woolen liner on the inside. So where they were going, they didn't need them. So we used to take them from them.

'That's What You Call a Short Round'

I must tell you a little story about my very first night in combat. The squad I went to was in a house, this was right on the front lines. There were open fields there, and they tell me there was a river not too far up, maybe a half mile, or maybe less, I don't know. The very first night, our staff sergeant, squad leader, said, 'You'll pull guard with me.' There were two of us, went up. And this other fellow pulled with another guy.

So our duty, our guard that night, was just on the outside of the house. There was a road, a dirt road, and we stood there for a while. All of a sudden, an artillery shell went overhead. It went and landed, now I know, behind us. It's funny how you get up there and you're disoriented, you don't know where, which direction you're going in or anything. And then pretty quick, another shell came the other way. So I asked Morgan what the situation was. And he said, 'That one that went that way, that's ours, artillery behind us. And the other one coming in was from the German side.' He called it harassing fire. You only get an artillery shell every once in a while, you know. Well it got so that you could hear the gun go off, and you could hear it whistle overhead, and you could hear it land. And I was kind of paying attention to that.

Then all of a sudden, there was one behind us. I'm listening for it to go overhead, and it didn't. It whined and it landed, probably, I don't know, maybe 100 yards from us. You know? And I said, 'Who fired that?'

He said, 'That's what you call a short round.'

I said, 'Well, you've got to watch out for the Krauts and your own people while you're out there.' Yeah. Oh golly.

*

I actually went on the front lines in February, I think it was the third of February, if I'm not mistaken. You know, you're kind of gung-ho. I think most guys are gung-ho going up there. But it doesn't take long that you realize, this is not John Wayne movies, you know. This is serious. You grow up an awful lot, while you're up there. I went up as a happy-go-lucky kid, and when I came out, I feel I was grown, you know what I mean? It's no fun. It's no fun. I do remember back in basic training, we used to go out on night patrols, compass patrols, find a certain spot, stuff like that. They had wire up for you, with bells on them. And you had to snip through it. Guys were all laughing and everything, it's a big joke, really, you know? I remember officers telling you, they used to chew us out.

'When you get over there', he called to them, 'Jerry doesn't fool around.' Meaning the Germans, you know. He was saying the right thing. It was truthful. I often wonder how some of the guys who weren't maybe as serious as I was, how they made out, wherever they went. So it's no joke. It's scary, when you're in combat; most of the guys, I found out, would do their job, and do the best they could.

Afterwards, hours later, and speaking only for myself, I used to, when things calmed down, I'd get the shakes. I've never felt like that before or after. It is a serious situation. If I had to do it over again, I would say, 'No.'

*

Let's see, so we went up through the Roer River. Well of course, the Germans were on the run. We were moving pretty fast, and the Germans were leaving; they knew your position. One of the worst things to me was when the artillery came in. They had some pretty good spotters somewhere. They'd come in and they would flood the area with artillery. There's hardly any running from artillery, so that's a scary situation. We had quite a few guys hit that way. At the same time, when we were chasing the Jerries running, they were sending up the Wehrmacht, which were the German professional soldiers. He was a good soldier. And the Hitler Youth, they remind me of the suicide bombers you have today. They didn't give a darn. They were crazy. They were. And you could fight them until you killed them all, really. And they very seldom would run. But some of them, 15 years old, 16 years old, even younger than that, probably.

Crossing the River

We got pulled back. We crossed; we came back to Holland. Exactly where we left from, I don't remember. But we came back into a small town in Holland, and we had a week of training there on the assault boats. This was in preparation for crossing the Rhine River. That was very interesting. They were like what today you'd call a, oh golly, what are they called? A jon boat, do you know what a jon boat is? It's just straight back and probably 15, 16 feet long. There was a bow, a squared-off bow in the front. They put two of them together, back-to-back, and they had what would you call them? The rings on the U-side, they'd back them together and you'd put a pin in there. So you had this boat that was double the length of one of them. The thing that surprised me was, you had an outboard motor on it, and there was a sailor. How he got over on the Rhine River, I don't know. But the Navy ran us across on these assault boats. Of course, the word was if the outboard didn't start, you start paddling. You know, it was a long way across that river. I think there was probably somewhere around 24 [of us in the boat] or something like that, you know. There again, we had thousands of guys going across. But some artillery did come in, and we had some casualties here and there, but not too bad.

On The Run

From there, we just went from little town to little town. Once in a while, you'd run across a company of men, or maybe even a battalion of Germans. But most of the time, it was just small groups. Like I said before, they were on the run.

We got almost surrounded, or cut off, one time. We jumped off at 4:00 in the morning. Again, I don't know what the name of this town was, but it was farm country. Well, there was a coal mine there, I remember that. And we stayed in a building at night, and early morning, probably 4:00 or so, we took off and went through the town, got off on the other side. It was foggier than heck. We climbed this hill; well this road kind of skirted the outside of that hill, on the outside edge, you know? We ran across a teller mine in the road. A teller mine is just a great big mine; it's an anti-tank mine. Someone saw it, and we had two TDs, tank destroyers, with us. They had stopped. The sun came through, and we got hit with everything the Germans had, everything, really. The only thing that saved us was that we were on the side of this hill, and they were in the woods. If the sun had come out a little bit later, or we didn't stop for those teller mines, if they'd have cut us off from behind, we'd have been annihilated. But hey, everything turned out okay, and they got on the run again, and we went after them. We had a few guys hit that day.

Most of that [fighting in Germany] was the same thing. Little towns, little skirmishes here and there, nothing too serious. We went all the way across, we went through Duesenberg and Dinslaken and other towns I don't remember. Essen. We ended up actually almost into Czechoslovakia at the end. Because a lot of the Germans that were on the run, they changed their clothes and just melded in with the civilians right there. Once in a while, you'd find some guy walking around, and we [would see] that their uniform, blue, it's called a bluish-green, it'd be sticking down below their short pants. You picked them up as a prisoner.

The war ended, and we went to Czechoslovakia; we were very close to Czechoslovakia. Took our training, jungle training, for the assault on Japan. We moved down to southern Germany in the mountains. Again, I don't know exactly where we were. But we had 21 days of jungle training; it rained for 15 of them. And it was just unbelievable, really. The training we got was a lot different than what we had had for Europe. Apparently, that came from experience they had over there from island hopping. One day, we were in tents, and a newspaper came out, the *Stars and Stripes*. I remember reading a little article that said that the United States had developed a fuel, I believe it said fuel, the size of a tennis ball, that would run a ship two and a half times around the world. I wish I had saved the article now. I said, 'Wow, that's a pretty good piece of fuel!' It wasn't long after that, they dropped the atomic bomb, and that was the beginning of that. Whew! We didn't have to go over there, because we had been told that we were going directly from Europe to the Pacific somewhere, no home, furlough, or anything like that. That was kind of a celebration when they dropped the first bomb. Then the second bomb, I said, 'Well, thank God for that.'

The Slave Laborers

I never really saw anything deep in the concentration camps. I saw, well, lesser camps, where some people were there. I remember the, I call them the pajamas, that they wore. They were striped uniforms, and they were all begging for food, and starved, really. When you could, you gave them something. But there was no organized thing to get these people repatriated, you know.

We came back into around near Dortmund, Germany. And we had a battalion, Hungarian, I remember, Polish, and Russian prisoners all together. We had two camps that we were trying to separate and get these people going back to their respective countries. I found that the Russians, you couldn't get too close to them, even the men, really. The Polish people were just kind of a happy-go-lucky people. They had been through quite a bit.

Now, there were some soldiers, but most had been brought back as slaves to work in the factories and things. We fed them, and every once in a while, they'd send out truckloads. I don't remember exactly where they were going, but we weren't involved with that. I felt very bad for those people, because they all seemed like very, very nice people. I remember the Poles very much, because we kept them in, okay, trying to keep them from going out, because they would go out and raid for food and other things.

The Farm Raid

This one camp that I was at, where I was on guard on the back fence. On the back fence it was a flat area, and the fence was down at the bottom of a hill, probably 60, 70 feet down that way. We'd tried to keep the people in the place. One afternoon I was there, and there were a couple of prisoners, or what do you call them, refugees, slaves, or whatever. They came up to me and they said, 'Hi.' And they would say it in German, 'Komrade.' One was asking me all about my M1, he wanted to know what it was all about, and he wanted to know if it was automatic, and he used the word 'automatisch.' I guess that's automatic.

Then they left, and then they came back before my tour of duty was up. They made me understand that they wanted to get out at night. I really didn't care, really. One of them, apparently, had worked for somebody not too far from the camp there. They wanted to know what time I came back on duty. I came on that night at 12:00, 12:00 till 2:00. I told them, as best I could, 12:00, could you be back before 2:00? God knows what they were going to do. But I got out there on the back fence, and in the dark, someone called me. They came up and I said, 'Okay.' Well, they all understood okay. Well, there weren't two of them, there were about eight or ten of them. They went down that hill and took off. It was probably 20 minutes to a half hour later, I could hear some shooting not too far from us.

Now, that stopped, and it's getting close. And it's like a quarter of 2:00. And I said, 'My God, they're going to come back and probably get shot by one of our own guys.' Pretty quick, I hear from down at the bottom of the hill, 'komrade, komrade.' 'Yeah, okay, okay.' Well, they came running up that hill, and they had the biggest pig you ever saw in your life. They had gone down to raid this family's farmyard, and they killed a pig and brought him in. You know, we never saw that pig or the remains of it or anything. They took it and they cooked it and they ate it! Then another night, we were all asked to go to some sort of a show that they had. These were the Polish people. They put on a little [stage] show, with the hand shadows and stuff like that. Somebody had told somebody there that I used to play the accordion. Well, before you know it, they had me up there on the stage and I'm playing the beer barrel polka, and the place isn't enough for us. Like I say, they impressed me as being just a happy-go-lucky people, really.

'They've Been Drinking with the Russians'

After that, well, I got sent to Nuremberg. Shortly after we sent most of these people back to their respective [former homelands], where they were going. I had them all separated, anyway. I can tell you another little story, too, while I was still there. We stayed in an airfield not too far from there. One night, I pulled guard at this little hospital, and there were German doctors and nurses there. I remember an elderly man coming to me, he was asking me for something in Russian. Apparently, he wanted a pill because, well, I didn't know what he was talking about. But I came on duty later that night, and they were bringing guys in that were sick. Throwing up, dead. Apparently, they had gotten into a high-octane gasoline at this airfield, and they were drinking it. Yeah. The next morning, we got pulled out and in formation, and there's Captain Mack again, he said, 'Has anybody here been drinking with the Russians?' Nobody responded. 'Anybody been drinking with the Russians? Take two steps forward.' Nobody moved. He said, 'Has anybody seen Ziggen or Dempsey?' No, no one had seen them.

He said, 'Well, they've been drinking with the Russians. Ziggen is blind and Dempsey is dead. Now is there anybody here that's been drinking with the Russians?' It was then that about a dozen guys stepped forward. They were drinking high-octane gasoline! Can you believe that? Geez. Terrible, terrible. I mean, these were things that kind of make you grow up, you know? I wasn't even nineteen yet.

Nuremberg

Well anyway, from there, I went to... they started the point system for guys to go home. Many of the older fellas, gosh, they had a hundred and some odd points, they'd been up from Africa all the way up. And they went and they disbanded the 79th Division, and the younger fellas like me were sent to the 1st Division, which was located in and around Nuremberg.

I got the duty of working with the Army engineers. They were photostatting copies of captured documents. And I ran a Photostat machine. That was a good duty. I worked the night shift, and I stayed right in Nuremberg, right by the Palace of Justice. I wished I had saved some of the copies of the things that the Germans did. I can tell you a couple of them.

The Documents

There was, well, these commandants of these slave labor camps, they had to be ruthless individuals. There was one paper we copied that said how they would take people out for a walk out of the camp, and they'd have a couple dozen of them, make them dig a big hole. Half of them would get in the hole, and they'd bury them up alive—the other half of the guys would bury their own friends alive. Another [document detailed] that the commandant of the camp said that they weren't shooting enough prisoners. So they had these people marched out to work, wherever they were going, and marched back in. If they came in without their hat on, they got shot. So of course, all these people would be very careful with their hats, and they'd march in. So the guards bringing them in would run up to them and take the guy's hat off and throw it out of line. Well, if you stepped out of line, you got shot, and if you got back at the camp [without the hat], you got shot. That's terrible, isn't it? These are the things that [the Germans documented themselves]; they apparently took pictures of these, wrote these up, and saved them. I don't know what they were going to do with them, but they were captured documents that they used in the trial.

Sergeant of the Guard

When that got done, when all the copies were made and the trial started, I went back with my company, and I pulled guard in the cell block. The cell block was sort of a center, like a star, and all these blocks went off this way [*gestures several radial corridors with hand*]. Well one of these blocks had the 21 bigwigs, Hermann Goering and Ribbentrop and Hess and all those guys. I pulled guard there for a little while. I was a staff sergeant at the time. I pulled guard on Albert Speer's cell, and Rudolf Hess. Then after that I was there for a short while. I became sergeant of the guard. I took my regular duties every other day for 24 hours. Luckily, I was asked to go up into the courtroom. I pulled guard with the courtroom guard at one of the visitor doors. After that, I was asked to go up onto the witness stand. That was very interesting, because from where we stood, we weren't too far from the interpreters. If they were speaking German, and you could pick out [the English translations], you know, so you could know what's going on, that was very, very interesting. Very interesting. I actually had, at that time, the latter part of the 21 original prisoners, like von Schirach, and Raeder, and Donitz, and Sauckel, right around that area there. It wasn't long, and I got pulled off of there, and they made me sergeant of the guard. I was moving up real fast. I stayed there until July of '46.

'Goering and I, We Didn't get Along'

I had a lot of contact [with these prisoners]. Goering, he was the highest-ranking German soldier there. He expected to be treated like he was a high-ranking officer. The rest of them, believe it or not, they used to bow down to him, let him go first and stuff like that. He and I didn't get along when I took over sergeant of the guard.

One of my duties was, during a recess, when I opened the door, I stood at parade rest right in the docket where he was right in the corner. I'm sure you've seen pictures of it. He would turn to me, and he asked me for some water. 'Vasser, bitte.' Okay. I go down to the Lyster bag, which was chlorinated, and I'd get him a little cup of water, and I'd bring it up to him. And he'd take a sip and he'd go, 'Bah, Americanich.' You know? He'd hand it back to me. Now there was no way of getting rid of the water; I used to have to walk down to the men's room on this side to get rid of the water and walk back up.

Mr. DiPalma later recalled that fed up with Goering's antics, he once met Goering's demands by replacing the contents of the cup with water from the toilet instead of the tap, which Goering found better than the chlorinated version. 'I guess I felt it was my little contribution to the war effort,' he added.

In the meantime, you know, I think he was just doing it on purpose, just getting rid of me. I think one of the things was that he didn't want to do any talking, didn't know if maybe I spoke German or stuff like that. I could understand a little bit. But what he didn't know is, we had some German-speaking GIs right there, and they picked up some stuff on him anyway.

Another time, at night when court was over, one of my duties as the sergeant of the guard was to run the elevator. The elevator was located behind a docket in one of the panels. The elevator carried six people: three prisoners, two guards, and myself, made it [one guard to one prisoner], going up or going down. Well at night, we had to get out of there and run and get our trucks to get back to our billet. Everybody would step back, and there's big confusion in the docket. [The Germans] let [Goering] go right through, you know. Well, one night, I grabbed ahold of Field Marshal Keitel, he was standing right there. I said, 'Come on, get in, get in.' And I dragged him in like that. He was indignant; he was going to let Goering get [in first]. I pulled somebody else in, and somebody else, and I left him, left Goering standing there, you know. I think that was one of the reasons why he would send me for water every day, he was getting back at me.

Another time everybody in the docket was stepping over one another, letting him get out first; they were going to lunch. He didn't want to cross the hallway where spectators were, he wanted to walk right across—he didn't want anybody to look at him. So this Captain Gilbert told us, 'Put him last.' Okay, so we put him last. Don't let him stand inside of the doorway. He would wait until everybody went by so he [would have to] walk straight across. Well, I pushed him out there one time, we carried a club, poked him in the back, you know. He turned around and he swung at me, and he hit me on the arm, so I gave him an awful belt in the kidneys. He never said a word to me [after that]. He didn't like me; I know he didn't like me. I had a couple confrontations with him, but other than Goering, the rest of them were all pretty good.

Albert Speer, many of them spoke English. I never heard Goering speak English. Albert Speer, he was Hitler's architect, if you remember correctly. I always felt sorry for him. He was the architect, but he kind of got, I think, using the right word here, sucked into being a Nazi, and he turned out to be a Nazi. Of course, this was all for glory, I guess, for himself. I think Hitler just used him. He was a very calm-speaking individual. Always spoke to the guards. He was quite an artist. He never did me, but some of the other guys that pulled guard on some of these cell blocks, on his cell, he used to draw pencil sketches of them, and they were good. Very, very good. Imagine something like that's worth a buck today. I don't have that.

Let's see, Streicher, he was a pain in the neck, complained all the time. Terrible, terrible. Going back just a little bit, when I pulled guard on the cell block, imagine standing there for an hour and watching the guy sleep through a little hole in the door, you know, it's awful monotonous. The guys used to talk to one another, and the other guys would get to laughing. Some of them [prisoners] didn't get much sleep at night. You kind of had to keep it down; when I was sergeant of the guard, sometimes you used to hear hollering down there, so I had to go down there and tell the guys to knock it off. Have you ever seen the old German pfennig? It's their penny. It's about as big as our half dollar. Well, one of the things they used to do at night, this wing had a terrazzo floor. These guys would roll these pennies down the terrazzo floor, and it sounded like a freight train coming down through there! [*Laughs*] I'm surprised that a lot of the German prisoners could stay awake in the courtroom the next day.

Another night, I was in the guard office, and I had a cot there, I was laying there. I could hear some screaming. I said, 'Oh my God!' I went down there and the guard at Streicher's door, out of monotony, had taken a piece of paper and folded it, and he had ripped a little man out of it, so that when you opened it up, it was a man with just legs and arms like that and the head. And from off his uniform somewhere, he had tied a piece of string [tied to the neck of the effigy]. You had the light on just outside of the cell, and he's swinging the thing in front of the light, and it's [silhouetting] on the wall, a man hanging. [*Chuckles*] Jeez. I really don't blame him for trying to get through the hours, standing there.

Rudolf Hess, I think he was sane. He was trying to act like he had a mental problem. When they wanted [fresh air], in their cell, they only had one window and it was high up. The ceilings were probably ten or twelve foot high, and there was a window, like you had in the old style of schools, with the hook on them. And there was just the awning type, but they open [that way]. There was a window stick that we used to use, and the sergeant of the guard was the only one who was allowed to handle the window stick, so when Hess called for a window [to be opened], he'd do this generally in the middle of the night sometimes, he'd call for the window stick. One night I went down there, and I went into the cell, opened the window, took the window stick, and waited outside. He used to stand in front of the window and look out, and he'd mumble something. It wasn't German, I think he was just faking, really.

Let's see, von Schirach, I pulled guard on the witness stand with him. He was head of the Hitler Youth. One day, there was quite a confrontation between him and Chief Justice Jackson. Of course, we could understand him. And he spoke decent English now, but most of his replies were in German. But through the interpreter, we could hear what was going on. They were arguing back and forth about the duties of the Hitler Youth. Well, they called a recess shortly after that, and he turned to me. I was on his left side. He turned to me, and he said, 'But the Hitler Youth is nothing more than your Boy Scouts.'

I said, 'Really?' He doesn't realize that I was a frontline soldier.

I said, 'I fought your Hitler Youth.' He never said a word [after that]. We found Hitler Youth that could take apart our BAR, our M1s, or any of our equipment. So they weren't Boy Scouts like he wanted to portray them.

I kind of felt sorry, though, for Admiral Donitz. I guess he was the bigwig as far as the Navy was concerned. One of the things they had him on was shooting prisoners. I guess, when his U-boats sunk a ship, these guys would go around getting rid of the ones that survived. Well, we never did that. But I do remember when I was on the front lines, and we were moving fast, we take no prisoners. I never had occasion to do anything about that. But that could've happened up in our area, too. Why would they get him on that, unless it was because he put out the order, maybe? I mean, I think the old story goes, all's fair in love and war, right? You break the other guy's leg so you cango see your girlfriend, right?

The rest of them were all just no problems, really. No problems. Alfred Jodl, he was a signer of the surrender terms. He didn't talk to anybody. Him and Keitel, they weren't Nazis, but they originally were Wehrmacht soldiers, and they were good soldiers. But of course, they turned into Nazis afterwards, you know?

*

I came home in July, yeah, about three months before the trial ended. [I was not present when Goering committed suicide]; I think [he died] the beginning of October, as I recall. Everybody was trying to get their autographs. In fact, I have their autographs. All but Hess. Every time you'd ask Hess for his autograph, he spoke good English, because he spent quite a bit of time in England, he said, 'after the trials.' Well, you know what our favorite saying was? 'You won't be here after the trials.'

The Return to Nuremberg

I was discharged at Fort Meade, Maryland. Yep, that was a happy day. I got a chance to go back to Germany two years ago. I went with my number three daughter, she writes children's books, and writes a few other little things, whatever she feels like doing. The day we got into Nuremberg proper, I wanted to go down to see the courthouse, if I could get there. It was raining, we got a cab and went down there. I was amazed at Nuremberg to start off with. When I was there, about one third of it was just demolished. But they've done a wonderful job of putting it together, they repaired the buildings. You could see where the stonework was a little bit different and stuff like that, and they saved an awful lot of it. I was surprised at the U-Bahn, the subway that they have there now. It is beautiful. It goes out of the city to the airport, and it goes all over the place. So we got to ride that over there. But getting back to the day that we went down to the courthouse, walked around the complex there. I told my daughter, I said, 'There's the gate that I used to go in every morning.' So we get down there, and the gate was open.

The building where the courtroom was, when we were there, you couldn't go [directly] into that building. You had to go into the main part of the palace, and then go upstairs, and come across. The courthouse, I mean, the courtroom was up on the third floor. But that door was open on the first floor. And there were people there. So I walked up and I grabbed this young fella and I said, 'Do you speak English?'

He said, 'A little bit.'

I said, 'Can we get up into the courtroom?'

'Well no, the last tour just went up.'

I said, 'Tour?'

'Yes, today's the first day that they started tours.'

I said, 'Well, I was a guard here during the trials.' Well, he went over and talked to this elderly gentleman, and the guy comes running over, and didn't speak a word of English. You know, he said to me and my daughter, 'Kommen, kommen!' And he ran us up these three stories, and we got into the courtroom. There was a guide, a tour guide, he was speaking in German. The fella went up and said something to him, and he continued with his speech. Then he said something about 'hauptmann.' The hauptmann is sort of a person that's a leader, or something like that. So there were maybe 18 people there, and they all turned and looked, and I said to my daughter, 'He must have told them that I was a guard here.' So anyway, when it got done, he said to me, 'Can you wait?' He spoke English also. He said, 'Can you wait till I show this film? I'd like to talk to you.'

I said, 'Okay.' Well, I have pictures of myself in the courtroom, but I've never seen myself on the film. And I saw it that day for the first time! Of course, it was all narrated in German. Anyway, after this got over with, this Wolfgang Meyer who was in charge of this thing, came to me and he asked all kinds of questions. So we were supposed to get out of there at 4:30, he kept me there till almost 6:00 asking questions.

*

I was sweating when I got done. A lot of the questions, I couldn't answer. But what they're doing now is they had set up a museum and they wanted as much information as possible, and they had different places that were on display. He said, 'We are opening up on November 4,' of, well, let's see, that'd be a year and a half ago. And he said, 'It'd be nice if you could be here at the opening.'

And I said, 'Well jeez, if I can, I'll try.' So my daughter, my wife, and myself, we bought tickets, and then September 11 came along, so we didn't go. Yeah. This thing that they call it, I have a pamphlet at home, it was called 'Fascination and Terror,' and they were trying to tell me how they were trying to show the good and the bad. I would've liked to have gone, but I think I'm going this year. I'd like to see that, yeah. It's nice that they, rather than be mad at Americans, would show that they probably were wrong, you know? Admit it and go on from here.

When I left the service, I worked for American Bosch. I used to hand lap the inside of an injection nozzle on a diesel, you know. That was an awful job. I never went back. I didn't know what to do.

Well my dad at that time was an inside crane operator. He worked an overhead crane. Of course, he was unionized. He said, 'Why don't you get into the union, and try and learn to run machines?' Stuff like that. I thought that was pretty good. So I did take an apprenticeship. I was an oiler on a crane, a helper. So I eventually got my license, and I was a crane operator, up until I retired.

*

I married in 1949, we had four daughters, and we have nine grandchildren. Like I said before, I was a happy-go-lucky kid when I went in. When I came out, I was grown up. We saw things that we don't see every day here in the States, or it wasn't totally like I was brought up. It makes me ... It made me, I should say, a little bit leery of everybody. You don't take people at face value. As a kid, anything an adult told me, that was it. But when I came back, I never trusted anybody. I think that's made me a better person. It tells you what the real world is, rather than a bowl of cherries, you know.

*

Leo DiPalma at the time of the interview, June 2002.

'I Think About Things Like That'

What's happening today, I think my experiences are nothing to what's going on now. I wouldn't want to be going in the service now, like our boys are doing. I hate to say this, but I have no qualms about any mistakes that we make now during the war. But I think even in that war, we didn't initiate it. It bothers me today when I read, well, we lose one guy or two guys or three guys. You know, we didn't start any of this here, so I don't feel bad when they have a problem. I do feel bad when a GI gets killed, even one.

I had a very good friend killed. When I went up, I was made a number two scout, number one scout, he had been up there a few months before me. In one little skirmish we had, he got killed. I never even saw him. That bothers me, it bothers me right now. He was one hell of a good kid. He was from Mississippi. That shouldn't be; he was married, and 21 years old, and had a child. He's gone. For what? It wasn't his fault. And there's many, many like that.

There were even, other than Clarkie, there are other guys that got killed. Older men with children, you know? Other than saying it's horrible, what else can you say? I met a guy from Boston, I remember him because when we came back to do this assault training, across the Rhine River, we were in the town of Applebee, Holland. I remember him going by, on his field jacket, he had a hub, a wheel, you know. And he had over it, 'Boston: the hub of the universe.' So hey, he's from Massachusetts, right? I'm from Massachusetts. So we got a little bit friendly and, well, he got hit with an artillery shell on that day that we crossed the Rhine River.

I think about things like that. You just can't forget it, really. It's not the way any of us in this country were ever brought up. I saw another guy die, same day, he had taken a piece of shrapnel in his leg up here, while we were in an artillery attack. Well, they had pinned us up against an elevated railroad. We managed to get back on the other side, but again, they had that position pinpointed for artillery. The German 88 was a very accurate artillery piece, and it was coming in, just clearing the railroad tracks, and getting us down below. I had gotten down into a brook, and I had dug into the brook, and dug on the bank. This other kid had actually got hit in the leg. And the medic went to him, and he said he was okay, put sulfur powder on him, bandaged the leg and covered him up for shock. He was dead in ten minutes, with just a wound in the leg.

We used to get training, of course, on shock, which I'm sure you've heard of. You believe it and you don't. As far as I'm concerned, one of President Roosevelt's sons said, I forget exactly how he put it. But [war is] an experience to go through [once], but never again. Words to that effect, I'm sure you've probably heard this. I hope it never, nobody ever has to go. I don't like war. It's too bad. But it seems like it's always necessary, isn't it?

PART FOUR

LAST THOUGHTS

Albert Tarbell later in life.

CHAPTER TWENTY-TWO

The Paratrooper V

It was time to wrap up the interview for the day, after almost three hours of non-stop testimony from a man who had an eyewitness view to some of the most important happenings of World War II in Europe, the first Mohawk paratrooper in the United States Army. He had some things to say about life after the war, and the therapeutic effects of opening up and sharing his wartime experiences.

Albert A. Tarbell

I was in Berlin until November. I think it was around November; I think I left there around November. I got orders to report to the trucking area the following morning, and a bunch of us were leaving for the States. So we had a party. We got two days' notice. They had a party for me at one of the German nightclubs. And oh, we were having a good time. At that time, that song came out, 'Sentimental Journey.' Oh, I had that band playing that over and over and over! And finally, the waiter came over, we had our own cognac with us. He said, 'There's a gentleman over there, an officer, and he'd like to join your party. He said you're having such a good time here.' It was a brigadier general from the Far East Command, on his way through, going back to the States, and he was going by the way of Berlin. He said, 'Is somebody going home?'

I said, 'Yes, sir.' I said, 'I'm going home.' Well, he sat down, and we had all kinds of drinks. Oh, we had a grand time there. Who would think a brigadier general would ask to join us regular soldiers, regular paratroopers? But he said, 'You're having such a grand time, I just had to come over and ask if I could join!'

Anyway, I ended up shipping out early in the morning, about 5:00. And who was there to meet us but General Gavin, to say goodbye to us. The last of the old guard was leaving the 82nd, coming back to the States. And he passed out Belgian fourragères to us, he handed us our Belgian fourragères.[39] He said, 'The rest of your awards will be in the mail,' and this and that. Yeah, so that was quite a send-off.

We got to Le Havre, and we got on the *SS America*, which was a luxury liner converted into the *USS West Point*, taken over by the Army in the service. And oh man, I had a couple thousand dollars in my billfold. Everybody had black market money, we had quite a bit of money. And whoa, they had some fierce card games there. I didn't even want to play [anymore], because I won over $1,000 in a poker game, American money. After that, I just didn't want to spend it, it looked so entirely different than your foreign currency you'd been getting all these years.

We had a hurricane in the middle of the Atlantic, and oh God, we were there for about two days in that storm. Oh, it seemed like a week, it seemed like a month; I thought it was never going to end. That ship would roll this way and that way and this way. One night, it rolled, and then it stopped, and then it rolled again. And all the barracks racks came falling down. I was sleeping in the grand

---

[39] *Fourragère*- award for distinguished military unit service, a braided cord worn on the left shoulder.

ballroom, right on down on the mezzanine floor, and oh, I thought we were going right over. Then it straightened back up. The ship would go right out of the water, come down, and the propellers would spin when they came out of the water. When it would hit, it would jerk! I mean, those sailors were working round the clock, those welders. And we said, 'How is this? Is this bad?'

'No, no, this is nothing!' And it seemed like the storm just died right down after that.

We finally made it back. We got back to Hampton Roads, where we left almost two years ago. And we came back to Fort Dix, and we were there just long enough for them to process us out. They wouldn't even let us keep our clothes, nothing, just a few things. I was lucky, I got through with three pistols. I had a permit for them. A sword, a couple knives, and a couple helmets; they took that. You know what I forgot to mention? That woman in the [house where we had the long R&R in France], when we were getting ready to leave there, they kissed us goodbye and shook hands. And here's this woman, come out in the other room, and she had my jacket for me. She had made a hood; she had lined the inside with fur from an old fur coat. Man, I was the envy of everyone for that! When we made that march, they thought I was a colonel or something! And she had it big enough it would fit over my helmet, it was all fur-lined—I wore that the rest of the winter, the rest of the war. I brought it back, I was going to keep it. Do you know, they took it away from me at Fort Dix? And then, they had the nerve to ask me to join the National Guard! I said, 'Well, I don't know.' I said, 'Let me think about it.' But then, I did think about it afterwards. But my wife wouldn't even let me join the Salvation Army after that, well, she was so glad to have me home. [*Laughter*]

*

I got home, I went back in the same trade that I was in, and I changed from there, I went into ironworking, [liked to be in the air]. My wife and I raised six kids and I kept working. I spent 34 years with the ironworkers, and I've been retired 18 years now.

I had a nice family. My son is a second-generation paratrooper. He's from Vietnam, and one of my daughters is an artist, so she had the Governor's Award, the first Mohawk woman to earn the Pataki Governor's Award.

*

I think [my service did change my life]. It brought me into my sphere in living; it gave me the knowledge of how to command men, too. At one time I had over 200 men and 14 foremen working for me. I think by being able to take orders and give orders and stuff like that, you know, you've got to give and take. That's one thing I learned. Our officers were some of the world's best. They ate with you. They lived with you. They fought for you.

The good thing about World War II was that we stayed as one group and the officers did not change every couple of months, like every six months you get a new batch of officers in. No, it was like this right from beginning to end, [our officers], they stayed with us. I think that made for better comradeship and I think for better soldiering, too.

'I Didn't Talk About the War'

For twenty-five years, I didn't talk about the war, just with one guy I served with. It was tough carrying that inside, I had some drinking bouts trying to drown it. That's why when my son Mike came home from Vietnam, I always got him on the side, to pump him for information, to get it out of him. The worst thing you can do is hold it inside; I had nobody to pump me for information, so I was always thinking about it. I could be driving home from work, look at the hills, and say, 'What a great place for fortification. They could have gun positions up there, and I could be ambushed, I'm wide open here.' For a long time, that kind of thing happened.

I could never sleep with my arms under the covers for many, many years—I think it had to do with that night we were counter-attacked in the Den Heuvel Woods, when I was in my sleeping bag. I had nightmares; my wife would have to wake me, then I would go back to sleep. I had nightmares right up until she died; they finally went away after someone told me to sleep on the side of the bed that she slept on. After that, I only had nightmares once or twice; to this day, I don't know why. Maybe it's because I worried so much about her, and what she went through, when I was in the service.[16]

'Tell the Children that I'm a Warrior'

In September 2006, Albert returned to Nijmegen to be greeted by the Dutch people who have not forgotten the men of 1944 and their heroic deeds. At the River Waal Crossing Commemoration, as one of the few surviving first wave veterans, he recited the Lord's Prayer in the native Mohawk tongue, bringing together the generations and the spirits of the men who had passed.

Later, he sent the schoolchildren of Nijmegen an Iroquois flag, and wrote to a Dutch friend to pass on some words to them:

> Through our laws as a guiding force, and through our heroes as an ideal, the Iroquois have persisted as a people. Heroes are important—they exist, and can help you to know who and what you are. They're like us of flesh and blood!
> Tell the children that I was a warrior.[17]

Albert Tarbell passed on August 25, 2009, at the age of 86.

The bodies of former prisoners are piled in the crematorium mortuary in the newly liberated Dachau concentration camp. Dachau, Germany, April 29, 1945. National Archives, public domain. USHMM.

CHAPTER TWENTY-THREE

Dachau and the Question

As I started this book, we passed the 76th anniversary of the liberation of Dachau.

Today, if the anniversary is brought up at all, many Americans might respond with a vacant stare. More might shrug and turn away. I suppose that is to be expected. But you know me. I just think that as a nation, sometimes we allow things to slip from memory at our peril.

It was real, and it happened. And as you have read, it was American GIs who overran this camp and many others in the closing days of World War II.

The men of the 42nd and 45th Infantry Divisions arrived independently of each other, here, in southern Germany, at Dachau, on this day. A concentration camp, they were told. Their noses gave them a hint of what they were about to uncover, miles before the camp appeared in sight.

Newspaper, April 30, 1945, that hung in my classroom for years.

Read the headlines, above. Note the sub-article:
> Boxcars of Dead at Dachau. 32,000 captives freed.

And so after some resistance, into the camp they entered. Life-changing events were about to unfold for the American soldiers.

For me, it's not about hero worship, or glorifying the liberator or any World War II soldier by placing him on a pedestal. Our time with them is now limited, mostly passed, but many of the liberating soldiers I knew pushed back at this, to the point of rejecting the term 'liberator'— 'It all sounds so exalted, so glamorous,' said one. But they will all accept the term 'eyewitness.'

Witnesses to the greatest crime in the history of the world.

So instead I think it is about honoring their experiences, their shock, the horror, the puking and the crying, the rage—and then, the American GIs recognizing that something had to be done. And they did suffer for it, for trying to do the right thing. Many tried to help by offering food to starving prisoners who just were not ready to handle it, only to see them drop dead. Or having to manhandle these emaciated victims who were tearing away at each other as food was being offered.

Some guys never got over it. How could you?

I have learned so much over the past few years from these guys, just through the way that they carried themselves and tried to cope with what they witnessed. In my World War II Studies and Holocaust class, we discuss these issues at length. I was so lucky to be able to teach it, to see our young people respond to learning and conserving and caring about the past. All I had to do was share my enthusiasm and expose them to the history.

Their history.

*

A few years back, I was privileged to teach a lesson to my high school seniors for NBC Learn, which was shared with other districts across the nation. Later, I stumbled upon this piece by the late author Tony Hays, who writes about his liberator father and his own encounter with the past.

Dachau Will Always Be with Us

Tony Hays

Dachau and the Question I had never been able to ask my father.

This is not so much an essay about writing as one about a writer's education, about one of those experiences that molds us, shapes us into storytellers. I read yesterday the story of Joseph C., whose father, a World War II veteran, left him with a special legacy from the war, from the hideous Nazi concentration camp at Dachau.

I feel a particular kinship with Mr. C.

My late father, Robert Hays, was the son of an alcoholic tenant farmer in rural west Tennessee. If the appellation 'dirt poor' fit anyone, it fit my grandfather's family. Daddy served in the Civilian Conservation Corps during the thirties. He and my mother, who was in the women's equivalent of the CCC, working as a nurse's aide at Western State Mental Hospital in Bolivar, Tennessee, met on a blind date in early 1940 and married in September of that year.

But just over a year later, Pearl Harbor happened. America was in the war. My father was among the first of those drafted in 1942. I won't bore you with the details, but he participated in the North African, Salerno, Anzio, and southern France invasions, saved by the luck of the draw from Normandy. But they slogged through France and on to Germany. On April 29, 1945, Allied troops liberated the Dachau concentration camp. I don't know whether he entered Dachau that day or the next, but that he was there within hours of the liberation is beyond dispute. A few months later, after more than three years overseas, he came home.

In later years, he would talk occasionally about the war, providing anecdotes that showed the chaos and random chance of battle. He spoke of driving through Kasserine Pass in North Africa just hours before the Germans killed thousands of Allied troops in a stunning attack. He spoke of a friend, defending his position from a foxhole, who was thought dead after an artillery shell landed right next to him. When the dust cleared, the friend was buried up to his neck in dirt but did not have a scratch on him. He spoke often of

Anzio, where he was wounded, and of the massive German air assaults on those soldiers clinging to that tiny sliver of beach along the Italian coast.

But he never spoke of Dachau.

Ever.

When he died in 1981, we found a photo in his wallet. An old sepia-toned shot like others he had taken during the war, pictures that he kept in an old brown bag. But this one was different.

It showed a pile of naked bodies. Well, really more skeletons than not, with their skin stretched pitifully over their bones. On the back, as had been his habit, was typed simply 'Dachau.'

I was confused. Why would he keep this one photo in his wallet all of those years? Especially a photo of a place and event that he never spoke about. It obviously had some deeper meaning for him than the other photographs. If it had been a shot of the building he was in when he was wounded (hit by an artillery shell), I could have seen that. A reminder of his closest brush with death. Yeah, I could buy that. But this macabre photo? That, I couldn't see.

So, for the next fifteen years, I remained puzzled.

Until the fall of 1996. I was working in Poland, and I had some time off. I took an overnight bus from Katowice, Poland, to Munich. It was an interesting trip all in itself. We sat in a line of buses at midnight on the Polish/German border, waiting for our turn to cross, next to a cemetery, as if in some Cold War spy movie. I remember passing Nuremberg and thinking that my father had been there at the end of the war. And then there was Munich.

I spent a day or two wandering through the streets, drinking beer in the Marienplatz. I'm a historical novelist, so the short trip out to Dachau was a no-brainer. Of course it was as much my father's connection with it as anything else that spurred the visit. But I'm not sure that I was completely aware of that at the time.

Dachau literally sits just on the outskirts of the Munich metropolitan area. I looked at the sign on the train station with a sadness, wondering for how many people that had been one of the last things they saw. It was only later that I discovered there had been another depot for those passengers.

The Dachau Memorial is a place of deep emotion. In the camp proper, mostly all that are left are the foundations of the barracks. One has been reconstructed to give an idea of how horrible life must have been. The camp was originally intended to hold 6,000 inmates; when the Allies liberated Dachau in 1945, they found 30,000. The museum and exhibits are primarily in the old maintenance building. I looked with awe at life-size photos of prisoners machine-gunned, their hands torn to ribbons from the barbed wire they had tried to climb in a futile attempt at escape.

I followed the visitors—I can't call them tourists—north to where you crossed over into the crematorium area. It was there that the full brunt of what had taken place at Dachau really hit me. A simple brick complex, it seemed so peaceful on the fall day that I stood before it. But as I read the plaques and consulted my guidebook, as I stepped through the door and actually saw the 'shower' rooms where the prisoners were gassed, as I stared into the open doors of the ovens, I felt a rage unlike any I had ever known consume me.

*

That night, I went to the famous Hofbräuhaus in Munich, to wash the images of the ovens away with some beer. I hadn't been there long when an elderly American couple sat at the table. They were from Florida, a pleasant couple. He had been a young lieutenant in the American army on the push into Munich. In fact, it had been his pleasure to liberate the Hofbräuhaus from the Germans.

Of course, I asked the question. 'Were you at Dachau?'

He didn't answer for several seconds, tears glistening in the corners of his eyes as his wife's hand covered his and squeezed. Finally, he nodded, reached into a back pocket and pulled out his wallet.

With a flick of his wrist, a photo—just as wrinkled, just as bent, as the one my father had carried—landed on the table. It wasn't the same scene, but one just like it.

Here was my chance, the opportunity to ask the question I had never been able to ask my father. I pulled the photo from my own wallet and laid it next to his.

'Why? Why have you carried it so long? To remind you of the horror of Dachau, of what had been done here?'

His face carried the faintest of smiles as he shook his head.

'No, son, to remind us of the horrors that we are capable of, to remind us not to go down that road again.'

The difference was subtle, but in that moment, I learned two lessons invaluable to a writer, subtle differences are important, and when you want to know the truth, go to the source.

As I sit here now and look at that same photograph, I realize that it was my father's legacy to me, of Dachau. Joe C.'s father left him something more tangible, a reminder of the same thing for the same reason, but more forcefully stated—a tiny box of human ash from the ovens.

Dachau is still with us, and I hope the legacy left by our fathers always will be.[18]

In a subsequent communication, Tony added, 'I left out another man, actually the one that the American couple came to see. They had wanted to meet someone who might have been in the German army and had been told that a fellow came in every night and sat at the table where I was sitting. Eventually, he did, a wrinkled old guy who spoke little to no

English. I knew some German, and so I translated as best I could. His name was Tony too, and he had been a teenager in the last days. He had been conscripted near the end of the war and had been taken prisoner by the Americans. He had been assigned to help clean up the hundreds of dead bodies at Dachau.

He cried as he told the story.'

The journalist and writer Tony Hays passed away in 2015.

Richard Marowitz, Al Cohen, Doug Vink
with captured souvenir,
Hudson Falls High School library, April 2000.

Richard Marowitz and Al Cohen talk to students
and display their artifacts.
Hudson Falls, NY High School, April 2001.

CHAPTER TWENTY-FOUR

War Stories

These stories were recorded around the library table after school, following the formal interview session, with just a small group of students and adults present, on April 28, 2000, just one day shy of fifty-five years to the day that the gates of Dachau were thrown open. Like with the bomber boys in Volume 3, being able to sit around a table and listen to them converse—good friends, unhindered and unscripted—was the thrill of a lifetime for all who were present. In closing, we ask you, the reader, to join us at the table one last time.

Somewhere in Germany, 1945

Richard Marowitz
Douglas Vink
Alvin Cohen

Rich Marowitz: The door slowly opened. There was a father, a mother, and a daughter, and they all had buckteeth. [*Laughter*]

That's not funny yet. I looked down at their little dog, and it had buckteeth! And that cracked me up. So the guys looked at me and they said, 'What the hell's the matter with you?' It's just funny. So we got them out of the way. And there's this big door in the floor that you picked up, and we picked it up and hollered downstairs, you know, in the basement. And we said to the folks, 'Is anyone down there?' And they were going like this [*makes hand motions*]. They were afraid to say so, but we knew there was someone down there, so one of the guys threw a grenade down there. And of what was left, twenty-five came out, we took them prisoner.

Now in scouting around the area, which was under sniper fire all the time, we pull in three SS troops. And the farms in Germany at the time, in the back yard they had this big square pit. This is where they put all the manure and they wet it down. It's not a healthy sight...

Doug Vink: It's not real appetizing. [*Laughter*]

Rich Marowitz: ...And they wet it down and there's always a lot of flies around. There must be some system underneath where they wet it down because all this drains into a tank. And they have a tank on the back end of the wagon, and they roll it out and they can actually spray the fields and fertilize them. So we stood these SS guys in that stuff, and we said, 'When you're ready to talk, we'll talk to you.' In the meantime the Germans were still sniping at us; we kept running back and forth in front of them because they were right in the alley where the sniper fire was coming from. We figured maybe they will hit their own guys, but it didn't work. [*Laughs*]

There was a house next to us where there was some sniper on the second floor who was just raising hell with us. And finally, we got him. We didn't know who the hell it was, but we got him. And we went up and took a look, we get into the house and went up to the second floor and this kid couldn't have been more than twelve years old! And the Hitler Youth wore, you know, short pants. One of the guys, he had little kids—eleven, twelve years old—in German uniforms. And we captured a couple of them one day. One of the guys in my platoon spanked the hell out of him and told him 'Now go home.'

I said to him, 'You idiot, he could turn around and shoot you.' But that was the colonel, he was just one hell of a guy.

Doug Vink: We were on the move once and hit the fire with the big guns. The tank gun got so hot that when our loader threw a shell in it, it only went halfway and swelled up. We're out there with a big stick, they had a long stick with a comb on it, you kept trying to pound it out. Anyway, they told us to stop right where we were to stay there. It was just outside a little German town. It was Easter Sunday. Here comes the townspeople with colored eggs and getting something for us to eat. And one's saying to me, 'There's [German soldiers] in the cellar.' So three of us get out and we go up, and we got the three of them. As we're bringing them back, I get back to the tank and I'm up in the turret and I watch and there's three more of them running across the field. Now I'm a first-class machine gunner; I have citations for being a first-class machine gunner. I couldn't hit one of them in the behind going across that field. They all got away.

One of these kids was a fifteen-year-old sergeant, fifteen years old! One was sixteen years old, and the other one was in his twenties. So there we are, a tank crew, broken down, and we can't do anything. And we got those three prisoners sitting there. Now the fifteen-year-old sergeant was the toughest guy you ever wanted to meet. Every time one of those other two tried to talk to us, he'd say something, and they'd stop. So the commander said to me, 'What the hell are we going to do with them?' It's been three days now we got them.

And I said, 'Nobody will take them!' I said that because nobody's coming up. We're waiting for the tank retriever to come to pick us up. So all of a sudden, here comes an American ambulance down the road coming out right from where the battle was. I get out in the middle and I stop them. I said, 'We've got three German prisoners here and we can't hold them because they're in the way.' Well, he said, 'Are they wounded?'

I said, 'Does it make a difference?'

'Oh, yeah, we only take wounded.'

I said, 'Give me a minute.' I went up and got my submachine gun. I hit the sergeant in the head. I said, 'Is he bleeding enough?'

'Yeah, bring him down.' And there he went. Well, we gave the kid a vacation. [*Laughter*]

Rich Marowitz: I'll tell you what, I had a bad experience. We had a captain from Louisiana that took great pride in the fact that he could speak fluent French. As a result, he spoke French to everyone—Germans, Hungarians, it didn't make a difference. He just wanted to try out his French. So he came with us one time. He was assigned there, and like I said before, the girls had the little white dresses. We got into this little village in the square and the church is always in the square. And this little girl in a little white dress, he goes over to her, and he starts talking. 'This is Alsace-Lorraine,' he said, he starts talking in French, and I could tell by looking at her she wasn't quite getting what he was saying, and she started to cry like hell. Now, in Alsace-Lorraine they speak this weird combination of German and French. Now Yiddish is a lot like German, that particular kind of German, and with a little bit of high school French, because I was still only eighteen at the time, I could make out what these people in this area were saying. So I turned around to one of my men. I said, 'That girl is going to call everyone out of church.'

He said, 'What are you talking about?'

I said, 'That kid doesn't understand what that idiot jerky captain is talking about.'

So he said, 'Are you sure?'

'Yes, I'm serious!'

Sure enough, the doors open up. It is Sunday morning, and everybody is coming out crying! They thought they were going to be shot! So someone said to me, 'Marowitz, go tell them to get back in church.' And the captain backed us up. You don't do that. There's no reason for it. War is war, but are you willing to pick on the kids and their mothers and old women?

Doug Vink: As Richard said before, you always find something funny. You had to...

This happened to us while we were in England. We were in a replacement depot waiting to be shipped over to go out where the guys got killed when they came on the beach at Normandy. And we were called as replacements, but you never sat still, even though you were in England. You figured 'oh well, I'll be going over there, let me take it easy.' No! We went on a road hike every day. Now this was the tank corps, and we still went on a hike. First, they give you infantry training before you ever become a tank man because once you lose a tank, you're definitely an infantryman. Nobody wants to lose a tank. But anyway, we were in England. So then they would take you for extra training on the tank, to make sure you're all up to date. Well, once you get to France, first thing they tell you is, 'Throw that damn book out the window! When you studied all this, forget about it—we don't do that!' You take all the tools off the tank, you buried them because you didn't want to be taking up tracks, you know, and be digging yourself out.

The funniest thing that happened to us in England, I don't know if anyone is familiar with the streets, streets are very narrow. Of course, they drive on the wrong side, but we're idiots. We don't know. We drove down the middle of the road. We got a tank—nobody is going to stop us! But then you come down to a dead end, and you got to go left or right, and there's all these little houses. We come down the hill one day, I said to the tank commander, 'I hope the driver knows we have to take a right.' Oh yeah, he knows!

Forgot to turn! Right across the street, right into the house, the gun sticking over the dining room table. And the commander yells to the girl at the table, 'Would you please pass the butter!' [*Laughter*]

Rich Marowitz: We were—one day, and I don't know what the river was. It was narrow, a canal or something, and there was this barge. Well, our job is to find out what the hell is going on. So we went out and checked on the barge. And there was this huge crate. Maybe its airplane motors or something like that, we cracked open one case. Champagne! We guessed maybe there were fifty bottles of champagne, so we cracked open another crate, and guesstimated that there was another fifty bottles of champagne. We got seven jeeps and we got seven cases of champagne, and we were heading back to headquarters because we were going to go reserve for two weeks. So we loaded up and we were sitting on top of the crate while we're going back, and we get back to headquarters and we immediately crack open a case. And we're preceding to get blind, and someone runs in from regimental headquarters and said, 'There's a town about 10 miles up, we don't know whether it's ours or theirs. Go find out!' So we were 28 drunken I&R men, and we're heading up there. Now to this day when we get together the standard topic of conversation is 'How long does it take for an I&R man to get out of a jeep?'[*Laughs*]

It's never been answered because you don't wait for the jeep to stop! If something fires, you roll out! The jeep is still going. It doesn't make any difference. The helmet goes one way, you go another. But you never drop your weapon, right? And nobody asked about the driver. How the hell does he do it? The old jeeps used a choke. He was driving with a choke, that was his gas pedal. And he had a scabbard on his side of the jeep with his rifle in it, and what he did was, he would hit the break, use his foot to hit the break; the right foot to hit the break, pushed the throttle in, and peel out and grab his rifle on his way and roll out! And the jeep found a place to stop, so, actually no one ever got hurt. You have to understand combat when you're on a jeep, you never use a windshield. That's always laying down and covered with canvas. Windows folded down because you didn't want to get hit with glass and you don't want to have reflections, either.

So this is what happens, now we got fired on, and we bailed out on the way, just outside this village. And we're looking up there, and nobody is firing, and I look over. I said, 'These guys look confused!' They look more confused than we were! They were all American tanks, so they stopped shooting. Then, they were checking us over more thoroughly, and one guy had eyeglasses and they finally realized we were Americans. And so they got up, and they had machine guns, they had machine guns outside of the tanks. And they said, 'We almost destroyed you! What the hell is the matter with you guys?'

I said, 'We're drunk.' We got back in the jeeps and went back. 'The Americans are here!' [*Laughter*]

Al Cohen: We were fighting in one town, and we had half the town taken. Still fighting from door to door and the rest of the town, and lo and behold, they found a still. And a lot of these guys are from Missouri, and they're moonshiners, so they drop their rifles and packs, and they're starting the still back up again. They had one hell of a time! [*Laughter*]

Doug Vink: Well I had a job one time, when I told you about when we were stopped outside Berlin to let the Russians take it. Well, after they took over Berlin, they moved us back all the way from Berlin to Frankfurt, and they built their puptents and they stayed there for a few months until the Russians got organized enough to come. So they gave all that land back to the Russians that we had captured, the Russians got all of that. So anyway, we were in this town. Down in the town was a winemaker. So the first sergeant said to me, 'I'm gonna give you some guards, and you're gonna live at the house with the winemaker.'

He said, 'It's your job to make sure that no civilian gets more than one quart a week.' It was being rationed to the civilians, but every morning I had a jeep full to take up to the camp. So that was great, we had the best of everything there. Those were the days that you remembered, when you were having a good time.

Rich Marowitz: After the war was over, they sent us to occupy Vienna. It was an international city, and I'll explain that in a minute. They issued a Vienna pass, it was written in French, Russian, English, and something else. I don't know. Anyway, and the town was split into four. And the smart thing to do was never to go to the Russian sector because you never knew if you were going to come back. They had a lot of these Mongolian characters there. Pockmarked faces and nasty looking, and you could smell them a mile away. And every once in a while you would find one in the back of the American Red Cross. They wandered over to where they weren't supposed to be. And I get a letter from my mother from where she used to go to her favorite candy store on Utica Avenue in Brooklyn; that's where we lived temporarily for a while. The owner had a daughter in Vienna who had married a German, and he had apparently protected her all this time. And she said that the wife wants to know that if she sends you a package, could you get it to her daughter, and she would enclose the address.

So I didn't really know what the hell to say and I really didn't get a chance because all of a sudden, the package showed up with the address, and I said to one of my buddies, 'Let's take a shot, we'll go over to the Russian sector.'

So we got over there. We got chased a few times. It was kind of dark by the time we found the apartment. There were no lights in the hallway. We counted the doors and felt for the number.

It was a small apartment setup. I knocked on the door and I heard this heavy German voice. 'Who's there?' And I tried to explain who it was. So then all of a sudden, the door crept open, and the first thing I saw was a gun. He saw an American soldier, and he said, 'Come on in.' And [the German husband's wife] was hiding in the bedroom. And then we sat down. Turns out, she was Jewish, and the man has protected her all this time from Germans, and Russians, and everything else. And we gave him the package and everything, and he said, 'How are you going to get back to your sector?'

I said, 'I haven't the slightest idea, but while it's dark we're getting the hell out of here!'

We took off and we got chased again and we got fired on, but it didn't seem as bad because it was dark. By this time we were so tired, I couldn't keep my eyes open. We found this little place like a little bed and breakfast, only she wasn't serving breakfast, but the place was spotlessly clean. And in Germany they had these big beds; when you got into bed, you disappeared, totally disappeared.

She said, 'I will let you stay here tonight, but you have to take your shoes off in bed!'

I said, 'I'll guarantee you we'll take our shoes off in bed!' So she let us stay the night, and we paid her. And we slept for just a couple of hours, and we got up and we got out and we got chased again, shot at again, and I immediately wrote to my mother, and I said, 'I am not taking anything more to her daughter! Just make sure...remember that! Don't make any promises!' And that was the last time I went back in there. The Russians would shoot at anything. They don't want you over there!

Doug Vink: They weren't allies to us!

Rich Marowitz: Russians are Russians; Russians are strictly for Russians, period. If you wanted to trust a Russian, that was your problem! Let me tell you something else. These guys will verify it because I guarantee you, they heard the same thing! Every time you captured Germans, what did they say? 'We'll help you fight the Russians!'

Doug Vink: That's right. They were ready at the end of the war—they said to Patton, 'We'll take our armies and join you and we'll go against Russia.'

Rich Marowitz: I mean you cannot believe how the Russians were hated by the Germans over there.

Al Cohen: Well, they wanted to hang Patton because he said we ought to keep going through Russia.

Richard Marowitz [*to students*]: You have no idea. When some people said they were going to deal with Russians… You don't deal with Russians! You think you're dealing with Russians, but you don't. They're going to do whatever the hell they want to do, whatever you say! You think you're dealing, but you're never dealing.

Doug Vink: Your division headquarters would get orders every day, and then they would filter back down the regimental command all the way to the battalion, down the company. You'd get a map. You'd get a map that you were supposed to do that much work that day. Well, with General Patton, maps didn't mean nothing. We'd be nine days off the maps! Gone! They wouldn't know where you were. But that's the way he was, but that's the way he accomplished some things.

He was up in the oil fields when they pulled him out. We were up there, right near Berlin, and we were told to stop. We could have been in Berlin about two weeks before the Russians arrived. Nope, they made that agreement at that Yalta Conference there. [Roosevelt] gave the place away.

But anyway, speaking about the Russians, they came into this town of Raunheim and they took over for months. They came in, and they had ragbags on their feet for boots. They were the most raggedy-looking things you want to look at! They had all of our equipment and our breech blocks, which is, your blocker slides back and forth to hold your big gun. Ours was always kept clean; we had every cleaning cloth. They were always kept polished, highly polished with oil. But the Russians had painted theirs green, just like the guns. I don't know how they fired! But anyway, my buddy—I had a buddy that I went through the whole war with then—I lost track of him for 35 years, but I found him last April. We've been back together. I said, 'You got any Mickey Mouse watches?'

'Yeah, well, I got a couple.'

I said, 'Well, I've got three.' The Russians are crazy over anything like that. Mickey/Minnie Mouse watch, anything.

I said, 'We're going to be leaving tomorrow and we're told to burn everything before we go. After the fire starts in all of the tents, I said, 'I got a guy down there who wants to buy the watches.' I said, 'But when I tell you to jump in that jeep and go—you jump in that jeep and go!'

He said, 'Why?'

And I said, 'You'll find out!' We went down and sold four watches for $150 each to the Russians. So I said to him now, 'Get the engine running!'

'Why?'

'Because this one here is a special one!' I wound it up.

The Russian said, 'Yes.' Gave me $150.

'Let's get out of here!'

My buddy said, 'What was so special about it?'

I said, 'It only runs five minutes!' [*Laughter*]

Al Cohen: When I first got to war trials and I was walking the prison wall, just like you see in any prison. A brick wall. And I'm walking along, and you carry the Tommy gun, and the standard operating procedure for that was, if anybody looks out of the courthouse into the exercise yard when the prisoners are in there, wave them off. Give them two waves. If they don't go, you can open up, and boy, everyone was waiting for us to open up. But the point is, down below on the ground floor where you could look through the barred windows, you saw cases of what looked like bottles of water. And every morning they would back up a two-and-one-half-ton truck, and you know how big they are, and they would unload vodka. By the end of the week that pile in that room was down to one or two cases. This went on, week after week. The Russians—they drank that like water!

Doug Vink: What I wanted really to tell you about, when I talk about the town of Raunheim, was that I was in charge of the wine cellar. At that time, we weren't allowed to fraternize with the people. We could get court-martialed for talking to them. Of course, guys like us were too stupid to realize that, so we talked to them. We were right in town with them. So anyway, one dark morning I got up, I was changing the guard. And I said to the fella, 'What's those voices up the street?'

He said, 'I don't know. The door just opened up there,' he said. 'Some people came out. They're not supposed to be on the street. There's a curfew.'

So I jump in the jeep. I said, 'You walk down the street and I'll go down the block and I'll stop on the other block.' So all of a sudden, the voices are coming, the voices are coming up fast. They get up close to me and I flash the flashlight on, and I said, 'Halt, who goes there?'

The voice booms out, 'It's all right. It's the colonel.'

I said 'Who?'

He said, 'The colonel, your battalion commander!'

I said, 'I'm sorry, sir. I'm gonna have to take you in.'

'For what?'

I said, 'Your order. Don't fraternize!' [*Laughter*] The next morning, that order was right out the window. From now on you can talk to anybody you want to talk to. We couldn't do it, but they could.

Adult Listener: You were in tanks and there have been all sorts of things after the war about how our tanks weren't very well protected. Did you know that?

Doug Vink: In them days? Oh, we knew it. We knew for the simple reason that when we first got over there and got the tanks, the most armor we had was six inches in the front and another eight around the gun. But that moved up and down, so if the Germans had their gun up, they could shoot under there, if they were good enough. They had four on the side. You had one on the bottom and two in the back, but then where the assistant driver was there was a big rack of .75 ammunition there. Now, that wasn't much there. Next to the gunner and next to the loader were other racks, and under the floor were racks. We only had one each under there. So then they came around and welded plates on the side just where the racks were, about where you were sitting in the tank.

Rich Marowitz: On the other hand, the Germans had a thing called the Tiger tank, the King Tiger. And that was scary even to look at. When we saw these tracks this wide [*makes marks with hands about three feet wide*], we got in the jeep, turned around, and went back the other way. There was nothing you could do. It was like throwing confetti at the Empire State Building.

Doug Vink: That was an eight-man tank! They'll light up anything! They'd light right up! They would light up brighter than anything. The King Tiger had five men in the turret. That was an eight-man tank! The only way you got them was to blow the bridges out behind them and call in the Air Force.

Rich Marowitz: If you ever go to Louisville, Kentucky, Fort Knox is just outside of Louisville. Right next to Fort Knox is Patton's Armor Museum. If you want to get scared to death, go to that museum. When we went into that museum, we went around the bend and we ran into this King Tiger tank. And it scared us then and there. One side was cut away and they had plastic over it so you could see in. There was a table of four guys playing poker in there, wasn't it? [*Looking at Vink*] I mean this was a monster, a total monster. Big 88 sticking out of it.

Doug Vink: We came up on one after the Air Force knocked it out. That was coming out of Bastogne. The Air Force had hit it. The piece of the gun laying on the ground was 22 feet long, and the piece sticking out of the torque was ten feet. That's not counting what was inside the torque. Just looking at them things...

Listener: They said one of the ways we were lucky is that most of them were on the eastern front.

Doug Vink: Most of them were. There weren't too many over here.

Rich Marowitz: There was enough for me, I'll tell you that right now.

Al Cohen: We went into a little town just outside of Frankfurt, which was supposed to have been taken. Well, you don't use heavy weapons, you find a tank group to go into a town to find out if there are Germans in there. You send him in [*points at Vink, the tanker*]. So anyway, we get into this town. It's supposed to have been taken. Can't find a GI, and people are hanging out white sheets, getting ready to give up. And to make a long story short, we hear tanks running around. So one of the fellas in our squad goes down the street and it turns down into another one, and we hear a tank down there. And they used to have sandboxes on the street in case of a fire to put the fire out. So he gets back. 'What happened? Where's our tanks?'

He said, 'Tanks, hell, that's Tigers!' We didn't realize they were King Tigers when we heard them. He said, 'I had to hide in one of those sandboxes for twenty minutes until they moved away!'

Rich Marowitz: The Germans really had this thing. When our guys went across the mountains, through the Siegfried Line, the call came up for muleskinners. Where they got all these stupid-looking animals I don't know, but they got them to carry stuff up the mountains. And jeeps had a hard time getting up. We got a bunch of weasels out. A weasel is a jeep with the half-tracks, treads. The Germans figured that the Americans wouldn't go over the top. You got to be stupid to go over the top, because it's so rugged. Well, they don't know how stupid the Americans are, so they brought their men down the sides, and we went over the top. [*Laughter*] Fortunately, all of their pillboxes were not manned. I say fortunately because the Siegfried Line was built many years before we got there. And you couldn't tell a pillbox when you were standing in front of it, because trees were growing out of it, everything was growing out of it. And if you were lucky, you spotted the little tiny windows that they looked out of and were shooting out of. We got round behind one. Got in it, it was unmanned. Prior to that, we were in this field in front of it where they wanted a clear view of fire, a 'field of fire,' so they cut down all the trees, and all that was left were stumps. So, you know, we were dodging behind the stumps, running around. And then we got in behind, and we walked in and I took one look into the abandoned pillbox, and I broke into a cold sweat. They had two machine guns set up; they were set up so that they could move them in either direction, by the numbers. By each machine gun was a framed picture with every stump in the clearing, and every stump had a number. And if they took the machine gun and went by that number, you were dead on that stump, if you were behind that stump or even near it, you were dead. So this was insane—it's a good thing, these Germans were... I don't know how we won the war. To tell you the truth, I don't know how we did it. We were just very lucky, and fortunately they ran out of stuff. They had better weapons and everything else.

Doug Vink: One other thing about our tanks. They had a top speed of 35 miles per hour—downhill! [*Laughter*] Downhill. I look at one of them today and wonder how the hell we ever got home in one of those things. Lost a lot of men, too.

Listener: Did you ever really get a good night's sleep?

Rich Marowitz: I don't remember. No one ever asked me before.

Doug Vink: No, once in a while you might have the chance to be in a house with no roof.

Al Cohen: One thing I wanted to mention before...If you watch *M.A.S.H.* on TV, the operating rooms weren't like that. Believe me. I lay on one table while they were working on me. The nurse next to me, she's humming and singing and she's putting a plaster cast on me and that's as close as I ever came to that.

Rich Marowitz: I was in the hospital for a while after the war. And those second lieutenant nurses were the cutest things I ever saw, they were just so cute. And talk about drugs. The lieutenant from headquarters brought me a great radio, and I was listening to music from the United States. Great bands and everything, and it pulled in everything. It was a great radio. And there was a guy a couple of beds up from me. A real jazz nut, and he said, 'Can I listen to it?'

And I said, 'Yeah, move into the next bed if you want.' He got discharged you know, and he came back a couple of days later with a big paper bag, and in the bag was a jar. He said, 'This is for you.'

I said, 'What is it?'

He said, 'Well, open it up!' So I open it up and I took out the jar and took one look at it, and this was one jar full of marijuana ready to be rolled! So I said to him, 'What are you, some kind of maniac?' I put it back, and it scared the hell out of me. I said, 'Get the hell out. I'm surrounded by officers here—I appreciate it, pal, but don't ever come back here with that crap again!' I was close to coming home. I didn't want to mess with that.

It was nearly five o'clock; our gathering was supposed to end at 2:30. As they packed up their gear, Richard summed up the day for the high school students.

"Now look at what you've learned today. You'll never find it in a book anyplace."

B-17 commander Earl M. Morrow, World War II Memorial, Washington, D.C., June 2016. Photo: Jessica Morrow Brand.

EPILOGUE

Americans Came To Liberate

Inscription at the World War II Memorial

"OUR DEBT TO THE HEROIC MEN AND VALIANT WOMEN IN THE SERVICE OF OUR COUNTRY CAN NEVER BE REPAID. THEY HAVE EARNED OUR UNDYING GRATITUDE. AMERICA WILL NEVER FORGET THEIR SACRIFICES."

PRESIDENT HARRY S TRUMAN
Address Broadcast to the Armed Forces, April 17, 1945

I left the early morning comfort of my hotel bed before I began my busy day in order to have some quiet time by myself. I settled into my walk in our nation's capital towards the Washington Monument.

I had been here only once before, in the sixth grade on a summer trip with my mother and her friend. We went up to the top and gazed down upon Washington, D.C. and the environs. A military helicopter went over, descending, and landed on the White House lawn. President Nixon was returning from a trip to Florida to visit his friend, Bebe Rebozo, I later learned. It was a thrill for a thirteen-year-old.

Fast-forward thirty-five years. I was in the middle of the first year of an all-expenses-paid study seminar, this first segment in the summer of 2008 a week-long introduction to becoming a 'Teacher Fellow' at the United States Holocaust Memorial Museum. That January I was asked to apply for this exclusive teacher program when staff learned of my work with American liberators and Holocaust survivors. I submitted multiple pages of documentation, including references from soldiers, survivors, administrators, and other teachers. That April, the principal called me down to the office for a chat. Now no one, including teachers, likes to be called to the principal's office. But he came around his desk with his hand out, and told me, 'Congratulations, I just got a call from the Holocaust Museum in Washington. You're going there in July!'

It would be the most intense study of my career to that date.[40] From early morning to late at night after dinner together, thirteen other teachers from across the nation and I were tasked with lectures from world-class Holocaust historians and scholars and behind-the-scenes tours with museum staff in all departments. We were being trained to be teachers of teachers, developing best practices to inform and educate others on the very complicated history behind the most horrific crime in the history of the world, a crime that our GIs would have first-hand knowledge of. But how could I return to our nation's capital, after those 35 years, and not go to the World War II Memorial showcased now right near the Washington Monument on the Mall?

The only way I would really have time to see it for myself would be if I got out of bed at the crack of dawn and walked over there

---

[40] *the most intense study of my career to date-* this experience would be followed by more intense study and travel to the authentic sites of the Holocaust; a 2013 three-week tour with the Holocaust and Jewish Resistance Teachers Program, and a 2016 three-week residency at the International School for Holocaust Studies at Yad Vashem in Jerusalem.

from the hotel before heading across the Mall to the museum. Fifty flags fluttered in the breeze as I strolled past the Washington Monument towards my destination, the sun delivering her first rays proclaiming another hot day. I had something to see. The inscription at the base of the flagpole as I entered this national shrine read,

"AMERICANS CAME TO LIBERATE, NOT CONQUER"

The Atlantic Arch and the Pacific Arch victory pavilions flank columns of bronze and granite representing every state and U.S. territory at the time of World War II; 4,038 gold-plated silver stars on the nearby Freedom Wall symbolize the loss of a hundred servicemen and women each. On this summer morning, it is a quiet place of reflection, a place to recall the efforts and sacrifices of so many families; the only other person here at this moment was a National Park service employee cleaning coins out of the magnificent fountains. Ground was broken on the Mall shortly after the 9/11 attacks on our nation; since it formally opened in 2004, thousands of World War II veterans have been flown in to the World War II Memorial, making, in many cases, a final pilgrimage to mark the years that forged their lives. The inscription on the Freedom Wall simply reads,
~HERE WE MARK THE PRICE OF FREEDOM~
*

Nearly 70 years after the war, scholars discovered that we are only beginning to understand the extent of the Holocaust. By 2008, researchers at the United States Holocaust Memorial Museum had cataloged some 42,500 Nazi ghettos and camps throughout Europe from 1933 to 1945. The figure was "so staggering that even fellow Holocaust scholars had to make sure they had heard it correctly; the documented camps include not only 'killing centers' but also thousands of forced labor camps, where prisoners manufactured war supplies; prisoner-of-war camps; sites euphemistically named 'care' centers, where pregnant women were forced to have abortions or their babies were killed after birth; and brothels, where women were coerced into having sex with German military personnel."[19]

So much for 'but we did not know!'

*

Leo DiPalma toured Nuremberg with his daughter in 2000. Shortly thereafter, she began to record her father's stories, which became his autobiography. The book caught the attention of Eli Rosenbaum, the United States' chief law enforcement officer responsible for bringing to justice and deporting Nazi war criminals. He praised DiPalma's efforts to remind people of the dangers of remaining silent in the face of evil. In 2009, in its replicated Nuremberg courtroom, the Virginia Holocaust Museum presented Leo with its inaugural Legacy of Nuremberg award and unveiled a wax figure of a Palace of Justice guard modeled after Leo, who then gave a riveting talk after being introduced by Rosenbaum. "When he talked to audiences about that, I think that [the idea that these crimes against humanity were perpetrated by human beings] comes through. It's easy, and it's more comforting, in a way, to think that [the perpetrators are] monsters; you know, [like], 'just be on the alert for monsters.' But that's not the message of Nuremberg."

Leo and his daughter gave talks to students and others for a few more years, until, as with so many of our veterans who offered their testimony as an example, it was just time to stop and rest. In 2018, with his wife having passed, he moved to a Massachusetts veterans nursing home, where he was loved and enjoyed the remainder of his days in the company of fellow veterans, relishing the visits from his family. In early 2020, his faculties now fading, his daughter Emily recalled, 'I just got this feeling that I needed to go see him, and I needed to go see him that day. I told him that he was a good dad and that I loved him, and I talked about our [Nuremberg] trip. And he looked up at me and he held my hand, and he smiled.'

Two weeks later, he was diagnosed with COVID-19; due to restrictions, she was unable to see her father again. 'It's kind of like a long pain that's just carried out. So, it's tough; but I knew my dad, and he wanted people to never forget what he did during World War II so that the rest of us could stay safe for the future. I feel like I need to carry that on; I'm honoring his life, not how he died.'

Leo DiPalma passed away at the age of 93 on April 8, 2020, as a result of the coronavirus outbreak at the facility.[41] Another daughter managed to see Leo a few hours before he died; she reported back to the family that a National Guardsman was posted outside of his door.

*

As Tony Hayes so poignantly discovered, Dachau and the memory of the experiences of our GIs—the trauma, the heartbreak, the good times, and the really, really bad times—should always be with us. One reader posted on my Facebook author page,

My father was a combat infantryman in WW II. He lived with PTSD for seventy years. I know he only told us a little of what happened, and he told us almost nothing, until the last few years of his life.

Before that, he would call his friend Paul, who was in the same unit as my father. Even after Paul died, he would drive one hundred miles to "talk to Paul" at the cemetery, because Paul was the only one he knew who understood what they had gone through. Only after Dad was unable to drive that hundred miles, did he really start telling us any significant part of what had happened.

---

[41] The coronavirus outbreak there left at least 76 veterans dead, devastating their families and resulting in charges against the facility's administrators.

These young men and women, caught up in the whirlwind of World War II, set the course of history by their deeds. Not all rose to the challenge, but the modest, the terrified, the sometimes bewildered-at-what-they-were-seeing young men and women slew the beast, and then tried to get on with their lives. Not everything gets packed away neatly, however, but I hope that by unlimbering their burdens to their interviewers, and now on these pages, we can return with them to the central theme of this series, to honor these lives so well-lived, and to remember their friends who did not make it home with them:

Dying for freedom isn't the worst that could happen. Being forgotten is.

MATTHEW A. ROZELL

THE THINGS
— OUR —
FATHERS SAW

ON TO TOKYO

THE UNTOLD STORIES OF
THE WORLD WAR II GENERATION

VOLUME VIII

THE THINGS OUR FATHERS SAW

THE UNTOLD STORIES OF THE
WORLD WAR II GENERATION
FROM HOMETOWN, USA

VOLUME VIII:
ON TO TOKYO

Matthew A. Rozell

WOODCHUCK HOLLOW PRESS
Hartford · New York

Copyright © 2022, 2024 by Matthew A. Rozell. Version 6.30.23 FIN. All rights reserved. No part of this publication may be reproduced, distributed, or transmitted in any form or by any means without the prior written permission of the publisher. Grateful acknowledgement is made for the credited use of various short quotations also appearing in other previously published sources. Please see author notes.

Information at matthewrozellbooks.com.

Maps by Susan Winchell.

Front Cover: "U.S. Marines in Landing Craft head for the beach at Iwo Jima on Feb. 19, 1945, during the initial landings." U.S. Marine Corps Historical Center. Public Domain Photographs, National Archives.

Back Cover: "Marine Aiming at a Japanese Sniper on Okinawa, 1945." National Archives, public domain.

Any additional photographs and descriptions sourced at Wikimedia Commons within terms of use, unless otherwise noted.

Publisher's Cataloging-in-Publication Data

Names: Rozell, Matthew A., 1961- author.
Title: On to tokyo: the things our fathers saw : the untold stories of the World War II generation, volume VIII / Matthew A. Rozell.
Description: Hartford, NY : Matthew A. Rozell, 2022. | Series: The things our fathers saw, vol. 8. | Also available in audiobook format.
Identifiers: LCCN 2022913755 | ISBN 978-1-948155-29-8 [hardcover] | ISBN 978-1-948155-27-4 [paperback] | ISBN 978-1-948155-30-4 [ebook]
Subjects: LCSH: World War, 1939-1945--Personal narratives, American. | World War, 1939-1945--Campaigns--Pacific Ocean. | United States. Marine Corps--Biography. | Military history, Modern--20th century. | Veterans--United States--Biography. | Military history, Modern--20th century. | BISAC: HISTORY / Military / World War II. | HISTORY / Military / Veterans. | BIOGRAPHY & AUTOBIOGRAPHY / Military.

matthewrozellbooks.com.

Created in the United States of America

To the memory of
~The World War II Generation~
and
~Thomas B. Vesey~

1930-2022
Korea Vet and Beloved Gentleman

"So much of war depends on ordinary soldiers, sailors, Marines, and airmen. Yes, you need brilliant people to lead them, but God, when I think of some of the things that happened because ordinary people just did the impossible, or the near impossible..."
—US Army Radioman, Pacific, World War II

THE THINGS OUR FATHERS SAW VIII: ON TO TOKYO

The Storytellers

FRANK J. CASTRONOVO

CHARLES M. JACOBS

PAUL ELISHA

JAMES A. SMITH, JR.

SAMUEL R. DINOVA

ALBERT J. HARRIS

UNKNOWN JAPANESE SOLDIER

JOHN H. KOLECKI

HENRY C. HUNEKEN

STEVE T. JORDAN

MITCHELL MORSE

THE THINGS OUR FATHERS SAW VIII:

TABLE OF CONTENTS

ON TO TOKYO

PART ONE	443
THE PACIFIC	445
THE PEARL HARBOR SURVIVOR	453
THE MARINE RIFLEMAN	471
THE INVASION RADIOMAN I	499
THE MARINE MECHANIC I	529
PART TWO	557
THE RUNNER	559
THE MARINE GUNNER I	583
'REVENGE FOR THE DEAD'	601
PART THREE	615
THE INVASION RADIOMAN II	617

THE BAR MAN	**643**
THE MARINE GUNNER II	**657**
THE B-29 RADIOMAN	**665**
PART FOUR	**685**
HACKSAW RIDGE	**687**
THE NAVY CORPSMAN	**709**
THE INVASION RADIOMAN III	**733**
PART FIVE	**741**
OCCUPATION DUTY	**743**
THE INVASION RADIOMAN IV	**757**
THE RESTING PLACE	**771**
ACKNOWLEDGEMENTS	**783**

Author's Note

I landed at Albany International Airport just as the evening was getting underway, returning from a trip to Toronto to re-interview an old Holocaust survivor friend of mine. It was a great trip, sitting with her in her living room, with the film director, cameraman, and one of Ariela's daughters. It was so good to see her after several years of meeting her at our soldier-survivor reunions, the last of which was in 2015 for the 70th anniversary of the liberation of the Train Near Magdeburg. But it was also good, given the extra stress of pandemic-era flight, to return home to upstate New York.

I still had an hour's drive north to the homestead where I pen these books. Two of my children currently share an apartment across the Hudson River from the state capital at Albany, in Troy, New York, so I decided to pay them an unannounced visit, but they already had plans, of course—they are young people, after all, and it was a beautiful Friday night.

I went up the hill to the old state highway that runs for fifty miles north and brings me almost to my door. City kids were out riding bikes in the street of their working-class neighborhood down by the river, others sitting comfortably on their stoops, watching the world go by. Troy, New York, is the home of Uncle Sam.[42] Also

---

[42] *the home of Uncle Sam* - "Uncle Sam is based on Samuel Wilson, who resided in Troy from 1789 until his death in 1854. Wilson and his brother owned and managed a meat packing business in Troy. They supplied a contractor, Elbert Anderson, for the federal government with beef, pork, whiskey and salt, which were sent to troops stationed nearby. Wilson, who also

known as the Collar City, a hundred plus years ago it hosted over two dozen shirt and collar factories. Irish and Italian men and women emigrated to work the industries, organize labor, build their churches, create their neighborhoods. Irish labor leader and future revolutionary James Connolly, executed by the British for his role in the famed 1916 Dublin 'Easter Rising,' even lived here for two years during the turn of the last century. Today, modern-day film crews flock here to use the spectacular architecture of that day as the backdrop for their turn-of-the-century dramas, such as *The Gilded Age* and *The Age of Innocence*. But there is another story, from this town, that needs to be told—the story of the sons who went off to fight the war as part of a federalized National Guard unit, drawn from the good stock at Troy and surrounding communities.

As I took my time leaving the heart of the city, I once again passed by St. Peter's Cemetery—rolling hillocks, beautiful trees and shrubbery, groomed pathways, the memorials adorned with mostly Irish surnames. I had never stopped here before, but then I noticed a historical marker. I turned around and entered the cemetery.

---

worked as an Army inspector, stamped on every barrel of goods he approved the letters, 'US/EA.' Following the death of Wilson, who was affectionately known as 'Uncle Sam,' a legend began. Dock workers joked that the 'US' of 'US/EA' stamped on inspected barrels stood for 'Uncle Sam.' Many of the men who worked in Troy and shipped the barrels became soldiers during the War of 1812, and ate the beef they had packed. They continued to spread the joke to other soldiers. The story grew until Uncle Sam and the United States became synonymous.
In 1961, the U.S. House of Representatives and Senate unanimously passed a law which proclaimed that Samuel Wilson of Troy, New York, was the progenitor of the nation's symbol, Uncle Sam, and that Troy is the official home of Uncle Sam. The bill was signed by President John F. Kennedy." Source: The City of Troy, New York - Home of Uncle Sam. Library of Congress, American Folklife Center. memory.loc.gov/diglib/legacies/loc.afc.afc-legacies.200003395/

So, this was where LTC O'Brien was buried. I knew I had to find him.

The sun was now about to set. I was the only person I could see in the cemetery; I drove and walked around for a good time, looking for the grave of a man I had learned of in writing my first volume on the Pacific, a posthumous Medal of Honor recipient killed in Saipan defending his men.

No luck. His burial site was just not standing out. So why is it that, aside from the roadside marker, this man who so heroically gave all for his comrades in arms, his country, is now seemingly a footnote to history for everyday Americans?

*

In this eighth volume in The Things Our Fathers Saw series, we return to the Pacific with the soldiers, sailors, airmen, and Marines who offer up their remembrances of comrades and friends, of baptisms by fire, of comraderies and sorrows from a generation we were lucky enough to get to know, who returned to tell us what they experienced, not so long ago. It has been my honor and privilege to observe and coalesce their interviews into the book you hold in your hands. The New York State Military Museum's Veterans Oral History Project came into being shortly after our own high school oral history project began; we gave our 200+ interviews to them and gleaned more from the recordings found there that were conducted at the same time we were doing our work. I have spent many days getting reacquainted, editing, researching, and writing to bring them back to life in the form of their own words, recorded for posterity by forward thinkers and questioners. So take these voices, pause, if you will, after each story, and think about what they did, what they went through, for future generations of freedom-loving peoples.

Matthew Rozell
July 7, 2022
The 78th anniversary of the banzai charge at Saipan
Washington County, NY

*Extent of Japanese Control in the Pacific, 1942,
featuring battles and locations in the book.
Drafted by Susan Winchell,
after Donald L. Miller.*

PART ONE

THE HARD ROAD BACK

'I'm going simply because there's a war on and I'm part of it and I've known all the time I was going back. I'm going simply because I've got to—and I hate it.

This time it will be the Pacific.'

—EXCERPT FROM ERNIE PYLE'S COLUMN, 'BACK AGAIN,' FEB. 6, 1945

Ernie Pyle shares a cigarette break with a U.S. Marine patrol on Okinawa during the Pacific campaign in World War II, April 8, 1945, ten days before his death. U.S. Marine Corps Photo, public domain.

CHAPTER ONE

The Pacific

There's nothing nice about the prospect of going back to war again. Anybody who has been in war and wants to go back is a plain damn fool, in my book.

I'm certainly not going because I've got itchy feet again, or because I can't stand America, or because there's any mystic fascination about war that is drawing me back.

I'm going simply because there's a war on and I'm part of it and I've known all the time I was going back. I'm going simply because I've got to —and I hate it.

This time it will be the Pacific.[20]

—excerpt from Ernie Pyle's column, 'Back Again,' Feb. 6, 1945

In 1949, a grave was opened on the tiny island of Ie Shima just off the northwest coast of Okinawa. Like many hasty wartime burials for men killed in action, this grave was one of many, side by side. It was time to bring the remains back home, time for a proper burial.

Ernie Pyle had seen a lot in his forty-four years, enough so that anyone looking at his photograph would guess they were looking at a man at least twenty years older. He was tired, haggard, and by the spring of 1945, looking thinner and gaunt. He suffered from bouts of depression.

He began his wartime correspondence career by visiting London during the Blitz in 1940. He was impressed with the resilience of the people, and wanted to know more, how everyday folks were coping, even thriving amidst the chaos of war. He was hooked, and so were his readers back in the States, who looked forward to more. His work led to his first book, and by the time he returned home, he was a household name. This surprised him. After all, he was writing about ordinary people. But then again, they were doing extraordinary things.

After a rest, he expressed an interest in going on an Asian tour, but the attack on Pearl Harbor put an end to that. Rejected by the Navy for being too small of frame, in November 1942 he packed his bags and headed to North Africa to cover the Allied landings. He was always close to the front lines, talking with soldiers, getting their names and stories right with little notetaking. At times, he witnessed the men he had been talking with subsequently killed in battle.

He followed the soldiers through the invasion of Sicily, then came back home to rest. His work took a personal toll, yet he found he was once again celebrated almost as a national hero, which led to the release of his second book, *Here Is Your War*. Uncomfortable with the acclaim and itching to be back with the men, he returned to the battlefront later in 1943, following the GIs as they slugged it out 'up the bloody boot' in the brutal Italian campaign.

Returning to England to cover the buildup to D-Day, he was tired but could not turn down an invitation to be present onboard General Omar Bradley's flagship *Augusta* to witness the Normandy landings firsthand, the greatest land-sea-air invasion in the history of the world. He followed the troops ashore, and at his peak, he was filing six columns a week. By now, he had also been awarded the Pulitzer Prize for his reporting, though no one seemed to know if he was ever even formally nominated. In the fall of 1944, he returned home again, utterly exhausted by what he had witnessed and had been attempting to process through his columns.

By the 1944 holiday season, he once again felt restless. By January he had made up his mind to go to the Pacific Theater. Although he did not really want to go, he felt that he owed something to the men fighting there. He told his now-estranged wife, 'I promise you that if I come through this one, I will never go on another one.'[21] In private, he confided to friends that he was not sure he would survive the war.

*

On Wednesday, April 18, 1945, Pyle accompanied a contingent of 77th Infantry Division soldiers as they were midway through operations to secure Ie Shima's airfield. A Japanese machine gun position opened up; he and his party jumped out of the jeep and scrambled into a roadside ditch. When Pyle lifted his head, he was struck in the left temple by a Japanese bullet and killed instantly. He was buried two days later alongside fourteen other men.

Ernie Pyle's death came just six days after the death of President Roosevelt. To the American public, both losses were sudden, and both were shocking, a double blow to a nation reeling from four years of war. Three weeks later, Nazi Germany formally surrendered, but the men fighting on Okinawa barely noticed. It was still all-out war in the Pacific.

Pyle had gone to the Pacific partially out of the nagging feeling that the soldiers, sailors, Marines, and airmen had been really overlooked, almost neglected in the big picture of what was really happening in World War II, by himself and the press in general. For some, this general attitude was symbolic of America's understanding of the war, even though World War II had started in the Pacific. It would now have to end there against a foe that was so fanatical, and so formidable, that it boggled the imagination, but as it began, the United States would be essentially engaging in two full-blown wars at the same time, taxing America's resources and families to the hilt. The sheer expanse of the Pacific Theater encompassed one-third of the Earth's surface; new methods and materials would have to be invented to drive the Japanese back.

Still, it was as if the fighting man in the Pacific was the proverbial red-headed stepchild of the American war. Only one quarter of the United States' sixty-six Army infantry divisions raised during World War II, coupled with six Marine Corps divisions, were committed to the Pacific. American fighting men were abandoned in the Philippines, suffering terribly at the hands of the conquerors. These forsaken soldiers, without hope, bitterly recited verses created by another war correspondent:

Battling Bastards of Bataan

We're the battling bastards of Bataan;
No mama, no papa, no Uncle Sam.
No aunts, no uncles, no cousins, no nieces,
No pills, no planes, no artillery pieces
And nobody gives a damn
Nobody gives a damn.[22]

The road back was rocky, and rough. It took seven months after Pearl Harbor to engage the Japanese on land at Guadalcanal, after the Japanese succeeded in almost total domination of the Pacific region. Late 1943 brought new amphibious landings where unforgivable mistakes were made, and hard lessons learned, but then more of a centralized island-hopping strategy began to crystallize. The summer of 1944 in the Central Pacific brought joint Army-Navy thrusts to within air-striking distance of the imperial Japanese homeland with attacks in the Marianas at Guam, Saipan, and Tinian, with horrific battles on the horizon for the reconquest of the Philippines, Iwo Jima, and Okinawa, not to mention the planning for the bloodletting in the event of the invasion of Japan itself.

Still, we need to keep in mind that there was no crystal ball, and our veterans' fears and anxiety, as well as their determination and resolve, is telegraphed in their own words after fifty or sixty-plus years in a way that is a frank testament to the times. Never before had Americans encountered an enemy like this. The ravenous Japanese war machine had to be stopped, pushed back, made to cry uncle, but even though they were reeling by 1944, they seemed to welcome death in battle as one of life's great honors. *Who crawls on their belly for a thousand yards in the dark, armed only with a knife? Who rushes a blazing machine gun nest with a sword or a stick, screaming at the top of his lungs? Who deliberately crashes their aircraft into a moving ship?*

What made people do this? How does the war-weary GI, Marine, or sailor fight *that* foe?

It has been seven months since I heard my last shot in the European War. Now I am as far away from it as it is possible to get on this globe.

This is written on a little ship lying off the coast of the Island of Okinawa, just south of Japan, on the other side of the world from the Ardennes...

For the companionship of two and a half years, death and misery is a spouse that tolerates no divorce. Such companionship finally becomes a part of one's soul, and it cannot be obliterated…

Last summer I wrote that I hoped the end of the war could be a gigantic relief, but not an elation. In the joyousness of high spirits it is so easy for us to forget the dead. Those who are gone would not wish themselves to be a millstone of gloom around our necks.

But there are so many of the living who have had burned into their brains forever the unnatural sight of cold dead men scattered over the hillsides and in the ditches along the high rows of hedge throughout the world.

Dead men by mass production—in one country after another—month after month, and year after year. Dead men in winter, and dead men in summer.

Dead men in such familiar promiscuity that they become monotonous.

Dead men in such monstrous infinity that you come almost to hate them.

Those are the things that you at home need not even try to understand. To you at home they are columns of figures, or he is a near one who went away and just didn't come back. You didn't see him lying so grotesque and pasty beside the gravel road in France.

We saw him, saw him by the multiple thousands. That's the difference.

We hope above all things that Japan won't make the same stubborn mistake that Germany did. You must credit Germany for her courage in adversity, but you can doubt her good common sense in fighting blindly on long after there was any doubt whatever about the outcome.[23]

—excerpts of the draft of Ernie Pyle's final column, found in his pocket upon his death [April 18, 1945]

On July 19, 1949, the National Memorial Cemetery of the Pacific in Honolulu, Hawaii, conducted its first five interments. One of them, lying now next to the men he had written about so well, was Ernest Taylor Pyle, 1900-1945.[24]

CHAPTER TWO

The Pearl Harbor Survivor

At age 82, Frank J. Castronovo sits in a chair at an armory on Long Island, New York, near his home of fifty-plus years, holding photographs and newspaper clippings, reminders of the things he saw, the experiences he had that he can't forget, the friends that he lost. He feels the need to speak up, to keep the memory alive. He wears a special medal around his neck.

"This medal was given to us at the 50th anniversary of Pearl Harbor. It was a Congressional medal only given to Pearl Harbor survivors. I wear this to every meeting and every parade. It shows Pearl Harbor and has President Roosevelt's famous words: 'This day shall live in infamy.'

This is from the local newspaper a few years ago, my picture and the speech I made, [titled 'A Salute to Veterans']"

"Frank Castronovo is a Pearl Harbor survivor and a veteran of Guadalcanal in the Solomon Islands. He enlisted in the Army July 11, 1940, and was discharged December 12, 1944. His words say it best: 'I shall never forget December 7, 1941, when the Japanese sneak attacked Pearl Harbor at five minutes to eight in the morning. Those gallant men on those ships never had a chance to defend themselves. I will live with this memory for the rest of my life.

At Guadalcanal we battled the Japanese until we secured the island. In my company alone, 35th Infantry, Company E, we lost nine men and about twenty-eight wounded. I am proud to write this in memory of my comrades.'"

*

Frank turns over more photographs in his hands.

"This is at Oyster Bay where we Pearl Harbor Survivors meet every December 7, and it was cold there, right by the bay. There are only a few of us left. The Elmont Memorial Day parade is coming up and we are the grand marshals at that parade. And this one, let me show you another one here—this is a month or two after the Pearl Harbor attack, when we got our first leave.

This is my friend Denman, then Ruggerio, and myself. Denman was later machine-gunned on Guadalcanal. Ruggerio died of natural causes just recently."

He gave this interview in May 2001 at the age of 82.

Frank J. Castronovo

I was born November 29, 1918, in the Bronx, New York. I can't tell you about my father because, as you might have read about, at that time in 1918 there was an epidemic going around called the Spanish influenza. My mom told me people were dying like flies, they couldn't bury them fast enough. People were lying on the sidewalk waiting to be buried, that's how bad it was. My father died eight days after I was born. My mother said he got to touch my fingers as a baby. That's the only thing I know about him. But my mom, she was the greatest person in the world. She raised six kids without a husband after that.

In 1929 the stock market fell, and I was about ten years old. I grew up during the Depression, from 1929 until 1940 when I went into the Army. People were helping one another. We had nothing, but whatever we had, we shared. It wasn't like today with the drugs and everything; it was about helping one another. If you had a dime, you were lucky. If you had a quarter, you were rich. If you had a dollar, you could yell it out and do whatever you wanted. A Coca-Cola was a nickel, White Castle burgers were six for a quarter, and all that kind of stuff. It was beautiful. The milk wagon came around and you'd steal a bottle of milk if you could get it. [*Chuckles*] I remember going shopping with my mother and for ten dollars we had three full bags of food, meat and everything. I think we ate better then than we do today. It was really nice as we helped one another and stuck together.

So 1939 came, and my mother got cancer, and a year later I lost her and she was the best part of my life. She was a great mom. What she did, women today should know. There were no refrigerators, no washing machines, no laundromats. Everything my mom did was by hand on the tub. She kept us clean as a whistle. She cooked, cleaned, and fed us kids.

Anyway, there was nothing around and I was 19, almost 20. My brothers were all married and one of my brothers was living in Pennsylvania. My brother Al took me to Pennsylvania and put me to work in a factory just to make a few dollars, but I didn't like it. Also, he had two children, and I felt I was in the way. I decided I wanted to enlist in the Army because I will never get this opportunity again to travel, and see what the rest of the world was about. I did the right thing and I'm glad I did it. I'm not sorry.

I enlisted in the Army on July 11, 1940. When I enlisted, they asked me where I wanted to go. The choices were Hawaii, Panama, or the Philippines. Well, I remembered all about the hula girls so I said I'll take Hawaii. [*Chuckles*] I'm glad I did, because of what happened in the Philippines [later after the Japanese invaded and many U.S. soldiers were taken prisoner], and so we went through the Panama Canal going to Hawaii.

I first went to Fort Slocum in New York City. I stayed there until they were ready to ship us to California. While I was there, waiting for the ship to come in, they sent us to Camp Drum, New York, way up next to the Canadian border, on maneuvers.

Our ship finally came in and took us to California. We got to California and spent a couple months there, waiting for our ship to take us to Hawaii. When we arrived, we had to stop at Alcatraz Island, where we helped unload supplies. Eventually our ship came in again and we were able to sail for Hawaii.

Hawaii

In Hawaii I went through basic training and I was there from November 1940 until they hit us in December 1941. If I'd had another six months I'd have been sent back to the States, as my two years would have been up. Then the Japanese bombed us, and that was the end of that.

[Training as a unit], we just learned how to march, how to respect the flag, how to get up in the morning. The first detail you had was on the 'honey wagon,' taking care of the garbage. You learned how to use a gun and how to dismantle it and put it back together. You learned how to dress, how to respect officers, and how to salute them. We respected [the soldiers who had been there a long time] a lot at first, but within a month or two you were one of them. As a matter of fact, pretty soon I had a buddy here and a buddy there. You are all away from home, so you become a family. They were from Pennsylvania, Carolina, Tennessee, New York, etc. But coming from New York you had to be careful because right away you had a bad name. [*Chuckles*] Oh yes, I [took some heat], I must admit. Some were very nice. But being a nineteen-year-old kid, I didn't realize that they would be still fighting the Civil War! I didn't believe in that; I didn't even remember who General Grant or General Lee was. But some of those guys had that embedded in their minds, like I do Pearl Harbor. If you were from New York, you were a Yankee. Luckily, I was able to handle myself because there was a lot of fighting going on. I said we were all GIs, and a lot of them were my buddies, but there were a few who resented you. We eventually got it sorted out and got along with each other.

The sergeants were like our fathers. The officers gave commands to the sergeants and the sergeants controlled us. If we went on maneuvers there would be a 1st lieutenant, a 2nd lieutenant, and maybe a captain.

'We were Going to Go To War With Japan'

Honolulu [before the attack on Pearl Harbor] was beautiful. You could go to town, have a drink. We only got $20 a month at that time and a Springfield rifle. From that $20 they took out for your haircuts and laundry, so there wasn't much left. So with what we had left we would go into Honolulu, if the Navy wasn't in. If the Navy was there, we didn't go because they took over the town. It was their time. When we went to town, we would have a few drinks and a good meal. we met people and some even invited us to their house. We met a lot of people that way. It was wonderful.

Before the war, a couple of months before they bombed us, they told us that we were going to be at war with Japan. They didn't say when or where it would start. They started giving us fixed bayonets and camouflage stuff. We were patrolling in trucks in 4-hour shifts looking for sabotage or anything that shouldn't be there, because they knew we were going to have war with Japan, and Hawaii would be one of the first places they would want to take. Once you conquer Hawaii, you are on your way to California.

We were looking for anything that shouldn't be there, like any kind of weapons or positions they were building, for anything suspicious. But we didn't see anything like that. Oh yes, it was nice. It was a beautiful climate. We in the military didn't mingle too much with the civilians. We made friends with people here and there but we had to keep our distance and be careful about what we said and who we mingled with. The natives didn't like us too much. There was jealousy about some of their women liking GIs. We had a few drinks, we had good dinners, and we met people. We played tennis once in a while or went to Waikiki Beach.

The night before the attack me and two buddies decided to go into town to have a little fun. Then we remembered the Navy was in. There was only one hotel, the Royal Hawaiian, and it was maybe three stories high. It was booked for the weekend. Every place was crowded. You had to fight your way to get a beer. I suggested to the guys that we should just go back to camp. So, we took the bus back to Schofield Barracks about ten o'clock that night. It was a good thing that so many of those Navy guys stayed in town that night. Otherwise, there would have been a lot more casualties during the attack.

After Pearl Harbor there was no more life; it was just 'go'. Everything was in blackout. It was at least a year after that before I saw lights again.

'Smoke, Flames, Explosions, Sirens'

It was December 7, 1941. It was a beautiful morning, early Sunday morning, when it was always very quiet there. There was nothing suspicious about it. Most were getting up to go enjoy the day off. We used to have lunch with Navy guys. They would come to our barracks or we would be invited to have lunch on their ships.

Where I slept in the Schofield Barracks was near the kitchen and I could smell the bacon, pancakes, sausage, and coffee. On Sundays you could sleep all day if you wanted to, but not me. I wasn't missing breakfast. That was the best meal of the day. I jumped up, grabbed my toilet articles, and headed up to the third floor to take a shower.

Just as I was about to shower, I heard this roar of planes coming over. It kept getting louder and louder, and closer and closer. All of a sudden it was right on me. I dropped everything and ran to the window. At that time the Schofield Barracks was like an island. There were no other buildings, no roads, no nothing. About a mile or two away was Wheeler Field and that's where the first bombs were dropped; they hit Wheeler Field. They hit the planes and the hangars. The Air Force men were running every which way, trying to get to the planes, trying to get out of the way, because you couldn't just stay there.

From there the Japanese went right into Pearl Harbor and dropped bombs. Then the next wave came over—I think they were four abreast—and the next wave and the next wave. For I don't know how long, a half hour or three quarters of an hour, it went from a beautiful morning to nothing but smoke, flames, explosions, sirens.

When those planes on the field were blowing up all over the place and the hangars were blowing up, I knew it had to be the Japanese; I was surprised and shocked, but I knew it had to be the Japanese.

I was out on the quadrangle outside the barracks, looking up at them. Each company, A through G, had its barracks and they surrounded a quadrangle. I was standing there like a dummy looking up at them; I was using some profanity, seeing one of the pilots smiling, and then he opened up with his machine gun and I hit the deck and was falling all over the place. Like a fool I had been just standing there looking up at him. I couldn't shoot at him because I had no ammunition. Our supply sergeant was in town. He was married. We were stuck without any ammunition. Even if I could, what are you going to do with a rifle anyway? These guys are coming over fast. You would have to be pretty good to hit one of them. Some who had ammunition did try.

We ran inside because we got the alert call. We all got together and the sergeant came and the captain was there. They told us to get ready to ship out. So we grabbed our stuff, lined up, and got ready to go to our positions. We went to the beaches. The artillery went up and the headquarters went up and so on, but you couldn't see much because of all the smoke. Though it was daytime it looked like night time, there wasn't much to see. When those battleships were hit and went up, it was nothing but flames and black smoke, huge clouds of black smoke. With explosions going off that was all you could see. There were bodies all over the place. We heard the ambulances, but our job was to get to the beaches and get to work. The next day we got equipment and materials and we started building and took our positions right away without the barbed wire. Every hundred feet was a machine gun position. We figured they were coming right back.

We set up the machine gun positions. They got their heads together pretty quickly. The sergeants and the officers did very good. They positioned us well. I give them credit. They knew what they were doing; it was a case of 'let's just do it.' I wasn't worrying about whether I was going to die. I was afraid, but I just put it out of my mind.

After that was cleaned up some, the next day the artillery was sent to positions and the coast artillery was set up in their positions, etc. The rest of us, the 19th, 21st, and 25th Infantry, had the job of stringing barbed wire along the beaches from one end to the other.

It took us a couple months—we expected the Japanese to invade us. Anyway, maybe every one hundred feet we had machine gun positions. I had mine and then the next, and on and on all over the island.

The Japanese did their job but they didn't follow through. If they had followed through, they would have wiped us out. We had a peacetime army, and we didn't have all of the equipment that we needed. We didn't have that many men. We could have held out a few days maybe. Later on, we started to get information about Japanese landings on Wake Island and others. Even when we were on the ship, we continued to get information on actions going on.

The worst part of the attack on Pearl Harbor was [what happened to those] gallant Navy men. The courage they had; they didn't have time to put their shoes on. They tried to get up on deck to man the guns. But it was too late, though they tried anyway. And it happened at five minutes to eight. I got up at ten to eight and in five minutes it all happened. Guys were getting ready to go enjoy the day playing golf or tennis, picnic, [or whatever]. Some were getting ready to go to eight o'clock Mass. That's when they hit. Many weren't just killed, they were murdered in their sleep. That's how I address it. It was cold-blooded murder, and I shall never forget it. We survivors will never forget it. It was a dirty sneak attack.

Guadalcanal

We expected an invasion, but that never happened. After we secured the island, they shipped new troops to the Hawaiian Islands, and we were sent on to other islands. Some went to Bougainville, some to New Caledonia, Guadalcanal, New Hebrides. My outfit ended up in Guadalcanal in the Solomon Islands. It took us 23 days to get there from Hawaii, because every eight minutes we had to change course because of submarines.

So we got to Guadalcanal, and there we had our hands full with the Japanese. They were positioned, ready, willing, and waiting for us. In those jungles you don't see anything. You just hope you are throwing grenades where they are supposed to be. Almost nothing was hand-to-hand. They had snipers tied in the trees. You had to be in their line of sight before they could fire. It was very still in the jungle so we watched for anything that moved. We would hear voices, and when we did, we threw grenades or fired mortars. We also had BARs and flame throwers. We weren't trained for jungle warfare; in Hawaii we were trained for open warfare, not jungle warfare. We learned the hard way. When we got there, it was do or die.

The Grenade

On Guadalcanal, before dark, we had to dig foxholes. There were two men to a foxhole. We were ordered to not move after dark no matter what. Anything that moved was the enemy. We couldn't smoke a cigarette. You couldn't even cough because it would give your position away—you had to put your face to the ground and cover your head to cough. And it rained every night there.

In the next foxhole a guy heard a noise and he panicked. He threw a grenade, which is what you are supposed to do, but not at night. The grenade flew up, hit a tree limb above them, and fell back into their foxhole. A fella [I knew], George Ferrara from California, lost both of his hands and had many shrapnel wounds. They couldn't move him, so the medics came and put a tent over him to treat him. They moved him out the next morning and got him to a hospital. I heard later that he survived but lost both hands and part of his leg. It was all because his foxhole buddy panicked and threw that grenade.

At night you used your rifle. The Japanese strategy was to fight at night, which was stupid. You can't see in the jungle to begin with so you can imagine what it is like at night. Our strategy was to stay quiet and don't move. If anything moved in front of you, you let 'em have it. Once when one of them came at us, there was just enough light to make him out and one of our guys opened up with a BAR and got him. But nobody moved. At night it was like fighting with your eyes closed. I don't know why they did it.

It was all up in the hills in the jungle. The hill we were on was Hill 27, [not far from Henderson Field]. We were in very heavy jungle. We had artillery and mortars; the artillery would blast away to clear the way for us to advance. The artillery guys knew where we were and we could tell approximately where the Japanese were. Sometimes we could even hear their voices. We also had mortars, which were very effective. Another thing was that our weapons were more powerful than what the Japanese had. Our grenades packed 48 steel fragments and exploded like a bomb. Thank God our weapons were more powerful. Even the rifles; if they didn't hit you in a vital spot, you could survive. It was the same with their grenades. If one didn't hit you directly, you could survive.

'It Didn't Take Us Long'

The Japanese were seasoned troops and knew how to handle it. But I am proud of us Americans. It didn't take us long to learn how to fight in the jungle. We had the Fiji natives who came to help us out. We didn't call them mountains, we called them hills. We were on Hill 27. Every night it rained up in those hills and it ran down the hills. It took us a day to get from the bottom to the top. Half of the guys couldn't make it because they had full field packs, ammunition belts, and rifles, and you had to crawl on your stomach. The Fiji natives led us and showed us how to get to the top. We finally got to the top and continued into the jungle. It took us between five and seven months to secure the island.

My company lost seven to ten men killed and 18 to 25 wounded. Three of my buddies, Nick, Denman, and Reynolds, were machine gunned right next to me. I was the target because Nick asked me to go down and fill our canteens and bring up more grenades. I said okay, and as I got up, the Japanese sprayed them. Don't ask me how I didn't get hit because I don't know! To this day I still don't know, but they got machine gunned and they all died. When I came home, I went to visit a couple of the parents because I knew where they lived.

Dog Tags

One day there were two Americans killed out ahead of our position that we couldn't get to. After four days we finally got clearance to move. The sergeant tells me to go up there and get their dog tags. For every guy that died you had to get his dog tag to verify that he was deceased. So I said a 'Hail Mary' and went up there, hoping they were still there. I got up there, and after four days, I don't want to tell you what that was like. I got their dog tags. There were two dead Japanese and the two guys from our regiment.

Then we just kept going day after day. The Air Force would bomb and we would advance, day by day. As a matter of fact, one of our Marines had found a diary on a dead Japanese. It was translated into English and it told the same story about how they were going day by day.

'Just Keep Going'

You don't think. You just do. You're young and gung-ho. What I was thinking, [I suppose], was that I just wanted to get this over with and get out of there. So, you just followed orders and the orders were to just keep going. Just when we were exhausted and trying to get a couple hours of sleep at night, 'Washing Machine Charlie' would fly over and wake us up. His plane sounded like a washing machine. Nobody knew where he came from. I remember passing out after four days without sleep.

When I got malaria, I was taken down off Hill 27 to the Red Cross medical tents. They were marked with red crosses so they would not be bombed. There I was, with a high fever, shaking like a leaf, with five blankets over me and an IV in my arm, when a couple Japanese planes came over and dropped bombs on that area. Everybody ran for shelter, but there I was, lying there hoping they wouldn't hit my tent. They weren't supposed to do that, but the Japanese did it anyway.

For food, we had K-rations, but I couldn't stand that. Once we had secured some of the island, I met this native. He was a wonderful person and I called him friend. The native men fish at night. They put out their nets, and in the morning, they pull them in with all the fish. Then they pick whatever fruits and vegetables they have, so I ate what they ate. That's why I survived those seven months before I got malaria. I was getting the vitamins that I needed that I wasn't getting from those rations. I lived with the natives, who loved us and hated the Japanese, who took their food and raped their women. With one of the natives, I used to go 'shopping.' By that I mean finding the local fresh fruits, vegetables, and fish, so I was getting a lot of vitamins and held up longer than a lot of others. But then finally I got the malaria very bad. My mind was not affected but my whole body was shaking like a leaf. They eventually flew me to a hospital in New Hebrides. That was much better than what we had at Guadalcanal.

*

We kept pushing them back toward Japan. MacArthur returned to the Philippines where the Japanese had done bad things. It was no wonder that the Filipinos hated the Japanese. When I was in Tennessee there were POW camps where the Italian and German prisoners were treated as well as we were treated. We hung around with them, had dinner with them, and treated them like human beings. Not the Japanese. On Bataan, they made the Americans march until they dropped dead. They raped and plundered the Philippine people. They were vicious and treacherous. They were good fighters and hard to kill, but they were bad. A lot of guys took souvenirs, and yes, I knew of a few who took gold teeth. What I really wanted to get was one of the officer's swords, but I didn't. They were really nice, but I was not interested in taking souvenirs as much as I was anxious to keep moving and get out of there. I have a diary that was given to me by a Marine, written by one of the Japanese telling about their day-to-day life on Guadalcanal.

Home

At New Hebrides, Mrs. Roosevelt came to visit the troops. We had lunch with her, and I sat right across the way from her. She interviewed me and she was a pleasure to talk to. She had a great sense of humor. She asked what she could do for me, like mail some letters, etc. I said if she could put me in an envelope, I could go with her. [*Laughs*]

From New Hebrides they sent me to a better hospital in Auckland, New Zealand. I was there for a couple of months. It was a beautiful country. They finally had to send me back to the U.S. to try to cure my malaria. I was sent to the Kennedy Hospital in

Memphis, Tennessee. There they asked for volunteers for a malaria study, and I volunteered. They drew blood every day for testing, and I was there for seven months. The reason I did that was that it relieved me from duty. I gave blood each day and was then free to go. From there they sent me to North Carolina. I don't remember how long I was there. They finally decided to discharge me, so they sent me back to Camp Upton in New York. I was discharged and came back home, December 12, 1944.

A couple months before I was discharged, I married my sweetheart whom I had met on the beach in 1939. We were just kids when we met. I was nineteen and she was sixteen. We kept in touch and fell in love through the mail.

My first job after I was discharged was working for the Port Authority of New York at the Holland Tunnel. I did that for about two years. But there wasn't much money in that, and we were raising a family. I left that and went to work in construction for about thirty years. Thank goodness for the GI Bill. With that you had a choice of going to college or buying a home. Having a family, I bought a home. We have that home today and I appreciate that. I still get a small pension since I was discharged, and we've been in that home for over fifty years. I appreciate what the government did for us. Without them I would never have been able to buy a home.

My wife's brother knew someone in real estate on Long Island who was selling these homes for the GI Bill. He suggested we look into it. So he took me out to Elmont to see the realtor. He showed us a home and we took it. All we needed was $800. I had $500 and a couple of my brothers loaned me the rest and we put the $800 down and bought the home and I was happy. The home cost $11,000 then. It is worth probably $150,000 today. We were moving to the country. There was nothing out there back then. I told my wife I was going to go hunting for small game. It was all woods around us. Pretty soon there were bulldozers and fast development.

I went from the bottom to the top. We adjusted to it and enjoyed it. We had a wonderful family. We had six children, three boys and three girls. They are all out there now, of course, though I lost one boy six years ago. I've had a wonderful life and now I'm enjoying my golden years.

'I Have Never Talked Much About It'

I had almost five years in. It was a great experience, a powerful experience, and one that I will never forget. I'm 82 now and I could still tell you what happened. I like to give speeches. I have given a couple speeches to the American Legion and to schools to enlighten them. I wanted them to know not what I did but what the ones who died did. I want the world to never forget, especially the newer generations, what all of those soldiers, sailors, and Marines did in places like Iwo Jima, et cetera. We risked and sacrificed our lives so that we could all be here today in this beautiful country of ours. I have belonged to the American Legion for twelve years now. I belong to the Pearl Harbor Survivors, and we meet every month. I keep in touch with everybody. And I have made the speeches to schoolchildren, and they were great. They surprised me. They would ask questions and I had to have the answers; they were sixth graders. When I talked about the natives, they asked how I could talk to the natives because they didn't speak English? I told them about Guadalcanal being controlled by England and how the English would send natives to school in England where they would learn the language. They spoke better than I did. You had to be on the alert. It was a great experience. I have never talked much about the war but when asked a question I have answered. But when I talk to these younger people, I want them to know what those men did, losing their lives for their country. I always speak for them.

Well, [my service] made a man out of me. I became a good family man because of my experiences. I was a kid who came from the Bronx and saw what life was all about. The people I met, the things I'd seen, the people I lost. It was a great experience. It really made a man out of me. I grew up overnight.

Frank J. Castronovo passed on July 6, 2014 at the age of 95.

CHAPTER THREE

The Marine Rifleman

A working-class kid from Troy, New York, Chuckie Jacobs became a United States Marine and a recipient of the Purple Heart after being wounded on Guadalcanal in the opening days of America's engagement with the Japanese on land. He went from high school to being schooled hard into how to kill. Unfortunately, being of Jewish descent, he was no stranger to discrimination, but like many of our men from the North Country, training in the Jim Crow-era South came as a rude awakening. He shared many stories about fighting across the South Pacific in the early days of the war as he gave this interview in the summer of 2001 when he was nearly 79 years old.

Charles M. Jacobs

I was born in Troy, New York, on December 29, 1922. I went to public school in Troy, and I went to high school in Troy, and I played football and basketball there. And I got into this war because I had to get into it. I enlisted on January 21, 1942, in Albany, New York. I lived in Troy and there was no Marine station in Troy, and I had to come to Albany to enlist. The way I got into this thing—I was a member of a Greek fraternity in high school that had chapters in Albany, Troy, Schenectady, and Hudson, New York. On

December 7 my group from Troy—six of us—went down to Hudson for a joint meeting with the Hudson, New York, boys. On the way back I was driving the car—it was my friend's 1931 Plymouth—and on the way back one of the fellas said, 'Turn the radio on.'

I turned the radio on, and we heard a little of what today they call elevator music, Benny Goodman and so forth. The program was interrupted, and the announcement came through that the Japanese had just bombed Pearl Harbor, there were many casualties, our Navy was shot up pretty badly, and the next day the president was going to declare war on the Japanese. To make matters worse, one of the boys with us had a brother and the brother was stationed at Pearl Harbor. Of course, he was beside himself with fear and anxiety over what had happened to his brother, and it was about three weeks before he found out that his brother was uninjured.

'I Feel Like I Have to Do Something'

I went home that night, and my folks were still up, and they asked me if I heard the news, and I said, 'Yes,' and they said, 'What are you going to do?'

I said, 'Well, I feel like I have to do something.'

I was taking a PG course at Troy High School to try to get a scholarship, which I never got, and I said to my folks that I would probably just end school right now and sign up at the Marine Corps. Do you know the reason for the Marines? Okay, I'll take you back to the eighteenth century. Back in the eighteenth century, they had sailing ships, and the idea when you had a sailing ship was to grapple them with these grappling hooks and pull them together and board them and kill everybody on board and take the ship and win the battle. The Marines were up in the crow's nest, up in the sails on the bars. The Marines were the sharpshooters and they used to shoot the officers of the enemy, so they had no leadership. That was their first purpose. Their second purpose was to go ashore and fight shore battles for the Navy. That's why the Marines were started back in the eighteenth century. I wanted to go into an outfit that I thought was a good tough outfit.

My mother said, 'Why do you want to join the Marines?' Because she knew what kind of an outfit it was, because her brother had run away from home and joined the Marines when he was a young man. He went from an enlisted man—he became a captain in WWII. He was practically blind, and he was running the officers' mess in Quantico, Virginia.

I wrote him a letter and I said, 'I'm thinking of joining the Marines now that the war has started.' I much admired him and his integrity and his honor and he came from being a private and became a captain. And it was a prestigious outfit, and I just wanted to be a Marine; I didn't want to be a soldier.

He wrote me back and said, 'I can't do anything for you.' I wasn't really interested in him doing anything for me; I was just interested in what his opinion was, and no matter what it was, I went down to Albany and I signed up at the Marine Corps Recruitment Office in Albany, New York. It was on probably the 10th or the 12th of January. As time went on, we passed the time of day—I left school, I told my coach and my teachers that I was all through. I had my diploma from June, and I was going into the Marines.

On the 21st of January my family—my brother, my mother, my father—got on a bus and we went from Troy to Albany. It was a very, very sad day because I left my family, and I didn't see them again for over two years. You know, I had been down to New York for a long weekend. But I had never been away from home before; when I left home, I was nineteen years old.

They put me on a train. I had a ticket that they gave me, and they sent me down to Parris Island, South Carolina, for boot camp. Now, I was in very good physical condition, but I was completely unprepared for boot camp. I was never subjected to harsh discipline by my parents; I never had any harsh discipline from any of my teachers because I usually did what they told me to do.

When I got to the Marine Corps it didn't make any difference what you were, or who you were, or how they felt—they really busted you up pretty good. I realized later the reason for this—the reason they worked on us like this—was so that we would be an army that was disciplined that could go in and fight a battle, because they no longer did battles where they had masses of soldiers trying to knock somebody out. It was a little more finessed. And you have to have people who will obey officers—who will obey non-commissioned officers—so this is the reason for that harsh treatment. We had to say 'sir' to everybody, everybody, on the base at Parris Island and Platoon 122—even the guy that did the cooking, or anybody. 'Yes, sir,' 'No, sir,' we had to say, and salute. But that got us ready for what came later.

'A Guy Who Wanted to Kill Somebody'

Well, we did our stint at Parris Island. We were there five weeks—they taught us close-order drill, they taught us bayonetting, they taught us weaponry, they gave us a rifle and wouldn't give us any ammunition yet, but they gave us a rifle. We had to know how to field strip it, we had to learn how to fight with bayonets, and they taught us how to kill people with our bare hands or with a knife. It was all things that I wasn't used to—this kind of thing. I was brought up in a decent home and there was never any talk of killing anybody, and all of a sudden from a nice young man I became a guy who wanted to kill somebody. And this is what I was taught in the Marines and that was what I had to do. At the time I was a little shocked. But I realized that this was what I had to do, because I did sign up, I am a Marine, and if the Marines have to do the fighting this way, this is the way I'm going to do it. And so we trained at Parris Island for that five weeks and about three days before Easter in April 1942, they told us to pack our gear; we were going to be transferred and we were going down to join a regiment.

They sent us to Camp Lejeune in North Carolina. They assigned me to A Company, 1st Battalion, 7th Regiment, 1st Marine Division, Fleet Marine Force—the United States now being in a state of war. And I finally had my assignment. I must mention I tried to get into the Marine Air Corps, but I wasn't accepted. I had to become a grunt, just a regular mud Marine.

Once we left Parris Island, we saluted everybody we saw, and everybody we saw, except the officers, said, 'It's not necessary to salute—only officers—you don't have to salute enlisted men.' We felt more like Marines then. They do tell you in the Marine Corps that you're the toughest guy on the street. Of course, it's not true, but we thought it was. We got to Camp Lejeune and there we started some real serious training—boat landings, invasions, jujitsu. We did a lot of hiking; we did a lot of squabbling amongst each other, and we finally figured we turned out probably halfway decent Marines. Then after a couple of months or a little bit less, one officer came into our tent and said, 'Pack up your gear, we're leaving.'

'Where are we going, sir?'

'I can't tell you that because I don't know either. Pack up your gear. We're leaving in twenty-four hours.'

Jim Crow

Twenty-four hours later we were down in Norfolk, Virginia, waiting to get on a boat. It was there that I saw one of my first signs of Jim Crowism, which really set me to thinking as good as this country is, there's some things wrong with it. I had a buddy who was from Georgia, and we got on the ship, and then we were given twelve hours' leave. We had to be back by midnight because we were going to sail. So we got on a streetcar, my friend Hig and I, and I got on the car first and there was a big heavy black man sitting in a seat all by himself and there was a very, very drop-dead gorgeous black girl sitting right in front of him. Of course, they weren't blacks then, they were Negroes.

I sat down next to the black guy. I pointed to the other seat, [near the black girl]. 'Here, Hig, sit there.' He had a funny look on his face, like he was ready to kill me.

Finally we got off the trolley car, and he says, 'Don't you ever have me sit next to a black girl like that, ever!' Only he didn't say 'black girl'; I never heard that 'N' word in my house. He finally got over his anger, though, but that was the first taste I had of Jim Crow. I thought it stunk, if you want to know the truth. It's not a way to treat people—very bad. I grew up playing basketball on a high school team, and football too, with a bunch of black guys and we smoked cigarettes with each other. They were all good guys. I had nothing against them. We weren't social friends, but I wasn't social friends with some other guys.

There was another Jim Crow incident [that I remember]. I was going on a train, and we had to stop in Washington. When I got off the train, everybody on it was white. And I got on the other train—because we had to change trains—I remembered my ditty bag was on the first train, so I ran back and [now] the other train was all black—all black people. I looked around and I said, 'I left something here,' and some guy said, 'Is that it right there?'

I said, 'Yeah, thank you very much, sir.' And he looked at me as if I said something wrong. I was just being polite. He was a guy. He was a black guy, but he was a guy. I never discriminated against people in any way.

Anyway, we got off the trolley car and we had a few beers. They weren't supposed to serve us, but they did. There were no girls around because there were so many sailors and Marines, so we went back to the ship, and we boarded the ship.

Shipping Out

The next day the ship took off around Cape Hatteras—one of the roughest pieces of water I ever saw. Guys were losing their breakfast and I think their lunch from the day before. It was pretty rough. Fortunately, it didn't bother me too much. I was able to eat and control everything. We went down through the Panama Canal and that was an interesting experience because you go on one level and the boat comes up and then you are talking to people on the dock. It was very, very nice. The food on board the ship wasn't too great. I walked into my bunk that was right on the water line and all I could think of was if a torpedo comes through this boat I am going to be blown to smithereens. And I figured to myself later, 'What am I worrying about because I'll never know the difference.'

'Island Paradise'

We got to where we were going—we were going to British Samoa. British Samoa was the next place that the Japanese were going to hit, according to what the brass thought, so we were there to defend British Samoa. And we got there and we trained, and we trained, and we trained, and they had a rifle range and we learned how to use our rifles better, we learned how to field strip them blind, we learned machine gunnery, we learned as many aspects of the war as they could teach us, and of course foxhole digging was my number one preference. We were pretty good at that.

At that time I was a rifleman. On Guadalcanal I had a rifle grenade, if you know what a rifle grenade is, and many people don't know. It's a rifle with a groove you put on the top and you put the grenade in and you put it on the ground and you pull the trigger and the thing comes out and goes over the hill and kills everybody on the other side theoretically. I never did get to fire it, but I did have it, and I did know how to use it. I used it, but I never fired it in combat.

British Samoa was like forty years behind the times. We went into a department store once—of course there wasn't much to buy. There were natives there—they wore the lava-lavas around them. They had some very strange toilet habits, but we put up with that. But they were okay; we didn't have any problem with them.

We did have one captain we had a lot of problems with, though. He was allegedly part of the Vitol Oil Company—I don't know if he was or not. He was about six foot seven and he had a stride that was very, very wide, and going up the hill the fellas at the bottom, at the back, they just couldn't keep up. And he gave us a bad time because we were doing this. I had the privilege of serving under a man by the name of Lewis B. 'Chesty' Puller, who was a Marine Corps legend, and this guy wasn't even in the war yet.[43] While this guy was berating us, Chesty came down and berated him. He let him have both barrels. When it came time to leave this island paradise, this captain was gone—he was sent someplace else.

'He Got Killed Last Night'

When we left that island, we were going into combat. In August we were on British Samoa. You see, we had been 1st Division, but when we came to Samoa we were detached, and we became the 3rd Marine Brigade. That was what we operated under with the whole

---

[43] Lewis B. 'Chesty' Puller (1898-1971) was a career Marine Corps officer and is the most decorated Marine in history, having been awarded five Navy Crosses, a Silver Star, and one Distinguished Service Cross, second only to the Medal of Honor.

regiment—called the 3rd Marine Brigade—because we had other people attached to us. We got put on ships and we didn't know where we were going, but we had a pretty good idea because we heard the rest of the division had invaded Guadalcanal because that's where the Japanese were and that was their stronghold. And I remember going on the ship and going over the ladder and we hit the beach. And of course, there wasn't anybody shooting at us because the Marines had a little base there and I can remember very distinctly, and I have to digress now. My father ran a dress factory in Troy and he had a lady working for him by the name of Mrs. Mulhalick, a very lovely old lady, and she brought her grandson up. Her grandson joined the Marines, and he was a sergeant. I never knew him, never met him, never knew what he looked like. As we were marching up to the lines, there was another group coming out. They hollered to us, 'Where are you guys from? What are you?'

We said, 'We're A17. What are you?'

'We're D25.' Whatever they were.

And I hollered out, 'Do you know a guy by the name of Bill Mulhalick?'

Some guy hollers, 'Yeah, he got killed last night!' That was the first real meaning of what a war is.

*

We went up and they gave us the airport to guard. I guess they didn't trust us on the line yet. So we guarded the airport and we asked, 'What's out there?'

'Well, nothing.'

'What do you mean nothing? Japs out there?'

'Of course. If anybody's out there, shoot him!'

Fortunately, nothing happened. The next day we were put in another position, moved up to the lines, and we were told to dig holes. So we dug our foxholes and I thought I had a foxhole about four feet deep. About two o'clock in the morning, we hear a 'putt,

putt, putt, putt, putt.' It was the Japanese version of a Piper Cub, but we called them 'Washing Machine Charlies.' Washing Machine Charlie came over and he would drop flares and light the place up like daylight and he would drop two or three of those, and then he would drop a few little bombs and then he'd go away. He was harmless. He didn't hurt anybody, or not too many. But the bad thing was, out in the bay, ten miles or nine miles out, was a Japanese cruiser, and he was throwing shells at us and that was the first time in my life that I was ever petrified. I was so scared my knees were knocking.

This is something that you get over. So I dug my hole deeper; I thought I had it about eight feet deep. I woke up the next morning—it was only [about a foot!] If a shell had landed near me, I would have been gone.

The Patrols

The next day, we started on patrols. We had various ones, sometimes we were just on a reconnaissance patrol, sometimes we were on a combat patrol, we did all kinds of patrols, and we got into firefights and guys got hurt, a lot of people got killed.

And after a while, you know, you get used to it. One of the first Marines that I knew that got killed was a guy by the name of Beamer. I don't know where he was from, but he went out in the woods to take care of some business, out into the jungle not far from our lines, and one of the guys saw movement out there, one of the Marines, and shot him. He died; he was dead. The war was beginning to come home to me now—that people have to die.

And on this one patrol, we went out—it was a combat patrol—of course we ran into problems. We ran into trouble, we ran into the Japanese, and we were having quite a fight and fortunately we kicked them out, we got them to run. My friend Higginbotham got shot, he didn't get killed, he got shot, but he left Guadalcanal. Strangely, I never heard from him again, he never wrote a letter; I never saw him again. Yet, we were pretty good friends.

After the fight I went around to see who got hurt. They had a little sort of a field hospital for the guys that got hurt and weren't dead. So I went over. There was this friend of mine, a guy by the name of Roe. He was lying on his stomach. I said, 'Where did you get hit?'

He said, 'I got hit in the butt.'

I said, 'Oh, that's good, you'll get to go home!'

He looked at me kind of funny, quizzically, and said, 'Yeah.'

So I went to sleep that night and it was quiet after that. I woke up the next morning to see how Roe was, and somebody said he died during the night.

I said, 'What did he die from?'

The corpsman told me, 'He wasn't only shot in the rear end, he had three bullet holes in his stomach, and he died.'

So friends of mine were beginning to have some problems. Higginbotham left, he was gone. I made friends with other people. As time went on, we started to get illnesses—jaundice, malaria, dysentery—we all got it. We all got malaria. This is the scourge that makes you practically useless while you have it, but when they manage to bring your fever down and break it, you're okay.

'Don't Worry About the Worms'

Living conditions on Guadalcanal were pretty rugged; there were no tents. We slept on the ground or in pup tents if we had a chance; most of the time we just slept on the ground. The food was abominable. We had no line of communication to get food or ammunition. It was very weak, the line was, and the food that we ate was sometimes Japanese rice and that was wormy, but somebody said, 'Don't worry about the worms—they're protein.' Living conditions were not good, but, hey, we didn't think anything of it—this was a war.

But I will tell you about the big fiasco. I said I served under Colonel—he became a colonel; he finally became a lieutenant general—Chesty Puller. At that time, he was a lieutenant colonel. He was our battalion commander, and he was away at a divisional meeting with whoever—I don't know. So, the man in charge was a fella by the name of Major Rogers. He was from Washington, D.C. He was in the reserve. In my mind, he wasn't too bright, because when he went into combat, he had his major's insignia on; he had shiny boots and a clean uniform.

The Beach

Anyhow, we were back in R&R coming off some patrol and the word came down that the Japanese were coming up the beach and at company strength—somebody go stop them. So who got it? A Company got it. So we all—they put us on Higgins boats and we went out and made the landing. Now this is significant to the story because when Higgins boats wait for you out in the bay, they go in a circle, and when one breaks off, all the others follow. We made our landing, we took the high ground; we didn't dig holes because there wasn't time. The Japanese were coming up; we're taking shots at them, and we discovered that there's not a company down there, there's a whole battalion! And we're a company of probably only 120 of us left. We were in big trouble. So we called for some artillery fire. Of course, the artillery was 75 mm, they only go three or four miles. The shells were landing among the Marines and not among the Japanese! We were getting it from our own men, from our own artillery, and we were getting it from the Japanese! So, somebody said, 'We better get the hell out of here! We're in trouble.' The first one to get killed was this major. He was walking around with those fancy boots on and the insignia; he took a shot right away. There was a young guy—I don't know from what company, he was a signalman—he got up on a stump and signaled the boats in the bay with the wigwag and they wouldn't come in! They stayed out there. I think he got a Navy Cross, because they were shooting at him, but nobody hit him. On the way down, we were all scared now; not scared to the point of panic, but we were trapped, we were going to get annihilated. There were just too many of them.

I was running down towards the beach and there was this Marine off to my left. I don't know who he was—he was probably with a machine gun company. I was here and a hand grenade went off and blew up. It hit me in the leg and knocked me—just like somebody threw a body block on me, and knocked me right off my feet and on my face. I crawled over and looked at him and he was gone. He was dead.

I figured I had to get to the beach. I did the best I could. I looked down at my leg and I said, 'I wonder if it's still there.' So I pulled up my pant leg and there was a little tiny hole in my leg and there was one hole in my pants. I figured it's a small piece. I got up to try to run, and I couldn't. I had to crawl and hop and everything else. I finally got to the beach, and we set up a perimeter. Meanwhile, those boats were still circling around in the harbor.

We had the perimeter up. The Japanese were attacking us lightly. I don't know why; we must have been holding them off pretty good. A young fellow by the name of Hittit—I don't know where he was from—stripped bare naked and swam out to the boats. They pulled him on board, and he said, 'Thanks for picking me up. Now go in and get the rest of the guys.'

I swear this is the truth. They said, 'No, there's too much shooting going on there!'

This was a war. He picked up a pipe wrench and he said to the coxswain on that boat, 'If you don't go in and get those men, you're going to get killed!' The boats went around and came in [to pick us up].

'I Would Follow Him into Hell'

One of my worst enemies, yet one of the best soldiers I ever knew, was a man by the name of Anthony P. Malinowski. He was my platoon sergeant. For one reason or another which I don't want to go into, he and I didn't like each other. Well, the truth is he didn't like me because of my religion, and I didn't like him because he didn't like me. So I got all the 'good' details—digging the trenches, desk duty, and everything bad he could give me. But I would follow him into hell because he was a good soldier, so I figure I got a better chance of living. He was a hero. He came down to the beach and he had a BAR, which is a Browning Automatic Rifle, which shoots a lot of bullets. He was shooting that, fighting the Japanese, and he got hit in the chest kind of hard. Before he fell down, he gave the BAR to somebody else. Another kid from New Mexico, we called him Tex-Mex, he was one of these dark-skinned guys, probably Indian descent from New Mexico, real nice guy, good-looking guy, good kid, nice boy, had a lot of fun. He got shot in the legs. He got beat up pretty badly. He said, 'Give me a BAR and give me some ammo and I'll hold them back.' And I guess he did, because then we got out. I never saw this guy again, so we assumed that he got killed too.

Once we got in the water, I was having trouble. My leg was numb. I finally got myself pulled up and into the Higgins boat. My company commander crawls up on the Higgins boat and he's got his .45 in his hand, and puts his hands up on the gunnel of the boat.

And, 'boom,' his pistol went off and he shoots himself in the hand! I thought that was pretty sad, but that wasn't the saddest part. He got onto the boat by himself, and he goes and he sits down over on the opposite side from me. There was a BAR sitting there and it had been shot, fired. It was hot and he sat on it with wet clothes. He jumped two feet up in the air. I laughed. He said he was going to court martial me.

I said, 'Well, there's no charge,' and I didn't worry about it, and he never did.

'This Guy's Dead'

They took us back to the base, and I said, 'Hey, this is great! I'm alive! Maybe I'll go home!' They took me back to the base. I couldn't get off the boat. I couldn't walk, so a couple of corpsmen came up and took me under the arms and brought me and put me down on a stretcher. I had given my jacket to somebody because he was cold. Now it's dark so I'm getting cold. I said to the corpsman, 'Can you get a blanket? I'm cold.'

And he says, 'Yeah.' So he went and got a blanket, and he threw it over me. I was lying there under the blanket. Some guy came over and kicked the stretcher and said, 'This guy's dead.'

'No, I'm not.' I sat up. 'I'm not dead.'

'Oh, go to the hospital.' So they took me to the hospital. The doctor examined me and looked at my leg and he said, 'Well, that doesn't look like much.'

I said, 'It hurts!'

He said, 'We'll give you something for the pain.' And he said, 'Nothing in there now.'

I said, 'When did it come out?'

He said, 'Well it bounced out.'

And I said, 'It bounced out where?'

And, well, he said, 'It went out the same hole.'

I knew he was lying to me. They were so hard up for men, they had to keep me there.

I couldn't walk. They kept me in the hospital about ten days. Ten days later I got out and my legs were swollen up and I could hardly walk from the sulfur drugs. And I went back to duty. And I missed out on one of the best shoots I ever missed out on, it was a wonderful shoot. The boys sat on the side of the hill and shot all the Japs who were trying to get out. We had them trapped. I wasn't even there. I couldn't walk. My captain told me to stay home, back at the base.

'I Was in Very Bad Shape'

After that I went from bad to worse. I got malaria, I got jaundice, and my leg started to get infected. I had a knot in my groin as big as your fist. Come December, I couldn't even stand up. I couldn't even sit up. I went from 175 pounds to about 125 and I was in very bad shape. So they said to me, 'You're relieved of duty. We'll take you down to the beach.' They took me down to the beach. I don't know what I was waiting for. And I woke up one morning and there out in the bay was a beautiful big white ship. It was a hospital ship. Some corpsmen came down and said, 'Do you need some help?'

I said, 'Yes, I can't walk.' So they took me and brought me right into the sick bay on the hospital ship and they unwrapped my wound. I had gauze around my wound, and I swear as they pulled the gauze off it stuck to the scab, which wasn't really scabbed over, it was just a little scabby. They pulled it and the blood shot twenty feet across the room. He said, 'My God, what happened to you?'

I said, 'I got hit with a piece of something—hand grenade.'

He said, 'Why didn't they take it out?'

'They told me it bounced out.'

He said, 'That's ridiculous. We'll fix you up.'

So that night on the ship I got another attack of malaria. I had 104.5; at 108 you're probably dead. But they broke the fever, and I was okay the next day. I was weak but I was all right. They started a [transfer] and they sent me to a hospital in Wellington, New Zealand. Nice country, nice people.

I was in the hospital, and I started to get better because they had taken the shrapnel out of my leg. The sinews and tendons were all wrapped around it. It was only a little piece but once they took that out, about ten days later, the bump in my groin, that went down, and I was feeling pretty good. So I was walking on the base one day. This was the Naval Hospital, of course, because everybody knows the Marines are part of the Navy; even our corpsmen are sailors. They didn't like it, but they were ours. I noticed on the bulletin board was a sign—'any Jewish serviceman who wanted to spend the Passover holiday with some New Zealand people, report to the chaplain.' So I reported to the chaplain. I think he was a Baptist. He said, 'I will send you to a rabbi who will assign you to a family.'

I said, 'Okay.' So I got my pass and everything, and I went down to see this rabbi, and I knocked on the door of the address he gave me and a man comes up—a big, tall man—and he had his collar on backwards. I looked at him and said. 'Gee, Father, I'm sorry, I must be in the wrong house.'

He said, 'No, I'm Rabbi 'So and so'; you're in the right house.'

I said, 'Why the collar?'

He said, 'In the British Isles, the British possessions, all clergymen wear their collar this way.'

I said, 'Okay, I can live with that. So we got talking and the second thing he said to me after my name is, 'Where are you from?'

'Well, I'm from a small town in upstate New York. You probably never heard of it.' This is down in Wellington, New Zealand.

He said, 'Where?'

I said, 'Troy.'

'Oh,' he said, 'Troy, New York,' and his eyes lit up.

He said, 'Do you know Rabbi Geffen?'

I said, 'Sure, he was my rabbi. He prepared me for my bar mitzvah.'

He said, 'I'm the man who talked him into becoming a rabbi. I'm going to give you a good home to go to.'

I said, 'Great.' So he sent me over to #6 Park Street, Thorndon, Wellington, New Zealand, to a man by the name of Jack Meltzer. He was a barrister—a lawyer—he was a lawyer for all the policeman in the country of New Zealand when they got into civil trouble. And he had a very nice home. It was 1942. He had a nice home; he had a wife, he had a sister-in-law and a mother-in-law and a daughter. Very nice people.

The first thing he said to me was, 'Do you want a shot of Dewars?'

I said, 'What's Dewars?'

He said, 'Scotch.'

So we had Passover—very nice—we had a Passover service. I went down to breakfast the next morning. I sat down and they gave me some toast and they gave me an egg and I knew that eggs were impossible to get—very, very difficult. They got maybe one egg a week a person, maybe, if they could get them.

I said, 'Gee, I don't want this egg, I get eggs all the time. Please, somebody else eat it.'

'You're our guest, you eat it.' I choked it down; believe me it was hard going down. And it was very nice.

They said, 'Why don't you come back next week—the end of the holiday.'

They were so nice to me I decided that there was something I had to do for them. I knew, because they had told me, that canned fruit was absolutely impossible to obtain in New Zealand in 1942.

They just couldn't get any canned pineapple, peaches, pears, anything, it was just unavailable. So I went back to the base and said I got to figure out a way to get them some canned fruit. And I really didn't know how to go about it because it involved theft.

I went down to the commissary, and I looked around and nobody's around, and there's a whole case of pineapple sitting there, canned pineapple, So I took that and I ran with it under my arms back to where my sea bag was, my duffle bag, and I threw it in my duffle bag. If I ever got an inspection, I would probably have gotten imprisoned or something. But it didn't happen that way. When I took that to them, they thought that I had given them a bar of gold. They were so happy.

Now, being Jewish has never affected me to any great extent. I always knew that we, the Jews, are a minority in this country and we have to give up some of the things that we cherish—not all of them, just some of them—to be able to get along in this country as human beings, and most of us do this. It hasn't affected me at all—only in two instances, the one with my platoon sergeant and then there was another instance; no sense in even going through it because this guy was a vicious guy, and he was also a coward. Malinowski, on the other hand, was a hero. I didn't like him, but he was a hero. There were a lot of guys that didn't like me, but most never really showed it, and a lot of guys did like me. It really wasn't a factor. Oh, I'm sure there was discrimination, but I found that out when I was going to school, that you've got to be what you are and just do the best you can. I got along with 98% of the people that I came in contact with, because that's the way I was trained. My father said, 'Don't insult anybody.' I only do it when I have to.

The Boxer

We had some recreation. At one time over on New Zealand the Marines had a football team. There was a guy by the name of 'Crazy Legs' Hirsch—he used to play for Notre Dame, I think. We used to go down and watch that, we used to play softball. Over on Samoa, we boxed. We put the gloves on with the Samoan guys and this guy kept telling me he's a champion, he's a champion. He kept coming at me. He said, 'Take it easy, take it easy. I'm taking it easy on you.' He hit me. I was never a boxer, but I knew a little bit about it, so I hauled off and I feinted him one way and he took the feint and I hit him in the jaw and knocked him right on his [ass]. He got up and ran away. That was the end of that fight.

There was a guy by the name of Flynn. Another guy and I were fooling around in the tent. We were wrestling; we knocked his rifle over. In the Marine Corps, the rifle is your god. You keep it clean at all times. It's the first thing you clean when you come off the field before you even clean yourself. This is an important thing—you've got to keep it working.

So, I knocked his rifle off on the ground. This guy Flynn said, 'Clean it.'

So I said, 'Okay,' and I picked it up and wiped it off. I said, 'That's good enough.'

He said, 'No, it's not.'

I said, 'Yes, it is.' So we started fooling around again, this other guy and myself, and knocked the rifle off again.

'Now pick it up and clean it and take it apart.'

I said, 'No, I won't take it apart! You want to make something out of it, come on outside!'

He was only a little guy about 135 pounds. I was 170. I [figured I] could kill him.

He said, 'No, no.' I thought he was scared of me. I felt pretty good, went back to my tent.

A couple of days later I'm reading *Ring Magazine*. You know what *Ring Magazine* is? I'm thumbing through the pages and there he is, 'Irish Frankie Flynn,' Number 7 welterweight in the country! I'm going to take him? So I ran over to his tent.

I said, 'Is that you?'

He said, 'Yeah.'

I said, 'Why didn't you take me outside? You would have killed me!'

He said, 'No, I can't. If a fighter hits somebody—these [fists] are weapons—and they hurt him, they are in big trouble. That's why I didn't go out with you.'

I said, 'Now I know! Thanks for not going out.'

So a couple of days later we were putting the gloves on, and he said, 'You want to put them on with me?'

I said, 'Yeah, under conditions,' and he said, 'What are the conditions?'

I said, 'That you don't get too cute.'

He said, 'Don't worry; I just want to practice bobbing and weaving.'

So we put them on, and I was swinging at him and I was missing like crazy, and all of a sudden he bobbed when he should have weaved, and I caught him with a left hook. He came at me and then he stopped, and he smiled and he said it was a good shot.

On Guadalcanal he was out on patrol, and he got shot in the back and he lost the use of his legs. And I felt so sad for Frankie Flynn. He was from Buffalo, New York, a nice guy; we were good friends after a while.

Cape Gloucester

A short time later, I was sent back to my outfit on an LST to Melbourne, Australia, and it was a different outfit. I was sent back to the same company, I was in the same platoon, I was in the same squad, but I didn't know anybody—maybe three guys—it had turned over so much with illness, disease, killed, wounded. But I made some new friends, and we made the Cape Gloucester landing and it was much the same as Guadalcanal; there was fighting and there was killing and there was dying. Everybody knows that this is what happens in a war.

In Cape Gloucester we were much more organized: we had backup, we had people to bring in food, people to bring in ammunition, they brought fresh troops in. And when we went to Guadalcanal, the Marines were—I wouldn't say we saved them—but they were in very tough shape because we were reinforcements. We were a whole regiment. In Cape Gloucester we went in as a big unit. We had lots of help. It was a much easier combat, the food was better, we had more time off because we had more people.

I was a mortarman on Cape Gloucester, I was a BAR man, and I was also a rifle grenadier. I did it all. I did shoot the 60-millimeter mortar. That was pretty interesting because you could lay back behind the lines a little bit. Of course, they could always break in through, too. I remember one incident; we had a spotter. There are things in the back of the mortar called increments. And you pull them off if you wanted to go a short distance, and you leave them on if you wanted to go a long distance—so many increments, so many feet. I used to know all that; I don't know it anymore. Our spotter told us what to do, and we did it. I dropped one in; I was the assistant. I dropped one in, and he said, 'Bullseye!' There were three Japanese soldiers running along and we hit right in the middle of them—got them all.

Stateside

After Cape Gloucester they sent us to a place called the Russell Islands. This was a small group of islands. I don't even know much about them. But they had a bulletin board. I'm a man of bulletin boards—the bulletin board got me to the Meltzers and got me two other things. I went to the bulletin board and there's a big notice and it said, 'All Marines with so many points can go back to the United States.'

I thought, 'How many points do I have?' And I read it out, what I had and what was required. I had, I think it was, eighty-six points and the requirement was like sixty, so I was number two on the list.

They put me on another ship and sent me back to San Francisco and Camp Pendleton and back to Albany. Years ago, the city of Troy had a Niagara Mohawk power coke plant—I don't know if anybody remembers it—but there was a smell from that, there was a terrible smell in South Troy, and in that taxicab going home, I smelled it and I knew I was home. So I had thirty days home, I had thirty days' leave. I had a good time. I only got malaria once and put in for an extension of leave. They gave me ten more days.

I reported back to Camp Lejeune, North Carolina. I was checked in by a sergeant who was taking the role and he said, 'Jacobs, Charles Jacobs?'

I said, 'Yes.'

He said, 'Are you Chuckie Jacobs from Troy?'

And I said, 'Yeah.'

He said, 'I'm Ikie Ring.' I didn't even recognize the guy. We played baseball against each other. He played for the tough guys from downtown. I played for the tough guys from up above.

He said, 'I have a good job for you.'

I said, 'Gee, thanks. What is it?'

He said, 'Just report to me every day.'

So every day I reported to him.

He [would then say], 'Get lost.' Great duty. Great duty. [*Chuckles*]

'He Had to Kiss It'

So anyhow, I was scheduled to go back overseas. Now, I'm not a fool—I figure the chances of coming out alive this time are little or none, or slim, or maybe—you know, who knows. But I figured I still wanted to serve my country. I wasn't going to fight it. I was going to go.

I came to a bulletin board. There on the bulletin board, it said, 'Any service personnel, any Marines, who think they want to go to college and become an officer—must be a high school graduate—report to so and so.' I scooted right down there. I told them I'd like to become an officer.

They said, 'You've got to take an IQ test.' I figured this is the end. But I took the IQ test and I failed it.

They said, 'You were so close, you only missed by one point, why don't you take it again?' I took it again and I sailed right through it. I passed it and the Marine Corps sent me to Colgate University and now I'm going to become an officer and a gentleman. And everything went fine at Colgate University. I got a military education. I got a year in.

Then one day we're standing in the chow line waiting to go to chow. We were all in uniform—we're still Marines—and there was a newspaper published that said the atom bomb has been dropped on Japan and mass destruction. So me with my big mouth, I said, 'I'll bet the war's over in ten days.'

One guy up there said, 'I'll kiss your ass if it is!'

I said, 'Huh?' Ten days later the war is over, and I was up in my room getting ready to go to class or doing something. The next thing I know there is a ruckus in the hall and here comes the whole company in and they grabbed me.

I said, 'What do you want?'

'Come on with us.'

They took me downstairs, and they got the guy that said he would kiss and brought him downstairs, and they took my pants off and he had to kiss it. This is a true story. I had a picture of it which I kept, but my mother had a flood in her cellar, and it's all gone.

The war ended. I was glad and I went to Bainbridge, Maryland, and got discharged, and the last thing I remember going through the discharge line—going through all the papers they have, you know the military has nine thousand papers—there was a guy sitting over at a little desk, a Marine all by himself, and he gives me the finger [*indicates index finger*]. 'Come here.'

I walked over and said, 'What can I do for you? I'm getting discharged.'

He said, 'Would you like to join the reserves?'

I said, 'Absolutely not!'

He said, 'Well, if another war erupts?'

I said, 'If another war erupts and my country needs me, I will be the first one to volunteer. I don't want to be in the reserves.' Of course, this is 1946 and in 1950 we had Korea.

'I Thought They Were Animals'

Having come in contact with the Japanese on several occasions, I thought that they were not too bright, some of them, but some of them were very smart. I thought that they were animals in some cases—maybe that's a little harsh term—but they did some awful jobs on some friends of mine and the one guy who was a captive of the Japanese. They actually had him on the block to cut his head off. They didn't, fortunately, but they did a lot of them. We had one

Marine go out on a patrol and he got separated from his group, or separated from his squad or whatever, and the Japanese captured him. We found him on the wire the next day with his hands and his legs cut off. Which I didn't think was very nice. Shoot him, shoot him. Don't do this; don't mutilate a guy. For a long, long time I had a resentment against the Japanese. I wouldn't buy a Japanese car.

Today, things have changed. The people who live in Japan today are not the same people. I figure maybe I killed their grandfather, you know. They're different people. I have even forgiven the Germans because they are not the same people that were so miserable to us. But this country was so good to us, so good to my family. One great-grandfather came over from Germany in 1850 or 1860 or somewhere around there and another one came over in 1880 and we found a haven here and it's been a pretty nice country.

'It's Not Your Job to Die for Your Country'

It was a very memorable war. It was the greatest experience of my life. I was taught early—I realized early, in the beginning, when you go to war, it's not your job to die for your country, it's your job to see that the other guy dies for his country, and we won. We saved democracy; we saved the world.

After the war I came home. I got out in January. The following spring, I met my wife, and the following year in '47, I got married, went to Union College in Schenectady and got my bachelor's degree. The GI Bill was the only way I could get to college. Two things I appreciate about World War II—I was able to get a college education, and I didn't get killed. Those are the two things that I really feel good about. We've had three children and each child has two children of theirs, so I have six grandchildren. I went to work for a liquor wholesaler, and I eventually became a sales manager. I've had a pretty good life. I can't argue too much.

My military career was a career, for me, of necessity. I had to go to war because I felt it was my duty as a citizen and a patriot of this country to go to war, [but] I still think war is not the big answer. I think war is a terrible thing—is it Sherman or somebody who said, '[War is] hell,' but it's more than hell. Hell's nice compared to war. You have to live in a muddy foxhole and dirty clothes and see your friends get shot. It's really a very uncouth, unfair, and undignified way of life, and if we could eliminate wars, I think we would all be better off. But I don't know if there's any way to do it. I don't know how. If I did, I'd make a lot of money.

I hope someday down the line somebody looks at this and sees it and says it did them some good, and they were happy to read it.

Charles Jacobs passed at the age of 87 on January 10, 2010.

CHAPTER FOUR

The Invasion Radioman I

A man of culture and letters, Paul Elisha is a vocal advocate for what he came to call an enlightened army. He speaks with a confidence that comes from first-wave battle experience that ranged from the blizzards and frostbite of the Aleutian Islands to the tropical atolls of the South Pacific and beyond, tempered by fifty-plus years of reflection and contemplation about what it all meant, and the lessons that we have not apparently learned.

He also had a front-row seat to one of the most famous events in that theater, when Douglas MacArthur returned to the Philippines in 1945. A veteran of eight separate amphibious landings, trained by Marine commandos, he is a battle-hardened yet gentle soul, a poet and musician, and an advocate for civil rights and civic responsibility; he even hosted his own classical music show on public radio. He was with war correspondent Ernie Pyle in the days before Pyle was killed; Pyle encouraged his writing and told him to apply to Indiana University, which he followed through with. He gave a series of interviews in 2000 and 2001.

"I stayed close to that sergeant of mine who was a tough guy. He said, 'You can stick with me.' And I did; the problem, of course, was that he really was tough and didn't care about going where it was dangerous. I felt if I stuck with him, I would come out all right. I think he joined the Army

probably in '39 or '40. He came in before Pearl Harbor. He would say, 'Think about the job. Think what you have to do, don't think about anything else, that will get you through.' Now, people who are into yoga say, 'Be in the moment'—that's what he [taught us]."

Paul Elisha

Before I entered the service on September 2, 1942, I was going to school at night, at the junior college, studying journalism, and working in the daytime at the Signal Corps Radar Laboratories. It was an adjunct of Fort Monmouth. They were working on a lot of hot projects for the war, and I was a telephone emergency procurement person. They would give you a list of suppliers, and a list of what they needed. You would call three of them that met the specs, then get the bids, and the low bidder and the guy who could deliver it fastest got the contract. Then you just fill out the form and go on to the next one. I was doing that because I was underage, wanted to join right after Pearl Harbor, but my parents would not let me. As soon as I was able to convince my father the following September, he signed the papers, and I enlisted.

The nearest place I could enlist at the time was Fort Dix, so I went down there and enlisted, and thought I could get back to Fort Monmouth, for Signal Corps, but I ended up at Camp Crowder, Missouri. We were the cadre, the first basic trainees at Camp Crowder. I went in September of '42, and was mustered out literally within a day, [three years later]. I came on September 24, 1942, and was mustered out at the same place at Fort Dix, New Jersey, on September 25, 1945. So it was three years. During the first three months that I was in the service, I got one furlough. I went home for six days, I think, or something like that. Then after that, I just kept going west.

Radio School

[The basic training I received] was on par with other soldiers at the time, but it was nothing like the training I got later at Camp Pendleton with the Marines. It was a quick thing, six or eight weeks, I forget which. Close-order drill, hikes, lots of pushups, KP, other things like that, some work details on the camp itself. And you got tested for various things so they could decide where they were going to send you. I was lucky because when I joined, early in the war, you could still ask for a branch of service. So when I asked for Signal Corps, they gave me a number of tests. I was also a musician; I played the violin and the drums. And typical of the Army, 'Aha, musician with good rhythm, good hearing, we'll make him a radio operator.' So they sent me to a civilian radio school, which had been taken over by the military, Coyne Radio School in Chicago. We lived in a hotel, and I went to radio school, and [studied] electronics, technology, and code. I was rated when I graduated as a high-speed radio operator. From the day I joined my unit, I don't think we ever used code. We always used voice. It just wasn't feasible in the field.

In January we graduated, but in December we were visited by a large group of high-level people, brass. They came through school, watched us at work. We were told they would be giving exams, and that those getting the highest scores would be getting a wonderful surprise. The rumors were rife, of course; the Army was going to build—on Top of the Mark, in San Francisco—a worldwide propaganda station.[44] And we were going to man it. I studied very hard,

---

[44] *Top of the Mark*- The InterContinental Mark Hopkins Hotel is a luxury hotel in San Francisco, built in 1939. The Top of the Mark was the nineteenth-floor glass-walled cocktail lounge with 360-degree views of San Francisco. "During WWII, servicemen would buy and leave a bottle in the care of the bartender so that the next soldier from their squadron could enjoy a free

and I think of the top ten, I came in fifth or sixth in the class. I was immediately assigned to this great surprise. As a going-away present, we received first-class Pullman accommodations to the west coast rather than a troop train. I remember a sergeant saying, 'I don't know about this. If they are giving us this, it must be pretty awful!' [*Laughs*] And it turns out we were the cadre for the 75th Joint Assault Signal Company.

The Joint Assault Signal Company

[The joint assault signal companies] were literally formed for a purpose. After Carlson's Raiders landed on Makin, that operation told them that for amphibious [operations] you needed [better] communications. Out of that raid came the feeling by Navy and Marine and Army people that if they were going to do any large-scale landings, they needed a unit that would coordinate all of the things that went into the landing and send the word back to the commander on the ships. So they knew whether they had to lay down fire, send in planes, send in more supplies, logistics, medical things, whatever they needed. And one of the things that came out of that commando raid was the idea that for full-scale landings, they needed a unit that would go in and coordinate all the needs and get

---

drink; the only requirement being whoever had the last sip would buy the next bottle. The soldiers gathered before shipping out for one last toast to the Golden Gate, believing that the bridge was good luck and would bring them home. As they sailed off under the Golden Gate, wives and sweethearts would draw together in the lounge's northwest corner, where they would tearfully gaze out the windows to watch them go. This corner became known as the 'Weepers' Corner.'" Source: www.historichotels.org/us/hotels-resorts/intercontinental-mark-hopkins-hotel/restaurants/top-of-the-mark.php

the word back to the ships, the idea of a joint assault signal company.[45]

They formed the unit, and put us together at Camp Pendleton, where Jimmy Roosevelt and the Raiders were.[46] So they picked a company strength unit, and they took us out to Camp Pendleton, California. I was one of six radio operators assigned to that, and they put us through a month and a half of training with Carlson's guys. At Camp Pendleton, we prepared for amphibious stuff. And then we became the 75th Joint Assault Signal Company—JASCO; that was the first JASCO ever formed. And the idea was that we were going to do a quick thing, go out to the Aleutians, then come back and train all the other JASCOs. It never happened; we got going and kept going across [the Pacific]. [*Laughs*]

Commando Training

We were formed at Fort Ord. The company was mustered, we got our officers, then after several weeks, we loaded onto trucks and went on down to Camp Pendleton, where we began our training. The first guys in 75th JASCO were Field Artillery, Air Force, couple of Navy people, and all the rest were related to the Signal Corps. The idea was that you had to cover all the bases. In an amphibious assault, the Navy is your artillery, and the Air Force is your artillery,

---

[45] *that commando raid*- Less than two weeks after the Guadalcanal campaign got underway in the Solomons, in mid-August 1942, just over 200 Marines of the 2nd Marine Raider Battalion under command of Colonel Evans Carlson and Captain James Roosevelt were landed on Makin in the Gilberts from two American submarines. The Raiders killed over 80 Japanese soldiers, at a cost of 21 killed and nine captured, who were later beheaded. The Japanese then heavily reinforced the Makin garrison. Source: Battle of Makin, en.wikipedia.org/wiki/Battle_of_Makin.

[46] *Jimmy Roosevelt*- James Roosevelt II (1907-1991) was the eldest son of President Franklin D. Roosevelt and Eleanor Roosevelt and was awarded the Navy Cross for his actions in World War II.

you have to handle the air strikes, the offshore shelling, and all communications on the beach and back to the ships. We would do that until the landing phase was secured, then they would pull us out and [have us] do the same thing somewhere else. You have all these Navy and Field Artillery types, it's a pretty unusual organization. And now suddenly you are being trained by Marine Raiders.

We were amazed when we saw what we were about to do, because these guys were typical of the Raiders, at that time, shaved heads, you know, daggers at the hip. They were nothing like the spit-and-polish Marines and soldiers you saw, they were pretty special people and they acted like it. And we lived with them for the next six to eight weeks. They put us through training in hand-to-hand combat. You would go out to the end of a pier with full battle kit, and they would kick you off the pier into the water, and you would have to get to shore with everything on. They had guys in the water in case you didn't make it. As I recall, looking back, it was pretty rough.

I remember the demeaning way which the [Marine Raiders] looked upon the Army. I can understand why there is still a lot of antipathy among the services. They didn't think we were going to make it. They were told to train us, and they did it. They kept saying, 'You guys can't do this.' I think a lot of that was probably by design. Because if you got angry enough, you could damn well do what they said you couldn't. A lot of us did exactly that.

As I recall, there were a number of times they would put you through a lot. We had a lot of hikes on rugged terrain up and down the coast. Our graduation from that course, they landed us at some godforsaken beach some distance from Camp Pendleton. We had to land, go inland to some particular spot, then make our way back, overland, cross-country, without being detected, to get back to a pickup point. You had to use any and all advantages you could create, scrape up, or whatever [to pull through]. Some of us they had to go out and get. I managed to get back. I was with a couple of guys who had come out of the CCC [the Civilian Conservation Corps]. We had a number of labor men, wiremen, who had come in from the CCC. [See], back in the late thirties before the war, if you got in trouble and had to see the judge, you could join the Army, join the CCC, or go to jail, so some of these guys were pretty creative when it came to getting back to camp. [*Laughs*]

Attack in the Aleutians

The rumors were all over the place. As a matter of fact, the interesting thing was that a lot of us felt sort of cheated after we heard [a rumor] that we were going to go into a couple of actions and then we would come back and be ensconced in California and train everybody else. We never did get to do that, I guess. One story that we heard was that we got so good at it, they couldn't let us go.

For a while, somebody said they were going to send us to Guadalcanal, [that] they were going to do a second landing on Guadalcanal. We had nothing to do with it. There was a lot of pressure to do something in the Pacific to raise the morale of the country. Since the Aleutians were the only piece of American territory that the Japanese had taken, it stood to reason that it would be great if we could take it back. I think that's why the strike was planned.

After Pendleton, we went back to Fort Ord. We did some maneuvers up and down the coast. Then we got on a ship, did some maneuvers, then moved by truck to San Francisco. We were loaded on some ships and went north. We stopped at Adak, [Alaska], I remember. We bivouacked on a tundra hillside for a couple days, and they gave us some equipment. We realized we were going into something.

As usual, there was a foul-up. We were told it was only going to take a week or two. We went in May. The weather was miserable.

We had field jackets, ordinary pants, and combat boots. We did not have heavy boots or anything else. As a result, there were a lot of guys who got bayoneted in their foxholes because they froze, they could not handle their weapons. The Japanese would come down at night and bayonet them in their foxholes, on Attu.

Actually, I landed with a group from the 7th Division, it was like a Ranger company, and our job was to land in a cove on the other side of the island away from the main landings. We were to climb up this mountain, go over the top, and come down to a place where we could actually see what was below. I remember setting up the radio with my buddy at the time, and tuning the radio to various frequencies, and picking up Radio Vladivostok, and hearing them play part of Tchaikovsky's *1812 Overture*. And then the rest of the invasion landed, the main thrust, and then the Rangers, who we had accompanied, came down from the other side.

You never knew, going in, what was there until you got there, despite all the recon, information, and everything else. I went into eight invasions and was literally in the first wave on every one of them. So I just stayed with it.

*Radio communications.
US Signal Corps manual, WWII.*

The SCR-284

Usually, we used what they called an SCR-284. It was about the size of a suitcase, on two folding legs. The lid would plop down and that'd be your workspace. The set was facing you in the rest of the suitcase. And then you have a cable going to a generator, which you turn; that was the worst job of the lot. We lost several people because the generator let out a squeal whenever you had to transmit and that gave away your position. You'd have one SCR-284, the large one with the generator. You'd have a couple of backpack radios. Then with you, you'd have a few people for fire support if you ran into a hard time supporting your communications setup you had when you dug in.

If it was possible, you might have a jeep with an SCR-284 on it. So you'd have a driver and a guy with him with a submachine gun or something. But they were combat units. Literally a small combat team, we call them. So, usually, we used people who ordinarily were jeep drivers, company clerks, or people like that. When we went ashore, they ended up as generator drivers. And then they didn't like it because they were sitting ducks. You know, we could lie down [a bit], man the radio or do the voice, whichever, but whoever was on the generator was up there cranking away, so that was not an enviable position to be in. The SCR-284 was a workhorse, you couldn't kill it. It had range, out to the ships, you know; it was a good 20 to 40 miles you could go with it.

During the last year and a half of the war, when production really got up to speed, and they were coming out with new things, and you had these walkie-talkies that you could depress the button to talk and listen. I can remember that they would go bad in a minute. But the 284s that we lugged in on our backs, which you worked with a hand crank generator, never broke down, they always worked. It was the later equipment that wasn't as good. They were not as precise as later equipment, but they were extremely rugged; they took tremendous amounts of punishment. I can remember stuff that would be dropped in the bottom of a boat. It would get full of sand.

We were doing many things. We found out that a lot of things that look great on paper don't turn out that way, as you well know. We found that we could not compartmentalize many tasks. We had forward observers who supposedly had their own equipment, and much of the time that stuff didn't work. So what would happen would be you'd get word back from front line positions saying, 'We need this fire immediately…', so we would get on the frequency and pass that along. We literally became a conduit for whatever was necessary.

Attu and Kiska

The landings at Attu were fine, but there was very poor preliminary intelligence for the Attu invasion. They really didn't have an idea of what the terrain we would be fighting on was like. Most of the guys got foot immersion. I remember the beach was not sand at all, it was thousands of little black rocks, and as a matter of fact, those rocks saved my foot. I got, I guess you would call it, frostbite in my right foot. Our lieutenant told a number of us to go down to the beach, see if you can find a quartermaster, get some dry boots.

I had to cut my boot off. There was a medical tent, and I saw a pile of boots outside. I saw guys go in, and they would throw the boot out. Well, very quickly we got the idea that they did not mess around, and someone with bad frostbite or gangrene, they took the foot off. I went down and cut my boot off. I stomped my foot on that beach rock until my foot was raw, but I got my circulation back. I got over to the quartermaster, got myself some boots, and got back up there.

The weather would change almost instantaneously at five-minute intervals. It could be raining one minute, it could be ice pellets the next, the sun would come out, it was incredible weather. It was almost nightmarish, being on top of the world. Visibility was miserable. That was the other thing—we literally were without air support because they could not fly in that weather. Once in a while they would try to get something up from Adak, but we relied on fire support from offshore, destroyers and cruisers. Once you landed, you were there and pretty much on your own.

At Attu, when we came down, once the landings had taken place and we joined the regular forces, the Japanese counter-attacked just about every night. We were behind a bank of tundra, dug in, and they came down. We were not supposed to be fighting, we were the support troops, but when an attack came everybody had to fire, you didn't lie there. I can still remember the lieutenant coming down and saying, 'C'mon, you guys, you're not here for the fun of it, get those damn M1 carbines working!' As a matter of fact, we had gone in with Garands to Adak. They took them away and gave us carbines. It was the first time we had them. I have to confess that I can still remember firing with my eyes shut the first few times I did it. I was with a crusty, tough sergeant, who had come from the logging camps up in Wisconsin, and he was with me through the entire war, and he said, 'You know, your best bet to getting out of this is to fire that thing at as many people as you can!'

The 7th Division, which really was sent into Attu, was hell for the people who went in. We weren't given the right clothes. We didn't have enough ammunition or logistics ashore. I watched a banzai charge come on Attu in which you just prayed that they didn't get to your foxhole because we were in the tundra, which is not like earth. It's this grass and it holds water, and we were frozen in there and the Japanese came down, many of them with bamboo poles with bayonets on them, and you could hear guys yell because they couldn't get to their weapons. They were frozen and they were just bayonetted and gutted in their foxholes by the Japanese who wore heavy clothing.

'Surviving Your First Combat'

I was pretty busy on Attu; most of us who were doing radios were kept very busy. And that was good, because as long as you didn't think about what you were doing, that got you through. It kept your mind on your work, you did as well as you could.

The feeling [of surviving your first combat experience] is incredible. It's top of the world, we can take anything, do anything. That existed until we found out we had to go back, then it was, 'Oh, shit.' [*Laughs*]. First of all, we were ill-equipped for that battle.

Nobody came back with anything; we left it all behind. As I recall, the general in charge of that operation was relieved. General Corlett was the new general in charge for the Kiska operation. After all, somebody had to pay the price.

One of the first things he did was to differentiate the troops who had tasted combat; there were not a lot of troops in the United States Army who had been in combat. He devised something called 'Corlett's Longknives.' All those who had been in the landings got these trench knives, which we were allowed to wear—a sidearm, so to speak. We would swagger around with these, and they gave us a new patch, a special patch, and that differentiated us from everybody else. Of course, everybody made directly for the nearest bar to bask in the glory. My trench knife went by the wayside, as all such things.

All the way there to Kiska, we expected the worst. They went through with the landings. Very quickly, we learned there was nobody there. Very quickly, they put us on a Liberty ship for almost a month, working our way south, all the way to Hawaii. They set us up in a camp behind Fort Shafter, in downtown Honolulu. We had to prepare for the Gilberts.

Liberty

In downtown Honolulu there was King Street, which you must have heard about by now. King Street was several blocks, near the water, which was literally run by the military. There was barbed wire around it, and it was a string of joints, mostly bars. The bars had other adjunct activity with it.

You went in one end; if you indulged in activity with the young ladies there, you got stamped [on the hand]. You did not depart until you cleared the prophylactic [line], which in those days was not a happy one. The military ran it; their object was to keep you fit for duty. They would give you a little tube of something which would burn like hell. You would go in the latrine and squeeze it. It burned like hell. I only did it once and I never did it again.

One guy in our unit, he was working on a PhD when he got drafted. He would locate a library, the Honolulu Public Library, and he would drag me down there. I got to know the library pretty well. We would go down to Waikiki to the restaurants. There was a theater, and inside there were palm trees and blue sky and stars. It was my first introduction to the tropics. It was my first time to see a centipede and a scorpion up close. At night, if you had to go to the latrine, you had to walk on these boards. If you stepped off, you might step on a scorpion; you would know it.

The Gilberts-Makin and Tarawa

The Marshalls and the Gilberts were nothing more than sand and palm trees and some low bushes. The one thing you worried about at night, believe it or not, were these crabs that had a large shell. They would cast a shadow and it would look like a helmet. [*Imitates crawling*] And they would scuttle, and the moon was very bright in the tropics, and you would see [what looked] like a helmet in the brush.

The one impression [of Makin] I carried back afterward was that I wish I had seen it under peaceful circumstances. It was one of the most beautiful settings I had ever seen. The moon was so bright at night you could almost read by it. I remember feeling badly that we'd messed it up. I realized it had to be done. But I thought I'd like to see it again sometime. I would like to go back to the route I took and see what's happened at all those places, and maybe react to it.

We were assigned to the 165th Regiment of the 27th Division, which of course was the old Fighting 69th.[47] It wasn't until the last week or two before the convoy left for the Gilberts when we trained with them. We went to the place, I am trying to remember, it was the other island. We did not join the regiment right away; they would isolate us. No more passes, we would study maps of where we were going. Our job was to provide communications for their training, so they would get used to working with us.

We boarded our ships, did calisthenics, had meetings with our non-coms and officers to go over the maps, to make sure we knew everything. We would not get the code until we were well out. You get to know people. That was my first introduction to [Marine General Holland M.] 'Howlin' Mad' Smith. He came aboard to talk to us. That was a transport; it was not a Liberty ship. I am trying to remember the name, but I can't. We fared pretty well, since we were communications people, we would 'spell' Navy personnel on the bridge. That way we would get the better food, which the Navy people always got. We could spend our time topside, more than down below where the troops were ordered.

I still remember gathering on the fantail. He is standing on a hatch cover, haranguing us about what we had to live up to with the Marines. He was not a very likeable character. He was addressing the Army troops, the 165th. We were going down with people who had done it all, the heroics, the whole business. He would begin his talk with a litany of all of the most famous engagements the

---

[47] *Fighting 69th*- The storied 69th New York Infantry Regiment, part of the New York Army National Guard, from New York City, has its roots in the Irish Brigade formed by Irish émigré revolutionaries. It has participated in four wars, beginning with the US Civil War, and 23 campaigns; it is said they were nicknamed 'The Fighting Irish' by Robert E. Lee himself. Source: 69th New York Infantry Regiment, en.wikipedia.org/wiki/69th_New_York_Infantry_Regiment.

Marines had been in, and he embellished it with how many men had died in each one. It amazed me that what he seemed to care about most was how glorious that was and, 'Here we lost 5,000 and here we lost 10,000,' and it was about how these men obtained glory for the Corps. I thought I wanted more humanity in a commander; I don't know what the military services are like today. There was not a lot of talk, free talk, among the men in general, as I recall, pro or con. Usually, talk was with one or two people that you would get to know better.

Landing at Makin

Men were taciturn about what they were going into. There was a reticence to show fear, or to let anybody else think that you did not understand what it was all about. I don't know if people are more loquacious today, or not. My sense was that these were people who, even among the draftees, realized they were there for a very serious job. And they were concerned, but most of their concerns were communicated to confidants, not out in the open.

I should qualify a lot of what I am now remarking with this: Once we had done Attu and Kiska, and had become this more or less special unit, taking others in, and we had been there, we knew what it was all about. We did not really associate that closely with the others. We were sort of separate and apart. You liked that, because it made you sort of special. Others looked to you like, 'They have been in combat.' I would say looking at my own unit, it had a great esprit de corps. We felt ourselves something apart because of the kind of work we did, and you develop that spirit. For instance, I can remember most of us sported beards. I used to get kidded about mine because of my age, but once we had been to Attu and seen combat, nobody told us to shave. We were the tough, grizzled veterans, and as long as we kept them trimmed, it was okay. It was sort of like a badge. We were those grizzled guys that had seen combat. I guess we became more and more grizzled with every operation.

'I'll See You on the Beaches'

We [prepared by] packing our kits. The sergeant would come down, see that everyone had what you needed, ammunition. We would meet with the communications chief and get the codes. Our preparation time was spent with specific housekeeping chores, which, in a way, was good because it kept you from dwelling too much on what you were facing. Always the commanding officer would come down and give you a talk. 'Do your best... Keep your head down.'

Then, over the loudspeaker, the orders to board the landing craft would begin, and we would go down the cargo nets into the boats. I met Father Joseph Meany, Chaplain of the 165th, who was aboard. The night before, he held services for all the men who wanted it, all three religions—Protestant, Catholic, and Jewish. I did not go to any of the services but a friend of mine went to Mass. I remember we had one fellow in our outfit who was a Quaker who really had a lot of trouble with guilt, because he'd gone against his parents' wishes to join us. Before every landing, he was sure he was going to be punished for that. Father Meany sat and prayed with him separately.

I still remember what he said before we went over the side of the landing craft. I sort of stood back and listened and the last thing he said was [*imitates Father's Irish brogue*], 'Now, let's go forth among the heathen and do our duty. I'll see you all on the beach when it's over. If I don't see you there, I'll see you in heaven. And for those of you who don't make it to heaven, the devil took you. Now, let's get to it!' He got wounded. I tried very hard not to think about stuff. I tried to focus on the maps and the codes. If I started to think about other stuff, I would start to get worried.

The tension would mount. You would see other guys more nervous, that would affect you. I have to say, the military at that time was not that politically correct as it is today. If you were from any ethnic minority, you took a lot of ribbing, some of it good-natured, some of it not. Being Jewish, I took some good-natured ribbing, and again, some that was quite hurtful. I soon learned from my interactions with the rest of the company that there were non-Jewish members of that group that expected you, because you were Jewish, to be yellow and inept. I was determined to disprove that. A lot of my responses and the way I reacted, looking back now, were colored by that. I was determined to never be seen in a situation of acting frightened, or worried, or anything like that. Some of that was bravado, I am sure, but I felt very good as long as I stayed close to that sergeant of mine who was a tough guy. He said, 'You can stick with me.' And I did; the problem, of course, was that he really *was* tough and didn't care about going where it was dangerous. He was from Two Rivers, Wisconsin. His name was Elmer Kominsky, and he came out of the logging camps. And believe it or not, I talked to him about three months ago. He's now in a nursing facility, because of arthritic knees. I felt if I stuck with him, I would come out all right. I think he joined the Army probably in '39 or '40. He came in before Pearl Harbor. He would say, 'Think about the job. Think what you have to do, don't think about anything else, that will get you through.' Now, people who are into yoga say, 'Be in the moment'—that's what he [taught us].

*

[Gearing up to land], what you do is go in large circles, each boat goes to its assembly area, you just keep circling around and around. The destroyer goes ahead to the line of departure, drops a flare in the water or a marking buoy. Then they come alongside and say,

'First wave, form up!' Then [the boats in the wave] string out [*gestures with arms in a wide line*]. Then the bombardment goes out. The bombardment lifts, and the first wave hits the line and goes for the beach. As I recall at Makin, a line of Navy TBFs or something came in and strafed like crazy. It began to look like it would be 'duck soup.'

Then the Higgins boats ground up on the reef. You could hear them trying to pull off. Then the [coxswains] said, 'I'm sorry, guys, you have to get off here.' They dropped the front ends and off we went.

The Tides

[The water was] about waist high. It varied with the terrain underneath you. As it turned out, you know, it was a good operation. We didn't lose as many men as we might have, but the Navy screwed up mightily; you know they misjudged the tides both at Tarawa and Makin Island. And if you know anything about the Pacific, an atoll is formed by several little islands around the lagoon. And if you want to get in and out of that lagoon, you have to know the tides pretty well because if the tide goes down beyond a certain point, the lagoon becomes inaccessible. What happened at Makin and Tarawa was that they misjudged the tide by several hours; there was a phenomenon that year with tides that made it difficult for the Navy to plot the exact time of tides. The Higgins boats went in, and they all scraped [the bottom]. On the coral reefs, they didn't want to rip the bottoms out, so they dropped the ramps right there on the reef. Let us off, the water is about up to here [*gestures to waist*], and we have to go several hundred yards to shore.

'The Only Thing That Saved Me'

What had happened was that the bombing and the shelling [were not terribly effective]. They later learned that the Japanese had built tremendous reinforcements on these islands and the shelling didn't do a great deal to destroy them. We had to wade in, almost a hundred yards, we got to within fifty yards of shore, there were little jetties out there, and the Japanese had placed machine guns, and they had a field of crossfire, and they were just whipping it back and forth. I still remember I was carrying that SCR-284, which was wrapped in this rubberized stuff. It was all waterproof, and evidently in the shelling beforehand, a bomb of some kind, their shell, had made a crater in the water. I stepped into that thing and went down just as the machine guns opened up, and right after that picture was taken that you're looking at there, the guys who had been on either side of me were lying in the water face down when I came up. The only thing that saved me was that I stepped in that hole and pulled myself up on that floating radio and kicked myself ashore. [Stepping into that shell hole] was the only thing that saved me at Makin.

I recall there were still [Japanese] shells landing on the beach. I heard a lot of fire, but you could not tell what it was. Things were so hectic going in you were not sure what you wanted to do, [but] you see that beach, and you want to get there and lie down. That's the first thing you wanted to do! Not make a target, you know?

I just pushed like hell and headed for the beach. We made it, found my sergeant, he said, 'All right, you guys, follow me!' We just went. The guys from the infantry were there, of course; they just formed lines, skirmish lines, and we started to set up, running the radio, that was our job. They set up a command post immediately. We began to run communications. As quickly as the lieutenant got the lay of the beach, he had our guys run telephone wires to the different landing parties, make sure we were in touch with them, so we could send their requests back. We were the initial communications center for the beachhead.

The 165th in Action

[Of course, I got to watch the 165th in action]; they were all around us. I thought—and this is why I got so upset after I heard about the Saipan thing—that these people were businesslike, orderly, conscientious, followed their officers' and non-commissioned officers' directions.[48] They went about the business of taking that island. They did what they were directed to do. As I understand it, in the post-mortem period, Howlin' Mad Smith was very angry,

---

[48] *I got so upset after I heard about the Saipan thing-* The Marines on Saipan were joined by the Army's 27th Infantry Division, a New York National Guard unit federalized in October 1940, and it was the 27th which would bear the brunt of the biggest banzai attack of the war. Before the final attack, the Marine commander expressed his unhappiness in front of war correspondents with the progress of the Army soldiers and had the Army general relieved of his command. In fact, in the attack to follow, three members of the 105th Regiment would be awarded the Medal of Honor, posthumously. A 27th veteran in Vol. 1 remembered: *"The 27th Division got stuck in the mountains fighting. We had to fight cave to cave, hand to hand sometimes. And we had a General Smith, Ralph Smith, one hell of a good man. And he was relieved by this Marine general, 'Howlin' Mad' Smith. From what I understood back then, the reason he was relieved of his command was that the Marines said we could not keep up with them. Well, Jesus Christ, they had tank support down in the lowlands, which we didn't have! They confiscated half of the 27th's artillery... and we were supposed to keep up with them! The best we had was 60 and 81mm mortars, and half the time you could not use them because of the terrain. There were mountains, gulches, hillsides, caves dug into them. That's the way it was; it was really rough going up through the goddamn mountains! As much as you tried, you could not keep up with them. You go past a cave so small you never noticed the opening. The next thing you know, you're getting shot at from behind."*

because it ostensibly took two days longer than he wanted for the island to be taken. But they followed Army procedure, they didn't throw their troops in there to be shot down. They followed envelopment and recon, things of that sort, all good, solid tactics, and it all worked. I mean, they were not overdue, they just didn't do it as fast as he would have liked to have had it done. But they did it and they took their casualties.

"Soldiers of the US Army's 2nd Battalion, 165th Infantry, struggle to shore on Yellow Beach on Butaritari Island, Makin Atoll, November 20, 1943." National Archives and Records Administration, public domain.

Makin Mary

Several hours after we had landed, the battle was going on. Out of the bushes came two local people, a young woman and her young brother. She must have been somewhere around seventeen or eighteen, I guess he must have been about twelve or thirteen. He had a loincloth of some sort on; she had a grass skirt, period. I don't know who it was, but anyway, she decided to help us. She got her kid brother to run the generator when the guy got tired. We gave her some K-rations. They just hung around. They did not get in the way. They did not bother anything; they were just sort of there. They felt safe near the command post. We later found out that one of the first things that happened when the place was secured was an order came ashore along with several hundred Navy skivvy shirts, [looked] like T-shirts. I don't know who originated this order, if it was Howlin' Mad or anybody else, but henceforth, all native female population would wear T-shirts. Well, the females loved this idea, and they went ahead and wore them tied around their heads. [*Laughs*]. Somebody came ashore for the occupation of the military government unit, and requested a meeting with the chief, the elder of the island. I'm told that in that meeting, he was told that the population would not walk around bare.

The chief said, 'You have to understand, our people have done this for centuries, they don't see anything bad.'

'Well, you can't flaunt that in front of our people.'

At which point, the chief supposedly said, 'I can vouch for my people if you can vouch for yours.' [*Laughs*]

Anyway, we were there for four or five days. I thought it was a very smooth operation. There were no major gaffes anywhere; it was wrapped up, the island was secured, it was only afterwards that we learned that the Marine commander was upset about everything. He felt it took them too long; I thought it had been an efficiently run operation. None of the communications that I heard actively going on [at the time] were from anybody upset, or that something didn't go according to plan, or anything like that. It was just a battle [plan] that was followed and worked out. Interestingly enough, when it was over, the media reports were all about the Marines and the Gilberts and of Tarawa, and it was almost a throwaway report of Makin. And in some of the reports, it was almost as if the Army had not been there. The Marines had one hell of a PR outfit working for them, and they used it. I think the Army was there to do their job.

[The Raiders had attacked Makin before we got there, of course.] We had known about that; they told us all about it in training. By the way, there was an interesting difference between Colonels Carlson, Roosevelt, and Howlin' Mad Smith. Throughout our training with Carlson's and Roosevelt's Raiders, it was emphasized to us—I can still remember the talk we got from Jimmy Roosevelt, in which he emphasized how badly they felt about the few casualties they had had on Makin. Those were too many, he felt. They had fifteen or sixteen, I forget how many men were left on Makin, killed in the operation. But he kept emphasizing that if you do your job right, it will keep you alive. Our object is not to get you killed, it's to keep you alive so you can do it again. And he kept emphasizing that. It was nothing like you heard from Howlin' Mad Smith, who didn't give a damn, he wanted to get this thing done, 'I don't care what it takes.' And it was a callousness about the well-being of the people in his trust, really, in his charge, that he was prepared to sacrifice them. I am not saying that everyone doesn't think 'so be it, so be it,' but that shouldn't be the objective. The objective should be 'let's do this and keep as many alive as we can.' And that was the glaring difference that I remembered between what I'd seen at Pendleton in my training, and this general.

Kwajalein

The battle for Kwajalein and its airfield under construction began to unfold on January 31, 1944. Using the lessons learned in the Gilberts, Kwajalein in the Marshalls was subjected to the most concentrated shelling of the war, with 36,000 shells from naval guns and ground artillery, followed by B-24 aerial bombings.[25]

Kwajalein was a larger island [atoll] than Makin, it was sort of in the shape of a T. As I recall, the object was going to land one group down on one end, and one group down at the other end. They were going to work toward each other, cut the Japanese in half or something. It never goes according to plan somehow in these things because you really never know what the enemy is going to do.

I also recall that it was the first place I ever saw the use of flamethrowers because they were dug in. Really, they had these things dug right down into the sand with coconut logs and coral and stuff all over them and you just couldn't root them out. We went along. We weren't supposed to root them out. Of course, we were communications, but because the island was so small, there really was no room for a lot of artillery; they brought some tanks into one of the columns, armored trucks in with some heavy stuff. But, in reality, they used naval bombardment all the way up to the coast as we went, and our people were the spotters.

Now, there's a whole different scene [on these atolls]; you know, there wasn't a single tree in the Aleutians, but here, you know, it was underbrush through palm trees, all the rest of it covered. And the Japanese, who had been living there for a couple of years before we got there, were very adept at using that. They used all kinds of tricks, and we were told about a lot of the tricks that might be used. But you still don't know until you see them. So, you know, at night, particularly, they would use little phrases like, 'Hey, Joe!' 'Hey, Joe!' You know, to get you to answer and come out. We learned from our friends the Raiders not to fall for that.

We operated purely with taps and hand signals, but never talked at night. We were also told not to shoot because it gave away your position. So, at night, most of us had large trench knives on hand, just in case someone needed them. The nighttime was the worst because of infiltration, and they were very adept at that.

On Kwajalein I had an experience that taught me that Japanese soldiers are not much different from American soldiers. I have a chip right here in this tooth [*points to his mouth*]. On Kwajalein, our positions, we dug in with V trenches. In a V, you had a guy at the point, and a guy at each end. [*Uses fingers to make a V sign*] The guy at one end of that V was hit, and at night, the Japanese intruder came in through that end. And I was whispering and trying to see what was happening down at that end.

I said, 'You okay?'

[The intruder] said, 'Yeah, yeah,' something like that. But something was funny, so I started crawling toward that end, and someone was crawling [towards me], and suddenly we came face to face. Immediately you try to think about what you were taught about hand-to-hand combat. I assumed the position and grabbed his arm and came across like that [*turns his trunk*], never thinking that he had a foot free, which came up and caught me in the mouth. We both fell back, and he ran back like hell that way and I ran like hell [the other way]. So I figured, he was just as human as I was, glad to get the hell out of there. [*Laughs*]

Kwajalein was four or five days. It was interesting because later, when I read some of the reports by Marines observers and PR people, they always played down Army operations by comparison, and we doubted the figures that became the final figures. The Army people came up with that because they told us going in there were like 2,000 Japanese on Kwajalein, but I remember when we left that island, we walked about almost three-quarters of a mile or so down to where the boats were going to pick us up, and there was this makeshift road, and alongside that road, the bodies were stacked four and five high like cordwood, many of them burned beyond recognition from the flamethrowers, but it looked like three times as many as they said were on there. If that was 1,800 Japanese, it was more like 4,000 or so. In many cases, they underestimated the number. I mean, it wasn't a horrendous miscalculation, but there always seemed to be more than they thought there was. Also, the state of [Japanese] preparedness was usually either they were better prepared than we thought, or they just were stubborn as hell.

And as I recall, I think there may have been maybe a half dozen survivors from that operation. Most of them committed suicide, so you always knew when the banzai attacks began that they figured it was over and they were just coming at you. There was that banzai charge of sorts on Attu, but they were in worse shape than we were. And there weren't enough of them to really make it a horrendous affair.

It was the first time that the Japanese outer defensive ring had been penetrated. Of the nearly nine thousand defenders, nearly eight thousand were killed, unfortunately including Korean forced laborers. U.S. military records do not distinguish between Japanese military and Korean slaves killed in the battle.

The Rats of Tobruk

After Kwajalein, we took a rest. They told us we were going to take a rest. We went to New Guinea, and MacArthur's people were doing the island hops from New Guinea, the Solomons to New Guinea/Buna, all that way. What had happened was that after they had taken Hollandia and set up a large supply base there, which we landed on, they decided on the leapfrog approach not to try to take everything. And they tried what they called a 'process of containment.' So what they did was they launched a strike at the northern end of New Guinea, and they drove the Japanese back into the interior and they set up a perimeter like Hollandia. And what they would do would be to send patrols out on that perimeter from time to time, just to keep the Japanese back, to let them know we were there, and so on.

The famed Australian 7th Brigade, the Rats of Tobruk, were pulled out of Tobruk after it fell. They said they were sending them home, but they sent them [to Hollandia] to do R&R patrols, and they would take a group of us and send two of us with each squad that went out on patrol as communications. So we went out with the Australian 7th Brigade members, and I heard they were wonderful guys. Fearless.

The Aussies were very casual about it all. As a matter of fact, I remember we were attached for communications purposes, and with each patrol that would go out there'll be like a patrol of 15 or 16 Australians on this perimeter at Aitape, New Guinea, and there would be four of us radio people sent along. The Japanese really never showed themselves in strength. They did a lot of sniper stuff and hit-and-run things. It was the jungle. They would love to climb up into trees and tie themselves up there, and they'd wait for whoever came along and hit you with sniper fire. If they missed, that was it for them because these guys were very blasé about it. If somebody says, 'Sniper!' or all of a sudden you hear a rustle or something in the trees, [they would just] turn around with one of those little Sten guns, just spray everything in sight. You'd see the bodies drop out of the trees.

Excellent fighters. They didn't flap easily, you know? They got the job done. I can still remember going along in a patrol. You might have just had a hit from a sniper or two and they returned the fire, got rid of them, and somebody would say, [*imitates Australian accent*] 'Oh, it's four o'clock, time for tea!' They'd stop everything, set up these little alcohol lamps, take out their canteens, and sit around on their haunches and brew a pot of tea, and the whole war would stop for tea! Well, we didn't mind it. We got along fine with them. The one thing we didn't like about them was that they drank warm beer. They would carry bottles of it along and they thought the Americans were crazy to drink cold beer. I remember that distinctly. We would josh each other a lot. They were easy-going people, the Aussies. Not like the British at all. They'd tell us all about Tobruk and we'd tell them about our battles. We'd swap battle stories and we got along fine with them.

Mr. Elisha's story will continue.

CHAPTER FIVE

The Marine Mechanic I

When we think about World War II, it's easy to overlook the personnel who kept the armed forces moving, the people whose knowledge, skill, and precision under pressure could mean the difference between life and death. James Smith was a Marine tank mechanic. He sits in a comfortable chair, decked out in his red commemorative Marine windbreaker jacket. It sports a round patch on the left breast that reads, in red lettering on a white background, *Iwo Jima Survivor, 1945-1990*, circling an embroidered outline of the famous Joe Rosenthal flag-raising image. He is also a survivor of the 3rd Marine campaigns at Guadalcanal, Bougainville, and Guam.

"My first experience with any kind of service trouble with the tank was on Bougainville. When we made a landing there, we had the light tanks, and when I came ashore, one of my tanks made a left turn to go down the beach and it came to a dead stop, and I was behind him... What had happened was that when that tank went into the water, it got hit in the back end with a wave, and water got into that engine compartment. Now, the engine compartment has a radial engine with an updraft carburetor on it.

The saltwater got down in the bottom of that engine compartment, and the updraft carburetor sucked that water up into the engine and killed it.

While I was working on that, I heard something behind me, and I looked back and it was a Zero coming right down the beach, strafing as he came down.

I was in the Pacific for twenty-nine months, from Guadalcanal, Bougainville, Guam, and Iwo Jima. At my age, I still haven't gotten to the point where I can get my mind to [understand] that it really happened..."

He gave this interview in February of 2003.

James A. Smith, Jr.

I was born in Wallington, New Jersey, and I'm going to be 82 this coming April. I went to two years of [secondary] school in Passaic, New Jersey, at Saint Nicholas School; it's a parochial school and I graduated there in 1935. We moved up [to northern New York] from New Jersey; moving back and forth from the city to the North Country and to high school up here for two years, for economic reasons, well, that's another story. [We were] a family of six and things were really tough in those [Great Depression] days, because we had come from the city, living 'The Life of Reilly,' so to speak, and then to come up here with no electricity, no [running] water, nothing, absolutely nothing, and my father was an ailing veteran from World War I.

I had originally come up in 1932 and lived with my aunt, came up for the summer vacation. Then, when I had gotten back to Jersey from that summer vacation, I had grown so much and browned up so much that everybody wanted to know where I'd been. It was called 'God's Country' as it is at times now; several people today still call it God's Country. But to us, it was really hell on earth because we were experiencing pioneer conditions! We had absolutely nothing to fall back on.

Nobody was working, so I left high school and went to work on a mink ranch in the [lower Adirondacks], north of Porters Corners. There was a mink ranch started up there by a gentleman from New York City, a Russian Jewish fellow, a well-educated man. I went up there just to work during the summertime to earn a few dollars. Well, earning that extra money like that was like a gold mine to our family. So, against my parents' wishes, I decided to stay there, left school, and decided to work the summer out. As the summer finally wore down, I was wondering what they were going to do with me, and they offered me a job to stay there in the mink ranch and to work there as an extra hand. Over a period of probably two years I learned the mink ranching business, the breeding and the feeding and the pelting. Learning to grade the mink furs was quite an education in itself; I was able to do that.

The Japanese Gentlemen

While I was there, we had five Japanese gentlemen come in from Japan. This is about 1939. What had happened was, they were looking to start some mink ranches in Japan. They were going through the yards and we were explaining the details of what we were doing, how it was done, and all the different details of maintaining a mink ranch.

When they got all through, they wanted to speak to me and I had a little bit of a conference in a corner with them. They asked me if I would consider going to Japan to start a mink ranch for them! They would make a ranch, and they offered me a home and a salary. Here I am, a young fellow, and I said, 'I'm going to go home and talk to my mother and father about it,' and spoke to them, and my father was all for it. He wanted me to go, he said it would be a great chance of traveling, opportunities like that. He said, 'This is great!'

But my mother, she was against it, she was one hundred percent against it! She was really dead set against anybody that looked 'Oriental.' I'd have to say that, because I think I asked her several times, 'What is your reasoning, Ma?', and I think it was from [the stereotypes put out] from Hollywood. She brought up the fact that in the pictures that were being made in those days—I don't know if you remember the old Chinese or Japanese movies at that time, there were different people brought into the movies in those days and all—and all she could remember about them was the 'hatchet man!' They called them that; I don't know if you are familiar with that term or not. She carried that thought in her mind all those years, and that's the first thing she thought about [when I asked about] going to Japan! So I didn't go to Japan. I turned it down, and it's a good thing, because I would have been in Japan when the war broke out.

'Where's Pearl Harbor?'

I remember Pearl Harbor very distinctly. I was in Paramus, New Jersey; I used to go horseback riding in those days before the war, and I was horseback riding with my uncle, Leo Smith. It was bitterly cold, and my Uncle Leo was really having a hard time. So I had a '38 Chevrolet Business Coupe.

I said, 'Uncle Leo, I'm going to the car to start it up for you and get it warmed up,' so that it'll be warm, because he was really freezing. I had an old Motorola radio that used to hang from the dashboard that I put in myself, and because it was on when I turned the ignition on, the radio came on. As I was waiting for the engine to level off, the news broadcast came up on the air on the radio that Pearl Harbor had been attacked. That was my introduction to Pearl

Harbor. It was the same old question [everyone had], 'Where's Pearl Harbor?' [We] didn't know where it was.

I've often thought about [what if I had accepted the offer to go to work in Japan]. I think, [after Pearl Harbor] the first thing I did think of is the fact that I would have been a prisoner of war. Not of war, but in a prison, being an American and being in Japan. I often wondered what my fate would have been. It's something that has bugged me over the years. I wondered just what I would have done, but after a while, I immediately got to thinking about [getting into the service].

'I Want You!'

I never thought too much about the military at that time, but my father, he had been a sergeant in the army and had been overseas. I [started] thinking about that, because I thought [with the war], it might be possible that I would be in the army. But on my trips back and forth to New Jersey—I was working in New Jersey now, traveling from New Jersey up to Saratoga, New York—on our way up on the Old [Route] 9W, there were a couple of these [billboards] with Uncle Sam on it, and I can see that finger— 'I want you!'—following along, just like he was pointing at me! I know it was a great sign; the more I saw it, [the more it was] asking me to join the Marines. So that kind of stayed with me for quite a while until I was clutching right along, and would you believe it, I got stopped by a state trooper. He pulled me over and he said, 'Where are you going in such a hurry?'

I said, 'I'm on my way up north to Saratoga Springs,' and I said, 'I'm working down below and traveling north on the weekends.'

Then I said, 'I'm considering enlisting in the Marines.'

'Well, look,' he said. 'I don't know where you got the gas from…' but as it was, I had a friend in New Jersey who had a gas station, and gas was eight cents a gallon. I used to carry a five-gallon can in the back of the car. So I had enough gas for my return trip; [he let me off.]

I was a mechanic. I was a mechanic all my life and every weekend I was up, if the car wasn't functioning right, I pulled the head off. It was a Chevy, it was easy to work on. I'd pull it apart and work on it, grind the valves, then throw it back together again; I was always trying to make an engine run at its peak, and get the best miles out of the gas. I was very conscious of that in those days, even to the point where I had drilled a hole into the intake on the carburetor on the manifold and had a ball bearing in there that would, as the vacuum pulled that ball bearing, it would bring it in and [allow] an extra mixture of oxygen or air to that carburetor, and that increased my mileage quite a bit. That was back in 1939-1940, right in that era of time when I was driving that car, and that's what happened to me on the way home with the war hanging over everybody's heads.

Well, within six months I had enlisted in the Marine Corps; I went in August of '42. Those posters had a direct bearing on it, really. I never thought about the Marines; I knew about the Army with my father, of course, and I was always wanting to be a flyer. When I was a kid, I used to travel to what is known as Bendix Airport now, but it was Teterboro in those days. I used to walk down there on the weekends and look at all the planes and all that. Just before the war, I was going to the Academy of Aeronautics in Carlstadt, New Jersey. It was a naval school run by the Navy, and would you believe, a lesson cost 25 cents a night to go in, and I took that course to go into aviation, but before the war broke out, they closed the school down. There was a Navy commander who was the instructor there, and they knew that we were headed for war; they pulled him out of there and they closed the school down. That was the end of that, but ironically, my son, Jim the third, was born with that instinct for flying. He ended up going to the Academy of Aeronautics in Long Island. It was an academy run by, I think, three World War II pilots. It's still there, the Academy of Aeronautics. But that's where my aviation career ended right there.

I went into New York City to enlist because I was familiar with the area a little bit and I would leave New Jersey. I went down there, and the lines were around the block to get to the recruiting stations! So I said, 'Well, enough of this!' I jumped in the car and went back to Jersey. That Friday, I drove up to Glens Falls and it was an old school up on South Street. There was a Marine recruiter up there in the school.

I went into the school and looked for him. There was nobody there but I finally located him, a recruiting sergeant.

He said, 'What do you want?'

I said, 'I want to enlist.'

He said, 'You sure you want to enlist?'

I said, 'I made up my mind. Definitely, I want to be in the Marine Corps.' So he gave me a quick physical, checked me real quick, and then took me down. They made a date and they picked me up on Broadway by the post office. There was a bus that came down through, they were picking up guys from way up in [the lower Adirondacks], North Chestertown, Pottersville, and bringing them down, coming through and picking up everybody to take to [the state capital], to Albany; that's where the main recruiting officers were, and they gave us a general physical there. I think there were about 15 or 18 people that had requested to be enlisted in the Marines. We were sitting out in the hall and they were going in and they went in alphabetical order. Being as I was on the end of the line, [I noticed] a strange thing was happening.

As the fellas came out, some of them were pretty well down in the mouth and I couldn't understand, I was wondering what was wrong.

I said, 'Boy, this has got to be some kind of an exam.' What was happening was they were flunking, and they were being sent from the Marine Corps down to the Army and the Navy. They were there, their offices were posted down through the hallways, and these guys were going from one to the other to find the one that would accept them.

So finally there were just two of us out of the eighteen, whatever it was that went in for the exam. I was the last guy in, and I went through all kinds of calisthenics, whatever, you know. They would take your blood pressure and your heart rate, all that, examine your hearing. He kept asking me something.

I said, 'I can't hear what you're saying.'

I said, 'I can hear you, but I can't understand you.' They had the window open, in those days there were a lot of trains in the lot there. They're all steam engines, of course, and they're making a lot of noise. But I said, 'Well, give me another chance. Let me try.' He kept at it, so I listened to him. He was standing behind me, in between the window and me.

As he was talking, I heard him say, 'Can you hear me talking?'

I heard him now, and I said, 'Why don't you close that window?'

He said, 'Listen, if you're in combat, you want to hear what's going on behind, because there's going to be a lot of noise. That's what we're looking for. We want to make sure your hearing is up to snuff.'

So he said, 'Okay, get the hell out of here.' He said, 'You're elected!' So there were just two of us out of the eighteen. I think they gave us a week to get our business in order and our lives straightened out, whatever it was, to get ready to go down.

Parris Island

We went down to Albany and boarded the train, and the trip down to Parris Island and the conditions were really bad—we couldn't wash, there's no shaving or nothing, and the trains were steam engines. I'll tell you, the soot was thick and hopping onto our bodies, in our hair, and all that. You couldn't wash, couldn't shave, nothing like that. When we got close to Parris Island, I was trying to shave, and I hit this part of my ear right there [*gestures to left ear*] with the train rocking and I started to bleed. I'm telling you, I bled like a stuck hog. I couldn't stop the bleeding! They were using everything to try to stop the bleeding. Finally, after a while, it did finally dry up there. But there's blood all over; you'd think I'd been in combat already now.

But anyway, that's what happened there. Over the next eight weeks was really some rigorous training. It was really, really rough. I compare it now with, I've been to Parris Island twice since then—the Marine Corps flew us as a detachment [*gestures to Iwo Jima Survivor jacket patch*], flew us down there a few years ago. Let me tell you something, those kids—when you go through the Marine Corps now, you got to be really in tough shape, you must really want to be in the Marine Corps, because it's no place for anybody just going in for the glory of it or whatever. It's tougher than what we had because they're pushing us through, [due to the war]. The boot camp training itself was very tough. Learning to use your rifle was the main object of the whole thing. The toughest part about the boot camp training was that we were training with the .03 rifle. That's a Springfield. We had been snapping in with that for several weeks, and right about two-thirds through boot camp, they brought the Garand rifle in. Here we are almost through with boot camp training, and they hand us a brand-new rifle! Fortunately for us, there was a young fella in our platoon who worked in the

Garand factory and he knew the Garand rifle. We were lucky because we had a class right in our barracks, right?

Our barracks were nothing but a big, long shack made out of green lumber. There was no paint, anything like that, it was just a long shack that housed a platoon of Marines. The fella that was in there, he worked in the Garand factory and he really saved our butts. So when we came out of that morning, we were way ahead of everybody with our rifles, and we learned to fire them. It was tough to make the adjustment from the two different rifles, but I was a firing 'expert' all through.

The day before [firing for] record, I got hit [in the face]; the back of the Garand rifle has got a square butt there, and the .03 didn't have that. I was so used to the .03 that I finally got hit. I got hit right here. [*Gestures to left eye*] The drill instructor said, 'You're doing fine, just keep up what you're doing.' But then all of a sudden, I have that black eye when I needed the points to make 'expert.' I couldn't keep it, my eye kept twitching from the pain here.

Boy, he kicked me right in the head. He called me everything. He said, well, I don't want to tell you what he was calling me, but it cost me. But I mean, I could still use my rifle very effectively. Unfortunately, I ended up with the Thompson submachine gun, which I didn't have too much training with.

Learning the Engines

But when we were getting ready to leave boot camp, there was one fella I had become pretty close friends with. His name is Ray Charlebois from Glens Falls. In fact, Ray worked up in the post office up there for many years. We were pretty good buddies, and we were standing and dressed in our uniforms and packs and everything, rifles, in the pouring rain, just like you've seen in the movies at one time or another. They're asking people what they thought they could do, whatever you thought you were good at.

He said to me, 'Go on, Jim, you said you're a mechanic. Why don't you?'

I said, 'I don't know. You read about these things where you'll [volunteer and] wind up with a wheelbarrow or something like that, all that kind of jazz.'

But I stepped forward; I was the only one in the platoon that stepped forward. I ended up in a tank battalion, a tank company, but the equipment we had then was like from the World War I days.

The 3rd Marine Division was activated in September 1942, training for combat to take the islands back from the Japanese. Smith's unit, the 3rd Marine Tank Battalion, would see heavy fighting on Bougainville, Guam, and later, Iwo Jima.

I ended up going to school in Camp Pendleton, that's where we ended up with our light tanks. We had to learn the whole electrical system of the tanks. It was an intensive, very quick course, because they were trying to get us moving out, because of the war and the way things weren't going that good, and they wanted to get into the Pacific to start taking the islands where they needed them the most. Actually, their main goal was to acquire an airstrip. That's what the story was for the islands, the airstrips. They wanted a place to get planes so they could use them to go forward and clear the way for as much as possible for us.

Some of the equipment was really bad. It wasn't anything that I would have liked to have gone to war with because nothing functioned right without being repaired, and it had to be repaired constantly. I noticed something in one of my tank battalion magazines, they were looking for anybody that had any experience with a

Guiberson diesel radial engine [for aircraft and tanks], which is a rare, rare bird. I have never heard of it since, but it was a diesel radial engine. It started with like a shotgun shell in the back—you put that into the chamber and the driver activates it with a toggle switch in the cockpit. That engine was a noisy thing, and it was loud, smoky, and we finally got rid of those. We ended up with some hand-me-downs from the army, some light tanks. They had the .37 millimeter [cannon] on them. They had the aircraft engine, it had a seven-cylinder Continental, and some had the Jacobson seven-cylinder radial engine.

Mud Marines

We did a lot of maneuvers. The tankers, we were classified as special troops. Our weapons were all automatic weapons. We all had .45 pistols and a Thompson submachine gun. [In convoys] on the way from San Diego until we first stopped off at New Caledonia, these ships were old banana boats, and we spent all of our time in the chow lines. From the minute you got up, you got in line for breakfast, and you got back in line again for lunch, whatever it was; you spent more time in lines, so that's why whenever I see lines, I get so disgusted and frustrated, it brings back all the things that were going on in those lines, and that's constantly what happened to us—a lot of our automatic weapons were stolen by the 'mud Marines' [while we were in these lines], the guys from the infantry. They were the ones that were in the frontlines, or whatever you want to determine as a frontline; in the jungles, there was no such thing as a 'frontline.' I mean, here we weren't in the trenches like in World War I. It was sporadic bunches of Marines here and there, trying to keep their lines together so that they weren't separated.

If they were separated, then they had to depend on radios. Most of the time it was just… you had to learn to take care of yourself.

You are going to take care of yourself [first]. We were trained to do that, because there were so many times where if you see somebody that's hit or wounded, whatever, you immediately want to stop and try to help them, it's a natural thing for a person [to want to help], and they told us not to do that. Don't stop to do anything like that. Somebody is trained to take care of somebody like that, and if you're not trained, you're not doing any good for that person, all you're doing is just causing [more] problems. If there is a hole in the line or wherever the firing is going on, you want to make sure that you're doing your job and not worrying about somebody. That may seem kind of tough to bear, even carry on your mind, on your conscience. But it had to be done that way. I remember a couple instances like that, especially on Guam, because I used to have to walk ashore with the mud Marines, I went ashore with our tanks. I was in 1st Platoon Maintenance, and I had six tanks to worry about.

The Early Landings

At Guadalcanal, we came in behind the 1st Division, the ones who made the initial landing there, for like a mopping-up operation. Now, ninety-nine percent of the time, people who were in the Marine Corps like me, we really didn't know what was going on. But actually what was happening was the same theme that will show up again later on in the Pacific campaigns, [again and again].

When we went down into Guadalcanal, when they made the statement that the island was 'secure,' that [implied that it] was the end of the fighting, but that was so wrong. It was unbelievable because there'd be, in some cases, several thousand Japanese loose on the island! They would form up in pockets or live in bivouac areas of their own. So with us coming up in behind [the 1st Division], it was a training area, [real] combat conditions, training people to learn how to fight a war in the jungle.

Jungle Rot

At Guadalcanal, a lot of us came down with a jungle rot on our feet. It came on with the rainy season—it rained for days on end, and we used to have to take our sea bags and dump them out and rotate our clothes so they wouldn't get mildew. Then there'd be jungle rot. It started to come out on our feet and there would be blisters; it's terrible, and I had them for a long time. After the war, I still was afflicted with it. I never went to the VA hospital for any help with it, but the only relief I could get from it in those days at Guadalcanal was, what I used to do is sterilize a razor blade and slice those blisters open and let the liquid out; it would relieve the itch, and then it would dry up. After a number of years, it finally disappeared from my system, whatever it was. Some of the fellas were really afflicted with it really bad to the point where they had to be taken right out. Their feet were in bad shape. the doctors used this [ointment] Merthiolate. It was a dark, purple-colored stuff like Mercurochrome. That's the only thing they put on it.

The other thing that some of the fellas were afflicted with was, I think they called it elephantiasis. It was from the mosquito and the infection ended up in the armpits and in the groin, in their testicles, and [those areas] would just swell up. They had to ship those Marines out. I remember they shipped them out to Oregon; a cold climate is the only place where they would ease this affliction. It would die down; what the medication was for it, I have no idea. But it was really a sad thing to see something like that happen from a mosquito bite.

US Marines in the mud at Bougainville. Marine in foreground center has been identified as Hans Wittmann, Company F, 2nd Battalion, 22nd Marines. US Marine Corps photo, public domain.

Bougainville

Operation Cartwheel, aimed at neutralizing the Japanese base at Rabaul, began in 1943. Rabaul was the principal Japanese forward operating base in the South Pacific at New Guinea, with tens of thousands of troops in reserve threatening the toeholds established at Guadalcanal and elsewhere. The Bougainville campaign, so named for the main island in that area, was part of this overall strategy.

Bougainville was really a tough situation, [because we landed and] you've got to maneuver with tanks. It was very difficult. On the Bougainville campaign, the thing that saved the whole campaign and really won the war there was the amphibious tractor. They call them the alligators, and they were indispensable. They were able to travel in the water. They carried a lot of ammunition, and they could travel in the jungle a lot better than the tanks could go. The tanks were a lot heavier than the amphibious tractor. The tanks, I worked on the tanks all the while. That was my job, to service the tanks, and the engines were the main thing that we had to be concerned about.

My first experience with any kind of service trouble with the tank was on Bougainville. When we made a landing there, we had the light tanks, and when I came ashore, one of my tanks made a left turn to go down the beach and it came to a dead stop, and I was behind him. I ran around to the front of the tank and I said, 'What's the matter?'

He said, 'It just stopped.'

So I said, 'Well, try it again.'

So we tried it; they had toggle switches for the starters. It would crank over okay, but it wouldn't start. Never even fired. So I went around the back, and when I got back to the back of the tank, the door is thick and they had bolts, they were inch-wide bolts. However, one of those bolts came out, I have no idea how there was a bolt missing. What had happened was that when that tank went into the water, it got hit in the back end with a wave and water got into that engine compartment. Now, the engine compartment has a radial engine with an updraft carburetor on it. The saltwater got down in the bottom of that engine compartment, and the updraft carburetor sucked that water up into the engine and killed it.

While I was working on that, I heard something behind me, and I looked back and it was a Zero coming right down the beach, strafing as he came down! I hauled my ass right out in front, I jumped in front of the tank, and I got down underneath the front of the tank and he went over. As he was banking, they got him—they hit him as he was banking, going down. He's going down the beach and strafing and they hit him, and I witnessed two of those kills. But when we were in Bougainville, the campaign was pretty much under control. The Army was coming in to take over the positions that we had taken. They took just about everybody that was available and that meant most of the division; we had to carry ammunition, barbed wire, and food, and put it in all the foxholes on the line before the Army could take over.

The worst part about it was that we were doing this, and when we got back, we're on the beach with all the confusion and things are going on and these poor guys were making like [it was] an invasion landing; they had people on the shore with the camera taking pictures of them making the landing on Bougainville. We've been there three or four weeks, and they were just coming in to take over.

The Seabees

The Seabees were the greatest bunch of guys you would ever want to be associated with. They did a lot to really hasten the war because those guys were Johnny-on-the-spot. They were patching up everything as fast as things were blown up. They were right behind, filling in the holes and cutting this and cutting that. They were into everything and they had everything.

Pappy Boyington was there with us on Bougainville. I saw his plane there, where they were bivouacked after the Seabees cleared the jungle up and built an airstrip. It's uncanny what those guys did with the equipment they had! They were right with us all the while. I could go on and on with the different things. We were stealing from them and they would steal from us.

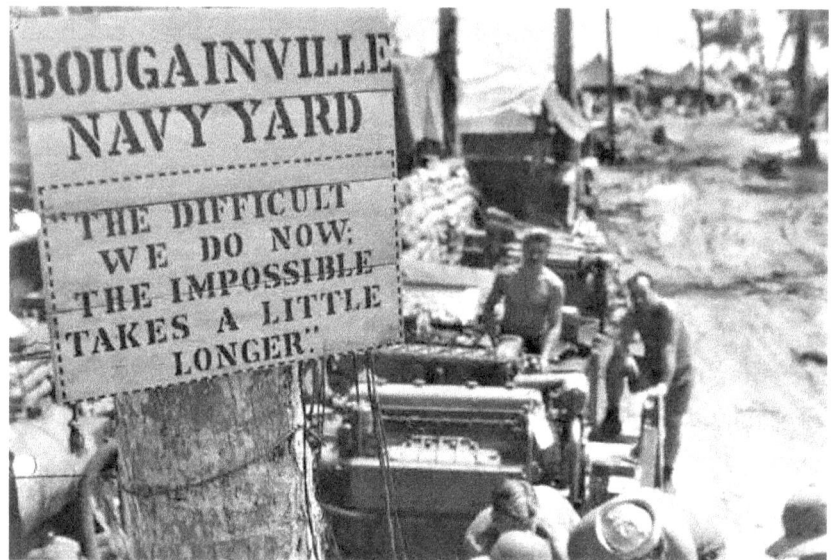

Construction Battalion Navy Yard on Bougainville with the Seabee Expression, 1943. U.S. Navy Seabee Museum

Keeping the Tanks in Order

We came back from Bougainville and got back to Guadalcanal, and we had hand-me-down Shermans. So what we really became was aircraft mechanics because here we have diesel now. They were General Motors 600 twin diesels and you know what they did? They sent in mechanics from Detroit to Guadalcanal, put up a couple of tents bigger than this room, and strung up two sets of diesel engines on racks.

They said to us, 'Take them apart.' So that's what we did. We tore the engines all down, detail stripped them. Then they told us to put it back together again, which we could do. But we couldn't start them; we didn't know the first thing about the injectors, and that's what they were using now. There was no electrical system, no ignition to worry about with the diesel. We had to learn how to adjust the injectors they had, what they call an injector rack.

Advertisement, World War II.

Each one of those racks had adjustments on of a locking nut with a tightening and adjusting screw on it. That was the heart of the diesel engine with us. You had to learn how to adjust those so that you got just the right type of spray into the engine, and also to control the governor. It had to be really fine-tuned, a very critical part of that diesel engine because if that governor went haywire, the diesel would run wild. It would go out of control, and it would blow itself up if you didn't shut it down. There was a big flap and if the driver senses something was wrong, he hit what we call the panic button at that solenoid flap to trip and shut off most of the oxygen to the engine. That's what a diesel thrives on, it's oxygen like any engine, and it will shut the engine down. That was our introduction to the diesel. It was just a matter of, as I said, adjusting those injectors because without those injectors running, there's a lot of loss of power.

In the Army, the Shermans, they had a Chrysler nine-cylinder radial engine, it's a big aircraft engine. Those things were easily blown up with a Molotov cocktail because we burned high-octane gas, which is what we burn in the light tanks.

But here now we were in diesel with these little twin engines, and it had clutches for both of those engines, and it had lockouts, a lockout like a choke. You pull that out and it disengaged that clutch from that engine, so if an engine got hit in combat, broadsided, and knocked out of commission, your temperature gauges would be telling the driver, over all the noise and everything, as soon as the temperature rose on the right or left engine. He would know immediately that there was something wrong with that engine, so he would pull the clutch lockout to see if it was running by his tachometer. If it wasn't running, he knew the engine was dead for whatever reason. But that other engine would pull that tank out of harm's way if it had to be taken out; it could get the crew out of there with that one engine. That was a beauty. It was a type of engine that could withstand most anything except for a broadside by an armor-piercing high-explosive round that would penetrate the hull and get to the engine. It was a good tank for what we used it for, and we used it more effectively in the later campaigns on Guam.

Guam

The [immediate] objective of all these landings [I was on] was to get supplies in on the beach, mostly ammunition, to get that in first. That's the first thing that's got to be done. Most of the time, with the tanks, we came in on the LCTs, or Landing Craft Tank. The LCIs were for the infantry, the Higgins boats, as they were called. Then there were the largest ships that were brought into the war a little later on, the big transport LSTs. They carried the tanks, trucks, all the heavy equipment. They had a huge opening on the front of the ship so that when they hit the beach they would drive up onto the beach.

On the LST, they had twin screws, and immediately, when they hit the beach, they reverse those to like an idling position. So, they kept the ship there, but it was also giving them a little pull off the beach, so that they wouldn't be stuck there. If it stayed there too long, the vacuum suction would hold it, and they would have a job getting it off. Now as they were unloading equipment, it lightens the ship, of course, it lightens the load. On Guam in particular, this caused a major problem, really. The water was a little deeper than other places, and when the LST would hit the beach, they would reverse the screws, but what was happening was it was pulling the sand from underneath the ship and creating big pockets in the ocean [floor], deep pockets.

When we were stepping off [our LCTs or LCIs], a lot of us would step off into those holes, and on Guam, it happened to me—I just went right out of sight. I had tools in my pack, and I had a rifle, because somebody had stolen my Thompson submachine gun, on that trip out from San Diego to New Caledonia. I had a rifle and I disappeared and went right down. When I hit the deck, the bottom of the ocean, I pushed myself back up again.

When I come up there was a [guy] who happened to be right there, and he put his hand out to me and pulled me out. He was there for just that reason; in fact there were a couple of guys, but I remember this one man who pulled me out.

"US Marines leap from their amphibious tractors for the sand dunes, Guam, July 20, 1944." US Marine Corps photo, public domain.

[On the way in], with all the confusion, there were a lot of dead Marines floating in the water. You were walking your way through, and the intense mortar fire was killing [us] on those beaches. The mortar fire was terrible.

I had a young fella with me who was new in the company. His name was Jasper Fane, and he had never been in combat. He was behind me, and when I turned around, I didn't see him. I stopped, I turned around, I was looking for him, and then I saw him step off the ramp and he disappeared. He went right out of sight. That fella was right there and then pulled him out. I waved to him, and I waited for him, and he caught up with me.

I said we had to look for a stream. That was our landmark, and we would go to the right of that stream, and that's where our tanks would have gone in. Well, we couldn't find any stream, the further we went down the beach.

I said, 'Jasper, the fellas are bunching up.' There was an officer standing on a 55-gallon drum and he had an old megaphone. He was hollering through that megaphone, 'Don't bunch up. Don't bunch up on the beach!' That's all he was hollering, 'Don't bunch up on the beach. Don't bunch up!' Some people start to disregard him, and they started to bunch up over to our left.

I said to Jasper, I said, 'Let's get out of here because there's a lot of mortar fire flying around and they're looking for targets. Let's move out of here!'

So we moved out up the beach, and they were dropping the 90 millimeters. One of them hit—it couldn't have been any more than fifty feet from me—so we hit the deck because I could hear it coming in, and I recognized the sound.

Jasper got hit. I don't know how he got hit; to this day I can't figure out how he got hit. He got hit in the leg, and I turned around and I said, 'Well, I'll try to get a corpsman.' I turned around, and to this day, I don't know what happened to him.

I went back up the beach, went back in the opposite direction. But just before that 90 millimeter hit, the Japs had spotted these guys bunched up and they laid a bunch of mortars in, and they got most of those guys. There were a lot of guys lying on the beach; some of the corpsmen were working there and the fire went through there and just tore everybody apart, right down that beach. It was—I don't even like to... in fact, at times, it just blacks out. I can't see those pictures anymore in my mind, of all those people that were being just blown apart after they had been lying there helplessly wounded.

So that's what happened there. There were a couple of Japanese officers too, lying there on the beach. I don't know why I remember all these things, or things like that. They were booby-trapped; really nobody was touching them. They lay right there; they were trying to psych us. It's—I don't know if you've ever been where there's been an accident, it's something that is really chaotic. There's so much going on that you wonder how anybody can get anything done because of the conditions, the things that are happening.

As we are standing there, those 90 millimeters are still coming. We got to the point where we were just standing around trying to get some direction, because here you are walking into a jungle. You don't know where you're going to be, if there's any place to meet, there's no direction whatsoever until you move in.

The Fever

On Guam, we used to set up ambush groups, two people in an ambush area, in different places in the jungle. I was in there with a Marine buddy of mine, Paul Ryan. He was a platoon sergeant; he became a gunnery sergeant after that. We had different things set up in the jungle where if anything rattled, we knew that somebody was out there that shouldn't be out there. It had to be about three or four o'clock in the morning, and all of a sudden, I heard him kind of groan a little bit.

I said, 'What's the matter, Paul?'

Boy, he said, 'I'm sick.'

The next thing I know he passed right out. Well, here I am. It's three or four o'clock in the morning, this guy's passed out, and I had no idea what was wrong with him. I finally got some word. There were another couple of guys a little further to the right. We had passwords we had to use at night, if you're going to do any moving, and they change it every day, every night, every morning, whatever, whenever. So I got word over and what was happening was that our relief was coming. It was a very timely thing, our relief coming in, and I said, 'Paul is unconscious.'

So they took him right out, dragged him right out, and left me there alone.

I said, 'Well, so here I am now, waiting, and no relief.' Finally, about two hours later, I started getting sick. I mean, I was really getting sick and I didn't know what was wrong with me, I had no idea what was wrong with me. I was feeling good and all of a sudden it hit me and I come down with it, the dengue fever, pretty close to two weeks that I was down with it. My teeth loosened up, hair fell out, your eyes you couldn't turn. If you want to look at anybody, you couldn't turn your eyes. You had to turn your whole body.

I was laid up for about two weeks just flat-out, didn't eat anything all day. All they fed us was aspirin, that's the only thing that they gave us at that time.

Zeroes

On the beach at Guam, it's about the third or fourth day and a Zero came and there was a dogfight going on with the Corsairs and the Zeros and we were watching that, crazy things happened. Two of the planes came down real low and they're all shooting at the first airplane and they wound up shooting at the Corsair Marine pilot and they hit him. Behind him was the Zero. This guy took a .50 caliber in his leg. He landed the Corsair on the beach and came out of there, and boy, let me tell you something, mister, he was calling out just about everything he could lay his tongue on. 'You call [yourselves] Marines?' But about that time, that Zero turned around, and he came back down the beach and was strafing.

As he was banking, there was a fella with a .50 caliber on this 6x6. He was pumping .50 caliber rounds into that thing just as perfect as you could. [A plume of black smoke appeared], just like you see in the movies, going right down the beach and crashing in the jungle. A colonel happened to be just watching all this. He took the guy's name and all that and he said, 'I'm going to put you in for a citation!' But I actually saw that, all those crazy things are happening, and you wonder how you survive.

Mr. Smith's story will continue.

Soldiers of the 27th Infantry Division review the bodies of dead Japanese soldiers following a banzai attack, July 1944. New York State Military Museum.

PART TWO

BANZAI

"I'm telling you the way I remember it, no bullshit. I remember it was like I was reborn again. I remember music. I could see the sun. My whole life changed in front of me, and when I came to, there were guys all around me. They were still fighting! The Japs were down around where I was, but they were in a little ways away, like from here to my driveway. They were still fighting them off!"

—US Army Infantryman, Saipan

CHAPTER SIX

The Runner

One of seven children growing up in Troy, New York, Sam Dinova was working with his father as a bricklayer when he volunteered for the Army in the autumn of 1940. After his one-year stint, he returned home, only to be called back after December 7, 1941. He would go on to be an unfortunate participant, wounded in the most horrific banzai charge of World War II.

"Everybody was screaming and hollering. I don't know what the hell was going on, I can't explain it to you—kids hollering, women screaming, machine guns firing and rifles firing. I grabbed my carbine, ran back with the other guys, and somebody hollered, 'Let's stop and all form a line and fight them back!' We did that, but they overran us. Now, when they overran us, there were [just] too many of them. We had these two kids in my outfit, one kid, one soldier—I don't know his name, they cut his head off with a saber! The other kid got hit, too—[these guys] were machine gunners—the other machine gunner got his head cut off, too."

He sat for this interview at his home in Troy, New York, in January 2003.

Samuel R. Dinova

[I was born in 1922.] I went to the eighth grade, and I stopped; I didn't graduate because I just didn't want to go to school [anymore]. I was fifteen years old; I went out to Idaho, I went in the CCC camp. You've heard of CCC camps?[49] I was supposed to be seventeen, but I lied about my age. For six months, we chopped trees, built roads, fought forest fires.

[When Pearl Harbor happened], I was home. I had already been in the Army—I went in the Army October 15, 1940—I enlisted, [see,] I wasn't quite eighteen. Then, you had to be twenty-one to get drafted. My friends were going in the Army, and they were going to be twenty-one or they were twenty-one. So, they went up to the National Guard before it was federalized, then when I joined it, October 5, the government federalized it, and that's why I went in.

'We're Going for A Year's Vacation'

We left Troy from the Troy Armory; we walked all the way down to Federal Street, then boarded the train at the Troy Depot. We lined up, the whole 1st Battalion, and we were loaded on the train, and we were headed for Fort McClellan, Alabama.

When we first got there—our captain had said when we left the Troy Armory, 'Bring your golf sticks, your swimming [trunks], we're going for a year's vacation.' [*Laughs*] We wound up way the hell out of the camp, it was up in the hills and we had to put tents up. That's where we stayed; I was there for almost a year, then we went on maneuvers. Then, June of '41 we went to Tennessee maneuvers. We came home and I went on a furlough, and after we got

---

[49] *CCC camps*-Civilian Conservation Corps; New Deal work relief program employing young men on environmental projects during the Great Depression.

back we were on the Louisiana-Arkansas maneuvers—that lasted quite a while. I remember the big artillery, the trucks were pulling the guns, the 175s, the 105s; I remember the tanks being out there. I don't know if it was Patton's outfit or what, but they had tanks out there. At night, it was raining, so I slept near the truck and tank. We got up and we had to fight. We were the Blue Army, and we fought the Red Army—that's the guys with the bands on their arms. We fought in Louisiana down around near Shreveport and Monroe. They were the Texas 36th Division that we were fighting; as a matter of fact, one of the guys was kind of a wise guy. He shot with the goddamn blanks, and it hit one of the guys—you know the flame came out—so one of our guys hit him with the butt of the rifle, one of our guys hit him with the rifle. We stayed there and then some of the guys were captured, and they were sent to Lake Charles, Louisiana.

When we got back in the fall—it was the end of September '41—they called me in the office, and they told me that I was going home. My year was up. See, I was not National Guard; I was Army. There was United States Army, National Guard, and draftees. Well, I had only signed for one year. So, when I got out, after a few days home, I went looking for a job. I had put my time in the Army. I didn't think there was going to be any war or anything. I was looking for a job and my brother—he was only a young kid then—he picked up the mail. Well, when Pearl Harbor happened, I was looking for a job. I was coming out of the Lincoln Theater, and I heard the kids running around with the paper, extras, they were selling the extra—Pearl Harbor was hit. I knew I was going to go back in the service. Yes, I was a civilian. But when they hit Pearl Harbor, I said, 'Oh, what happened?'

A few days later I got a letter from Cluett Peabody to go to work.⁵⁰ Here I am, I didn't know I was supposed to get a letter from them to go to work, [but then], I got a letter from the War Department—they called me back; on January 14, I got the notice to report back to active duty. They gave me five days to be there by the 19th of January 1942. So now when I went in, I got the notice. We shipped out by rail out of Albany Depot down to Camp Upton, New York. We were assigned to this barracks. I met different guys there the week or two I was there, you know, I got talking to guys, they were from all over New York State. Then this guy—he was with a tank outfit, and he got called back in the service and he was always clowning around—he wouldn't let me in the men's room. I had to wash up because I had to go on KP.

I said, 'Come on, will you, I have to get going!'

He said, 'All right, come on in.' I went to look into the latrine, there was a guy, he committed suicide. What he did—he grabbed the wastepaper basket, and he got the rope from his barracks bag—the barracks bags used to have ropes on them; I don't know if you remember that. He threw it over the rafter, and he hooked it, and he kicked the barrel out and bang, he went down. He committed suicide.

I had to go on KP that day. I dipped out spuds, potatoes, about 2,800 guys [we had to feed]. They were from all over. While I was doing that, we had to clean up the mess hall and all that. I didn't get out of there until about nine or ten o'clock at night. The next day they had me on guard duty. The civilians were going to see their sons off, going back in the Army. They had a lot of civilians up in Camp Upton. I forget now if they gave me a club or not, you know,

---

⁵⁰ Cluett Peabody & Company, Inc. of Troy, New York, was a manufacturer of shirts, detachable shirt cuffs, and collars. Troy had an early industrial history, and later, for its standing in the garment industry, became known as the 'Collar City.'

a billy club. I had to stop the people from going into the mess hall and things like that. I did that. At night I was on guard, and it was awful cold out there in January, so I used to go into—they had a little shack in there with coal furnaces, and Joe Louis the fighter was down there, too; he was stationed there when I was there. They called us out one morning; they told us to fall out. They called the sergeant to come out and he called you by your name and you went out onto the company street. And then they told us we were shipping out and we had to get ready, and we had to go down to the depot. I don't know how far the depot was from the camp.

Jungle Training

We went down to the camp and we shipped out. We went to California. We went down to Camp Haan, California, down near Riverside. We were there for a few days and they shipped us right to Fort Ord. We went over to Ford Ord, we stayed there and did training, going out in the field with the mortars; now we had regular mortars.

We went to California. We were out regular drilling every day like we did down in Alabama, you know, close-order drill, going out firing our guns and mortars and things like that, machine guns. [Then the 27th Infantry Division] shipped out to Hawaii, I think it was March 10, 1942.

On the barracks bag, they had a code word marked 'plump,' and we were supposed to be headed for the Philippine Islands. That's what I was told, I don't know how true that was. In the meantime, the Japs already took the Philippines, and we wound up going to Hawaii. We got off of that ship and we went on another ship called the *USS Republic*. It was a captured German ship in the First World War—the way I was told. I'm telling you everything that I know. So, from there on we went to the big island; we drove all around those islands, we did [more] training there. And then we went to Oahu where Pearl Harbor is; we were staying in tents.

We went on thirty-mile hikes, we did jungle training, amphibious training, and I know one time we went out up in the mountains and we had mules bringing us food. A couple of them went down—they fell off the cliff! We were on the edge, narrow passes there. And we stayed up there and we fired our mortars, and we started a forest fire with the mortars; we had to go down and put it out. I remember that. And then one day they took us over to Maui from Honolulu where we got on a ship; we had simulated landing. They had airplanes come by and throw down paper bags of flour, simulating that they were a bomb. They had these [landing craft]—they came down with a ramp on the side, landing craft infantry, LCIs—you came down and ran up, you know, they got as close as they could in the water, and we got off of them, falling in the sand and all that, with your rifle and all that shit there.

We took more jungle training. I'll never forget the day I burned my hand on the damn Browning Automatic, BAR. I don't know what made me grab the goddamn thing, and my hand got all blistered up. It was so white from the heat. The BAR, that was a good gun. We fired them, we fired a Tommy gun, we fired a pistol and the mortars and everything like that. And they took us out to a little village off of the shore to the ocean. They had like a lagoon. You had to swim with all your equipment on. A lot of guys were throwing it off—they were going down; you had to swim at least seventy-five yards with your equipment on, and as a matter of fact, I don't know how the hell I did it. I'll never forget the day a couple of guys went down, and they had these Navy divers go down after them, and they got them all right. Another guy went down, and he never came up; the Navy guy drowned down there. We did that and then they started trying us out with just the small haversack pack, a little bit at a time, with different equipment on. Then they had us go out to the ocean, out a little way, and they had like a wall, and they had the cargo nets and they had us go up and down on these cargo nets.

Shipping Out

After that training, we went back to the company and we used to go out to the field every day, training. As a matter of fact, I was in the hospital there for a couple of weeks. I had an operation on my leg. And we got the orders to pull out. We were shipping out—where, we didn't know. One of the guys told me, and I told him to get the lieutenant to get me out of there. I didn't want to stay up in the hospital; I wanted to go with my outfit.

We left Schofield Barracks on the side where nobody could see us, in these little freight trains; they used to carry sugar cane. We got in there, so many in a car, and they brought us all the way to the back of the island where nobody could see us. They brought us right into Pearl Harbor, where we got on the ship in Pearl Harbor. I think it was June 1, 1944.

We sailed out. I remember over the loudspeaker—June the 6th, the invasion of Europe started, Normandy. They announced that over the speaker.

Now when we were going out, I remember one night I was staying out on deck, sleeping on the deck, and I could see in the distance big flashes—must have been the Navy ships shooting at the shore because we were up near there. Then the next day, they got us, they assembled us on the deck of the ship, ready to go over the net. We started to go out, but they called us back. I was up on [the top of the cargo net] there and I could see the island, and the next thing I knew there was a flash. The [Japanese] had an ammunition dump and everything went up. Big balls of flame and all that stuff flying in the air. We pulled out of there.

In mid-June 1944, just over a week after the Normandy landings in France, 20,000 Marines of the 2nd and 4th Divisions landed and suffered heavy casualties. Reserves of Marine battalions and the Army's 27th Division followed a few days later. Guam, Saipan, and Tinian were seen by planners as essential stepping stones in the conquest of Japan, hastening defeat through economic deprivation of war materials and construction of long-range bomber airstrips. Awaiting them on Saipan were almost 40,000 Japanese troops controlling the high ground, every yard of the landing beaches cross-registered for devastating artillery fire. After nearly a week of Marine combat, it was time for the Army to bring in its reinforcements. The men of the 27th Division were tasked with the duty.

Saipan, <u>Stars and Stripes</u>, July 1944.

The Landing

They put us on [for the landing]; we went in on the 17th. See, we were supposed to be [reserve troops] for Guam—that's what they said, but we went in on the 17th of June, 1944. So, as we got in the Higgins boats, they made these circles, and they lined up going in. We got in so far; we couldn't go any further on account of the coral reef. They had these [amtanks], they went in the water—I don't know what the hell they called them—and we had to jump off on a beach. The Higgins boats couldn't go in or they'd rip the bottom up.

So, we got in there, and when I first got there, I saw a jeep with the blood plasma giving it to Marines who were on the beach, and then I saw three Marines—they were dead. One guy had a tank on him, a flame thrower, and he was shooting it at that cave where the Japs were coming out, and you could see some of the Japs on the ground. They were dead, scorched.

As we moved in that morning, we went up so far, all of a sudden we hit the ground, we got an air raid or something—you could hear the motor of the plane, and pieces of shrapnel were falling on the ground. They were shooting up at it, then we moved out. As we moved out, we moved into this area and the airport was there, Aslito Airfield.

So, we went in the airfield—I don't know who had it first, the Marines, or the Japs took it away from the Marines, but we got in there and I was digging a hole. The Japs used to put their planes in bunkers there so they wouldn't be spotted by the air. They weren't on the field; I didn't want to get near where the planes were; I didn't want to get near because I figured if the Japs came in, they could roll grenades. So, I dug in and the next thing I know, we were fighting. Well, anyway, while we were in there fighting up near the airport, the report came this guy got killed. A guy from Lansingburg [outside of Troy], Swede Johnson, they called him, he got killed. And then we pulled in, we dug our holes at night, and another kid [who would be killed later], Ciccarelli, I was near him when we hit this big cave. We were out there in front with our rifles, and we got them out of there. There were women and kids—old, old lady, old man, carrying the kids on their shoulders—and there were some Japs. They had G-strings on them, nothing on them, you know, to cover their privates. And they were sent behind the lines.

So I'm telling you what I did. That evening, we pulled up to this area, where the 165th, of the Fighting 69th, already had the foxholes dug, and we were supposed to take their holes that night. And this one guy that was in our outfit, he was a regular Army guy, he was a wise son of a bitch. He was from Arizona. He was made sergeant in our company, and he was picking on all the guys. So he happened to jump into the hole where all that shit was. Oh, was he mad as a banshee, smelled like hell! He was hollering and screaming like hell. [*Laughs*]

I say we went back in the holes right away because there was a Jap Zero dogfighting with one of our planes. You could hear the machine gun chatter; he came down and started strafing us. I leaped and [hit the ground], and I hit my chest on the frigging coral they had; I scratched my chest, I'll never forget that day. And [the pilot of the Japanese Zero], he lands down in the field there, and the guys opened up. We had guys there with .50 calibers down the field, and they opened up and they killed him. I didn't see this; this is what I was told. But I know they were fighting in the air; I could see the planes.

Coming in from the beach, when I got off the [amtank] to come in and land, I saw one of our airplanes. The tail was up in the air and the motor was in the ground, and a parachute was all loose and was on top of the tail of the airplane. And I was right there, me and a few other guys, and I was [poking] around near the cockpit. The plane was all scorched—I don't know if he got knocked down, shot down, or if he crashed or whatever happened. But it was in the ground, sticking in the air. So, I went to dig, I had that little pick mattock, and I was digging near his head, but I didn't see any head; it was just black ashes—I found just bone, skull, that's all I found there. I dug down a little bit and I pulled off his tag. His tag was near the skull and that was all black. The Navy has round tags; we got the flat one, they got the round one, and on that tag, it said, 'Paul Danna, United States Navy Reserve.' Well, then when I was digging farther down, you could see it was all charred, it was all ashes. His whole torso was all black and everything, so we started to scrape around that. We started digging a hole, and then we put what remains we could in there. Now what happened was, I got a stick; don't ask me where we got the stick and pieces of wood. We made a cross on it, we tied it with shoelace tight as we could, and we put the tag on there so the Graves Registration could pick it up.

Before we dug in that night, I went looking into [this concrete bunker]. I had my carbine outside, leaning against the thing, and the guys were scrounging around. And we found opium, rubbers, different things; guys were picking stuff up. They found rubbers. I found a nice silk handkerchief; I gave it to some guy about twenty-five years ago. Embroidered right on the handkerchief [was an image of] a Jap having intercourse with this geisha girl. It was a nice silk handkerchief.

In the meantime, we heard a big explosion. We went out, I grabbed my carbine—it was right on the end of the door there. One of our outfits, it was the 165th, dropped a mortar shell short; it hit in our area, and it killed a guy in my company—he was from Connecticut, Skiba—he was one of the replacement guys that came in from the Christmas Islands—and then there were two or three guys from B Company who got killed. There was a lot of confusion over that.

So now, that night, we dug in there. The next thing I heard while we were dug in—now, it's dark, it's pitch black—I heard a noise, a flutter, and something hit down right near my foxhole. I'll never forget that; I don't know what it was, I didn't look, I didn't get out of the foxhole, because you didn't know what they'd do; your own men might shoot you. It might have been a dud—whatever it was, I don't know. There was a roadway, and during the night, the Japs were trying to get out. They had these trucks, and our machine gunners opened up. You could hear them screaming— [our guys] opened up and they killed a bunch of them. The next morning you could see them all, leaning all over the trucks and everything, and then we pulled out of there.

We went up in this area where Mt. Tapochau was, where the banzai attack would come from, where they all came down. Now, we pulled up into that area, and we had these panel trucks with speakers on them telling the people to give up, we'd take care of them. There was a Jap general up there—he told his people that if they gave up, he would kill them. So, we pulled into that area; we dug in.

That day we were watching for snipers and out came women and kids, they had religious people on that island. They called them Chamorrans. These people were awful religious. We used to burn down the houses—they lived in shacks, the Japs took them over, you know. And one of the guys in my outfit was grabbing the gold teeth out of the [dead Japanese] with his bayonet. These [Chamorro] people were awful religious—they had the Blessed Mother in their shacks—they were like saints, and the Japs were raping the women and all that. They did everything. Well, we saw them coming out, and kids were bleeding, and we took them to the medics who were bandaging them up; some got hit with mortar shells, or whatever it was.

When I first came in, I did see a big, big wire fence. It must have been barbed wire, and they had had these Japs in there. Wiry little Jap soldiers, they were about my size, nice-built guys. They had them in there—we took them prisoners. The Japs had, in the mountain, a door cut out of the mountain. I don't know if it was square or what, but they used to open it up, pull a gun down, and shoot down into the ocean, shoot at the ships. And when we did find out, we knocked it out. At first, we didn't know where it was coming from, but they found out. I know that.

We're coming up this trail, and we're down near Tanapag Harbor, and this was before we got to the mountain, and there was a lagoon. I'll never forget—I saw a couple of soldiers, they had an old, old man. Why I say he was old, he had the goatee on him. He was a Jap from the navy—he might have been a naval officer or something, an admiral or whatever you call him, and they were on him with the gun, with the rifles.

We took a break down near this road and I'll never forget that day. Tokyo Rose was on; we were listening to her. In the meantime, we were waiting to move up to where the mountain was. We were in this area and Lieutenant Stark—he was from Ohio, he was a nice guy—he says, 'Sam, I'm going to make you a runner.'

I said, 'No, no, I don't want to be a runner,' because the guys who got out of the foxhole at night, they'd think you might be a Jap and they'd shoot you; they killed a couple of guys in the Signal Corps outfit who were attached to us. He was going to make me a runner and I didn't want to do it. But I was a runner anyway, this was when we moved out.

A jeep came down to the CP, where the officers were talking, you know they had their spot, and they were told to tell Lieutenant Ryan to stay put—in other words, not to move—but in the meantime, we were already starting to move out.

He says, 'Captain Callan, tell Lieutenant Ryan to stay put with the mortars.'

Now if he had done that, we would have been all right, but what happened was, [the captain] said, 'We're already moving out.'

So, up we went to the foot of the mountain and dug in. Up on the top of the hill I could see a big fire, just like they had a bonfire up there, and they were shooting down at us and you could hear the guns going off and they'd be peppering us every once in a while.

During the night, I was called out to the CP. There was Emmet Callan, our company commander there, Lieutenant Tuger, Lieutenant King, Earl O'Brien, and another officer, I don't know, there were four or five of them. I had to deliver a message, and then I came back to the company.

On July 7, after three weeks of fighting, the most horrific suicide charge of the Pacific War was about to get underway. Backs to the sea, rather than resort to surrender, the Japanese general ordered a full-scale frontal assault targeting a gap in the 27th Division's lines between the 1st and 2nd Battalions of the 105th Regiment. Over six thousand screaming Japanese soldiers, sailors, and even civilians broke through the lines; one officer likened it to a western movie cattle stampede that just would not end.

When I got back, about four o'clock in the morning—I was in my foxhole about four o'clock in the morning, four, four-thirty, in that area. Next thing you know, the sky lit up, it looked like today, you see how sunny it is out there—it was like daylight, it was like twelve o'clock in the afternoon at four-thirty in the morning, and you could see these women, kids, soldiers! They had bamboo poles with bayonets on them, shovels, picks, pitchforks—they had everything. These were civilians, with soldiers too. They came down on us; our machine gunners were out, and they started killing them—there were so many of them! I was at the foot of the hill. I couldn't get out of my foxhole because they were raking the dirt [with fire], and it was going in my hole. Then, me and these other two guys [got out]—where they went, I don't know.

Everybody was screaming and hollering. I don't know what the hell was going on, I can't explain it to you—kids hollering, women screaming, machine guns firing and rifles firing. I grabbed my carbine, ran back with the other guys, and somebody hollered, 'Let's stop and all form a line and fight them back!' We did that, but they overran us. Now, when they overran us, there were [just] too many of them. We had these two kids in my outfit, one kid, one soldier was from—I don't know his name, he lived in this little town outside of Rochester called Lyons, New York. They cut his head off with a saber! The other kid got hit, too— [these guys] were machine gunners—the other machine gunner got his head cut off, too. He was from Lexington, Kentucky; his name was Carneel.

When they did that, we had formed a line, and we started to fight them, but they still came at us; we had to push back. I ran down to the railroad track; it carried the sugar cane to the factories. Now, that night, it rained, I forgot it had rained. My carbine, the end of the thing had some mud in it. I threw a couple of shots, I just took a shot to clean it out. That was down near the railroad tracks, near the bunker I was looking up over. So, when I did that, they kept coming; I was shooting at them.

I ran down by the ocean. I don't know where the hell [I was]—I could see different guys running, and I saw one of the medical officers—he was with a guy from my company—he was on one side and he was running. Then I didn't see; everybody was for themselves. You couldn't help your brother if you had to; if your brother was there, you had to leave him. I saw the back of the officer's shirt and it was all blood, he got hit in the back, and then I ran down by the ocean, down the shoreline. They had a big silver-colored thing in the ground; it must have been a mine. I jumped over it and got behind a coconut tree, where I met two guys from Pennsylvania. So these two guys were with me, and we stayed behind this coconut tree, while the guys were running out in the ocean, swimming out in the ocean to get away from the Japs. The Japs were shooting all around; they circled around us—too many! There must have been at least five thousand of them. And we were only two battalions, 1st and 2nd Battalion. Then these guys got up, and they ran; I heard they got killed after. You know, [later] they're making the count for the guys that were killed, who got wounded. In the meantime, I'm behind this coconut tree. I got up over the coconut tree, and I crawled out towards the Japs.

They had big weeds—this big, tall grass. I met another guy there with my company. He was from Wichita, Kansas; his name was Ganz. I don't know what happened to him; when I crawled out, I lost him. I crawled back, I wiggled back to the same position I was in before.

Wounded

[The Japanese then] let [loose with] a barrage of mortar shells or artillery—whatever they threw at us—and then they hit the beach. I remember seeing the black dirt, sand, everything in the air. Next thing I know, I don't remember anything; I got hit in the leg. When I got hit in the leg, I got knocked out.

I'm telling you the way I remember it, no bullshit. I remember it was like I was reborn again. I remember music. I could see the sun. My whole life changed in front of me, and when I came to, there were guys all around me. They were still fighting! The Japs were down around where I was, but they were in a little ways away, like from here to my driveway. They were still fighting them off. I remember Lieutenant Stark—he was the medical officer—he put the sulfur drug on my leg, because my leg, when it was hit, you could see all of the flesh out of that hole where it had come out, all the guts from my leg, it was a mess. I lay there—I couldn't do anything. My leg wouldn't go, it was just dead. So, he put the sulfur drug on me and everything.

'They Had Baker Propped Up Against the Tree'

One guy runs by me—he's dead now, he used to live near me, too. When they had Baker propped up against the tree, he put a cigarette in Baker's mouth, lit it for him, and took off.[51] He went right by me, this Carlo, he's dead now. He came by me, and I gave him my rifle, [thinking], 'what the hell am I going to do with it,' not realizing, you know, I've got to use it myself. I gave him my rifle.

There were guys next to me, there were two brothers, and one of them—I don't know [what happened to the other that day]—but the one brother was killed. He got shot, he was next to me, he was shot in the head; this is after I was wounded. See, I lay on the ground, they kept coming, the soldiers—the American soldiers. They were fighting them off; they were right near me. This kid who got killed, his name was Bernhardt, he was from Petersburg. His

---

[51] *they had Baker propped up against the tree-* "Private Thomas Baker, also hailing from Troy, was a rifleman in Company A of the 105th. Baker had distinguished himself earlier in the campaign on Saipan by single-handedly destroying an enemy strongpoint that was holding up his company's advance. He exhausted his ammunition and used his rifle as a club. After he bashed his rifle apart on several Japanese attackers, Baker and a couple of his buddies pulled back. Baker was hit, and a fellow soldier began carrying him. When the soldier carrying him was hit, Baker insisted to be left behind. His buddies propped him up against a tree, lit a cigarette for him, and gave him a pistol loaded with eight rounds. After the battle, his buddies found him dead, with the empty pistol still in hand and eight dead Japanese bodies around him." Source: Decuers, Larry. *Banzai Attack: Saipan*. The National WWII Museum, July 7, 2020. www.nationalww2museum.org/war/articles/banzai-attack-saipan

other brother made it all right, and after the war, he went to California.

The lieutenant, the medical officer who put the sulfur drug [on my leg], he was there [with me at the time]. We stayed there until it got dark, around seven or eight o'clock, whatever time it was. I lay there and Nick Grinaldo—he dragged me and somebody else, he dragged me under a tree with all the wounded guys. I was next to Eddie Boudoin; he died here about almost a year ago, he had a plate in his head, shrapnel had hit him [that day] in the head. Then there were other guys, I don't know, I was out of it.

That night after I was under this tree, another soldier in my company got killed. He went out, he was all right until he went down to a little ravine to get water for the guys. When he went down, a mortar shell hit him there. He got killed. He was from Gary, Indiana—Mike Sabo. As a matter of fact, my brother [found his name]; he was in the Pacific, too. He was in the Navy and when he went to Hawaii after the war, he looked at the monument and he saw all the guys who were killed and wounded in the 27th, and I mentioned it to him about the guys in my outfit that got killed. He had the names, and he took a picture of the names on the stone, and he told me about it. My brother's dead now. He fell off of a roof. He was cleaning the roof of his house down in Florida. He's cleaning, and his wife says, 'Don't do it, the guys are coming to clean.' He was always a workaholic, always working, and his foot got caught in the rung of the ladder, tipped back and smashed his head on the driveway. He's the one who took a picture of this Mike Sabo, this guy from Gary, Indiana, who got killed getting the water.

What happened that night—it got to be around seven o'clock, eight o'clock. The [amtracs] were coming up to the edge of the ocean on the shoreline where the beach is. Guys were running out. The [landing craft] didn't have any guns on them, they carried personnel. Amtracs, they called them, and the guys were all jumping in, and they're getting on that, getting in the thing, and as they [were running for the amtrac], I grabbed this one guy—he and another guy in C Company—they grabbed me. I told them, 'Get me out of here!', because if the Japs could see me, they would have killed me, you know, when they ran by. So, they dragged me out and there was no room in the [amtrac]. So, they put me—they got a motor about half as big as this room—on the hood. The heat was bothering me, so a guy threw a field jacket on the hood of the thing, and I got on it. As we pulled out, the Japs were shooting at us.

The next thing I know, we go down this big, big open area, it looked like three football fields. I'm half out of it. A guy came up with the jeep, and they took me and another guy off [the amtrac], they shot me with morphine, put me on the jeep. They strapped us up on a jeep and they took us to this big open field.

Christ, like I told you, the next morning I was out of it. Everything was blurry. I was hurt, but I didn't know how bad I was. That night, they were operating right out of a big, big truck. Two-and-a-half-ton truck—they were operating right out of there with a light in there, emergency operations.

'He Swung the Sword'

I lay there all night long, and the next morning a guy came over to me, Sal Farina, he looked like Wallace Beery, he was a rugged-looking guy. I never told you about him, should I tell you about him? Well, when the Japs chased us down that morning—they pushed us—our tanks came up and they didn't have the hatch open, and he kept hitting his hand on the tank to tell them the Japs were all around us, and to get up and start shooting them with the machine guns. When he was doing that, a Jap came out of the bushes. The Jap came up—and I'm not making this up or anything, no bullshit—the Jap came up and swung the sword like that at him. [*Gestures with arms*]

Sal didn't know it, but he happened to see it from the corner of his eye, and he went down like that [*makes ducking motion with head*], and the sword went over his head. He told me that himself, he told me what happened when [the Jap] swung the sword at him—he missed him, and Sal let out a yell, 'AGHHH,' like that, like a big scream. And it's a good thing because that scared the Jap. One of the naval officers—he told me all this himself, and it's no bullshit, either—came up, and he shot the Jap.

The Replacement

Going back when I was on the ground there that morning, this soldier came by me, I think with a little chunk out of his arm, a bullet wound. He was with one of these new guys that came from the Christmas Islands; nobody knew him, though I knew him casually because we were shipping out and these guys were coming with us. Well, he was with us a couple of months. He was a machine gunner. Well, that morning when they broke through, he starts shooting at them with the machine gun, the water-cooled. Sal was his sergeant, the guy that the Jap tried to hit with the sword. He told him, 'Get out of here!', because they had killed a lot of them, but the gun froze up on [the kid], it warped from the heat. So, Sal got out of there. Before the kid could get out, he got killed. Those guys didn't know him. This kid I'm talking about, this soldier, he was with the 43rd National Guard Division from Connecticut—they broke it up, and they put so many in each of our regiments, that is how I got to know him. I didn't know him that well, but anyway, later, one of the nephews wrote to the 27th Division to say, 'I wish I knew somebody that knew my uncle.' The nephew was from New Haven, Connecticut—I imagine the kid's sister lived there—and that was his uncle.

Nobody up in the post knew him, they asked me, 'You know this guy?'

I said, 'I knew him a little bit.' Nobody knew him! They didn't know who he was! He was one of the new replacements. A mortar shell hit him and ripped his whole shoulder out. This kid here, he didn't get a chance to get out. He and Sal were firing the machine guns on the Japs, Sal got out, and by the time he got out the kid got killed. Now Sal—I saw him. I was on the ground in a big field hospital where they operate in the big trucks. Oh, it was a big field, guys were dying there, wounded. He says to me, 'Are you going to be all right?'

So, I didn't see him anymore. The next thing I knew, a couple of guys were picking me up; I thought they were Japs. They were Koreans, you know, they had Koreans on that island; the Japs had them do all the dirty work. So, anyway, they picked me up and they put me on a hospital ship, the *USS Samaritan*. I was on that hospital ship, and they were burying guys who died, throwing them off the ship after we left, and they took me to New Caledonia.

I lay in New Caledonia—I got there the later part of July. As a matter of fact, we were right by the island of Truk, where the Japs had that island. But they abandoned it, [we] didn't invade it. And when I got down, the Navy guy took me off, put me in the ambulance, and took me to the 29th General Hospital in New Caledonia. I forgot to tell you about—I was pulling guard duty. There was an open pass, this was just before the big banzai raid came. This guy lay next to me. He was from the 106th Infantry, and I was on guard. I was all dirty, needed a shave and everything—filthy.

I said, 'What's your name?'

He said, 'I'm from the 106th.' He said, 'My name is [so and so]. Where are you from?'

I said, 'Troy, New York.'

He said, 'I'm from Albany!'

I said, 'No kidding.'

'I'm in the 106th,' he said. 'I got a brother-in-law named Joe Merola from Troy; used to be the bread man, used to make the Italian bread.'

I said, 'Shit, I've known him all my life!' He was surprised. Then when I came out of the service, when I got discharged, I saw Joe Merola down in the neighborhood and I was telling him how I ran into his brother-in-law while we were fighting. I didn't know that guy from Adam.

And the next thing I knew I was on a hospital ship. They operated on me, and I got to New Caledonia, and I was convalescing. Then they put me on an airplane, and I went to Espiritu Santo. I was only a few miles from where the guys were stationed—my outfit, the guys that didn't get killed. Then they brought in all new replacements. I didn't know who they were. I was completely out now. I was in a different outfit, all new guys. Then they trained them and they went to Okinawa, then from Okinawa they came home. They went to Japan and they came home on the point system. I was over there thirty-two months.

[They sent me to] the hospital for a few days in Hamilton Field, California, and from there they shipped me to Lowry Field, Colorado, and then I was shipped to Washington. Two women picked me up, they were WACs. They had me down near Hagerstown, Maryland—that's outside of Washington. They put me in the ambulance, and I went down to Martinsburg, West Virginia. That's where I was in Newton D. Baker General Hospital. Then I went to Camp Atterbury, Indiana. They checked me over and they sent me home for three months. They said, 'Go on home for three months. You're still in the service, though.' They figured why [have me] convalesce in the hospital when I could do that at home. They said, 'Come back in September.' This was in the summer. I'd come back right after Labor Day. I went back.

They said to me, 'No, we can't let you out yet.' They sent me home again—three more months. And I got out December 22, about three days before Christmas 1945. But it was a long stay in the different hospitals and then I was hopping around. They were giving me treatment, whirlpool, they couldn't do anything. I have a big scar on my leg, a big hole there. [*Points to leg*]

Home

At first, I was so weak when I came home, I couldn't eat. I didn't want to be near anybody. I [normally] weighed one hundred twenty-eight, one hundred thirty pounds, but then when I was wounded, I went down to about ninety pounds. My aunt used to get two raw eggs—she said, 'I'll build him up,' and she mixed it with a shot of vermouth, and I drank it. It did build me up, though. See, I was small, but I was wiry.

My leg—this is the leg that got hit [*points to left leg*]—was big as that [*circles thumb and forefinger*], to the bone. All the flesh was up in here [*motions to thigh*]. That's an awful big scar; I'm lucky I didn't lose my leg, but I can hardly walk now. I got a bullet here that didn't go through [*motions to right lower leg*]; I have a scar there. Then when I was crawling after I got hit, I was hit [again] in the back. It's a good thing I got it in the back—I can show you, about the size of a nickel; the scar's there. As a matter of fact, when I went into St. Mary's Hospital quite a while ago, and they did an x-ray of my kidney, and they said, 'You have a foreign body in there.' They thought it was a tumor or something.

I said, 'No, oh no, I remember.' Yes, it was a foreign body, it was a piece of the metal!

[When I got home, I ran into fellow soldier] Joe Mariano. He told me when he came home—I asked him, I said, 'Joe, [what do you recall from that morning] when the Japs chased us?'

He said, 'I wasn't hit.' He was [fortunate]. They surrounded the medical department, they surrounded the headquarters, they completely surrounded, there were so many of them. It was hand-to-hand fighting.

He said, 'Sam, I don't want to tell you—where I live here, if you go up [the block] about a quarter of a mile, [and picture] dead Americans and Japs all on the ground, and a lot of the guys I saw the night before were there, dead.'

He said, 'I wouldn't touch anything because I don't know what was boobytrapped or what. They were all dead on top of one another!'

I hope I'm getting some of my stories accurate. But it is the truth.

Mr. Dinova was the recipient of the Bronze Star and the Purple Heart, among other decorations. He passed away on December 4, 2010, at the age of 88.

CHAPTER SEVEN

The Marine Gunner I

Albert Harris was born at home, the youngest of three siblings. When the war broke out, he enlisted in the Marine Corps, trained as a machine gunner, and saw action in the Marshalls and the Marianas, and at the battle of Iwo Jima. He was fast friends with his two other gun crew members, one of whom was subsequently killed the first day at Saipan, and the other near the end on Iwo Jima; he mourned them all his life.

In 1947, he and some fellow Marine buddies joined the Marine Reserves; it had a good baseball team, and they wanted to play together, however, when the Korean War broke out, he was recalled to active duty, training new recruits in his specialty, the .30 caliber air- and water-cooled machine guns. He served eight years as a Marine; after that, he never touched a gun again.

"There were some Japanese soldiers apparently up in the cave underneath where we were standing. A lot of other people were hidden in these caves all along. But they had gotten the people afraid of us, probably terrified of [us] coming. So, we went down there, we sent scouts down there [first]. A couple of them got killed by the snipers, so we pulled back to the cliff line and then had the Japanese speakers try to convince the people that

we weren't going to harm them. But I would imagine [they were] like, 'Who are they kidding?' There was nothing much we could do at that point. The killing just started. I saw whole families standing on a rock, right along the ocean, and explode a grenade, and then maybe a survivor would crawl off into that water. [But as an eighteen or nineteen-year-old in combat], I think by that time, I was a little deadened about anything shocking me. I thought much more about it in years after."

Albert J. Harris

I was born in Harris, New York, which is a small hamlet down between Monticello and Liberty. I lived there until I was through high school. I went to high school in Monticello and from then on, I moved to New York right after that in Brooklyn. I was in Brooklyn at the time the war started in '41.

My first thought [when I heard the news about Pearl Harbor was] I was wondering where the hell Pearl Harbor was, like everybody else. I don't remember any particular emotions really at the time. I didn't know much about the world; I wasn't following the world situation. I didn't know there had been a crisis for a couple of years. I was just existing in New York. So outside of trips down to the city to ballgames and things like that, yes, it was my first time really away from home.

During '42, I realized I better start looking for some spot. I was very vulnerable at 18 years old and single, so I shopped around. I didn't particularly want to go into the Navy, because I thought I might not enjoy life aboard ship; you're sort of confined there a good part of the time. The Army had no appeal. I don't know. It's just I was 18 years old, and I wasn't thinking things out too well at the time. I probably made a foolish move, but I just went and hit on and tried the Marines.

I enlisted and I was called up on December 7, 1942. They made a big thing of it at the time. There's a [recruiting station] on Lower Broadway, the room was full of people, and it made the front page of the *Daily News* and the *Post* and everything that day. Then we went into oblivion. [*Laughs*] We left to go down to Parris Island.

'Your Ass Belongs to the Marine Corps'

Parris Island was twelve weeks of hell. You just kept thinking that you were going to die and that seemed like a terrible prospect. But you're on the base about two minutes or less, and you already become molded in their image. They come down on you like just unbelievable. It was very hard.

They tell you not to worry about the people at home, [because] they forgot about you already. You better give your soul to the Lord because your ass belongs to the Marine Corps. They did everything they could to make your twelve weeks miserable. It had its moments, but I didn't think too much about it. I was too busy doing what they told me to; it was good training and discipline. It was massive training in discipline and that was the whole name of the game anyway. They just made you aware that you belonged to them. Then they started to build up pride and the fact that you were in an elite unit and that you better live up to the other people and stuff like that. But what they did, they did very well and did it fast. You got to know the basics of being a Marine. To tell you the truth, I didn't do that much socializing. I didn't have time to find out much about anybody. I didn't make any close friends.

Training to Be a Marine

Then they shipped me up to Camp Lejeune, which is in North Carolina. That's the east coast Marine training base. At that time, they were just forming the 4th Marine Division. I was one of the first people that came into the 4th Marines. We were there, just a nucleus of people, probably a month or two, that's all. Then they moved us across the country on a troop train to Camp Pendleton, California. At Camp Pendleton, they formalized the whole outfit. I became an assistant machine gunner in the 24th Marines, 4th Division, K Company.

Then I started to build relationships with the other people in the platoon. You never had much chance to socialize with the rest of the regiment. I wouldn't have known the rest of the regiment probably if I fell over them. But I did get to know people in the company. Our company was, of course, about two hundred, two hundred and fifty people. I knew them by sight and the people in my platoon were very close, of course.

Our sergeant was a post-[World War I] Marine, he was solidly of the old-school type. He wasn't a bad guy. He didn't work out too great in combat, but he wasn't bad, just ordinary. He knew what had to be done in the way of training. You see, the problem with the training at that time, they didn't have much to go by. By this time, it was obvious that they knew that the Marines were going to be strictly a Pacific force and they were fighting an enemy that was nothing like [we would face in] World War I. That's the only basis they had of how to train people, World War I, which was trench warfare. So, they trained us and spent a lot of time on things that were ridiculous, but they had to keep us busy. I remember I took a long time, two or three weeks [learning] semaphore [signaling]. In the islands out there if you raised a semaphore flag, you'd have been long dead before you got the second flag up there. It was useless stuff.

They trained very little live ammunition training—none. I never threw a live grenade. I was the assistant gunner on the .30-caliber machine gun, but the only thing I did was carry the ammunition, I never fired it on the range. They trained us on how to take apart the water-cooled, and how to carry it with the big tripod and everything. We never used it in combat. You couldn't use a water-cooled in the islands, carry a water-cooled machine gun. So, we used the air-cooled .30.

I'll tell you, all the training they did, it was kind of worthless because I think I would have learned how to dig a hole by myself or climb down the net of a ship. I could have figured that out without them telling me. But again, it goes back to their strong point and that was command and discipline. You've got to realize that you obey what you are told to do. There was no… you knew where you stood. They had to do something to pass the time. I see now a lot of times on the History Channel they show the Marine training, and it's so much more sophisticated now than it was then. But, it worked. We were young, probably most of the people were eighteen years old average; even the junior officers might have been twenty-four, twenty-five.

'Awed By the Destruction'

We were at Pendleton up until January 13, 1944. It was about a year. We shipped out from San Diego. We stopped at Pearl Harbor. At the time, it was still a mess. In fact, we stopped there for a couple of days to pick up the rest of the convoy. I remember they gave us a day off just to stretch our legs. They had planking going from our transport across the side of the *Oklahoma* and from *Oklahoma* to Ford Island where they had a little recreation for us. That was my first visit any place outside the United States was walking across the *Oklahoma*. It probably still had bodies in it at that time.

I was awed by the destruction. Of course, what they had released at the time to the general public didn't cover the situation. But anyway, we were only there for a few days. Then the whole convoy went out and we landed on the Marshall Islands.

The Marshalls

Following the heavy Marine losses at Tarawa in November 1943, military planners cautiously approved plans for an island-hopping campaign to break the outside Japanese ring of defense, beginning in the Marshall Islands, a grouping of nearly 100 small islands over 2,000 miles southwest of Hawaii, the largest of which is Kwajalein, over six miles long and two and a half miles wide. Within the atoll were two smaller objectives, Roi and Namur, in the north, and Kwajalein Island itself in the south. The 4th Marine Division would assault Roi-Namur, and the Army 7th Infantry Division would attack Kwajalein.[26] *The Marine attack took place on February 1-2, 1944.*

We attacked Roi-Namur, which was the first pre-war Japanese island. It was only two days, I think, to take this atoll. The atoll is very big, like a big pearl necklace made up of little islands. They moved the convoy in to the attack ships, which we were on. That morning early, they put us into the LCVPs—the tracked vehicles—and started to circle us around to get the waves together.[52] Then, when it was going to be the H-Hour on D-Day, they start straightening up the lines—I was in the first wave going in—they make these lines to get them just in the right order that they want. Then, so you go past the destroyer escorts, maybe we're a couple of thousand feet off the shore. As we went by them going into the shore, I remember looking up at them and having the sailors waving at us and thought Holy Christ, what have we gotten into here? [*Laughs*]

---

[52] *LCVPs—the tracked vehicles*- Mr. Harris may actually refer to a version of the LCTs—Landing vehicle, tracked, colloquially known as Alligators, and also known as amtracs, or in the armored versions, amtanks.

That was the first time I realized I should be someplace else. This is terrible. It looked like two-to-one [odds that] you won't come back.

Our particular ship landed in a pretty good spot—we didn't land right in front of the pillboxes, so it wasn't too bad. I jumped off. They're quite high, the [LCTs]—and I was so loaded up when I jumped off with gear, everything from gas masks to strips of ammunition. I was the 'instrument corporal,' theoretically. Nobody knew what that was, but I had all that crap. I had range finders and I had maps and I had binoculars like Rommel. [Loaded with all that stuff], when I went off the [landing craft], I went flat on my face in the surf. That was my first invasion.

'Lose It And It's Your Ass'

[My new classification], that was another thing going back to the old World War I philosophy. Everybody in the squad had a job, and that's all they knew, such as assistant gunner, or instrument corporal, and runners, all these World War I things that meant something. So, they told me I'd be the instrument corporal. That sounded good. I was only a PFC. I thought instrument corporal, I get a promotion. But, no, there was no promotion. Nobody did anything until we were about two weeks from sailing, leaving California, and suddenly all this fancy gear started to come in labeled for the 'instrument corporal!' I had this range finder that looked like a golf bag in a beautiful leather case. I had no idea even how to open the case! Why would we need a range finder on an atoll? I had another instrument which came in a smaller leather case, something to do with map making. I had a stopwatch. I had a pair of binoculars that big in a case again. I had a map case. And all my regular equipment, and my gas mask, too.

I said to the sergeant, 'What am I going to do with this?'

He said, 'I don't know, but you hold on to it! Lose it and it's your ass!'

I carried all this crap; I threw them away, first thing. Nobody asked me about it. That was the end of the 'instrument corporal.' I guess they felt they could win the war without instrument corporals. [*Laughs*]

The fighting at Roi and Namur was brutal. Massive explosions set by the Marines to destroy blockhouses killed nearly two dozen of their own. That night, a banzai charge decimated the Japanese; when the fighting was over, only eight-seven of the enemy were left alive, just two percent of the occupying force of 3,500. The Marines lost 190 men killed in action.

That [action] lasted two days. The Army 7th Division took Kwajalein itself, which is on the southern end of the atoll. It was very successful. Their losses [were high]; we only lost two hundred killed. In fact, we had a Medal of Honor winner—a guy named Sorenson who fell on a grenade and apparently saved the lives of some in our company.[53]

The 'Instrument Corporal'

Then they put us back aboard ship, and we went back to Maui which was to be our training ground. That was about [two] thousand miles back. So, the whole division was put into a tent camp which they had built on the side of the volcano. Have you ever been to Hawaii? They have a big volcano called Haleakala. They put this massive tent camp there, and that was our training grounds for

---

[53] Richard K. Sorenson [1924-2004] was one of only four surviving Marine MOH recipients [out of 27] who received the honor after shielding their comrades in arms from grenades with their own bodies.

about the next about four or five months. Then we went off again, to attack Saipan and Tinian. [With the lessons they learned in our first invasion], I think the only thing they had to learn was that they didn't need an 'instrument corporal'...[*Laughs*]

Now, one important thing that they did learn, not from that operation but from the one just before, was made by the 2nd Marine division. That was Tarawa. In Tarawa a lot of the landing boats got hung up on the coral, and people had to wade in. They were decimated.

This time, for our invasion, they had gotten a hold of all of these tracked vehicles which would go over the coral. So, everybody got in. That was a very important thing about them. But the position that the Japanese were in by this time was always defensive, and they were dug in. I never saw a live Japanese in my four battles. I never saw one live one.

Saipan

On our way to Saipan, they told us quite a bit about the contour of the island, of what we could expect; they had a mockup of the island on the ship. They told us whatever they knew about it, which was limited, but I would say that we had all we needed. The overall commander of that operation was [General] Holland Smith.[54]

---

[54] *Holland Smith*- Holland McTyeire "Howlin' Mad" Smith [1882 -1967] was a 'Marine's Marine,' the overall commander of the land-based Saipan operation. He harbored no love for the Army or the 27th Division's commander, General Ralph Smith [1893-1998], as discussed by veterans in Volume 1 of this series. Before the final attack, the Marine commander expressed his unhappiness with the pace of Army progress in front of war correspondents and had the Army general relieved of his command. This action, coupled with Marine General Smith's unrelenting criticism even after the war, badly exacerbated interservice relationships. Ralph Smith was exonerated by an Army inquiry shortly after his command was relieved. He lived to be 104,

I was with the reserve regiment. We came in about, I think, H-hour was about 11 o'clock—we landed at about five. We landed below Garapan, which was one of the large cities. Well, they weren't very large. By the time we landed, things were very quiet. Maybe it was a little later than that because it was starting to get dark. My platoon was in amongst a bunch of what looked like gas tanks or barrels. I remember I was looking at my squad leader, who was right in front of me. His shoe was practically right in my face, and things were very suspiciously quiet. All of a sudden, we heard that first shell coming in. That first shell, it exploded somewhere near me and I was looking at his shoe, and a piece of shrapnel took the heel of his shoe right off in front of me! Then, they just kept pouring them in on us.

'The Most Horrible Moment of My Life'

I remember somebody yelling to get out of there, because there's gas around there, but we didn't know where to get! Nobody's giving any orders or anything, but people started to move forward. This was the most horrible moment of my life. As you move forward, it looked like all of the World War II [movies] that you ever saw in your life were happening all around you, all of these explosions. I was in a daze. I went, I don't know how much further. We just kept moving forward.

Finally, we came to a ditch—a curved ditch—and somebody said, 'Get down in the ditch!' We plopped in there. All night long there was firing, and people were hit in the ditch. If you had wounded, you didn't know where to go. I didn't have the foggiest idea where the beach was or where to take anybody. You just felt if you were

---

and in all that time only once broached the subject of their tensions in an interview in the 1980s, but only to defend the actions of his men on Saipan.

moving around, you were going to get killed. So, I remember that went on all night. The whole thing—the whole episode from the time of the first shell, practically, is just like a dream. On Roi-Namur, we hadn't experienced anything like that. So, I was not really prepared for this.

The casualties were horrible. I remember that at just about dawn, I looked up from the trenches. It had quieted down a bit. I saw this Marine, sort of sitting up over the trench; I thought what's he doing up there? I looked up, and saw that he was decapitated.

By the next morning, it had quieted down. What had happened, the Navy—of course we had a lot of Navy all around us—was now able to see where the artillery was coming from up in the mountains, so they started to control them. We were able to start moving again. We had a couple more barrages but not as bad as [the beginning]. Saipan was very tough. It was physically demanding.

Our first night, we lost half of our people, either dead or wounded. The only thing we had left was what we carried. I didn't have a pack or anything. I just had my ammunition and a belt and my carbine and water. That was it. The organization was scattered. Nobody knew where anybody was because of the barrage. It took a while for that to get all organized again.

'The Place Was Full of Bodies'

They finally brought food in; the beach wasn't that far away, once they could stand up on it and do things. It was twenty-five days or so, of really a lot of things happening. It was the heat of the place. It's on the equator. It was in June and July, so it was hot. The place was full of bodies, [and the dead] bodies caused maggots, and the maggots caused flies. During the day, you couldn't even put any food up in your mouth or anything, because the flies would cover your spoon. You couldn't go to the bathroom, because they'd be after that. You'd have to wait until night to have a bowel movement. You'd walk along, and the flies would get on every little scratch you had. You'd have five or six of them trying to get to the blood. You just had to walk along like this [*waves his hand in front of his face*]. That went on for most of the time.

The fear was worse at night, but the Japanese [there] didn't move around at night, and as it turned out, didn't fire much at night because they were afraid of the counter-fire. I know on our gun, we had to keep awake all night, so we did one hour off and one hour on, all night. It was bad. The thing about it too—the island was full of civilians. They got hurt too, badly.

Running Into the 27th Division

Once, in the middle of the island—we were going to the west coast through this trail—we [ran into the 27th Division]. They were coming in another direction, and somebody told me who they were—just two roads that passed there, in the day. They looked like they were older people than us. Old, they were probably twenty-two or twenty-three years old, but they seemed so much older than us. I guess they were just shifting positions between the two divisions. [But] communications, when you're just a soldier, you don't know much what's going on. All I knew about what was going in the battle was what I could see.

Soldiers of the 27th Infantry Division with Japanese souvenirs on Saipan. New York State Military Museum.

An interesting thing happened there. About the fifth day on the island—as I mentioned there was a monstrous convoy that brought us there. There were battleships, transports, supply ships, repair ships. The whole harbor was full of ships. So, we were up on this high ground at this point about the fourth or fifth night. They were still there. When it got bright the next morning, we looked out and there was nothing in the harbor but a few little harbor boats! You thought, my God, are we doing that bad they just left us here? I knew we weren't doing very good, but…[*Chuckles*]

What had happened was that the Japanese fleet had been sighted and they had left for a big battle called the 'Turkey Shoot of the Marianas,' where they destroyed practically the air force of the

Japanese.[55] That was what they pulled out for. That Japanese convoy was heading for the Marianas to probably shell us.

Marpi Point

At the end of the battle, [I witnessed] the most eerie, bizarre thing that I ever saw in my life. Up at the end there was a place called Marpi Point. We were there for two or three days, just watching people commit suicide, civilians basically jumping into the water, blowing themselves up with grenades, having their own soldiers shoot them.

What had happened was the end of the island was covered with a shrubbery very tight, like a hedge. It was also coral, and it was pockmarked with these holes, so people could get in these holes all along there. Then there was a cliff just about a thousand feet from the edge, which had caves in the underside. There was a path going down into the flatland, before you got into the water.

There were some Japanese soldiers apparently up in the cave underneath where we were standing. A lot of other people were hidden in these caves all along. But they had gotten the people afraid of us, probably terrified of [us] coming. So, we went down there, we sent scouts down there [first]. A couple of them got killed by the snipers, so we pulled back to the cliff line and then had the Japanese

---

[55] *'Turkey Shoot of the Marianas'-* In the Battle of the Philippine Sea, June 19-20, 1944, the last major carrier battle of the war, American aviators destroyed nearly 400 Japanese planes to a loss of just 23, an action that became known as 'The Great Marianas Turkey Shoot'. Three Japanese carriers were also lost in their attempt to disrupt the landings in the Marianas and deal the punishing blow to US naval forces that had been the hope since Pearl Harbor. This, coupled with the losses sustained in the Battle of Leyte Gulf, put an end to Japanese carrier-based ambitions in the Pacific. One of the pilots later debriefed exclaimed, "Why, hell, it was just like an old-time turkey shoot down home!" Potter, E. B., *Admiral Arleigh Burke*, Naval Institute Press, 1990. 154.

speakers try to convince the people that we weren't going to harm them. But I would imagine [they were] like, 'Who are they kidding?' There was nothing much we could do at that point. The killing just started. I saw whole families standing on a rock, right along the ocean, and explode a grenade, and then maybe a survivor would crawl off into that water. [But as an eighteen or nineteen-year-old in combat], I think by that time, I was a little deadened about anything shocking me. I thought much more about it in years after.

The Little Girl

On about the third or fourth day after, I went down on a patrol to this big cave that was underneath; it was bigger than this room. It was carved out, and it was full of bodies—piles of Japanese bodies in the middle of it—a [huge] stack of them, with ten million flies! I remember because we carried a few [of them]. I remember, in fact, that I carried a little girl back, [still living], to the lines. She must have been about five or six. She had a shrapnel wound in her cheek, right through it, but she wasn't whimpering or anything. I remember I returned her to the civilians there, or to the Red Cross or whoever it was, but it was horrible. I remember, in the whole war, there couldn't have been a much more bizarre thing, and [all that] after Saipan was secured.

Tinian

We hung around there for a few days getting a couple of hot meals. Then we went back aboard ship, the same ship we came in on. It pulled up out in the ocean a little ways because Tinian, our next objective, was only three or four miles away. So, we went out just far enough to make another invasion and the next morning we came back and invaded Tinian.

It was very different because [the Japanese] expected us to land down on the part of the island where the beach was, at Tinian Town. We surprised them by landing on this very small beach on the upper end, a small, very rocky area. In fact, instead of landing us as a couple of people in a row, they landed us in company formation, one company right behind another. There was very little opposition. It put us in a good position. That night they had a banzai attack, but it didn't hit right in front of my line [like the one on Saipan]. The Japanese were decimated again by it; I remember when we finally moved out, walking through piles of bodies. They were lined up. They came up there from Tinian Town where they expected us to land. The troops came up during the night and just made that attack.

After that, there was just a scattering of resistance the rest of the way down, until you got to the end of the island. This was about seven days later. Then we were pretty well held up quite a while in a rocky area. We took a lot of casualties there. As I remember, tanks had to be finally brought up. Again, they're all firing, but you never knew where they were firing from. They were firing from cover.

[Still], we were in good shape; our losses [here] weren't that terrible. We had losses but we were in fairly good shape, [but] by this time, it just felt like 'God, we're going to be here forever!' There was never any thought about when you'd get back, or get home. You felt, 'well, this is my life, I guess, this is the way I'll spend my days.' The whole war looked at that point like if the Japanese were going to fight for every isle and every spot like this, there's no way [we are going home].

I remember we were on a patrol, sort of just a mop-up type thing, and there were five or six of us who went through this wooded area. We came into a clearing and there was a whole family of Japanese who had hung themselves. Apparently, they fastened a rope and then just sat down. There was a mother, father, and two kids hanging and bloated, strictly because they were, I guess, in fear of these invaders and they had probably been told [that bad things would happen]. Even with something like that, at this point, what could you do? You just looked at it blasé, and that was part of the day. It's the type of thing that now, fifty years later, you think about harder than you did at the time, but it doesn't bother me, I don't know, [though,] it puts a lot of things in perspective.

After Tinian, we went back, this is a very long trip back to Maui—it took almost a month and a half. We had prisoners; they had picked up some prisoners, so we had them in the hold. You never saw them. The only way you saw them was [if they died], once or twice a day they'd bury them at sea by sliding them down the plank.

'Nobody Knew Who the Guy Was'

I'll tell you as far as treatment of the Japanese prisoners and the dead, we never made any attempt to identify the bodies, who they were. All the Japanese that went into a shallow [grave] were covered over [with earth] by a bulldozer. They're all missing in action, all the Japanese dead [we buried], or else they were sealed in the caves they were in when they were blown up. I helped bury a lot of Japanese, but I never saw any attempt to identify anyone, even though I'm sure that they had identification on them. [I suppose that bothers me] now when I hear we are trying to get the North Vietnamese to give us all sorts of records on our dead and everything; I think we're being a little hypocritical here.

We went back to Maui to just get our replacements to fill in the ranks and did normal marching and training and stuff. A lot of time, the poor guys [brought in as replacements] were brought in right during a battle, and shoved in the line without knowing anybody.

That was very typical. That's the way a lot of them arrived. A lot of them came in and died and nobody knew who the guy was.

Mr. Harris's story will continue.

CHAPTER EIGHT

'Revenge For the Dead'

In 2011, I received a letter at my school address from a local citizen who was aware of my work with students and World War II veterans. In it, he enclosed a translated transcription of a Japanese soldier's diary on Saipan, which was apparently found after the battle, presumably recovered from his body following the final banzai charge previously described by veterans in this book and in Volume I, the largest banzai charge of the war. The World War II vet whose possession it wound up in "serviced the Enola Gay the morning of the bombing mission." Unfortunately, the original seems to have disappeared. The translated typewritten transcription is presented here for the first time and serves as a window into the thinking and character of this unknown Japanese soldier, apparently serving with a medical detachment; as the fighting grows more intense, it is clear he understands his fate.

The American Landings

11 June 1944

The second air raid since landings on Saipan Island. Same as before, bombing was carried out in large pattern bombing and receiving terrific bombardment right after noon and toward evening. The raid occurred while we NCOs were cooking, and we didn't have a chance to take cover in the air raid shelters. Although our AA put up a terrific barrage and our planes intercepted them, it seemed that the damage was considerable. Charan Kanca and Tinian areas were burning terrifically.

12 June 1944

Same as yesterday the enemy appeared. Spent the day in the air raid shelter and it seems that I have the dengue fever.

13 June 1944

Also today the enemy appeared and bombed. Each squad dug air raid shelters by order of the commander. In the afternoon, enemy fleets appeared offshore and commenced furious naval bombardment. Seems as if the bombardment was centered around Charan Kanca and Garapan.

The hospital was hit and burning. During the night our 2nd Company supplied material to the hospital. 1st Lt. Omur and 2nd Lt. Yamaguchi of the hospital units are in high spirits. We carried the patients and supplies to the air raid shelters.

14 June 1944

Toward the later part of the day, naval bombardment and bombing was prevalent. Today we transferred to the air raid shelter on the left side of the valley. In the evening we prepared to move medical supplies and tents, commencing moving at 12 o'clock, however, it was so far that it took us till dawn. On this day, enemy troops and supplies have landed and the time had come at last.

15 June 1944

During the evening the unit commander and a large part of the NCOs departed for the Saipan Shrine for the treatment of patients under terrific fire. Lt. Kunieda performed bravely and courageously treating the patients under naval barrage, and he should be considered an ideal model for the medical section. We administered medical aid to one of the patients and it was the first time that we had carried out medical treatment since our landing on Saipan Island. Under the terrific bombardment, an impressive ceremony for our country was carried out in Saipan Shrine. During the night, we transferred the patients to the 3rd Company on top of the hill. Upon returning, immediately departed for the rocks.

16 June 1944

Due to movements of the previous day, I was tired, so I rested in the air raid shelter.

17 June 1944

I and other NCOs plus five men were ordered by the commander to secure medical supplies. Today the enemy planes were in their glory, bombing and strafing at will.

19 June 1944

Today the order was given for the distribution of duty. I was placed in the pharmacists section, commanded by Lt. Yamaguchi.

20 June 1944

The enemy strafing is becoming heavier and because of naval gun fire I stayed in my shelter all day.

21 June 1944

Due to approach of strafing, bombing and artillery fire, we endured to dig shelters.

Moving the Patients

22 June 1944

Today the enemy attack was more furious, while carrying out duty below the cliffs, the artillery of the enemy found its mark and caused several casualties. During the evening we transferred the hospital unit to the top of the mountains.

23 June 1944

Today the enemy barrage is increasingly terrific. Through treatment of the patients cannot be accomplished. We obtained water and food for the patients, who did not appreciate it.

24 June 1944

Terrific assault by the enemy. They were overshooting the hospital, but one finally landed 10 meters from our dugout and regrettable though it is, we received a few casualties.

25 June 1944

Because of unfavorable conditions and near the vicinity, the unit received orders to move near the vicinity of Tata-Hoke, during the night, removed some patients to same. It is generally regrettable, but we had to abandon some supplies.

26 June 1944

Spent the night below the cliffs with the patients. Condition is becoming increasingly unfavorable and because of concentration of artillery fire, took cover among the trees. No casualties. During the evening, the unit received orders to move to Donney.

Some of the patients were committing suicide with hand grenades.

27 June 1944

Slept good last night because of the Saki we took last night. Upon being awakened by Capt. Watanabe, immediately departed for Donney. Proceeded to Donney under terrific fire by artillery. We received heavy casualties due to the concentration of fire by land units and tanks. Took cover on top of the mountain.

Preparing for Banzai

Was ordered by hospital commander to prepare for purpose of attacking the enemy with rifles, hand grenades, or bayonets on sticks. I was ordered by Lt. Yamaguchi to burn medical supplies. Because of furious fire by the enemy, one tank was destroyed and the enemy withdrew. It was decided that the severely wounded would be evacuated to Tata-Hoke by way of the mountain pass. On the way we were separated from Lt. Yamaguchi and lost our way and came out by the seacoast.

28 June 1944

We found the main strength of the company and were relieved to hear that Lt. Yamaguchi was safe. Suddenly we received a terrific bombardment as we were resting near the 'Y' junction. We immediately dropped to the ground and were covered by dirt and sand. I received a slight wound across the forehead. When the barrage subsided there were cries of pain and calls for help around the area. Took to the forest, assembled and waited. During the night received another barrage. Quenched our thirst with rainwater.

29 June 1944

'Sadness, Pity and Anger'

Dug foxholes due to scare of the previous night. Stayed in them till the afternoon and again received a terrific bombardment. When the firing was over everything was desolated. Took up our duty of treating patients again. During the night orders were received to proceed to Tata-Hoke, but the trip was hampered by a terrific rain squall. Under the flare lighted road we continued to Tata-Hoke. When we reached the Y junction, there was a feeling of sadness, pity, and anger, and we received a blessing to resolve and gain revenge for the dead.

30 June 1944

Toward the morning we reached the Tata-Hoke area. Immediately started on the construction of air raid shelters and received a rain of bombs from enemy planes. Stayed in the shelter all afternoon. Toward the evening did my duty as a medic. Ate rice for the first time since the 25th and regained my strength. Felt like stamping the ground and tears came to my eyes. On this day the hospital received concentrated fire and numerous casualties occurred. I received a slight wound on the thigh of my left leg.

1 July 1944

While working, everyone seemed to regain his strength and upon seeing this, I was greatly relieved. Stayed in the air raid shelter due to the concentrated artillery fire. During the let up, rice was cooked, which had a taste most undesirable. After eating, fixed dugout and attended to the medical supplies.

2 July 1944

At dawn, I visited the place where my friend lay dead with a bayonet wound through his head. Covered him with grass and leaves, after returning ate a breakfast of hard tack and pickled prunes. While eating, heard gun fire and orders were issued for security positions, however, no attack was received and so returned to the shelter. During the evening, took care of medical supplies and fixed up the shelter.

3 July 1944

At daybreak, the sound of enemy artillery and rifle fire reached throughout the valley. Immediately took up security position. The rifle reports seemed more terrific than yesterday, however, the situation cannot be comprehended. If the enemy approaches, the whole unit will repulse them and with every weapon at hand.

Toward the end of the day, took refuge in the dugout with Lt. Yamaguchi due to attack and fire from ground units. Later tried to transport rations under the command of Lt. Yamaguchi but failed due to enemy fire and actions. Today the casualties were the men in the pharmacists section.

'My Foxhole is My Grave'

4 July 1944

Different from yesterday; today is extremely quiet. Near noon the terrific artillery barrage and rifle reports came nearer, so immediately took the battle position. After the rifle fire subsided and nothing happened, at nine o'clock commenced moving toward the top of the mountain, but was greatly hampered by flares.

I was bothered by my wounded leg. Orders were given by the unit commander to fight in this bivouac area. Dug in with all my might. My foxhole is my grave. Heard that orders were issued by the commanding officer for all men to take part in the last assault.

5 July 1944

Lt. Matsumia came into our dugout saying, 'As long as I am going to die, I want to die with the pharmacist section.' He joined us, also [saying], 'If this is going to be our grave, let us make it clean,' so after reveille, we attended to cleaning up the area.

While waiting in the area in our hole after breakfast, the furious assault of the enemy began and the second company under the command of Lt. Matsumai formed into three squads and took up positions on top of the mountain.

Seeing that we were surrounded in the front and the rear, we were being approached by the enemy with the determination of annihilation. We fired at the enemy from the rear, but with the determination of killing and doing away with them. The enemy was advancing rapidly along the road.

We drank coffee and Saki while waiting for further orders. The order was issued for each company to carry out night attacks. Lt. Yamaguchi went to work with Col. Omura and the pharmacist section, bade the final farewell among themselves and awaited the commencement of the movement. Men committed pathetic suicide due to severe wounds. The Lt. and the pharmacist section bade farewell and was promised to meet at the Yakumi Shrine after death.[56] I, with Lt. Yamaguchi, was absorbed into the command section and was very happy. At last, under his command and Capt. Watanabe, the weaponless unit commenced night attack. As the units began movements, communications between the units could not be taken.

6 July 1944

Received an artillery barrage during the morning and took refuge among the rocks. As each round approached nearer and nearer, I closed my eyes and awaited it. Rifle reports and tanks seemed nearer and nearer, and everyone took cover within the forest and then the machine guns could be heard over our heads. I thought it was the end. We got ready to charge out with hand grenades, when ordered to take cover by the Capt. When I looked around the side of the rock I was hiding behind, I saw the hateful face of the enemy shining in the sunshine. With a terrific report the rock in front of my face exploded and the sergeant that had joined us last night was killed, also the corporal received wounds in his left leg. However, I could not treat the wounds, even though I wanted to. Everyone

---

[56]*Yakumi Shrine after death*- The author almost certainly refers to the Yasukuni Shrine, "a Shinto shrine in central Tokyo that commemorates Japan's war dead. The shrine was founded in 1869 with the purpose of enshrining those who have died in war for their country and sacrificed their lives to help build the foundation for a peaceful Japan. The spirits of about 2.5 million people, who died for Japan in the conflicts accompanying the Meiji Restoration, in the Satsuma Rebellion, the First Sino-Japanese War, the Russo-Japanese War, the First World War, the Manchurian Incident, the Second Sino-Japanese War and the Pacific War, are enshrined at Yasukuni Shrine in the form of written records, which note name, origin and date and place of death of everyone enshrined." Source: Yasukuni Shrine, JapanGuide.com. www.japan-guide.com/e/e2321.html.

hugged the ground and remained quiet, waiting for the opening in the enemy. As I stood up to get a rifle from one of the dead, a bullet hit between my legs and I thought that I was hit but glancing down, to my happiness, nothing was wrong.

A report was heard, and I looked around and Cpt. Ite, lying on his back with a rifle in his hand, had been killed. After fierce counter fire, the enemy was repulsed. I approached the body of Ite, who had a bullet hole through his left temple with his eyes partly open and his lips tightly clenched. I'll take Ite's revenge; so, taking Ite's rifle, which he had tightly in his hands even after death, I waited for the enemy to attack.

'Please Cut Skillfully'

Cpl. Yasuhire also had wounds in both of his legs. Pathetically he was saying, 'Please cut skillfully.' Matsumai with the sweat pouring down his head, took one stroke, two strokes, and on the third stroke he cut off the corporal's head.

The reports of the rifles outside subsided. Soon, however, reports commenced roaring in the frontal area. I pocketed the scroll written by Cpl. Onos' hand, and commenced moving to join the friendly troops by opening a bloody path. However, because of firm enemy security measures, this could not be carried out; this friendly force was the vehicle unit which we were supposed to meet at Mt. Tapochau. Soon a squall began, and everyone was drenched.

7 July 1944

While shivering from the wetness, orders were issued to move. Facing down [toward] the north, bowing reverently to the Imperial Palace, and bidding farewell to my parents, aunt, and wife, I solemnly pledged to do my utmost.

With Sgt. Hasegawa and Cpl. Watanit [we] departed for the rocks and came out of the forest. It is regrettable that we have separated from Lt. Yamaguchi because we promised that the place would be the same. Between the enemy bombardment we approached the cliffs where before we received the enemy barrage. We tried to reach the shore, but couldn't, on account of the rocks and cliffs.

The enemy is surrounding us in all directions. Helpless, we took cover in the forest. At the crack of dawn, enemy activity commenced on the road below the cliffs with vehicles, tanks, and walking soldiers.

'The End Has Come'

At last the end has come. We have separated from our unit staff and members of the 2nd company consisting of Sgt. Haswgawa, Cpl. Watanit, and Narusi and myself. And with the patients of the transport units, our group consisted of less than ten men.

Even though we have no weapons, we want to attack and with the determination of dying for the Emperor, both my parents, my wife and my aunt. I am grateful for I am 26 years old, thanks to the Emperor, that I have lived to this day. At the time that my life is fluttering stray like a flower petal to become part of the soil.

Since the enemy landing, to have fought against the enemy endeavoring with the utmost power in carrying out my duty and thus becoming a War God, I am very happy. It is only regrettable that we have not fought enough and that the American devil is stomping on Imperial Soil. I, with my sacrificed body, will become the white caps of the Pacific and will stay on this island until the friendly forces annihilate the hateful enemy and come to reclaim the soil of the Emperor.

Dear Kieko—Please live with courage. My sincere regards to Mother and Father.

Dear Brother—Take care of the family, wife and aunt. Take my revenge.

Dear Sumiko—Even though I am ending on this southern island, your brother is firmly convinced that you will continue in my place.

Dear Aunt and Uncle—thanks for your hospitality. I regret that I cannot repay you. Please take care of Sumiko.

8 July 1944

I am glad that I can die on the seventh anniversary of the Sino-Japanese incident.[57] I firmly believe that the enemy will be annihilated and will pay for the certain victory of the Imperial Land.

[END OF DIARY]

---

[57] *seventh anniversary of the Sino-Japanese incident*-Japanese expansionist aggression triggered the full-blown war with China known as the Second Sino-Japanese War [1937–1945]. The 'Marco-Polo Bridge Incident' of July 7, 1937 marked the start, culminating in many Japanese atrocities committed in the following months and years.

General Douglas MacArthur wades ashore during initial landings at Leyte, Philippine Islands. Army Signal Corp Photo, National Archives. Public Domain.

PART THREE

'I HAVE RETURNED'

"People of the Philippines: I have returned. By the grace of Almighty God our forces stand again on Philippine soil—soil consecrated in the blood of our two peoples. We have come dedicated and committed to the task of destroying every vestige of enemy control over your daily lives, and of restoring upon a foundation of indestructible strength, the liberties of your people."
—Gen. Douglas MacArthur, Landing in Leyte, Oct. 20, 1944

CHAPTER NINE

The Invasion Radioman II

The decision to invade the Philippines was discussed in Hawaii in July 1944 by the top brass and President Roosevelt. Admiral Nimitz initially favored blockading the Philippines and invading Formosa; MacArthur pressed for his 'return to the Philippines as promised,' with landings at Leyte. The Seventh Fleet would be tasked with naval and logistical support. The attack would go forward in October, with a preliminary assault at Peleliu. On September 15, 1944, the 1st Marine Division and Army troops began the attack on Peleliu after three days of heavy bombardment by Navy gunships. Peleliu hosted a major Japanese airfield that, in the planning stages, was deemed a major threat to any U.S. advance on the Philippines. The island was heavily defended, and casualties were very heavy. The 1st Marine Division lost 1,252 killed and over 5,700 wounded or missing. The 81st Infantry Division, sent in to relieve the Marines, lost over 540 dead and 2,700 wounded or missing in action. The battle remains controversial since it was never used as a staging area for the invasion of the Philippines or any other subsequent operations, though it did draw some Japanese troops away from the Philippines. Nearly 10,700 Japanese were killed on the tiny island.[27]

Paul Elisha had completed four first-wave invasions. After R&R, the men of the 75th Joint Assault Signal Company prepared for the return to the Philippines.

Paul Elisha

Normally, [our initial assaults] like Attu, Kiska, Makin, Kwajalein, were all fairly short operations. The first one at Attu was a month-long operation, but nobody knew it was going to take that long, so we were stuck in it until the end. Normally, in a larger operation like with the Philippines, we would stay until the battle was, let's say, twenty miles inland, and they would pull us out once all of the support and logistical people came ashore. They would pull us out and we would get ready to go on the next one.

Aitape was in June, we did that for a little over a month. Then we went back, I think to Manus, where we got ready for Leyte. They'd send you into a place where there was a PX or a service club. You did lots of drills, lots of calisthenics training. Always training, you'd go out on amphibious training exercises. That's what the R&R was all about. They didn't want us to get rusty.

Leyte

For Leyte, we were again attached to the 7th Division, I think it was, and we were in the first wave at Leyte Gulf. Getting ashore was not nearly as bad as making it at Kwajalein. First of all, the Japanese had more room to maneuver. When you hit a small coral atoll, they were there to throw you off immediately. So it was a tough landing. Leyte, as I recall, going in was not as bad as we thought it was going to be. Once we got ashore, we caught mortar fire and some machine-gun fire. There were some counterattacks. As I recall, the immediate objective when we landed on Leyte was the town of Tacloban, where there was an airstrip. The objective was to get to Tacloban so they could capture that airstrip and bring in the air support. I think in about two days, we were close to Tacloban. Once we got 18 or 20 miles in so they could land artillery, you were just about beyond the range of battleships' [guns and communication], so that was it and they pulled us back.

Abandoned

The Americans had landed successfully over 200,000 men. The Japanese Navy set into motion a complex 'oceanic banzai charge' to destroy the landing fleet and isolate the Americans now on land.[28] The Japanese Navy was converging from three different directions to take the gamble at destroying the invasion fleet. From October 23-26, 1944, complex maneuvering over thousands of miles and several sub-engagements wound up in the nearly complete destruction of the Japanese fleet. The Battle of Leyte Gulf was the largest naval battle of World War II.

The thing that complicated Leyte was that when they did pull us back to the beach, just after the landings at Leyte, the Battle of the Philippine Sea took place.[58] I don't know if you remember that or not. That was a major naval battle of the Pacific War. When they found out that the Japanese task force was bearing down, and actually they didn't know about it until the last minute because it came through the Straits between Leyte and Luzon rather than seaward.

---

[58] *The Battle of the Philippine Sea-* It was indeed a major battle, sometimes referred to by air veterans of the battle as the Great Marianas Turkey Shoot, totally destroying Japan's capacity to conduct carrier operations. However, this occurred on June 19-20, 1944, before Mr. Elisha's arrival. He is certainly referring instead to the great Battle of Leyte Gulf, the dates and details of which coincide exactly with his time on Leyte. In his defense, this battle is sometimes referred to as the SECOND Battle of the Philippine Sea.

So the Navy didn't want to get caught bottled up in there. So every ship was yanked out of there, even the LSTs around the beaches. What happened was they were told to dump everything they had. The beach suddenly became this massive chaotic place with piles of ammunition and all kinds of supplies and everything. The Navy just took off!

At the conclusion of the three-day Battle of Leyte Gulf, a sinister new development began to harry the weary American crews. Out of the skies came suicide planes, armed with bombs, often closing on a target in pairs, intent on crashing into ships. The kamikazes, or 'divine wind,' took their inspiration from the typhoons that had saved Japan from Mongol invasions centuries before.

Kamikazes

You may recall, if you've read any of the histories of the Philippine invasion, that shortly after just two days, I think, after we landed there, the Japanese sent a fleet up through the Straits there to hit the invasion force. So they pulled out. Well, you realized you were on your own now. As a matter of fact, for a while, it was an alert because they thought that if the land force got word of it, they would counterattack. What did happen, however, was we were subject to some pretty intensive kamikaze attacks by air. We were on the ground; the Japanese from Manila and other places sent air strikes in with kamikaze pilots.

What [the Navy] did was, they dumped everything on the beach. So they pulled the LSTs, everybody else out, and they went out to meet them, and so we were fairly certain the aircraft carriers were gone. We had just a couple of destroyers cruising offshore. And so, the Japanese pretty much had the air over the island to themselves, and they sent kamikazes in. Now, in Okinawa, they were really bad.

But our first experience was on Leyte when they came in on the beaches.

We'd been told that there were such things and to expect them, but until they happen, you don't know what they're like. As a matter of fact, the day that we were pulled off of Leyte, we were up toward a small village called Manaoag, as I recall, which was inland about a mile and a half, and we had a little encampment there and then they told us we were leaving to get ready for the Luzon invasion. They were pulling us back and they had some LSTs up on the beach and we were to go back and go aboard. Just as we got to the beach, the siren went off for an attack, and in came the Japanese planes. I remember there were several of us—eight of us, I think—and two or three of us dove under a big truck that was pulled up on the side of the road when we came down to the beach. We dove under this truck. The other four or five raced like hell and ran up the ramp of the LST. As luck would have it, one of the kamikazes came down and dove right into the fantail of that LST. It blew the back end right off and two of our guys were killed in that. We were just lucky that we dove under the truck.

They just pulled everything out of the belly of this LST and dumped it on the beach and pulled out. So, here was this huge dump of ammunition and we were just across the road. We'd set up our radio and stuff at the command post. And all of a sudden, we heard the siren and the code red for a raid, and they came in and one of them just dove right down into that fat pile and all hell went up [*throws both arms in the air*]. We went up in the air, radio, everything else. And I had this arm that was broken, [*clamps right hand on left forearm*], this arm had just what they called a 'greenstick fracture,' [*moves opposite hand to right arm*], but I could move it and you couldn't do anything. I remember another guy and I laid behind a stack of #10 rations. It was about four cartons this way and about that high [*gestures with arms*], and we just lay behind it for hours and the bullets were just going, you know, you didn't dare stand up. And then, finally, I remember a warrant officer came along with two other men and he said, 'There's a cart loaded with 155 mm shells over there and we got to get it the hell out of here because when that blows, you know everything is going to go.' So the four of us with the warrant officer went and we just pushed this cart. I remember there had been a group of Black troops who were transporting people, unloading at the time, and one of them came and helped us move that thing. I've always wondered what became of him, because without him, we'd never have done it. And I'm sure nobody ever wrote him up in a book, but we got it moved.

'You Don't Want to Get Stuck Here'

Then, we just threw ourselves back down behind those #10 rations and waited for the firing of bullets to stop. I ended up in a field hospital, with both arms in splints, and one of my buddies, about four or five days later, came in and said, 'God, you don't want to get stuck here.'

He said, 'We're getting ready to go down to Luzon. You better hurry back!' I can't explain this, but there is a feeling, if you stay with your own group, you're better off than if you're a free agent out there somewhere. God knows what'll happen to you. It's like the devil you know is better than the devil you don't. So I went AWOL from the hospital. It was broken, it was healing. It was wrapped, and then they splinted it. [I didn't have much of a problem with] my CO; I had the feeling he was trying to kill me anyway. But I remember the night before we went down to get on the ship to go to Luzon, I was sitting on a cot, and we had by then set up tents. The battle for Leyte was practically over and we were down near the beach when he came in and he threw this thing at me, which turned out to be a Purple Heart medal, and he said something like, 'I don't know why I am giving you this.'

He said, 'Don't think that arm is going to get you out of anything.' He said, 'That'll teach you to go AWOL.'

The Luzon Campaign

The Luzon campaign was not an easy campaign either, I recall, largely because the plan of attack was changed. Originally, when the maps we were given, we were landing in Lingayen Gulf. If you look at the map of the Philippines, there are two sets of hills and mountainous terrain down the sides of the island. Then there's a valley in between. The original plan is to hit the beach at Lingayen Gulf and run right down that valley to Manila. Cut the island in half. Also because there were both civilian and military prisoners in Manila being held in prisons and stuff, they wanted to liberate those people. MacArthur wanted to capture Manila intact if he could. For some reason, toward the end, before we landed, we got other maps and instead of going down the valley, we went down the coastal areas and some of that was literally hill to hill to hill.

I can remember outside of Baguio, which is called the summer capital of Luzon because it's up in the hills, I can remember there was one large mountain. We were there for communications, and for fire support. We must have gone on to that mountain at least three or four times and got thrown off three or four times before they actually secured it. Heavy casualties, really; there was a rumor going around. One of the rumors was that many of the wealthy landowners who own plantations in the valley were close personal friends of MacArthur's. He was trying to do as much as he could for their plantations not to be torn up. If that's so, we paid a hell of a price for that territory. I always felt there were a lot of unnecessary casualties in Luzon.

624 | WORLD WAR II GENERATION SPEAKS III

"An abandoned Japanese baby is adopted by front line medical unit of the 27th Div. The baby was found with a scalp wound, in the arms of its dead mother, by a tank crew during the fighting below Mt. Tapochau." Saipan, July 1944. New York State Military Museum.

The Baby

It's impossible for you to see death and that kind of human degradation and not be affected by it. I can remember in Leyte, we had left the village of Manaoag and we were advancing toward Tacloban. We set up communications and across the road, all of a sudden there was a commotion. Of course, coming from the village of Tacloban, trying to reach the American lines were civilians, once the Filipinos heard the Americans had landed. They began streaming toward the beaches to greet us. They were waiting to be liberated and I remember my sergeant said, 'What the hell is going on over there? See what that's all about, Elisha.' So I ran across the road, I had my carbine just in case. One thing you have to be very careful of in places like the Philippines where there were a lot of civilians was that the Japanese didn't try to get in among them. The commotion was about a ditch where a shell had landed on the side of the road, and there was a woman lying in the ditch and she was giving birth! So there were some units going by toward the front, and they had medics with them. I yelled for a medic, and one of the medics came over and he helped this woman give birth.

I remember I was standing there, and I shouldered my carbine, and I'm keeping people away. I said, 'Keep away. Keep away. Stand back.'

Then, all of a sudden, I hear this, 'Whaa.'

And then the medic turns around, he says, 'Here, take this.'

He had it wrapped in something, I don't know, a khaki towel or something, and he handed this baby to me while he finished up with her. I'm standing there in the middle of this. You see guys on stretchers waiting to be taken back, and you could hear the gunfire and everything else, and here you're standing with a newborn baby in your arms. You know that affected me tremendously. But all of these things, you know, I think what affects you most is that you see life and death in such basic terms. Cheek by jowl, [close together, side by side] as it were, and that is bound to affect you.

'I Have Returned'

I personally witnessed what turned out to be one of the biggest publicity events of the war. There was a historic newsreel of MacArthur's landings at Luzon and Leyte, keeping his promise, 'I shall return.' I think [the view of MacArthur is] overblown because he had a tremendous PR staff.

Several of us had just come back; they had finally taken the town of Tacloban, where the airstrip was. That was the first priority, and that's when we were supposed to be pulled out, because they had to land planes there so they could bomb the rest of the Philippines and Okinawa. They finally took that airstrip and Tacloban, and we were relieved.

They said, 'Go back to get some hot meals and showers,' and we were standing on the beach, watching a bulldozer push this sand out into the surf. And there was a little knot of men, and Kaminsky, our sergeant, asked, 'What's going on here? What are they doing there?'

They said, 'Well, they are pushing the sand out, so the general won't get his feet too wet when he comes ashore.'

We could see this boat waiting offshore, and then it came up and they dropped the door. And these guys came off with Thompson machine guns at the ready, you know, and then MacArthur behind them. And just before this happened, there were a whole bunch of photographers and press people and PIOs— 'Public Information Officers.' And this major came down and shooed everybody off to one side.

He said, 'The general does not like this profile, go to that side!', you know, they set the whole thing up. And then, he's coming ashore, everybody with the guns at the ready, and then he stops on the beach there. There is the body of a dead Japanese, and he kicks it over and he says, 'That's the way we like to see them.' And we just... you know, I could just see 'Willie and Joe,' and what they would have said.[59] [*Chuckles*]

After Luzon, we prepared for Okinawa.
Mr. Elisha's story will continue.

---

[59] *'Willie and Joe'*-American cartoonist Bill Mauldin's scruffy GI infantry characters, who offered their down-to-earth take on the stark realities of war in humorous fashion in *Stars and Stripes* and elsewhere from 1940 to 1948.

UNCLE SAM

The Marine Mechanic II

Iwo Jima, or 'Sulfur Island,' was eight square miles of sand, ash, and rock lying 660 miles southeast of Tokyo. It could serve as a refueling stop for the B-29s and B-24s that were now flying almost daily out of the fields in the Marianas to bomb the Japanese mainland.

In late November 1944, aerial bombardment of Iwo Jima with high explosives began and continued for a record 74 straight days. The 21,000 Japanese defenders survived this with scores of underground fortresses connected by sixteen miles of tunnels stocked with food, water, and ammunition. The surface was covered with concrete pillboxes and blockhouses housing some 800 gun positions.

On February 19, 1945, the attack began as the landing ships brought the Marines towards the beaches of blackened volcanic sand. A total of 27 Medals of Honor were awarded for individual acts of heroism under fire at Iwo Jima. The island was deemed secure on March 25—25 days longer than planners had counted on. Nearly 7,000 Americans and 19,000 Japanese died at Iwo Jima.

It was the Marines' costliest battle ever.

James Smith

Iwo Jima

We were on the way up to Iwo Jima, see, we were a floating reserve; the 3rd Division weren't supposed to land there. As we were approaching the island, there were three LSTs on starboard and port sides as we were going up through, just kind of floating along nice and easy. No big rush to get anywhere. Then, we were attacked by the kamikazes; on the port and the starboard sides, they got hit.

It was in the early morning. We were at chow, breakfast. They had worked out a scheduled system for people eating because they didn't want everybody eating at the same time. So as it happened, it was foggy, and this kamikaze hit [one of the ships] on the right and another Zero came over. He couldn't have been fifty feet over our heads—I could see the pilot, he came right over, and he missed our ship, misjudged by fifty feet. If he had come down, I wouldn't be here today. But he went right over the bow, right into the drink; whether he was hit by us, I don't know, because he was so close that you couldn't even get a weapon on him.

Yeah. Well, we were hit by the kamikazes the day before the flag raising, and they had lost, I think, half a dozen doctors on the starboard LST. We were offshore and they were getting ready to send in different sections of the division and to help out because things were going bad to worse. Everybody was champing at the bit, and here we are out here, and we want to go in and do something. It was so bad, everything was starting to get rough, and the beach was cluttered from the mortar fire—if you were there, you could just envision a thousand people on the beach with the equipment, trying to get out of that sand, out of that volcanic ash. We were offshore, as I said, and watching. Then somebody said, 'There goes the flag!'

But that was the first flag. The second flag, I didn't see, but the first flag I did. It was so rough that they brought the guys back and they got back on board the ship again. It was so bad, they couldn't get in. It was really bad. It was unbelievable, what was happening there, because from what I've read in my history books, a lot of these people came right out of boot camp off to Iwo Jima. Now, I can't imagine what was going through those guys' heads. Here we are, we've been in the Pacific for over two years now, and had come through three campaigns, and here we are up here now [just] floating and not able to do anything. I had found out later that they were actually trying to keep our division [intact] for the invasion of Japan. I don't know whether it was true or not, but that's the scuttlebutt that was going around.

"Trapped by Iwo's treacherous black-ash sands."
Mount Suribachi in background.
National Archives. Public domain.

Now, the whole division didn't go in, but at the same time, we went in whenever different sections were needed, whatever they needed. The Sherman tanks had a .75 on them. As far as the all-around use of the tanks, Bougainville, [with the jungle], was the worst. It got better as you traveled up the island of Guam. It was a lot better and they were very effective; some of the tanks were equipped with flamethrowers, and on Guam, they used them quite a bit. We didn't have too many flamethrowers in our company. We were B Company, and A and C may have had some other newer tanks that were equipped with the flamethrowers to use up there on the different caves. We used them quite a bit up on Iwo, too. On Guam, we used a lot of bulldozers. We had a bulldozer, what we call a retriever tank, with a big bulldozer blade on it.

We finally brought in all of our tanks, and we had sixteen tanks in the three battalions of tanks—A, B, and C Battalions. We lost all of our tanks. The Japanese used 500-pound aerial bombs that were buried all through where the tanks might travel. We lost a lot of them that way. I think we had one tank left, and what we were doing at the time was salvaging parts from other tanks that were knocked out.

Tank Retrieval Under Fire

We were assigned to pull out some tanks for parts. Schwintek, Bob Reevey, and myself took a tank retriever to go up on the second airstrip to pull one of the tanks out. It had hit a landmine, and one of our fellas was still in one of the tanks. We couldn't get him out because he was in such a dazed and shocked condition that nobody could get near him, because he had his .45 out. He was the assistant driver, and he was sitting there, and he thought that everyone who came near him was Japanese. They tried to talk to him, and finally they did get him out after he passed out. He's still alive today in Massachusetts.

There was another tank beyond us that we were trying to get to. We had hooked up the cables and we were going to tow the tank out, and as I straightened up, I looked at the airstrip, and here came a bunch of mortars. They spotted us, and they started to lob the mortars at us. I quickly unhooked, pulled the pins on the cables, and hollered out to Ray Bebob, the retriever driver, and we jumped up on the tank, and they chased us right across that step. To this day, I don't know how we made it; I really don't know how we did. The Lord was on our side out there because as we were clutching along, they were just dropping [shells] behind us. They were on our sides and behind us, but they just didn't get zeroed in on us the right way; we were ducking from all directions and I can remember Schwintek saying, 'What are you ducking for, Smithy?' I just looked at him.

We just laughed at one another, and we got back okay. So this fella Schwintek I'm talking about, was awarded the Silver Star. He was formerly an MP on the beach at Guam and things were going pretty good except on our left there was a place called Sunita Bluff where the 3rd Regiment, I think, was having a bad time. They were losing people by the score there because it was a place where they had to go up, and the Japs were rolling grenades down. They tore the company all apart and the corpsmen were trying to pick up survivors, putting them in the trucks they had right there.

Now, these guys are working under fire all the time. This isn't like, 'Okay, fellas, wait a minute, [stop shooting], we got to pick up this guy,' it wasn't that way. They were under fire all the while, and unfortunately when the driver got hit, he was killed. This fella Schwintek was an MP. He jumped into that reconnaissance truck and drove the truck out of harm's way, and got the guys out of there.

Later on during another campaign, we were supposed to make another campaign landing, Kavieng was the name of the island. We got all loaded up for that and came back to Guam. So to keep the morale up, what they did was they put on the parades and paraded all the tanks, cleaned up and refurbished. Then they had a formation fall out, and then they start calling people out of the ranks and they awarded him the Silver Star for what he did, evacuating that reconnaissance truck with all those injured, wounded guys onboard.

Hit on Iwo

I did get hit on Iwo therewith, I think it was the Japs were using anti-aircraft guns on us too. If they could depress them enough, they would shoot across and they hit our machine shop.

One of the mechanics, Dan Tupper, was a second platoon maintenance man. Colonel Withers was in charge of our tank battalion at that time.

We had a machine shop. I was working on a tank up on a second airstrip and they got hit, and I got blown against the tank I was working on and got cut over my eye. But I just went down and picked up my tools, and went back to work again. Our corpsman, his name was Mendez, he said, 'You're bleeding.'

I was, 'Well, that's all right. I hit the tank. I don't know what it's from but just forget about it.'

'Well, let me take care of it.'

I was lying there in this hole with him, and he was cleaning my face off and the Japs had, I think they called it a spigot. It was a huge mortar. You could hear it; when they launched that it sounded like an old rusty gate opening. I knew that one of them was coming. But they didn't have much direction with it, because over half of them would end up in the ocean, would end up on the other side in the water. I was then on my back and one of those went over and of course, everybody scatters and heads for the hole. They don't know where it's going to land and I was lying there and I said, '6-8-9-4-2.'

He said, 'What the hell's the matter with you?'

I said, 'I just read the number on that mortar.'

I was on the island from February 22 to March 16. I was there pretty close to a month.

Going Home

We went [back to Guam] in an LST that had been hit by a kamikaze but was still usable. We made about seven knots, just enough to steer it from Iwo back to Guam; where my bunk was there was a hole in the side of the boat, and probably you could put a tank through it.

The thing that I remember most about before the invasion of Iwo was that we had the old *Saratoga* aircraft carrier with us. She was on our starboard side, and I used to be interested in aviation. I was always up very early up on topside—in fact, I slept topside quite a bit; I just lay there and watched those guys take off in the morning when they were taking off and flying in and going in close air support and it was quite a feeling.

Many months, in fact, after we had got back from Iwo, we knew we were going home, and we had our sea bags packed for about a week and they told us that there was some scuttlebutt around that one of us mechanics was going to stay behind to break in some new mechanics. Nobody knew anything about who it was going to be. So when the company fell out that following morning, they're calling off the names to pack sea bags, and then we're going, but they didn't call out my name. I was stunned; I was staying. I said, 'Oh my God, it's me!' I went right out, in fact, I ran, down to this tent where this really new second lieutenant was. I went down and I charged into that tent like a bull, and I said, 'Lieutenant, let me see that sheet!'

So I must have had an awful look on my face, because he handed me the sheet without even asking why I wanted it. I looked at it, I went down the page, and there was my name! We had been told that I'd made sergeant and it was still listed as corporal. I said, 'There's my name, Corporal James A. Smith, Jr!' He looked at me and I said, 'That's my name and you didn't call it up.' I turned around and shoved off, went back up the hill.

The guys said, 'What happened?'

I said, 'He just went over my name.' There was a Jesse R. Smith in A Company, there was a Dolph N. Smith in there somewhere. [Someone] said, 'Well, we're all [going to be] made sergeants now.'

I said, 'Listen, I'm going home. I don't care what they're making me.'

Jim Riley, our warrant officer in charge of the men, came back and said, 'I got some bad news for you guys.'

'Where are we going now?' The first thing we're thinking is, we're stuck here again.

He said, 'There's only one sergeant rating [available]. It's come through for you [three] guys, but I don't know what to do. So I don't know who it's going to be, guys. So let's cut cards.'

So we cut cards—I just cut the cards and looked back and this fella by the name of Packy, a good friend of mine, had the high card. So he makes sergeant; we didn't care. At that time we just wanted to go home—enough is enough. So we got on board; they put us on a brand-new aircraft carrier called the *Kwajalein*. We got on board that ship.

Boy, when we left our camp to go onboard, it was like driving down into New York City, that island had changed so much. It didn't look at all as if we had come in and made the landing there, you couldn't recognize it. It was like a city had been born! There were roads, the Seabees had built a core highway down through there, a three-lane highway down through the town off the beach. It was like seventh heaven, we couldn't believe it, didn't know where we were, didn't know where to go. It's a good thing we're on this truck that took us to the aircraft carrier; it was like a dream.

We got out to sea, and to wash our clothes, we used to tie all of our clothes on a rope to wash them in the ocean. We got really clean, really salty. So that's where the term came from, salty Marines. We were standing there on that fantail and washing the clothes and this fella comes walking up behind us. He was standing there and we had a lot of ropes, a lot of clothes we were dragging in. Out of all the ropes on the end of that fantail, whose rope does he pick on? Mine. He pulls my clothes up, and he drops the rope. I said, 'Hey, mate, what the hell do you think you're doing?' He just looks at me.

I said, 'Whoa, wait a minute. You're going to lose my clothes. What's the matter with you?' He just looked right straight through me—he just had that blank stare and looked right straight through me. I knew something was wrong with him and he just stared at me.

He turned around and he walked away. When he turned, I saw that he had some holes in his head. He was an officer, but he wasn't wearing his bars, whatever his rank was, and he just walked away. Well, we found out that we had some people who had lost it and they were onboard ship with this [condition], walking around and they didn't even know who they were. That's how bad some of them were. I don't know where he was from.

I was onboard the carrier on the way to Hawaii when [President Roosevelt] passed away. It was in April, my birthday was April 5, and I was onboard ship when we got that word. It was kind of a shock when you hear something like that; it's really disturbing to think that somebody like that didn't live to see the end of the war, the results of what we had done. That's a part that kind of stayed with me, thinking about when he was leading a country in war and all, and to pass away before he saw the end results of it.

'It Saved a Lot of American Lives'

I often think about [the dropping of the atomic bombs on Hiroshima and Nagasaki]. That's kind of a tough one. I think of the stories that we had heard later. There was a rundown on what the Japanese were doing to prepare for our invasion of Japan. In this book I read, in some of the pictures and some of the stories, they had 5,000 kamikaze planes on the ground waiting for us. They had planned to line the beaches with the women and the children. I think about that part, it keeps coming back to me [in thinking] about when that bomb was dropped.

I hate to say it, but I was glad to hear that [the bombs] had slowed them down, in trying to stop them to get our message through. That it's useless [to continue to fight on]. Why should they go on fighting and not give up? I have so many mixed emotions about that, it's hard to pin. I don't like to say I'm glad it was dropped, because I know how many people have suffered because of it, and are still suffering because of it. But it saved a lot of American lives. I wondered how many millions of our people would have been slaughtered on the beaches; we would have lost an awful lot of people. It truly saved a lot of people's lives, because I know there would have been a terrible amount of slaughter on the beaches with their people there and our people too. I mean, it would be tough for our guys to go ashore and face women and children.

The Japanese soldiers were good. The thing that they had on their side is, they just didn't care about living. I mean, they were just fanatics, it was unbelievable, the slaughter, what they did. [Climbing up and] banging on tanks—it's hard to describe why a person would do that, he has to be out of his mind. But most of the time they were full of sake. They did a lot of drinking and I think that's what drove a lot of them, they were so psyched that they got so wound up. I mean, they would just charge into a tank that was shooting, lead flying, and they would walk right into it. You and I, we wouldn't do anything like that. You would try to protect yourself, you want to survive, you want to do your job and survive, but they just didn't care.

It was unbelievable what they did. Some of the atrocities that they did on our Marines [was so bad that] you wouldn't want to hear about it. I still have a bad feeling about them. I can't shake it off. I really can't. [But another thing is] that whatever they accomplished something at times, they seem to me to be winning, and all of a sudden, their winning would stop, that sometimes they just didn't follow through. They would stop.

I know that some of them [were scheduled to meet us]; we were scheduled to go back to Guam for the 50th Anniversary Landing, the liberation of Guam. Unfortunate as it was, my mother at that time was very ill and she ended up in the hospital three or four times. So we had to cancel our trip to Guam, but some of the fellas went, they took a lot of pictures. In one incident, they had some little boys [there whom they befriended]. Well, they got back to Guam, and lo and behold, some of those people are still living and they came forth. They took pictures with them, and they had it posted in a newspaper on Guam, and they sent me pictures of these people who were kids, now 60-65-year-old people.

*

I've stayed in contact with all those guys that are living. I think there are about 35 people, maybe it's right in that figure somewhere who would be left in the original company. I write cards. I handwrite a message to every one of them every Christmastime. If [someone] answers back, I write the widows, there are a lot of widows. I write to them, and they keep in touch. A little story behind that fella, Schwintek. For over 50 years I'm writing him letters, at Christmastime, short letters, but I never heard a word from him. This past December, I finally received a card from him, and it was written by his granddaughter. She wrote on the card that it was good to hear from me and that [he was] so glad that I've kept writing. So I wrote another letter back to him. I haven't heard from him. I don't know what's happened. I don't know whether I have to wait another fifty years; it's a long time ago.

The Truck Accident

I'll tell you about one incident that crops up from time to time, and just about three years ago, it was finally resolved for this one Marine on Guam.

We were on the beach probably about a week or more, and our tanks formed up on a line, and they were shooting at different targets, whatever. They relieved some of these fellas to bring them back so they can have some warm chow. I was working on a tank. I was underneath one of the tanks dropping what we call an inspection plate; I was going to change the starter. Don't ask me how I remember these things.

Suddenly heard some terrible screaming. The hair stood on the back of my head, I thought it was a banzai, I thought some Japanese had broken through and were coming through the bivouac area. I crawled out from underneath the tank and stood up, and I can still hear the screaming. I looked off to my left and there was a sort of a hill, the road went up and turned. What had happened, this 6x6 truck, they had a bunch of guys on the back of it. They were loaded with the fellas that were from the tanks, and they were taking them back up the hill. As they got halfway up the hill, the fella who was driving the truck, it stalled on him. Of course, with those engines, they had a vacuum brake system on them. If the engine stalled, there was no vacuum for the brakes, but there's always a reserve so that you could stop the truck. But the truck driver got excited or something, he turned the wheel and turned it into the bank. When he did that, it rolled over. It had about probably a dozen guys in the back of that truck. That's what the screaming was. The truck tipped over [and trapped the guys underneath], and one of our tanker men is [dead]; unfortunately one of the stakes went right through him, pinned him right to the ground. Now, these fellas are underneath the truck, and we came running up, and to this day I don't know how we did it—we just picked that truck up. We picked that truck up and turned it, to let those guys out. My friend Tom Murphy was underneath. He said the only thing that saved his life was that there were a lot of packs in that truck and he said, 'It cushioned the blow for us.' But there were at least twelve guys underneath that truck and one of the fellas was killed and the other fellas were pretty well mangled up. His name was Miller. He was killed, and for the rest, there was some real bad results of that accident.

'He Hugged Me, And He Started to Cry'

One of the fellas who was a truck mechanic, Frank B., for years he and I both played guitar and we used to entertain the troops back then, but he would never show up at the division reunions. Over the years he'd write, but then he didn't write at all. Finally, I called him up when we were at Savannah at a reunion; he lived close to that area. I had a phone number and called and I talked to him. He said, 'Yeah. I'll come to the next one. I'll come to the next reunion.' He was always promising. So finally the next reunion was in Philadelphia and he said he was coming. He kept saying he was coming. When we got to the hotel, the rooms were all filled up. We had quite a bit of a problem with that, but I kept checking at the desk.

I talked to the woman at the desk, and she said, 'He's here. He's in the hotel.' We're trying to find him. I called his room and a fella answered, I found it was his grandson who was there [with him].

I talked to him, and I said, 'Where's your grandfather?' I told him who I was.

'Well', he said, 'he's downstairs somewhere, Jim.' I don't know how he knew my name but evidently Frank had been talking about us. He said, 'He's downstairs somewhere.'

So I hung up the phone, and I walked into the hospitality room. As I walked to the hospitality room, I saw two or three of our guys, and here comes Frank walking. We just grabbed each other. Now, this is a long time.

I said, 'Frank, how the hell are you? Why did you wait so long?' Now we kept talking back and forth and he kind of looked around.

I said, 'What's the matter, Frank?'

He said, 'Hey, can I talk to you alone?'

I said, 'Yeah, what's wrong?' So we sat down on a bench.

I said, 'What's the matter, Frank?'

He looked around and I said, 'For God's sakes, what's wrong? You look like there's a ghost behind you or something.'

He said, 'You remember that accident with that truck?'

I said, 'How can I forget that? So what's that got to do with you?'

He said, 'I was a truck maintenance man.'

I said, 'Yeah, so what?'

He said, 'I heard somebody said that those brakes failed on that truck. That was one of my trucks.'

Now [I realized that] this fella carries this guilt. All those years he thought that that truck flipped over because it was his fault. He carried that guilt all those years.

He said, 'I overheard somebody saying it was on one of Frank's trucks that the brakes failed.'

I said, 'Frank, those brakes didn't fail on that truck. The fella just stalled the engine. There was nothing wrong with the brakes on that truck. He rolled it into the bank and the truck flipped over. The brakes did not fail.'

Well, he took a hold of me, and he hugged me and he hugged me, and he started to cry.

I said, 'For God's sakes, Frank, all those years you were holding it.'

He said, 'It just about killed me to think that it was my fault.'

I said, 'But it wasn't your fault, Frank. Those brakes did not fail.'

'Boy', he said, 'you don't know how glad I am that I came to this reunion to find out. I'd have taken that to the grave with me!' That's another side story, about Frank.

'So Many Stories'

I'm active in the Marine Corps League. I've been involved in that for many years, was commandant over a number of years back. I'm serving as a chaplain now; whenever one of our members passes, we have a little ceremony for them. There aren't too many of us left; I'm the oldest one of the detachment. We are active in this respect, [but] we don't have anybody to work with anymore; there's only four or five of us that attend our meetings. I think we had three Vietnam veteran Marines. Tragically, two of them committed suicide.

I don't know if I mentioned before, I'm a musician. So I'm involved musically too; I had a band for over 50 years. Some of these people are musicians too, some of the wives, these widows, are playing and singing like I am. I could go on and on; I've got more stories than you can shake a stick at. Some of the fellas are completely blank. There's so many stories that I get goosebumps just thinking about all the things that happened, and [the fact] that I can still remember them. In my own mind, I wonder sometimes at the fact that I can remember all the things that happened.

[I have learned a lot about what we were really doing since those days]. I don't think I'll be any kind of a strategist or whatever, but from my experience being in the campaigns, and then doing a lot of the reading, and most of all, watching The History Channel, I can [better understand] what we were doing there, and it's crazy [to think about it].

My wife said to me, 'Why do you watch?'

I said, 'There are so many things that happened that we were completely unaware of. There are so many things [to tie together], if you only just stop and think about [them].'

I was in the Pacific for twenty-nine months, from Guadalcanal, Bougainville, Guam, and Iwo Jima. At my age, I still haven't gotten to the point where I can get my mind to [understand] that it really happened, that I was [part of it all], that I was able to survive all those campaigns and not [really] get a scratch.

James A. Smith, Jr. passed away on April 8, 2015, having just celebrated his 94th birthday.

CHAPTER ELEVEN

The BAR Man

A lifelong resident of western New York, educator and author John Kolecki was a Marine Corps BAR man who was wounded twice during the Battle of Iwo Jima. He was awarded the Purple Heart and Bronze Star for his actions.

"We had to look for a cover, and I spotted sort of a made-up Japanese foxhole with some rocks arranged. I didn't want to jump in because sometimes these places were booby-trapped, you know, but I had to take a chance, so I jumped in there and to the side of me, as I jumped in, there was a dead Japanese soldier. Apparently, somebody shot him right through the head. Now, there was enough room for me to kind of crawl up to him, which I dared to do, because I had no choice, and he had a little picture of a girl that he had placed among the rocks; it must have been the wife or the sweetheart of this dead Japanese soldier. And so, I had a dead companion for the night with a picture of his girlfriend or wife, I don't know. I spent the night with a dead Japanese soldier. Yeah, that was something sad."

He gave this interview in 2006 when he was 85 years old.

John H. Kolecki

I was born in North Tonawanda, New York, on August 14, 1920. I was a graduate of North Tonawanda High School and I was in my junior year at Canisius College when I volunteered to join the Marine Corps.

[When Pearl Harbor happened], I believe I was at my girlfriend's home. It was a Sunday afternoon; either I was there for brunch or lunch, I'm not sure. Oh, I was very much surprised. I didn't think that anything like that could happen in our times. Although, I was intrigued with the negotiations going on in Washington because, at that time, there were two Japanese ministers that went to Washington to negotiate some kind of an agreement dealing with lifting the embargo on scrap iron and on oil. And somehow that the Japanese economy was very adversely affected by our [punitive economic] actions in the Far East.

Soon, I was jealous of all the other guys that were going into the service, and I was still a student, and I was left alone. And that kind of put me in some bad straits. I didn't feel good. So, there was a speaker that arrived at Canisius College and there was some assembly, and I was impressed with the Marine Corps speaker, so I decided to join the Marine Corps. I believe it was in 1942 but I wasn't called to active duty until about maybe four or five months later.

'I Had A Premonition'

I went to San Diego for my boot camp. It was rather strenuous, but I didn't mind the rigorous demands that were imposed on me. Actually, the first two weeks were the hardest. Then the third, fourth, fifth week, we spent three weeks on the firing range where the pressure was somewhat off the recruits. The totality of basic training was seven weeks. We had a choice of whichever services we want to go, either into artillery or infantry, whatever. And I joined the paratroops, I wanted to go to the paratroop school. [See], I was a pilot; I actually had a private's license. I could have joined the Air Force, but for some reason I had a premonition that I would die in an airplane, but I wouldn't die on the battlefield. So, I abandoned my hopes of being a pilot to become a paratrooper, and I joined the paratroops at Camp Gillespie in California. And strange thing happened that in the course of my training, the paratroop program was abandoned. So, consequently, here I was ready to get my wings, so to speak, and the program was canceled, [along with] the 4th Paratroop Battalion, which I was in; the 4th Paratroop Battalion was [to be formed as] the nucleus of the 5th Marine Corps Division.

I never got to [make a jump]; I got as far as folding the parachute. I did a lot of running, believe me. The calisthenics and the exercises and the running that we had to do were quite extensive, quite demanding. But I accepted the challenge, then the paratroops school was disbanded. I went to Camp Pendleton where they were forming the 5th Marine Corps Division.

From there, we went to Hawaii, the main island, and there was Camp Tarawa where we did extensive training. Even at one time, we had maneuvers under round fire, real fire. And from Camp Tarawa, we then went aboard ship and took us just over a month before we hit Iwo Jima. We stopped at several places. We stopped at Kwajalein, Saipan, and Tinian. And then finally, we assaulted the island.

'You Won't Have a Scar'

We were in the first wave at Iwo Jima. And I remembered just before I hit the beach, somebody offered me a chewing gum, of all things. Why not? I took the chewing gum and we landed on shore, and I hopped over the side. I was a BAR man, by the way, Browning Automatic Rifle. I hit the beach and was running very hard. It was sort of an ash, deep black and gray sand; [getting] traction was very difficult. I made it up to a slope and I placed my BAR and I hurried to my friend, Pak. 'Pak, bring me the ammo.' Just as I turned, Pak gave me the ammo; a bullet grazed my eye and the top of my nose. Had I been looking forward, I probably would have lost both of my eyes and the bridge of my nose. Fortunately, I turned to my right [just at that instant], and that kind of saved my life.

But a stupid thing happened. A corpsman immediately gave me a shot of morphine and bandaged both eyes so that I couldn't see. Somehow, I crawled into a deep shell hole, you could even put a little cottage in there. It must have been from a 16-inch naval gun, I assume. After a while, I said, 'I got to take a look and see what's going on.' I was feeling some slight pain because the morphine immediately took action. I lifted my right eye and I looked at the crest of the shell hole and there's a huge floating Japanese mine there! How did it get there? I don't know.

I tried to crawl out of the shell hole, but I couldn't. So, some other Marine came by, saw me, they start yelling, 'You get out of here before that thing explodes!' And he gave me a hand. He took his sling off his rifle and handed it to me [to grab onto]; he got me out and then I was escorted to the beach, and I ended up on the hospital ship.

I was on the hospital ship about a week or more. Well, being aboard ship, they treated my eye and nose with some kind of compresses, so I questioned the nurse.

'Why don't you apply sulfur powder?' That's what we were using at that time on any wound. Sulfur powder was the thing.

She says, 'No, we have to put these on,' like Vaseline compresses. She says, 'We want the wound to heal from the inside out. This way, you won't have a scar.'

So, I went along with it, 'Okay.' Well, about the third or fourth day, I was ambulatory aboard ship. In fact, the chaplain came to me and says, 'John, I see you walking around. Would you serve as an honor guard? We're going to have a burial at sea.'

I said, 'Of course, Father. Sure.'

So, this was a very sad situation. Here they put this dead Marine into a plastic bag with some weights, which I assume were at the feet, and they headed out with him on something like a stretcher. They put the colors, the flag over the corpse. The taps were played. And then the chaplain read a verse from the Bible he said, and then, gingerly, we kind of lowered the stretcher. The deceased was dumped into the blue Pacific. It was very sad. The whole thing was over in about five, eight minutes. And I sometimes think about being the honor guard at that very, very sad funeral. When I go to funerals today, it's a half-day event. Flowers and the coffin, and all that lamenting and services of some sort, and here was a boy that died, and the parents didn't even know what it was all about, what happened. Yeah, very sad.

Well, anyway, to make a long story a little longer, I bumped into a friend of mine from my platoon aboard ship. Tucker was his name, and he told me he got wounded through the calf of his leg. He showed me his beautiful wound. So, we had lunch together. We conversed about things going on, and then about the sixth or seventh day, the announcer came out and said, 'Now here this. Here this. Any Marine desiring to return to shore with the doctor's permission may do so.' So, he looked at me and I looked at him and we were briefed that the whole operation would be over in seven days, and there might be three additional days mopping up the fanatics.

I said, 'Okay, you want to go, Tucker?'

'All right, let's go.'

So, he went to the doctor. The doctor gave us the okay. We went back ashore. And I had the hardest time finding my outfit, but I finally did. An artillery observer told us, 'The 27th Regiment and Company B is in this direction.' We finally got there.

'The Horrors of War'

As I was trying to get in touch with my platoon, I really saw behind the lines the horrors of the war, of the combat. That's where I saw many of our GIs being stacked like logs, under a lean-to before they were buried. There were all kinds of dead Japanese soldiers in trenches where they committed hara-kiri; their modus of operation was that they would take a grenade, put it under their chin, pull the pin, and blow their heads off. I saw many dead Japanese defenders with their arms blown off and their heads blown off or they would take a rifle and take their sandal, whatever—they mostly seemed to be wearing sandals—and they would put the toe into the trigger mechanism. Put the rifle under the chin and blow their heads off, rather than surrendering, which would be, well, most humiliating and dishonorable. And there were scores of these dead Japanese defenders, and I understand that only about four hundred surrendered after the battle out of 22,000 defending Japanese soldiers. The rest were killed, and they were buried in mass graves anywhere. Yeah, very sad.

'A Dead Companion for the Night'

I had an operatic experience, too, [on Iwo Jima]. Night was closing in, and we were moving up on the front lines and somehow the Japanese spotted us and started peppering us with mortar shells. So, naturally, we had to look for a cover, and I spotted sort of a made-up Japanese foxhole with some rocks arranged. I didn't want to jump in because sometimes these places were booby-trapped, you know, but I had to take a chance, so I jumped in there and to the side of me, as I jumped in, there was a dead Japanese soldier. He was clean-shaven. He had a clean uniform. He just had a trickle of blood on the side of his head. Apparently, somebody shot him right through the head. Now, there was enough room for me to kind of crawl up to him, which I dared to do, because I had no choice, and he had a little picture of a girl that he had placed among the rocks; it must have been the wife or the sweetheart of this dead Japanese soldier. And so, I had a dead companion for the night with a picture of his girlfriend or wife, I don't know. I spent the night with a dead Japanese soldier. I was kind of safe, and I felt safe, too. Yeah, that was something sad.

We had replacements that sometimes lasted a day or two. In my platoon, five lieutenants were either shot or wounded. Lieutenant Stan Holtz, who was our original platoon leader, had been killed on D-Day. I became a squad leader; the corporal of our squad became the platoon leader. So, the replacements that followed, they lasted a day or two, and it seemed that they were primary targets of Japanese snipers. Some of these platoon leaders, I never got acquainted with them, I don't even remember their names.

The Japanese were very crafty soldiers. Their camouflage was something unique, something they could be proud of, really. To spot a live Japanese soldier was not easy because they were camouflaged and they had all kinds of foxholes, caves that they jumped out, fired a few rounds, and they would hide. I liked the BAR very much but, you know, in combat, I don't think I fired more than five rounds. The only Jap that I saw, Japanese soldier, I saw him in a trench, and I saw his helmet and he threw a grenade at me. And it wasn't a shrapnel grenade, it was a concussion grenade, and it bounced around, it exploded, but nothing happened. I tried to shoot at him, but he was so fast. I fired after he had gone already.

The Explosion in the Cave

Now, there was an incident towards the end before I got wounded the second time. Our platoons surrounded a cave, and a Japanese officer came out with the white truce flag, and he starts mumbling something, and eventually, we caught on, he wanted a translator. So, some half an hour or something later, an American translator started to communicate with this Japanese officer. And what we were told was that there were sixteen men in this cave, and they're going to come to a decision what they're going to do. So, this Japanese officer says, 'I'll be back at eleven o'clock in the evening, and we'll see whether we're going to surrender or not.' Well, there was a bushido code that every Japanese soldier's supposed to tell American soldiers before he dies.

So, we figured, 'Well, maybe they'll surrender. Maybe they won't. Maybe they'll come out and make a banzai charge against us rather than surrendering.' Because they were fanatical fighters. The Japanese did not honor themselves in surrendering to the Americans. Well, anyway. So, I was stationed above the cave and the rest of the platoon were outside the immediate area of the cave because if they come out and banzai charge, we got to have room to fire and that's so we don't fire at each other; that could be done very easily. Well, eleven o'clock came and nothing happened. And we began to whisper, 'What are they going to do?'

So, we sit tight. It must be about maybe after 11:00 and there was a volcanic explosion. I guess what they did was they stalled for time to get any kind of explosives together, figuring they're going to commit hara-kiri and they'll take us along with them.

It was a humongous explosion, really; the mouth of the cave was like a huge shotgun, the blast came out with dust and fire. I just curled up and nothing happened to me, but there were some guys who just were so shell-shocked they could not speak, the ones that were close to the mouth of the cave. I remember this Olmsted; he was a corporal. The guys had to carry him [*shakes arms vigorously*], his nerves were gone—I could see a person suffering from shell-shock. The blast was so terrific, so frightening that you think you're going to die, or you might even feel that you are dead. I've seen it with my own eyes.

Another night, there was a case where some Japanese soldiers were left behind our lines. And then, in the middle of the night, might have been one or two o'clock in the morning, one tried to run back to his line. I didn't even fire because I didn't see him. Of course, when he ran from behind our lines, hoping to reach his lines, he took a chance because they would sporadically shoot these flares, parachute flares. I didn't see him, but the Marine next to me, he says, 'I got a shot at him.' And the next morning, he said, 'They got this fella who tried to run for it.' The strange part was, we had a dog on the front line, and the dog never sniffed him out. He somehow got through but never made it back to his lines.

Friendly Fire

I had some very unusual experiences under friendly fire. We made several assaults on the ridges, and before we made an assault, they would soften up the ground with mortar shells or artillery. [The second time that I was wounded], I happened to be in a foxhole, and one of the shells, I think, landed too close. I was curled up, and the shrapnel hit me above the wrist and in my leg, my thigh. Another time we moved up on the ridge, and someone goofed back at the lines, and they thought we were Japanese, and we got peppered with American artillery and that was horrendous, it was unbelievable what artillery could do.

After the dust cleared, it was unbelievable. The havoc that that artillery barrage can create. We lost seven men; we lost our executive officer. It was a very, very unfortunate, sad situation that our boys opened up on us. It was some kind of a snafu, but it didn't last long. It probably lasted a minute, but when you're under fire like that, you think it will never let up. It was a terrible experience. After the barrage lifted, and the assault was made, I got up and the corpsman just escorted me back behind the lines and, fortunately, he waved down a jeep and he took me to the field hospital. And at the field hospital, the doctor looked me over, put me aboard the plane, and I ended up in the Guam hospital. And I was there for a week, and later, I was flown to Hawaii, Honolulu. I stayed there and about four days afterwards, I rejoined my unit on the main island at Camp Tarawa.

'Drowning in His Own Blood'

I was wounded twice, so I was entitled to a furlough, so I went home for ten days, and then came back [to Camp Pendleton], and they didn't know what to do with me because I had been recommended for officer's training and the war was coming to a close. So, they put me in charge of a recreational hall, ping pong and pool table, at Camp Pendleton. So, I was on duty eight hours and two days off. I didn't have enough money to enjoy the weekends off, so I would go to LA. There was a Catholic Church, cost me a dime or twenty-five cents, I don't recall, for a bed, a towel, and clean sheets to spend the night. So, naturally, I went to LA as often as I could, and the way I got there was mostly hitchhiking. Sometimes I took the train, but the train was packed, standing room only, unbelievable how congested public transportation was from Pendleton to LA. So, I preferred hitchhiking. At least I had a little elbow room, you know. And usually, the truckers were pretty good, and even civilians sometimes picked up Marines and took them to LA.

I might have been at the recreation room [when I heard about the death of President Roosevelt]. I thought more about the guys, [frankly], the friends that I lost in combat than I did about the president [when he died], really. I had some very close personal friends and I saw one of them get shot in the neck and I saw him die. I couldn't do anything about it. The corpsman came, started applying a bandage to prevent the bleeding. He tore it off. He's shaking. I think he actually died probably drowning in his own blood. He died a terrible death. So, my thoughts were more on what happened at the battle. Of course, I knew the president died; the word was out already. The war's practically over. The Germans and Italians were surrendering. I was thinking more of going home than anything else.

I do remember I had a reaction [to the dropping of the atomic bombs]. Now, I recalled my high school chemistry teacher. We discussed atomic energy, and he gave us a very cursory explanation of the atomic bomb.

He says, 'Once they perfect this separating the atom, only an ounce could blow up a city block.' And there was quite a discussion. And so I associated that lecture, that one ounce of split atoms blowing up a city block, with that bomb, blowing up a city. I had a very vague idea what the atomic bomb was, and I tried to imagine what the city would look like after the atomic bomb.

Going Home

At the time the war ended, I was already on my way hitchhiking to Pendleton, back to camp, when the announcement came. Oh, that was a good time. Great celebrations, yeah. It was a great relief. And I had enough points, you know. They had a point system and I think I was six points shy of being discharged from the service. So, something happened that later, they even lowered the points, and I was discharged in November of 1945; I came home a little after Thanksgiving. And so, when that happened, I went on a visit to Canisius where I was matriculating just before I went in the service and the dean spotted me. I remember Father Sullivan said, 'Oh, John. Good to see you.' I never knew he knew my name.

'I see you're back in school.'

I said, 'No, I just came in to see if I could bump into some of my old cronies.'

'You mean, you haven't registered?'

'No, I was late two weeks.'

'You come in Monday. You're registered.'

I said, 'Well, there are some courses that I need to take that are not available.'

'Don't worry about it. You just come on Monday. You're registered. You're starting school on Monday!'

So, I'm back. The following year, in March, I got my sheepskin. Because I was twice wounded, I was [covered] under Public Law 16, entitled to forty-eight actual months of education. Canisius is only eight or nine months a year. So, I had all those forty-eight months to chew up. So, I went back to Canisius, got my B.S. Then I went to Niagara, got my master's degree and Master of Arts.

Then I got a grant to study. You know, when they launched the Sputnik, there was a cry for more Russian language, so I went to an adult education course also and I took Russian. I had a little bit of Russian, so I applied for this federal grant, and they accepted me. The federal government sent me to Northwestern University for the summer. And then the following year, the second part of the program, they sent me to Indiana University to study Russian language and culture, and the second part of the Indiana program was five weeks in the Soviet Union. So, I was an exchange student in the Soviet Union in 1963. That's when that Vietnam War really got [underway].

Well, anyway, I spent five weeks in the Soviet Union and the program entailed visiting several universities, museums, art galleries, conversing with Russian students. The Russian students wanted to speak English and we wanted to speak Russian, because they wanted to sharpen their English, and we wanted to sharpen our Russian. I was fortunate to be one of the sixty-four students that were chosen under this program to go to the Soviet Union. I came back. Now there was a New York State grant to study Russian. So I applied, and I got that state grant, and it was offered at Canisius College. So I went there, continued with my Russian language. And it was in the summer of '66, I was an exchange student for the second time to the Soviet Union.

I spent the entire summer. It was sixty-some days. I had a good time, but some of the students had a hard time acclimating themselves, and [for them], some of the food that was served was not palatable. I'm of Slavic descent, so I'm used to sour cream, and I'm used to buttermilk and sauerkraut, pig's feet, and all of that. You know, for breakfast, they would serve, not orange juice, they would serve kefir, which is like sour milk, as a breakfast drink. For me, I drank sour milk, buttermilk, and it didn't bother me. Some of the students complained about the food, but we were treated very, very well by the Communist hosts. And we went to various art galleries, and we visited several cities. We didn't stay long. We spent some time in Kyiv, in Leningrad, in Sochi.

We went as far east as Baku on the Caspian Sea. I still recall we were going by bus, and we were outside the city limits, and you could smell naphtha. You could smell the oil. And when we got closer to the city, there was a forest of oil derricks, all wooden ones; they were not steel. Wooden derricks. You know, they need it to pump the oil from the ground. Yeah. And the architecture was sort of a mixture of European and Asiatic; you could tell by even the fences that they had. They were unusual and the buildings were different. It was a very enlightening experience for me under these programs that I participated in.

I went back to school to Niagara. Got my M.A., and then I still had so many months left. So I went back to Canisius, got another master's degree in education. I ended up being a schoolteacher at the North Tonawanda and in the Sweet Home school systems, and I also taught in the evening division at the Niagara County Community College, Russian language, Western Civ 101. I didn't know too much about western civilization or whatever, but I knew enough for me to get by.

'People Who Detest War'

I'm a life member of the American Legion, and I'm a life member of the Disabled Veterans. Sometimes Hollywood portrays an unfair picture of what battle is like, with the exception of the truest image of combat, I think, which was the movie called *Saving Private Ryan*. To me, it was pretty close, very close, true to life in combat, yeah. For example, in our company there were three platoons, one hundred forty-four Marines. When I returned to Camp Tarawa after I was wounded, the second time, just nineteen of us made roll call out of the original one hundred forty-four, [so] I can empathize with [the conscientious objector]. I can empathize with people who detest war, because I wouldn't want my son to go through the same thing that I went through.

John H. Kolecki passed away on December 31, 2008, at the age of 88.

CHAPTER TWELVE

The Marine Gunner II

Albert J. Harris

Iwo Jima

We left for Iwo Jima probably about November. The convoy took quite a while forming. Once we were aboard ship, we knew where we were going. By that time, we had a pretty good guess anyway because they had been bombing Iwo for about two months. A lot of talk was that we were going to Truk, if you've heard that name, but that was a big base that we eventually bypassed.

It took a long while to get up there. [In my first sighting, it] was pretty awesomely bad! It wasn't very picturesque. We landed again as a reserve regiment. We came in, again, about six o'clock at night; we were sort of hanging around all day waiting to get on boats—the landing boats.

When we went in, the Japanese commander had built such an intelligent defense. The upper part of the island was honeycombed with caves—completely a network of unbelievable caves. The lower part, the lower one-third was the landing area, and Mt. Suribachi was at the end. He let almost two divisions of Marines get on the island with only a modest amount of resistance. Then he just massacred the guys on the beach for four days; he stopped the front lines from going any further through his line-of-caves network. For four days, people were on the beach. The beach was only about the size of one hole on a golf course! You had all these bodies and anything you threw there is going to hit something. [*Pauses*]

Oh yeah, Iwo. I never saw a tree on Iwo. The part where all the caves were looked like a massive rock pit that had been hit by an atom bomb. No organization to it. Bodies. Small boulders. Big boulders. Cliffs.

The beach was like, on both sides there, black sand, sort of [more] like—I don't know if you could call it sand, it was more of a black gravel. When you stepped in it, it made a very big [footprint] like an elephant.

'Somebody Made A Big Mistake'

I came ashore at the time I had been transferred to the battalion intelligence section. I was what they called the 'intelligence scout.' Theoretically, I was supposed to find material of intelligence value. It didn't work out. I ended up being a 'gofer' for the colonel in charge of the battalion whose name was Vandergrift. He was the son of the Commandant of the Marine Corps. He was a wild man. I think he was trying to live up to the name. He was a lieutenant colonel. Anyway, I had two guys in my little group when I came ashore. The shore, you couldn't believe it because they had hit a lot of boats coming in, so the shore was just amazingly [crowded] with every sort of debris, and junk, and bodies, and everything.

I came ashore about when it was just getting dark again. I fell on the ground just as soon as I got out of the water, orientating myself; there was a guy lying there right next to me, with his rifle out and everything—I looked at him and he had been shot at some point during the day, right through the helmet [*points to his forehead*]—he was looking perfectly normal, no blood. I didn't see anything [to indicate he had been killed], but he was dead.

Now, we didn't see any of our guys that were supposed to be with us, or any in our company. So, we ran ashore about two hundred feet or so, three hundred. I told the guys, dig in a little spot. I dug a hole next to [the dead guy]. Other people start to dig in all around us, [and soon], the whole place was full of guys digging in. That's where we were for three days because the front-line troops had been held up on the other side of the airport. Somebody made a big mistake by putting that many people on shore. But the Japanese who were firing from the upper artillery and mortars, they couldn't miss. Any time they fired a mortar, it could hit some of us.

I remember once during the night—this was in the midst of a barrage—his thing came flying in on me, I felt it and I felt a face. I thought, oh my God, if this is the face, I've had it, but it was part of a gas mask that resembled a face. That's what I felt.

'That Was My Last Visit to A Cave'

After three days, I didn't know where the company was; I wasn't going to walk round looking for them. They weren't looking for me, that's for sure. I finally did locate them, where I was supposed to be. Then I went a number of times up to the lines with the colonel and the other times I went with my group just trying to find things that were of intelligence value, but actually it turned out we were just souvenir hunting, [really]. We went down a number of caves, foolishly. One time, we went down, just the three of us in this cave, it was covered with branches and everything, so it was camouflaged, but it had steps down into it, carved out of the stone. Stone wasn't easy to carve. So, I went down maybe ten steps, and there was a dead Japanese in the middle of the steps, so I walked over him. I have a flashlight and I have a .45 that I borrowed. I went down the cave, then right ahead of me it went about thirty feet and then curved. It was full of boxes and stuff. Then off to the right and left there were other caves. So, I am looking at all the caves and everything, I raise the flashlight and I am sure that I saw a face looking around the corner at me. So, I shot at it and the whole [place] lit up! I started backing up out of the cave, like a western, up backwards all the way, up past the dead body. That was my last visit in a cave. Holy Jesus! Then I heard later on that people got in real trouble in these caves, just foolishness.

'I Hope It's Our Guys!'

I could see that flag raising, but it really didn't make much of a difference to us at the time. It wasn't any strategic value; I think now when I heard more about the flag raising and read about it, I think I must have seen the original where they just put up a flag and the boats made all the noise. We didn't know what was going on. Suddenly, we looked back; it was about a mile back from the front line. We looked back and saw the people on top of Suribachi. I thought, 'I hope it's our guys!' That's all I thought about, and apparently a couple hours later, they did the famous Rosenthal shot. It was symbolic.

I didn't know that was a famous photograph until months later. I think I was two to three years back home before I realized what an impact the thing really had. It was a sensation. It was a perfect thing. People considered that the end of the battle and everything, but it wasn't the end of the battle. It had nothing to do with the end of the battle, but it was symbolism that counted.

'You Didn't Get a Cake'

I was on Iwo about a month. I celebrated my 21st birthday on Iwo—a very mild celebration. You didn't get a cake. [*Laughs*] No, no. They kept me alive. It was funny. The way it turned out, I think this is true for a lot of people there, I could have gone ashore on Iwo or any of the others carrying a six pack of beer and a ukulele and it would have done just as good. I spent the war being a 'shootee,' not a 'shooter.' [Unlike] in the war movies, there were no firefights going on where you're shooting [after aiming]; I never saw anybody aim. You just had to aim at caves, or you had to send the flamethrowers in. You had to protect the flamethrowers while they went in; you didn't see the [enemy on Iwo].

Then they took us back and the same routine again back to Maui, and I know we were supposed to go into the invasion of Japan, probably early the next year. I got a little break; they sent two people who had been in the division awhile over to temporary duty working in Pearl Harbor. I worked there for a couple of months and that's where I was when the war actually ended.

I was on guard duty in this prisoner of war camp in Pearl Harbor on Ford Island [when the war ended]. Not much reaction. We were no place that anybody celebrated. The people who were celebrating that you see in a newsreel were people that had never been any place; they wouldn't be sitting around in Times Square if they had been in a war.

[Now], at the time, I was very happy that [the bomb] had happened, because I could just visualize what an invasion of Japan would be, and comparing it [to my experience], they would have fought for every little village on the whole [Japanese] islands. I have had a lot of thoughts on it later; I realize it was a decision and you can't quarrel with [it, but] I sort of wondered why they ever dropped the second—the Nagasaki one. That never made any sense to me at all.

After about a couple of weeks, they brought us back to the camp again with the regular unit. They brought us back on an escort carrier to San Diego. We were then brought back up to Camp Pendleton. We were there a few days, and then broke up. So, when we broke up after all this time together, there was nothing. Nobody said 'goodbye'; I never said goodbye to any of the people I was with. I was by myself. I didn't know anybody when I was going through the discharge.

After three days, I caught a train up to New York; the only one meeting me at Penn Station was some bum. I got the early train, and that was it. That was the end of my war. Two months [later], I went to work for the New York Telephone Company. I was with them for twenty-five years, then I went to AT&T and retired from AT&T.

'I Never Saw a Hero'

The war years, they shaped my whole life. I think I was able to accept things better, I could put things and people in perspective much better. Items that might upset other people, I could roll with them, for better or for worse. I didn't have the drive maybe of a lot of other people. Whatever my life became, it was shaped by those years completely. It's a satisfaction, I guess, knowing that you can put up with things and were able to accept it and you didn't do anything to be ashamed of.

In my experience, here I was in four battles, some of the most vicious of the whole war, and I never saw a hero. I never saw one hero! I saw people trying to stay alive, doing their job, doing what they were told. I never saw anybody above and beyond the line of duty. I read about all of these wonderful things everybody was doing and thought, 'What's happening to me?' [*Laughs*] I mean, even the Persian Gulf, which lasted two days, and maybe a hundred battle casualties, yet they came up with all these medals. Even the Oklahoma City bomber got a medal—Bronze Star. It must have been a different caliber of people, or they are a lot more talented [in] writing up their citations. But that's beside the point.

'My Ten Minutes of Fame'

I never really talked too much about it. I didn't have a very active social life before, and I didn't really have a lot of friends. Most of my friends were also in the service in other services. [Those guys] shared a lot of that type of thing.

Back in 1950, I went [to a reunion] in New York. I haven't been to any of the others. It would still help to go, but I don't travel much and it's fewer people that I would know. Of course, they're dropping off, but it was an experience. I don't like to be an old soldier. I don't think I ever had any psychiatric-type problems associated with being in a war; I like to talk about it when somebody wants to hear it.

I really didn't develop many profound thoughts when I was in there. It was just life; it was the way the ball had bounced in my life. For the first time, I was with more people; I came from a small town and I never had a lot of people to associate with, and suddenly I am living with these people for long periods of time, and I've got to say it was kind of enjoyable.

I saw things that are history now. On that little, teeny island, I had my ten minutes of fame, with no fame. [*Laughs*]

Albert Harris passed at the age of 89 on October 4, 2013.

B-29 Superfortress bombers near Mount Fuji, Japan, 25 July 1945. National Archives. Public domain.

CHAPTER THIRTEEN

The B-29 Radioman

Strategic bombing raids to Japan began in earnest from the newly liberated Mariana Islands as the fighting ended in the early summer of 1944. By summer 1945, wave after wave of the sleek new B-29 Superfortresses began to arrive in the skies over Japan. A quantum leap in aviation technology, the B-29 was much longer, wider, and faster than previous heavy bombers, and capable of carrying a much larger bomb load over vast expanses of ocean.

The coupling of the B-29 with the development and deployment of incendiary 'firesticks,' six-pound cylinders filled with napalm, or gelatinized gasoline, was a very serious development that brought death and destruction on a scale never before seen in warfare. Veteran Sam Kamerman described his impressions as a young man on this new, top-secret weapon of destruction, giving insights into some of the earliest fire-bombing missions over Japan.

"About a hundred and fifty miles from Kobe—anywhere between a hundred and fifty, two hundred miles—one of the crewmen in the nose over the intercom says, 'What's that spot out there?'

I had to manipulate around to get up front, but I got up front, and at approximately twelve-thirty, one o'clock there is this little orange dot. You can't tell distance at night, but there's this little orange dot. Nobody knew.

I said, 'What the heck is that?' It's all black, then there's this little orange dot. It could be a plane, it could be a light, it could be anything. As we keep going to the target, this little orange dot starts getting larger. I'm back in my seat and somebody hollers out, 'Kobe is burning!' Approximately a hundred and fifty miles away you can see a fire; you can't believe it...

When we get to the target, the bomb bay doors open; everything's burning. We're over the target. At this point, there comes up a smell that was awful. It was [burning] debris, and also bodies."

This interview took place in 2005, sixty years after the missions, when he was approaching 82 years of age.

Sam L. Kamerman

I was born on March 16, 1923, in the Lower East Side, New York City. I had two years of high school. That was it.

[I heard about Pearl Harbor when] I was in the park playing basketball with a bunch of fellas. I was eighteen years old, I guess. This is a Sunday, around one o'clock or so. In comes Harry, into the park. All of these young kids are playing basketball. He hollers, 'The Japanese just bombed Pearl Harbor!' You know what all of us did? We all asked each other, 'Where is Pearl Harbor?'

I enlisted because all the fellas around me, my age, were being drafted. I didn't want to go into the Army or be in the dirt kind of thing, so I enlisted into the Army Air Corps, in New York City. I went to Miami Beach for basic training. Two things I remember, I got KP twice down there and I did pots and pans. These pots were like three feet high; for seventeen hours I'm digging into the pots.

Somebody didn't like me. I caught this twice in the month's time that I was there.

Flight Training

From there, I went to Madison, Wisconsin, Truax Field, radio school for a couple of months, and then I went to the Sioux Falls, South Dakota, radio school for about five months. Upon graduation, an officer came into the classes.

He said, 'We need flying operators.'

I was not interested.

He said, 'You get an extra stripe.'

I still was not interested.

He said, 'Well, you get fifty percent [more] flying pay.'

I still wasn't interested.

He said, 'Well, there's no KP,' and that did it. [*Raises hand*] Don't laugh. This is the truth. KP, I got out of it; that was it.

I went down to Philadelphia, a special school, radio school. Learn a little of EIR, voltage and capacitance, resistance, that kind of stuff. We also learned Morse code. Being a flying radio operator, you had to know your Morse code. From there I went back to Madison, Wisconsin. From there, I was sent to Salina, Kansas. This was the 20th Air Force, the 58th Bomb Wing. When I got there, I went on one or two practice flights in a B-17. The first time I was uncomfortable, because I was looking out the window all the time and just enjoying the sights.

I got my flight gear. The flight gear was very, very impressive stuff. You get a summer flying suit. You get a winter flying suit. You get a .45 caliber gun. You get a watch. You get goggles. You get a parachute; it just keeps coming and coming.

So, now I'm part of the 58th Bomb Wing. I'm attached to them. They send me down to Great Bend, Kansas. I'm there for about two months. From there, they send me to a place called Marietta, Georgia. I'm there for like another couple of months, this is all part of the 58th Bomb Wing. From there, I went to Walker Army Air Force Base in Kansas.

After I was there about six, eight weeks, this officer says to me, 'You don't have to volunteer, but we need flying radio operators to go overseas.' At this point, I've been in the service like seventeen months or so, a year and a half.

I said to the officers, 'Let me get a furlough [first] so I can go home. I'll come back.'

He said, 'We can't do that.'

In one of the best moves I ever made, I said no.

'I don't want to go.'

A couple of weeks later, this 58th Bomb Wing—which was the first B-29 outfit, by the way, the very first combat outfit—they went to the China-Burma-India area. They flew out without me.

Two weeks later after they leave, I'm sent to Pratt, Kansas. This is a new bomb wing, the 73rd Bomb Wing, and I am now part of a combat crew. Well, the B-29s at this point, for testing, were very unreliable. Most of our B-17 combat training had to do with B-17s. This is from about April to around August. This is about a five-month thing. I was in with a very nice crew. By the way, in this crew, which is eleven crewmen, we had four New Yorkers in my particular crew.

We flew in all kinds of weather. It was lightning. It was thunder. What are you doing out in this weather? We flew one combat training mission that was approximately seventeen hours in the air. We left Kansas, we flew to the Caribbean, then flew east over Cuba. From there, we flew north over the Atlantic to Massachusetts, then we flew approximately to Michigan, and then back to our base; it was a long, long time. This was one of the few times I flew with an oxygen mask, because the B-29 was the first bomber in World War

II that had a pressurized cabin. It was quite an experience being up at 25,000 feet with the oxygen mask, and tapping away at a speed of like, five, six words per minute. You can't type fast in an airplane, not that I was any good or special at it. You don't recognize the shaking but when you want to do something, [the airplane] lets you know its shaking. I was commended on this particular flight for being in touch with the Army Airways Communication System.

Our commanding general, by the way, was a New Yorker, Rosie O'Donnell, you ever hear of him?[60] He ended up a real big deal. Now, we finished our training and we're all going home on furloughs from Kansas, to New York, for me. A B-17 on a training mission was going from Pratt, Kansas, to Mitchell Field, New York City. We flew into Mitchell Field, it took us about five hours or whatever, instead of the forty-eight hours. Coming back, me being a kid, and knowing I am going overseas, I wanted to stay home a little longer so I took extra time; on the last day, I went back to Mitchell Field hoping to catch some kind of a ride. Sure enough, I got lucky, so as not to be AWOL—there was a B-17 going to Kansas. This plane is dropping me off in Kansas, but not my base. I got up on a highway and thank the Lord, the people there were wonderful. You get out there and they'd pick you right up, 'Where you going, soldier?' I got back to my base about eleven o'clock at night, an hour before I'm AWOL.

Now we're getting ready. We finish our combat training. In the 73rd Bomb Wing, there's the 497th Bomb Group, the 498th, the 499th, and the 500th Bomb Group. There are ten crews in each squadron, three squadrons to a group. We've got one hundred twenty combat crewmen in a big hangar place in Harrington,

---

[60] *Rosie O'Donnell*-General Emmett E. 'Rosie' O'Donnell Jr. [1906-1971] led the first B-29 attack against Tokyo, and served as Commander in Chief, Pacific Air Forces from 1959 to 1963.

Kansas. All these crews are going there to pick up a new B-29 Superfortress.

A Pioneer Crew

For the Pacific, I consider myself [part of] a pioneer crew. It's a [phrase] I made up because we were the first ones. Each crew will eventually get a new B-29 Superfortress. We get ours. We get in. We take off. In about an hour and a half, we blow an engine! I get in contact with the home base. I let them know we are making an emergency landing in a place called Kingman, Arizona. The funny part about this is that, at this time, this plane is top secret! When I went home, I never mentioned that I was flying in a B-29. They didn't know about a B-29 anyway, and I never mentioned that I'm involved with that.

We made the emergency landing in Kingman, Arizona. When we get to the stand where the plane ends up, we have about thirty, forty MPs around the plane. Nobody's allowed to get near the plane, because it's top secret. When I walked down, I felt like I was somebody who came in from outer space. This is the feeling. Of course, they're all looking at us. We had different types of jackets at the time, they made us look pretty exclusive, so [that contributed] to the feeling.

Two days later we have a new engine. We go to California. From California, we go to Hawaii. From Hawaii, we went to a place called Kwajalein, which is a little atoll, all they got is an airfield, anything else you can forget about. From there we went to Saipan, and the beginning of where we are going to be involved, somewhere in late October 1944.

The B-29 was much larger than the B-17. It went further, it flew higher, it flew faster, and in reference to bombs, we had two bomb bays that were tremendous. The B-17 had a small, little bomb bay.

I was the radio operator, but I didn't know too much about what was happening. I had to read up [on it later] to find out. They didn't give me enough medals. [*Laughs*] With all I went through, I said, 'All right, that's their game.'

Let me see, where was I? We got in some training missions. We bombed Truk Island, it was Japanese-held at the time. Now in November, approximately November 23, 24, 1944, we go on the first ground-based bombing mission of Tokyo. Two and a half years before [our mission], Doolittle bombed Japan. Now we are going on the first one [since then]. We didn't do a good job at the beginning, but we let them know they were in a war.

'We Got Clobbered'

We went over, there was flak; there's always flak, and as a rule, there's always fighters. Not only were we the first ones, but our particular group was also A Group; we were like the first ones to go over targets. We got clobbered. We got clobbered.

The next day, the day after this, in this country it was plastered all over the papers. I have it here. [*Pretends to read headline*] 'B-29 Superfortress bombs Tokyo!' This was great for the public, you know. You read this, and you say, hey, we're going after them, that kind of stuff.

We had eleven in our crew, and [almost] all of us were from up north, but the pilot was from North Carolina; I can't think of the name [of the plane] offhand. It never got a splash, like today you'd see these books and they have beautiful [nose art] paintings and all, and loads of different good names.

On January 27, we had another mission. We were the first group, the 497th, to go over. In this mission, we had seventeen planes, and most of our missions at the beginning were to try to knock out the airplane plant in Tokyo. On this particular mission—

and this is the week after Curtis E. LeMay took over our outfit—You've heard of him, Curtis LeMay?[61] When LeMay came into our outfit, he made changes. All of us cursed this guy all to hell. We cursed him all to hell. We were bombing at 25,000 feet; he brought us down to 16,000. These are daylight raids. Then, he brought us down in night raids to approximately 6,000 feet. Everybody was cursing this guy. I even said what's this guy up to, [but] this is the best thing that ever happened to us. He had the answers for us. He came up with the incendiary bombing; this was a big thing. We were one of the small percent. My crew was one of the small percentages, approximately ten percent, of the crews that flew on these five missions, because they were tough missions on the plane, it was tough for the engines to handle.

---

[61] *Curtis LeMay-* (1906-1990) Andrew Doty, a B-29 tail gunner featured in Volume I of the series, recalled: '*General Curtis LeMay, head of the 20th Air Force, concluded that individual B-29s, flying in at 5,000 to 8,000 feet at night, would be far more accurate than if they bombed from 25,000 to 30,000 feet. They could burn out large areas of the Japanese cities, 'de-house' the population, and destroy the many cottage industries that supported the war effort.*
Another major advantage was that the bombers would not have to make the long, demanding climb to high altitudes that strained the engines and drank up fuel. Nor would they have to assemble in formation and jockey about on the way to the target. Consequently, they could carry twice the bomb load. Engine maintenance would be reduced, which would result in more bombers over the target.
LeMay's decision had dismayed the B-29 crews. The low-level raids obviously were much closer to ground anti-aircraft and searchlight batteries and left less room for crewmen to bail out if their plane was shot down. Many B-29s were seen to catch fire, explode, and plunge to earth. The incendiary raids against major cities were not welcomed by the airmen.'

Over The Target

Over the target, the Japanese fighters shot down two planes. [Don't forget, that's] an average of eleven men per plane. A third plane sort of lingered on the side somewhere, we never saw this one again. The fourth plane [lost] ditched a couple hundred miles off Japan. They never saw them again. That was four planes. The fifth plane made an emergency landing on Saipan. The crew was all shot up. So, out of seventeen planes on this mission that my crew was on, we lost like thirty percent. I figured it out—two more missions like that, and we're not around. That's all it took. That was the fear.

The fighter opposition was fierce, we have it in a book. Five hundred and fifty fighter attacks just on our seventeen planes; we got away with that. I didn't know it at the time, but we got away with that.

The Incendiary Blitz

I'm going to jump to March 1945. The middle of March was what they called the incendiary blitz—March 9, 11, 13, 16, 19. We hit Tokyo, Nagoya, Osaka, Kobe, and back to Nagoya. This first one over Tokyo, March 9, is considered one of the most horrific bombing missions of any war. We burnt out like sixteen square miles on that one. Fifteen point eight, sixteen square miles, what's the difference, two-tenths of a square mile? Eighty thousand plus died. A hundred thousand injured. A million homeless. Ridiculous kind of numbers, but this is what actually took place.

I'm the radioman on my ship. We're getting close, about a hundred and fifty miles from Tokyo. At this time, I'm not doing my job properly, because I'm listening to music. Wah-wah, you know that music, I'm the only one listening because I'm the radioman on the radio frequency. I'm listening to it, and all of a sudden it cuts out. I look at my equipment. I try to figure out what happened. There's nothing wrong with my equipment. I figured it out. I got on the intercom and said, 'Radio to crew. Tokyo Radio just went off the air.'

They knew we were coming. We were a plane by itself at this time. They knew it. We're coming over to take photos, that was one of the missions, a photo mission. They just went off the air. There's a procedure. A plane comes close, they go off the air.

As I said, we were an A group. Many times, we were the first, or the early ones, to go over. When you go over Tokyo early, you drop your bombs, your incendiaries, and you leave. You may not even see anything burning, because you're the early one. We did this with Tokyo, Nagoya, and Osaka.

'Kobe is Burning!'

Going to Kobe, we were one of the latter planes. About a hundred and fifty miles from Kobe—anywhere between a hundred and fifty, two hundred miles—one of the crewmen in the nose over the intercom says, 'What's that spot out there?'

I had to manipulate around to get up front, but I got up front, and at approximately twelve-thirty, one o'clock there is this little orange dot. You can't tell distance at night, but there's this little orange dot. Nobody knew.

I said, 'What the heck is that?' It's all black, then there's this little orange dot. It could be a plane, it could be a light, it could be anything. As we keep going to the target, this little orange dot starts getting larger. I'm back in my seat and somebody hollers out, 'Kobe is burning!' This is a hundred and fifty miles out! You can't believe it! Approximately a hundred and fifty miles away you can see a fire; you can't believe it.

Now we are in the latter part of the mission. There's been, I don't know, three hundred planes that dropped their firebombs on this area. When we get to the target, the bomb bay doors open; everything's burning. We're over the target. At this point, there comes up a smell that was awful. It was [burning] debris, and also bodies. We're at six thousand feet approximately; we're very low. Now at this point—and this is all in books, but here I'm not quoting books; this is what happened to me—we get the turbulence from this big fire. It comes up into the plane, and this plane gets shook up. This is a big plane and my top gunner, he hurt his head because it shook so much where he was sitting. When it shook so much, my question was, where did we get hit? We're supposed to get hit because of this [lower-level mission], but we didn't get hit. Turbulence coming up—you've flown, you've heard about turbulence, but you don't know what turbulence is! This thing is out of [control]...

[Now], they give cockamamie stories about one of the planes was turned over [by the turbulence]. I don't believe that. One of the things in reference to telling these stories is there is a tendency to fabricate. I don't fabricate. I know what I've been through—what I saw, I should say.

We were on these missions, one after another. You're not sleeping. They give you a [pill] that you take before you get to the target, Benadrex, I think it was—I remember one time my eyes were like this! [*Chuckles, holds hands apart wide*] Everything looked so beautiful. We're right near the target. And when you come back, they're giving you a shot of whiskey, so you can relax. You've got [it] coming up. You've got [it] coming down. You're not getting the proper sleep, whatever it took. Curtis E. LeMay, who was our boss then, at the end of the five missions, he said, 'My boys are a little tired.' What an understatement. For a young guy, I said, 'Why am I feeling like this? Why am I feeling so lousy?' This kind of thing can take its toll. A round trip [from Saipan to Japan and back] was thirteen hours.

We got flak, we got fighters, it was all there. I can tell you one time, we're over the target, and I hear a 'ping' and my navigator is right pretty close, and I look at him and say, 'What happened?'

You can't talk. The noise is tremendous. You can't communicate. I said, 'What happened?'

He said, 'I don't know.' When we got back to the base I immediately jumped out; there was a nice big hole there right by the bomb bay, very close to us. The holes were there in many planes. The flak was up there. Like they say in the movie, you look out the window and you can walk on the stuff. As long as you can see it, you're all right. It's when you don't see it, it comes up, bam, it could hit you, it could hurt you, but it wasn't like it was in Germany. In Germany, the Eighth Air Force, I'm glad I was never involved with that. They got [plastered].

At the beginning [I wore a flak vest], yes, but it was so cumbersome. The first time or the second time you wear it. You throw it right down there where you're at and leave it there. [You think], all right, if they are going to kill me, let them kill me.

We flew for five months without fighter protection because the fighters couldn't go from Saipan to Japan and back; we had to wait until they captured Iwo Jima. Once they captured Iwo Jima, there were many B-29s that made emergency landings there. The Marines and the Army who sacrificed their lives on Iwo Jima, it was for a good 'B-29 cause.' The B-29 people, it saved a lot of us.

I was on a crew [where actually] very little happened. I didn't even catch a cold. I was sitting at a desk; I could have sat at that desk the whole war with all that going on, and not look out. I remember looking out, one time. Somebody said there's a plane way out there, at two o'clock. I got up into the Plexiglass where the navigator shoots his stars. I looked at about two o'clock and there's this plane just staying ahead of us.

I heard somebody holler, 'He's turning!' That's when I took a look, and there's this plane coming right at us. I'm watching and, again, you don't hear anything. I see on the wings there's this orange stuff coming out; it's a matter of split-seconds. I realized, with this orange stuff, he was shooting at us!

There was another incident that's very hard for somebody to believe. I had to read about the same incident to know [more about it]. It's a nighttime mission, and we're over Japan, and we're heading towards a target at five, six thousand feet. I'm up in this Plexiglass, and I'm looking around—it's all dark out there. But I notice at about ten-thirty, a plane—it had to be fairly close to us and going in the same direction. The first thing you say to yourself, B-29. But I took a better look. This was a two-engine plane.

I said, 'Well, we don't have any. What is this all about?' This plane was staying ahead of us for about five minutes, that I observed. Then I went back to my desk. Then I read about what it was all about, I didn't know at the time. This plane was sending [information] back to the base in Japan about our altitude, our speed, all the information, but I had to read about it. I didn't understand this particular thing [at the time]. Somebody would say, come on, it's your imagination. I know I saw this thing for about five minutes.

We dealt with 'kamikazes,' as they say. The Japanese had a squadron of what they called 'rammers,' who were not [technically] kamikaze people. They came in and tried to hit the tail a certain way to hurt the plane. They, in turn, would parachute out. I read a book on that; this is what they did. They rammed the plane, whereas the kamikaze went in just to blow up.

Now another thing. In April '45, the kamikazes were clobbering the Navy in the area there. They flew out of the southern tip island, the southernmost island of Kyushu. They hurt the Navy a lot at this time, so we went in, we bombed their air bases in Kyushu. Three days later, they'd have the holes filled in. You couldn't do too much about it, but one of the funny stories I tell is that my crew bombed 'USA.' On one of our missions over Kyushu, the name of the [Japanese] air base was 'U-S-A.' We bombed the USA; I consider it amusing. [*Chuckles*]

The number [of missions completed] for our outfit to go home was thirty-five missions. We were one of the small percent that flew only thirty missions. When they told me, 'This is your last mission,' I knew I hadn't flown thirty-five and, as a kid, I'm not opening my mouth. If they're telling me I'm going home, I'm going, I'm not going to question them. [But] after looking at it, we were involved with rough stuff.

I can tell you I met my radar man about ten, fifteen years later. He was at some Army air base. I sit here, he sits there, and we were talking about 'the good old days.' After we finished, I left him, and I said to myself, 'Was he in the same war I was in?' He had a different story altogether; this is what you have to deal with. Maybe you were right, maybe he was right. You know where I learned that? I learned that from somebody who said to me the dog can only see from this angle [*gestures low*] and we see from this angle [*gestures high*]. [It all depends on] where your perspective is. This is what happened.

Saving the Crew

One time—this is like January 3, 1945—my pilot's friend ditched his plane between Iwo Jima and Saipan. He went on a mission, came back, couldn't make it, and into the drink he went. They had an idea, the radioman or whatever, of the [last] position. The next morning, my pilot comes in and he says, 'Sam, get your chute.' 'Get your chute' means you are going on a flight. He says to me, 'Get the chute and get in the plane.' This is a plane where two new engines have just been put in.

There's about six or seven of us in the plane. He needed a plane to try to find his friend, but if the people upstairs knew about it, they'd hang him for it; these things aren't 'dumbo' kind of things.

We got in the plane. I'm always in the front. This particular time—we have a tunnel in a B-29 Superfortress. It's a crawl-through tunnel—when you crawl through, it's just about like this [*motions narrowly with hands*]. You can't see anything on your right. You can't go back. If you have a case of claustrophobia, it'll kill you. I'm halfway through; I'm moving. I'm moving. Very funny. I went through this thing twice. I went to the side gunner's spot, [looking out]. There was another side gunner there, and all the officers were up front.

What was my pilot doing? [It's] hundreds of square miles and he's just circling and circling, doing smaller circles for an hour, hour and a half. I'm in there, I'm looking out; I can only tell you, don't be in a life raft in the middle of the ocean—it's worse than a needle in a haystack, and with an airplane, you're moving quick, two hundred miles an hour. What's below, you just don't see.

Very luckily, somebody said, 'Down below!' From where I was, I looked down, and in a split-second, I saw a life raft. I thought there were six or seven people in it, crewmen. That was it. We circled around; I never saw them again. He called in a destroyer or sub in the area, and because of my pilot, they saved about six or seven crewmen. There's more of a story to it, but they were saved. I was very proud of my pilot.

Close Calls

One mission we went out very close to Japan. We flew about nine hours, and we aborted a mission, which means that we flew and flew and when we got close to the island, we had a malfunction of the engine. If you're having trouble with an engine, you don't want to go over the target in a bombing formation, because when you fall back, they're going at you. You can forget about it. They just look for somebody to have a little problem, then they leave everything else, and they go for this one. So, we aborted. We dropped the bombs in the ocean, and we came back.

Another time, we're coming back from a target. Now, we have some bombs hung up, the bombardier couldn't release them. These are big bomb bays; it's twelve, fifteen feet from the front of the bomb bay to the rear of the bomb bay. These bombs happened to be stuck way in the rear in an awkward spot. Our bombardier comes and opens the bomb bay door. This bomb bay door [*gestures with hands*] is open, we're flying over the ocean. All you've got down there is water, water, and more water. He's climbing out, and if he slips, he's gone. Any kind of fall, that's the end of him. He's going along the side of the fuselage. There's a little ledge of about nine inches, and he's moving along this little edge. He's moving toward the back of the bomb bay to get to the bombs. It's hard to believe. At this point, my stomach couldn't take it. I had to stop looking. He released the bomb, came back, because if you're going to land, these things are subject to going off. They're still armed and they have to be released. I don't know too much about armament. He did a great thing there.

I was back in the States by the time the atomic bombs were dropped. I finished my last mission the end of May. It was all top secret. They were on Tinian, we were on Saipan. My crew, my outfit, made it easy for these guys, because we took all of the clobbering. I'm not putting them down, but we took all of the clobbering, and they came along. By the time they got there, who's attacking them? They're not being attacked. How far is Tinian from Saipan? There's a little inlet; it's about three to five miles. I saw Tinian when

I went down to the beach to soak on the beach. One time, I looked at Tinian and I see a plane taking off. I'm watching. This is like three miles away. I see another plane taking off and I say, 'Oh, they're going on a mission.' Another plane, and I'm watching for a while. This one plane takes off and instead of going up it goes down, down, down. There's a big splash. I don't hear it. I'm too far away. That's all there is to it. That was all there is to it. When the engines don't give you enough power, you're not going up, so you're going to go down. This is one of the things that happened.

We didn't live in barracks, we lived in Quonset huts on Saipan. In my Quonset hut we lost one crew that went on a mission and never came back. Then we lost a second crew. They come, and they go.

When we finished our combat missions, we were put into tents from our Quonset hut. They're keeping us away from the combat flyers, we've finished our missions. Now at this point I'm figuring we go back in a couple of days. They kept us there for like a month. I myself said I don't understand why they kept us there. We're finished. Put us somewhere where we can start heading back. They didn't do anything about it. Later on, I read a story of a crew that finished just about the same time, or maybe a little ahead of us, they got into a B-29 and were flying back to the States. They flew from Saipan to Kwajalein; from Kwajalein, they were supposed to go to Hawaii. This crew that just finished missions over Tokyo, over Japan, they crashed in the ocean! Now, from this I deduced that the wing doesn't want to lose any more men. So, this is one of the reasons I feel that they kept us there. When they finally make a move, I'm the first one they pick in the crew, and they put me in a B-29 to go back to the States. The officers and all the enlisted men, they all stayed; I don't know how long they stayed. After reading this story, I thought I was a guinea pig. I was the only one.

'I Kissed The Ground'

I hit California the 5th of July, 1945. I got off this plane, and, like they do in the movies, I kissed the ground. After that, I never flew in the service again.

I went to work in November of '45. I didn't use the GI Bill, and let me say to all of you people, use the GI Bill. That's one of my negative moves. When I got out of the service, I did a little night school work.

I would say the whole crew lost contact with each other until they started with the reunions; the first reunion that I went to was like ten years ago. Our bombardier was there, one of the gunners, my radar man, and myself. We were the only ones at that time. Since then, our radar man passed away. Our bombardier became a lieutenant colonel, eventually. When he goes out of the house, he gets in the car, he doesn't walk much. The other one seems to be in a senior type of home, something like that. He says he's happy there. I spoke to both of them around the holiday time. I move around but not easy. I'm hoping to go to Florida maybe. Maybe one of these cruise ships, but I'm single, they don't want singles. It's a negative thing to be single. To go with another fellow, oh my goodness, that's so tough, they got their own way of doing things, they're self-centered, my goodness. A couple of months ago, I went away with another fellow my age who I got along with quite well. By the time we got back, I didn't want to speak to him at all. I'm saying to myself, 'I know it's not me.' I'm only too glad to bend with somebody, it's not me. [*Laughs*]

Aftermath of March 9–10, 1945 Tokyo raid. Ishikawa Kouyou.

Over sixty Japanese cities had been incinerated by the B-29s. Howling firestorms devoured civilians and workers in sheets of flames, burning hundreds of thousands to death.

When asked after the war about the morality of his orders to the crews of the B-29s, General LeMay responded, 'We knew we were going to kill a lot of women and children when we burned [Tokyo]... Killing Japanese didn't bother me much at the time. It was getting the war over with that bothered me.'

'We had to kill in order to end the war,' one pilot remembered. 'We heard about the thousands of people we killed, the Japanese wives, the children, and the elderly. That was war. But I know every B-29 air crewman for the next two or three years would wake up at night and start shaking. Yes, [the raids] were successful, but horribly so.'[29]

Sam L. Kamerman passed away on October 16, 2014, at the age of 91.

PART FOUR

OKINAWA AND BEYOND

"We tried to coax them to give themselves up. Some of them killed themselves with hand grenades and others went to a cliff at the end of the island and just jumped down on the rocks and were killed. Mothers with little children in their arms did that. So they were really committed people.

We were lucky. By rights, if you look at the odds, we had had eight combat landings, and a number of us were literally in the first wave of every landing. We would talk about it. The last couple I remember we were saying, 'You know, if we come out of this one, it's a miracle,' because we were pushing the odds."

—US Army Radioman, On His Final Landing At Okinawa

CHAPTER FOURTEEN

Hacksaw Ridge

Situated less than 350 miles from mainland Japan, sixty miles long and nearly 900 square miles, the island of Okinawa hosted perhaps 120,000 defenders on paper, but once taken, American planners reckoned it would be big enough to support 800 heavy bombers to rain hell on the enemy for the planned Operation Downfall invasion of Japan, scheduled for November 1945. As the winter of 1945 gave way to spring, it was clear to the Japanese that the island had to be held at all costs. Taking it was not going to be simple or easy. The logistics for the largest combined amphibious operation in the Pacific War took months, and over half a million Americans were to be committed to the battle in the newly created Tenth Army, a hybrid force that included the Army's 7th, 27th, 77th, and 96th Infantry Divisions and the Marines' 1st, 2nd, and 6th Divisions supported with nearly 20,000 naval personnel on land. From the sea, troops were ferried and supported by the nearly 300 ship armada of the US Fifth Fleet, which included the firepower of 18 battleships, 39 aircraft carriers, and 3,000 aircraft, and almost 250 British Commonwealth planes.[30]

Early morning on Easter Sunday, 1945, the invasion of Okinawa began. The first of four initial divisions of Marines and soldiers to hit the beaches that Easter morning were somewhat perplexed, however, to find little or no opposition. Others noted the irony of the date: besides being Easter Sunday, it was April 1—April Fools' Day. The defenders were waiting. Japanese troops had by now fixed on defense-in-depth tactics and chose to consolidate defensive positions in a rough and precipitous area in southern Okinawa, known as the Shuri Defense Line, with its treacherous escarpment riddled with the defenders' tunnels and caves.

Henry Huneken was committed to the battle with the reinforcing 77th Division. He became acquainted with a young man from Lynchburg, Virginia, who wanted to serve his country but as a devout Seventh-day Adventist, refused to carry a gun and was trained as a medic. Desmond Doss became the first conscientious objector to war to be awarded the Medal of Honor.

"The Japanese were using that as an artillery observation outpost, and they had the natives dig a network of caves and tunnels, three stories deep, in that thing. And that's why we could not cross it. Every time fellas got to the top, [the Japanese] had machine gun crossfire up there, and they just mowed them down.

I came ashore early in the morning and I saw six litters lying there, with the ponchos covering them, [glistening from the] moisture from during the night. They were just beginning to steam up from the sunshine, and I thought to myself, 'Oh, for heaven's sake, what am I doing here?"

Henry C. Huneken

My name is Henry Huneken. I am eighty-two and a half years old. I was born 2-2-22 near Bremen, Germany. And I came to the United States, my parents brought me here when I was almost five years old, in 1926.

My educational background is the public school system of New York City; I didn't quite finish high school. In 1939, I went on a trip to Europe to visit my grandparents, and while in Europe, I saw that there was a lot of activity, militarily, and I thought it would be best that I get out. So I left and I came back.

I enlisted in October of 1942 in the United States Coast Guard. And I was in the Coast Guard Station in New York City and what we did was called port security; we boarded every ship that came into the harbor and acted as security. The port security system was brought into being because of the *Normandie* fire; on the ship *Normandie*, the French liner, they were doing what they call 'burning' with acetylene torches and the sparks ignited and the ship caught fire, and when the New York City Fire Department tried to put it out, they poured so much water on it that it capsized, right in the dockside.[62] And that was the reason why they enacted this port security system.

Now in the port security system, I was stationed in three different places. I was on Ellis Island for a while guarding the hospital nurses there; I walked to the seawall with a rifle that wasn't even loaded. And I was also stationed in Stapleton, Staten Island, at age 18, and that was where we had our detail boarding all the ships.

Now, I had requested that I be advanced in rank to a quartermaster, and one day I got notice to come over to the 3rd Naval District. And I went with the hopes that I would be promoted at that point. Instead, they handed me a discharge. It was an ordinary discharge, and it was for the 'convenience of the government,' and the reason for that was at the time, the Coast Guard was overcrowded, so for

---

[62] *Normandie* fire-The luxury French ocean liner was docked in New York when the Vichy government, loyal to Germany, came into power following the fall of France in June 1940. The Navy seized the liner to convert it into a troop ship; in the process of converting it, it caught fire.

whatever reason they could find, they were discharging personnel and I was one of them that was chosen.

I asked the officer at the Coast Guard what I should do, and he said, 'Well you'll have to go back to your draft board.'

'Greetings from Uncle Sam'

I said, okay, so I went back to my draft board and about two months later, I got a notice from Uncle Sam. It said, 'Report for physical, Grand Central Palace' on Madison Avenue, I think it was.

I went over and they said, 'Well, what would you like to go into? What branch of the service?'

The Coast Guard during wartime is part of the Navy. So I said, 'I'd like to go into the Navy.' And he said, 'Okay,' and they stamped my papers.

I went down with thirty-three men to the Naval District Office on Church Street. And they read off thirty-two names and they didn't read my name off. So, I went up to the fella and I said, 'Look, what am I, an orphan? I'd like to know why my name wasn't called.'

He said, 'Well, what's your name?' So we went in to see the officer of the day, and the officer of the day said, 'You're no longer fit for naval duty.'

I said, 'Well, what do I do?'

He said, 'Well, I guess you have to go back to your draft board.' So, I went back to my draft board again, and I couldn't get a job because I had a 1-A classification. But in the meantime, I got another letter, 'Greetings from Uncle Sam,' and I went down to Grand Central again. And this time there was no question as to what branch of the service I would like. So they stamped it 'Accepted Army' and that's how I was drafted into the Army.

I went to basic training in Camp Blanding, Florida. That's an infantry training camp for fourteen weeks and my designation was as a rifleman. And while down there, we were out on bivouac and we were notified that we had a hurricane coming, and they had to pull 17,000 men off the field because of that hurricane threat.

Shortly thereafter, I had an interview with a major down there who was J-2, which is Intelligence in the Army, and we had a discussion. And he said, 'I understand you're a German.'

I said, 'Yes, I am.'

So he said to me, 'What would you do, if we send you when the first wave goes?'

I said, 'Well, there's not much I can do, I'd have to defend myself, but I'd rather not be sent to Germany.' [See,] I passed the interpretation test. They wanted to have me go to Germany, but I didn't want to because I had relatives there, so on and so forth. So they sent me to the Pacific—just two of us out of those 17,000 men that I trained with. The other men all went into the Battle of the Bulge, but this Chinese fella and I were sent to the Pacific. And we went on a long troopship, and we went all the way down to New Guinea because the islands had not been taken at that time. We took a very slow trip, and we had no escort; we were alone and we would inch our way up. And finally, we landed on the island of Leyte, which was still not declared secured.

The 77th Division

I was put into what they call 'replacement depot' there on February 2, which was my birthday. And about three or four days later, I was assigned to a company in the 77th Division because they had just come down from the mountains after the operation; they had been on Guam before that. They had taken the island of Guam and then they were assigned to go into Leyte. I'd be of the 307th Infantry in the 77th Division.

The 77th Division had gone through many different kinds of training. They went through mountain training, they went through desert training, they went through, I don't know, just about any kind of training that they could possibly have, because it was like an experimental division, they had a lot of older men in it, up to the middle 40s, I think. But they began to weed them out, so by the time they went overseas, they were pretty well prepared for anything, you know, and they were called a 'hot' division.

Our commanding general was General Andrew D. Bruce. And we were known over in the Pacific as Bruce's Butchers, most of us coming from the New York-New Jersey-Connecticut area. The officers were mostly southern, but the enlisted men were mostly from the New York metropolitan and tri-state area.

Leyte

On Leyte, I was shot at a couple of times by Japanese who had gone into the hills and stayed there. What happened on Leyte, they were building like recreation rooms and mess halls out of bamboo for us. And we engaged the local natives to go up into the mountains and cut bamboo. We loaned them our six-wheeler trucks and they went up there and they cut the bamboo. But they were being sniped at by the Japanese [hiding up there], so they wanted protection. So they sent a couple of us GIs up there with rifles, but we didn't know that there were any Japanese up there. We would put our rifles by the truck, and we'd wander off into the neighborhood someplace. So I was shot at a couple of times.

The Run-Up to Okinawa

At that point already, they start to prepare for the Okinawa invasion. That was almost a 24-hour deal, unloading ships, loading ships. I loaded the great big 155 mm artillery shells, they were heavy. I came back with a hernia, incidentally. I don't know whether it was from that, or the fact that I carried a flamethrower for one day where I had to take it and throw it on my shoulder, but I came back with a hernia, and that's why I'm getting a slight pension, 10% pension.

That was about a month's time. In that time, we were preparing, and we also went out and we did a little bit of what they call amphibious training. [We were] climbing down the rope nets into the troop carriers, the landing craft, and it got a little bit rough out there sometimes, then we [actually] boarded the ships. I don't remember what day it was that we left, because we were assigned to take five little, small islands to the southwest in the China Sea before the initial invasion began of Okinawa, so we arrived there on the 26th of March and the invasion began on April 1.

My regiment took these five small islands, the Kerama Islands. I was not sent ashore, my company happened to be a reserve, so we did not go in. And then we went back onboard ship and every night the whole division would pull away from the islands, except for the people who remained on the island after they were taken for [garrison duty].

The Kamikazes

We went back into the China Sea and at that point, we got very heavily bombarded by kamikaze planes. The ship to the right of us was hit; this plane went right into the bridge, and I think about 72 officers and men were killed just by that one plane. One of the wounded happened to be Winthrop Rockefeller, who became the governor of Arkansas later on. I had quite a few interesting episodes with him, we used to go beer drinking together.

The ship on the left also was hit. And one evening, we had an alert and we were told to go below. I was reading a book from Bob Hope, and I was sitting on the railing, and I couldn't see myself going down below so fast, so I stayed up there and I looked up. And as I'm looking up, I see this plane coming directly towards us. The gunnery crew of that ship was not very accurate, they were not very good trying to hit the sleeve of that target plane in training back in the Philippines.

'Wow, this is going to be something,' I thought. At that point, I froze; this plane was coming directly in, but all of a sudden, there was a terrific explosion and the 5-inch gun on the tail end of the ship had hit that kamikaze plane directly on the nose and it just disintegrated—the pieces fell on the deck around me. It was headed right towards me!

Hacksaw Ridge-The Maeda Escarpment

The Japanese plan on Okinawa was to let the Americans come ashore and move towards the south and then clobber them, surround them and then do them in. And we got ashore, we were finally committed because the 96th Division was so badly decimated that the generals began to ask themselves, why are they not advancing; they had lost an awful lot of men. So we were finally committed, and it was my first experience getting up to the front lines.

They had advanced to this escarpment, which was a high elevation of rock and coral that ran most of the way across the center of the island. And the Japanese were using that as an artillery observation outpost, and they had the natives dig a network of caves and tunnels, three stories deep, in that thing. And that's why we could not cross it. Every time fellas got to the top, [the Japanese] had machine gun crossfire up there, and they just mowed them down.

I came ashore early in the morning and I saw six litters lying there, with the ponchos covering them, [glistening from the] moisture from during the night. They were just beginning to steam up from the sunshine, and I thought to myself, 'Oh, for heaven's sake, what am I doing here?'

But it took us nine days to take that position. First of all, we got these cargo nets from the ships from the Navy, and we tied them up there. And this fellow Doss was instrumental in helping to tie them up. Having been in the Coast Guard, they called on me as well to tie these cargo nets up to the top, so the soldiers could climb up there with their equipment and try to storm these positions up on top.

Well, like I said, took us nine days. Every time we went up there, we had over 80 percent casualties, in my company as well.

One night we were up there with my squad, and we were in three foxholes. I was in the middle foxhole and three other fellas were in the foxhole to my right and the squad leader was in the foxhole to my left. The sun was going down, and the mailman came up and he gave me a whole stack of letters from Ursula, my wife. I started to read them because there was a little bit of a cutout on the side of this escarpment, and we had piled a couple of rocks up on the edge [for cover], to make it a little bit higher.

He came up and he said, 'You have anything else you'd like?'

I said, 'Yeah, I'd like you to bring me a pair of dry socks.'

He came back a little bit later, he brought some dry socks, and he also brought a couple of doughnuts, I remember. And then I sat there, and I was reading the letters. I must have gotten about 25 or 30 letters at one time.

'Help Me!'

Now it got dark, and they threw up flares, and we would look out all the time. And all of a sudden, there was an explosion in the foxhole next to me; they had thrown a hand grenade in there. And while I'm looking—I'm looking out over Buckner Bay up there, I could see the ships out there—I see this form in the ground crawling up to me. And he saw me, and he said, 'Huneken, help me, help me, help me!'

It was our BAR man, Mike Revak. And he had taken a hand grenade almost on his lap and his leg was shattered, it was really turned around. He was a big guy, he was about six foot, and I couldn't pick him up, I couldn't lift him. So I took him by the belt, and I pulled him into where we were able to evacuate him that night. I cut open his pants leg and I sprinkled some sulfanilamide on him, but he lost the leg anyway. I never saw him again after that. I found out later that he lost all his genitals and lost the leg.

We were told to consolidate our position where the squad leader was. We had two Japanese wooden ladders that were tied together, two 24-foot ladders, and they went to the top, because this whole thing was a sheer cliff of forty feet that we had to go up on the cargo nets and on ropes. Then we consolidated our opposition to that; we waited, and we waited, and it was pretty dark already by now, must have been about eleven o'clock.

Japanese Infiltrators

My squad leader, his name was Harvey Gilliam, tapped me on the shoulder and he said, 'Huneken, get down and get a little bit of rest.' He says, 'Twelve o'clock, come back up and relieve us.'

I said fine. I went down, my foot was on the top rung of that ladder already, because we had a feeling that they were crawling up on us, which they were, and which is what finally happened.

I had just gotten down, about 11:15, something like that, when all hell broke loose up on top and they raided, you know. The Japs wore split-toe sneakers. The Japs, they just crawled; it took them almost four hours to crawl that distance. When the flares went up, we would look out and we'd watch every stone, every rock, and if the stone moved, we knew it was a human being. If it wasn't a rock, it had moved, that's the only way you could make out the figures. Anyway, they raided, they charged with bayonets attached to the bamboo poles, and they got Gilliam in the stomach, and it cut him open. And he just dropped, and I think there were five guys that were left up there. One of them was a New Mexican fella who spoke Spanish, and I can't remember his name. Anyway, he came at me out of a cave, or a cut in the rocks, down below, and I had my rifle at the ready—I was going to pull the trigger and he said, 'Amigo, amigo!' He said, 'Don't shoot, it's me!' So that's how his life was spared. It was just a matter of a split-second, okay?

And then we all scooted around to a great big rock, there were about seven of us. We had a medic, I can't remember his name, but it was not Doss; Doss was in the company command post [at that time]. Anyway, [this medic] stayed with us and he gave my squad leader, Harvey Gilliam, morphine shots all night long. Which kept him quiet, and he didn't utter a sound, because if he had made a sound, the Japanese would have known where we were. We had left everything up there. All the hand grenades, everything that we pulled up all day long and used all day long, they would have thrown down on us, but nobody knew where we were exactly.

'Burn Them Out'

Another incident on the escarpment, how we finally took this position knowing that it was three stories down. We had a V-shaped trough built about 20 feet long, up to a hole, because they're coming out of these holes all the time, up on the top. We poured five-gallon cans of gasoline in it, and it would go down into the hole, then somebody would have to crawl up and throw a phosphorus grenade in there and blow the whole thing up. That's what we did several times. But they came right back up out of those holes again because they just went off into the side passages, and they would come right back up out of them again. This one time, my captain, Captain Vernon, refused an order from the colonel [via] radio contact with the regimental command post.

He said, 'I found a cave.'

And the colonel said, 'Blow it.'

The captain said, 'I can't; I don't know what's under there.'

So he refused the command, and the colonel said, 'I want you to blow it.'

He says, 'No, sir. I'm sorry, I refuse,' because we all would have gone up.

Later on, the colonel came up, and the way they finally took this position is, they took flame-throwing tanks coming around from the front, from the other side. [It had a steep slope], it went down to a 40-foot precipice, and then they finally shot flamethrowers into the holes and everything, which finally burned them out. And then we were slowly able to advance. We were pulled back off the line at that point to about fifteen miles back, where the giant 155mm guns were the gun emplacements, and they put us right in front of those things, and every time they went off, we jump two feet high, for heaven's sake. Because your nerves get a little bit tight, you know.

Then we got replacements, because we had quite a few losses. We got one young kid, 17, 18 years old, right fresh out of high school, and then we were sent back up on the line again. We don't even have a chance to train with them or anything. We were sent back up on the line because they were trying to advance towards Shuri [Castle]; the city was Naha that was off towards the right. On both sides of this, we had another division; on the operation of Okinawa, there were four divisions of infantry and two divisions of Marines. Now, the Marines seem to have gotten most of the credit for that operation, which bothered us all through the years, but they have a good PR system, the Marines.

'Fix Bayonets, No Round in the Chamber'

So we never got our due, although the second time that we were put on the line, we advanced, and we were given the orders. We are going to make a night attack deep into the Japanese territory. And the orders, the way they came down to us were, 'You'll fix bayonets and there will be no round in the chamber.' In other words, they didn't want any noise in that night attack because that was unheard of. Nope, I don't think any American infantry outfit has ever made a night attack like that. But we did, we had two companies, I was in Company B, and Company E. For that we got a Bronze Star, every member of the company. For the escarpment, we got a presidential citation. Those are the medals that I earned over there.

After that, the whole Okinawa campaign was over at the end of June. That was three months, March, April, May—no, that's almost four months, because we were taken off the line about the middle of June and sent back into a rest area. And from there we went back to the Philippines.

Desmond Doss

Desmond Doss became the first conscientious objector to be awarded the Medal of Honor. As a medic assigned in 1944 to 2nd Platoon, Company B, 1st Battalion, 307th Infantry, 77th Infantry Division, he was first awarded two Bronze Stars with a 'V' designation 'for exceptional valor in aiding wounded soldiers under fire on Guam and the Philippines.'

*Desmond Doss, on top of the Maeda Escarpment,
Battle of Okinawa, May 4, 1945. US Army photo, public domain.*

Desmond Doss was a conscientious objector, and he was a medic. And little by little—see, his Sabbath is Saturday, according to his religion. So, while in training, he had shoes thrown at him, he was berated, he was called down because he wouldn't work, he refused to work on a Saturday, he wanted to go to church. He was a Seventh-day Adventist. He was taken out of the company several times, but he liked the fellas in the company, even though they were not too pleasant to him, so he kept coming back. And when they went to the island of Guam, they began to realize how conscientious this fellow was in performing his duty as a medic. He would go under all kinds of adverse conditions of pulling these fellas and attend to them, you know, in combat.

And the same thing happened on Leyte; by that time, they were pretty well convinced that he was the right guy.

And when it came to Okinawa, he and I were the main ones that tied up these cargo nets up on the top that enabled the fellas to get up there. And for the nine days that we were there, I went six days and six nights without sleep there when we were in that operation because if you fell asleep, you were dead. You could maybe get a five- or ten-minute catnap, that was about the extent of it. Anyway, Desmond Doss very often would go up the rope ladders and go out where fellas were hit, sometimes very badly. And he would pull them in, pull them in right under the machine gun fire and everything. He had nothing, he had no fear. That was his belief in God. So he saved quite a few guys' lives, that's what his Medal of Honor citation states, that he's saved 75 men's lives.[63]

---

[63] *he's saved 75 men's lives-* Desmond Doss's [1919-2006] Medal of Honor citation, personally presented at the White House by President Harry S. Truman on October 12, 1945, reads:
"Private First Class Desmond T. Doss, United States Army, Medical Detachment, 307th Infantry, 77th Infantry Division. Near Urasoe-Mura, Okinawa, Ryukyu Islands, 29 April – 21 May 1945. He was a company aid man when the 1st Battalion assaulted a jagged escarpment 400 feet high. As our troops gained the summit, a heavy concentration of artillery, mortar and machinegun fire crashed into them, inflicting approximately 75 casualties and driving the others back. Private First Class Doss refused to seek cover and remained in the fire-swept area with the many stricken, carrying them one by one to the edge of the escarpment and there lowering them on a rope-supported litter down the face of a cliff to friendly hands. On 2 May, he exposed himself to heavy rifle and mortar fire in rescuing a wounded man 200 yards forward of the lines on the same escarpment; and two days later he treated four men who had been cut down while assaulting a strongly defended cave, advancing through a shower of grenades to within eight yards of enemy forces in a cave's mouth, where he dressed his comrades' wounds before

Every once in a while, he got a fella down like that, he would tie ropes under their arms and lower them down. When we got them down below, they would ask for volunteers; we needed four men to carry a litter, and I volunteered quite often because it meant getting back to the base hospital and staying off the line for maybe half an hour, an hour. And you'd have to, of course, go back again, but that little rest there was so helpful sometimes.

After the night attack, let me see if I can recall this, he went out and he tried to get a couple of guys in, and a mortar round struck right close by him and shattered his arm. So he took a carbine, and took the stock out of it, and made himself a splint out of that, to

---

making four separate trips under fire to evacuate them to safety. On 5 May, he unhesitatingly braved enemy shelling and small arms fire to assist an artillery officer. He applied bandages, moved his patient to a spot that offered protection from small-arms fire and, while artillery and mortar shells fell close by, painstakingly administered plasma. Later that day, when an American was severely wounded by fire from a cave, Private First Class Doss crawled to him where he had fallen 25 feet from the enemy position, rendered aid, and carried him 100 yards to safety while continually exposed to enemy fire. On 21 May, in a night attack on high ground near Shuri, he remained in exposed territory while the rest of his company took cover, fearlessly risking the chance that he would be mistaken for an infiltrating Japanese and giving aid to the injured until he was himself seriously wounded in the legs by the explosion of a grenade. Rather than call another aid man from cover, he cared for his own injuries and waited five hours before litter bearers reached him and started carrying him to cover. The trio was caught in an enemy tank attack and Private First Class Doss, seeing a more critically wounded man nearby, crawled off the litter and directed the bearers to give their first attention to the other man. Awaiting the litter bearers' return, he was again struck, this time suffering a compound fracture of one arm. With magnificent fortitude he bound a rifle stock to his shattered arm as a splint and then crawled 300 yards over rough terrain to the aid station. Through his outstanding bravery and unflinching determination in the face of desperately dangerous conditions Private First Class Doss saved the lives of many soldiers. His name became a symbol throughout the 77th Infantry Division for outstanding gallantry far above and beyond the call of duty."

hold his arm straight. Then they wanted to evacuate him, and they put him on a litter. I wasn't there at that time, [but] while he was [being made] ready to be evacuated, they brought another [hurt soldier] in and the guy seemed to be pretty well wounded. Doss looked up at the medic, who was tending to both of them. And he said, 'Look, I'll roll off, and you take him back on it.' And they took him, he rolled off the litter, and they put the more heavily wounded guy on it. This is the kind of guy he was. And that's why he was recommended for the medal.

More Losses on the Escarpment

I remember one time we were on the escarpment where Colonel Hamilton came up. We were walking out, and they had just poured the gasoline down there, and there was a young lieutenant that came up early in the morning, just up from stateside. He just got off the ship and came down—he was a demolition expert. And they had poured the gasoline in, then I was up there with the fella by the name of LaPrade, who was a French Canadian who came from Maine, and we were close enough to rub elbows. And all of a sudden, before the lieutenant was even at the edge to throw his phosphorus grenade in there, there was a tremendous explosion, the dust and everything flying all over the place. And all of a sudden, this guy [who had been] next to me was missing. He was [found] lying on the ground, he died of a concussion; I saw the blood coming out of his nose and out of his ears. He was dead [but the blast] didn't affect me [then], but I still can't hear that well to this day.

Our captain was killed too, Captain Vernon. After we made this night attack, we kept advancing south towards the Shuri Castle, and he was in a foxhole. And we told him he should move his foxhole because the Japanese knew that he would have had a command post there, and they were [probably] zeroing in on it with knee mortars.

Now, the knee mortars are not something that you put on your knee, they put it on the ground, and they could put those things on a dime. When they pull that cord, you just knew that was going to come. And we told him to move his position, and he said, 'No, everybody knows I'm here and the company...'

He wanted to stay there, and he took one right on the head. A young fellow, 26 years old, the nicest guy I've ever met, Captain Vernon. And the executive officer who was with him, he was killed too, and also in the same foxhole was Captain Vernon's orderly, Samuel Dolce; he came from Rochester. I saw him many years afterward. Well, he was pretty well burned. He was pretty well scarred up.

I also kept a diary, which I never did get back from the guys that were doing this story on Desmond Doss, but that was pretty much the end of the operations on Okinawa—like I say, it took three months.

'Old People and Children'

We went on a little bit of patrol duty, I don't want to go into that [too much], because it involves some things that we're not very proud of, although it had to be done.

I was interested in photography, though I had no film. One of those lieutenants in my company had film and he had a camera, and he asked me to go along with the patrol to take some pictures of the countryside, of the houses, and whatnot. So, I went along, and I came across some brushwork at the side of the road, and I saw a little footprint in the mud there—by that time we had gotten the rainy season, it was really rainy and very nasty—I saw this little footprint and all this brushwork in front of us.

I didn't know it was a hole. I went back to the lieutenant that was leading the patrol and I said, 'I found these footprints.'

I said, 'What do you want to do about it?'

He said, 'Blow the hole.' So they put a satchel charge in, and then they blew the hole, but in there were nothing but old people and children.

But [who's to know]? The Okinawan people were used by the Japanese to bring supplies up to the front lines to them. They used them to carry ammunition, they used them to carry food. So that's why we didn't take any chances. There were no prisoners, very few prisoners were taken on the island of Okinawa. It was either you or I—I mean, that's the way it was, and the Okinawan people even were told that we're going to rape them and this and that. They were taking their children and throwing them off cliffs, and they would jump after them. It happened quite a bit.

Ernie Pyle

Ernie Pyle was with my regiment when he was killed. That affected us more than when we were notified of the death of President Roosevelt. We just said then, 'Well, let's get this all over with.' But when Ernie Pyle was killed, that really affected us because Ernie Pyle indirectly was responsible for the Combat Infantry Badge, and $10 a month extra for combat infantrymen. Yeah, we really felt bad when [he was killed]—he's buried in Hawaii, and I went to see his grave with my wife. He had gone all through Africa, Italy, Europe, always on the front lines with the GIs, always, and he comes to my regiment and is shot right through the head by a sniper. He was like the curious young fellas from high school, they raise their head, they looked around, and quite a few of them were hit by snipers right between the eyes.

At that time of [the atomic bombs], I was back in the Philippines. It was August, I believe. Well, we thought that's the end of the war. It's got to be, because these people, they can't put up with something like that, and it was a good thing that it did happen, because the 77th Division was slated to go right into Tokyo. And the Japanese would not have given up, the women, as well as the men, they were preparing to put up a very stiff fight.

Return to Okinawa

When we left the island of Okinawa, I think there were about 200,000 people living on the island. When I went back in 1981, there were a million and a half people on the island of Okinawa. The Japanese have turned it into a regular resort, because of the beaches and so on, and they travel it quite extensively. But unfortunately, [when we were back as part of a documentary film on Desmond Doss][64], we were not able to do much traveling. We went back to the escarpment, and they filmed up there and they filmed with Doss, showed exactly [where things happened]. And at the final day of filming, they sat us on four chairs up on the escarpment facing north. And all of a sudden, the director of the film said to the four of us GIs, he said, 'Turn around.'

We didn't know what to expect. We turned around, and there were these seven little Japanese [men] coming up the draw, in civilian clothes, naturally. Our hearts almost fell, you know, because to see these [guys]... two of them were ones that had been right on the escarpment, and the others were just veterans from other areas.

We had a dinner that night, or a couple of nights later, where they all attended. And it was supposed to be in our honor, but we sat and ate at the back of the room. Anyway, the Japanese were there [with us], we had a chance to talk to them through interpreters, and it was quite interesting to hear them talk about what they went through there, too. Yeah, they had a rough time, too. They

---

[64] *documentary film on Desmond Doss-The Conscientious Objector,* which in turn inspired the film *Hacksaw Ridge* [2016].

had about 150,000 troops, and we had about 150,000 troops. It was pretty equal as far as that goes.

After I left Okinawa, we went back to the Philippines, back to Cebu, which is an island right next to Leyte. And it was at that point that I was transferred to IX Corps. So I went from the 77th Division to IX Corps, because I had been to business school and I typed, I took shorthand, so they made me a company clerk. With IX Corps, I went up to the island of Hokkaido, to the city of Sapporo. And I was up there for four months, as part of the Army of Occupation.

Psychologically, the war affected me throughout my life because I had many sleepless nights with it. You know, these things come back to you. I've had many sleepless nights to this day. As a matter of fact, as I got older, they became more prevalent. But I feel that I'm as normal [as the next guy].

Henry Huneken became a salesman, cabinetmaker, carpenter, and building inspector after the war. He passed in 2019 at the age of 97.

CHAPTER FIFTEEN

The Navy Corpsman

He sits in a chair before his interviewers in a darkened room two days before Thanksgiving, summoning forth memories that have clearly haunted him on some level from nearly sixty years in the past. Steve Jordan came to the 22nd Marine Regiment [22nd Marines] of the 6th Division as a corpsman in the Pacific—the same outfit that Joe Fiore [*The Pineapple Kid, Volume I*] was a part of—although not of his own choosing, having picked the Navy over the Army when it was time to enlist. Later, in the reserves, he was called up for Korea, and here he also recounts his participation in the sub-zero Battle of the Chosin Reservoir.

He gave this interview in 2003.

Steve T. Jordan

I was born in Schenectady, New York, October 13, 1924. I just got through freshman year in high school, and then I quit because the war started, and I enlisted at age eighteen. I was in school, but I had no idea where Pearl Harbor was. Most people didn't. We were all going to leave school and enlist, and I guess three or four of us did.

I don't know [why I picked the Navy], I just didn't want the Army, and I thought the Navy would be good. You know, get on a ship and it would be a pretty clean life, that kind of thing. I went through boot camp up in Sampson, New York, early in November 1942. There was a lot of construction going on, and it was in the wintertime, and it was cold and muddy, you know. It was all new to everyone, so it wasn't just me that was walking around, 'wow,' you know, just amazed; it was everyone. We had a couple of boats, but we didn't do much in them, because the winter came quick, and it was a bad one. When on a range, we fired .22s. I had never seen a rifle like it before. It looked like a pipe on the end of a stick, you know. And we were taught how to tie knots and this kind of thing. And that's about the only equipment [training] we did, [besides] some splicing and fitting pins and stuff like that. That's normal seamanship, you forget right after you've done it. [*Laughs*]

Hospital Corps School

I went in there in November, and I got out of there, I think, the end of December. They were pushing us right through. What they did is, they put us in a drill hall, and they said, you know, 'this gang over here, and this middle gang, and another gang, over there.' They said, 'You guys are staying here, and you're going to cooks' and bakers' school.' The next bunch was going to Little Creek, Virginia, they went into the armed guards. The third bunch, they said, 'You guys are going to Portsmouth, Virginia,' and that was the group I was in. I had no idea what it was, you know, until we got to Portsmouth, Virginia, and it was Hospital Corps school! I had to think that one over, I didn't know if I wanted to do that or not. I guess I made up my mind, and I got up the nerve to go to the old man and say, 'Look, I want out of this thing,' and he so much as told me, 'Hey kid, you're in it, and the only way out of it is in a wooden overcoat, so make the best of it!'

So that's what we had to do. It was all the medical stuff. Medical therapeutics, and nursing and first aid, and all that kind of stuff. Doing splints, and carrying people, and all this. And when you got a rate, you were a pharmacist's mate, and to me it didn't relate at all because we didn't do anything with, you know, we gave pills, but a doctor said, 'Here, you give these pills.' We never figured it out ourselves.

We trained there for about eight weeks; I had more training after that. I got out of Hospital Corps school, I went to Norfolk, Virginia, the naval operating base; there was a hospital there and I did a lot of medical work. I handed out tennis balls, and [archery equipment], bow and arrows, and all that kind of stuff; golfing equipment, you know, I had a shed, and all the stuff was in it, and I'd get the patient's name, you know, and that's what I did. But every once in a while, I had to stand watch in some ward where someone was really sick or something. They would give you a rundown of what you had to do, okay. But somewhere along the line, I goofed up because I got shanghaied out of there and I was sent to Camp Lejeune, North Carolina. And there was quite a few of us that went to that, where we went through field medical training school, which was doing what we knew how to do, what we were taught to do in Corps school, [but] out in the field under combat conditions.

I could get a carbine, or a .45, and I chose a carbine until I found out after that it shoots curves—you don't get good distance with it. Later on, I picked up a Garand and that's what I carried.

It's hard to remember how long I was there. It wasn't very long, because we went through all the training, from the infiltration course to the rifle range a couple of times, and all the medical stuff, and then we had classes where you sat in a hot metal building and some Marine officer would give you the history of the Marine Corps and the rocks and shoals, that kind of stuff. It was very boring, you know. He would even fall asleep as he was giving us this stuff, but it was a requirement, you know. But when you think about it, it was good, you know. And the [instructor] who did it was a WWI veteran; he was a major, I think.

After Lejeune I went aboard ship, the *USS Clay*, it was a transport, an APA, and it was a shakedown cruise, and I went aboard as a troop. We were in a replacement battalion; we were in the 39th Replacement Battalion. We rode a train from Lejeune to Norfolk, and then got on the ship, and we went through the Panama Canal and went to Pearl Harbor. We were in a convoy, but they were dragging a target, and there were planes shooting at the back of the target; they were doing a lot of training on the way over. It was a nice ship, it was brand new, but it had a lot of things wrong with it. We didn't realize it, but the crew did.

[When we arrived in Hawaii], we went into some kind of a 'repo depot' where everyone came in, and if they needed a machine gunner, or a cook, or something like that, they would pull them out because it was a mixture of corpsmen and Marines and all that. So then I was told I had to go aboard this ship with some other guys, and we got on this transport, and we took off and we went out into the Pacific, out into the islands. We went to this island that had just been attacked before we got over there, and it was in the Marshall group. I believe it was Roi-Namur. We joined an outfit there, the 22nd Marines there, and I stayed with them for the whole of World War II.

[We dressed in Marine fatigues but wore a Navy rate on the arm.] When I first went there, it was just a red cross, and we wore it down low; that signified we were a corpsman. At the beginning, I was a hospital apprentice, 2nd class, which is equal to a corporal.

So I wore a corporal's stripes, but just on my left arm, and we wore the red cross below it.

At first, [we were not treated by the regular Marines so well], it was nothing but arguments and fights and ridicule, you know, 'swabbie' this and that and the other thing. But we had a couple of sailors that beat up a few Marines, and the old man [had it out for us]; he said, 'I got to find this sailor who beat up four of my Marines!' He was a tough guy. But after we were with him a while and went into training with him, we became friends.

The Invasion of Guam

Our first landing was on Guam. Guam, we were on it for fifty-eight days; [before that], we floated around. See, there is Saipan, Tinian, and Guam. And we were going to hit Guam, but Saipan was having a hard time, so they kept us on reserve. So, we floated around the Pacific for [quite a while]. We got attacked by some Bettys; they came in and they carried a torpedo. Me and this other guy were playing cards, sitting on a spud locker, you know, and this thing came and flew right between our LST and the one right next to us, and [the torpedo] was just skipping the top of the water. And I said, 'Wow, what the hell was that?', and then we see the meatballs on the wings. [It was close]. Phew, I tell you, you can't dig in out there! But we were lucky, we got through it all right. They shot it down, and another came back the next day and raised some more hell.

Then Saipan started to go pretty well, so we went to some other island, I don't remember which one it was. We got some mail, and we got some beer, stayed there overnight, and then a couple days later, we made the landing. First, I was on a transport, and then we transferred from the transport to an LST. We had to sleep topside because there wasn't enough room for everyone. Well, we went to the tank deck and got in the amphibious tractor; I got on this amphibious vehicle. You were assigned to which one, and I was assigned to go in this one that was [commanded] by a major, and he had a jeep on it. I was assigned to him, and he was killed there.

Well anyhow, we started off, you know, we got our wave to go. And we were between, I think, the second wave and the next one. We got out and we made a turn, and all this amphibious tractor does is go round in circles because one of the wheels wasn't working! You know they run on those tracks, even turn in the water, so we were just going around in circles. So now they had to transfer us from that one to another, but the jeep stayed in that one; I mean, we ended up without a jeep. But anyhow, by the time we got on the beach it must have been the third or fourth wave was hitting. And there were a lot of casualties, there were a lot of amphibious tractors that were hit, there were a lot of guys that were in the water, and we were busy taking care of them for the longest time. But then they had another outfit come in, some more corpsmen, and some more Marines came in. The ones that made the initial landing, which included us, we had to start moving; we had to catch up with our troops and move. Well, the major had what we call the 'OP' party, it was the observation party, so we'd have to get up and see what the Japs were doing. You know it was maybe fifteen, sometimes there was twenty-five in a group. He was a pretty gung-ho character, I'll tell you. We took a hell of a beating at a place called 'Road Junction 15' in Guam, and that was on the way to what was left of the Marine Corps barracks. We had a lot of guys killed.

At that Road Junction 15, it was just one of those things we walked right into. They had crossfires set up, and boy, they slaughtered us. [*Pauses, folds arms across chest, looks down in silence for a few seconds, composes himself*].

After we got to the Marine barracks and took over, I got sick—I had the chills and all this business. See, like I said, we were out floating around for fifty-eight days, and we ran out of Atebrin. And there was a lot of malaria and a lot of dengue fever and crap like that, that affected all of us. So I got sent down to the beach and they put a tag on me, they said, 'Go on down to the beach and get some juice and get some rest and then come back when you're feeling better.' You know, the old man told me that, so I said, okay.

I went down to the beach and there was a hospital there, there was a second separate hospital. See we were a bastard [unit] off of the 22nd Marines, we weren't in a division, we were just a regiment. We were with the 4th Marines and the 11th Marines, so we were a brigade, the 1st Provisional Marine Brigade. So anyhow, the hospital was a second separate hospital, and I was staying there. So they gave me a can of juice and they started me on a regimen of Atebrin and right about then the Japs pulled a counterattack; they were knocking off the hospitals on the beach. So they evacuated us all out to the ocean, you know, we got aboard ships. And I got on this ship, well it was an APA. All I remember is that Cesar Romero was a chief on there, it was a Coast Guard thing, I think. I never saw him, but that's what they said, 'Cesar Romero,' and I said, 'Boy, that's great.'[65] But anyhow I ended up back in Pearl Harbor, because we went here, and we went there. Every ship we went to looked down and said, 'We'll take him, him, and him,' and they'd lift you up, lift the litter up off the boat we were in, and they'd pick out who they were going to take, because they were doing triage there.

---

[65] *Cesar Romero*-Cesar Romero [1907-1994] was the self-proclaimed 'Latin from Manhattan' Cuban-descended actor perhaps best known by his shipmates for his role as the Cisco Kid in six westerns in the years leading up to his enlistment in 1942 in the US Coast Guard, eventually serving aboard the assault transport *USS Cavalier* as an apprentice seaman in the invasions of Tinian and Saipan, finishing his enlistment with the rating of chief petty officer.

Well, I looked bad, because I had a lot of blood on me—but it wasn't mine, it was everybody else's. So I got picked on one ship [first] and it was that Cesar Romero's ship. So they were doing operations there, and this doctor said, 'You sit there on the floor,' on the deck, it was in the mess hall, and they were working on everybody, you know. And that's the first time I ever saw that operation [aboard a ship]. I've seen it in the field, the aid station, but never on a ship. So finally this doctor says, 'So where were you hit?'

And I said, 'I wasn't hit,' you know, and he's calling this other doctor saying, 'Look it, he's got blood in his ears.'

He said, 'It's a sign of a concussion.'

I said, 'Wait a minute, I'm a corpsman.' I said, 'This is other people's blood, I wasn't hit!' I got that blood on me somehow, from my hands or whatever.

They stuck me in a ward, and they gave me a shot, and that was the end of it for a while, and I ended up back in Pearl, which was all right. So while I was there, I said, 'Hell, I've got nothing else to do,' my appendix started bothering me, so they took it out. Just one of those things, where the doctor had said, 'You're going to work today,' you know, I'd been there a while. So I get out there to work in a tomato patch, you know, we were hoeing the plants up. Jeez, I got this pain in the gut. So I go see the doctor, and he says, 'You're goofing off.'

I said, 'No, I'm not, I really got a pain!' So he checked me out and he took a blood test, and that's what it was. I had appendicitis. So they took it out, and I took it easy for a while.

Then I got back to the 22nd. They had gone to Guadalcanal, that was our home base where we would set up. So I caught a ride on a ship, and I hitchhiked. I had my records—I carried my own records. They said, 'Get on whatever ship you can, and they'll take you there,' eventually. So it took a while, but I ended up on the Canal, and I ended up in 3rd Battalion and I didn't like that because I was in 2nd

Battalion. Finally I got that squared away and got back to where I belonged.

Okinawa

Then we trained for the next operation. We didn't know what it was, but it was Okinawa, and we landed there. That was April 1. Easter Sunday, April Fools' Day, and it was the whole nine yards, that whole same day—we had an unopposed landing, I think they sucked us right in—and it was easy, and then we went up north. We went the hell up north; we went to the northern tip of Okinawa and we were like 350 miles from the southern tip of Japan, and with nobody on our left flank. So we stayed up there for a while, and then, I guess it was the 27th or the 25th Army Division was having a problem down south. The 1st Marine Division was also down south, and these guys were tied in next to them. So they got the word to us, and they loaded us on trucks and down we went, and we replaced the 1st Marine Division. Man for man, hole for hole. They moved over, and they took out the 27th and gave them a break. And that's when we started getting into a lot of combat. We ran into Sugar Loaf Hill, and that was a mess. And that's when the major got killed.

'He Was Left There to Die'

A couple of days before he was killed, we were on a hill. We were OP'ing it up, 'snooping and booping'; we were watching the Japs and this and that, and all of a sudden, some Jap appeared on top of this hill. It was all rocks and coral, and he had a satchel charge, you know, it was a wooden box with a detonator on it. And he threw that, and it came down and luckily it landed right in between all these rocks. But it blew up, [and for us] it was all concussion—it didn't have any shrapnel, or anything like that, but it blew the shit out of all of us. You know, we were all dopey and crummy there for a while. When it blew this coral, the major got hit in the leg, I think it was the left leg, so I had to take care of that for him. I had put a 12-inch battle dressing on him because he was hit in about four different places. Like I said, he was a gung-ho son of a bitch.

'That's too much of a battle dressing!' He said, 'I can't move around with that, I got to be able to move around!'

So I said, 'All right, okay,' and I pulled some of the stuffing out of it; you know, I did what I could. I got him fixed up and then he was all right.

It was like two or three days later and we hit Sugar Loaf Hill [again], and the first group of the 22nd went up and got kicked right off of it. There was a lot of casualties. I think it was that night or the next night, there was a lot of action going on and we were at the foot of this thing. And the major took volunteers, you know. So we were all there, and I was going to go with him.

He says, 'You go back and stay at the bottom of the hill, I don't want you coming up the hill with us.' [*Arches forward quickly in his seat, looks down, gets briefly emotional...*] He was killed up there... [*Snaps back into composure*] He was a good Marine, [but] I didn't like that man. I'll tell you why I didn't like him. There was one of the guys that we all knew, he was a good guy, and he got the left cheek of his ass blown off. And there he was, lying there, and they had gauze over him, you know, to keep the flies and crap off him, the blowflies. A lot of his insides were sticking out, he'd had it, and they just had him lying there.

They had him pretty well doped up and everyone there would lie to him, you know, [he'd ask], 'How bad is it?'

'Oh, you're all right, you're gonna be okay.' [*Pauses, looks down again briefly*] He was left there to die.

But [the major] comes over, and he picks up the gauze and he says, 'Jesus Christ, you bought the farm!' And you know, that got to me, and I got in some trouble.

I said, 'You're an asshole!' and I yelled at him—I never got any more rate after that, you know, I [had] made second class, but that was the end of it. I don't know whether he had anything to do with it, [because] he was dead a short while after that. Maybe it's my imagination, because I didn't like the man for that reason, I figured, hey, this is a well-educated guy, a major, and he's acting like, well, just what I called him, an asshole.

*

'A Long Trip Home'

Anyhow, we stayed on Okinawa a hundred and ten days and then we got sent back. We went to Guam and that was our home base. It was a year to the day from the time we invaded Guam to the time we came back. So it was quite a celebration. You know, they had the booze out, you know everyone was there to welcome us. So we stayed there, and then I had enough time to come home. See, by then, there were just no ships going home, and then the war ended, so we were sitting there and then this one morning this guy calls me. And he's like, 'Hey, Greek, look down in the bay!'

Great big flattop [is sitting there] [*spreads arms apart*]; it was the *Bonhomme Richard* and they put us on it. [Now it was going to be used] as a ferry boat to bring the guys home, and this was the first trip it made. Jeez, they threw away airplanes and ammunition, they were throwing them over the side, you know, because the war was over! And we were running with lights on, and it was great.

We did everything by alphabetical order, so I slept in the J section, down in the hangar deck, in a square that was marked off with a white J in the middle. In the morning when I got up, I'd fold up that cot and go to another spot where there was another J and stow my gear there. So we had to do that every day, and the rest of the day, we did all kinds of stuff. We chipped paint, you know, we hung around. There wasn't much to do, and it was a long trip home because we took a long route. We got to Treasure Island, in San Francisco, and we came under the bridge, and some of those planes took off from the *Bonhomme* and flew under the bridge upside down! Anyhow we got a little liberty, and I came home and got discharged.

The Reserves

I was in the reserves, I joined the 1st Engineer Company in Albany. It was a Marine Corps engineer company, and some of the guys that I had been in the 22nd Marines with were in it [with me]. So I figured, well, we'll go play cards together and we'll drink a few beers and have some fun; we'll go to Camp Lejeune in the summertime and all this. And we did this, up until August [1950]; I forget what day it was. We were activated, they activated the unit. We marched down New Scotland Avenue [in Albany]; we had been in the Christian Brothers Academy high school rifle range there, that was our home base, and we marched from there all the way down to the train station. The mayor from Schenectady was there, and the city manager, and [Albany] Mayor Corning was there; all the dignitaries were there to see us off. And I remember every one of them, they all took turns saying, 'These men are not going overseas, they're going over there to Camp Pendleton to train those Marines that are going to go overseas.' Yeah, you believe that one, and well, I'll tell you another one.

So we got to Pendleton, and we went right into training again. So I told you before that in 1943, I went through that school at Camp Lejeune and became a field medical technician. Now, a Sergeant Crow was in charge of us. He was a good guy.

He said, 'How many of you guys went through field medical training school?' And I'm thinking to myself, I'm not going to tell him I went through it, you know, let him find that out, and I can get some more training, which I thought I should have.

We started through that stuff again, but halfway through that training, we were at the rifle range and Crow comes down and he said, 'You fall out,' and he called a couple other guys who were pulling the same thing I was. So we were told that we had to go on the next draft because we had already had that training.

He said, 'I know what you were doing,' and he said, 'That's okay,' and he agreed with us.

So anyhow, we went overseas. We got to Japan. We got kids that had snuck through; they were going to go to Christian Brothers Academy [high school], that's how young they were. I was 24, almost 25, when I got recalled, but some of these kids had never been through boot camp! All they knew was what they were taught at the [school] rifle range. Some of them snuck through; they did a pretty good job, they got most of them through boot camp, so they did get the basic training, and I'm happy for that because you had to have it. I strongly believe if you don't have that, then you don't belong out in combat.

On to Korea

So anyhow, we got to Japan, and they outfitted us out. Everybody went out and got drunk and did their thing, and then a couple of days later we were on a ship that took us to Korea. I got there November 12, 1950, and joined the Dog Medical Company. Now this is altogether a different life than I had had with the Marine Corps before.

Before, I was in a company, I was part of a group. Now I'm with a rear echelon kind of an outfit that moves in two sections. One section moves up, and then the other one moves up, and you set up a hospital. I got assigned to that and we were in this place called Chipyong-ni. We were just across from the 38th Parallel. That was after the Wonsan landing, it was a little north of the Wonsan harbor, and then the winter started coming in. And we didn't have any winter gear other than sweaters and some long underwear—stuff like that, and your greens—we didn't have any parkas or gloves, or anything like that. So they had to scrounge up stuff like that for everybody. And we got those shoepacks, they called them Italian mountain boots. They were an awful thing, they were big. If you wore a size ten shoe, or a nine, you were [now] a size twelve shoe, and it had a great big felt insole in it. So you got two pairs of insoles; one pair you kept inside your shirt, next to your body, and a pair of socks, heavy socks. The other pair was in your shoes, so when you changed, you just changed those socks. Well after about a week, you start smelling like hell. Anyhow, those things were always wet. You marched, your feet got wet, and there was no way to get them out of there. You had to dry them somehow. So you had to go through this ritual every night to dry your stuff. That's what caused most of the guys to get frostbite and get their feet screwed up. Mine are screwed up [due to diabetic complications], but they're not bad, there are a lot of guys worse off than me. You know how I feel? I can get along without [the VA doctors], really. There are guys that should be taken care of and thank God most of those guys are being taken care of. So I don't need that, I can take care of myself.

So anyhow, we started off on November 12 and we started going north, and we'd go in like two sections: I was in section one. We'd get on these trucks, on the six-by-sixes, and the tents were on there, and the 55-gallon drums of fuel oil. You know, everything you needed was in there. And you would go up and the first thing you did was put up a hospital tent. And that was 100 feet long, the first one, and then you would add to it as you go on. Then we would put up the pyramidal tents, you could put six guys in them. We put up those for the doctors and the officers, then finally we would get a chance to put our own up. And then a couple of days later the next group would come up with the remainders. Most of the tents were heated; where you had a lot of guys, you had the little tin stove. It could either run on oil or it could run on wood, or coal, or whatever you had, but it got so cold up there we were mixing gasoline with the oil and that was taboo and that was bad. A few tents burned up, but you had to do something. It was really cold up there.

The Chosen Reservoir

On November 27, 1950, Mao Zedong ordered a Chinese force of 120,000 to attack and annihilate 30,000 United Nations troops in North Korea. The surprise attack began a seventeen-day battle in subzero temperatures. A fortuitous UN breakout and withdrawal followed to the port of Hungnam, and the United Nations pulled back completely out of North Korea after inflicting heavy casualties.

We were always moving. The first group would move out and you may be at a place for a couple of days, you may be there a week. When we got up to the reservoir, up to the Chosen Reservoir, we were there a long time, I think it was maybe two weeks, I don't know. We didn't have it as bad as the guys up in there.

So our division went up there, and the 7th Marines were at Yudam-ni, which was northwest, I guess, from us. Then north from us was Hagaru-ri, and the 5th Marines were there and some of the 7th Marines, they were moving around. And some of the 1st Marines went up there, cause we traveled with the 1st Marine Regiment. So we set up at Kodari, which was, I think, twelve miles down the road from Hagaru-ri, and that's where we were. And a couple of times I went up to Hagaru-ri, me and another guy, with a jeep and a trailer because there was a water point up there. We didn't have a water point where we were, and we needed water for the chow lines. So a lot of times when you went up to Hagaru-ri, you had to stay there at night because they didn't want you on the road at night by yourself.

So we stayed, and a few nights we got hit. I think around the 27th of November, all hell broke loose, the old crap hit the fan that night. It was bad all over. And we started getting casualties and you couldn't believe it, the way they were coming in, my God! My job was, I worked outside, and when these guys would come in, we would bring them into the receiving tent and then somebody would take over from there. I didn't do any first aid to anybody there—I was just a pair of hands, and I had a gang that worked with me. Anyhow, that was my job, to unload these guys and then when they were going out, if they were leaving, I had the book. As we put a guy or two guys on a Bell & Howell helicopter, you know, the glass bubble above the skids, where you had half of a Stokes stretcher that had fabric on it to keep the guy warm, and it had a cover for it. So you put two guys on, one on each skid, and they had a little glass [window] where they could look out; they could see the rotors going around or something. But anyhow we would load these guys on, and then I would get their names, make sure that I had everything, and then they would take off.

I stayed there until we got out of the reservoir; we walked out. I don't know how far that was from where we were. It was quite a ways; we had to walk from Kodari to the railhead. What happened was the 7th Marines came from Yudam-ni to Hagaru-ri, and then they came down to Kodari, and then they started on down to go to Hungnam, the seaport, because that's where the ships were that were going to take us out. Then the 5th Marines came through us and went on down and then the 1st Marines fought the rear action on the way down. But the 5th Marines and the 7th were up on the ridges, and they kept the main supply route open so we could get out of there. Anyhow, they said, once you get down to the railhead, you can probably ride on a truck but until that time we had to walk.

It was a long walk, and it was cold; it was like twenty, thirty below zero. As long as you were moving, it didn't bother you. So by eleven o'clock at night, we get down to the railhead.

They said, 'Okay, you can get on the trucks now,' so we got on the trucks, and we started out. I don't think we went two or three miles and the truck in front of us got hit. It was carrying ammunition, so, oh boy, everything was cartwheels coming out of there, you know, all these explosives going off. So we got the hell off of the truck we were on, and it was a good thing we did, because there was 55-gallon drums of aviation fuel on that truck, and we didn't know it, but there were only three of us on the back of that truck.

Anyhow, they ambushed us, and we were lying in this ditch all night until the next morning. That's when my feet really frosted up, because my feet and my socks became wet. The next morning we got going again and we ended up down in Hungnam. They gave us something to eat and then we went aboard the ship.

Then we ended up down in Pusan. That was something, they just kept feeding us breakfast. All the time we were on that ship, all we were getting was breakfast, but it was good.

Chesty

You've heard of Chesty Puller? Well, Chesty had the 1st Marines, and he was right with us most of the time, you know. I knew who he was, you know, you would see him every day and say, 'Good morning, General,' or something, but I didn't shoot the shit with him or anything. But I was out on the strip there, where we had

TBFs or these Navy fighter bombers that would come in and they would take casualties out and I think you could get around six or eight people on them as long as they weren't stretcher cases; as long as they were ambulatory, you could stuff them in there. So we had those, we had some Piper Cubs, where you could put one guy in it, and we had the Bell helicopters that you could put two guys on. If they come in with a Sikorsky, that meant one stretcher case. You had to stick them in through one window and they stuck out the other side, and then you could have some guys go in there that were ambulatory. So anyhow, I worked for Doctor Adams, the guy who was in charge of all the moving of the patients and getting them out to the ships and stuff. This one day, we were out on the field, and he called me and there was a guy with him. So I went over, and it was Chesty Puller. Chesty said, 'Did Captain Barber go out?' So I look in the book, and I said, 'Yeah, we got him out yesterday. I put him on a Sikorsky, he was one of those guys that was jammed in.' Now we had the book and I had initialed it where I put him down, because it was important that you did those things.

So Chesty says, 'Thanks, Aspirin, now I believe it.' And I found out what had happened. He had asked Doctor Adams—of course I got the book, so Adams doesn't know. And he said, did Captain Barber go out? Adams said, 'Yeah, I think so,' and Chesty says, 'I don't care what you think, did he go out?'

The Stolen Cigars

I always had a lot of respect for Chesty. He was a good guy. I'll tell you an incident that happened one time. We had some real thieves in the medical company. Some of these corpsmen, they could get anything you wanted. They went out and they took a jeep, and they went to some Army place, and they got this big cardboard box and they brought it up to Dog Med and we opened it up, and it was full of boxes of cigars! And these were boxes of fifties, so everybody had cigars, everybody; they didn't charge anybody anything. So somehow the Army got ahold of the numbers that were on the jeep, wherever the hell they stole the cigars from.

This colonel and a couple of captains come up and they were at the 1st Marines, raising hell, and they wanted to find out who the hell stole their cigars. So Chesty didn't want to have anything to do with this kind of crap, he's sitting at his desk, with his shirt pocket full of cigars, the hot loot. I had to bring these two corpsmen, because they worked for me, I had to bring them down there, you know. So I go down and Chesty says to these two, 'Okay, I'm going to take care of everything.'

So this colonel keeps saying, 'Well, what are you going to do, are you going to take some kind of action?'

Chesty says, 'This is my command; I'm going to take the action I see fit.'

So here we are, in the asshole of the world, and he tells this Army colonel, he says, 'These men are restricted,' and that was the only punishment. But Jesus, there he is sitting with those cigars in his pocket, and he didn't smoke cigars! He would cut them up and put them in his pipe, then he would light them and smoke them that way. [*Chuckles*]

The Greek Air Force

After we got down from the Chosin, we started out again in the spring. I don't remember, it might have been around this place called Inje. I'm not sure, I lost track of where we were. Doctor Adams, the guy that I worked for, he knew I was Greek, see, and he said, 'We got the Greek Air Force coming in and they got a C-47 and they're going to come in.' Now, we don't have any communications with them, but we'll lay out panels. I had myself, and a black kid; there was an Army outfit there now and they were all blacks. And they had these very good ambulances, boy, they were better than anything we had. They had good heaters in them, and they could really hold a lot of people. So we had this black kid, and come to find out he was from Troy, New York. So he and I became friends. So we go out to the airstrip in the morning, and we lay out the panels and then we would wait there. These Greeks would come around, they would do a loop, they would fly around, and when they would see the orange panels lying out, they would land. When they made that loop, we would radio back and say, 'Okay, start moving the casualties,' because they were like twenty miles away, maybe twenty-five. So they'd start them out in those good ambulances that were well heated, and they would line up and they could take something like forty-something and put them on those C-47s.

And they were stacked in there, man, they had the straps hanging down, you know, and the stretchers would go in. Then they would take off with them.

Those Greeks would always say, 'Come with us, come with us!'

'What do you mean come on with you?'

'We are going to [a couple other places], then we end up in Japan and then we come back and do this route again.'

I said, 'Look, I'm not going with you guys. I mean, one of these days, somebody's going to come looking for me and I'm not going to be around, and then my wife's going to get a letter, 'Your Steve is gone,' or whatever.'

They finally understood, but they would bring me back a bottle of whiskey or something from Japan. They were good guys. You know what's funny about it? Most of them could speak English. They could speak English so well they had the limey accent, because that's where they were trained.

The Chinese on the Mountain

So it was a good job, I enjoyed it. But one day we got out there and it was me and the black kid and a guy named Gunther, we used to call him 'Gunny.' And somebody else, I forget who the other guy was, but we went out there and were laying our panels out and these Chinese opened up on us. They were up on the side of the hill, in the woods there. They opened up on us, there were only four or five of us out there, whatever the hell it was. Then this other guy came with a jeep, he was going to help. He gets out of the jeep, and we were trying to yell to him, but he was quite a ways away from us. And Jesus, didn't he get shot. He gets hit right in the head, aw, man, it killed him just like that.

We had already radioed back and then they sent a squad of Marines down, and they went up and they went through, and they cleaned those guys out. But that was the only time we really got harassed on the airstrip like that. Most of the time we were all right.

When we were at Kodari, we could see the Chinese up on the mountain there. Now, the only way you could see them is if they turned around and faced you, because then you would see that their faces were dark. They were wearing white parkas and their rifles were white, everything was white. And you couldn't see them, they would move around up there, and you wouldn't see them until they turned around and faced you and then you could see a dark face. And it was a game of, you know, 'Don't bother us and we won't bother you,' and that's the way it went for the longest time. But every once in a while, we would get up in the morning and there would be three or four Chinese sitting outside of our tents there at Kodari, and their feet would be huge. They were wearing those goddamn sneakers. We had trouble with the shoes we were wearing, but these guys were wearing sneakers and their feet were just frozen solid. And they were in bad shape, and they couldn't take that cold any better than we could.

I don't care what anybody says, a lot of guys would say, 'Oh, they're tougher than us or they can withstand that cold, and we can't.' You know, that's a lot of bull. I don't know. And a lot of times they would turn our prisoners loose. When the going got too rough for them, and the Marines were on hot pursuit of their butts, they would turn our guys loose; they would shag ass but leave the Marines there. And that's how we got them back, and they hadn't been too bad to them. In most cases, they were pretty good to them. They gave them rice to eat; you had to eat what they did. They would have a big sock hanging around their neck full of rice. How the hell they ate that stuff, I don't know.

Blood

In Korea, there was more whole blood [available]. In World War II, it was mostly plasma, I never saw much blood. Of course, I wasn't in the rear. We carried plasma. We carried two units; one was the dry unit, and the other was the water unit, and you had to mix them together. Luckily, I always had some Marine that would carry one of my units and I would carry the other one. We would put it together when necessary. It was tough because when a guy is wounded, all his veins, they flatten out, and it's hard to get one. The kits that they had in World War II, the needle they had, it was like an eight-penny nail, for Christ's sake, it was big. And it wasn't very sharp, and you had to stick a guy three or four times to finally get it into him. In the Korean War, I think the needles were better than what we had in World War II. But there was the whole blood, and that was a problem when it was cold, it would stiffen up. What you had to do was put mineral oil on the tygon tubing, and you would hook the guy up, and then you would have to have some guy strip it, like you're milking a cow, to push the blood through, otherwise it would congeal. I don't know, I heard some of the doctors say, 'Thank God there was this freezing,' because wounds would freeze up and there wasn't as much loss of blood as there was in World War II.

'The Chosin Few'

Anyhow, that was a hundred years ago, as far as I'm concerned. I belong to the 'Chosin Few,' and it's a lot of good guys, but there are a lot of these guys, that's all they have in life, is that [time]. I feel sorry for them, really; I mean, that's all they do. I've got one guy, he constantly calls me up [to talk about it]. And I keep thinking, 'Jesus, don't you have another life?' Two weeks out of your life was up there in the Chosin, and that's all the hell you got left?

'You Play the Hand You're Dealt'

I don't know, thank God I was not wounded. Somehow, I got through two wars without being wounded, though I did come close a few times. I think [my time in the service] put me behind quite a bit. Not so much during World War II, because I didn't have anything else to do, okay? But during the Korean War, I was married, I had a two-year-old kid. I was working for the Knolls Atomic Power Laboratory, and I went and I told them, 'Hey, my reserve unit got called and I'm going to have to go.' We were on active duty as of August 7, I guess it was. This guy, I can't remember what his name was, he's all, 'Oh, you can't go!' I was on a fire department, we had this special training, you know, because we were the first people in a situation where we might find a fire, or where there was radioactive material, you know, stuff like that. And we were being trained for all this, so we had kind of an important job to do. So this guy says, 'They can't take you.'

I said, 'Fine, one way or the other.'

Then he comes up and he says, 'You got to go.'

He said, 'I thought I could get you out of it.'

I said, 'Well, you thought wrong, Uncle Sam is thinking different.' And my attitude was, hey, I signed up for this. I was free, white, and twenty-one, and I knew what I was signing. I knew what I was getting into, and if I had to go, I had to go, and I would make the best of it.

You play the hand you're dealt.

Steve T. Jordan was 89 when he passed on May 5, 2014.

CHAPTER SIXTEEN

The Invasion Radioman III

Paul Elisha

Okinawa

We were told it was going to be a rough one. First of all, it was going to be different than any of the other islands. It was the northern Pacific. The Japanese had a long time to prepare. I personally landed with the 2nd Marine Division; we were attached to them for the landing. Some of my units went with [another] infantry division, which also landed with a pincer movement. They were landing on different parts of the island.

There, the landing was a really tough landing because, for one thing, it's a very mountainous island. The Japanese really dug in caves. They also had the heaviest artillery we'd ever come up against, 220 caliber guns, and they were on the sides of the opposite mountain. They'd shoot over the mountains at you.

Humor gets pretty dark with each passing campaign. You're making jokes, toward the end, about life and death. I can't remember any specifics, but I know of this. You know when the humor would really get going toward the end like when we were going into Okinawa, which was really a rough landing. As you'd hit the line of demarcation where the landing craft would speed up and streak for the beach, we would be down and the guys would say, 'Hey, you're got yourself soiled. You got your diapers on?' and stuff like that. Guys would josh back and forth with all kinds of black humor, so to speak. You did it because you were scared shitless, mostly. You never got over that feeling. That last dash to the beach, you do it with your heart in your mouth always because once that ramp is down, there's nowhere to go but straight ahead.

They let us come ashore, but almost immediately after landing, they opened up with everything they had. So the beach was really messy. Mortars as I recall, 220 caliber shells, and a lot of machine-gun fire. It was rough to get off the beach. We did our usual thing. We found a fairly sheltered area, dug in, set up the radio, and began sending messages back for fire support for whatever was needed. Eventually, they did get off the beach and we stayed with that.

It was a tough day, the toughest of any that I recall. I know I read one official account that said that it wasn't so bad, that they let [us] land, but it was a bad landing. They were all bad landings, but they were good if you could walk away from them.

Meeting Ernie Pyle

I was on Okinawa for, I would say, a couple of weeks. After I was there a few days and we got pulled back for rest and a hot meal, I had an interesting experience because I was also serving in a dual capacity for the unit. I had been asked to be a combat correspondent for *Yank Magazine.*

When we had gotten pulled back, I got called to the CO's office and he said, 'I'm going to need you for a couple of days.'

I said, 'What for?'

He said, 'Seems there's this guy, this reporter. What's his name, Pyle? Ernie Pyle is here. They need somebody to take him around to the different units around the island and for interviews. So, while he's on this side of the island, you're it.'

Next thing I know, they introduced me to this little guy and it's Ernie Pyle—*the* Ernie Pyle.

He was great. I spent two days with him, we got to talk a lot. Of course, I took him to some of the different outfits. We had a jeep and a driver, and he interviewed them, and as a matter of fact, I was with him when he got on the boat. You know, they sent a small party over to this small island called Ie Shima, which was just off of Okinawa. And he thought that would be an interesting thing to go on, because they told him it was just going to be a small operation. They didn't even know how many [Japanese troops there were], or if there was anybody over there. They were just a few people going to mop it up, and a sniper killed him.

Oh, he was so much like an ordinary GI. First of all, he hated being everywhere he went. He really didn't like it at all, but he did it. He did this because he had to, you know, and he rarely did it unless it was in the context of setting the stage for what he was doing. He talked to officers, but he was really the enlisted man's journalist. He talked to ordinary dog faces, you know? And they loved him for it because he told it like it was. [He was a good reporter] basically because he got all the facts straight. He did not accept handouts from the brass. He would talk only to the enlisted people, very rarely talked to some brass; there had to be people with them, the enlisted people. He got the unvarnished facts from the GIs. He also knew how to find the human interest in every story, but I literally was one of the people that sort of walked with him down [to them]. They were loading up to go to Ie Shima, which was going to be a clean-up operation, just a couple of patrols really and he went with them. I helped put his gear aboard the landing craft. That's the last I saw of him.

*

I remember one of the treks when I was taking him from one place to another. We got to talking, and he asked, 'What are you going to do when you get out of here?' You know, when this is over.

I said, 'I don't know, I'll probably go on with my writing and stuff.'

He said, 'Check out Indiana University. Great school', he said, 'it's really good.'

Well, as it turned out, when I got out of the service, I sent four letters of application: one to Northwestern, one to the University of Kentucky, one to NYU, and one to Indiana. And they accepted me, Indiana accepted me, so I ended up there. I was the first recipient of the Sigma Delta Chi Ernie Pyle Memorial Award for reporting at IU. I sat at his desk at the Indiana University *Daily Student* in my senior year. And so there's an eerie connection that I have with Ernie Pyle.

*

We idolized [FDR]. I was on Okinawa when Roosevelt died. By the way, that was a strange situation because it's just about—I'm trying to remember the juxtaposition, I can't remember if it was just before or just after, but Simon Bolivar Buckner Jr., the [Commander] of the Tenth Army, the general who ran that operation in Okinawa, was killed on Okinawa... And so that was an eerie feeling, and for me even more so... [because] you had Buckner, Roosevelt, and Ernie Pyle.[66] It was almost as if everyone died all at once. Great grief. I witnessed men openly crying, and for us, especially in the 75th JASCO, we were particularly moved because while we were in Hawaii, before we went off between the Makin and Kwajalein assaults, Roosevelt came to Hawaii to meet with MacArthur and

---

[66] *Buckner, Roosevelt, and Ernie Pyle*-FDR died on April 12. Ernie Pyle was killed by a sniper on April 18. Buckner was killed on June 18 when a Japanese artillery shell landed nearby, and fragments struck him in the chest.

Nimitz, and one of the things that occurred there was that we were the honor guard.⁶⁷ We were chosen as the honor guard, and they did a special thing where his open car was pulled up for a review, and we were the honor guard for that, and he gave us a presidential unit citation for what we had done up to that point, and it's one of the medals I never collected.

GI Reporter

If you were a GI and you were a reporter, it wasn't like being a [civilian] correspondent like those other people were. You still have to do what you have to do, and as a matter of fact, some of the officers looked on it as, you know, you're looking to get something extra special. 'You, who do you think you are?' You know, that sort of thing. I got a byline and I still somewhere have my letter of commendation when it was over saying, 'you guys have done a great job and we thank you for it' and et cetera.

We were censored. We had received a set of instructions on how-to, you know, what not to write, and you were supposed to follow them. We pretty much did. You know, we weren't out to scoop the US Army in those days and there were some differences, really strong differences compared to what would come later. Let's say [as opposed to] Vietnam and those wars, everybody really believed in this, in that war, and you didn't want to do anything to foul it up. You know, you did what you had to do. And I think that,

---

⁶⁷ *Roosevelt came to Hawaii to meet with MacArthur and Nimitz-* Pacific Strategy Conference, July 1944. Admiral Leahy and General MacArthur were also present. "MacArthur decided to upstage Roosevelt by arriving in a long open limousine with elaborate motorcycle escort, accepting the welcome from the cheering crowd. Even before he arrived at Hawaii, he was already unhappy for being forced to leave his troops to attend this 'picture-taking junket,' as he commented." Source: Pacific Strategy Conference, World War II Database, ww2db.com/battle_spec.php?battle_id=75.

even among correspondents, that was pretty much the rule. I got to meet some of them, but, you know, they're very hazy right now. You have to understand that there wasn't a great deal to see. This was the thing with Ernie Pyle. He sought out enlisted men to talk to; the average war correspondent during WWII went with the brass, they got their briefings on things. They weren't allowed that close to the action, really. I would say D-Day was probably the most participatory action they got into.

[As a reporter for *Yank*] we weren't able to tell anything ahead of time, but after the fact, you could write it up. You could interview people, you could write up events that took place in any of the campaigns you were on, and then you would submit them, of course, to the *Yank* people, who would run them through the censor. Then they'd end up in *Yank Magazine*. It was like *Stars and Stripes*, except instead of a newspaper, it was a magazine format. I enjoyed it because it gave me a chance to write. I did it until I went home.

Pushing the Odds

The Japanese soldier was tough as nails. Committed, literally committed. The only time I recall seeing any prisoners at all was after Kwajalein, I think there were five or six that were taken, and that's because they were wounded and hadn't the resources to kill themselves. Everywhere else they would fight until they were beaten and then they would die. On Okinawa, for instance, when we finally isolated them at the far end of the island, we had bullhorns and translators who tried to tell them. By the way, in Okinawa, there were also Japanese civilians who were sent there to colonize the place and they were with the troops. We tried to coax them to give themselves up. Some of them killed themselves with hand grenades and others went to a cliff at the end of the island and just jumped down on the rocks and were killed. Mothers with little children in their arms did that. So they were really committed people.

*

We were pretty lucky; I'd say we had about somewhere between thirty and forty percent casualties, but many of those I found out later; you'd see a guy taken away and you wouldn't know what became of him. I later found out that not as many were fatal as many other units were. We were lucky. By rights, if you look at the odds, going into that many landings, we had had eight combat landings, and a number of us like myself were literally in the first wave of every landing. We would talk about it. The last couple I remember we were saying, 'You know, if we come out of this one, it's a miracle,' because we were pushing the odds.

Mr. Elisha's story will continue in the final section.

PART FIVE

FINAL THOUGHTS

"I think that a commander is faced with a decision of what must be done at that given moment to achieve an objective and end that battle or that war. You cannot expect him to think, 'Well, we're going to kill all those people,' when he's looking at his own people being killed at the same time. I mean, what's a good killing, and what's a bad killing?

We should have thought of all that before we began at all."

—US Army Radioman, World War II

CHAPTER SEVENTEEN

Occupation Duty

We are gathered here, representatives of the major warring powers, to conclude a solemn agreement whereby peace may be restored.

The issues involving divergent ideals and ideologies have been determined on the battlefields of the world, and hence are not for our discussion or debate.

Nor is it for us here to meet, representing as we do a majority of the peoples of the earth, in a spirit of distrust, malice, or hatred.

But rather it is for us, both victors and vanquished, to rise to that higher dignity which alone befits the sacred purposes we are about to serve, committing all of our peoples unreservedly to faithful compliance with the undertakings they are here formally to assume.

It is my earnest hope, and indeed the hope of all mankind, that from this solemn occasion a better world shall emerge out of the blood and carnage of the past—a world founded upon faith and understanding, a world dedicated to the dignity of man and the fulfillment of his most cherished wish for freedom, tolerance, and justice.

—REMARKS BY GENERAL DOUGLAS MACARTHUR, SURRENDER CEREMONY

On September 2, 1945, Admiral "Bull" Halsey's flagship *USS Missouri* was in Tokyo Bay awaiting the arrival of the Japanese delegation with General MacArthur and Admiral Nimitz aboard, positioned in the exact spot where Commodore Matthew C. Perry had anchored on his first visit to Japan in 1853, and flying his original 31-star flag. The Japanese delegation was escorted promptly aboard at 9:00 a.m. and at MacArthur's invitation, signed the terms of surrender. In the United States and Europe, it was six years to the day that the bloodiest conflict in human history had begun.

Mitchell Morse was just fifteen years of age when the United States declared war on Japan. He enlisted in the spring of 1944, after an earlier admission into the Army Specialized Training Reserve Program, which he did not like. Still, he found himself an officer in Japan just as the fighting ended, as part of the Army of Occupation. A free spirit, he relates his experiences commanding an all-Black detachment, the racism his soldiers encountered, and his opinion of the now-conquered people of Japan, including a tearful reunion four decades later with the Japanese teenager who served him as a houseboy.

Mitchell Morse

I was born March 10, 1926, in the infamous place, Brooklyn, New York. I was with a friend in Brooklyn [when I heard about

Pearl Harbor]. We both used to breed tropical fish, and we were waiting on one of his fancy guppies to give birth. And we were sitting looking into his fish tank when we heard it come over the radio; it seemed like total insanity to me. Totally unexpected and a real shocker.

I was in college at the time, at age fifteen. I went into the Army Specialized Training Reserve Program, and I spent three months in Princeton. I had a lousy record there since it was mostly science, which was not my bag. And from there I went into basic training on April 9, 1944, at Fort Bragg, North Carolina.

It was pretty awful. Aside from the physical rigors, which I was not used to, I couldn't get used to the attitude southerners had towards anybody who was not from the South. And my biggest shock was when one of the guys who I was taking basic training with, apparently, he had owned a dry-cleaning store, and he enthusiastically told us the great joy he had when some black guy came in and wanted to know where his clothing was, and it wasn't ready. And the man said something about it, and he took such a great pleasure in physically throwing him out. And then, going into bus stations, and seeing the isolated restrooms. And the way it was, just quite a culture shock for somebody from New York.

During basic, I decided it was much better to be an officer than an enlisted man, so I applied for OCS. Before that, the government had started a new program whereby they were taking ten people from throughout the services, all over the country, into West Point, directly, without the usual senatorial approval and recommendations and so on. I applied for that. I figured that's even better, four years in college, by then the war will be over, and I'll spend a couple of extra years in the Army and be on my way.

Training to be an Officer

Well, I almost got through to it; I was narrowed down to the last handful in Fort Bragg, and then, probably because I was a smartass in those days, I was not accepted. So the next best thing was to get to be an officer another way. So I applied for OCS and was accepted; I went to Fort Benning, Georgia, Benning School for Boys. That was tough physically, very rigorous; I think I was eighteen at the time. Most of the guys had been in the Army for some time. A lot of them had been in combat overseas as enlisted men, then came back to try to get a commission. I was, if not the youngest, one of the youngest in the entire class. We started the class with 300 and graduated with a class of 150.

[The training was] exceptional. The physical training was excellent, and whatever training you can get for leadership was excellent too, although I don't think that's something you can [really] train somebody for—either it's within or it's not.

I spent a year in Camp Gordon, Georgia. That was a lot of hard work, but that turned out to be fun; I enjoyed that a great deal. Giving classes in hand-to-hand combat, I weighed about 135 pounds and one of my good buddies was 6' 3", much larger. He used to attack me from the rear with a knife and I would flip [him] in moving my shoulder, much to the surprise of all the trainees, and much to my surprise as well. I used to take a particular delight [in that].

'An Education Beyond Belief'

[After that training], the war was still on in the Far East and the islands, and I received orders to go overseas to fight in these various godawful island battles. I got to Fort Ord in California, and they give you a last-minute physical inspection before you ship. I'd had my shipping orders already, but they discovered I had a hernia, maybe from carrying a footlocker in one hand and a duffle bag over the other, whatever the reason was. So they pulled me out, stuck me in the hospital, operated on me, and by the time I was out of the hospital, the war was over.

Instead of going into combat, I spent about ten or eleven months in Japan [as part of the occupation force]. That was an experience, an education beyond belief. First of all, to discover that the Japanese were not the horrible people, that the everyday man in the street was not the horrible person we were trained to believe. We went over there, obviously, 'to civilize them.' That's what we were trained to do, to go over there and teach them what the world was all about. But the average Japanese [person] was a very kind, gentle soul. And I liked most of them, and I had a very close feeling for the country at large and the culture at large. Being a believer in reincarnation, I kind of figured well, maybe I'd been here in a previous lifetime.

I was a second lieutenant. I didn't get to be first lieutenant until they kicked me out of the Army, well, not kicked me out, but finally got out of the Army.[68] I never got promoted while I was in Japan because I was a bit of a cut-up, so when I was due to be promoted, the colonel and I didn't get along too well, so he always passed me by.

'They Thought I was Sent from Heaven'

At first, I was a company commander of an infantry platoon in the 34th Regiment of the 24th Infantry Division. And being where we were, in order to facilitate the cleaning of the men's clothes, there was a Quartermaster Mobile Laundry Detachment which used to service the entire regiment, clean the clothes and so on.

---

[68] *got out of the Army*- Mr. Morse served in the Army Reserve until 1983.

Well, the lieutenant in charge of the quartermaster detachment had to go home on emergency furlough. His mother was in a hospital, severely ill, so they needed somebody to take over temporarily. Being in the infantry, hearing 'quartermaster,' I immediately volunteered, and being the most recent arrival to the regiment, I was put in charge. I stayed right on the same base, and I was put in charge. And the name of this, to give you an idea of the time, was the "354th Quartermaster Mobile Laundry Detachment 'parentheses' Colored". That was part of the official designation. So here I was, commanding officer of a laundry detachment with all black guys, I guess, no, I don't know what you'd say nowadays. In those days it was 'Colored,' now it's 'Black' or 'Afro-American.' In any event, I had this crew with whom I got along famously; I used to play poker with them. Officers had a liquor ration, and I got a certain amount of beer and a bottle of booze every once in a while, which I gave to my guys, because I didn't drink, so they thought I was sent from heaven. [*Laughs*] Used to shoot craps with them too. I forgot all the terminology but some of the [craps vernacular] was just great, for when you 'speak to the dice.' That was an experience unto itself, a total education.

When they were by themselves doing their job, [morale was] terrific, but we were attached to a Southern regiment. And we used to get monthly rations, so many candy bars, so many cans of beer, so many soap, this and that. And when the rations came in, everybody would get in a long line; it would snake tail all the way out. I forget who was in charge of the PX, some major from down South. And no matter how long the line was, how early they got there, he always made my guys get at the end of the line. So if there were a hundred of my guys there, and they got on a line, then another hundred [white soldiers] came, [this major would] make my guys get to the very tail end of the line. It reached the point to where I got into a fist fight with him over this. Which you're not supposed to do with [your superior officer], I hate to use the term 'superior officer,' he was [downright] inferior; he just happened to be a higher-ranking officer.

Of course, my guys then felt like I was family. 'Hey, Lieutenant, do you want us to get him for you?' You know, they'd have left him lying somewhere; nobody had ever fought their battles for them before. So their morale was pretty good. As I said before, I gave them my liquor ration and beer ration, whatever it was, used to play poker with them.

The Japanese Houseboy

I was nineteen at the time, and I acquired my Japanese houseboy, Yukihiro Miada. He was sixteen, I was nineteen, but I was the big honcho. He drove me crazy, though. He'd shine my shoes, he'd hold my shirt while I dressed, and I almost dropped him a couple of times because when I got out of the shower, he insisted upon toweling me down. This was just too much, I couldn't stand it. But he was absolutely adamant about it.

During that period of time, a good buddy of mine who was still with the infantry regiment I had been with, he and I were at a track meet at a nearby town, meeting with another regimental track team. We arrived there by train, and in the train station there were a number of Japanese war orphans, just sort of living in the station, waifs with distended stomachs from not eating enough, and so on. So when we arrived, all we had with us was some chewing gum and candy, which we gave to these little boys. Two days later, we came back, and there they were, chewing on the same chewing gum. So, through an interpreter, we found out that they had no parents, that they were lost during the war, so we took [two little boys] back with us, and they lived with us for many months until we both came back to the States.

When we got them, they were all scruffy with distended stomachs, and then we fattened them up, had little suits made for them by the local tailor, and they lived with us for a while. That was an exciting experience. And Miada San, we gave him the nickname of Jacko. Jacko not only took care of me, but he also took care of the two little boys. So that was an experience unto itself.

An Extended Stay

Under the point system then you got rotated based on the number of points. About a month or two before I was supposed to come home, the colonel in charge of the regiment called me up and said, 'Morse, you're short on training officers, I want you to train [more guys].'

I said, 'I'm sorry, Colonel, can't do that, I'm responsible for $500,000 worth of equipment,' and I gave them all the excuses why I couldn't do it. Well, there had been a Seabee outfit not too far away, and when they were disbanded and all went home, they left a lot of vehicles around. So I picked up a jeep, and the motor pool, painted it OD for me, and put 354th Quartermaster Mobile Laundry Detachment [logo] on it. So I had my own vehicle, but all of a sudden that jeep, which I had acquired several months before, [became a problem]. The colonel was going to bring me up on court-martial charges for stealing a jeep, which I'd been using for months and months; it was common knowledge. And with officers, it's a general court-martial, so it's serious stuff. So, I had my choice of a general court-martial or spending thirty days confined to officers' quarters or barracks; the thirty days went past the time I was supposed to come home. So I had to stay there an extra three weeks because he was going to teach me a lesson, which he did.

Transitioning to Home

Anyhow, I'd already registered to go back [to school], because I had finished two years of college before I enlisted. I was one of those precocious kids, I got into college at 15. So by the time I enlisted, just before I was eighteen, I'd finished two years of college. So when I went back, I got discharged in Fort Dix. I went back to school because of the two years before, I accumulated enough credits for one more year while having gotten the credits from Princeton University and then for OCS and they gave you credits for various things. So I only had one year and an extra course to go to graduate, which I did. And I got a job and married a year later at the age of 21, married to the same beautiful lady who came in [today] with me. That was fifty-three years ago. So, at the age of 21, I had been working for a year, and graduated from college and spent 33 months in the Army. So, it was a very busy youth that I spent, very productive.

When I started out in college, I was majoring in accounting. Which, for me, was kind of strange, but in those days, you majored in what you thought you could make a living at. So after much discussion with my parents, we decided, well, accountants always make a living; even during the Depression, accountants made a living. So I started out majoring in accounting. While I was in the Army, I realized that was not for me. So I went back to school, I switched to foreign trade, graduating with a BBA, bachelor of business administration, majoring in foreign trade. I got a job with an import-export company, spent six years with this company and somewhere along the way decided that was not the way I wanted to spend the rest of my life, either.

Then I had this revolutionary idea, revolutionary for a Depression baby. What would you like to do? Well, what I'd like to do is be a sculptor. Yeah, but you're not good enough to make a living being a sculptor. Well, what's next? A painter? No, you're not good enough to be a painter. So I did the next best thing. I decided if I couldn't sell my own paintings and sculptures, I'd try to sell somebody else's.

In 1953, I started the first traveling art gallery in the United States on wheels. I bought a brand-new station wagon—it was a Chevy, three thousand bucks—and I went around to the different artists in Greenwich Village and I got art on consignment. [At that time], after the war, there was a lot of construction going on all over Long Island, nearby Connecticut, nearby New Jersey, so I made flyers on a mimeograph machine and I went around myself to all these new developments, and on foot I stuck a flyer in every mailbox. I would get calls from people, and I would go to the house, and assuming for your house you needed a painting in the living room, I'd run in and out 10-20 times, holding paintings up over the sofa until you saw something you liked. Through this, I got recommendations, now I picked up a couple of interior designer accounts. Now I was steady with repeat business; by this time the station wagon was so full you could barely see out the back, and we had two infants only eighteen months apart. We'd drive around, Ellie was next to me, I'd be driving, she'd be in the front seat, and we took the two kids with us with all these racks of paintings bouncing around; once we stopped for a traffic light, and things kept sliding over the top, and hit one of us in the back of the head.

We started getting worried about the kids in the car so we said, 'Well, it's time, we're gonna have to plant roots somewhere,' so we picked what we considered to be an affluent town where I'd done a lot of business, a general area where we opened up a retail shop [specializing in what] was called 'wall décor,' all kinds of things for [the home, and it all grew from then on].

'From Smart-Ass Boy to A Man'

[My World War II experience] turned me from a smart-ass boy into a man. It was miserable, and it was horribly rotten, but very beneficial. It was very positive, absolutely. Japanese people are different, and I have the same opinion today—the average Japanese, the man on the street, is a kind, gentle, considerate soul, but it's the upper echelon corruption there that makes everyone here seem like they're amateurs. In Japan, everything is, you know, one hand washes the other, and they take care of each other, and the average person has no say, but they keep voting for the same political group for over fifty years now. Everything is done for the protection of the entrepreneur, the big businessman, and that's why it's been so difficult for our companies and European companies to open anything up over there; they place so many restrictions, so many barriers, that it makes it impossible.

Reunion

Forty-one years [after the war], my daughter became a member of what the Japanese call the JET program, Japanese-English Teachers. She had been teaching English as a second language in Manhattan, in the World Trade Towers. And she found out about this opportunity to go over there. They were recruiting teachers from all over the world, but they wanted native-speaking English, so that the children could learn the vernacular—not just the stiff formal textbook English—which most of the teachers taught and spoke themselves. They got them from the United States, England, New Zealand, Australia, all the English-speaking countries. So she'd been over there about a year at the time when we decided to go over and visit.

We were touring here and there, and I arranged the schedule so we could go to the old town where I had been when Jacko was my houseboy. And I remembered his address from then, because for several years after I came back, we had corresponded, though of course with time we lost track of one another. I remembered that and I still remember the address to this day, 569 Yushiro [Street]. So we took a detour to Himeji, and we had a Japanese interpreter. We went to the town hall to try to find him, a really remote possibility.

[The dwelling at] 569 Yushiro Street had burnt to the ground years ago, and now there was a gasoline station there. But the people at the home office in Himeji were incredible. The chief of the whole village hall, the town clerk or whatever he was, he had three people going through all the old records. They tracked down everybody who had lived on that block at that time, called them all up, and served us tea in between, fussed all over us. About two hours later, one of them located where Jacko's brother lived. He gave us the phone number. We left there and we were really excited about the possibility of finding him, but we couldn't get through to the brother for some time. I don't know, the family must have been out working.

Finally, late in the day, about three, four o'clock, we got through, using the interpreter, of course. We spoke to Jacko's sister-in-law and got his telephone number. Hurray, my God, it looks like we're getting close to finding him, forty-two years later. So, we left a message with his sister-in-law [giving her] the hotel we were staying at, which I think was in Osaka, and to please call us there; I had to leave the following morning, and I didn't want to be this close without seeing him! We don't hear from him all afternoon. Then, lo and behold, we're in our room getting dressed to go down and have dinner, and the phone rings; he called up! I'm jumping up and down with joy; I get all teary just thinking about it. It turns out he was downstairs in the lobby, with his wife. [*Gets emotional, asks for the camera to be turned off momentarily so he can compose himself*]

So, we went downstairs and had a fantastic reunion, we had dinner together, and his English, although not perfect, was excellent. And he had been from—I found out later on—a well-established family. His father had been a Japanese military officer. His older brother had gone to the military academy and Jacko had been destined to go to the military academy, but the war ended, and he ended up with me instead.

After that, we were in touch with him on a regular basis, and a year later, my daughter married a Japanese high school English teacher. And if anybody would have told me when I was there earlier that I would have a Japanese son-in-law, and two Japanese grandchildren, I'd have had them committed in a straitjacket. Remember I went over there to 'civilize' those people, me and everybody else [in the Army of Occupation].

Jacko came to the wedding; he was part of our side of the family. I don't know if you know it, but Japanese weddings, even if they have 500 people, for the actual ceremony, there are only fifteen people from each side of the family, maximum of thirty people, no matter how many people are waiting outside. So Ellie and I were there, my son was there, a Japanese art dealer friend with whom I was doing business with in New York. Jacko was there with his daughter and wife, from our side of the family. We went back the following year, for the birth of our first grandson, and Jacko was there again, bouncing my grandson on his knee, and like an uncle, perhaps. So that story had a very happy ending.

Of course, ever since then, we've been going back. See, in the past twelve years, we've been there about sixteen times. Totally unexpected, as I say, when I was there, and if anybody would have suggested the possibility to me, of what would have happened years later, I would have had myself or them committed.

CHAPTER EIGHTEEN

The Invasion Radioman IV

Paul Elisha

After Okinawa, we went back to Luzon, which is actually outside of Manila. They put us in a tent encampment there and we were waiting for orders. And as a matter of fact, we had begun map readings, so we were restricted to the encampment. They covered this with barbed wire and sent MPs to guard the area. Well, once you started looking at the maps of the next place you were going to go, that became sensitive. Literally, I remember the day that they dropped the bomb on Hiroshima. We were reading maps of Tokyo Harbor when the bomb was dropped.

We knew—the word went like wildfire, you know. But particularly for us, we were again going to be in the first wave to land and we were going to be the communications people for that landing. We would have gone right into Tokyo Harbor; we began to get orientation for what would have been the landing on Japanese soil itself. I don't think many of us would have come back from that.

*

[We had known the war was winding down]. You hear reports, you know it. For instance, we knew VE Day came when we were up to our eyeballs in battle on Okinawa. In some ways, you get more apprehensive because you're this close to what you think could be the end, and what you say is, 'Shit, if I get it now...' That's really miserable. It's a funny thing. I've thought about this, and I have no idea what it's like now in combat. But one of the things I can never remember is the people I was with not doing 150% of the job they were sent there to do on every single operation. I mean, you would go beyond. You would rack your brain on how to get it done better, how to do it better. For me, I have to say this, as you can tell I have a great affection for the man who was the sergeant of my unit. He said an interesting thing. I don't know how he got this wisdom because he'd never been in combat before. He'd been in the service because he was a National Guardsman who got mobilized.

He said, 'Look, Elisha. Let me tell you something. You keep your mind on what the job we got to get done here is and that'll get you through. Don't think about all the other stuff, what might happen. This is what's got to happen. Stick with me.' He was hell for leather, by the way. He got rid of his carbine, he got himself a Thompson submachine gun which he always carried into battle. He was always in the thick of where the fighting was, and I was like within a foot of him at all times. After a while, there are like, what would you call it, talismans? For some reason, he was my immortal sergeant. My talisman. I felt as long as I stuck with Elmer, I'd make it back. Now, we both made it back, but what I would do largely, at the moment of greatest fear, is to concentrate on the job having to be done, and it worked.

[Our biggest motivation in combat] was getting it over with. The other thing our lieutenant used to say was, 'Just remember, the quicker we get these guys out of here, the quicker we beat them and take this place, the quicker we can go home.' He would say that before every landing. If you kept that in mind, that was your motivation.

[You depended on your buddies a lot.] We worked in teams, always. At night, especially in the initial stages of the campaign, we would set up our perimeters and they were all foxholes. Either you were singly very close together or you were two people and two people and two people. So, you've learned to work together. The other thing was on most of the ones in Attu, Kiska, Makin, Kwajalein, and Aitape. When we landed, the first couple of nights silence was the rule and you did not use your weapon. The order was, 'You do not use your weapon unless you absolutely must as a last resort.' You had a knife which you were to use, or you were to use the butt of the weapon, but you didn't shoot because that could set off a whole bunch of stuff and nobody would know where anybody was. Anyway, so not being able to use conventional methods, you had to rely on all sorts of things, which meant you relied on each other, whatever signals you set up, whatever code you set up.

'The Style of the Times'

In my unit, I was one of four people who were Jewish. There were guys that I literally went through hell with. We would share foxholes, we would repel banzai charges together. When it was all over, they call me 'Jew boy.' Oh, yeah. 'Hey, Jew boy. You're going to town tonight?' It was discrimination, tinged with some camaraderie. But for instance, after Okinawa, I can remember back when we went back to the Philippines, and we were waiting to see if we were going to go to Japan or not. We were in a big tent, and I can remember a poker game started. One of the staff sergeants by the name of Noyer, who was one of the Jews with me, was in that poker game and they began to talk about going home and getting civilian clothes. One of them said, 'We'll go to one of those sheeny shops in Brooklyn,' because Noyer was from Brooklyn, 'and see if we can get a good deal, jew him down on a suit of clothes.' Then they began talking about different experiences of how they were gypped by Jews. A fight broke out in which I was a party, and there were like two or three of us against twenty. My sergeant, Elmer Kaminski, came in and knocked some heads together and told them off, in effect saying, 'These guys saved your ass not too long ago! What the hell's the matter with you assholes?'

Those things did happen. By the way, we had with us two Navajo Indian radio operators also. Code talkers. They were great. They would talk back and forth in their language. So that way, we knew that we weren't going to be intercepted. I got to know one of them pretty well largely because several times, I helped him home when we were still in the States and when we were in Hawaii. We used to help each other a lot that way. If somebody had a little too much to drink or something, we'd see that they all got home okay. They were both called 'Chief,' naturally. One of them was fairly garrulous and he got along fairly well. But you know, it was the same kind of bigoted camaraderie that I had to put up with. 'Damn Indians, can never hold your liquor,' and stuff like that. 'Dumb Indian.' Things of that sort went on. Thinking about it now, we had some Polish guys that they call 'polacks' and 'square heads.' But you know what? These things went on between groups in the whole outfit. It was almost like a style of the times; these were the times, let's put it that way. There were those times, but then there were other times when the hell was so hellish, you shared it, and religion, [race], had nothing to do with it anymore.

Home

We were put aboard ship. Well, by the time we got aboard the ship, we were waiting to hear. They use the points system. Of course, we had been in so many combat landings. Our officers told us we'd get back among the first and we did. I think I forget how many points you needed but I had like 141 points or something like that.⁶⁹ So then they took us down to the harbor. They put us aboard the ship, we went blackout and in convoy from Manila to Hawaii. At Honolulu, they put us aboard a ship that had been a cruise ship. It had lights strung from stern to bow and all the lights aboard went up, and we went from Honolulu to San Francisco.

[Arriving in San Francisco], I remember we went ashore, and we met a cab driver. We were taken to an area where they said, 'You're going to be here for a few days,' and they gave us passes, clean uniforms, got us all our combat ribbons and we went into town. I remember the cab driver at the gate at the Presidio, one of us said, 'We got to get some money. We haven't been paid.' The cab driver said, 'Are you kidding? You guys won't be able to buy a drink.'

He was right. That city was wide open waiting for us. I remember I wanted to sit at a table because we had eaten so much on the ground and out of cans. I wanted to sit at a table. I remember I wanted to sit at a bar and order a drink and look around. So all the way across the Pacific we kept saying, 'When I get back, I'm going

---

⁶⁹ *Adjusted Service Rating Score point system*-Witnessing the frustration incumbent with the Army's failed demobilization efforts at the end of World War I (where entire divisions were sent home at once, rather than individuals based on merit/time served) as General Pershing's Chief of Staff, General George C. Marshall ordered up a study for a more objective, timely methodology for getting the troops home in late 1943. It called for the following:
One point for each month of Army service
One point for each month in service abroad
Five points for each campaign
Five points for a medal for merit/valor
Five points for a Purple Heart
Twelve points for each dependent child (up to three)
Source: Bamford, Tyler. *The Points Were All That Mattered: The US Army's Demobilization After World War II.* National WWII Museum, August 27, 2020. www.nationalww2museum.org/war/articles/points-system-us-armys-demobilization

to the Top of the Mark and have a drink in the bar.' And we did. We went to the end of this bar, and it was just gorgeous.

Then they took us to the outside of LA by truck after a few days. We waited there a week and you'd wait for your number to come up. We were near an airfield and what they were doing was, they had a bunch of old C-47s with bucket seats. As Air Force guys were being mustered out, they give them a plane to fly back to the East Coast. They load forty guys aboard. That's how they sent you back. We went back to New York that way. By the way, it took 21 hours on a C-47. We went from LA to Denver to Kansas City to New York.

Believe it or not, I was with several other guys who got mustered out on the same day. We were from the same unit and one of them was from Brooklyn, the other one was from Rochester, New York. They said, 'Hell, we're not going home right away. We're going to New York City and tie one on!' So I joined them and actually went to New York City for two days and had a ball and then we went our separate ways. I went home to Asbury Park, New Jersey.

Adjusting to Civilian Life

Separation, for me, was kind of hard. There was a bond that took place, and, you know, you thought that you were suddenly in a different world.

I called my parents. I told my father I had a stop to make first. Didn't quite tell him where, [but it was to celebrate with my buddies in New York]; I told him when I'd be home. By the time I got home, there was a huge party, get-together in my hometown, and that was it.

I had trouble with my mother who didn't understand who I was yet, who thought it would be just like the day before I went away. There was some difficulty there. Well, they wouldn't leave you alone and they wouldn't allow—they didn't realize that you had a [different] life for three years, making literally life-and-death decisions. And now, you didn't want anybody to tell you where to go, and what to do, when to do it, when not to do it, and everything else. They were just being who they were, but she didn't realize that I'd gone far beyond that.

My father realized this because he had been in combat in World War I. He pretty much left me alone. He took me out for a drink a couple of times. Just the two of us, man to man. So I had difficulty with my mother, and with many civilians who didn't understand. I got in big trouble with a cousin of mine. I still remember, he gave a party in New York City, which I went to. I haven't even bought a civilian suit yet. I had my ruptured duck insignia on. And there was this guy who had been a 4-F, a lawyer. Here was this apartment down at University Place in New York and jammed with people. Great cocktail party.

This guy came up to me and looked at all the ribbons and everything and he says, 'I guess you had a pretty rough time, didn't you?'

I said, 'Well, yeah.' Like this, I didn't really want to talk to anybody about it.

He said, 'Why do you think you had it rough? You know, we couldn't get a can of Bumblebee salmon for three years.'

Something just hit me, and I came up from the floor, literally. I decked him. Of course, he was a good friend of my cousin. Everybody sort of looked and said, 'See, that's what they're coming back like.'

I could see these people talking. 'Look at him. Look at him.'

I left the party. I went a few doors down the block to where there was a bar and saw a couple of GIs in there. I went in like, you know, to be at home.

I still remember I embarrassed my father terribly. I lived in the small town of Bradley Beach, about a mile from Asbury Park. My father was in a store there where he worked. I came to have lunch with him, and we were coming out of this store to go across to a luncheonette. Then just about that time, a car backfired, and I did a full splat right down like that. In the middle of the street. It was a reflex. I heard this *Bam!* and I just went down. I hit the dirt and he looked around.

'What the hell's the matter with you like that?'

'What do you mean what the hell's the matter with me?' I was embarrassed as hell but...

I had gotten out in September, joined what they call the 52-20 Club, [began to] get my bearings, and began writing letters to colleges. Then by January, I'd gotten an acceptance to Indiana University. I went out there for the January term. I graduated from IU in August of '48 on the GI Bill, and I worked on the side as a tutor and did odd jobs or whatever to help. You got 75 bucks a month. You know? And I got to sit at Ernie Pyle's desk at the Indiana *Daily Student* in my senior year. The Sigma Delta Chi was giving a prize and they decided to name it the Ernie Pyle Memorial Prize, and I was the first winner. So now you know it was just good to be back to see it all. You know that you had a feeling, that's what you were fighting for. You get back and just enjoy it all.

'I'm Not Going to Be A Part of It'

I found out that it was not easy to be a working musician in New York. So I took a job in a newspaper on Long Island, and then a friend of mine said, 'You were in the Signal Corps; you're a writer.' They're looking for people from Fort Monmouth, and I became a civilian public information officer attached to the signal school in 1950 at Fort Monmouth. I stayed for four years. I was there during the McCarthy-Army fiasco. That, in some ways, bothered me more than the war did. Well, I had pride during the war. [Now], I sat in a lot of strategy sessions, where, you know, I said, 'Well, what are we going to do now?' [The feeling was], you know, 'Let's man the guns. Let's go to work on this,' and I don't know, 'We have to cooperate in every way.' You felt like you were helping him ferret out all these Reds, but there weren't any, you know, not really. They never brought anybody to trial or anything like that. They ruined a lot of lives, and [McCarthy came here] with Roy Cohn and held a lot of public meetings and [went around to] high schools around Fort Monmouth with everything but the 'Sieg Heil' afterward, you know, and I was really upset about it. And finally, I went in to see the CO of the unit. I was with the Reserve Officers Training School. That was my public information job, and I said, 'You know, I can't handle this. I just can't be a part of it."

He said, 'Well, our hands are tied, there's nothing we can do.'

So I tendered a letter of resignation. My parents were beside themselves because they thought it would seem as if I had resigned at the time that it would look like I had been one of those ferreted out, so I said, 'No, I'm not going to be part of it.' I went in, I got a letter of commendation going out. No repercussions, ever. I had done too much good work. [*Chuckles*]

Lessons of War

I don't think there was a person in my unit who would have argued with [Truman's decision]. You know? I have always believed, along with Harry Truman, that in many ways, he felt that he was saving more lives than were expended. And if, in a war of that kind, you had to choose between whose lives you were going to save, you would choose your own. The other thing is, if you think about it, the Japanese started that war. We didn't go attack Tokyo, they attacked us. I don't feel glad about the death of anyone, whether they be Japanese or German or anyone else. I think that war is senseless and death by war is probably the worst possible kind of death for anyone, and we should look for every way we can to keep it from happening.

[Today], I have a great sense about it, and I know all the arguments about us. What we did to Dresden, for instance, and the fire bombings and what we did to Hiroshima and the other Japanese city, Nagasaki. But wartime, once the war has begun, I think splitting hairs over so-called ethical questions is an exercise in futility. Largely because we didn't start the war. Nobody talked about ethics when Hitler leveled the city of Amsterdam and Rotterdam with Stuka dive bombers. All of these things, the Japanese—just look at what happened on the Death March to Bataan. I think that a commander [in chief], and even the commander of a small unit, has a horrendous decision to make. He's faced with a decision of what must be done at that given moment to achieve an objective and end that battle or that war. You cannot expect him to think, 'Well, we're going to kill all those people,' when he's looking at his own people being killed at the same time. I mean, what's a good killing, and what's a bad killing? We should have thought of all that before we began at all.

Someone could say, 'Well, the real culprits are the people who allowed Hitler to become what he was, and Hirohito and Tojo to become what they were.' But it was done. I think that's the lesson that for me is the strongest. When I see lessons not being learned today, and I don't give a damn about whether or not there's a stable government in Iraq, but when I see the war [end] and [victory declared while leaving] the mechanism in place for the next war as with Saddam Hussein, I mean that's unconscionable. Because somebody else is going to have to go clean up that mess, and that means other Americans will someday have to fight and die, which is exactly what happened.

I'm hoping that somebody in Afghanistan or wherever it is, we will take note right now of all these lessons that we learned in a war and do something to make certain it doesn't happen again. But once it's happening, for a person to stop and say, 'Well, you shouldn't do this because that's unethical,' but this is okay because that's a 'clean killing' [is not relevant anymore]. Like we talk [now] about 'clean' and 'dirty' bombs.

'You Have to Have Been There'

World War was an experience. Well, I can understand what Hemingway meant when he said that for most men, it's an experience unlike none other that they will ever have in their lifetime. He was absolutely right. No matter what your experience is, it's nothing quite like it. It's almost difficult to really explain it so that someone else can feel it. You have to have been there. It's the only way I know. I can understand the attitudes of many people who have not. I can also not understand some attitudes of people who have, and still haven't learned the lessons. Having gone through it now, I wouldn't take anything for what I gained from it. I would have to say that if necessary if the time came, I would probably do it again for my country under the same kinds of circumstances.

My perspective now is interesting to me because I've had such a long history as a political writer, a student, and an observer of politics. Looking back, men in war don't think a great deal about politics; as they say, for the ordinary infantryman, his entire scope is fifty feet in front of his foxhole, and back then, you really had that sense and thinking. Thinking back about it, that sergeant of ours I mentioned so much, Elmer Kaminsky, when you used to ask him for opinions, he would say, 'You know, I don't think too much about it. They got higher-paid folks than me making those decisions.' I'm sure all of us that survived have since become a lot more critical, politically, than we were then.

I believe in an enlightened army. I believe in an enlightened populace; I think they fight better for what they believe in, but then it behooves the leadership to make sure that they only have to fight for things that are deeply believed in and at critical times, and all other times, if they are adventures, we should stay the hell out of them.

The 'Greatest Generation'

I don't know if [we were] the 'Greatest Generation' or not, having been a part of it. I think about it. I've done a lot of reading about the Civil War, and I wonder if they weren't the greatest generation or if they didn't think of themselves as that, and rightly so when you think about it, and I've done a lot of reading about the Revolutionary War. When you think of what those people went up against, to establish an idea, which became a nation, I'm wondering if *they* weren't the greatest generation. So I think it may be a bit presumptuous. Yes, I think the world was on the brink of near extinction, at least civilization as we knew it was, and in many ways, we were a great generation, and I was proud to be part of that. But I'm not so sure I would say we were the 'greatest.' I don't know.

Looking back, one of the things that I've come to believe is that wars—maybe Napoleon was right, that the victor is the one that makes the least mistakes—war is really a series of mistakes; that's how you get into them, and looking back on some of the operations I went through, it's amazing that we got through them and that we won, which more and more brings me back to the fact that so much of war depends on ordinary soldiers, sailors, Marines, and airmen. Yes, you need brilliant people to lead them, but God, when I think of some of the things that happened because ordinary people just did the impossible, or the near impossible... That's really what I think about war and why we need to do everything we can to keep from getting into them. But one of the things I have to say is that I have the greatest respect for the people who give their lives to military service. In this democracy, we couldn't maintain a democracy without it. I know there are people who believe, you know, we could do without the military. No, you couldn't.

You need to always be there for whatever the needs of that democracy are with the military, just as the ordinary citizen has to be there. But I do believe that because of our history as a participatory democracy, and the whole idea of the citizen army and citizen soldier, we don't have enough respect for the people who fill those roles. I think you come to have, you know, those in the professional military. I understand they have an elitist feeling about what they do, but I still believe that we need to maintain proper respect for the people who drop everything and come when their country calls.

I was proud to do it and I'd probably do it again.

Paul Elisha passed away at the age of 92 on August 16, 2015.

"New York Army National Guard Lt. Col. William O'Brien, commander of the 1st Battalion, 105th Infantry Regiment, leads his unit in the relief of another outfit during the battle of Saipan, June 18, 1944. O'Brien would receive the Medal of Honor posthumously for his leadership and actions during the largest Japanese suicide charge of the Pacific Theater July 6-7, 1944." Credit: New York State Military History Museum. National Guard, Public Domain.

EPILOGUE

The Resting Place

With many casualties and ammunition running low, Lt. Col. O'Brien refused to leave the front lines. Striding up and down the lines, he fired at the enemy with a pistol in each hand and his presence there bolstered the spirits of the men, encouraged them in their fight and sustained them in their heroic stand.

Even after he was seriously wounded, Lt. Col. O'Brien refused to be evacuated and after his pistol ammunition was exhausted, he manned a .50-caliber machine gun, mounted on a Jeep, and continued firing.

When last seen alive he was standing upright firing into the Japanese hordes that were enveloping him. Sometime later his body was found surrounded by enemy he had killed.

— MEDAL OF HONOR CITATION

The late spring sun was setting in the idyllic cemetery I had passed so many times without stopping before. I kept looking for the resting place of this lieutenant colonel I had read about. In the end, I had to refer to GPS coordinates and photographs on the internet of a past military remembrance ceremony at his grave to find it.

Back in Section 7, Lot 23, after 20 minutes of searching, I finally found a simple brass marker embedded flat to the ground, no formal headstone or memorial other than a simple homemade wooden cross painted white, and two small American flags rippling in the breeze, side by side. No wonder I missed it.

WILLIAM J O'BRIEN
MEDAL OF HONOR
LT COL US ARMY
WORLD WAR II

The Congressional Medal of Honor Society notes:

"O'Brien joined the Army from his birth city of Troy, New York, and by June 20, 1944, was serving as a lieutenant colonel in the 1st Battalion, 105th Infantry Regiment, 27th Infantry Division. On that day, on Saipan in the Mariana Islands, he braved enemy fire to reach several American tanks which were unknowingly firing on their own troops. The next week, on June 28, he oversaw and personally led an attack on a Japanese-held ridge. On July 7 his battalion came under attack from a much larger enemy force, the largest banzai charge of the Pacific War. He refused to leave the front lines even after being wounded and continued to rally his men until being overrun and killed. He was posthumously awarded the Medal of Honor on May 9, 1945, for his actions throughout the battle for Saipan."[70]

---

[70] William J. O'Brien's (1899-1944) full Medal of Honor citation reads as follows: "For conspicuous gallantry and intrepidity at the risk of his life above and beyond the call of duty at Saipan, Mariana Islands, from 20 June through 7 July 1944. When assault elements of his platoon were held up by intense enemy fire, Lt. Col. O'Brien ordered 3 tanks to precede the assault companies in an attempt to knock out the strongpoint. Due to direct enemy fire the tanks' turrets were closed, causing the tanks to lose direction and to fire into our own troops. Lt. Col. O'Brien, with complete disregard for his own safety, dashed into full view of the enemy and ran to the leader's tank, and pounded on the tank with his pistol butt to attract 2 of the tank's crew and, mounting the tank fully exposed to enemy fire, Lt. Col. O'Brien personally directed the assault until the enemy strongpoint had been liquidated. On 28 June 1944, while his platoon was attempting to take a bitterly defended high ridge in the vicinity of Donnay, Lt. Col. O'Brien arranged to capture the ridge by a double envelopment movement of 2 large combat battalions. He personally took control of the maneuver. Lt. Col. O'Brien crossed 1,200 yards of sniper-infested underbrush alone to arrive at a point where 1 of his platoons was being held up by the enemy. Leaving some men to contain the enemy he personally led 4 men into a narrow ravine behind, and killed or drove off all the Japanese manning that strongpoint. In this action he captured 5 machine guns and one 77-mm. fieldpiece.
Lt. Col. O'Brien then organized the 2 platoons for night defense and against

Bill O'Brien was born in 1899. His parents are here. He died in this most horrific banzai charge of World War II, in which the 1st and 2nd Battalions of the 105th Infantry Regiment, 27th Division front line lost 650 killed and wounded, but also took over 4,300 of the enemy to their deaths.[31]

And he was not the only MOH recipient, posthumous, from this town who died on Saipan that day; in Part Two of this book you also learned about the actions of 28-year-old Thomas A. Baker, 'propped up against a tree.' And what of the dentist-turned-combat doctor from Minnesota from this same 105th Infantry Regiment, Captain Ben Lewis Salomon?[71] He was another of the officers killed

---

repeated counterattacks directed them. Meanwhile he managed to hold ground. On 7 July 1944 his battalion and another battalion were attacked by an overwhelming enemy force estimated at between 3,000 and 5,000 Japanese. With bloody hand-to-hand fighting in progress everywhere, their forward positions were finally overrun by the sheer weight of the enemy numbers. With many casualties and ammunition running low, Lt. Col. O'Brien refused to leave the front lines. Striding up and down the lines, he fired at the enemy with a pistol in each hand and his presence there bolstered the spirits of the men, encouraged them in their fight and sustained them in their heroic stand.

Even after he was seriously wounded, Lt. Col. O'Brien refused to be evacuated and after his pistol ammunition was exhausted, he manned a .50 caliber machine gun, mounted on a jeep, and continued firing. When last seen alive he was standing upright firing into the Japanese hordes that were then enveloping him. Some time later his body was found surrounded by enemy he had killed. His valor was consistent with the highest traditions of the service."

[71] Captain Ben Lewis Salomon's (1914-1944) Medal of Honor Citation reads: "For conspicuous gallantry and intrepidity at the risk of his life above and beyond the call of duty. Captain Ben L. Salomon was serving at Saipan, in the Mariana Islands on July 7, 1944, as the Surgeon for the 2nd Battalion, 105th Infantry Regiment, 27th Infantry Division. The Regiment's 1st and 2nd Battalions were attacked by an overwhelming force estimated between 3,000 and 5,000 Japanese soldiers. It was one of the largest attacks attempted in the Pacific Theater during World War II. Although both units fought

in the charge, but not before inflicting perhaps one hundred deaths of the enemy protecting his wounded patients, and posthumously awarded the Medal of Honor in 2002 for his heroic defensive actions.

Three MOH citations, one action, one infantry regiment. That kind of selfless self-sacrifice is rare; in fact, as retired New York Army National Guard Lt. Col. Paul Fanning noted on the seventy-fifth anniversary at the foot of O'Brien's grave, 'There is nothing like this in our Army history, where three men all sacrificed themselves in such a way to save the lives of their fellow soldiers.'[32]

*

Today, literally as I string together these last few words to reflect upon these men, the last living World War II Medal of Honor

---

furiously, the enemy soon penetrated the Battalions' combined perimeter and inflicted overwhelming casualties. In the first minutes of the attack, approximately 30 wounded soldiers walked, crawled, or were carried into Captain Salomon's aid station, and the small tent soon filled with wounded men. As the perimeter began to be overrun, it became increasingly difficult for Captain Salomon to work on the wounded. He then saw a Japanese soldier bayoneting one of the wounded soldiers lying near the tent. Firing from a squatting position, Captain Salomon quickly killed the enemy soldier. Then, as he turned his attention back to the wounded, two more Japanese soldiers appeared in the front entrance of the tent. As these enemy soldiers were killed, four more crawled under the tent walls. Rushing them, Captain Salomon kicked the knife out of the hand of one, shot another, and bayoneted a third. Captain Salomon butted the fourth enemy soldier in the stomach and a wounded comrade then shot and killed the enemy soldier.
Realizing the gravity of the situation, Captain Salomon ordered the wounded to make their way as best they could back to the regimental aid station, while he attempted to hold off the enemy until they were clear. Captain Salomon then grabbed a rifle from one of the wounded and rushed out of the tent. After four men were killed while manning a machine gun, Captain Salomon took control of it. When his body was later found, 98 dead enemy soldiers were piled in front of his position. Captain Salomon's extraordinary heroism and devotion to duty are in keeping with the highest traditions of military service and reflect great credit upon himself, his unit, and the United States Army."

recipient, Iwo Jima Marine veteran Hershel 'Woody' Williams, is lying in state in the US Capitol Rotunda, having recently passed at the age of 98, symbolizing the passing of the World War II Generation's MOH recipients and indeed, the passage of this entire generation of veterans. When he was awarded the medal personally by President Truman, he felt conflicted, which he expressed in an interview later:

'I no longer just represented me. I now represented the Marines who protected me, Marines who sacrificed their lives doing that… If I had written that recommendation for the Medal of Honor—which I didn't, my commanding officer did—I would have never used the word *'alone.'* I sort of resent that word in my citation. It says, *'He went forward alone.'* That's not correct. Four Marines were protecting me, and two of them were killed while they did it. So I have said from the very beginning that it does not belong to me. It belongs to them.'[33][72]

---

[72] Woody Williams' (1923-2022) Medal of Honor citation reads: *"For conspicuous gallantry and intrepidity at the risk of his life above and beyond the call of duty as Demolition Sergeant serving with the First Battalion, Twenty-First Marines, Third Marine Division, in action against enemy Japanese forces on Iwo Jima, Volcano Island, 23 February 1945. Quick to volunteer his services when our tanks were maneuvering vainly to open a lane for the infantry through the network of reinforced concrete pillboxes, buried mines and black, volcanic sands, Corporal Williams daringly went forward alone to attempt the reduction of devastating machine-gun fire from the unyielding positions.*
Covered only by four riflemen, he fought desperately for four hours under terrific enemy small-arms fire and repeatedly returned to his own lines to prepare demolition charges and obtain serviced flame throwers, struggling back, frequently to the rear of hostile emplacements, to wipe out one position after another. On one occasion he daringly mounted a pillbox to insert the nozzle of his flame thrower through the air vent, kill the occupants and silence the gun; on another he grimly charged enemy riflemen who attempted to stop him with bayonets and destroyed them with a burst of flame from his weapon.

He also battled the demons that our veterans pick up on the battlefield, the ones that never truly leave them, haunted by the friends he had lost, the men he had killed.

They once walked among us as humble giants of humanity. Some of these survivors, like Woody, a career counselor of veterans, went on to dedicate their lives to others. As I've stated before, they were our neighbors, our teachers and coaches, shopkeepers and carpenters, millworkers and mechanics, nurses and stenographers, lawyers and loggers, draftsmen and doctors, people from every walk of life, high school dropouts and college graduates. They were the World War II Generation, and there was a time after the war when we just simply took them for granted. They were ordinary people who did extraordinary things, on the battlefield, and in their lives that followed. It is my hope that this series brings us closer to this part of the American character that we really can't afford to forget.

Maybe it is presumptuous of me to be quietly disturbed that Bill O'Brien, MOH, has a final resting place that doesn't call attention to the man or his deeds, that a Medal of Honor recipient doesn't even have an upright stone. But maybe that's the way Bill would have wanted it; this generation was like that. Maybe the family felt the same, in their quietly overwhelming private grief. And maybe it's just really none of my business, after all. But I just can't move on without sharing this story, because it is our story, too, the story of America. Like Woody said, 'I no longer just represented me…'

His unyielding determination and extraordinary heroism in the face of ruthless enemy resistance were directly instrumental in neutralizing one of the most fanatically defended Japanese strong points encountered by his regiment and aided in enabling his company to reach its' [sic] objective. Corporal Williams' aggressive fighting spirit and valiant devotion to duty throughout this fiercely contested action sustain and enhance the highest traditions of the United States Naval Service."

You don't have to search for the cemeteries or final resting places to learn to appreciate what that generation did. You've taken the time to listen to their stories. Say their names, and the names of their fallen friends, and they will live forever. [73]

---

[73] *and they will live forever*- As this book was going to press, I received an email from a reader of my previous books. It arrived just as I was finishing this chapter, and, with his permission, I would like to share what my reader expressed about his grandfather's pain and trauma, and a grandson's yearning to know him better.

RE: THE THINGS OUR FATHERS SAW

8.1.22

FROM: Dennis M.

"Mr. Rozell, I have always been fascinated by World War II and the history behind it. I am 51 years old, and my grandfather fought in the Pacific, and like most of his generation, he never spoke of it. I know he struggled with PTSD his whole life and I unfortunately learned more about his military career when he passed than I had known when he was alive.

According to my father, my grandfather was a really intelligent man before the war and was well respected in the community that they lived in a small town in western Minnesota. He was my mom's father and from the little bit I was told, he was not a front-line soldier but with all the casualties they suffered in the beginning, he volunteered to be a machine gunner and I know he was wounded five times. Being [as] he grew up in a small town and also where racism was unfortunately more prevalent back then, my mother told me they were raised to look at people the same, no matter what their color was, and the only reason I bring this up [is because] I was told when he was wounded on two of those occasions, Black soldiers helped save him.

He was awarded multiple medals, but unfortunately, *he threw them all overboard on his way home from the war* [*author emphasis*], and no one in the family knew this until after his death. I was only 17 years old when he passed away and I would have loved just to sit down and talked with him about his military experiences and service, but unfortunately that was never to be.

Because dying for freedom isn't the worst that could happen. Being forgotten is.

He was just one [of] million[s] of men drafted and pulled from their lives to go and serve in the military and do their duty until the war ended. My father told me the war changed him for the rest of his life, after it was over, and I often wondered what kind of man he would have been like had he not like millions of other men had to go to war and seeing the horrific experiences of it.

He was unfortunately an alcoholic his whole life after the war and my father said the war is what caused this; although this is going to sound crazy to say, he was a 'good' alcoholic, if there is one, in that he always treated us grandkids with love and kindness—you rarely knew he was intoxicated, although when you are young and naïve, we could never tell because he was always so good to us.

There were a couple of letters he wrote while he was overseas [that didn't tell much] with how they censored mail back then—and I am sure not to make my grandma worry—but the only time he mentioned anything about fighting in the war [was] where he wrote that at night they never got much sleep, because they always had to worry about the Japanese trying to sneak into their fox holes.

I just wish I would have known more about his military career and what medals he earned while serving overseas. Thank you again for preserving their stories for future generations before all of these great men and women are gone as I love reading the stories that these men and women have shared in a time when everyone from that generation pitched in and did their part for the war effort and unfortunately some of them made the ultimate sacrifice.

Sincerely, Dennis M."

IF YOU LIKED THIS BOOK, you'll love hearing more from the World War II generation in my other books. On the following pages you can see some samples, and I can let you know as soon as the new books are out and offer you exclusive discounts on some material. Just sign up at matthewrozellbooks.com

Some of my readers may like to know that all of my books are **directly available from the author, with collector's sets which can be autographed** in paperback and hardcover. They are popular gifts for that 'hard-to-buy-for' guy or gal on your list.

Visit my shop at matthewrozellbooks.com for details.

THE THINGS OUR FATHERS SAW ® SERIES:

VOICES OF THE PACIFIC THEATER

WAR IN THE AIR: GREAT DEPRESSION TO COMBAT

WAR IN THE AIR: COMBAT, CAPTIVITY, REUNION

UP THE BLOODY BOOT-THE WAR IN ITALY

D-DAY AND BEYOND

THE BULGE AND BEYOND

ACROSS THE RHINE

ON TO TOKYO

HOMEFRONT/WOMEN AT WAR

CHINA, BURMA, INDIA

ALSO: A TRAIN NEAR MAGDEBURG

ABOUT THE AUTHOR

Photo Credit: Joan K. Lentini; May 2017.

Matthew Rozell is an award-winning history teacher, author, speaker, and blogger on the topic of the most cataclysmic events in the history of mankind—World War II and the Holocaust. Rozell has been featured as the 'ABC World News Person of the Week' and has had his work as a teacher filmed for the CBS Evening News, NBC Learn, the Israeli Broadcast Authority, the United States Holocaust Memorial Museum, and the New York State United Teachers. He writes on the power of teaching and the importance of the study of history at TeachingHistoryMatters.com, and you can 'Like' his Facebook author page at AuthorMatthewRozell for updates.

Mr. Rozell is a sought-after speaker on World War II, the Holocaust, and history education, motivating and inspiring his audiences with the lessons of the past. Visit MatthewRozell.com for availability/details.

About this Book/ Acknowledgements

*

A note on historiographical style and convention: to enhance accuracy, consistency, and readability, I corrected punctuation and spelling and sometimes even place names, but only after extensive research. I did take the liberty of occasionally condensing the speaker's voice, eliminating side tangents or incidental information not relevant to the matter at hand. Sometimes two or more interviews with the same person were combined for readability and narrative flow. All of the words of the subjects, however, are essentially their own.

Additionally, I chose to utilize footnotes and endnotes where I deemed them appropriate, directing readers who wish to learn more to my sources, notes, and side commentary. I hope that they do not detract from the flow of the narrative.

First, I wish to acknowledge the hundreds of students who passed through my classes and who forged the bonds with the World War II generation. I promised you these books someday, and now that many of you are yourselves parents, you can tell your children this book is for them. Who says young people are indifferent to the past? Here is evidence to the contrary.

The Hudson Falls Central School District and my former colleagues have my deep appreciation for supporting this endeavor and recognizing its significance throughout the years.

Cara Quinlan's sharp proofing and suggestions helped to clean up the original manuscript.

Naturally this work would not have been possible had it not been for the willingness of the veterans to share their stories for posterity. All of the veterans who were interviewed for this book had the foresight to complete release forms granting access to their stories, and for us to share the information with the New York State Military Museum's Veterans Oral History Project, where copies of the original interviews reside. Wayne Clarke and Mike Russert of the NYSMMVOP were instrumental in cultivating this relationship with my classes over the years and are responsible for some of the interviews in this book as well. Please see the 'Source Notes.'

I would be remiss if I did not recall the profound influence of my late mother and father, Mary and Tony Rozell, both cutting-edge educators and proud early supporters of my career. To my younger siblings Mary, Ned, Nora, and Drew, all accomplished writers and authors, thank you for your encouragement as well. Final and deepest appreciations go to my wife Laura and our children, Emma, Ned, and Mary. Thank you for indulging the old man as he attempted to bring to life the stories he collected as a young one.

NOTES

—THE INTERVIEWS—

Source Notes: **Abbott Wiley**. Interviewed by Wayne Clarke, February 19, 2013, Valley Falls, NY. Deposited at NYS Military Museum.

Source Notes: **William Millette**. Interviewed by Michael Russert and Wayne Clarke, April 30, 2004, Latham, NY. Deposited at NYS Military Museum.

Source Notes: **Harry Rosenthal.** Interviewed by Michael Russert and Wayne Clarke, January 16, 2001. Syracuse, NY. Deposited at NYS Military Museum.

Source Notes: **Jacob N. Cutler.** Interviewed by Michael Russert, August 8, 2002. Queens, NY. Deposited at NYS Military Museum.

Source Notes: **Sydney Cole.** Interviewed by Toby Ticktin Back, August 7, 1989, Buffalo, NY. Interviewed by Wayne Clarke and Kathleen Mathews, April 9, 2009, Buffalo, NY. Deposited at NYS Military Museum.

Source Notes: **Nicholas F. Butrico.** Interviewed by Michael Russert and Wayne Clarke, February 3, 2003, Congers, NY. Deposited at NYS Military Museum.

Source Notes: **Albert A. Tarbell.** Interviewed by Michael Russert and Wayne Clarke, January 16, 2003. Syracuse, NY. Deposited at NYS Military Museum.

Source Notes: **Richard M. Marowitz.** Interviewed by Michael Aikey and Wayne Clarke, October 8, 2001. Latham, NY. Interviewed by Matthew Rozell, April 28, 2000, for the Hudson Falls HS World War II Living History Project, Hudson Falls, NY. Deposited at NYS Military Museum.

Source Notes: **Timothy J. Horgan.** Interviewed by Christopher Smith, December 3, 2005, for the Hudson Falls HS World War II Living History Project. Glens Falls, NY. Deposited at NYS Military Museum. Chris also contributed to this transcript and analysis.

Source Notes: **Lawrence E. Bennett.** Interviewed by Michael Russert and Wayne Clarke, January 8, 2003. Newburgh, NY. Deposited at NYS Military Museum.

Source Notes: **Augustine John DiFiore.** Interviewed by Michael Russert and Wayne Clarke, March 20, 2003. Brooklyn, NY. Deposited at NYS Military Museum. Student Reanna Rainbow contributed to this transcript and analysis.

Source Notes: **Robert C. Baldridge**. Interviewed by Michael Russert and Wayne Clarke, August 4, 2004. Lawrence, NY. Deposited at NYS Military Museum.

Source Notes: **Rudolf F. Drenick**. Interviewed by Michael Russert and Wayne Clarke, November 18, 2003. South Setauket, NY. Deposited at NYS Military Museum.

Source Notes: **Charles J. Zappo.** Interviewed by Michael Russert and Wayne Clarke, May 17, 2007. Buffalo, NY. Deposited at NYS Military Museum. Student Joseph Marine contributed to this transcript and analysis.

Source Notes: **Alvin M. Cohen.** Interviewed by Michael Aikey and Wayne Clarke, August 8, 2001. Latham, NY. Interviewed by Matthew Rozell, April 28, 2000, for the Hudson Falls HS World War II Living History Project, Hudson Falls, NY. Deposited at NYS Military Museum.

Source Notes: **Emilio J. DiPalma.** Interviewed by Michael Russert and Wayne Clarke, June 28, 2002. Cambridge, NY. Deposited at NYS Military Museum.

Source Notes: **Douglas Vink.** Interviewed by Matthew Rozell, April 28, 2000, for the Hudson Falls HS World War II Living History Project, Hudson Falls, NY. Deposited at NYS Military Museum.

Source Notes: **Frank J. Castronovo.** Interviewed by Robert von Hasseln and Wayne Clarke, May 25, 2001. Freeport, NY. Deposited at NYS Military Museum.

Source Notes: **Charles M. Jacobs.** Interviewed by Michael Aikey and Wayne Clarke, August 8, 2001. Latham, NY. Deposited at NYS Military Museum.

Source Notes: **Paul Elisha.** Interviewed by Robert von Hasseln, December 12, 2000. Interviewed by Michael Aikey and Wayne Clarke, July 16, 2001, November 28, 2001. Latham, NY. Deposited at NYS Military Museum.

Source Notes: **James A. Smith, Jr.** Interviewed by Michael Russert and Wayne Clarke, February 20, 2003. Saratoga Springs, NY. Deposited at NYS Military Museum.

Source Notes: **Samuel R. Dinova.** Interviewed by Michael Russert and Wayne Clarke, January 7, 2003. Troy, NY. Deposited at NYS Military Museum.

Source Notes: **Albert J. Harris.** Interviewed by Michael Aikey and Wayne Clarke, July 30, 2001. Latham, NY. Deposited at NYS Military Museum.

Source Notes: **Unknown Japanese Soldier.** Diary entries, July 11, 1944, to July 8, 1944. Saipan. Translated transcription mailed to Matthew Rozell by Terry Barber, Fort Ann, New York, in a letter dated December 12, 2011. It was acquired by him from his wife's aunt, whose deceased husband was a veteran of the Pacific war. The original diary's whereabouts are unknown.

Source Notes: **John H. Kolecki.** Interviewed by Michael Russert and Wayne Clarke, February 22, 2006. Buffalo, NY. Deposited at NYS Military Museum.

Source Notes: **Henry C. Huneken.** Interviewed by Michael Russert and Wayne Clarke, August 5, 2004. South Setauket, NY. Deposited at NYS Military Museum.

Source Notes: **Steve T. Jordan.** Interviewed by Michael Russert and Wayne Clarke, November 25, 2003. Saratoga Springs, NY. Deposited at NYS Military Museum.

Source Notes: **Mitchell Morse.** Interviewed by Michael Aikey and Eric Scott, April 11, 2001. Kingston, NY. Deposited at NYS Military Museum.

NOTES

[1]. For more on the V-1, see www.museumofflight.org/Exhibits/fieseler-fi-103-v1.

[2] 12,500 tons a day- Hickman, Kennedy. '*World War II: Operation Market-Garden Overview.*' ThoughtCo, Aug. 28, 2020, thoughtco.com/world-war-ii-operation-market-garden-2361452.

[3] Childers, Thomas. *World War II: A Social and Military History. Part II, Lecture 20. Operation Market Garden and the Battle of the Bulge.* The Teaching Company. 1998.

[4] Miller, Donald L. *The Story of World War II.* New York: Simon & Schuster, 2001. 329.

[5] MacDonald, Charles. *A Time for Trumpets-The Untold Story of the Battle of the Bulge.* New York City: Morrow. 2002.

[6] Lippman, David. *Operation Plunder: Crossing the Rhine.* Warfare History Network. warfarehistorynetwork.com/2016/09/15/operation-plunder-crossing-the-rhine

[7] Obituary. *Alexander Drabik, 82, First G.I. To Cross Remagen Bridge in 1945. New York Times*, Oct. 2, 1993.

[8] Ludendorff Bridge. Wikipedia. en.wikipedia.org/wiki/Ludendorff_Bridge

[9] Operation Paperclip- Ossad, Steve. *The Liberation of Nordhausen Concentration Camp.* Warfare History Network. December 31, 2019. warfarehistorynetwork.com/2019/12/31/the-liberation-of-nordhausen-concentration-camp/

[10] Operation Paperclip- Ossad, Steve. *The Liberation of Nordhausen Concentration Camp.* Warfare History Network. December 31, 2019. warfarehistorynetwork.com/2019/12/31/the-liberation-of-nordhausen-concentration-camp/

[11] Van Lunteren, Frank. *Blocking Kampfgruppe Peiper: The 504th Parachute Infantry Regiment in the Battle of the Bulge.* Philadelphia and Oxford, Casemate Publishers. 2015. 192.

[12] Gavin, James M. *On To Berlin: Battles of an Airborne Commander, 1943-1946.* New York, Viking Press. 1978. 286-288.

[13] Wöbbelin. Holocaust Encyclopedia. United States Holocaust Memorial Museum. encyclopedia.ushmm.org/content/en/article/woebbelin

[14] Gavin, James M. *On To Berlin: Battles of an Airborne Commander, 1943-1946.* New York, Viking Press. 1978. 286-288.

[15] Childers, Thomas. *World War II: A Military and Social History. Part III, Lecture 28, The Race for Berlin.* The Teaching Company, 1998.

[16] Some text from final paragraphs from testimony found in Michael Takiff's *Brave Men, Gentle Heroes: American Fathers and Sons in World War II and Vietnam.* New York: HarperCollins, 2003. 258.

[17] 504th Parachute Infantry in WWII. Facebook page post, March 7, 2006. facebook.com/504thPIR

[18] Hayes, Tony. *Dachau Will Always Be with Us.* March, 2015. Accessed at getitwriteblog.wordpress.com/2015/03/12/dachau-will-always-be-with-us/

[19] Lichtblau, Eric. *The Holocaust Just Got More Shocking. The New York Times,* March 1, 2013.

[20] Pyle, Ernie. *Back Again.* Wartime Columns of Ernie Pyle, The Media School Indiana University. sites.mediaschool.indiana.edu/erniepyle/1945/02/06/back-again

[21] Lancaster, Marc. *Ernie Pyle killed on Ie Shima.* World War II on Deadline, April 18, 2021. ww2ondeadline.com/2021/04/18/ernie-pyle-killed-ww2-correspondent

[22] Hewett, Frank. *The Battling Bastards of Bataan.* 1942.

[23] Pyle, Ernie. *On Victory in Europe.* Wartime Columns of Ernie Pyle, The Media School Indiana University. sites.mediaschool.indiana.edu/erniepyle/1945/04/18/on-victory-in-europe/

[24] Lancaster, Marc. *Ernie Pyle killed on Ie Shima.* World War II on Deadline, April 18, 2021.

ww2ondeadline.com/2021/04/18/ernie-pyle-killed-ww2-correspondent

[25] Toland, John. *The Rising Sun: The Decline and Fall of the Japanese Empire 1936-1945*, Random House, 1970. 470.

[26] Chapin, John C. *Marines in World War II Commemorative Series, Breaking the Outer Ring: Marine Landings in the Marshall Islands*. National Park Service. www.nps.gov/parkhistory/online_books/npswapa/extcontent/usmc/pcn-190-003124-00/sec2.htm

[27] The Peleliu operation is further discussed and remembered by veterans in Vol. I of this series, Voices of the Pacific.

[28] Miller, Donald. *The Story of World War II.* New York: Simon & Schuster, 2001. 416.

[29] Miller, *The Story of World War II.* 458-61.

[30] *Tenth Army*- Source: Battle of Okinawa. wikipedia.org/wiki/Battle_of_Okinawa. Cross-referenced.

[31] Valenza, Andrew, N.Y. Guard Soldiers Remember Medal of Honor Recipients, New York National Guard. July 9, 2019. www.nationalguard.mil/News/Article/1898451/ny-guard-soldiers-remember-medal-of-honor-recipients

[32] 'There is nothing like this in our Army history'- Paul Fanning, New York Army National Guard Lt. Col., Ret., quoted in Valenza, Andrew, N.Y. Guard Soldiers Remember Medal of Honor Recipients, New York National Guard. July 9, 2019. www.nationalguard.mil/News/Article/1898451/ny-guard-soldiers-remember-medal-of-honor-recipients

[33] *Woody Williams quote*-Tuthill, Matt. *Living Legend: the Story of Hershel "Woody" Williams*. Chef Irvine.com, chefirvine.com/magazine/living-legend-the-story-of-hershel-woody-williams.

www.ingramcontent.com/pod-product-compliance
Lightning Source LLC
Chambersburg PA
CBHW070039080526
44586CB00013B/859